Amanda López-Betanzos

GYN/ECOLOGY

GYN/ECOLOGY

THE METAETHICS OF RADICAL FEMINISM

MARY DALY

With a New Intergalactic Introduction
by the Author

BEACON PRESS : BOSTON

Beacon Press
25 Beacon Street
Boston, Massachusetts 02108

Beacon Press books
are published under the auspices of
the Unitarian Universalist Association of Congregations.

Printed in the United States of America

99 98 6 7 8 9 0

Library of Congress Cataloging-in-Publication Data
Daly, Mary.
Gyn/ecology, the metaethics of radical feminism : with a new intergalactic introduction / Mary Daly.
p. cm.
Includes bibliographical references and index.
ISBN 0-8070-1413-3
1. Feminism. 2. Feminism—Moral and ethical aspects. 3. Social ethics. I. Title.
HQ1154.D312 1990
305.42—dc20 90-52596

The First Passage:

To my mother and foresister, Anna, whose vision extended beyond the boundaries imposed by patriarchal institutions—who always encouraged me to do my *own* work, and who opened the way for the Labyrinthine Journey

The Second Passage:

To Jan Raymond, scholar of deepest integrity, true doctor of philosophy—trail-blazing Amazon/Searcher whose labrys/spirit awakens in other women the awareness of their own equality to the A-mazing task

The Third Passage:

To Denise Connors, courageous Voyager, who has witnessed and understood—more profoundly than anyone I have known—the murder and dismemberment of the Goddess, and who survives to Re-member, Spark, and Spin

We are grateful to the following poets, publishers, and copyright holders for permission to reprint material in this volume:

From *Beginning With O* by Olga Broumas, Copyright © 1977 by Olga Broumas, by permission of Yale University Press; from *The Hand That Cradles the Rock* by Rita Mae Brown, by permission of the author; "Song to My Mama" and "Scars" by Meg Christian © 1974 by Meg Christian (Thumbelina Music BMI), All rights reserved. Used by permission; from *Trilogy* by H. D., Copyright 1944 by Oxford University Press, Copyright © 1973 by Norman Holmes Pearson, Reprinted by permission of New Directions Publishing Corporation; from *Collected Poems 1909–1962,* by T. S. Eliot, Copyright, 1936, by Harcourt Brace Jovanovich, Inc., Copyright © 1963, 1964 by T. S. Eliot, Reprinted by permission of Harcourt Brace Jovanovich, Inc., and Faber and Faber Ltd.; from *A Woman Is Talking to Death,* published by Diana Press, 4400 Market St., Oakland, Ca. 94608, copy available by mail, Copyright © Judy Grahn 1974, 1977, by permission of the author and Diana Press; from *New York Head Shop and Museum* by Audre Lorde, Copyright 1974 by Audre Lorde Rollings, Broadside/Crummell Press, Detroit, Michigan; from *Mother India* by Katherine Mayo, by permission of Harcourt Brace Jovanovich, Inc., the Katherine Mayo Estate, and Jonathan Cape; from *Lady of the Beasts* by Robin Morgan, Copyright © 1962, 1968, 1973, 1974, 1975, 1976 by Robin Morgan, Reprinted by permission of Random House, Inc., Robin Morgan, and Georges Borchardt, Inc.; from *Monster* by Robin Morgan, Copyright © 1961 by Robin Morgan, Reprinted by permission of Random House, Inc.; "Mountain Song," words and music by Holly Near, © 1977 Hereford Music, All Rights Reserved, Used by permission; from *Movement in Black* by Pat Parker, Copyright © Pat Parker 1978, and from *Womanslaughter* by Pat Parker, Copyright © Pat Parker 1976, 1978—both published by Diana Press, 4400 Market St., Oakland, Ca. 94608, copies available by mail—Reprinted by permission of the author and Diana Press; "For Strong Women" by Marge Piercy, Copyright Marge Piercy, 1978, by permission of the author; portion of "A Work of Artifice," first appeared in *Leviathan,* from the book *To Be of Use* by Marge Piercy, Copyright 1969, 1971, 1973, 1974 by Marge Piercy, Reprinted by permission of Doubleday & Company, Inc., and Harold Matson Company, Inc.; from "Sharon in the Field" by Evelyn Posamentier, by permission of the author; Lines from "Diving into the Wreck" and "Waking in the Dark" from *Diving into the Wreck, Poems, 1971–1972,* by Adrienne Rich, Copyright © 1973 by W. W. Norton & Company, Inc.; Lines from "Natural Resources" and from "Toward the Solstice" from *The Dream of a Common Language, Poems, 1974–1977,* by Adrienne Rich, Copyright © 1978 by W. W. Norton & Company, Inc., All with the permission of the author and the publisher; from *Snapshots of a Daughter-in-Law* by Adrienne Rich, by permission of W. W. Norton & Company, Inc., and Chatto and Windus Ltd.; from *Bee Time Vine & Other Pieces* by Gertrude Stein, Copyright © 1953 by Alice B. Toklas, by permission of Yale University Press; from *The Crisis of the Seventeenth Century* by H. R. Trevor-Roper, Copyright © 1967 by H. R. Trevor-Roper, Reprinted by permission of Harper & Row, Publishers, Inc., and Harold Matson Company, Inc.; from "The Ballad of Merciful Mary" and "The Witching Hour" by Willie Tyson, by permission of the author; from "The Hive" by Jimmy Webb, © 1968 Canopy Music, All Rights Reserved, Used by permission of Warner Bros. Music; from *Three Guineas* by Virginia Woolf, Copyright, 1938, by Harcourt Brace Jovanovich, Inc., renewed, 1966, by Leonard Woolf, Reprinted by permission of Harcourt Brace Jovanovich, Inc., the Author's Literary Estate, and The Hogarth Press.

CONTENTS

Their origin and their history patriarchal poetry their origin and their history patriarchal poetry their origin and their history. . . .
Patriarchal poetry makes no mistake. . . .
Patriarchal Poetry is the same as Patriotic poetry is the same as patriarchal poetry is the same as Patriotic poetry is the same as patriarchal poetry is the same.
Patriarchal poetry is the same.

Gertrude Stein,
from "Patriarchal Poetry,"
Bee Time Vine and Other Pieces

Their origin and their history patriarchal scholarship their origin and their history.
Patriarchal scholarship makes no mistake.
Patriarchal Scholarship is the same as Patriotic scholarship is the same as patriarchal scholarship is the same as patriarchal poetry.
Patriarchal scholarship is the same.

Myself,
Gyn/Ecology: The Metaethics of Radical Feminism

I have dreamed on this mountain
Since first I was my mother's daughter
And you can't just take my dreams away
Not with me watching.

You may drive a big machine
But I was born a great big woman
And you can't just take my dreams away
Without me fighting. . . .

No you can't just take my dreams away.

Holly Near,
from "Mountain Song," sung by Meg Christian,
Face the Music (Olivia Records)

NEW INTERGALACTIC INTRODUCTION

In the year 1975 my world split open, in the most Positively Revolting ways imaginable. That year marked my entry into a New Realm of Qualitative Leaping through galaxies of mind-space. I was Moving far out on my Spiraling Intergalactic Voyage, which I Re-Call as beginning *in utero,* or perhaps even aeons before that traumatic period.

1975 was the year I began writing *Gyn/Ecology*. It was a Startling, Stunning Time, consisting of Moment after Moment of Spinning Integrity. I believe that this book could not have been written earlier, because before that Time there was no context which would have allowed for the possibility of its becoming. But that year was marked by a convergence of many events which hurled me into utterly New dimensions of thinking, living, loving, writing, be-ing.

At this point it is important to explore that context.

THE WATERSHED YEAR

During the first week of January 1975 I embarked on a bizarre adventure which was typical of the Time.* I had been invited to deliver a paper at the Second International Symposium on Belief in Vienna, which was sponsored by Cardinal König of Vienna and the Agnelli Foundation. The participants in the symposium were world-renowned theologians and sociologists of religion. Nearly all were males, and most of the papers were pedestrian, pedantic, and—in a word—dryasdust.

Since the situation could not have been more incongruous, I decided to be congruous with its incongruity by wearing my usual cords and boots. I sported a terrifying Tiger T-shirt, which I

* This is the Time which I Now Name "The Third Spiral Galaxy" of my Voyage. I develop this theme in a New work entitled *Outercourse: The Be-Dazzling Voyage* (San Francisco: Harper San Francisco, 1992).

thought was appropriate for the subject of my paper, "Radical Feminism: The Qualitative Leap Beyond Patriarchal Religion."*

Among those in attendance when I read my paper was Cardinal König himself. The appearance of his eminence inspired me, in a perverse sort of way, to be as ferocious as possible. With unmitigated gall—or maybe simple forthrightness—I explained that my presence there was an experiment, questionable and problematic to myself. Not wishing to bore myself by returning to "square one" for the benefit of this august assembly, I succinctly summarized my previous thought in twenty-three theses and moved on from there.†

Since Cardinal König came to hear my paper (I don't recall that he showed up for any others that day), subsequent interchanges with his eminence were entertaining and memorable. My friends Emily Culpepper and Robin Hough, who happened to be vacationing in Europe at the time, also came as staunch supporters and accompanied me to the Cardinal's palace, where a reception was held for the Symposium participants. Robin served as my unofficial photographer—since the Cardinal had an official one there—so that I would have my own pictorial record of the event, particularly of shaking hands with his eminence while verbally sparring with him, smiling the whole time.‡ I also have photos of myself smoking cigars with Emily. The cigars had been passed out on silver trays, together with champagne, by female servants in black uniforms to the men present. We simply could not refuse the opportunity to help ourselves.

After the reception, Emily, Robin, and I went out to a Viennese Weingarten, and the next day we took off by train for Venice, where we happily drank delicious wine ("Lacryma christi del vesuvio"—"Tears of Christ of Vesuvius") in the Piazza San Marco. A couple of days later I made a complicated series of

* A shortened version of the paper was published later as "The Qualitative Leap Beyond Patriarchal Religion" in *Quest: A Feminist Quarterly* (Spring 1975).

† See "The Qualitative Leap Beyond Patriarchal Religion."

‡ Of particular interest was the conversation I had with König in the course of our handshaking and smiling for the benefit of photographers. It went like this: König: "So, you teach at Jesuit-run Boston College!" Daly: "Yes and they would like to get rid of me but they cannot." König: "I am not so sure about that!"

plane connections in stormy weather and arrived back in Boston just in time to teach my 4:30 class in Feminist Ethics.

I felt buffeted by swirling energies, then, as the spring semester of 1975 was beginning. There was much excitement in the air. For me, personally, there was the smouldering knowledge and expectation that the new edition of *The Church and the Second Sex* would be coming out any day, with its "Autobiographical Preface" and "New Feminist Postchristian Introduction." It was like waiting for a New Time bomb to be released into the atmosphere.

In addition to that expectation, there was my anticipation of Boston College's decision regarding my application for promotion to the rank of full professor. I had applied in the fall of 1974, and now, in January, word of the university's decision was due momentarily.

By any and all standards of academia/academentia this was a highly appropriate time to have applied for the full professorship. I had published (in addition to dissertations) two major books—*The Church and the Second Sex* (first brought out by Harper and Row in 1968) and *Beyond God the Father: Toward a Philosophy of Women's Liberation* (Beacon Press, 1973). By the fall of 1974 the latter was used as a college text in universities and seminaries across the country and was excerpted in several publications. In addition I had made contributions to more than ten books and had published more than twenty articles in professional journals as well as in feminist periodicals. I had done substantial committee work in a variety of areas, had given more than seventy public lectures, and had presented papers to learned [*sic*] societies. I was listed in a dozen or so *Who's Who* Dictionaries and Encyclopedias. I also had seven degrees, three of them doctorates.

I mention these tedious details of qualifications because the university's decision, unbelievably, was negative. My students and many other supporters demanded an explanation, so the department chair "explained" to interviewers from *The Heights,* the student newspaper (February 10, 1975): "She has made no significant contribution to the field. In terms of achievement, Mary's case seemed to rest on *that book* [*Beyond God the Father*], and it is not a distinguished academic achievement." At a subsequent meeting (February 24) the university's attorney made an astonishing analogy between my case and that of Erich Segal, whose popular novel *Love Story* was not considered a scholarly work entitling him to promotion in the classics department at Yale.*

Feminists from all over the United States protested Boston College's absurd denial of my promotion. On February 27 we created a Stunning event, a kind of Meta-response to the whole situation—a Forum on Women in Higher Education, held in Roberts Center, a large gymnasium at Boston College. About one thousand women packed the gym, as Robin Morgan began the Forum with the battle cry "Sisters, we meet on bloody Jesuit ground." Nine women educators from various "fields" then spoke, most of whom related experiences of discrimination, denial of tenure, and firings at universities across the country. This event revealed to all of us present that Radical Feminists teaching in all departments were being purged from universities.†

The revelations of this Forum, combined with Boston College's disparagement and attempted erasure of *Beyond God the Father* as well as *all* of my work—and indeed of my very be-ing—fomented enormous explosions in my psyche. They unleashed my powers and hurled me further on my Intergalactic Voyage.

* Cited by Janice G. Raymond from the proceedings of that meeting in "Mary Daly: A Decade of Academic Harassment and Feminist Survival," in *Handbook for Women Scholars: Strategies for Success,* ed. Mary L. Spencer, Monika Kehoe, and Karen Speece. (San Francisco: Americas Behavioral Research Corporation, 1982), 84.

† Of special significance was the fact that Jan Raymond, who had gone through Boston College's Ph.D. program in Religion and Ethics with me as her adviser and who was currently writing her doctoral dissertation with me as her director, was denied even an interview for a faculty position in ethics at BC. Questioned by interviewers from *The Heights* (February 10, 1975) whether Raymond's association with Daly was the actual reason for the denial of an interview, the department chair is reported to have said: "Yes, in the sense that she approaches most subjects from a basically feminist perspective." He went on to say that the department would be out of balance if two people were approaching things from a feminist, anti-Christian perspective. (The theology faculty consisted of more than thirty members at that point.) As Jan Raymond proclaimed at the Forum: "My final and greatest sin was female identification and bonding. I performed the unforgivable act of studying seriously—of identifying professionally—with a woman."

I was thrown into greater and greater freedom. Since *Beyond God the Father* had been super-scholarly and yet had been called "unscholarly" by the cynical and deceptive fathers of reversal, I was now liberated into the possibility of qualitatively Other Daring Deeds. It was not the case that I would become *less* scholarly. Indeed, I was now free to become even more so—and to leap creatively further into the Background.

Moreover, the True Horror Stories of the Radical Feminists driven out of academia that year kindled my Righteous Rage, which was/is Creative Rage. I knew, then, fully, that my scholarship and originality would never be rewarded within the "system," that my Rewards would be utterly Other, chiefly in the work itself and in what this communicated to other women.

The wide foreground context of this Watershed Year was the media's foreclosure on feminism. This was typified in a cover story in *Harper's* magazine entitled "Requiem for the Women's Movement." The picture on the cover was of a woman in mourning, wearing "widow's weeds." The intended message was obvious.*

There was, however, a Deep Background context: Despite signs of regression, the Movement was Moving, Spiraling farther and farther. More and more women were "coming to consciousness," that is, waking up and awakening each other from the patriarchal state of sleeping death. Moreover, there was a widespread eagerness—a profound Lust—for Leaping beyond the patriarchal constrictions of Mind/Spirit/E-motion that were still holding us back. Indeed, the Women's Movement was not dead. It had, to some extent, gone underground/undersea, but/and it was, as it now is, vibrant/alive with expectation and hope.

Despite erasure by the media and other patriarchal institutions, there was by 1975 a substantial body of feminist writings, as well as artwork, music, films, and organizations of all kinds. And despite the widespread purging of Radical Feminists from academia, Women's Studies existed and was expanding—and some few Radical Feminists did manage to survive on the Boundary

* Periodically throughout the 1980s and into the 1990s, the media masters have continued to hum the same boring refrain, for example in *Time* and in *The New York Times*.

of academia and of Women's Studies itself. In addition there was a large women's Network, which was rapidly becoming international/global. This had not yet settled down too comfortably into "women's communities," nor had the massively passivizing effects of the therapeutic establishment or of New Age style "Goddess Spirituality" blunted the Radical Impulse.*

The dream of a "Feminist University," too, was alive and well among women in 1975. A manifestation of this was Sagaris, a feminist summer school held in Lyndonville, Vermont (at which I taught courses during the first session). In many ways, no doubt, this experiment "failed," but even as a flawed incarnation of the dream, it created a Memory of the Future—a hope that Something Else could be.

In 1975 also my Lesbian Life-Time took on a New dimension. Complex and tumultuous from the start, my experience of ecstatic connectedness at this Time made it possible for me to Spin *Gyn/Ecology* so that it flourished in ways that previous books had not. No doubt, had there not been such a Be-Dazzling connection I would have written a book during that time, but it would, I am sure, have been less alive and daring than *Gyn/Ecology* became, as it Unfolded into its own shape of be-ing. It was in the rich, ecstatic, powerful Aura (O-Zone) of my connectedness with Denise that my writing flowed and sparkled, deep into the Hag-Time of night and early morning. In the Time before sunrise the landscape/seascape/skyscape of this book opened up to me, as I was Heard into the right words by the Sparking and Spinning of that Boon Companion who arrived in Tidal Time.

Doorway after doorway of my imagination was flung open as I raced through the labyrinthine passages of my own mind, Facing and Naming the myths and actual atrocities of Goddess-murder all over this planet and their interconnectedness—and A-mazing the masters' mazes in order to Dis-cover and Celebrate Gynocentric Ecstasy.

* Nor has the Radical Impulse yet been defeated. Many Furies and Harpies are committed to the task of fanning its flames so that ever greater combustions/conflagrations will continue to Self-ignite.

THE SPINNING AND WEAVING OF THIS WORK

As I began the researching, that is, Searching, for this Work in the summer of 1975, the process involved reading and taking notes on all sorts of materials on plain eight-by-eleven-inch white pads and filing them in manila folders according to topic. It was clear very near the beginning of this undertaking that the basic theme of the book would be the Soul Drama, or Otherworld Journey, involving encounters with demons who are personifications of the deadly sins and who block gateway after gateway of the Journey. The difference between the classical patriarchal description of the "otherworld journey" and mine is fairly simple: In *Gyn/Ecology* the demons that block the Ways of Voyaging Spinsters are manifestations/incarnations of patriarchy itself.* As A-mazing Amazons with our Labryses we cut them down and move deeper and deeper into the Otherworld, which—since we *are* Other—is our Homeland.

My files of notes increased fantastically in magnitude and in multitude. Within a few weeks or a few months—I am not sure which—the actual writing began. It was quite near the beginning of this writing process when the Moment of the title of this book arrived. It popped into my mind, seemingly out of nowhere. The spelling was not immediately clear to me, even though the sound of the word was clear. It would be, I knew, either *Gyn-Ecology* or *Gyn/Ecology*. Within a short time it became clear that the slash, not the hyphen, was right. I really wanted to slash the male-controlled/woman-controlling "science" of gynecology. The slash was also visually extendable into a Labrys, and indeed this possibility was Realized on the cover of this book.

Eventually I had a footlocker brimful of folders and also had several chapters written. These were in the order of the Deadly Sins as I had Re-Named them, and the titles of the original chapters were as follows: Chapter One, "Flying Fetuses: Processions from Womb to Tomb"; Chapter Two, "The Games of the Fathers: Prostitution and the Younger Professions"; Chapter Three, "A Broom of One's Own: On Escaping from the State of Possession"; Chapter Four, "Aggression: The Reign of Ter-

* See pp. 30–31 of this book.

ror''; Chapter Five, ''Obsession: Broken Hearts, Purple Hearts, Sacred Hearts.''

By the time I had reached the middle of the original Chapter Five I realized that I had taken on an enormous task. I was only in the process of writing a first draft and had just begun work on the fifth of the eight Deadly Sins of the Fathers and I already had several hundred pages. Clearly this book would require a *long* time to write.

In May 1975 I had applied for a Rockefeller Foundation Humanities Grant, and in March 1976 I was awarded a very substantial grant from that foundation. Since I was on unpaid leave of absence from my teaching job at Boston College, this grant was literally a life-saver. It allowed me the time to write this lengthy work and to pay much-needed research assistants.

So *Gyn/Ecology* Unfolded and Unfolded. I began to contemplate the possibility that it might become a work of nine volumes. I do not say this as a joke or by way of exaggeration; it is indeed what I thought. Then I thought that there would be three volumes, of which *Gyn/Ecology* would be the first. I had a general idea that this book would deal chiefly with the first three Sins on my list of Deadly Sins of the Fathers, which are Processions, Professions, Possession (deception, pride, and avarice). I thought the second volume would be about the next two Sins, namely, Aggression and Obsession (anger and lust.)* The third volume, I then believed, would be about encounters with Assimilation, Elimination, and Fragmentation (patriarchal gluttony, envy, and sloth).† I did not yet realize that the writing of *Gyn/Ecology* itself would take three years.

As I began the rewriting of *Gyn/Ecology,* that is, the second draft, something, or rather, somethings, Strange started to happen. For one thing, the whole shape of the work Shifted radically. Indeed, the entire writing process became a Stunning experience

* These did become the core theme of *Pure Lust: Elemental Feminist Philosophy* (Boston: Beacon Press, 1984), which was published five and one half years after *Gyn/Ecology*.

† These are to some extent challenged in *Websters' First New Intergalactic Wickedary of the English Language,* Conjured in Cahoots with Jane Caputi (Boston: Beacon Press, 1987). They are really taken on in *Outercourse: The Be-Dazzling Voyage*.

of *Shape-shifting*. This word is, I think, accurately defined in the *Wickedary* as

> transcendent transformation of symbol-shapes, idea-shapes, relation-shapes, emotion-shapes, word-shapes, action-shapes; Moon-Wise Metamorphosis.*

Moreover, in the Shape-shifting process the writing became more and more condensed. Whole pages sometimes became one paragraph or perhaps one sentence. The Fire and Focus were intense, burning away what seemed to be unnecessary words, forcing me to create New Words.

Often the New Words arose as a result of chases through the dictionary, which involved the uncovering of etymologies, definitions, and synonyms, which in turn led to further word-hunts and Dis-coverings.†

Clearly, then, the chapters changed; the outline changed; I changed. I sometimes broke into incantations, chants, alliterative lyrics. As I wrote in the original Introduction to this book:

> At such moments the words themselves seem to have a life of their own. They seem to want to break the bonds of conventional usage, to break the silence imposed upon their own Backgrounds. They become palpable, powerful, and it seems that they are tired of allowing me to "use" *them* and cry out for a role reversal.‡

There was nothing contrived about this process. I did not sit down and think that this work required a "different style" and then attempt to create it. I simply risked leaping into the process of gynocentric writing, which meant that the work, in a real sense, created itself.

Part of the Peculiar phenomenon of the writing of this book was its Timing. My Muse or Muses invariably waited until evening to arrive and stayed around until I was more than ready to

* *Wickedary*, p. 96.

† A simple example is the Dis-covering of the fact that, according to *Webster's*, the word *fashion* is etymologically linked to *fascist*. This is indeed thought-provoking.

‡ See pp. 24–25 of this book.

collapse with fatigue. Since the inspiration tended to become stronger during the wee hours of night, I struggled and fought against the temptation to stop just when the Spinning was at its Beginning.

Although I was not in a "trance" when writing *Gyn/Ecology,* I was in a special mode of creative consciousness, which stemmed, in part, from a will to overcome all phallocratically imposed fears and *Move* on the Journey of Gynocentric Creation. The fears that haunted me were legion. I was worried, at first, that no one would publish such an Outlandish book, and then that even if it did find a publisher, it would receive only horrendous reviews or dead silence from the critics. I was haunted by the spectre of being considered "off the wall" because of its Outrageous style and ruthless unveiling of patriarchal myths and atrocities. I was afraid that noncomprehending editors would say the style was "gimmicky."* Of course, I was expecting the worst.†

However, I had a Network of friends, so it was not possible to imagine—for too long a period of time—that I was a cognitive minority of one. Moreover, after I had written some of the New material I experimented with presenting it in my public lectures at colleges around the country. The results were positive and en-Couraging, so I was spurred on to become an ever more Positively Revolting Hag. Indeed, the emergence of *Hag*-related words, as well as such Names as *Crone, Spinster, Harpy, Fury,* and other New Words, was an integral part of the writing process, and when I spoke these aloud to women I was committing Acts of Be-Speaking. I was speaking the words into be-ing. Nor was I alone in this process. Wild women Heard me into Be-Speaking, and together we were forging a Metalanguage that could break through the silence and the sounds of phallocratic babble.

* A couple of New York editors who had seen short sections of the manuscript did, in fact, write very negative comments to me, which, however, did not succeed in dis-Couraging me. The positive flow of my Muse was much stronger than their negativity.

† I could not then guess that *Gyn/Ecology* would be received so warmly and so widely immediately upon publication. Nor could I have guessed that this positive response would endure.

Somewhere on the Journey of writing *Gyn/Ecology,* especially when I was working far into the night, a sort of formula came to me, which could be called a *mantra,* or perhaps more accurately a Witch's Self-determining Spell. The words, as I Re-Call them, were: "No matter what happens to me afterward (or, as a consequence) I WILL write this book." The Spell carried me through the dark nights of my soul's Journey and onward into more Be-Dazzling adventures.

A comparable phenomenon had happened a few years before in the process of writing *Beyond God the Father*. Then the mantra/Spell had been simply: "I have to turn my soul around." What this meant, in part, was that I had to turn my soul away from what I called "beta," that is, the tedious, time-consuming, mind-consuming foreground junk that was pushing to pre-occupy me, such as worrying about schedules, paying bills, shopping, et cetera, ad nauseam. Often in the afternoons I could literally see beta trying to push itself through the door. Of course, on a deeper level, "turning my soul around" referred to an enormous break-through phenomenon.

When I came to the writing of *Gyn/Ecology* I still had to keep the everlasting attacks of beta at bay, of course. But I had by then already turned my soul around, that is, I had begun the Metapatriarchal Journey already during the Time of *Beyond God the Father*. Now the task was a more intensified turning. It was the task of Weaving connections in such ways that I was in fact Spinning the integrity of my own be-ing and knowing, experiencing vertigo, and moving into uncharted Realms.

This leads me to the important subject of the Intergalactic context of *Gyn/Ecology*.

THE INTERGALACTIC CONTEXT OF GYN/ECOLOGY

Re-membering my own Voyage as a Radical Feminist philosopher, I am intensely aware of the struggle to stay on my True Course, despite undermining by demons of distraction and fragmentation that have always attempted to pull me off course. These I gradually Dis-covered and learned to Name as agents and institutions of patriarchy, whose intent is to keep me—and indeed all living beings—within the stranglehold of the foreground, that is, fatherland. My True Course was and is Outercourse—moving beyond the imprisoning mental, physical, emotional, spiritual walls of the state of possession. Insofar as I am focused on Outercoursing, naturally I am surrounded and aided by the benevolent forces of the Background.

This Voyage could also be called *Innercourse,* since it involves delving deeply into the process of communication with the Self and with Others—a process that demands profound and complex Passion, Re-membering, Understanding. It could also be called *Countercourse,* since it requires Amazonian Acts of Courageous Battling. However, its primary/primal configuration is accurately Named *Outercourse,* for this is a Voyage of Spiraling Paths, Moving Out from the state of bondage. It is continual expansion of thinking, imagining, acting, be-ing.

I Now see the Spiraling Paths of my Outercoursing Voyage as made up of Moments which have Momentum, hurling me beyond foreground limitations. They are Acts of Leaping through portals into the Background. I think that whenever a woman Leaps in this way she brings others with her, by example, by inspiration. Her Courage is contagious. Hence Moments/Movements of Outercourse are Political/Metapolitical.

Like stars, Moments are born. They happen in the Twinkle of an Eye/I.* In my experience, one Moment leads to another. This is because it has consequences in the world and thus Moves me to take a Leap to the next Moment. My focus as a Voyager directs the interactions among the Moments.

As seen from my Present perspective, the Paths of my Voyage constitute four Spiral Galaxies. Where/When then does *Gyn/Ecology* appear in the previously uncharted Realms of this Voyage? To answer this question briefly, it emerged near the beginning of the Third Spiral Galaxy. To explain this, it is important to look at the larger Intergalactic context.

Like the spiral galaxies of the universe,† the galaxies of *Outercourse* are in perpetual motion. At a certain point in this

* Conversation with Jane Caputi, Newton Centre, Mass., June 1988.

† A *spiral galaxy* (of the universe) is defined as "a galaxy exhibiting a central nucleus or barred structure from which extend concentrations of matter forming curved arms giving the overall appearance of a gigantic pinwheel" (*Webster's*).

whirling progression, the Voyager is enabled to take an especially Momentous Qualitative Leap and thus begin a New Galaxy. Since the Focus and Momentum are from the same Source/Force, the New Galaxy Moves in harmony with the preceding one.

The First Spiral Galaxy of my Voyage, which began whenever I began and continued—in terms of foreground time—through 1970, consisted of Moments of Prophecy and Promise. That part of the Voyage involved overcoming foreground illusions about "the future" and Realizing the opening of my Background Future. This was the Galaxy in which *The Church and the Second Sex* was written.

The Second Spiral Galaxy swirled through the years 1971–1974. This consisted of Moments of Breakthrough and Re-Calling. It was the Time, especially, of Seeing into and through the foreground "past" into the Background Past—beyond the phallocratic myths and symbols. It was a Time of Naming the lies about women's history and Re-Calling our own Archaic Origins. This was the Galaxy of *Beyond God the Father* and of the writing of my "New Feminist Postchristian Introduction" to *The Church and the Second Sex*.

The Momentum of these Moments hurled me into the Third Spiral Galaxy, which consisted of Moments of Spinning Integrity. This Swirled from early 1975 into the late 1980s. *Gyn/Ecology*, which was completed in 1978, was my first Major work of this Time, and it was followed by *Pure Lust* and *Websters' First New Intergalactic Wickedary of the English Language*.

Moments of Spinning Integrity Moved me out of the foreground present into the Present. *Gyn/Ecology*, as participating in this Time of the Third Galaxy, incorporates also the Background Future and Past, for as my vision and be-ing in the Present changed/changes, the Past and Future also change.*

It is from the vantage point of the Fourth Spiral Galaxy, however, that I can Now look at *Gyn/Ecology* and understand it in

* For example, by the Time of *Gyn/Ecology* such words as *Postchristian* had become unimportant to me. Such a term had focused attention on where I had been rather than on where I now had arrived. It seemed that to keep stressing it would be comparable to a woman's dwelling on her divorce and identifying as a "divorcée" long after the event had occurred.

New ways. This is the Galaxy of Time Traveling. It is a Metagalaxy or Megagalaxy made of Moments of Momentous Re-membering. By Time Traveling I can retrace earlier Moments, as with a pen of light. The earlier Moments take on New significance and assume richer meanings as I revisit them in the Fourth Dimension. It is in this way that I Now See, Hear, Touch *Gyn/Ecology*. I know it, and I know it again, in an ever-widening Spiral of Re-membering.

GYN/ECOLOGY AS A WORK OF PIRACY

From my perspective of Momentous Re-membering I Now see *Gyn/Ecology* as a daring Piratic enterprise. Having been a Pirate for many years, I have Righteously Plundered treasures of knowledge that have been stolen and hidden from women, and I've struggled to Smuggle these back in such a way that they can be seen as distinct from their mindbinding trappings. After Voyaging for a while, I began (in the Second Galaxy) to Reclaim these treasures by Naming them in New ways, in order to render their liberating potential accessible to women. For example, many years ago, in *Beyond God the Father,* I plundered the christian idea of "the Second Coming" and transformed it to mean "the Second Coming of women." Since then, I have moved on to far more Daring and Disreputable Deeds.

In *Gyn/Ecology,* as in *Beyond God the Father,* I took on the massive symbol system of patriarchal religion. My tackling of these symbols in both books involved abstract analysis. I used my highly evolved Craft of philosophical and theological reasoning, arguing on the enemy's own turf. I also used theoretical analysis to confront patriarchal strategies, such as reversal, erasure, particularization, and universalization.

In *Gyn/Ecology* I went beyond the scope of *Beyond God the Father*. First, the analysis is not restricted to christianity but extends to the universality of patriarchal religion itself. Second, the synthesis of abstract reasoning and Metaphoric expression expands and intensifies as New Words proliferate. Moreover, since I had decided to "go the whole way" with Radical Feminism, the Way was wide open for A-mazing and Spinning, in other words, for exorcism and ecstasy. So my symbol smashing broke down barriers to creative thought, and my Focus became Fierce.

In *Gyn/Ecology,* then, I Plundered vast amounts of material from the patriarchal thieves. In the case of myths and language, I worked to Smuggle back to mySelf and other women meanings that have been hidden, buried, reversed, as well as New meanings. This involved the creation of more and more New words, New Images. For example, I retrieved the word and image *Argonaut,* which Rightly applies to/belongs to women.

I wrote to expose the atrocities perpetrated against women under patriarchy on a planetary scale and to show the profound connections among these Goddess-murdering atrocities. To this purpose I Dis-covered the Sado-Ritual Syndrome.*

As I Plundered and Smuggled back the information about worldwide atrocities, this required investigation of patriarchal resources. It was an agonizing process. I had to look at the horrible material—which often included photographs of the maimed women, especially in the cases of footbinding and genital mutilation—read it over and over again, write about it, rewrite early drafts about it, proofread it over and over. The horrors burned

* Since *Gyn/Ecology* was published, the agents of patriarchal evil have invaded women and nature with more and more virulent attacks. Their tentacles have grown and multiplied. I have found that the seven-point Sado-Ritual Syndrome (explained on pages 130–33 of this book and applied throughout the Second Passage) continues to work very well as a tool for analyzing the escalating horrors of the sadosociety and for showing the connections among them.

To list a few of these ''developments'': A ten-billion-dollar pornography industry has developed and continues to escalate; its images of the torture, murder, and dismemberment of women and girls are everywhere, ''inspiring'' more and more rapists and sex murderers to copy these images. Woman battering and incest are alarmingly widespread. The reality of these horrors has always existed under patriarchy, but in recent years there has been an increase not only of information about them but also of the ''practices'' themselves. There has been an upsurge of international trafficking in women. Women of color are the primary victims of this atrocity as well as all other crimes. The demand for child prostitutes is enormous, especially around military bases and as ''tourist attractions.'' The new reproductive technologies have developed at an alarming rate, taking on forms that reduce women to subhuman ''subjects'' of experimentation. The torture of animals in laboratories and in agribusiness beggars description. And the Life-killers continue to kill the earth and its inhabitants.

themselves into my brain; yet this knowing had to happen and be communicated.

As I uncovered the connections I began to Spin ever more Wildly, and my Journey became more ecstatic. I was Fired by the white heat of accumulating Rage, which hurled my Pirate vessel around and ahead to the Ecstatic be-ing of the Third Passage.

This brings me to the subject of my Craft as a Pirate, particularly as it applies to *Gyn/Ecology*.

MY PIRATE'S CRAFT

My Time Traveling adventures and my life as a Pirate have been possible because of my Craft. The word *craft* means, among other things, skill and cunning. Wild women sometimes refer to our strength, force, skills, and occupations as Witchcraft. My own particular Craft involves writing and the forging of philosophical theories.

Craft is etymologically related to the verb *crave*. As Voyager I have Spiraled and continue to Spiral with my Craft because I crave something, because I have a strong longing for something. That "something" is the free Unfolding and expansion of my be-ing. Propelled by Wonderlust, by Wanderlust, my Quest *is* the expansion and communication of my be-ing.

I have come to see that taking charge of my Craft has been one of my primary/primal tasks as a Pirate, for this is overcoming the "woman as vessel" motif that prevails in Stag-nation. As I explained this motif/theme in *Gyn/Ecology,* women under phallocratic rule are confined to the role of vessels/carriers, directed and controlled by men. Since that role is the basic base reversal of the very be-ing of Voyaging/Spiraling women, when we direct our own Crafts/Vessels we become reversers of that deadly reversal. In this process we become Crafty.

My reversing of patriarchal reversals in *Gyn/Ecology* involved/required functioning in what might be called "a subliminal mode." This way of thinking/writing probably would not have been possible for me if I had not spent years studying medieval theology and philosophy, and writing dissertations in these fields, at the University of Fribourg, Switzerland, the medieval city in which I lived and studied for seven years. For there I learned to think and write in a theological/philosophical language that could not say what I was trying to say. So in my dissertations I was writing in code without realizing that I was doing this.

Much later, when I was writing *Gyn/Ecology,* that experience of having been obliged to think subliminally was very useful. Having "caught on" in some deep way to the multileveled nature of discourse, I was enabled to reverse the process I had learned in Fribourg and decode patriarchal texts, thus exposing their hidden messages.

My writing of the dissertations strengthened my ability to go to the heart of a problem, to draw the logical conclusions, to articulate my arguments in a way that is inherently clear in itself—which is quite a different matter from being a good "debater" who merely argues to score points but does not seek the truth. Years later, when writing *Beyond God the Father* and especially *Gyn/Ecology* and *Pure Lust,* I could draw upon these skills and the confidence that came with them. This was very important for the process of these books because free creativity, the knowledge that overreaches itself, needs to be Fiercely Focused.

To put all of this in a somewhat oversimplified way, the increasing Powers of my Craft required first learning the rules extremely well in order to break them with precision.* So my training as a Thomist theologian and philosopher became my Labrys, enabling me to cut through the man-made illusions and to Dis-close the deceptive deadly devices that are used by the academics, media men, and other culture controllers of patriarchy—devices such as erasure and reversal. As I saw more and more through their deceptive strategies, my work became Wilder while I continued to draw upon my rigorously cultivated precision.

My Craft Spiraled on through the writing of *Gyn/Ecology,* breaking down barriers to Seeing connections and opening the

* It is important to stress that this study of medieval theology and philosophy was by no means the acquiring of a mere instrument of destruction. For me it has been a way of positively reclaiming what was deep and valuable in the tradition so that it could function as a viewer into the Background.

way for Dis-covering the Treasure Trove of symbols and myths that have been stolen and reversed by the patriarchal thieves.

When I broke through to the Dis-covering of these Treasures I was able to examine them, play with them. When I tore them free from their dead casings of patriarchal theological systems they sparkled and Sparked me to make up my own Metapatriarchal Metaphors. These Metaphors carried my Craft, so that I felt like a gull sailing with the Great Wind which kept calling and carrying me over the shining sea of mind/spirit space which I Now Name the Subliminal Sea. It is important to understand how the creation of *Gyn/Ecology* is related to this Subliminal Sea.

GYN/ECOLOGY AND THE SUBLIMINAL SEA

As a Crafty Pirate I have dared to sail the vast Realm of mindspace which is the Subliminal Sea. This contains deep Background knowledge, together with countless contaminants—the man-made subliminal and overt messages disseminated through the media and other channels for the purpose of mind manipulation.

Reflecting upon my travels in the First Spiral Galaxy I Re-Call the experience of be-ing pushed/directed by a Great Wind. Traveling in that early Time involved sailing the surface of the Subliminal Sea, Sensing its depths, while not being overtly conscious of the contents of those depths, at least not to a sustained degree. Occasionally I had conscious glimpses, and these were enough to keep me on Course. I could feel through my Craft the swishings and swirlings that rocked the boat, so to speak. Some of these, I think, were the result of E-motions and psychic sensations that smoulder in Undersea Volcanoes, just under the threshold of conscious awareness. These eruptions were my Moments of Prophecy and Promise.

In the Second Galaxy, the intensified Momentum of my Craft warmed the surrounding waters. Droplets of those Subliminal Sea waters rose into the air, forming a Mist containing vital subliminal information. So when my Craft entered this Mist I began to See/Hear consciously Messages from the Subliminal Depths. I crossed the Limen/Threshold into Moments of Breakthrough and Re-Calling. From my Present perspective (that of the Fourth Galaxy)

I can see that I was then beginning my work as Pirate of the Mist.

In the Third Spiral Galaxy, the Time of *Gyn/Ecology,* I continued sailing into the Mist, but now with the style and flair of an Argonaut. I began to See a New Light through the Mist. This occurred more and more as I became active in the practice of Spinning, in the arts of knotting and unknotting, and Realized the Vertigo of creation. The Light that I began to See and by means of which I could See I would Now call Be-Dazzling. That is, it has the power to eclipse the foreground world with the brilliance of Background Be-ing.

GYN/ECOLOGY AS A VERB

In the original Introduction to this book I wrote:

> Writing this book is participating in feminist process. This is problematic. For isn't a book by its definition a "thing," an objectification of thinking/imagining/speaking? Here is a book in my hands: fixed, solid. Perhaps—hopefully—its author no longer wholly agrees with it. It is, at least partially, her past. The dilemma of the living/verbing writer is real, but much of the problem resides in the way books are perceived. If they are perceived/used/idolized as Sacred Texts (like the bible or the writings of chairman Mao), then of course the idolators are caught on a wheel that turns but does not move.*

To put it another way, I have always seen *Gyn/Ecology* as part of a Movement, including my own Voyage, which has continued since that writing and continues, because I am not a noun, but a verb. When I set it free so it could *be* in the world, I did not see it as a work of perfection. For some women it could be an Awakening shock, for others a Source of information, or a springboard from which they might Leap into their own A-mazing Searches, Words, Metaphors.

Above all, I was acutely aware that I had not done or written everything. I had not written the Last Word. (Otherwise, how

* See p. 22.

could I ever write again?) Rather, I had set free this book, this bird, in the hope that its song would be Heard and that it would harmonize with the works of other women, whose melodies, of course, were coming from different Realms of the Background. I looked forward to the profusion of New Creation, which I believed could emerge from women of all races, cultures, classes—from women all over this planet, speaking/Be-Speaking out of our various and vital heritages. I thought of our rich and radiant Diversity.

And this has happened and is happening, because our Time has come. Particularly Moving to me, personally, is the work of women of Ireland, that Treasure Island which I recognize deeply as the wellspring of my Background, my ancestral home. Especially Gynergizing on a global scale is the New abundance of creation from women of color.

Explosions of Diversity do not happen without conflict, however. One of the responses to *Gyn/Ecology* was a personal letter from Audre Lorde, which was sent to me in May 1979. For deep and complex personal reasons I was unable to respond to this lengthy letter immediately. However, when Lorde came to Boston to give a poetry reading that summer, I made a point of attending it and spoke with her briefly. I told her that I would like to discuss her letter in person so that we would have an adequate opportunity to understand each other in dialogue, and I suggested places where we might meet for such a discussion. Our meeting did in fact take place at the Simone de Beauvoir Conference in New York on September 29, 1979. In the course of that hour-or-so-long meeting we discussed my book and her response. I explained my positions clearly, or so I thought. I pointed out, for example, in answer to Audre Lorde's objection that I failed to name Black goddesses, that *Gyn/Ecology* is not a compendium of goddesses. Rather, it focuses primarily on myths and symbols which were direct sources of christian myth. Apparently Lorde was not satisfied, although she did not indicate this at the time. She later published and republished slightly altered versions of her originally personal letter to me in *This Bridge Called My Back* and in *Sister Outsider* as an "Open Letter."

It continues to be my judgment that public response in kind would not be a fruitful direction. In my view, *Gyn/Ecology* is itself an "Open Book." I regret any pain that unintended omissions may have caused others, particularly women of color, as well as myself. The writing of *Gyn/Ecology* was for me an act of Biophilic Bonding with women of all races and classes, under all the varying oppressions of patriarchy. Clearly, women who have a sincere interest in understanding and discussing this book have an obligation to read not only the statements of critics but also the book itself, and to *think* about it.

GYN/ECOLOGY AND RAGE

Gyn/Ecology can be Seen/Heard as a Thunderbolt of Rage that I hurled into the world against the patriarchs who have never ceased to massacre women and our Sister the Earth. I wrote it in a Time of Great Rage, when women were Wildly Moving, Sinspired by their Creative Fury.

Rage is not a stage. It is transformative focusing Force that awakens transcendent E-motion. It is my broom, my Fire-breathing, winged mare. It is my spiraling staircase, leading me where I can find my own Kind, unbind my mind.

Rage, however, can be displaced. In reaction to the Absolutely Righteous Rage of women of color against racism, some women retreat into passivity, hostility, and guilt,* often displacing energy into targeting scapegoats. The latter can become de-energized, losing the ability to focus Rage. The winners in this game, of course, are the patriarchs themselves, who, by the way, invented it. Having embedded Self-hatred and horizontal violence into women, they leave us to our own devices for becoming distracted into destroying ourSelves rather than engaging in an honest and thoughtful battle against racism and woman hating.

So may this New Intergalactic Introduction be my clarion call to us all: That we refuse this destruction by refusing to be distracted any more from the Gynergizing Focus of our Rage. I think it is High Time that Gyn/Ecological Volcanic Rage be Dis-covered again and again.

* Conversation with Emily Culpepper, Newton Centre, Mass., May 1990.

GYN/ECOLOGY AND SPIRALING INTO THE NINETIES

The Impossible/Possible Dream of Radical Feminism has never died. It is true that for many, especially in the course of the decade of decadence we have just Survived, it seemed to fade. What happened, in fact, is that it receded, somewhat, into the depths of the Subliminal Sea. But Sister Pirates, who are also divers, have worked to retrieve it. Moreover, it is Surfacing again, seemingly of its own accord. I think that our Time is coming round again, as we enter the Nineties.

However, this re-surging of the Dream is no mere passive event, no spectator sport. It must be Realized. This is a Tremendous Challenge. I think that as Voyagers we now face the Challenge of entering the Age of Cronehood of Radical Feminism. It is probably the case that the so-called "first wave" of feminism, in the nineteenth century, did not surge into the Age of Cronehood, even though there lived individual Crones, such as Sojourner Truth and Matilda Joslyn Gage. For as a collective Movement, feminism became "stuck," and there was not the possibility then of fully seeing the multi-racial, multi-class, and indeed planetary dimensions of the Women's Movement. Nor was it possible to know that our Sister Earth is in mortal danger.

In the "second wave," although there has been a dreary expenditure of energy reinventing the wheel, we are moving toward understanding that a Qualitative Leap into Cronehood is necessary for Survival.

It is a desperate time, but desperation, too, can be a gift. Desperation combined with Furious Focus can hurl a significant New Cognitive Minority of women into the Age of Cronehood, the Time of Realizing the Fourth Dimension. While feminists have always been a minority under phallocratic rule, the New Cognitive Minority includes women who constitute a memory-bearing group—Crones who have "been around" and can Re-Call earlier Moments and who can *bear* the memories, learn from them, and open the way for change.

There is, of course, imminent danger of succumbing to psychic numbing. We could continue to drift as vessels driven by men in power. But we have the Power to Choose. We *can* seize the decade by taking charge of our Crafts. We *can* Move.

So I am hurling *Gyn/Ecology* out again. It is as it was, and as it is. I have Moved on and am Moving further on to the creation of Other books. I hope that in its richness, as well as in its incompleteness, *Gyn/Ecology* will continue to be a Labrys enabling women to learn from our mistakes and our successes, and cast our Lives as far as we can go, Now, in the Be-Dazzling Nineties.

APPENDIX TO NEW INTERGALACTIC INTRODUCTION

GYN/ECOLOGY IN THE LIVES OF WOMEN IN THE REAL WORLD

Bonnie Mann

I began using *Gyn/Ecology* in my work with battered women because it is a book that faces the big Questions,[1] Questions about life and what it means to live it as freely and furiously as any woman can. For battered women who escape, who risk everything for the chance to live, getting down to the reality of the big Questions is what can make the difference between living and living hell.

It started this way. A woman in her early fifties who had been battered for more than thirty years found the Courage to Leave.[2] It took months of fleeing and fighting. The court battle and custody battle were vicious. She won finally, the dust settled, he went on to the next woman, she went slowly mad. In and out of the state hospital for the first time in her life, she dropped forty pounds, slipped into a deeper despair than any she had known. One day after two hours of heavy, desperate conversation, she said to me, "Bonnie, the problem is I just don't know who I am."

I saw the chasm opening up in front of her; the first "earthquake"[3] is so often the hardest. I too was shaken. Who could a woman be after so many years of being made into no one? No longer his after having been his so utterly. Another woman, not battered half so long, had said, "He had done everything to me. He had killed a lot of me."[4] What if a woman meant to turn to herSelf finally but found only a holograph?[5] Had he

Bonnie Mann is a Radical Feminist philosopher and activist who worked in the battered women's movement in Northampton, Massachusetts, for five years. She is currently pursuing a doctorate at State University of New York at Stony Brook and is active in the antipornography movement.

killed too much of her? That woman who had raised children, stayed sane, practiced the particular strength of the survivor for years, turned to a deceptive play of light on a flat surface, behind which there was no one to be found.

"My world revolved around him," one woman said. "He was center but he made it that way. He was like center object. I had to constantly do everything for him. If it wasn't working his way, that's when the battering started." Sometimes a woman is so much destroyed that she must reach beyond the confines of her own life story in order to Re-member[6] who she is.

The clarity of one woman's insight—"I just don't know who I am"—forced me to stop and think: How to rise to this challenge and confront this deepest of Questions in a group for battered women? I had been told repeatedly by well-meaning feminists that these women weren't "ready" for a radical analysis, that radical feminist works like *Gyn/Ecology* were "elitist" or would "alientate" women. Many of the women who came to the group had not finished high school and would not be able to "relate" to such work. But this woman exposed, for me, the reversal:[7] The real problem was not whether battered women were ready for a radical analysis of male supremacy but whether those of us working in the Movement were ready for such radical Questions.

Mary Daly had written of "the wild questions" in *Gyn/Ecology:* "Males have posed the questions. . . . They have hidden the Questions. The task for feminists now is con-questioning, con-questing for the deep sources of the questions."[8] *Gyn/Ecology* had opened the passage to the "wild questions" for so many women, myself included. I began using it in the group for battered women as a way to open a passage to the Background,[9] to Dis-cover[10] the "threads of connectedness"[11] with which a woman might weave a new context in which to understand her life and live it. With the varied levels of formal education in the group, reading *Gyn/Ecology* together was impossible, but teaching it was not. Passages could be read aloud, central themes presented and discussed in the concrete terms provided by the common experience of battering. This was a way to confront, finally, "the confusion that is evoked in all women as a result of sensing simultaneously both the invincible reality of Female Process itself and its erasure/fragmentation."[12]

Any battered woman who is still alive is, at some level, in the Process of struggling for freedom. At the same time she experiences the trap of the everyday, a more or less constant bending to his will, the demanding details of daily necessity that make anything *not* confined to the context built around him seem illusory. Daly's insistence that we can and must Dis-cover new time and space, that there is something profoundly positive beyond what men have done to us, moves us to the edge of a radical Question like "Who am I?" Her work insists that this Question be asked not as therapeutic self-indulgence but as an existential leap into free space, where man is not center object. This leap involves a radical and concrete shifting of loyalties to women, and this space is political insofar as it is a space from which it is possible to wage persistent attacks on the political system of male supremacy, that is, to fight concretely for women's freedom.

In a free space like the space provided by a group for battered women, it is possible to cultivate the practices of remembering/Re-membering that are essential to our struggle. Seeing no way out, the battered woman must actively forget the reality of the violence in order to survive within the confines of the world the batterer creates with himself at the center. To continue to live in the world of women's everyday lives in patriarchy, she must continuously forget what she continuously learns about what that world means for her. Every battered woman's advocate knows the frustration of talking with a woman engaged in this process of forgetting. A particular beating shocks her into a moment of truth—she tells it in detail, she does not deny that he intended to hurt her, that every moment of the attack was meant. A few days later her memory has failed her—perhaps he did not mean to hurt her so badly, perhaps he really did stumble and push her into the wall inadvertently, perhaps he didn't know he might have killed her. Stepping out of the world that revolves around him requires remembering what he did, writing it all down while it is still fresh, rereading it (often in disbelief) a few days later when the "memory-censor" has already begun to block out the details.

Real Surviving, really "living beyond, above, through, around the perpetual witchcraze of patriarchy,"[13] requires an even more difficult act of Re-membering. A woman must become capable of telling the story of her life in a way that literally puts the pieces together, that discloses and creates meaning, that constructs the possibility of a real future in which she, and all women, will be free. This act must go far beyond a woman's own life story in the immediate sense. Here she is excavating the threads of connectedness that link her life to the lives of women already long dead and not yet born, to the lives of women tortured in other ways in other places, and to a deep and powerful sense of the possibility of her own and all women's freedom. Real Surviving is an "extremist action," taken "in a situation of extremity";[14] it is political conscientization[15] that gives us our past, and simultaneously our future.

A cultivated practice of making connections enables a woman to re-tell her life story with an acute awareness of the ways in which the man who was "center object" did not ultimately determine the meaning of her life. As one woman, Barbara, put it, "My former husband tried to take my life. From that day forward I felt different inside myself. It's almost like all women are weeping. It's really weird. It's a sense of connectedness. But there's something that changes, not just me but the universe. . . . It's the Background, it's something way deep."

When Daly introduced the distinction between foreground and Background in *Gyn/Ecology,* she introduced a way for women to understand their own experiences of fragmentation. Often battered women would say to me, "I haven't been myself in years" or "He doesn't want me to be me." The ordinary language expresses the ordinary experience, the ordinary breaking of the spirit, women's experience of the male supremacist demand for female Selflessness. The foreground/Background distinction sets this experience in context, so that women can "discern the pattern of the whole,"[16] see "the total context of deception."[17]

Speaking of her deep rage toward the man who beat her for nearly fifteen years, Sal said, "I know now that was my Background coming out but I would put the foreground over it again as soon as it came out; it was like hush up, shut up, you're only in deeper and I would put the foreground back on." Battered women engaged in the process of Re-membering themSelves know that the fathers' foreground fixes them in a certain state of paralysis:

> . . . if you really dig deep in your inner self you know you hated [the battering]. And when I was living in the situation, I lived in the foreground. I know it now. It was like, live with everyday basis—feeding the kids—and then deep down inside if now I stop and think about it I know I hated it . . . but foreground kept just playing more than Background. I never went in deep after it. It'll change (I would say in my mind) everything will work out. The kids are eating supper tonight, the kids are going to bed, everything's going smoothly . . . the Background came out but you pushed it back again.

The knowledge that she "hated the battering" is the knowledge that she resisted on some level; even though the foreground "kept playing more," the Background still came out, she was still more than what he did to her.[18]

This discovery means everything to a battered woman (to any woman in a male supremacist world). If there is more, more than what he made her (not) be, there is hope, and this hope moves to the center where the man is no longer "center object." The moments of hope, the "moments of be-ing"[19] she Re-members, bring her to the "eye of the cyclone,"[20] the "symbolic way of entry into the Otherworld,"[21] which is "a world other than patriarchy."[22] She enters a space that is Other because patriarchal norms, values, and violence are no longer expected or accepted as "just the way things are." The journey into the Otherworld involves finding our way back to reality,[23] and women's sense of reality *is* Otherworldly in male supremacist contexts.

The "Otherworld" is in fact much more this-worldly than the world he kept her in ever was. She suddenly experiences her feet on the ground. It is that precious sense of being treated as if one were real, finally. This experience is often initiated simply by being in the presence of other women. One woman described her first contact with feminists as "like friendship being born." Another woman put it this way: "I found out that all the things I went through are not in my head but they really occurred." It is a simple experience that has profound consequences—"Everything made you realize it's true, it's accurate. What you're saying, nobody thinks it's a farce. I mean, I could sit there and say Henry kicked me, Henry called me an asshole, and everybody believes you. They made you realize you weren't wrong. It was reality all the way." Reality-all-the-way is Dis-covered and created in a context of Sisterhood, a bond between women that "has at its core the affirmation of freedom."[24] This Sisterhood makes it possible for us to hear the Questions women are asking in a new way. The sense of reality it provides dis-spells the irreality of a world where man is center object.

Daly teaches that "the metapatriarchal journey begins with hearing the dissonant voices of the foreground and dis-spelling them."[25] I cannot begin to recall the number of battered women who reported literally hearing the batterer's voice in their heads telling them what to do. One woman who had been beaten for putting the handles of the silverware up instead of down in the dish drainer told of hearing the man's voice months after she had escaped. Every time she put the handles up in defiance, she heard him screaming at her and re-lived a moment of terror. Dis-spelling the voice of "that man in your head"[26] requires a deeper hearing, requires that we "hear new voices—our own voices."[27] *Gyn/Ecology* gives so many women the joy of hearing the first clear sounds from the Background.

Just inside the passageway to the Otherworld, the everyday world of male violence, of male supremacy, is exposed in sharp relief. For battered women unwinding the psychic winding sheets, such a "shift of the center of gravity"[28] is essential to expose the methodical reversals. A battered woman calls the police for help and she spends the night in jail. A battered woman goes to court to renew a restraining order and finds that the judge has rescinded the order that he refrain from abusing her and has issued a new order that she refrain from abusing him. A battered woman reports to the authorities that the batterer is abusing her children, and the authorities file a report blaming her for the abuse. The man who beats her says he doesn't, or that she likes it, or that he'll never do it again; in reality he does, she hates it, he'll do it as long as he can.

From the perspective of the Otherworld, an elsewhere where he is not center object, a battered woman sees the reversals as systematic. They *do* mean to drive her crazy. Hearing the sound of her own voice and other women's voices for perhaps the first time, she is moved to confront the actual scope of the deception that kept her in "her place." The normalization of patriarchal atrocities against women is seen as a central strategy of male supremacy. As Daly notes, "When everything is bizarre, nothing seems bizarre."[29] Or as Sal put it, "You always say, 'Oh, he was good tonight,' or this type of thing, or 'He behaved himself tonight,' when in reality he was an asshole but it was so much better than being beaten even though he sat there and screamed at you, called you names, demanded this, demanded that." Sal's insight is that the extreme violence serves to normalize an every-day level of abuse, to make it seem that "he was good tonight."

One of the most important discoveries for women in the battered women's group was that male supremacy also normalizes itself in much more subtle ways. Daly's term "noxious gas"[30] was a name for the hard to distinguish yet deadly degradations. Speaking of her efforts to establish an "equal" relationship with another man after having left the one who battered her, Cheryl described the persistent inequality of the relationship: "It's like smoke, it comes in under the door." This sort of noxious gas chokes a woman just as surely as more overt violence, though it is harder to name. *Gyn/Ecology* opened up the possibility for us to identify and name the most subtly treacherous aspects of the foreground "reality" in which battered women are trapped.

It became clearer to me as I continued to use *Gyn/Ecology* and other radical feminist works in groups for battered women that the source of the desperation in the desperate realization "I just don't know who I am" is "a silence that breaks us."[31] This deep silence is not the one that is broken over and over again in the now commonplace rituals of "breaking the silence." A mere public confession of victimization, or a public declaration of pain or anger, does little to break through to the unthinkable Questions. Breaking this silence requires that a woman confront the prospect of herSelf without any man or male ideology as center object. It requires confronting the prospect of women's freedom and setting ourselves to the task of bringing it into the world. Breaking through to the wild Questions is "an extreme act, a sequence of extreme acts."[32]

I turned to *Gyn/Ecology* as a sourcebook in my work with battered women because battered women turned to me with wild Questions, Questions that could be answered only as *Gyn/Ecology* was written, out of the "lived experience of be-ing."[33] In such a context a book can never become the focus "as a thing, a noun"; if it does not "spin as a verb"[34] it is useless. Barbara reported that her first response to hearing Daly's work read aloud was, "Oh my god! I'm a radical feminist!" She continued:

I used to—when I'd go in the bookstore and I'd see books about radical feminism—I'd have this fear. And I'm a great reader, but oh I wasn't going to read that! And I always had this great fear that, oh, they would just be angry books. I don't know, I would have this awful fear. And then when Bonnie was reading stuff from *Gyn/Ecology* I thought, "God, why have I been so afraid of those books," . . . and if anything there's a connectedness. That really did help me, that *really* helped me because up until that point I felt like no other woman thought this way, that I was terribly radical and alone.

The reaction of many women to the material presented from *Gyn/Ecology* was, "Why didn't we know this?" "How could this knowledge have been kept from us for so long?" There is another side to these Questions of course, and that is: "We know it now because some woman took it upon herself to write." A deep sense that a gift had been given, a deep sense of the responsibility one bears to receive such a gift well, emerged among us one day as we grappled with the outrage of not having known. As Sal explained it:

She actually showed you man's opinions and you could see right through it and she would put it right down. Everything Bonnie read out of Mary Daly about the abuse, it all compares to the same thing you're probably thinking except it's being expressed in a book. You can really relate to the book. It's not like picking up a book and it's all how many numbers, how many people have been beaten, how many this, it's down to reality and that's what I really enjoyed about it.

Getting down to reality is the mark of any great feminist book. This is how a book like *Gyn/Ecology* goes beyond itself, moves among women in ways its author may not have imagined, exceeds whatever its particular limitations might be as a work in feminist theory (and all great books have such limitations). The crucial point in this context is not whether a book is "scholarly," or whether it fits nicely into the confines of stylistic norms, or even whether one "agrees" with it entirely. All of these fade to the level of pseudo-questions and pseudo-concerns in the face of the way such a book gives women new access to the world, gets down to the reality of women's lives, and opens passage to a new time and space.

When a woman tells her life story, the vantage point from which she is able to tell it, to understand and explain what she did, and the depth at which other women are able to hear it, to hear the meaning of her actions, determine ultimately the meaning of her life. A book has a similar sort of life story. The meaning of radical feminist theory, in one woman's words, is this:

> It makes you feel like you're not the only one. It makes you feel stronger that you're not the only one, and want to do something about it. I mean, we sit there in group and we're like, "What can we do?" "What can we do?" You know, how can we stop it? Even though there's only a few of us, it's like everybody's got the willpower that we want to do something. . . . [It] brings us back to reality that something has to be done.

When a woman gets down to reality she is "coming into knowledge of her anger, which means getting ready for action."[35]

The reality that something has to be done, that we have to do it, emerges as the specific historical context in which works like *Gyn/Ecology* are received well or not. What matters most is how deeply we hear the wild Questions, the Questions women are asking. "We can spin only what we hear, because we hear, and as well as we hear."[36] Ultimately the meaning of radical feminist theory is only what we *do,* how we shape the context in which it comes to life, how we carry the quest for women's freedom into the world.

NOTES

1. See Mary Daly, *Gyn/Ecology: The Metaethics of Radical Feminism* (Boston: Beacon Press, 1978), p. xv.
2. For an in-depth treatment of what such Courage means for women, see Mary Daly, *Pure Lust: Elemental Feminist Philosophy* (Boston: Beacon Press, 1984), pp. 280–85.
3. See Daly, *Gyn/Ecology,* pp. 409–13.

4. All direct quotations are taken from interviews with women who attended the Necessities/Necesidades group for battered women, Spring 1985. Interviews were conducted and transcribed by Kathy Miriam, a Sister radical lesbian feminist whose encouragement, extraordinary intelligence, and commitment were key elements in the development of the group itself and this essay.
5. Daly, *Gyn/Ecology*, pp. 50, 56.
6. See Mary Daly, *Websters' First New Intergalactic Wickedary of the English Language* (Boston: Beacon Press, 1987), pp. 92–93.
7. As Daly notes, reversal is a "fundamental mechanism employed in the world-construction and world-maintenance of patriarchy," so fundamental in fact that it is literally everywhere. See *Wickedary*, p. 93, for a complete definition.
8. Daly, *Gyn/Ecology*, p. 345.
9. Ibid., p. 3.
10. Ibid., p. xiii.
11. Ibid., p. 389–92.
12. Ibid., p. 322.
13. Daly, *Wickedary*, p. 96.
14. Daly, *Gyn/Ecology*, p. 17.
15. My use of *conscientization* is taken from the work of Brazilian pedagogist Paulo Freire, particularly *Pedagogy of the Oppressed* (New York: Continuum, 1970). *Conscientization* names the process of coming to consciousness of oneself as a member of an oppressed class and as a potential actor in history.
16. Daly, *Gyn/Ecology*, p. 19.
17. Ibid., p. 20.
18. D. Workman, "Beyond Victimism," unpublished paper, 1985.
19. Daly, *Wickedary*, p. 146.
20. Daly, *Gyn/Ecology*, p. 392.
21. Ibid., p. 402.
22. Ibid., p. 1.
23. Ibid., p. 4.
24. Ibid., p. 369.
25. Ibid., p. 405.
26. Kathy Fire, "Crazy," Folkways Records, 1978.
27. Daly, *Gyn/Ecology*, p. 405.
28. Ibid., p. 390.
29. Ibid., p. 17.
30. Ibid., pp. 3, 29.
31. Ibid., p. 22.
32. Ibid., p. 21.
33. Ibid., p. 23.
34. Ibid.
35. Ibid., p. 337.
36. Ibid., p. 424.

PREFACE

This book voyages beyond *Beyond God the Father.*[1] It is not that I basically disagree with the ideas expressed there. I am still its author, and thus the situation is not comparable to that of *The Church and the Second Sex,* whose (1968) author I regard as a reformist foresister, and whose work I respectfully refute in the New Feminist Postchristian Introduction to the 1975 edition.[2]

Going beyond *Beyond God the Father* involves two things. First, there is the fact that be-ing continues. Be-ing at home on the road means continuing to Journey. This book continues to Spin on, in other directions/dimensions. It focuses beyond christianity in Other ways. Second, there is some old semantic baggage to be discarded so that Journeyers will be unencumbered by malfunctioning (male-functioning) equipment. There are some words which appeared to be adequate in the early seventies, which feminists later discovered to be false words. Three such words in *Beyond God the Father* which I cannot use again are *God, androgyny,* and *homosexuality.* There is no way to remove male/masculine imagery from *God.* Thus, when writing/speaking "anthropomorphically" of ultimate reality, of the divine spark of be-ing, I now choose to write/speak gynomorphically. I do so because *God* represents the necrophilia of patriarchy, whereas *Goddess* affirms the life-loving be-ing of women and nature. The second semantic abomination, *androgyny,* is a confusing term which I sometimes used in attempting to describe integrity of be-ing. The word is misbegotten—conveying something like "John Travolta and Farrah Fawcett-Majors scotch-taped together"—as I have reiterated in public recantations. The third treacherous term, *homosexuality,* reductionistically "includes," that is, excludes, gynocentric be-ing/Lesbianism.

Simply rejecting these terms and replacing them with others is not what this book is about, however. The temptation/trap of mere labeling stops us from Spinning. Thus Goddess images are truthful and encouraging, but reified/objectified images of "The Goddess" can be mere substitutes for "God," failing to convey that Be-ing is a Verb, and that She is many verbs. Again, using a term such as *woman-identified* rather than *androgynous* is an immeasurable qualitative leap, but Spinning Voyagers cannot rest with one word, for it, too, can assume a kind of paralysis if it is not accompanied by sister words/verbs.

The words *gynocentric be-ing* and *Lesbian* imply separation. This *is* what this book is about, but not in a simple way. In *Beyond God the Father* I wrote:

> For those who are . . . threatened, the presence of women to each other is experienced as an absence. Such women are no longer empty receptacles to be used as "the Other," and are no longer internalizing the projections that cut off the flow of being. Men who need such projection screens experience the power of absence of such "objects" and are thrown into the situation of perceiving nothingness. . . .
>
> In this way, then, women's confrontation with the experience of nothingness invites men to confront it also.[3]

The primary intent of women who choose to be present to each other, however, is not an invitation to men. It is an invitation to our Selves. The Spinsters, Lesbians, Hags, Harpies, Crones, Furies who are the Voyagers of *Gyn/Ecology* know that we choose to accept this invitation for our Selves. This, our Self-acceptance, is in no way contingent upon male approval. Nor is it stopped by (realistic) fear of brutal acts of revenge. As Marilyn Frye has written:

> Male parasitism means that males *must* have access to women; it is the Patriarchal Imperative. But feminist no-saying is more than a substantial removal (re-direction, re-allocation) of goods and services because access is one of the faces of power. Female denial of male access to females substantially cuts off a flow of benefits, but it has also the form and full portent of assumption of power.[4]

The no-saying to which Frye refers is a consequence of female yes-saying to our Selves. Since women have a variety of strengths and since we have all been damaged in a variety of ways, our yes-saying assumes different forms and *is* in different degrees. In some cases it is clear and intense; in other instances it is sporadic, diffused, fragmented. Since Female-identified yes-saying is complex participation in be-ing, since it is a Journey, a process, there is no simple and adequate way to divide the Female World into two camps: those who say "yes" to women and those who do not.

The Journey of this book, therefore, is (to borrow an expression from the journal *Sinister Wisdom*) "for the Lesbian Imagination in All Women." [5] It is for the Hag/Crone/Spinster in every *living* woman.[6] It is for each individual Journeyer to decide/expand the scope of this imagination within her. It is she, and she alone, who can determine how far, and in what way, she will/can travel. She, and she alone, can dis-cover the mystery of her own history, and find how it is interwoven with the lives of other women.

Yes-saying by the Female Self and her Sisters involves intense work—playful cerebration. The Amazon Voyager can be anti-academic. Only at her greatest peril can she be anti-intellectual. Thus this book/Voyage can rightly be called anti-academic because it celebrates cerebral Spinning. If this book/Voyage could be placed neatly in a "field" it would not be this book. I have considered naming its "field" Un-theology or Un-philosophy. Certainly, in the house of mirrors which is the universe/university of reversals, it can be called Un-ethical.

Since Gyn/Ecology is the Un-field/Ourfield/Outfield of Journeyers, rather than a game in an "in" field, the pedantic can be expected to perceive it as "unscholarly." Since it *confronts* old molds/models of question-asking by being itself an Other way of thinking/speaking, it will be invisible to those who fetishize old questions—who drone that it does not "deal with" *their* questions.

Since Gyn/Ecology Spins around, past, and through the established fields, opening the coffers/coffins in which "knowledge" has been stored, re-stored, re-covered, its meaning will be hidden from the Grave Keepers of tradition. Since it seeks out the *threads of connectedness* within artificially separated/

segmented reality, striving "to put the severed parts together," [7] specious specialists will decry its "negativity" and "failure to present the whole picture." Since it Spins among fields, leaping over the walls that separate the halls in which academics have incarcerated the "bodies of knowledge," it will be accused of "lumping things together."

In fact, *Gyn/Ecology* does not belong to any of their de-partments. It departs from their de-partments. It is the Department/Departure of Spinning. Since the Custodians of academic cemeteries are unable to see or hear Spinning, they will attempt either to box it out or to box it in to some pre-existing field, such as basket weaving.[8] Cemetery librarians will file and catalogue it under *gynecology* or *female disorders.* None of this matters much, however, for it is of the nature of the Departure of Spinning that it gets around. Moreover, it is of the nature of Women's Movement that we are on the move. Eventually we find each other's messages that have been deposited in the way stations scattered in the wilderness.

The cerebral Spinner can criticize patriarchal myth and scholarship because she knows it well. Her criticism has nothing to do with "jumping over" tough discipline of the mind. The A-mazing Amazon has no patience with downward mobility of the mind and imagination. She demands great effort of herself and of her sisters.* For she must not only know the works of The Masters; she must go much further. She must see through them and make them transparent to other Voyagers as well.[9] To borrow an expression from Virginia Woolf, she must take a "vow of derision":

By derision—a bad word, but once again the English language is much in need of new words—is meant that you must refuse all

* WARNING: This book contains Big Words, even Bigger than *Beyond God the Father,* for it is written for big, strong women, out of respect for strength. Moreover, I've made some of them up. Therefore, it may be a stumbling block both to those who choose downward mobility of the mind and therefore hate Big Words, and to those who choose upward mobility and therefore hate New/Old Words, that is, Old words that become New when their ancient ("obsolete") gynocentric meanings are unearthed. Hopefully, it will be a useful pathfinder for the *multiply mobile:* the movers, the weavers, the Spinners.

methods of advertising merit, and hold that ridicule, obscurity and censure are preferable, for psychological reasons, to fame and praise.[10]

Who and where are "the deriders"? The reader/Journeyer of this book will note that it is not addressed only to those who now call themselves members of "the women's community." Many women who so name themselves are Journeyers, but it is also possible that some are not. It seems to me that the change in nomenclature which gradually took place in the early seventies, by which *the women's movement* was transformed into *the women's community,* was a symptom of settling for too little, of settling *down,* of being too comfortable. I must ask, first, just *who* are "the women"? Second, what about *movement?* This entire book is asking the question of movement, of Spinning. It is an invitation to the Wild Witch in all women who long to spin. This book is a declaration that it is time to stop putting answers before the Questions. It is a declaration/Manifesto that in our chronology (Crone-ology) it is time to get moving again. It is a call of the wild to the wild, calling Hags/Spinsters to spin/be beyond the parochial bondings/bindings of any comfortable "community." It is a call to women who have never named themselves Wild before, and a challenge to those who have been in struggle for a long time and who have retreated for awhile.

As Survivors know, the media-created Lie that *the women's movement* "died" has hidden the fact from many of our sisters that Spinners/Spinsters have been spinning works of genesis and demise in our concealed workshops. Feminists have been creating a rich culture, creating new forms of writing, singing, celebrating, cerebrating, searching. We have been developing new strategies and tactics for organizing—for economic, physical, and psychological survival. To do this, we have had to go deep inside our Selves. We have noted with grief that meanwhile another phenomenon has appeared in the foreground of male-controlled society: pseudo-feminism has been actively promoted by the patriarchs. The real rebels/renegades have been driven away from positions of patriarchally defined power, replaced by reformist and roboticized tokens.

This book can be heard as a Requiem for *that* "women's movement," which is male-designed, male-orchestrated, male-legitimated, male-assimilated.[11] It is also a call to those who have been unwittingly tokenized, to tear off their mindbindings and join in the Journey. It is, hopefully, an alarm clock for those former Journeyers who have merged with "the human (men's) community," but who can still feel nostalgia for the present/future of their own be-ing.

ACKNOWLEDGMENTS

The task of writing "acknowledgments" becomes increasingly perplexing and ridiculous. There is no way that I can adequately name or measure the contributions of other Hags, Sisters, Spinsters, Crones, to the creation of this book. In the preface to *Beyond God the Father* I discuss women's oral tradition and comment: "My references to conversations are meant to be a reminder of that tradition, as well as an effort to set precedent for giving women some of the credit due to them, finally." This whole thing has gotten out of hand, however, for five years have passed since then, and there are many more women from whom I have received encouragement and gynergy through their written communications, their conversations, their sustaining power of presence. The creation of this book has occurred in the context of a Network of Spinsters hearing forth each other to new speech. It is impossible to express all my debts.

Jan Raymond has generously shared her valuable class lectures and materials and given indispensable criticisms of the manuscript. Her work has been so intertwined with my own for so long that it has often been impossible to tell whose ideas are whose. Michelle Cliff has been a witty sharer of ideas as well as an excellent copy editor. Charlotte Cecil Raymond has been such an understanding, helpful, and gracious editor that I hereby unchristen her with the honorable epithet: "Hag."

Denise Connors has been a Spinner of ideas woven into this book from its beginning. Conversations with her have sparked new visions, and these, together with the countless books and journals which "jumped off the shelf" into her hands and onto my desk deeply affected the course of the Journey. Pat McMahon has been a truly Haggard helper, contributing beyond the bounds of justice. Jennie Cushman provided assistance when it was badly needed. Helen Gray has been a staunch and supportive sister. Pat Green has been a true friend, whose differing perceptions are a reminder that the women's movement is not monolithic.

Emily Culpepper has shared experiences of earthquakes and discoveries of new horizons as our paths have met on the Spinning Journey. To say that her criticisms have been invaluable is an understatement. Jane Caputi has been an extraordinary helper with daring and unique ideas and a gift for finding books and articles no one else would have dreamed existed. Peggy Holland has been an inspired Searcher, always providing original suggestions, including the idea for the labrys and dolphins on the jacket of this book. Eileen Barrett has been a most helpful espionage agent, contributing information from the dark recesses of medical libraries. Susan Leigh Star provided important material and insights for the manuscript in its early stages.

Linda Barufaldi contributed inimitable Barufaldian comments and criticisms upon various drafts of the manuscript. Conversations with Andrée Collard have generated whole sets of ideas and images. Discussions with Fran Chelland have helped me to stay in touch with what has been sustaining to my spirit in the classic philosophical tradition.

Adrienne Rich has been ineffably encouraging and enspiriting. She has helped the process of this book in ways that I cannot begin to count. Through her own work and sharing of criticism she has given the inspiration which only such a boundary-breaking poet and warrior could provide in the course of our uncommon quest for "a common language." Nelle Morton has been a guiding spirit, reminding me always of the unutterable importance of images. She hears me forth to new speech, and because of her I can never forget that "in the beginning is the hearing."

The writing of this book required free time. The Rockefeller Foundation provided a Humanities Grant which not only enabled me to take an extensive leave of absence from teaching at Boston College, but also to do the necessary travel for this project and to provide salaries for secretarial and research (search) assistants. In particular, I thank two women at the Rockefeller Foundation, Sonia Teshu and Dr. D. Lydia Brontë, Associate Director of the Humanities Program, for their invaluable aid in connection with the complexities of grant procedures.

I wish to express my gratitude to the foresisters whose spirits inspired me to break the barriers of silence and of sound, and to keep on writing. Among these are Matilda Joslyn Gage, Virginia Woolf, and many whose names I do not know, many of whom were probably burned as witches.

Finally, in fairness, I thank my Self.

GYN/ECOLOGY

INTRODUCTION

THE METAPATRIARCHAL JOURNEY OF EXORCISM AND ECSTASY

> All mother goddesses spin and weave. . . . Everything that is comes out of them: They weave the world tapestry out of genesis and demise, "threads appearing and disappearing rhythmically."
>
> Helen Diner,
> *Mothers and Amazons*

This book is about the journey of women becoming, that is, radical feminism. The voyage is described and roughly charted here. I say "roughly" by way of understatement and pun. We do not know exactly what is on the Other Side until we arrive there—and the journey *is rough*. The charting done here is based on some knowledge from the past, upon present experience, and upon hopes for the future. These three sources are inseparable, intertwined. Radical feminist consciousness spirals in all directions, dis-covering the past, creating/dis-closing the present/future.

The radical be-ing of women is very much an Otherworld Journey. It is both discovery and creation of a world other than patriarchy. Patriarchy appears to be "everywhere." Even outer space and the future have been colonized. As a rule, even the more imaginative science-fiction writers (allegedly the most foretelling futurists) cannot/will not create a space and time in which women get far beyond the role of space stewardess. Nor does this colonization exist simply "outside" women's minds, securely fastened into institutions we can physically leave behind. Rather, it is also internalized, festering inside women's heads, even feminist heads.

The Journey, then, involves exorcism of the internalized Godfather in his various manifestations (his name is legion). It involves dangerous encounters with these demons. Within the christian tradition, particularly in medieval times, evil spirits have sometimes been associated with the "Seven Deadly Sins," both as personifications and as causes.[1] A standard listing of the Sins is the following: pride, avarice, anger, lust, gluttony, envy, and sloth.[2] The feminist voyage discloses that these have all been radically misnamed, that is, inadequately and perversely "understood." They are particularized expressions of the overall use of "evil" to victimize women. Our journey involves confrontations with the demonic manifestations of evil.

Why has it seemed "appropriate" in this culture that the plot of a popular book and film (*The Exorcist*) centers around a Jesuit who "exorcises" a girl who is "possessed"? Why is there no book or film about a woman who exorcises a Jesuit? [3] From a radical feminist perspective it is clear that "Father" is precisely the one who cannot exorcise, for he is allied with and identified with The Possessor. The fact that he is himself possessed should not be women's essential concern. It is a mistake to see men as pitiable victims or vessels to be "saved" through female self-sacrifice. However possessed males may be within patriarchy, it is *their* order; it is they who feed on women's stolen energy. It is a trap to imagine that women should "save" men from the dynamics of demonic possession; and to attempt this is to fall deeper into the pit of patriarchal possession. It is women ourselves who will have to expel the Father from ourselves, becoming our own exorcists.

Within a culture possessed by the myth of feminine evil, the naming, describing, and theorizing about good and evil has constituted a maze/haze of deception. The journey of women becoming is breaking through this maze—springing into free space, which is an a-mazing process.

Breaking through the Male Maze is both exorcism and ecstasy. It is spinning through and beyond the fathers' foreground which is the arena of games. This spinning involves encountering the demons who block the various thresholds as we move through gateway after gateway into the deepest chambers of our homeland, which is the Background of our Selves. As Denise Connors has pointed out, the Background is the realm of the wild reality of women's Selves. Objectification and alienation take place when we are locked into the male-centered, monodimensional foreground.[4] Thus the monitors of the foreground, the male myth-masters, fashion prominent and eminently forgettable images of women in their art, literature, and mass media—images intended to mold women for male purposes.

The Background into which feminist journeying spins is the wild realm of Hags and Crones. It is Hag-ocracy. The demons who attempt to block the gateways to the deep spaces of this realm often take ghostly/ghastly forms, comparable to noxious gases not noticeable by ordinary sense perception.[5] Each time we move into deeper space, these numbing ghostly gases work to paralyze us, to trap us, so that we will be unable to move further. Each time we succeed in overcoming their numbing effect, more dormant senses come alive. Our inner eyes open, our inner ears become unblocked. We are strengthened to move through the next gateway and the next. This movement inward/outward is be-ing. It is spinning cosmic tapestries. It is spinning and whirling into the Background.

The spinning process requires seeking out the sources of the ghostly gases that have seeped into the deep chambers of our minds. "The way back to reality is to destroy our perceptions of it," said Bergson. Yes, but these deceptive perceptions were/are implanted through language—the all-pervasive language of myth, conveyed overtly and subliminally through religion, "great art," literature, the dogmas of professionalism, the media, grammar. Indeed, deception is embedded in the very texture of the words we use, and here is where our exorcism can begin. Thus, for example, the word *spinster* is commonly used as a deprecating term, but it can only function this way when apprehended exclusively on a superficial (foreground) level. Its deep meaning, which has receded into the Background so far that we have to spin deeply in order to retrieve it, is clear and strong: "a woman whose occupation is to spin." There is no reason to limit the meaning of this rich and cosmic verb. A woman whose occupation is to spin participates in the whirling movement of creation. She who has chosen her Self, who defines her Self, by choice, neither in relation to children nor to men, who is Self-identified, is a Spinster, a whirling dervish, spinning in a new time/space. Another example is the term *glamour,* whose first definition as given in Merriam-Webster is "a magic spell." Originally it was believed that witches possessed the power of glamour, and according to the authors of the *Malleus Maleficarum,* witches by their glamour could cause the male "member" to disappear. In modern usage, this meaning has almost disappeared into the Background, and the power of the term is masked and suffocated by such foreground images as those associated with *Glamour* magazine.

Journeying is multidimensional. The various meanings and images conjured up by the word are not sharply distinguishable. We can think of mystical journeys, quests, adventurous travel, advancement in skills, in physical and intellectual prowess. So also the barriers are multiple and intertwined. These barriers are not mere immobile blocks, but are more like deceptive tongues that prevent us from hearing our Selves, as they babble incessantly in the Tower of Babel which is the erection of phallocracy.[6] The voices and the silences of Babel pierce all of our senses. They are the invasive extensions of the enemy of women's hearing, dreaming, creating. *Babel* is said to be derived from an Assyrian-Babylonian word meaning "gate of god." When women break through this multiple barrier composed of deceptions ejaculated by "god" we can begin to glimpse the true gateways to our depths, which are the Gates of the Goddess.

Spinsters can find our way back to reality by destroying the false perceptions of it inflicted upon us by the language and myths of Babel. We must learn to dis-spell the language of phallocracy, which keeps us under the spell of brokenness. This spell splits our perceptions of our Selves and of the cosmos, overtly and subliminally. Journeying into our Background will mean recognizing that both the "spirit" and the "matter" presented to us in the fathers' foreground are reifications, condensations. They are not really "opposites," for they have much in common: both are dead, inert. This is unmasked when we begin to see through patriarchal language. Thus, the Latin term *texere,* meaning to weave, is the origin and root both for *textile* and for *text*. It is important for women to note the irony in this split of meanings. For our process of cosmic weaving has been stunted and minimized to the level of the manufacture and maintenance of textiles. While there is nothing demeaning about this occupation in itself, the limitation of women to the realm of "distaff" has mutilated and condensed our Divine Right of creative weaving to the darning of socks. If we look at the term *text* in contrast to *textile,* we see that this represents the other side of the schizoid condensations of weaving/spinning. "Texts" are the kingdom of males; they are the realm of the reified word, of condensed spirit. In patriarchal tradition, sewing and spinning are for girls; books are for boys.

Small wonder that many women feel repugnance for the realm of the distaff, which has literally been the sweatshop and prison of female bodies and spirits. Small wonder that many women have seen the male kingdom of texts as an appealing escape from the tomb-town of textiles which has symbolized the confinement/reduction of female energy.* The kingdom of male-authored texts has appeared to be the ideal realm to be reached/entered, for we have been educated to forget that professional "knowledge" is our stolen process. As Andrée Collard remarked, in the society of cops and robbers, we learn to forget that the cops are the robbers, that they rob us of everything: our myths, our energy, our divinity, our Selves.[7]

Women's minds have been mutilated and muted to such a state that "Free Spirit" has been branded into them as a brand name for girdles and bras rather than as the name of our verb-ing, be-ing Selves. Such brand names brand women "Morons." Moronized, women believe that male-written texts (biblical, literary, medical, legal, scientific) are "true." Thus manipulated, women become eager for acceptance as docile tokens mouthing male texts, employing technology for male ends, accepting male fabrications as the true texture of reality. Patriarchy has stolen our cosmos and returned it in the form of *Cosmopolitan* magazine and cosmetics. They have made up

* We should not forget that countless women's lives have been consumed in the sweatshops of textile manufacturers and garment makers as well as in the everyday tedium of sewing, mending, laundering, and ironing.

our cosmos, our Selves. Spinning deeper into the Background is courageous sinning against the Sins of the Fathers. As our senses become more alive we can see/hear/feel how we have been tricked by their texts. We begin unweaving our winding sheets. The process of exorcism, of peeling off the layers of mindbindings and cosmetics, is movement past the patriarchally imposed sense of reality and identity. This demystification process, a-mazing The Lies, *is* ecstasy.

Journeying centerward is Self-centering movement in all directions. It erases implanted pseudodichotomies between the Self and "other" reality, while it unmasks the unreality of both "self" and "world" as these are portrayed, betrayed, in the language of the fathers' foreground. Adrienne Rich has written:

> In bringing the light of critical thinking to bear on her subject, in the very act of *becoming more conscious* of her situation in the world, a woman may feel herself coming deeper than ever into touch with her unconscious and with her body.[8]

Moving into the Background/Center is not navel-gazing. It is be-ing in the world. The foreground fathers offer dual decoys labeled "thought" and "action," which distract from the reality both of deep knowing and of external action. There is no authentic separation possible.

The Journey is itself participation in Paradise. This word, which is said to be from the Iranian *pairi* (meaning around) and *daēza* (meaning wall), is commonly used to conjure an image of a walled-in pleasure garden. Patriarchal Paradise, as projected in Western and Eastern religious mythology, is imaged as a place or a state in which the souls of the righteous after death enjoy eternal bliss, that is, heaven. Despite theological attempts to make this seem lively, the image is one of stagnation (in a stag-nation) as suggested in the expression, "the Afterlife." In contrast to this, the Paradise which is cosmic spinning is not containment within walls. Rather, it is movement that is not containable, weaving around and past walls, leaving them in the past. It moves into the Background which is the moving center of the Self, enabling the Self to act "outwardly" in the cosmos as she comes alive. This metapatriarchal movement is not Afterlife, but Living now, dis-covering Life.

A primary definition of *paradise* is "pleasure park." The walls of the Patriarchal Pleasure Park represent the condition of being perpetually parked, locked into the parking lot of the past. A basic meaning of *park* is a "game preserve." The fathers' foreground is precisely this: an arena where the wildness of nature and of women's Selves is domesticated, preserved. It is the place for the preservation of females who are the "fair game" of the fathers, that they may be served to these predatory Park Owners, and service them at their pleasure. Patriarchal Paradise is the arena of games, the place where the pleas of women are silenced, where the law is: Please the Patrons. Women who break through the imprisoning walls of the Playboys' Playground are entering the process which is our happening/happiness. This is Paradise beyond the boundaries of "paradise." Since our passage into this process requires making breaks in the walls, it means setting free the fair game, breaking the rules of the games, breaking the names of the games. Breaking through the foreground which is the Playboys' Playground means letting out the bunnies, the bitches, the beavers, the squirrels, the chicks, the pussycats, the cows, the nags, the foxy ladies, the old bats and biddies, so that they can at last begin naming themselves.

I have coined the term *metapatriarchal* to describe the journey, because the prefix *meta* has multiple meanings. It incorporates the idea of "postpatriarchal," for it means occurring later. It puts patriarchy in the past without denying that its walls/ruins and demons are still around. Since *meta* also means "situated behind," it suggests that the direction of the journey is into the Background. Another meaning of this prefix is "change in, transformation of." This, of course, suggests the transforming power of the journey. By this I do not mean that women's movement "reforms" patriarchy, but that it transforms our Selves. Since *meta* means "beyond, transcending," it contains a built-in corrective to reductive notions of mere reformism.

This metapatriarchal process of encountering the unknown involves also a continual conversion of the previously unknown into the familiar.[9] Since the "unknown" is stolen/hidden know-ing, frozen and stored by the Abominable Snowmen of Androcratic Academia, Spinsters must melt these masses of "knowledge" with the fire of Female Fury.

Amazon expeditions into the male-controlled "fields" are necessary in order to leave the fathers' caves and live in the sun. A crucial problem for us has been to learn how to re-possess righteously while avoiding being caught too long in the caves. In universities, and in all of the professions, the omnipresent poisonous gases gradually stifle women's minds and spirits. Those who carry out the necessary expeditions run the risk of shrinking into the mold of the mystified Athena, the twice-born, who forgets and denies her Mother and Sisters, because she has forgotten her original Self. "Re-born" from Zeus, she becomes Daddy's Girl, the mutant who serves the master's purposes. The token woman, who in reality is enchained, possessed, "knows" that she is free. She is a useful tool of the patriarchs, particularly against her sister Artemis, who knows better, respects her Self, bonds with her Sisters, and refuses to sell her freedom, her original birthright, for a mess of respectability.

A-mazing Amazons must be aware of the male methods of mystification. Elsewhere I have discussed four methods which are essential to the games of the fathers.[10] First, there is *erasure* of women. (The massacre of millions of women as witches is erased in patriarchal scholarship.) Second, there is *reversal.* (Adam gives birth to Eve, Zeus to Athena, in patriarchal myth.) Third, there is *false polarization.* (Male-defined "feminism" is set up against male-defined "sexism" in the patriarchal media.) Fourth, there is *divide and conquer.* (Token women are trained to kill off feminists in patriarchal professions.) As we move further on the metapatriarchal journey, we find deeper and deeper layers of these demonic patterns embedded in the culture, implanted in our souls. These constitute mindbindings comparable to the footbindings which mutilated millions of Chinese women for a thousand years. Stripping away layer after layer of these mindbinding societal/mental embeds is the a-mazing essential to the journey.

Spinsters are not only A-mazing Amazons cutting away layers of deceptions. Spinsters are also Survivors. We must survive, not merely in the sense of "living on," but in the sense of living beyond. Surviving (from the Latin *super* plus *vivere*) I take to mean living above, through, around the obstacles thrown in our paths. This is hardly the dead "living on" of possessed tokens. The process of Survivors is meta-living, be-ing.

THE TITLE OF THIS BOOK

The title of this book, *Gyn/Ecology*, says exactly what I mean it to say. "Ecology" is about the complex web of interrelationships between organisms and their environment. In her book, *Le Féminisme ou la mort*, Françoise d'Eaubonne coins the expression "eco-féminisme." [11] She maintains that the fate of the human species and of the planet is at stake, and that no male-led "revolution" will counteract the horrors of overpopulation and destruction of natural resources. I share this basic premise, but my approach and emphasis are different. Although I am concerned with all forms of pollution in phallotechnic society, this book is primarily concerned with the mind/spirit/body pollution inflicted through patriarchal myth and language on all levels. These levels range from styles of grammar to styles of glamour, from religious myth to dirty jokes, from theological hymns honoring the "Real Presence" of Christ to commercial cooing of Coca-Cola as "The Real Thing," from dogmatic doctrines about the "Divine Host" to doctored ingredient-labeling of Hostess Cupcakes, from subliminal ads to "sublime" art. Phallic myth and language generate, legitimate, and mask the material pollution that threatens to terminate all sentient life on this planet.

The title *Gyn/Ecology* is a way of wrenching back some wordpower. The fact that most gynecologists are males is in itself a colossal comment on "our" society. It is a symptom and example of male control over women and over language, and a clue to the extent of this control. Add to this the fact, noted by Adrienne Rich, of "a certain indifference and fatalism toward the diseases of women, which persists to this day in the male gynecological and surgical professions." [12] And add to this the fact that the self-appointed soul doctors, mind doctors, and body doctors who "specialize" in women are perpetrators of *iatrogenic disease.** That is, soul doctors (priests and gurus), mind doctors (psychiatrists, ad-men, and academics), and body doctors (physicians and fashion designers) are by professional code causes of disease in women and hostile to female well-being.† Gynecologists fixate upon what they do not have, upon what they themselves cannot do. For this reason they epitomize and symbolize the practitioners of other patriarchal -ologies, and they provide important clues to the demonic patterns common to the labor of all of these. In their frantic fixation upon what they lack (biophilic energy)*† and in their fanatic indifference to the destruction they wreak upon the Other—women and "Mother Nature"—the phallic -ologists coalesce. Their corporate merger is the Mystical Body of knowledge which is gynocidal gynecology.

Note that the *Oxford English Dictionary* defines *gynecology* as "that department of medical science which treats of the functions and diseases peculiar to women; also *loosely,* the science of womankind." I am using the term *Gyn/Ecology* very loosely, that is, freely, to describe the science, that is the process of know-ing, of "loose" women who choose to be subjects and not mere objects of enquiry. Gyn/Ecology is by and about women a-mazing all the male-authored "sciences of womankind," and weaving world tapestries *of our own kind.* That is, it is about dis-covering, de-veloping the complex web

* The technical term *iatrogenic,* used to describe the epidemic of doctor-made disease, is composed of the Greek words for physician (*iatros*) and for origins (*genesis*).

† Clearly, some women sometimes are helped through emergency situations by priests, ministers, gynecologists, therapists—but this is largely in spite of the institutions/professions within which they work. A great deal of the work of such exceptional professionals consists in repairing damages caused by their colleagues and by the methods of their professions. One serious liability associated with their ministrations is the conditioning of women to depend upon them rather than upon our own natural resources. It should not be necessary to repeat this distinction throughout this book, which criticizes patriarchal institutions and those who conform to them.

*† By *biophilic* I mean life-loving. This term is not in the dictionary, although the term *necrophilic* is there, and is commonly used.

of living/loving relationships *of our own kind*. It is about women living, loving, creating our Selves, our cosmos. It *is* dis-possessing our Selves, enspiriting our Selves, hearing the call of the wild, naming our wisdom, spinning and weaving world tapestries out of genesis and demise. In contrast to gyne-cology, which depends upon fixation and dismemberment, Gyn/Ecology affirms that everything is connected.

Since "o-logies" are generally static "bodies of knowledge," it might at first glance seem that the name *Gyn/Ecology* clashes with the theme of the Journey. However, a close analysis unveils the fact that this is not so. For women can recognize the powerful and multidimensional gynocentric symbolism of the "O." [13] It represents the power of our moving, encircling presence, which can make nonbeing sink back into itself. Our "O" is totally other than "nothing" (a fact demonically distorted and reversed in the pornographic novel, *The Story of O*). As Denise Connors has pointed out, it can be taken to represent our aura, our O-Zone.[14] Within this anti-pollutant, purifying, moving O-Zone, the aura of gynocentric consciousness, life-loving feminists have the power to affirm the basic Gyn/Ecological principle that everything is connected with everything else. It is this holistic process of knowing that can make Gyn/Ecology the O-logy of all the -ologies, encircling them, spinning around and through them, unmasking their emptiness. As the O-logy of all the -ologies, Gyn/Ecology can reduce their pretentious façades to Zero. It can free the flow of their "courses" and overcome their necrophilic circles, their self-enclosed processions, through spiraling creative process. It is women's own Gyn/Ecology that can break the brokenness of the "fields," deriding their borders and boundaries, changing the nouns of knowledge into verbs of know-ing.

THE SUBTITLE OF THIS BOOK

By the subtitle, *The Metaethics of Radical Feminism,* I intend to convey that this book is concerned with the Background, most specifically of language and myth, which is disguised by the fathers' foreground fixations. Merriam-Webster gives as one of the definitions of the prefix, *meta:* "of a higher logical type—in nouns formed from names of disciplines and designating new but related disciplines such as can deal critically with the nature, structure, or behavior of the original ones (*meta*language, *meta*theory, *meta*system)." Despite the dullness of dictionary diction, there are clues here. I would say that radical feminist metaethics is of a *deeper intuitive* type than "ethics." The latter, generally written from one of several (but basically the same) patriarchal perspectives, works out of hidden agendas concealed in the texture of language, buried in mythic reversals which control "logic" most powerfully because unacknowledged. Thus for theologians and philosophers, Eastern and Western, and particularly for ethicists, woman-identified women do not exist. The metaethics of radical feminism seeks to uncover the background of such logic, as women ourselves move into the Background of this background. In this sense, it can be called "of a higher [read: deeper] logical type." It is, of course, a new discipline that "deals critically" with the nature, structure, and behavior of ethics and ethicists. It is able to do this because our primary concern is *not* male ethics and/or ethicists, but our own Journeying.

This book has to do with the mysteries of good and evil. To name it a "feminist ethics" might be a clue, but it would also be misleading, pointing only to foreground problems. It would be something like arguing for "equal rights" in a society whose very existence depends upon inequality, that is, upon the possession of female energy by men. The spring into free space, which is woman-identified consciousness, involves a veritable mental/behavioral mutation. The phallocratic categorizations of "good" and "evil" no longer apply when women *honor* women, when we become honorable to ourselves.[15] As Barbara Starrett wrote, we are developing something like a new organ of the mind.[16] This development both causes and affects qualitative leaping through galaxies of mindspace. It involves a new faculty and process of valuation. None of the dreary ethical texts, from those of Aristotle down to Paul Ramsey and Joseph Fletcher, can speak to the infinitely expanding universe of what Emily Culpepper has named "gynergy." [17] Indeed, the texts of phallocratic ethicists function in the same manner as pornography, legitimating the institutions which degrade women's be-ing. Gyn/Ecological metaethics, in contrast to all of this, functions to affirm the deep dynamics of female be-ing. It is gynography.

There are, of course, male-authored, male-identified works which purport to deal with "metaethics." In relation to these, gynography is meta-metaethical. For while male metaethics claims to be "the study of ethical theories, as distinguished from the study of moral and ethical conduct itself," [18] it remains essentially male-authored and male-identified theory about theory. Moreover, it is only theory about "ethical theories" — an enterprise which promises boundless boringness. In contrast to this, Gyn/Ecology is hardly "metaethical" in the sense of masturbatory meditations by ethicists upon their own emissions. Rather, we recognize that the essential omission of these emissions is of our own life/freedom. In the name of our life/freedom, feminist metaethics O-mits seminal omissions.

In making this metapatriarchal leap into our own Background, feminists are hearing/naming the immortal Metis, Goddess of wisdom, who presided over all knowledge. In patriarchal myth she was swallowed by Zeus when she was pregnant with Athena. Zeus claimed that Metis counseled him from inside his belly. In any case, the Greeks began ascribing wisdom to this prototype of male cannibalism. We must remember that Metis was originally the parthenogenetic mother of Athena. After Athena was "reborn" from the head of Zeus, her single "parent," she became Zeus's obedient mouthpiece. She became totally male-identified, employing priests, not priestesses, urging men on in battle, siding against women consistently.[19] Radical feminist metaethics means moving past this puppet of Papa, dis-covering the immortal Metis. It also means dis-covering the parthenogenetic Daughter, the original Athena, whose loyalty is to her own kind, whose science/wisdom is of womankind. In this dis-covering there can be what Catherine Nicholson named "the third birth of Athena." [20] As this happens, Athena will shuck off her robothood, will re-turn to her real Source, to her Self, leaving the demented

Male Mother to play impotently with his malfunctioning machine, his dutiful dim-witted "Daughter," his broken Baby Doll gone berserk, his failed fembot. The metaethics of radical feminism means simply that while Zeus, Yahweh, and all the other divine male "Mothers" are trying to retrieve their dolls from the ashcan of patriarchal creation, women on our own Journey are dis-covering Metis and the third-born Athena: our own new be-ing. That is, we are be-ing in the Triple Goddess, who is, and is not yet.[21]

THE TRADITION OF THIS BOOK: HAG-OGRAPHY

Hagiography is a term employed by christians, and is defined as "the biography of saints; saints' lives; biography of an idealizing or idolizing character." Hagiology has a similar meaning; it is "a description of sacred writings or sacred persons." Both of these terms are from the Greek *hagios,* meaning holy.

Surviving, moving women can hardly look to the masochistic martyrs of sadospiritual religion as models. Since most patriarchal writing that purports to deal with women is pornography or hagiography (which amount to the same thing), women in a world from which woman-identified writing has been eliminated are trying to break away from these moldy "models," both of writing and of living. Our foresisters were the Great Hags whom the institutionally powerful but privately impotent patriarchs found too threatening for coexistence, and whom historians erase. *Hag* is from an Old English word meaning harpy, witch. Webster's gives as the first and "archaic" meaning of *hag:* "a female demon: FURY, HARPY." It also formerly meant: "an evil or frightening spirit." (Lest this sound too negative, we should ask the relevant questions: "Evil" by whose definition? "Frightening" to whom?) A third archaic definition of *hag* is "nightmare." * (The important

* *Nightmare* is said to be derived from the Middle English terms *night* plus *mare,* meaning spirit. The first definition given in Merriam-Webster is "an evil spirit formerly thought to oppress people during sleep." Another definition is "a hag sometimes believed to be accompanied by nine attendant spirits." For Hags this should be a friendly gathering.

question is: Whose nightmare?) *Hag* is also defined as "an ugly or evil-looking old woman." But this, considering the source, may be considered a compliment. For the beauty of strong, creative women is "ugly" by misogynistic standards of "beauty." The look of female-identified women is "evil" to those who fear us. As for "old," ageism is a feature of phallic society. For women who have transvaluated this, a Crone is one who should be an example of strength, courage and wisdom.

For women who are on the journey of radical be-ing, the lives of the witches, of the Great Hags of our hidden history are deeply intertwined with our own process. As we write/live our own story, we are uncovering their history, creating Hag-ography and Hag-ology. Unlike the "saints" of christianity, who must, by definition, be dead, Hags live. Women traveling into feminist time/space are creating Hag-ocracy, the place we govern. To govern is to steer, to pilot. We are learning individually and together to pilot the time/spaceships of our voyage. The vehicles of our voyage may be any creative enterprises that further women's process. The point is that they should be governed by the Witch within—the Hag within.

In living/writing Hag-ography it is important to recognize that those who live in the tradition of the Great Hags will become haggard. But this term, like so many others, must be understood in its radical sense. Although *haggard* is commonly used to describe one who has a worn or emaciated appearance, this was not its original or primary meaning. Applied to a hawk, it means "untamed." So-called obsolete meanings given in Merriam-Webster include "intractable," "willful," "wanton," and "unchaste." The second meaning is "wild in appearance: as a) *of the eyes:* wild and staring b) *of a person:* WILD-EYED." Only after these meanings do we find the idea of "a worn or emaciated appearance." As a noun, *haggard* has an "obsolete" meaning: "an intractable person, especially: a woman reluctant to yield to wooing."

Haggard writing is by and for haggard women, those who are intractable, willful, wanton, unchaste, and, especially, those who are reluctant to yield to wooing. It belongs to the tradition of those who refuse to assume the woes of wooed women, who cast off these woes as unworthy of Hags, of Harpies. Haggard women are not man-wooed. As Furies, women in the tradition of the Great Hags reject the curse of compromise.

The Great Hags of history, when their lives have not been prematurely terminated, have lived to be Crones. Crones are the long-lasting ones.* [22] They are the Survivors of the perpetual witchcraze of patriarchy, the Survivors of The Burning Times.† In living/writing, feminists are recording and creating the history of Crones. Women who can identify with the Great Crones may wish to call our writing of women's history Crone-ography.[23]

It is also appropriate to think of our writing in this tradition as Crone-ology. *Chronology,* generally speaking, means an arrangement (as of data, events) in order of time of occurrence or appearance. In a specific sense, however, it refers to "the classification of archeological sites or prehistoric periods of culture." Since the history of Hags and Crones is truly Prehistoric in relation to patriarchal history—being prior both in time and in importance—haggard women should consider that our Crone-ology is indeed our chronology. In writing/recording/creating Crone-ography and in studying our own Prehistoric chronology, we are unmasking deceptive patriarchal history, rendering it obsolete. Women who refuse to be wooed by patriarchal scholarship can conjure the chronicles of the Great Crones, foresisters of our present and future Selves. In Greek mythology, the crow is an oracular bird. Whether or not an etymological connection can be demonstrated, the association between Crones and oracular utterances is natural and obvious. As unwooed women unearth more of our tradition, we can begin to hear and understand

* The status of Crones is not determined merely by chronological age, but by Crone-logical considerations. A woman becomes a Crone as a result of Surviving early stages of the Otherworld Journey and therefore having dis-covered depths of courage, strength, and wisdom in her Self.

† *The Burning Times* is a Crone-logical term which refers not only to the period of the European witchcraze (the fifteenth, sixteenth, and seventeenth centuries) but to the perpetual witchcraze which is the entire period of patriarchal rule.

our own oracles, which have been caricatured as the "screeching" of "old crows."

Hag-ographers perceive the hilarious hypocrisy of "his" history. At first this may be difficult, for when the whole is hypocrisy, the parts may not initially appear untrue. To put it another way, when everything is bizarre, nothing seems bizarre. Hags are women who struggle to see connections. Hags risk a great deal—if necessary, everything—knowing that there is only Nothing to lose. Hags may rage and roar, but they do not titter.

Webster's defines *titter* as follows: "to give vent to laughter one is seeking to suppress: laugh lightly or in a subdued manner: laugh in a *nervous, affected, or restrained* manner, especially at a high pitch and with short catches of the voice [emphasis mine]." Self-loathing ladies titter; Hags and Harpies roar. Fembots titter at themselves when Daddy turns the switch. They totter when he pulls the string. They titter especially at the spinning of Spinsters, whom they have been trained to see as dizzy dames. Daddy's little Titterers try to intimidate women struggling for greatness. This is what they are made for and paid for. There is only one taboo for titterers: they must never laugh seriously at Father—only at his jokes.

There is nothing like the sound of women really laughing. The roaring laughter of women is like the roaring of the eternal sea. Hags can cackle and roar at themselves, but more and more, one hears them roaring at the reversal that is patriarchy, that monstrous jock's joke, the Male Mothers Club that gives birth only to putrefaction and deception. One can hear pain and perhaps cynicism in the laughter of Hags who witness the spectacle of Male Mothers (Murderers) dismembering a planet they have already condemned to death. But this laughter is the one true hope, for as long as it is audible there is evidence that someone is seeing through the Dirty Joke. It is in this hope that this Hag-ography is written.

THE SILENCING OF WOMEN AND SILENT SPRING

This is an extremist book, written in a situation of extremity, written on the edge of a culture that is killing itself and all of sentient life. The Tree of Life has been replaced by the necrophilic symbol of a dead body hanging on dead wood. The Godfather insatiably demands more sacrifices, and the fundamental sacrifices of sadospiritual religion are female.

The sacrificing of women requires the silencing of women, which takes place in myriad ways, in a maze of ways. A basic pattern of these ways is Self-splitting, which is initiated by the patriarchally powerful and which the victims internalize and continue to practice within the caste of women. Women are silenced/split by the babble of grammatical usage. Subliminal and subtle Self-splitting is achieved by the very pronouns we are trained to use to designate our Selves. Julia Stanley and Susan Robbins have written of the peculiar history of the pronoun *she,* which was introduced into Middle English as a late development. During the Middle Ages, *he* had come to be both the female and the male pronoun. After *she* was introduced, it referred only to females, while *he* became "generic," allegedly including women. This transition in the history of the pronoun *he* was hardly insignificant:

> Since the female pronoun always designates females—while the male pronoun designates all humans as well as all males, patriarchal language, as manifested in the pronominal system of English, extended the scope of maleness to *include* humanity, while restricting femaleness to "the Other," who is by implication nonhuman. Any speaker internalizing such a language unconsciously internalizes the values underlying such a system, thus perpetuating the cultural and social assumptions necessary to maintain the patriarchal power structure.[24]

When women become aware of the manipulable ambiguity of the pronoun *he,* we have perceived only the foreground of grammatical silencing techniques. Just as it would be a mistake to fixate upon the pseudogeneric *man* and assume that terms such as *people* and *person* are "real" generics (a falsehood disclosed by such expressions as "people and their wives") so it is a mistake to fixate upon the third person singular. As Monique Wittig has shown, the pronoun *I* conceals the sexual identity of the speaker/writer. The *I* makes the speaker/writer deceptively feel at home in a male-controlled language. When she uses this pronoun, she may forget that *she* is buried in the false generic *he*. The fact is that the female saying "I" is alien at every moment to her own speaking and writing. She is broken by the fact that she must enter this language in order to speak or to write.[25] As the "I" is broken, so also is the Inner Eye, the capacity for integrity of knowing/sensing. In this way the Inner Voice of the Self's integrity is silenced; the external voice babbles in alien and alienating tongues. And when the Self tries to speak out of her true depths, the pedantic peddlers of "correct" usage and style try to drown it in their babble.

Women are silenced/split by the embedding of fears. These contrived and injected fears function in a manner analogous to electrodes implanted in the brain of a victim ("patient") who can be managed by remote control. This is a kind of "silent" control (as silent as the pushing of a button). Women may feel that they are free from certain fears ("liberated") and then bend to the unacknowledged power of these fears with mental knee-jerk responses. A brief analysis of responses to a few of these instilled fears should unmask the methods of "silent" control which silence the voices of women's deep Selves, while allowing the "liberated" false selves to babble freely.

For example, the cliché, "She lacks a sense of humor"—applied by men to every threatening woman—is one basic "electrode" embedded just deeply enough into the fearful foreground of women's psyches to be able to conduct female energy against the Self while remaining disguised. The comment is urbane, insidious. It is boring and predictable if seen through, devastating if believed. The problem is that the victim who "sees through" this dirty trick on one level may "believe" the judgment literally on more vulnerable levels. It is perfectly consistent with patriarchal patterns that this device is used especially against the wittiest women, who are dismissed as "sharp-tongued." The Godfather is the Father of Lies and favors the most blatant lies.

In the Land of the Fathers, the more blatant the lie the greater its credibility, for it is then most consistent with the general pattern of bizarre beliefs. Our ability to overcome the power of such particular fear-instilling lies depends upon our ability to discern the pattern of the whole. Gyn/Ecology requires a constant effort to see the innerconnectedness of things. It involves seeing the totality of the Lie which is patriarchy, unweaving its web of deception. Since the totality of the patriarchal Lie is *not* integrity, since it lacks the complexity of real integrity, it tends to fall apart quickly once we see its pattern, once we dare to face "the whole thing." Moreover, since it depends entirely upon the reality which it distorts and demonically reflects, our seeing through patriarchy is at the same time learning to see the Background, our stolen integrity/energy/be-ing.

Once we are attuned to the fact of instilled fears and of how they are used to keep women in line, we can detect the patterns over and over again. As we isolate each fear and examine it, we can see that our overcoming it depends upon seeing it in context: seeing through The Whole Thing. Consider, for example, the instilled fear of becoming like one's mother (matrophobia).[26] Repeatedly we find daughters who repudiate the particular kind of victimization they see in their mothers' lives, only to live and die out an apparently opposite but really only slightly variant form of the same dis-ease (for example, the life of a Cosmo Girl as opposed to that of a staid suburban housewife). Embedded fears of being labeled "sick," "selfish," or "sexless" all function in similar ways. If the victim does not see the pattern, she will react to the particulars by becoming mindlessly "normal," murderously "selfless," moronically "sexy." In these various ways, her Self is silenced.

Fear of the label "lesbian" has driven many into matrimony, mental hospitals, and—worst of all—numbing, dumbing normality. It has driven others into heterosexist "gay pride" protests promoted by and for men, into butch-femme matings modeled on matrimony, into aping the genital fixations of porn peddlers, pimps, priests. Lesbians/Spinsters/Amazons/Survivors can defeat the embedded fears only by acknowledging the total context of deception plotted by the male supremacist script-writers. Spinning, A-mazing, Surviving is coming out of the shadows into a fullness of light which reduces the "spotlights" of the fathers' fixations to invisibility/impotence. In her own light the Self sees/says her own light/insight. She sees through the lurid male masturbatory fantasies about made-up "lesbians" who make out in *Playboy* for men's amusement. The Self expels them, together with other embedded "seminal ideas." Images of the macho female prison guard, the "rejected" old maid, the bad mother, the "happy" bunny-bride, the Totaled Woman—all are interconnected implanted fears that can be silenced only when women dare to see the connections among them and to see/name our Selves.

Overcoming the silencing of women is an extreme act, a sequence of extreme acts. Breaking our silence means living in existential courage. It means dis-covering our deep sources, our spring. It means finding our native resiliency, springing into life, speech, action. Many years ago Rachel Carson published her book *Silent Spring*. She was an early prophet foretelling ecological disaster. Her book was greeted with noise and babel but despite the awards and praise, essentially it received the silent treatment. Like the mythic Cassandra, who was cursed by Apollo ("the god of truth") to be disbelieved when she prophesied truth, Rachel Carson, whose credibility was weakened by her sex, was greeted with superficial attention and deep inattentiveness. Ecologists today still deny her recognition, maintaining dishonest silence.[27] Meanwhile the springs are becoming more silent, as the necrophilic leaders of phallotechnic society are carrying out their programs of planned poisoning for all life on the planet.

I am not suggesting that women have a "mission" to save the world from ecological disaster. I am certainly not calling for female Self-sacrifice in the male-led cause of "ecology." I am affirming that those women who have the courage to break the silence within our Selves are finding/creating/spiraling a new Spring. This Spring within and among us makes be-ing possible, and makes the process of integrity possible, for it puts us in touch with the intuition of be-ing which Jan Raymond has called the intuition of integrity.[28] This intuitive, dynamic integrity enables us to begin seeing through the mad reversals which have been our mindbindings. It empowers us to question the sacred and secular "texts" which have numbed our brains by implanting "answers" before we had a chance to question and to quest. Our dis-covery of the Spring within us enables us to begin asking the right questions. There is no other way to begin. The hope which springs when women's deep silence—the silence that breaks us—is broken is the hope of saving our Selves, of delivering our Selves from the Sins of the Fathers and moving on from there. Since this Spring of women's be-ing is powerfully attractive to our own kind (womankind), we communicate it even without trying. Thus by breaking the imposed silence we help to spring other prisoners of patriarchy whose biophilic tendencies have not been completely blighted and blocked. The point is not to save society or to focus on escape (which is backward-looking) but to release the Spring of be-ing. To the inhabitants of Babel, this Spring of living speech will be unintelligible. If it is heard at all, it will be dismissed as mere babble, as the muttering of mad Crones. So much the better for the Crones' Chorus. Left undisturbed, we are free to find our own concordance, to hear our own harmony, the harmony of the spheres.

THE PURPOSE, THE METHOD, THE STYLE OF THIS BOOK

Writing this book is participating in feminist process. This is problematic. For isn't a book by its definition a "thing," an objectification of thinking/imagining/speaking? Here is a book in my hands: fixed, solid. Perhaps—hopefully—its author no longer wholly agrees with it. It is, at least partially, her past. The dilemma of the living/verbing writer is real, but much of the problem resides in the way books are perceived. If they are perceived/used/idolized as Sacred Texts (like the bible or the writings of chairman Mao), then of course the idolators are caught on a wheel that turns but does not move. They "spin" like wheels on ice—a "spinning" that in no way resembles feminist process.

We cannot avoid this static kind of "spinning wheel" by becoming anti-literate, anti-cerebral. "Feminist" anti-intellectualism is a mere reaction against moronizing masculinist education and scholarship, and it is a trap. We need creative crystallizing in the sense of producing works—such as books. Like crystal balls, Glowing Globes, these help us to foretell the future and to dis-cover the past, for they further the process itself by transforming the previously unknown into that which we explicitly know, and therefore can reflect upon, criticize. Thus they spark new visions. This creative crystallizing is a translation of feminist journeying, of our encounters with the unknown, into a chrysalis.[29] This writing/metamorphosing/spinning is itself part of the journey, and the chrysalis—the incarnation of experience in words—is a living, changing reality. It is the transmission of our transitions. Feminist process must become sensible (in actions, speech, works of all kinds) in order to become. The journey requires the courage to create, that we may learn from lucid criticism, that we may re-member the dismembered body of our heritage, that we may stop repeating the same mistakes. Patriarchal erasure of our tradition forces us to relearn what our foresisters knew and to repeat their blunders.

The warped mirror image of creative Hag-ography is standard patriarchal scholarship, which merely re-searches and re-covers "women's history." Insofar as this book is true to its original impulse, it is a written rebuttal of the rite of right re-search. It is part of the metapatriarchal journeying of women. Hopefully, it will not merely "survive" as a thing, a noun, but will spin as a verb, as a gynocentric manifestation of the Intransitive Verb.

Elsewhere I have advocated committing the crime of Methodicide, since the Methodolatry of patriarchal disciplines kills creative thought.[30] The acceptable/unexceptional circular reasonings of academics are caricatures of motion. The "products" are more often than not a set of distorted mirrors, made to seem plausible through the mechanisms of male bonding. On the boundaries of the male-centered universities, however, there is a flowering of woman-centered thinking. Gynocentric Method requires not only the murder of misogynistic methods (intellectual and affective exorcism) but also ecstasy, which I have called *ludic cerebration*. This is "the free play of intuition in our own space, giving rise to thinking that is vigorous, informed, multi-dimensional, independent, creative, tough." It arises from the lived experiences of be-ing. "Be-ing is the verb that says the dimensions of depth in all verbs, such as intuiting, reasoning, loving, imaging, making, acting, as well as the couraging, hoping, and playing that are always there when one is really living." [31]

Gynocentric writing means risking. Since the language and style of patriarchal writing simply cannot contain or carry the energy of women's exorcism and ecstasy, in this book I invent, dis-cover, re-member. At times I make up words (such as *gynaesthesia* for women's synaesthesia). Often I unmask deceptive words by dividing them and employing alternate meanings for prefixes (for example, *re-cover* actually says "cover again"). I also unmask their hidden reversals, often by using less known or "obsolete" meanings (for example, *glamour* as used to name a witch's power). Sometimes I simply invite the reader to listen to words in a different way (for example, *de-light*). When I play with words I do this attentively, deeply, paying attention to etymology, to varied dimensions of meaning, to deep Background meanings and subliminal associations. There are some woman-made words which I choose not to use for various reasons. Sometimes I reject words that I think are inauthentic, obscuring women's existence and masking the conditions of our oppression (for example, *chairperson*).[32] In other cases my choice is a matter of intuitive judgment (for example, my decision not to use *herstory*).*

At times I have been conscious of breaking almost into incantations, chants, alliterative lyrics. At such moments the words themselves seem to have a life of their own. They seem to want to break the bonds of conventional usage, to break the silence imposed upon their own Backgrounds. They be-

* I prefer the power of the term *Prehistory* to name the prior importance of the interconnected significant events of women's living and dying. *Her-story,* I think, shortcircuits the intent of radical feminism by implying a desire to parallel the record of men's achievements. It fails because it imitates male *history*. Inherently, it has an "odor" of mere reactive maneuvering, which is humiliating to women. It conveys an image of history's junior partner. The point is not simply that this term is "etymologically incorrect." It is enlightening to compare this term with such woman-made constructs as *man-ipulated* or *the/rapist,* which are also "incorrect," but do succeed in targeting/humiliating the *right* objects.

come palpable, powerful, and it seems that they are tired of allowing me to "use" *them* and cry out for a role reversal.* I become *their* mouthpiece, and if I am not always accurate in conveying their meanings, that is probably because I haven't yet learned to listen closely enough, in the realm of the labyrinthine inner ear.

Another delicate area has been the use of pronouns, especially the choice between *we* and *they* to refer to women. Elsewhere I have stressed the importance of the pronoun *we* and avoided the "objective" *they*. Obviously, there are times when the use of *we* would be absurd—for example, when referring to the women of ancient Greece. However, there are other instances when I have to play pronoun usage by ear. As the Journey progresses, and as the extent of the risk of radical feminism becomes more evident, it becomes clear that there are women, including some who would describe themselves as "feminists," with whom I do not feel enough identification to warrant the pronoun *we*. Sometimes, since the ambiguity about whether to use *we* or *they* is not clearly resolvable, there are difficult choices. Since pronouns are profoundly personal and political, they carry powerful messages. Despite the fact that many writers and readers ignore this pronominal power, subliminal clues are transmitted and received. At times my choice of *we* or *they* is a means of realizing my identification with, or separation from, certain roles and behaviors. At other times I use these pronouns interchangeably in reference to the same subject out of a sense of balance which is simply "playing by ear."

My use of capitalization is "irregular," conforming more to my meaning than to standard usage. For example, I consistently capitalize *Spinster*, just as one normally capitalizes *Amazon*. I capitalize *Lesbian* when the word is used in its woman-identified (correct) sense, but use the lower case when

* They appear also to want to break the silence of silent reading, demanding to be read out loud. Attentive journeyers of this book will notice that this is most likely to happen in the course of the First and Third Passages.

referring to the male-distorted version reflected in the media.* *Self* is capitalized when I am referring to the authentic center of women's process, while the imposed/internalized false "self," the shell of the Self, is in lower case. In writing of the deep *Background* which is the divine depth of the Self, I capitalize, while the term *foreground,* referring to surface consciousness, generally is not capitalized. I have not created or followed rigid rules about this matter, but simply have tried to convey meaning accurately/forcefully. Thus, when I write *State of Possession,* the capitals are meant to convey that this is not only an individual or internal condition, but a kind of society. At times I choose *not* to capitalize when this would be required by standard usage. The reader will see what I mean when she encounters such an expression as *the patriarchal god* (as contrasted with *The Godfather*). I have no need to consistently capitalize *christian* or *god,* being much more inclined to capitalize *Crone* and *Goddess.* This is obviously a matter not only of "taste" but of evaluation. I generally do not bother to change proper names which are conventionally capitalized. Thus I relegate such cases as the terms *Apollo, Christ,* and *Zeus* to their conventional upper cases. One could spend too much energy worrying about such matters. As Gertrude Stein remarked:

> Sometimes one feels that Italians should be with a capital and sometimes with a small letter, one can feel like that about almost anything.[33]

I do not generally put the terms *feminine* and *masculine* in quotation marks. I use both of these terms to refer to roles/stereotypes/sets of characteristics which are essentially distorted and destructive to the Self and to her process and environment.[34] Thus, if the terms *feminine* and *masochist* are

* I prefer to reserve the term *Lesbian* to describe women who are woman-identified, having rejected false loyalties to men on all levels. The terms *gay* or *female homosexual* more accurately describe women who, although they relate genitally to women, give their allegiance to men and male myths, ideologies, styles, practices, institutions, and professions.

used synomously this has nothing to do with the deep reality of the female Self, but with patriarchally imposed, Self-denying masks.

There is also the matter of the use of sources. The primary sources of this book are women's experiences, past and present. Its secondary sources are male-authored texts from many "fields." I use the latter in various ways. Sometimes I use them to expose their limitations, to display and exorcise their deceptions. Sometimes I use them as springboards. At all times I am acutely aware that most of these books and articles were written at the expense of women, whose energies were drained and ideas freely and shamelessly taken over. The following "acknowledgments" from Edwin Newman's *Strictly Speaking* are slightly more obvious than the average, but convey the typical situation:

> This book is dedicated to my wife and daughter. My wife's contributions have been so many and varied that it is not possible to list them. There would be no book without her. My daughter supplied many suggestions, much encouragement, and through the years, tolerance of my kind of humor above and beyond the call of duty. Jeanette Hopkins provided the impetus for the book and edited it. Carol Bok did the typing and the research. To both of them my deep thanks. Mary Heathcote was the invaluable copy editor.[35]

As Andrée Collard has said of male authors: "He not only copies her ideas; he also holds the copy-right." [36] Finally, I must add that in using male sources, at no point have I acted in the position of "disciple" citing an authority. I have tried, righteously, to use the materials available to me under the prevailing conditions, deploring, as scholars should, the necessity for resorting to such secondary re-sources.

NAMING THE ENEMY

This will of course be called an "anti-male" book. Even the most cautious and circumspect feminist writings are described in this way. The cliché is not only unimaginative but deadeningly, deafeningly, deceptive—making real hearing of what radical feminists are saying difficult, at times even for ourselves. Women and our kind—the earth, the sea, the sky—are the real but unacknowledged objects of attack, victimized as The Enemy of patriarchy—of all its wars, of all its professions. There are feminist works which provide abundant examples of misogynistic statements from authorities in all "fields," in all major societies, throughout the millennia of patriarchy.[37] Feminists have also written at length about the actual rapist behavior of professionals, from soldiers to gynecologists.[38] The "custom" of widow-burning (*suttee*) in India, the Chinese ritual of footbinding, the genital mutilation of young girls in Africa (still practiced in parts of twenty-six countries of Africa), the massacre of women as witches in "Renaissance" Europe, gynocide under the guise of American gynecology and psychotherapy—all are documented facts accessible in the tomes and tombs (libraries) of patriarchal scholarship.[39] The contemporary facts of brutal gang rape, of wife-beating, of overt and subliminal psychic lobotomizing—all are available.[40]

What then can the label *anti-male* possibly mean when applied to works that expose these facts and invite women to free our Selves? The fact is that the labelers do not intend to convey a rational meaning, nor to elicit a thinking process, but rather to block thinking. They do intend the label to carry a deep emotive message, triggering implanted fears of all the fathers and sons, freezing our minds. For to write an "anti-male" book is to utter the ultimate blasphemy.

Thus women continue to be intimidated by the label *anti-male*. Some feel a false need to draw distinctions, for example: "I am anti-patriarchal but not anti-male." The courage to be logical—the courage to name—would require that we admit to ourselves that males and males only are the originators, planners, controllers, and legitimators of patriarchy. Patriarchy is the homeland of males; it is Father Land; and men are its agents. The primary resistance to consciousness of this reality is precisely described in *Sisterhood Is Powerful*: "Thinking that our man is the exception, and, therefore, we are the exception among women." [41] It is in the interest of men (as men in patriarchy perceive their interest) and, in a superficial but Self-destructive way, of many women, to hide this fact, especially from themselves.

The use of the label is an indication of intellectual and moral limitations. Despite all the evidence that women are attacked as projections of The Enemy, the accusers ask sardonically: "Do you really think that *men* are the enemy?" This deception/reversal is so deep that women—even feminists—are intimidated into Self-deception, becoming the only Self-described oppressed who are unable to name their oppressor, referring instead to vague "forces," "roles," "stereotypes," "constraints," "attitudes," "influences." This list could go on. The point is that no agent is named—only abstractions.

The fact is that we live in a profoundly anti-female society, a misogynistic "civilization" in which men collectively victimize women, attacking us as personifications of their own paranoid fears, as The Enemy. Within this society it is men who rape, who sap women's energy, who deny women economic and political power. To allow oneself to know and name these facts is to commit anti-gynocidal acts. Acting in this way, moving through the mazes of the anti-female society, requires naming and overcoming the obstacles constructed by its male agents and token female instruments. As a creative crystallizing of the movement beyond the State of Patriarchal Paralysis, this book is an act of Dis-possession; and hence, in a sense beyond the limitations of the label *anti-male,* it is absolutely Anti-androcrat, A-mazingly Anti-male, Furiously and Finally Female.

THE CHART OF THIS VOYAGING/WRITING

In traditional accounts (Eastern and Western) of the Otherworld Journey there are gates through which the soul must pass. The soul is obliged to say the correct words in order to pass the wardens at each Passage.[42] I have already suggested that in women's metapatriarchal Otherworld Journeying the wardens are the demonic powers of patriarchy, which assume ghostly forms (that is, are difficult to perceive) and function as noxious gases. Women who are able to name our Selves are thereby empowered to name the demons at each Passage.

When we say their names, they—in effect—drop dead. To put it another way, the gases drop down (condense) into a merely messy puddle.

These warden-demons can be seen as personifications of the Eight Deadly Sins of the Fathers. It is significant that in the traditional listing of the "Deadly Sins," Deception is not usually named. This nonnaming is an indicator of the pervasive deceptiveness of male-constructed "morality," which does not name its own primary Deadly Sin. Deception is in fact all-pervasive. It keeps us running in senseless circles. It sedates and seduces our Selves, freezing and fixing Female Process, enabling the fathers to feed upon women's stolen energy. The Paternal Parasites hide their vampirizing of female energy by deceptive posturing, which takes the form of Processions (religious, military, judicial, academic, etc.).

For this reason, I choose to use the term *Processions* to name the deception of the fathers. At every turn, the Voyagers of this book encounter Processions of Demons wearing multiform masks. We exorcise them, expelling their deceptions from our minds, ousting these obstacles to our Ecstatic Process. Processions both display and disguise the Deadly Sins of the Fathers. The deception they engender glues the Sins into conglomerates, reversing them, re-presenting them as Virtues.

The following list, which not accidentally may resemble a sort of incantation, is a new naming of the Eight Deadly Sins of the Fathers. Although any listing is necessarily linear, it is clear that these malfunctions (Male-Functions) are interconnected, that they feed into each other.

Processions
The basic Sin of Phallocracy is *deception*—the destruction of process through patriarchal processions, which are frozen mirror images of Spinning Process.

Professions
Deadly *pride* is epitomized in patriarchal professions, which condense the process of know-ing into an inert and mystifying thing ("body of knowledge").

Possession
Androcratic *avarice* is demonic possession of female spirit and

energy, accomplished not only through political and economic means, but, more deeply, through male myth.

Aggression
The malevolence of male violence (which is, in fact, usually dispassionate) is misnamed *anger,* masking the fact that women are The Enemy against whom all patriarchal wars are waged, and muting righteous female anger.

Obsession
Male *lust* specializes in genital fixation and fetishism, reflecting a broken integrity of consciousness, generating masculine and feminine role constructs legitimated by sadospiritual religion.

Assimilation
Gynocidal *gluttony* expresses itself in vampirism/cannibalism —feeding upon the *living* flesh, blood, spirit of women, while tokenism disguises the devastation of the victims.

Elimination
Misogynist *envy* tends inherently toward the elimination of all Self-identified women, accomplishing this end through the re-conception/re-forming of some women into Athena-like accomplices.

Fragmentation
Patriarchal *sloth* has enslaved women, whose creativity is confined by mandatory menial labor and by deceptively glorified subservient social activities, resulting in "busy" and enforced feminine sloth.

Each of these Sins of the Fathers is more than a sum of abstractions. Each is incarnated in the institutions of patriarchy and in those who invent, control, and legitimate these institutions. Thus women's journey of Self-centering becoming, passing through the "gates of god" which block us from our own Background, means confronting these deceptive incarnations/demons, naming them and naming their games.

Our Journeying past these watchful wardens is not linear. A-mazing their mazes involves spinning through them, at multiple times in multiple ways. Since their names are legion, there is not one simple once-and-for-all name for the demons. Their lecherous litanies are like passages of Unholy Scripture which they repeat over and over again, and which have many levels of deception, not perceptible all at once. They become more perceptible as we learn to name our Selves, become our Selves, more adequately. Concomitant with the a-mazing struggle, which is exorcism, is the ecstatic process of Spinsters dis-covering the labyrinth of our own unfolding/becoming. Passing through the male-made mazes is not simply a preliminary lap of the journey. It makes way for and accompanies the Ecstatic Labyrinthine Journey of Survivors.

In this book I will chart/describe this a-mazing and spinning voyage. That is, I will write about fundamental "blind alleys" of the masters' maze, which hide the Passages of the Labyrinthine Way of Ecstasy. I will be concerned with dis-covering the fathers' Processions and with breaking away from them. The Voyage will involve encounters with the other seven Deadly Sins/Demons as well. These encounters are recurrent and in random order, as the Demons appear and re-appear at various points, attemping to block our way.

The Voyage of this book moves through three Passages. As the terrain changes so also does the style of the explorer, her movement, her language. In The First Passage there is an exuberance of dis-covery as the Voyager breaks through the barriers of obsolete myths which block vision. There is the constant surprise of seeing what is on the other side of the hill and on all sides as the scope of vision broadens and deepens.

In The Second Passage there is a soberness and focused attention as the Explorer encounters the Unnatural Enemies of Female Be-ing in their multiple postures of Indecent Exposure. There is a focused intensity as she marks the snares laid by the deadly game trappers, analyzing the archetypal atrocities in order to unmask the lethal intent of the death dealers.

In The Third Passage, having perceived the *intent* of the gynocidal gamesters, she moves deeper into the Otherworld—which is her own time/space. Her style reflects her new-found capacity to recognize their intent in its seemingly innocent and chillingly familiar manifestations (their chivalry, their help, their care, their art, their romance, their respect, their rewards, their blessings, their love). This new knowing—her Beatific Vision—encourages her to invent new modes of Be-ing/Speaking, which are Spooking, Sparking, Spinning.

My charting and describing are inspired by many foresisters. Since all who have embarked on this journey are "contemporaries" in the only sense that matters, the century or span of decades measured by patriarchal time in which "his" history places each of us is far less relevant than our own network of communication. All women who define our own living, defying the deception of patriarchal history, are journeying. We belong to the same time and we are foresisters to each other.

Here, in this volume, my charting and describing is inspired in a particular way by the words of one foresister, Virginia Woolf, who in her profoundly anti-patriarchal book, *Three Guineas,* asks:

> What are these ceremonies and why should we take part in them? What are these professions and why should we make money out of them? Where, in short, is it leading us, the procession of the sons of educated men? [43]

In this prophetic book, published in the 1930s, she shows connections among the absurd professional processions, displaying their deception, their morbidity and meaninglessness. She advises us to "break the ring, the vicious circle, the dance round and round the mulberry tree, the poison tree of intellectual harlotry." [44] The circle of processions and of professions is linked to possession. Of women's dilemma, she writes:

> Behind us lies the patriarchal system; the private house, with its nullity, its immorality, its hypocrisy, its servility. Before us lies the public world, the professional system, with its possessiveness, its jealousy, its pugnacity, its greed. The one shuts us up like slaves in a harem; the other forces us to circle, like caterpillars head to to tail, round and round the mulberry tree, the sacred tree, of property. It is a choice of evils. Each is bad.[45]

Yes, and each is part of the *same* system of patriarchal possession, whose primary property is female life.

The writing/journeying of this book passes/spins through the phallocratic maze. Yet the Other side of this Otherworld

Journeying is dis-covered at every turn. This is the ecstatic side. It involves speaking in various modes: Spooking, Sparking, Spinning. Although there is no "one-to-one" correlation between the exorcising and the ecstatic movements, there is a kind of moving pattern, a spiraling of counterpoints, a harmony of hearing and speaking. Our acts of exorcising are Rites of Passage, by which we win the rights of passage.

In the process of encountering and naming the Male-Factors who freeze process into processions, hoard knowing within professions, and kill creativity by possession, I point out clues which, as they are recognized, disclose the living process which has been hidden, caricatured, captured, stunted, but never completely killed by the phallocentric Sins. These clues point to a force which is beyond, behind, beneath the patriarchal death march—an unquenchable gynergy. They serve as raw material for a process of alchemy. We transmute the base metals of man-made myth by becoming unmute, calling forth from our Selves and each other the courage to name the unnameable.

THE FIRST PASSAGE

PROCESSIONS

Divine Scripture uses, in relation to God [the trinity], names which signify procession. . . . The procession of the Word in God is called generation: and the Word Himself proceeding is called the Son. . . . Besides the procession of the Word in God, there exists in Him another procession called the procession of love.

Thomas Aquinas,
Summa theologiae

There it is, then, before our eyes, the procession of the sons of educated men, ascending those pulpits, mounting those steps, passing in and out of those doors, preaching, teaching, administering justice, practicing medicine, making money.

Virginia Woolf,
Three Guineas

The preacher says the proper things
And then the rusty alto sings
And now they'll all get roaring drunk
Pretending they're essentially alive,
While the proud procession leads her to the hive.

Jimmy Webb,
from "The Hive," sung by Meg Christian,
I Know You Know (Olivia Records)

PRELUDE TO THE FIRST PASSAGE

Patriarchal society revolves around myths of Processions. Earthly processions both generate and reflect the image of procession from and return to god the father. According to christian theology, there are processions within the godhead, which is triune. The son, who is the second person, is said to proceed from the father, and the holy ghost is said to proceed from the father and the son. Moreover, all creatures proceed from this eternally processing god, who is their Last End, with whom the righteous will be united in eternal bliss. Thus, in this symbol system there is a circular pattern/model for muted existence: separation from and return to the same immutable source.

Christians, according to this tradition, participate in the "supernatural" processions through the sacrament of baptism.[1] That is, they officially join the army of believers. Significantly, the word *pagan* is derived from a late Latin term *paganus*, meaning civilian, "because the Christians reckoned themselves soldiers of Christ." [2] The processions of christians, then, are profoundly connected with military parades, mythically as well as historically. What is ultimately sought by this "salvation army" is reconciliation with the father, for the human species has been alienated from him through the fault of the first parents, Adam and Eve, whose Original Sin has been transmitted to all. Thus the mythic christian procession toward god presupposes belief in possession by evil forces, release from which requires captivity by the church. Consequently the sacrament of initiation (baptism) explicitly contains a rite of exorcism, blatantly belying the fact that this is really a rite of entrance into the State of Possession.

Western society is still possessed overtly and subliminally by christian symbolism, and this State of Possession has extended its influence over most of the planet. Its ultimate symbol of processions is the all-male trinity itself. Of obvious significance here is the fact that this is an image of the procession of a divine son from a divine father (no mother or daughter involved). In this symbol the first person, the father, is the origin who thinks forth the second person, the son, the word, who is the perfect image of himself, who is "co-eternal" and "consubstantial," that is, identical in essence. So total is their union that their "mutual love" is expressed by the procession (known as "spiration") of a third person called the "Holy Spirit," whose proper name is "Love." [3] This naming of "the three Divine Persons" is the paradigmatic model for the pseudogeneric term *person,* excluding all female mythic presence, denying female reality in the cosmos.

This triune god is one act of eternal self-absorption/self-love. The term *person* is derived from the Latin *persona* meaning actor's mask, or character in a play. "The Processions of Divine Persons" is the most sensational one-act play of the centuries, the original *Love Story,* performed by the Supreme All Male Cast. Here we have the epitome of male bonding, beyond the "best," i.e., worst, dreams of Lionel Tiger. It is "sublime" (and therefore disguised) erotic male homosexual *mythos,* the perfect all-male marriage, the ideal all-male family, the best boys' club, the model monastery, the supreme Men's Association, the mold for all varieties of male monogender mating. To the timid objections voiced by christian women, the classic answer has been: "You're included under the Holy Spirit. He's feminine." The point is, of course, that male made-up femininity has nothing to do with women. Drag queens, whether divine or human, belong to the Men's Association.

This mythic paradigm of the trinity is the product of christian culture, but it is expressive of *all* patriarchal patterning of society. Indeed, it is the most refined, explicit, and loaded expression of such patterning. Human males are eternally putting on the masks and playing the roles of the Divine Persons. The mundane processions of sons have as their basic but unacknowledged and unattainable aim an attempted "consubstantiality" with the father (the cosmic father, the oedipal father, the professional godfather). The junior statesman dreams of becoming The President. The junior scholar dreams of becoming The Professor. The acolyte fantasizes about becoming The Priest. Spirated by all these relations is the asphyxiating atmosphere of male bonding. And, as Virginia Woolf saw, the death-oriented military processions display the real direction of the whole scenario, which is a funeral procession engulfing all life forms. God the father requires total sacrifice/destruction.

Patriarchy is itself the prevailing religion of the entire planet, and its essential message is necrophilia. All of the so-called religions legitimating patriarchy are mere sects subsumed under its vast umbrella/canopy. They are essentially similar, despite the variations. All—from buddhism and hinduism to islam, judaism, christianity, to secular derivatives such as freudianism, jungianism, marxism, and maoism—are infrastructures of the edifice of patriarchy. All are erected as parts of the male's shelter against anomie. And the symbolic message of all the sects of the religion which is patriarchy is this: Women are the dreaded anomie.[4] Consequently, women are the objects of male terror, the projected personifications of "The Enemy," the real objects under attack in all the wars of patriarchy.

Women who are willing to make the Journey of becoming must indeed recognize the fact of possession by the structures of evil and by the controllers and legitimators of these structures. But the solution is hardly "rebirth" (baptism) by the fathers in the name of male mating. Indeed, this "rebirth"—whether it is accomplished by the officially acknowledged religious fathers or by the directors of derivative secular organizations (e.g., television, schools, publishers of children's books)—is the very captivity from which we are trying to escape, in order to find our own origins.

Radical feminism is not reconciliation with the father. Rather it is affirming our original birth, our original source, movement, surge of living. This finding of our original integrity is re-membering our Selves. Athena remembers her mother and consequently re-members her Self. Radical feminism releases the inherent dynamic in the mother-daughter relationship toward friendship, which is strangled in the male-mastered system. Radical feminism means that mothers do *not* demand Self-sacrifice of daughters, and that daughters do not demand this of their mothers, as do sons in patriarchy. What both demand of each other is courageous moving which is mythic in its depths, which is spell-breaking and myth-making process. The "sacrifice" that is required is not mutilation by men, but the discipline needed for acting/creating together on a planet which is under the Reign of Terror, the reign of the fathers and sons.

Women moving in this way are in the tradition of Great Hags. Significantly, Hags are commonly identified with Harpies and Furies. Harpies are mythic monsters represented as having the head of a woman and the body and claws of a vulture, and considered to be instruments of divine vengeance. As Harpies, Hags are workers of vengeance—not merely in the sense of re-venge, which is only reactionary—but as asserting the primal energy of our be-ing. The Furies were believed by the Greeks and Romans to be avenging deities. As Harpies and Furies, Feminists are agents for the Goddess Nemesis.

As Harpies and Furies, Feminists in the tradition of the Great Hags are beyond compromise. It is said of the Goddess Demeter after her daughter Korê (named "Persephone" after being abducted by Hades and brought to the underworld) was stolen from her, that she compromised. She had stated flatly that she would not allow the earth to bear fruit again unless her daughter was returned to her. But, according to the patriarchal myth, when Zeus decided that Persephone should live with her husband (Hades) for three months of the year and pass the other nine months with her mother, *Demeter set aside her anger* and bade the soil be fertile. But Persephone had tasted of the pomegranate; she was *possessed* by her husband, and every year when the cold season arrived she went to join him in the deep shadows.[5] The myth expresses the essential tragedy of women after the patriarchal conquest. The male myth-makers presented an illusion of reunion between Demeter and Persephone-Korê. The compromise can be seen as forced upon Demeter, but it was fatal for her to undervalue the power of her own position and set aside her anger, just as it was fatal that she taught the kings of the earth her divine science and initiated them into her divine mysteries. The patriarchal Greek myth-makers (re-makers) constructed a typical phallocratic plot when they (through Zeus) seduced her into the apparently satisfactory—even triumphant—compromise. However, the fact that the daughter was *allowed* to return for a "period of time" says everything about patriarchy.*

Those who live in the tradition of the Furies refuse to be tricked into setting aside our anger at this primordial mutilation, which is the ontological separation of mother from daughter, of daughter from mother, of sister from sister. Women choosing Hag-ocracy refuse to teach divine science to the kings of the earth, to initiate them into our mysteries. Hag-ocracy is the time/space of those who maintain a growing creative fury at this primal injustice—a fury which is the struggle of daughters to find our source, our stolen original divinity.

The history of the footbound women of China (which will be discussed at length in The Second Passage) provides us with a vivid and accurate image of the way in which women have been coerced into "participating" in the phallocratic processions. The footbound daughter was *bound* to repeat the same procedure of mutilation upon her own daughter, and

* Women are constantly tempted to measure reality in terms of the measurements of Father Time, which are linear, clocked. This is a trap. Our gynocentric time/space is not measurable, bargainable. It is qualitative, not quantitative. Because we refuse to be possessed by patriarchal myth we live in a different kind of duration, which has multifarious rhythms. The fathers who control the Clockwork Society try to consume this, our Lifetime. The Time Keepers' Lie consists in claiming that "free time" can be cut off neatly from sold or bargained time (the nine-to-five schedule, the constant availability demanded of the housewife). The Masters mask or deny the fact that this division is a fundamental fragmentation. This brokenness must be healed during alleged "free time," when the wound-up captives of Father Time waste wounded energies "unwinding." Furious women must begin by seeing through the Time Keepers' Lie and daring to defy the Time Keepers' schedules. The more we do this, the more we "find time" for our Selves. Hags' spirits soar out of the cells of the Clockwork Prison when we defy the Lie, leaving their "frame of reference," de-riding their boundaries. Otherworld Journeyers are precisely time/space travelers, seeing through the senseless circles, the pointless processions of the hands on the Grand Fathers' clocks.

the daughter upon *her* daughter. To visualize the procession of generations of crippled mothers and daughters, hobbling on three-inch-long caricatures of feet, moving slowly, grotesquely, painfully in meaningless circles within the homes (prisons) of fathers and husbands—their owners—is to *see* the real state of women in patriarchy. To understand that this horror is still going on, assuming insidious forms of *mindbinding* and *spiritbinding* in every nation of this colonized planet, is to begin to comprehend the condition of women caught on the Wheel of Processions, clutched by the clockwork hands that circle the surface of the Time Keepers' clocks.

Furious women know that patriarchy is itself a continual resurrection of the past, a series of processions. No social revolution, however "radical," that falls short of metapatriarchal movement can break the circles of repetition. Only Hags—that is, Furious women—can kick off spiritbindings. This is possible, for mind/spirit has a resiliency that feet, once destroyed, can never have again. The bindings can be burned. Virginia Woolf knew this:

> And let the daughters of educated men dance round the fire and heap armful upon armful of dead leaves upon the flames. And let their mothers lean from the upper windows and cry, "Let it blaze! Let it blaze! For we have done with this 'education'!" [6]

Keeping the fire burning, saying No to Processions, means facing something that is very hard to look at: Deadly Deception through male myth—the subject of the following chapters.

CHAPTER ONE

DEADLY DECEPTION: MYSTIFICATION THROUGH MYTH

I wish that more people could fly into space. It would make for a lot better world.

Donald K. Slayton, Astronaut

I would like to take part in a flight that could continue for a long time around the earth.

Alexei Leonov, Cosmonaut

A man's world. But finished.
They themselves have sold it to the machines.

Adrienne Rich,
from "Waking in the Dark,"
Diving into the Wreck

We are the hollow men
We are the stuffed men
Leaning together
Headpiece filled with straw. Alas!
Our dried voices, when
We whisper together
Are quiet and meaningless
As wind in dry grass
Or rats' feet over broken glass
In our dry cellar

T. S. Eliot,
from "The Hollow Men,"
The Waste Land and Other Poems

Despite all the evils they wished to crush me with/
I remain as steady as the three-legged cauldron.

Monique Wittig
Les Guérillères

Patriarchy perpetuates its deception through myth. Before considering specific myths or conglomerates of them, it is important to look briefly at language about them. On the banal level of everyday cliché, one often hears: "It's only a myth (or story, or fairy tale, or legend)." The cliché belittles the power of myth. The child who is fed tales such as *Snow White* is not told that the tale itself is a poisonous apple, and the Wicked Queen (her mother/teacher), having herself been drugged by the same deadly diet throughout her lifetime (death-time), is unaware of her venomous part in the patriarchal plot.

On a level that passes as "sophisticated," scholars from various fields generally agree on certain components of what they perceive to be myth. Myths are said to be stories that express intuitive insights and relate the activities of gods. The mythical figures are symbols.[1] These, it is said, open up depths of reality otherwise closed to "us." [2] It is not usually suggested that they close off depths of reality which would otherwise be open to us.

The language of Mircea Eliade is fascinating. Declaring that myths are "paradigmatic models," he asserts that "what men do on their own initiative, what they do without a mythical model, belongs to the sphere of the profane; hence it is a vain and illusory activity, and in the last analysis, unreal." [3] In case the totality of this stagnation is not evident, the following passage is explicit:

> This faithful repetition of divine models has a two-fold result: (1) by imitating the gods, man remains in the sacred, hence in reality; (2) by the continuous reactualization of paradigmatic divine gestures, the world is sanctified.[4]

Such lines contain the essence of the patriarchal view of myth. To participate in "reality" is to repeat mythical models, to *reactualize* them continuously. The myth-masters do not admit that these paradigmatic models stage "reality" and program the audience to be performers of "vain and illusory activity." Breaking out of the circles of vain and illusory processions requires exactly the initiative which patriarchal myth stifles and which theorists such as Eliade deplore.

No one has so magnificently satirized the absurdity and horror of this deceptive repetition as Virginia Woolf. Having seen through the emperor's old clothes, she describes "educated men" in their public capacity:

> Now you dress in violet; a jewelled crucifix swings on your breast; now your shoulders are covered with lace; now furred with ermine. . . . Now you wear wigs on your heads . . .[5]

She observes that the ceremonies which take place when men wear such uniforms are even stranger than the uniforms themselves, that men perform the rituals always together, always in step, always in the uniform proper to the man and the occasion. Moreover—and this is crucial—the paradigmatic procession/parade by which males act out male-centered myth is the military parade.

The ceremonies, with the required uniforms, decorations, gestures, are all parts of the deceptive, "sacred" processions by which the patriarchal processors participate in their paradigmatic myth. Woolf spells out the fundamental clue to the meaning that is masked by the deadly deceptive processions. She ponders:

> What connection is there between the sartorial splendours of the educated man and the photograph of ruined houses and dead bodies? Obviously, the connection between dress and war is not far to seek; your finest clothes are those that you wear as soldiers.[6]

Here is the high creativity that sees interconnections between apparently disparate things. The basic march, in measured body movements, is a death march. The radical disease is necrophilia.

Woolf's insights concerning this acting out of man-made myth are extremely important in more ways than one. First, as I have just shown, she makes explicit the meaning of the myth: "ruined houses and dead bodies." Second, she gives us clues that help in deciphering the deception of patriarchal analysis of (male) myth. When a philosopher such as Jaspers asserts that myths express "intuitive insights," and when a theologian such as Tillich asserts that these "open up depths of reality and of the self otherwise closed to us," they deceive us with statements that are both true and untrue at the same time. The unstated presupposition of these statements is that the myths being discussed are patriarchal myths. The patriarchal myth-makers/legitimators desperately wish that the Otherworld would be "otherwise closed to us." Since the Female Self is the Otherworld to the patriarchs, their intent is to close us off from our own Selves, deceiving us into believing that these are the only doorways to our depths and that the fathers hold the keys.

Since a radical feminist analysis reaches the point of recognizing patriarchal myths as lies in the deepest sense, as distortions of our depths, one could easily conclude that traditional definitions should be dismissed. Yet this conclusion is too simple. Woolf's analysis of the ceremonies which are the "acting out" of phallocratic myth show that they did indeed give her material for "intuitive insights," and that she could use them to open up "depths of reality." Needless to say, these were not the insights intended by the myth-makers and uniformed myth perpetuators. Yet she *did* elicit insights by seeing through them. So also do women elicit insights by seeing through such obvious myths as the second birth of Athena from the head of Zeus, or the birth of Eve from Adam's rib. We do this by reversing their reversals—a complex process which involves much more than swinging to a simplistic conclusion that "opposites" of male myths are the "depths" we seek. For example, to conclude that "womb envy" is the key to phallocratic deception and to fixate upon female biological fertility would be just another way of falling into the trap of demonic deception. To remain there is to stay boxed into the fathers' house of mirrors, merely responding to the images projected/reflected by the Possessors. After recognizing these mirror images Hags must break through the looking glass into the Otherworld, our world, where we can learn to see with our own eyes.[7]

In order to reverse the reversals completely we must deal with the fact that patriarchal myths contain *stolen* mythic power. They are something like distorting lenses through which we *can* see into the Background. But it is necessary to break their codes in order to use them as viewers; that is, we must see their lie in order to see their truth. We can correctly perceive patriarchal myths as reversals and as pale derivatives of more ancient, more translucent myth from gynocentric civilization. We can also move our Selves from a merely chronological analysis to a Crone-logical analysis. This frees feminist thought from the compulsion to "prove" at every step that each phallic myth and symbol had a precedent in gynocentric myth, which chronologically antedated it. The point is that while such historical study is extremely useful, we can, whenever necessary, rely upon our Crones' clarifying logic to see through the distortions into the Background that is always present in our moving Self-centering time/space. As the women said in *Les Guérillères*: "Make an effort to remember. Or, failing that, invent." [8] The first definition given in Merriam-Webster for *invent* is "to search out or come upon: FIND, DISCOVER." Only after this do we come to such definitions as "to think up" and "to create." Women can discover and create our myths in the process of a-mazing tales that are phallic.

Thus the deception in Eliade's analysis becomes obvious. For what women who have the courage to name our Selves can do is precisely to act on our own initiative, and this is *profoundly* mythic.* From the point of view of male myth-

* When I speak of gynocentric myth and feminist myth-making I do not refer to tales of reified gods and/or goddesses but to stories arising from the experiences of Crones—stories which convey primary and archetypal messages about our own Prehistory and about Female-identified power.

masters this inventiveness is "profane," a term which Eliade defines as "vain and illusory," and which sociologists define as the sphere of "routine experience" and of "adaptive behavior." Those caught in the circles of deceptive processions will of course call female myth-breaking and myth-making "profane." For in fact feminists breaking the code of distorted phallic myth are breaking the routine, the vanity, the illusions, the adaptive behavior of the death marchers caught on the wheel of their "paradigms." The call to female profanity is the call to the sacred realm, our Background.

The term *profane* is derived from the Latin *pro* (before) and *fanum* (temple). Feminist profanity is the wild realm of the sacred as it was/is before being caged into the temple of Father Time. It is free time/space. This Prehistoric sacred is prior to the patriarchal sequestered "sacred" not merely temporally but, more importantly, in range and depth. Since it is not confined within the walls of any spatial or temporal temple, it transcends the "accepted" dichotomies between the sacred and the profane. The feminist journey into the wildly sacred Background is movement into wholeness/integrity.

It may be helpful to look further into a few of the most "accepted" ideas of the sacred in Western religious thought. I have already indicated that there is a generally accepted classification of the contents of human experience into two opposed categories, the sacred and the profane. This dualism is essential to the analysis of such theorists as Malinowski and Durkheim.[9] Essentially the same division is affirmed in the works of Max Weber (particularly in his treatment of "charisma") and of Rudolf Otto (in his discussion of "the holy").[10] While there are variations among these theories, they affirm basically the same split. In rejecting rigid splits associated with the patriarchally defined categories of "sacred," "charismatic," or "the holy," I am not saying that feminist analysis makes no distinctions. I am saying that we have to be free to dis-cover our own distinctions, refusing to be locked into these mental temples. To try to fit metapatriarchal process into these categories is attempting something analogous to fitting natural feet into footbindings which at first deform and later function as needed supports for contrived deformity.

The point is not that the terms used by "authorities" are necessarily always "wrong." Thus some of the terms used by Durkheim to describe his idea of "the sacred" might also be chosen by a woman dis-covering her Background—for example, the term *strength-giving.*[11] However, certain points should be kept in mind, especially by women with academic "backgrounds." First, such terms do not *belong* to Durkheim et al. We do not need such "authorities" for legitimation. While it may be hard to unlearn the lessons of academia—especially hard for those of us who earned "honors" for learning them—it is honorable to unlearn them. Second, such terms have different meanings in a gynocentric context. The strength which Self-centering women find, in finding our Background, is our *own* strength, which we give back to our Selves. The word *strength-giving* is only materially the same, only apparently the same, when used by women who name the sacred on our own authority. For the patriarchal "sacred" can be recognized as strength-sapping by women who choose to be our own authors, authoring our Selves.

I hasten to add that sometimes the words used by women to describe mythic depths dis-covered in Self-centering/spinning will not coincide even apparently or materially with those used by male authorities on (male) myth. Thus the terms *awe* (G. Van der Leeuw) and *dread* (Rudolf Otto) do not, I think, ring true to feminist breaking through to the Profane world of our mythic reality.[12] Furious women may be dreadful to the Holy Father(s), but our tendency is to become dreadless, as we become attuned to the nature of patriarchal religious dread.

When I use the term *mythic* to describe the depths of metapatriarchal Self-centering/be-ing, I mean to convey that the Dreadful Selves of women who choose the Wild Journey participate in the source of what the pale patriarchal myths reflect distortedly. Our participation is hardly a comfortable repetition of "paradigms." There is a sense of power, not of the "wholly other," but of the Self's be-ing. This participation is strength-giving, not in the sense of "supernatural elevation" through "grace" or of magic mutation through miracle drugs, but in the sense of creative unfolding of the Self. Metapatriarchal mythic a-mazing means repudiating saintliness and becoming wholly haggard, Holy Hags. As such, women are "wholly other" to those who are at home in the kingdom of the fathers. Dreadful women are "quite beyond the sphere of the usual, the intelligible, and the familiar." [13] Indeed, women becoming "wholly other" *are* strange. Myth-living/loving Hags are members of the "Outsiders' Society." [14]

The mythic wholeness/holiness of Dreadful women unmasks the estranged State of Patriarchy. The State of Estrangement is typified in the new art named "holography"—three-dimensional photography. Holographs—three-dimensional pictures projected onto flat photographic plates—give the illusion of wholeness.[15] Such deceptive "wholeness" is patriarchal holiness. It really is the absence of Self. This is flat, surface existence, deceptively giving the impression of depth. When I use the term *mythic* to describe the Background journey, I am attempting to speak of dimensions hidden by the all-pervasive "holographs" which are the distorted reflections of true depth. Holographs, then, typify the contents of patriarchal myth. Thus myth-breaking is breaking the projector of these illusions—dis-covering the realm of radiant energy where the Self lives and moves.

I suggest that a primary pursuit of those who wield power is and has been, since the inception of patriarchy, the manufacture of such holographs, which in turn program hollow men who ceremoniously live out the paradigmatic roles prescribed by the myth-masters.* Indeed: "The more hollow the more hallowed" should be the fathers' slogan. In writing of "hollow men" I am not referring specifically to males; rather I am using the pseudogeneric term, *men,* deliberately. For

* T. S. Eliot's poem, "The Hollow Men," exquisitely expresses the barrenness experienced by his breed:

Those who have crossed
With direct eyes, to death's other Kingdom
Remember us—if at all—not as lost
Violent souls, but only
As the hollow men
The stuffed men.

women are included in the invitation to hollowness, and insofar as they succumb they cease to be female-identified and become purely feminine: adorable and deplorable, but never really horrible, never Dreadful.

The creation, that is, the reduction, of reality to holographs is effected through various means. In the following section I will analyze an example of such reductionism from "the news." Since "the news" on the calendar of Father Time is always really "the olds" ("New news is old news," one could say), the fact that the example is a few years old is totally irrelevant.

HANDSHAKES IN SPACE: A CELESTIAL HORROR SHOW

In July 1975, a space spectacular was manufactured and described by newscasters as a "technological miracle." This was the famous "first international docking in space." It was in fact an act of international intercourse; it was, to use Jan Raymond's expression, "a lecherous link-up"[16] of the American spaceship "Apollo" with its Russian counterpart "Soyuz" (meaning: "union"). An official news release out of Houston, referring to the mating as "androgynous," explained that the U.S. ship played the "male" or active role on Thursday (July 17) by inserting its "nose" into the "nose" of the Russian ship. To even the score, the crafts reversed roles on Saturday (July 19). Warming to his subject, the author of the news release declared that an earlier Apollo docking "was a purely male-female arrangement—a probe that fit snugly into a receptacle."[17] While their ships enjoyed androgynous sex in space, their astronauts and cosmonauts satisfied themselves with handshakes, the traditional symbol of brotherhood. The essential point is that despite the sex-role reversals of the copulating crafts, the real bonding was all male. As one of the news releases from the space center at Houston put it: "The meaning of the mated hands circles the globe."[18] Male monogender bonding does indeed circle the earth, choking her in its grasp.

Heeding some of the technological details of the male mating involved in that celestial spectacular can help us fathom the craven craving for pomp and splendor manifested in all patriarchal processions. The heroes, acting completely under the direction of computers (their masters), were forced to *crawl* from ship to ship. Upon their glorious return, they also had to crawl out.[19] Although they managed to crawl successfully, they were affected by the noxious yellow gas emitted from their craft. In a chronic state of anxiety about loss of control over their excretory functions, they reportedly took Lomotil tablets, an anti-diarrhea medicine, "just as a prophylactic." The space food, praised by cosmonaut Leonov for its "freshness," was in fact packaged in tubes, cans, and plastic bags, anchored to the table with elastic bands.[20] Such inglorious details unmask the real roles of the heroes in this technologically miraculous circling. Here then is a clue to the need for "sartorial splendour" in the "processions of the sons of educated men." Robotized, the sons of their own machines, the processors are more controlled than controlling. Above all, they are not free. This uniformed sartorial splendor then (spacesuits, priestly and judicial robes, professorial and surgical gowns) is workmen's compensation. It is pitiable consolation for the unacknowledged knowledge that the processions ultimately are nothing more significant than a computer-controlled crawl.

FROM ROBOTITUDE TO ROBOTICIDE: RE-CONSIDERING

Where do women "fit in" to this space of stale male-mating, this world of wedded deadlock? We are supposed to fit in to the "family pictures"—such as those displayed by the space heroes on their craft—and into the pictures shown on television and in the printed media. In the televised pictures of the return, the wives were shown smiling in frantic euphoria (perhaps with the help of modern medicine) while their masters displayed far less enthusiasm at greeting *them*. Women are supposed to "fit in" to this picture, *as pictures,* that is, as projections.* At the present stage of technology, the "presence" (absence) of women is re-presented in the form of photographs, or of televised two-dimensional images. The direction of phallotechnic progress is toward the production of three-dimensional, perfectly re-formed "women," that is, hollow holograms. These projections, or feminine nonwomen, the replacements for female Selves, could of course eventually be projected in "solid" form—as solid waste products of technical progress, as robots. Eventually, too, the "solid" substitutes could be "flesh and blood" (not simply machines), produced by such "miraculous" techniques as total therapy (for example, B. F. Skinner's behaviorism), transsexualism, and cloning. The march of mechanical masculinist progress is toward the elimination of female Self-centering reality. Whether or not our re-placements are materially "hollow" or "solid" is not the ultimate issue. These are simply different ways of describing the absence of Female Depth, of spirit, in feminine nonwomen conceived by male mothers.

I will call this hollow/solid depthless state *robotitude*. It is comparable to a term coined by Françoise d'Eaubonne to describe the state of servitude of women in a phallocratic world: *"feminitude." Robotitude,* however, stresses the reduction of life in the state of servitude to mechanical motion. Moreover, it is not gender-specific, and thus indicates that the robot state is not restricted to women. It is not. However, the differences between female and male robotitude are crucial.

Women are encouraged, that is, dis-couraged, to adapt to a maintenance level of cognition and behavior by all the mythmasters and enforcers. The false molds, or forms, implanted in our minds during our first months and years of existence are comparable to the "sanctifying grace" or "supernatural life"

* This situation is not changed at all by the fact that, since the "Handshakes in Space" event, a few women have been appointed to fly on space shuttles of the future. An Associated Press news release, published in the *Boston Globe,* January 17, 1978, announced that "6 women, 3 black men and an Asian [are] among 35 candidates to fly on the nation's space shuttles in the next decade." Such tokenism functions to hide and reinforce stereotypes. The forms and functions of tokenism will be discussed throughout this book.

believed by catholics to be infused into the soul at baptism. The added "fixes" injected continually by society's mind-controllers can be compared to the "actual grace" which catholics believe they receive through other sacraments. While men also receive false molds and follow-up fixes to reinforce their supernatural, that is, unnatural, state in patriarchal society, the grace/serum injected is different. Fatherly fixes are essentially ego-inflating for men, whereas those administered to women are depressants. The stark contrast between "uppers" for men and "downers" for women can be noted in all manifestations of culture, including almost all contemporary films (with rare notable exceptions such as *Harold and Maude*). The depressants administered to women may be falsely experienced at times as "highs," but these restrain the authentic Self, pinning her down with a double cross.

Simone de Beauvoir writes in *The Ethics of Ambiguity* that in the history of individuals it appears that adolescence is a time of choice. Then she adds:

> Doubtless this decision can always be reconsidered, but the fact is that conversions are difficult because the world reflects back upon us a choice which is confirmed through this world which it has fashioned. Thus, a more and more rigorous circle is formed from which one is more and more unlikely to escape.[21]

This passage describes very well the situation of women surrounded by the Deceptive Processions, suffocated by the circles of false "choices" which they impose. De Beauvoir names very well what real choice means:

> To exist . . . is to *cast* oneself into the world. Those who occupy themselves in restraining this original movement can be considered as sub-men [read: sub-women]. They have eyes and ears but from childhood on they make themselves blind and deaf, without love and without desire.[22]

Women fixed on the double cross of deception are made to make themselves blind and deaf. The blindness and deafness, as well as the dumbness and encircled paralysis imposed upon them, are different from such defects in males who hold institutional power, who have restrained "the original movement" toward be-ing. For the latter, psychic cripples though they are, and however much their choices have been conditioned, have assumed the role of deceivers/controllers. Their egos are supported, although in an ultimately self-destructive way.

The "decision," writes de Beauvoir, can always be reconsidered. It is important to ask what this reconsidering means for women. The term *consider* is derived from the Latin *considerare,* meaning literally, "to observe the stars." For women to re-consider our earlier paternally prescribed tendencies, deceptively mis-named "decisions," is nothing less than daring to see, name, and reach for the stars. It is reclaiming our original movement, our Prehistoric questing power which has been held down by the inner/outer artificial ceilings/sealings of the State of Servitude. De Beauvoir writes that "life is occupied in both perpetuating itself and in surpassing itself; if all it does is maintain itself, then living is only not dying..."[23] This maintenance level of "only not dying" is what I am calling robotitude. The problem is to get beyond the maintenance level, for "a life justifies itself only if its effort to perpetuate itself is integrated into its surpassing and if this surpassing has no other limits than those which the subject assigns himself [herself]."[24] Clearly, as the Handshakes in Space Show demonstrated, the heroes of phallotechnic society do not demonstrate any such surpassing, but only a caricature of it. Circling in their spacecraft, their womb-tombs in the sky, they illustrated the paradigmatic myth of Processions from womb to tomb, of separation and return, re-turning and re-turning.

Women surpassing the circles of these circlers, daring to see the stars for ourselves, are casting our Selves into the world. This means breaking the casts into which we have been molded and breaking away from the cast/caste condemned to act out the roles prescribed by masculinist myth. Re-considering the imposed choices of the past means acknowledging that a spell has been cast upon us, that we have been framed by the pictures of patriarchy, robotized by its rituals. De Beauvoir has written:

The oppressed has only one solution: to deny the harmony of that mankind from which an attempt is made to exclude him [her]. . . . In order to prevent this revolt, one of the ruses of oppression is to camouflage itself behind a natural situation since, after all, one cannot revolt against nature.[25]

Women can carry out the re-considering process by refusing steadily to allow the fact of struggle between the sexes to be camouflaged, that is, by denying false "harmony of mankind." This means living in a state of ultimate risking. Breaking away from false harmony, women begin to hear the healing harmony of Hags, the cacophony of Crones. It is of ultimate importance that we break out of the pictures by which we have been framed, out of the chorus into which we have been cast. Re-considering requires roboticide, destroying the false selves. The original movement is the Self's cosmic questing power. Restraining it is "only not dying"; regaining it is ultimately the only thing that matters.

It is hard to see/name the fact that phallocracy reduces women to framed pictures/holograms/robots. The see-ing, nam-ing of this nonbeing is essential to liv-ing. As Linda Barufaldi, a postchristian Feminist, has said: "It's like the Beatific Vision."[26] Explaining her remark, she added that in her adolescence she had always been puzzled by her catholic instruction concerning this belief (in an ultimate vision of the christian god). For according to catholic teaching it is impossible to have the Beatific Vision in this life. She now realizes that this was a typical reversal: for a woman to see through the patriarchal god is to begin to live, finding her own divinity. Another postchristian Feminist theologian, Emily Culpepper, remarked that this see-ing of women reminded her of the reversal contained in the idea of "gallows humor"—an expression meant to convey that there is an experience of seeing through the absurdity of everything only when one is condemned to die. This notion, she now recognizes, reversed the fact that seeing through the controlling (male) myths is the beginning of living.[27]

The state of robotitude is marking time hopelessly, a pure repetition of mechanical gestures. Beginning living means that the victim sees and names the fact that the oppressor obliges her to consume her transcendence in vain, changing her into a thing.[28] No kind of tokenism in a transcendence-sapping system will free our Selves from the spell of patriarchal myth. As long as that myth (system of myths) prevails, it is conceivable that there be a society comprised even of 50 percent female tokens: women with anatomically female bodies but totally male-identified, male-possessed brains/spirits. The myth/spell itself of phallocratism must be broken.

It may at first seem "natural" for women to reason that one can break the spell by demonstrating that "achievement" on male terms is natural to them. But after this is seen through, we encounter the problem of unmasking and moving beyond the mediocrity of such achievements without falling into opposing forms of mediocrity. Moreover, revolting against the tyrants of a phallotechnic world is revolting not only against their pseudonatural "life," that is, maintenance level of existence, but also against their pseudosupernatural state, against their myths and technological miracles.

Revolting Hags/Crones are repudiating robotitude, which is an imposed state of idiocy, a kind of cretinism. The term *cretin,* according to Merriam-Webster, is derived from a French dialect term meaning "kind of deformed idiot found in the Alps." The root of this term is the Latin *christianus* (christian). This term was used "to indicate that such idiots were after all human." Revolting/re-considering requires deicide; leaving the State of Idiocy implies the death of the cretin god. It also implies repudiating inclusion in the pseudogeneric "after all human" condition of cretinism. Re-considering is denying this false harmony, breaking its bonds, bounding into freedom.

FLYING FETUSES: MYTHOLOGICAL/ TECHNOLOGICAL NECROPHILIA

A few years ago one Robert Byrn, a 40-year-old professor of criminal law at Fordham University, took it upon himself to represent all human fetuses between the fourth and twenty-fourth week of gestation scheduled to be aborted in New York City municipal hospitals. Byrn was himself represented by attorney Thomas Ford, who made the following statement: "The fetus might well be described as an astronaut in a uterine spaceship." [29] As Ellen Frankfort aptly comments:

> It takes a certain kind of imagination to assume guardianship for something lodged within another's body—a rather acquisitive proprietary imagination that fits right in with the conception of a woman as a spaceship and the contents of her womb as an astronaut.[30]

The astonishing Byrn incident and the analogy made by his attorney merit some attention for the light they throw upon the deceptions of male myth. Since an astronaut is perceived as the captain of a "vessel," there is a desire to see the fetus as controlling the woman. Moreover, the image of the astronaut in a spaceship is interesting also because in this image the "captain" is very much controlled by other males outside the spaceship (for example, politicians, economists, scientists, flight surgeons, engineers). This makes the analogy particularly "appropriate" in its perverse way, for the fetus is maintained in control of the woman by males outside (for example, politicians, legislators, priests, doctors, social workers, counselors, husbands, "lovers"). Moreover, the analogy involves deceptively circular reasoning, making it doubly appropriate in this doublethink context. For here, a biological event—the presence of the fetus in the uterus—is imaged as "like," that is, imitative of, a technological event—the presence of an astronaut in a spaceship. This elicits an obvious question: *Is* the astronaut in the spaceship an attempt to imitate the situation of the fetus in the uterus? Elsewhere I have shown that there is (unacknowledged) evidence in ethical writings on abortion of a widespread male tendency to identify with fetuses.[31] This merits further analysis.

There are clues about the source of this fetal identification syndrome (which is frequently fatal for women unable to obtain needed abortions) in Frankfort's description of Byrn as "a childless man who seeks to guard unwanted fetal tissue." [32]

Males do indeed deeply identify with "unwanted fetal tissue," for they sense as their own condition the role of controller, possessor, inhabitor of women. Draining female energy, they *feel* "fetal." Since this perpetual fetal state is fatal to the Self of the eternal mother (Hostess), males fear women's recognition of this *real* condition, which would render them infinitely "unwanted." For this attraction/need of males for female energy, seen for what it is, is *necrophilia**—not in the sense of love for actual corpses, but of love for those victimized into a state of living death.

Frankfort's description of Byrn as "childless" also merits scrutiny. For it is the condition of *all* males to be childless, and there is evidence that this condition is experienced as disturbing to those who are obsessed with reproduction of the male self (which should not be confused with any genuine desire to care for and energize another being). Indeed there are male authors who are very willing (perhaps too willing) to attest to the anxiety of males over their childless state. Philip Slater, for example, writes of "this vulnerability of the male in the sphere of worldly immortality which gives rise to the concept of the 'external soul,' so prominent in magic and mythology."[33] According to his view, a woman need not guess whether something of herself continues on in a new organism, for she can see the child emerge from her own body:

> Thus if one translates "soul" in these stories as "that part of me which will live on after I die," the woman initially holds her "soul" within herself. It is only the man whose "soul" always resides outside of himself.[34]

Thus "as men have been lamenting for centuries, his immortality is out of his own control."[35]

According to this view, then, males identify the "immortal" soul with biological offspring, and women should feel fortunate in their role as incubators, shells, hotels, youth hostels, homes, hatcheries for human souls. I have already suggested that it is

* *Necrophilia* is defined by Merriam-Webster as "obsession with and usually erotic attraction toward and stimulation by corpses, typically evidenced by overt acts (as copulation with a corpse)."

dangerous for women to accept reductionist theories about the male propensity for "womb envy." Thus it should arouse suspicion that Karen Horney's "womb envy" theory (with which she countered Freud's proposition of "penis envy") has been eagerly adopted by some liberal males (for example, Philip Slater). The problem with such a theory is that the implied criticism stops short of being a genuine feminist analysis. Hags must learn to double-double unthink (Andrea Dworkin's phrase)—that is, to go past the obvious level of male-made reversals and find the underlying Lie. Thus it is a pitfall simply to reverse "penis envy" into "womb envy," for such theories trick women into fixating upon womb, female genitalia, and breasts as our ultimately most valuable endowments. Not only disparagement, but also glorification of women's procreative organs are expressions of male fixation and fetishism. These disproportionate attitudes are also demonically deceptive, inviting women to re-act with mere derivative fetishism, instead of deriding these fixations and focusing upon the real "object" of male envy, which is female creative energy in *all* of its dimensions. Male hatred of women expressed in such fetishized forms hides the deeper dimensions of envy, which remain unacknowledged. Thus we hear one male say of another's "project" or invention, "That's his baby." We also hear men describe the books, papers, articles of other men as "pregnant" with meaning. Such deceptive expressions provide clues to the deeper levels of deception. They suggest that the procreative power which is really envied does in fact belong primarily to the realm of mind/spirit/creativity. Yet this envy is not necessarily a desire to *be* creative, but rather to draw—like fetuses—upon another's (the mother's) energy as a source. Thus men who identify as mothers (that is, supermothers controlling biological mothers) are really protecting their fetal selves. They wish to be the fetuses/astronauts and the supermothers/ground commanders, but not the biological vessels/spaceships which they relegate to the role of controlled containers, and later discard as trash.

Ultimately these two roles—male fetus and male supermother—are connected (even identical), since both roles are contingent on a parasitic relationship to women. The male "mother's" spiritual "fecundity" depends upon his fetal (fatal) fettering of the female to whom he eternally attaches himself by a male-made umbilical cord, extracting nutrients and excreting waste (as he does also with "Mother Earth"). The penis, of course, is both a material and symbolic instrument for the restoration and maintenance of this umbilical attachment.

It is impossible to miss symptoms of this male fertility syndrome in the multiple technological "creations" (artificial wombs) of the Fathers—such as homes, hospitals, corporate offices, airplanes, spaceships—which they inhabit and control. Moreover, these male-constructed artificial wombs are ultimately more tomb-like than womb-like, manifesting the profoundly necrophilic tendencies of technocracy. Here Erich Fromm's description of necrophilia is applicable, although misleading. Writing of the *Futurist Manifesto* (1909) of F. T. Marinetti, he states:

> Here we see the essential elements of necrophilia: worship of speed and the machine; poetry as a means of attack; glorification of war; destruction of culture; hate against women; locomotives and airplanes as living forces.[36]

What is described here is a mechanization of life, a robotizing regression, *the* patriarchal pathology, which exposed itself in the mid-seventies in the Heavenly Homosexual Hitching as a metapathology.* But Fromm's description is deeply decep-

* The necrophilic mentality of the space programmers was exemplified in Dr. Wernher von Braun, the German-born space scientist, whose rocketry enabled the United States to make the first manned landing on the moon. When von Braun died in June 1977, an earlier "triumph" of his career was drawn to public attention. As the *Boston Globe* reported on June 18, 1977: "Almost three decades earlier, he headed the German effort that culminated in the notorious V-2 rocket bombs sent against Britain by Hitler in the final year of World War II. More than 1,000 of the weapons landed on London and its suburbs. At the end of the war, von Braun and 120 associates from the German rocket center at Peenemuende on the Baltic Sea surrendered to the Americans, after fleeing to southern Germany to avoid capture by the Russians. They were hired by the U.S. Army to work on rocketry in the United States." An article in the *Boston Globe*, June 19, 1977, gives some indication of the horror of the V-2 rockets, citing a 68-year-old pharmacist who

tive, for, although some essential elements of necrophilia are noted, the core cause, "hate against women," is mentioned only as a detail on an itemized list, rather than being shown in its prior causal relationship to the other times. Woman hating is at the core of necrophilia.

Thus it was utterly appropriate that the American spacecraft in the Celestial Spectacular of 1975 was named "Apollo." For Apollo was the personification of anti-matriarchy, the opponent of Earth deities. His name is said by some to have been derived from *appollunai,* meaning destroy.[37] Jane Harrison points out that he is the death-dealer, most deadly of all the gods.[38] She also shows that he is a woman-hater.[39] Moreover, Kerényi points out that Apollo's real enemy was a female creature, a dragoness named "Delphyne"—a name connected with an old word for womb.[40] Apollo killed her immediately after his birth.[41] With perverse appropriateness, his temple was built at a place named "Delphi," functioning as his artificial womb. Significantly, upon this temple was engraved the maxim: "Keep woman under the rule."

Although Apollo was fathered by Zeus and had a mother—Leto—he could well be described as "not of woman born."[42] Fittingly, he was born in a place of Not-Earth, a floating island in the sea named Delos. Fittingly, too, he encouraged matricide. Slater observes that "the myth of Apollo seems to express an infinite process [*sic*] of doing and undoing, of affirmation and negation of the maternal bond."[43] The more accurate term, of course, would be *procession,* for this is a deadly circle.

It should also be noted that the myth of Apollo functioned

---

lived through the blitz: "The V-2 rockets were the worst. When the V-1 types came over you could hear them. But you never heard the V-2s. Imagine just walking along the street and then 'bang'—with no alarm, no warning or anything. That's what it was like." Shortly before von Braun's death the scientists intoned: "We are now coming into an era of space research that one might call the humanitarian era in which man will use the tools and capabilities of space." When his death was announced, President Carter eulogized him: "He was not only a skilled engineer but also a man of bold vision. His inspirational leadership helped mobilize and maintain the effort we needed to reach the moon and beyond" (*Boston Globe,* June 18, 1977).

to legitimate male homosexuality in ancient Greece: "Apollo had relationships with many youths, the first of whom was Hyacinthus; the summer festival *Hyacinthia* commemorated this relationship."[44] Another scholar cites an inscription hewn on the rock wall beside the temple of Apollo Carneius on the island of Thera (Santorin) in the Aegean. It reads: "Invoking the Delphic Apollo, I, Crimon, here copulated with a boy, son of Bathycles." We read that "the sacred place and the name of Apollo make it plain that . . . we are being told about a sacred act, steeped in solemnity and honor."[45]

The mythic associations of the "union with Apollo" displayed in the space spectacular were deceitfully manipulated. Clearly, the culture does not plan spectaculars to legitimate "gay liberation." The astronauts and cosmonauts were obviously "family men" with "family pictures." What *was* legitimated was male power bonding, while the erotic component in male mating was concealed and denied. The fact that the erotic component was present on a mythic level but concealed made the apparently nonerotic power bonding message more effective. While overtly promoting the oppressive ideal of the nuclear family, this space spectacular subliminally appealed to erotic fantasies allegedly taboo in heterosexist society. This deceitful taboo titillation tactic is employed widely in patriarchal propaganda, reaching hysterical heights in the hidden messages of advertising.

The products of necrophilic Apollonian male mating are of course the technological "offspring" which pollute the heavens and the earth. Since the passion of necrophiliacs is for the destruction of life and since their attraction is to all that is dead, dying, and purely mechanical, the fathers' fetishized "fetuses" (re-productions/replicas of themselves), with which they passionately identify, are fatal for the future of this planet. Nuclear reactors and the poisons they produce, stockpiles of atomic bombs, ozone-destroying aerosol spray propellants, oil tankers "designed" to self-destruct in the ocean, iatrogenic medications and carcinogenic food additives, refined sugar, mind pollutants of all kinds—these are the multiple fetuses/feces of stale male-mates in love with a dead world that is ultimately co-equal and consubstantial with themselves.

The excrement of Exxon is everywhere. It is ominously omnipresent.

THE ILLUSION OF "DIONYSIAN" FREEDOM

There have, of course, been male reactions against a state of consciousness which is perceived as "the tyranny of Apollo." Nietzsche expressed this reaction, and more recently it has been a theme song of some christian theologians, such as Sam Keen, who writes: "Western culture has become increasingly Apollonian, and the time has come when the rights of Dionysus must be reasserted."[46] According to this view, the influence of Apollo has dominated Western theology and religious institutions, which for the most part have been identified with the status quo, putting their weight behind maintaining their "present boundaries." Oddly, the "Dionysian" approach is seen by such theologians as "revolution" and as "a radical solution."[47]

Any careful scrutiny of patriarchal Greek myth makes clear that Apollo and Dionysus are simply two faces of the same god. Thus the proposals for "revolution" have the dreary resonance of a revolving door, re-sounding the same message. The "solution" consists in seeking absolution from the crime of worshipping a false god by gazing for awhile at one of his other masks. What is sought is merely variety on the level of appearance—since genuinely radical change would involve the fearsome courage to cut through all the masks, facing Nothing.

Since Dionysus is so commonly set up as the mystifying mythic "complement" of Apollo and offered as an androgynous alternative to the stereotypically rigid Apollonian masculine model, his story requires some scrutiny. Jane Harrison points out that "the word Dionysus means not 'son of Zeus' but rather 'Zeus-Young Man,' i.e., Zeus in his young form."[48] Dionysus was in fact (in the fact of myth) his own father. To anyone aware of the meaning of Christ ("the Word incarnate") in christian myth, the parallel is inescapable. Christ is believed by christians to be the incarnation of the "Second Person of the Trinity," and thus consubstantial with the father. Therefore, Christ, too, pre-existed himself and was simply a later manifestation of "Zeus (Father)-Young Man." Christian theologians who have been reveling in "Dionysian" theology will, of course, be the first to grant that Christ incorporates elements both of Apollo and of Dionysus. In glorifying the "Dionysian element" they see themselves as celebrating a release from one-sidedness—from stereotypic Apollonian/masculine rigidity, as finding "a dancing god." The emerging (still christian) theology is one "of the spirit, leisure, play, listening, waiting, feeling, chaos, the unconscious."[49] All of this, of course, sounds like a description of "positive" aspects of stereotypic femininity. It is important that we dis-cover the connections between apparently contradictory phenomena, namely the femininity of Dionysus, which male theologians and philosophers reacting against Apollo identify with and glorify, and the strange (but familiar) "fact" that he is his own father.

G. Rachel Levy informs us that "in the ritual of Dionysus the Son eclipsed the Mother."[50] Any feminist can see the ominous implications of this eclipse. In its light (darkness) we can perceive the significance of the "radical" male re-turn to the Dionysian mask of the male god. Slater is very explicit about this "solution" to male identity problems:

> What is unique about the Dionysian solution is that the maternal threat is welcomed, and boundary-loss actively pursued. Instead of seeking distance from or mastery over the mother, the Dionysian position incorporates her.[51]

Dionysus does not have to run away from his mother or struggle against her. His victory is total.

Semele, the mother of Dionysus, is the Totaled Woman. When she was six-months pregnant Zeus struck her with thunder and lightning, and she was consumed. Graves sums up the sequelae:

> But Hermes saved her six-month son: sewed him up inside Zeus's thigh, to mature there for three months longer; and, in due course of time, delivered him. Thus Dionysus is called "twice-born," or "the child of the double door."[52]

Thus Dionysus's mother was already dead long before he was born. Zeus dispenses with the woman and bears his own son.

But there is more to the convoluted plot than this. For some of the myth-masters held that Semele had been impregnated by drinking a potion prepared by Zeus from the "heart" (probably meaning phallus) of Dionysus, who had pre-existed her. (According to some, he had previously been borne by Persephone, who had been raped by Zeus.)[53] Thus Dionysus is his own father, reborn and self-generated.[54] Since he (Zeus-Young Man) is identified with Zeus who bore him, he is also his own mother. Thus Semele can be seen as epitomizing the patriarchal ideal of mother as mere vessel. Moreover, the apparently contradictory aspects of Dionysus—his self-fathering and his femininity—coincide. In the "light" of these elements of the Dionysian myth we can well be suspicious of male fascination with the all too feminine Dionysus, for his mythic presence foreshadows attempts to eliminate women altogether.

This femininity of Dionysus should be seen also in connection with his glorification as boundary-violator, as the one who drives women mad. A clue to the meaning of this maddening boundary violation is unwittingly provided by Norman O. Brown, who writes of Dionysus as "the mad god [who] breaks down the boundaries," abolishing repression. According to Brown: "The soul that we call our own is not a real one. The solution to the problem of identity is, get lost."[55] This Dionysian temptation to "get lost" is not unfamiliar to women, whether our "background" has been christianity, imported Eastern spirituality, liberated liberalism, "the people's struggle," straight suburban society, the orgiastic sexual avant-garde, or all of the above. This is the seductive invitation to "lose the self in order to find it." Whether the loss takes place through the glorified pain of feminine christian masochism or through the "pleasurable" torture of S and M rituals, or through determined devotion to Higher Causes, the result is the same: female annihilation. Although countless women are seduced into this tragic loss of Self, the fabricators of the destructive plot are male.

To Dionysus was attributed the ability to shatter cognitive boundaries in women, that is, the capacity to drive women mad—which he did whenever possible. Madness is the only ecstasy offered to women by the Dionysian "Way." While the supermasculine Apollo overtly oppresses/destroys with his contrived boundaries/hierarchies/rules/roles, the feminine Dionysus blurs the senses, seduces, confuses his victims—drugging them into complicity, offering them his "heart" as a love potion that poisons.

The rituals of romantic love as well as those of religion draw women into the "ecstasy" of Self-loss, the madness which is literally standing outside our Selves, being beside our Selves. In contrast to this, radical feminist ecstasy is Self-centering moving beyond the boundaries of the fathers' foreground. This is finding the Self. Indeed, we break the credibility of the contrived Apollonian boundaries—such as the false divisions of "fields" of knowledge and the splits between "mind" and "heart." But in this process we do not become swallowed up in male-centered (Dionysian) confusion. Hags find and define our own boundaries, our own definitions. Radical feminist living "on the boundary" means this moving, Self-centering boundary definition. As we move we mark out our own territory.

The Dionysian solution for women, which is violation of our own Hag-ocratic boundaries, is The Final Solution. To succumb to this seductive invitation is to become incorporated into the Mystical Body of Maledom, that is, to become "living" dead women, forever pumping our own blood into the Heavenly Head, giving head to the Holy Host, losing our heads. The demonic power of Dionysian deception hinges on this invitation to incorporation/assimilation, resulting in inability to draw our own lines. To accept this invitation is to become unhinged, dismembered. Refusing is essential to the process of the Self's re-membering, re-fusing.

The madness which is the Dionysian Final Solution for women is confusion—inability to distinguish the female Self and her process from the male-made masquerade. Dionysus sometimes assumed a girl-like form.[56] The phenomenon of the drag queen dramatically demonstrates such boundary violation. Like whites playing "black face," he incorporates the oppressed role without being incorporated in it. In the phenomenon of transsexualism, the incorporation/confusion is deeper. As ethicist Janice Raymond has pointed out, the majority of transsexuals are "male to female," while transsexed females basically function as tokens, and are used by the rulers of the transsexual empire to hide the real nature of the game.[57] In transsexualism, males put on "female" bodies (which are in fact pseudofemale). In a real sense they are separated from their original mothers by the rituals of the counseling process, which usually result in "discovering" that the mother of the transsexual-to-be is at fault for his "gender identity crisis."[58] These "patients" are reborn from males. As Linda Barufaldi suggested, this fact was symbolized in the renaming of the renowned transsexual of tennis, Renée (literally, "re-born") Richards, whose original first name was Richard.[59] The rebirthing male supermothers include psychiatrists, surgeons, hormone therapists, and other cooperating professionals. The surgeons and hormone therapists of the transsexual kingdom, in their effort to give birth, can be said to produce feminine persons. They cannot produce women.[60]

The seduction of women—including feminists—into confusion by Dionysian boundary violation happens under a variety of circumstances. A common element seems to be an invitation to "freedom." The feminine Dionysian male guru or therapist invites women to spiritual or sexual liberation, at the cost of loss of Self in male-dictated behavior. Male propagation of the idea that men, too, are feminine—particularly through feminine behavior by males—distracts attention from the fact that femininity is a man-made construct, having essentially nothing to do with femaleness. The seductive preachers of androgyny, of "human liberation," dwell upon this theme of blending. When they put on the mask of Dionysus, the Myth-Masters play the role of Mix-Masters. "Mixing Up the Victim" is the name of their mime.

The illusion of Dionysian freedom, then, drives women into madness. As defined by Honor Moore, M-A-Dness is Male Approval Desire. She writes:

> M-A-D is the filter through which we're pressed to see ourselves—if we don't, we won't get published, sold, or exhibited—I blame none of us for not challenging it except not challenging it may drive us mad . . .[61]

It is true that the Apollonian mask of god drives women into madness, but this is the madness of one who sees the face/mask of the Destroyer, and who desires his approval because she *knows* she needs this in order not to be raped, maimed, starved to death, imprisoned, murdered. This is a clearheaded M-A-Dness. But the Dionysian method is to break the boundaries that make such methods in our madness possible. Dionysus, the "gentle-man," merry mind-poisoner, kills women softly. Male Approval Desire, under his direction, lacks a sense of distance from The Possessor. The Dionysian M-A-D-woman desires the approval of her god because she loves him as herself. She and he, after all, are two in one flesh. She and he are of one mind. She has lost her Self in his house of mirrors, and she does not know whose face she sees in her beatific visions.

Thus Dionysus drives women mad with his femininity, which appears to be a relief from the stern masculinity of Apollo. Kerényi points out that Dionysus "was called Pseudanor, 'the man without true virility'—not to speak of all his joke names such as *gynnis,* 'the womanish,' or *arsenothelys,* 'the man-womanly.'"[92] This is the ultimately deceptive glorification of femininity, convincing women that it is desirable for men and also desired by them, luring females into forgetting the falseness of femininity, blinding us to the fact that femininity is quintessentially a male attribute.

BOUNDARY VIOLATION AND THE FRANKENSTEIN PHENOMENON

The most basic and paradigmatic form of boundary violation is, of course, rape. Patriarchy as the Religion of Rapism legitimates all kinds of boundary violation. It blesses the invasion of privacy, for example, by such governmental agencies as the FBI and the CIA, christening this invasion "Intelligence." It extends its blessing also to the violation of life itself by scientifically "created" pollution, by the metastasizing of a carcinogenic environment—epitomized in the ever-expanding cities of the dying—and by the hideous weapons of modern warfare. The creators of artificial death belong to the same funereal fraternity as the various male supermothers—creators of artificial life and manipulators of existing life. As boundary-violators, all participate in the mythic paradigm of Rapism. All march in the same funeral procession, and the knowledge they share in common is mortuary science.

Mary Shelley displayed prophetic insight when she wrote *Frankenstein,* foretelling the technological fathers' fusion of male mother-miming and necrophilia in a boundary violation that ultimately points toward the total elimination of women. Her main character, Doctor Frankenstein, expressed a bizarre necrophilic "maternal instinct" in making the monster whom he later repudiated, fled from in terror, and was destroyed by in agony. Unable to be a "mother" (creator) the mad scientist in the story constructs his "child" from parts of corpses. While in the process of making his monster, he muses about his project:

> A new species would bless me as its creator and source; many happy and excellent natures would owe their being to me. No father could claim the gratitude of his child so completely as I should deserve theirs. Pursuing these reflections, I thought that if I could bestow animation upon lifeless matter, I might in process of time . . . renew life where death had apparently devoted the body to corruption.[63]

Mary Shelley here unmasks the mentality of the technological "parent." For it is precisely the case that no mere *father* could realistically claim the right to such gratitude as that desired by the "single parent" monster-maker, the scientific sire. Doctor Frankenstein's inordinate wish for such gratitude is a symptom of the "external soul" syndrome discussed earlier. For such gratitude would imply perpetual indebtedness of the creature for the gift of life itself and "prove" that the monster-maker possessed an animating force or "soul." This character illustrates the hysteria of the manic mother-mimer who experiences his inherent male sterility as unbearable barrenness.

Today the Frankenstein phenomenon is omnipresent not only in religious myth, but in its offspring, phallocratic technology. The insane desire for power, the madness of boundary violation, is the mark of necrophiliacs who sense the lack of soul/spirit/life-loving principle with themselves and therefore try to invade and kill off all spirit, substituting conglomerates of corpses. This necrophilic invasion/elimination takes a variety of forms. Transsexualism is an example of male surgical siring which invades the female world with substitutes. Male-mothered genetic engineering is an attempt to "create" without women. The projected manufacture by men of artificial wombs, of cyborgs which will be part flesh, part robot, of clones—all are manifestations of phallotechnic boundary violation. So also the behaviorism of B. F. Skinner and "physical control of the mind" through the use of implanted electrodes by such scientists as Delgado, are variations of monstrous male "motherhood." Having implanted electrodes in the brain of his "child" (brainchild), the Master Mother has it firmly tied to his electronic apron strings.[64] The list can be extended to include other Master Mothers, such as physicians and surgeons (especially in gynecology/obstetrics and in neurosurgery), psychiatrists, therapists, and counselors of all kinds.

The pseudocreative power of boundary violation (the Dionysian specialty) is clearly an invasion of women's bodies/spirits and of all our own kind: earth, air, fire, water. This is *real* violation/invasion and requires that Hags make our Selves impermeable to the invaders' violations and exorcise the effects of their presence. Our understanding is often muddied, however, by the patriarchal propensity to erect artificial boundaries (the Apollonian specialty) and then to "violate" these as "enemy" territory. Wars among nations, corporations, administrations belong to this category of invasion and defense. This sort of "violation" belongs to the arena of boys' games and essentially has nothing to do with women's priorities. Yet, countless women are in fact killed, maimed, and raped in these war games, and the energy of millions more is sapped and diverted by loyalty to one "side" or the other of these idiot battles. The adequate response of Furious Women is refusal to be tricked into pouring our energy into false loyalties. Our sane surviving requires seeing through male-made, maddening artificial boundaries, as well as deriding male "violation" of these false boundaries. Furious women will refuse to follow the man-made model of Dionysus's sister, Athena, the brain-child of Zeus, who is obsessed with abetting and supporting the Battles of the Boys. For we can see that she is M-A-D with Male Approval Desire.

Since the twice-born Athena is now legion, having been reproduced over and over by xerox cloning (conditioning), she may not be able to feel her true condition as did Doctor Frankenstein's monster in Mary Shelley's tale. She may not be *able* to feel wretched, helpless, alone, and abhorred, "apparently united by no link to any other being in existence." [65] Since she is a Self-suffocating shell, a figment of her bizarre father's imagination, she hides depth from the Self. But behind the foreground of false selves, of fathers' favorites, there is the deep Background where the Great Hags live and work, hacking off with our Dreadful double-axes the Athena-shells designed to stifle our Selves.

Predictably, the smothering Mothermen of the Apollo and Dionysus Club will try to graft back on to our psyches the Athena-parts hacked off by Hags. Our hope lies in our power to know what these prostheses and cosmetics really are. The artificial faces, limbs, conditioned responses, are dead matter molded into "life-like" imitations of women, labeled "The Real Thing." It is essential that we be aware of the shifting methods of the ghoulish gynecologists, these sons of Frankenstein, whose specialty is "the science of womankind."

CHAPTER TWO

DISMEMBERMENT BY CHRISTIAN AND POSTCHRISTIAN MYTH

What have they dared,
sucking at man's wounds for wine,
celebrating his flesh as food?
Whose thirst has been slaked by his vampire liquor,
whose hunger answered by his ghostly bread?
Who have they dared to hang on that spine instead
and then deny, across millennia?
Whose is the only body which incarnates creation
everlasting?

Robin Morgan,
from "The Network of the Imaginary Mother,"
The Lady of the Beasts

I will use my wife as an extension of myself.

President Jimmy Carter,
Interview in *Time,* January 3, 1977

. . . this crime has been committed
Not once, but 100 times told.
It began when I was but a young girl.
As you see, I have now grown quite old.
It is not a crime you have recorded
In your volumes trimmed with gold.
I do not speak of the rape of my body,
I refer to the rape of my soul.

Willie Tyson,
from "The Ballad of Merciful Mary,"
Full Count (Lima Bean Records)

We are, I am, you are
by cowardice or courage
the one who find our way
back to this scene
carrying a knife, a camera
a book of myths
in which
our names do not appear.

Adrienne Rich,
from "Diving into the Wreck,"
Diving into the Wreck

Hags must understand the recipes of patriarchal mind poisons prevalent today, analyzing their ingredients and the ways in which these are combined. We must learn to recognize, avoid, expel these poisons from our environment, for they are designed to paralyze Voyagers, to prevent our spirits from soaring beyond Processions. Therefore this chapter will focus upon modern modes of mythic mystification in the West. This will require an analysis of hebrew, christian, and postchristian male myth.

REFINED MINDBINDING: CHRISTIAN MYTH

I have shown that the christian trinity legitimates male mating (Prelude). This trio, which might be named "The Legiti-Mates," united with their offspring (Incarnation), Christ, and with his corporation, The Mystical Body of Christ, attempt to incorporate the world. Christian myth, like refined sugar, has been "purified" of the cruder elements that were present before its processing. Just as refined sugar sweetly damages the body, purified myth seductively deceives the mind. We might consider the following passage in Matthew's Gospel (13:13–14), in which Jesus says:

> The reason I talk to them in parables is that they look without seeing and listen without hearing or understanding. So in their case this prophecy of Isaiah is being fulfilled:

You will listen and listen again, but not understand, see and see again, but not perceive.

Of course no one—neither the chosen elite nor the flock of followers—was really meant to understand. However, whereas the "chosen" disciples willingly abandoned themselves to christianity, there were others—the mysterious "they"—who, intent on survival, rejected the divine invitation to ultimate Self-destruction. Hags/Witches must know that *we* are "they"—that is, the intractable, willful ones, deliberately "dull of hearing," resisting these paralyzing parables. Patriarchal myth is refined in christianity so that Hag-ocracy will decline. Sugar-coating its necrophilic intent, it attempts to seduce Hags to resign our Selves and sign our own commitment papers to the institution of the Double Cross, doublethinking our Selves into total numbness and dumbness.

Trinitarian Reversals

Christian myth obviously did not spring out of nowhere. This idea is believable only to those who deny that it *is* myth, that is, part of the processions of patriarchal myths. My purpose here is not only to point out some cruder parallels/sources in chronologically antecedent androcratic myth, but also to uncover clues to Crone-logically antecedent myths and symbols, which have been stolen and reversed, contorted and distorted, by the misogynist Mix-Masters.

I have already discussed the christian trinity as the paradigm of processions, representing the closed system of eyeball-to-eyeball self-congratulatory communion among the fathers and sons. It is the model merger, the central committee, the consummate conglomerate. Generously, theologians, have allowed women some vague identification with the third person, if we will accept the false implication that the femininity of the holy ghost has anything to do with females.

The irony involved in this invitation to assimilation can be better appreciated if we are aware of the omnipresence of the Triple Goddess in early mythology. Athena, for example, had been the Triple Goddess.[1] Moreover, Plato identified Athena with Neith, who was the skin-clad Triple Goddess of Libya and who belonged to an epoch in which fatherhood was not recognized.[2] The pre-Hellenic Triple Goddess is sometimes identified as Hera-Demeter-Korê, and in Irish myth there is the Triple Goddess Eire, Fodhla, and Banbha.[3] There was also in Hellenic mythology the Triple Moon Goddess, whose different local titles were Thetis, Amphitrite, and Nereis.[4] The list could go on. The basic pattern was, according to some, Maiden, Nymph, and Crone, and according to others, Maiden, Mother, and Moon. Jane Harrison points out that figures interpreted to be "mother and daughter" are, in fact, often older and younger forms of the same person.[5] This threefoldness is by no means a mere family model. It has temporal, spatial, cosmic meanings.

The fact is that the ancient world knew no gods. Fatherhood was not honored. As patriarchy became the dominant societal structure, a common means of legitimation of this transition from gynocentric society was forcible marriage of the Triple Goddess, in her different forms, to a trinity of gods. Thus Hera was taken by Zeus, Demeter by Poseidon, Korê by Hades.[6]

When we see the Triple Goddess in the Background of the various trinities of gods which foreshadowed the christian trinity, other christian symbols fall into perspective as dim derivatives. Thus, in the Pelasgian creation myth, Eurynome, the Goddess of All Things, assumed the form of a dove and laid the Universal Egg. Her Sumerian name was Iahu meaning "exalted dove." * This title later passed on to Yahweh as crea-

* Upon hearing about the Goddess's name, Iahu, Eileen Barrett pointed out that as a child, when joyful and excited, she had often spontaneously exclaimed a word which sounded similar to this Sumerian name, i.e., *Ya-hoo!* She also commented upon the practice, during hebrew religious ceremonies, of refraining from pronouncing out loud the name of Yahweh when it occurs in the text being read. She suggested that the similarity in sound between the words Yahweh and Iahu may have been perceived, at some time in the distant past, as "giving the show away." This is one Crone-logical hypothesis about the traditional silence. Hag-ologists should note that in Merriam-Webster the name YAHU is listed as a "transliteration of the Hebrew tetragrammaton YHWH as some modern scholars believe it was pronounced before the Jews ceased to pronounce it about three centuries B.C.: YAHWEH."

tor.* [7] When we see the traditional symbol of the holy ghost as a dove in the light of this Background, its absurdity becomes obvious. One is tempted to speculate about how "he" could lay an egg.

Then, too, there is the ritual position of the fingers of the catholic priest giving a blessing. The thumb, index finger, and middle finger are raised, while the other two fingers are turned down. This position is said, of course, to represent the christian trinity. Originally, it was the "Phrygian blessing," given in the name of Myrine, the great Moon-Goddess of Asia Minor, known also as Marian, Ay-Mari, Mariamne, and Marienna. She was the counterpart of Neith, who of course was Athena, before she was reborn from the head of Zeus.[8] When we realize that Myrine was Mother of the gods, that is, the Background of which the christian trinity is a distorted mirror image, the gruesome reversal involved in the "honoring" of Mary as "Mother of God" (the god whom she adores) is evident.

There is more to be considered concerning the triplicity of the Goddess. Kerényi alludes to the astonishing fact that one of the names of the Goddess was Trivia—a name used equivalently with Hecate, Artemis, and Diana. The classical figure

* As Graves points out: ". . . the mythographers were forced to admit that the Creator of all things might possibly have been a Creatrix. The Jews, as inheritors of the 'Pelasgian,' or Canaanitish, creation myth, had felt the same embarrassment; in the *Genesis* account, a female 'Spirit of the Lord' broods on the face of the waters, though she does not lay the world egg . . ." (See Robert Graves, *The Greek Myths* [Baltimore, Md.: Penguin Books, 1975], I, 4, *2*). This "embarrassment" is reflected in such works as *The Hebrew Goddess,* by Raphael Patai (New York: Ktav Publishing, 1967). Despite all the evidence, Patai insists that "the legitimate Jewish faith . . . has always been built upon the axiom of One God" (p. 21). The adjective *legitimate,* of course, removes embarrassing facts as illegitimate. Patai, at the close of his Introduction, presents the following depressing and deceiving prophecy: "It will be there [in Israel] . . . , if at all, that she will re-emerge, in who knows what old-new image, to mediate, as of old, between man and God, and to draw the faith-bereft sons with new bonds of love to their patiently waiting Father" (p. 28). Happily, no Daughter or Mother seems to be involved here, and certainly not The Goddess.

of Hecate, Goddess of Witches, was built upon a triangle, with faces turned in three directions (later replaced by three dancing maidens). The Hecate statutes were set up at the crossing of three roads; hence the name, Trivia. The idea of the crossing of the three roads was of course cosmic, for such crossings point to the possibility of dividing the world into three parts—which the ancients did. Thus Hesiod in the *Theogony* acclaims the Goddess as the Mistress of three realms —earth, heaven, and sea—a dominion which was hers long before the order of Zeus.[9] Even in the Middle Ages, crossroads, specifically the places where three roads converged, were believed to be locuses of preternatural visions and happenings. In Sweden, for example, sacrifices were made to elves at "three-road meetings." In the Highlands of Scotland, divination was believed possible if one sat on a three-legged stool at the meeting of three roads when the clock struck twelve on Halloween (the witches' Sabbath). Such beliefs have by no means completely disappeared.[10]

In light of the cosmic significance of the term *trivia* as the crossing of three roads and of the Goddess who bears this name, the contemporary meaning of the term in English should be examined. The English term, which according to Merriam-Webster is derived from the Latin *trivium* (crossroads), is defined as "unimportant matters: TRIFLES." The adjective *trivial* is defined as "COMMON, ORDINARY, COMMONPLACE . . . of little worth or importance: INSIGNIFICANT, FLIMSY, MINOR, SLIGHT." Of course, according to patriarchal values, that which is "commonplace" is "of little worth," for in a competitive, hierarchical society scarcity is intrinsic to "worth." Thus gold is more important than fresh air, and consequently we are forced to live in a world in which gold is easier to find than pure air.

The bizarreness of this mind-set/mythos becomes evident when we realize that the christian trinity is dogmatically declared to be "omnipresent." This omnipresence is never equated with triviality, needless to say. Yet, there is an apparent contradiction in the fact that androcracy, which makes scarcity an inherent requisite for great worth, finds it fitting to name its allegedly infinite, perfect, supreme god "omnipresent." The apparent contradiction fades when we re-consider the implications of the fact that patriarchy is the Religion of Reversals. The "omnipresent" god is not in fact "commonplace," because he is no place. Correctly named, his "omnipresence" is omniabsence. His absence everywhere is named as "presence" everywhere, and the "presence" consists precisely in this false naming. The ubiquity of false naming masks the ominous Absence which is the essence of the patriarchal god. It confers upon him infinite worth in the rarified realm of Reversal Religion's value system. The infinite absence of divinity in the patriarchal god is the ultimate scarcity—rarified to the point of Zero. Here is the hidden meaning of his being called "Omega," which decoded, says Ultimately Nothing.

The Goddess's name, Trivia, then, should function as a constant reminder of patriarchal religious reduction of real, multidimensional presence to the Nothingness which is created by the fathers in their own image and likeness. Whenever Hags hear the terms *trivia, trivial, trivialize,* these should function as reminders of the omnipresence of Reversal, whose ultimate meaning is re-versing of life-engendering energy, symbolized by the Goddess, into necrophilic Nothing-loving. In the Land of the Fathers, women are trivial, concerned with trivia, deserving to be trivialized. In the Prehistoric Background of Hags, the time/space of Trivia, women are free to find the cosmic triviality of our own complex creative power.

Transformations: From Tree of Life to Torture Cross

This cosmic energy is symbolized in the Tree of Life, the Sacred Tree, which is the Goddess. Helen Diner points out that the tree "belongs to the cult of all Great Mothers and, like them, is sacred." [11] The tree, however, can hardly be limited to a symbol for biological fertility. It represents a cosmic energy source. In ancient Egyptian art, the Tree is depicted as bringing forth the Sun itself.[12] This Cosmic Tree, the living Source of radiant energy/be-ing, is the deep Background of the christian cross, the dead wood rack to which a dying body is fastened with nails. As Diner succinctly states: "In Christianity, the tree becomes the torture cross of the world." [13]

Thus the Tree of Life became converted into the symbol of

the necrophilic S and M Society. This grim reversal is not peculiar to christianity. It was a theme of patriarchal myth which made christianity palatable to an already death-loving society. Thus Odin, worshiped by the Germans, was known as "Hanging God," "the Dangling One," and "Lord of the Gallows." Neumann remarks that "scarcely any aspect of their religion so facilitated the conversion of the Germans to Christianity as the apparent similarity of their hanged god to the crucified Christ."[14] In the cheerful German version, the tree of life, cross, and gallows tree are all forms of the "maternal" tree. As we shall see in The Second Passage, Germany remained particularly faithful to this mythic S and M tradition, which was acted out with fervor during the witchcraze and during the Nazi holocaust.

The christian culmination of the Tree of Life is analyzed by Neumann in the following manner:

> Christ, hanging from the tree of death, is the fruit of suffering and *hence* [emphasis mine] the pledge of the promised land, the beatitude to come; and at the same time He is the tree of life as the god of the grape. Like Dionysus, he is *endendros,* the life at work in the tree, and fulfills the mysterious twofold and contradictory nature of the tree.[15]

The bland "objective" scholarly style dulls the reader's capacity to cut through to a realization of the horror of phallocratic myth. Hags should certainly question *why* such "fruit" of the tree of death is equated to a pledge of the "promised land," for the situation hardly looks promising. We should also question how he could be the life at work in the tree, since the "tree" is obviously dead and he is on his way to the same state. As for the "mysterious . . . and contradictory nature of the tree"—the confusion here is mind-boggling. For a tree *is* mysterious but it is *not* contradictory. What is contradictory is Reversal Religion's reduction/reversal of the Tree of Life to a torture cross. In this pseudocosmos of contradictions anything can make "sense." Thus we are told that the Cross is a bed. It is not only Christ's "marriage bed," but also it is "crib, cradle, and nest." It is the "bed of birth and . . . it is the deathbed."[16] When we recall that Christ incorporates the femininity of Dionysus—the role to which females in patriarchy are supposed to conform—the equation of marriage bed and deathbed does, of course, make a certain kind of sense. Appropriately, one might classify the equation as unintended "gallows humor."

Veiled Vampirism

The transformations in the Tree of Life symbolism unveil the fact that in christian myth Christ assimilates/devours the Goddess. Whereas the Goddess had been the Tree of Life, Christ becomes this. Moreover, as the "life at work" in the tree, he becomes its juice/sap. When we consider that the tree had been the body of the Goddess, the violence of this assimilation becomes more perceivable. The "gentle Jesus" who offers the faithful his body to eat and his blood to drink is playing Mother Goddess. And of course the fetal-identified male behind this Mother Mask is really saying: "Let me eat and drink you *alive.*" * This is no mere crude cannibalism but veiled vampirism.

In connection with this "blood-drinking" syndrome of christian ritual, it is important to look at the origin of the "chalice" which contains the wine believed to be transformed into Christ's blood.† In his *Dictionary of Symbols* Cirlot offers the confusing idea that the chalice is "a sublimation and a consecration

* In 1975 the book *Alive,* by Piers Paul Read—the story of the Andes survivors who ate the frozen bodies of their dead companions—received the Catholic Book of the Year Award from the Thomas More Association. In the book the survivors justify their eating human flesh on the basis of the gospels and the ritual of the catholic mass. Their interpretation was accepted by priests who are theologians and canon lawyers.

† We should also note Ernest Jones's admission that "in the unconscious mind blood is commonly an equivalent for semen." See Ernest Jones, *On the Nightmare* (London, 1949), cited in H. R. Hays, *The Dangerous Sex: The Myth of Feminine Evil* (New York: G. P. Putnam, 1964), p. 152. This of course evokes yet another set of images embedded in the ritual. Moreover, we have already seen, in connection with the Dionysian myth, that the image of the heart can function as a symbolic cover or substitute for the phallus.

of the cauldron as well as of the cup." [17] To Crone-ographers aware of the significance of the cauldron in prepatriarchal history it is obvious that the symbol is not "sublimated" and "consecrated," but rather ripped off, reduced, reversed, reveiled. Neumann has pointed out that "the magical caldron or pot is always [in early imagery] in the hand of the female mana figure, the priestess, or, later, the witch." [18] Adrienne Rich lucidly shows the significance of the fact that pottery-making was invented by women and taboo to men. She shows that the cauldron is associated with the Mother Goddess, the Priestess-Potter, the Wisewoman, and Maker, and—generally—with women as transformers:

> Thus, not power *over others,* but *transforming* power, was the truly significant and essential power, and this, in prepatriarchial society, women knew for their own.[19]

What happens, then, when the cauldron of women-identified transforming power is stolen, that is, reversed by christian myth into the chalice, a symbol of the alleged transforming power of an all male priesthood? [20] Just this: patriarchy asserts its *power over* others in the name of the male god by using the ancient symbol of nonhierarchical, gynocentric transforming energy.* The priest is playing priestess. Hiding behind her symbol, he attempts to change wine into "sacred" blood—the christian version of Male Menstruation.† However, in this case there is none of the original creation associated with the

* This is grotesquely illustrated by the protestant hymn, "Have Thine Own Way, Lord":

> Have thine own way, Lord! Have thine own way!
> Thou are the Potter: I am the clay.
> Mold me and make me after Thy will.
> While I am waiting, yielded and still.

† The hebrew tradition also manifests considerable confusion about menstruation. Thus, discussing the biblical laws, Neusner writes: "The menstruating woman or the leper is not dangerous outside of the cult. These people are unclean—which means *only* that they cannot come to the Temple until purified." (See Jacob Neusner, *Invitation to the Talmud: A Teaching Book* [New York: Harper and Row, 1973], p. 17).

cauldron/chalice, but rather the christian chalice becomes the focus of a cannibalistic/necrophagous ritual. The contents of the cup—the blood of the slain Christ—are consumed by the pseudopriestess.

The "Virgin Birth"

In order to become the Goddess, the male god, manifested in Christ, had to be reborn. This theme was of course present in the story of Dionysus, who pre-existed himself and was reborn from the thigh of Zeus. However, this was a cruder story than that of Christ, who did not even require a paternal thigh from which to be reborn, and whose mother (Mary), unlike Semele, did not need to drink a potion containing his "heart." In the christian myth, the second person of the eternal trinity pre-existed his own incarnation as Christ. The holy ghost, the third person, who was consubstantial with him, impregnated Mary spiritually. So spiritual was the whole affair that Mary remained a virgin, according to christian theologians, before, during, and after his birth.[21]

It should not be imagined that Mary had any real role in this conception and birth. Although some christians like to call the "virgin birth" a paradigm of parthenogenesis, it is not that. As Helen Diner points out, it is really the opposite of parthenogenesies, for in the myth of the Virgin Birth, Mary does nothing, whereas in parthenogenesis the female accomplishes everything herself. Of the christian myth she writes: "Thus the Virgin, in the extreme spiritual religion called Christianity, means only the vessel waiting in purity for the bearing of the Savior." [22] Commenting upon the "Virgin Birth," Anne Dellenbaugh points out that this myth stripped all women of their integrity, for the female was transformed into little more than a hollow eggshell, a void waiting to be made by the male.[23] Dellenbaugh goes on to point out important associations between parthenogenesis and cloning. Her point is that a deliberate effort is being made to remove creativity from women and re-establish it in the realm of male domination and control. Thus, the christian "Virgin Birth" is a link between primordial mythic parthenogenesis and technological attempts to establish the "father" as the one "true parent" through cloning.[24]

It is understandable that most people would be confused not only by the christian myth of the "Virgin Birth," but also (and consequently) by the deceptive pious equations of this myth with parthenogenesis. The deception is redoubled by the language of scientists and scientific popularizers concerning parthenogenesis. For these "authorities" use misleading language to erase the fact that when parthenogenesis takes place the eggs develop independently of sperm. They refer to such stimulating agents as magnesium chloride, salt, or even simply cold temperatures as "the father" when female animals (for example, sea urchins, turkeys, and rabbits) reproduce without males.

An illuminating illustration of the deceptive reversal thinking of christianity combined with technological doublethink is provided in the following statement by Robert Francoeur, a catholic ex-priest and specialist in experimental embryology:

> If this is the situation among the other animals, as far as natural and artificial parthenogenesis goes, is it possible that women may occasionally be *victims* of a *virginal conception* [emphases mine]?[25]

Since many feminists are actively interested in exploring the possibilities of parthenogenesis, it may strike the reader as strange to see women who (possibly) conceive parthenogenetically described as "victims of a virginal conception." The language of Francoeur the scientist contains an implicit recognition of the hidden implications of christian myth. I suggest that his language reflects christian doublethink. For the mind of the catholic scientist has been impregnated by the christian reversal of parthenogenesis—the "Virgin Birth." The catholic Mary is not the Goddess creating parthenogenetically on her own, but rather she is portrayed/betrayed as Total Rape Victim—a pale derivative symbol disguising the conquered Goddess. Because of this mythic deception, parthenogenesis, but not "normal" impregnation, is illogically linked with victimization.

The rape of the Goddess in all of her aspects is an almost

universal theme in patriarchal myth. Zeus, for example, was a habitual rapist. Graves points out that Zeus's rapes apparently refer to Hellenic conquests of the Goddess's ancient shrines.[26] The early patriarchal rapes of the Goddess, in her various manifestations, symbolized the vanquishing of woman-identified society. In the early mythic rapes, the god often assumed a variety of animal forms; the sense of violence/violation is almost tangible. In christianity, this theme is refined—disguised almost beyond recognition.

The rape of the rarefied remains of the Goddess in the christian myth is mind/spirit rape. In the charming story of "the Annunciation" the angel Gabriel appears to the terrified young girl, announcing that she has been chosen to become the mother of god. Her response to this sudden proposal from the godfather is totaled nonresistance: "Let it be done unto me according to thy word." Physical rape is not necessary when the mind/will/spirit has already been invaded.[27] In refined religious rapism, the victim is impregnated with the Supreme Seminal Idea, who becomes "the Word made flesh."

Within the rapist christian myth of the Virgin Birth the role of Mary is utterly minimal; yet she is "there." She gives her unqualified "consent." She bears the Son who pre-existed her and then she adores him. According to catholic theology, she was even "saved" by him in advance of her own birth. This is the meaning of the "Immaculate Conception" of Mary—the dogma that Mary was herself conceived free of "original sin" through the grace of the "savior" who would be born of her. This grace received in advance, described by theologians as "grace of prevention or preservation," is something like a supernatural credit card issued to a very special patron (matron). Mary's credit line was crossed before she was even conceived. Double crossed by the divine Master Charge system, she was in a state of perpetual indebtedness. Still, as I have explained elsewhere, despite all the theological minimizing of Mary's "role," the mythic presence of the Goddess was perceivable in this faded and reversed mirror image.* [28]

* In order to understand the Background of Mary, Hags should recall that she was known as "the new Eve." This leads us to look into

Rebirth of the Divine Son

The ultimate rape of the Goddess, however, required something more than this refined confinement in the figure of Mary.

---

the Background of Eve who, in hebrew myth, was a dulled-out replacement for Lilith, Adam's first wife. Patai writes of Lilith as portrayed in the Talmudic period: "When Adam wished to lie with her, Lilith demurred: 'Why should I lie beneath you,' she asked, 'when I am your equal since both of us were created from dust?' " (See Raphael Patai, *The Hebrew Goddess,* p. 210.) Any Crone-ographer, of course, can recognize this as a watered-down version of what Lilith really might have said, which would hardly have been an argument for mere "equal rights." As for Eve, constructed from Adam's rib—Peggy Holland has pointed out that this is an interesting mythic model: the first male-to-constructed-female transsexual. Patai affirms that it was Lilith who persuaded Eve to eat of the Tree of Knowledge and he acknowledges that Lilith was a Hag (pp. 210–13). According to Cirlot, Lilith, in the Israelite tradition, corresponds to the Greek and Roman Lamia. (See J. E. Cirlot, *A Dictionary of Symbols,* trans. by Jack Sage [New York: Philosophical Library, 1962], p. 180.) Graves puts more of the pieces together, indicating that Lamia was the Libyan Neith, also named Anatha and Athene. (See Robert Graves, *The Greek Myths,* I, 61, *1.* Graves adds that "she ended as a nursery bogey" (which is, of course, the fate of all Hags/Crones/Witches in patriarchal myth). Lilith is also identified with Hecate, the lunar goddess and "accursed huntress." After pointing this out, Cirlot remarks: "The overcoming of the threat which Lilith constitutes finds its symbolic expression in the trial of Hercules in which he triumphs over the Amazons" (*Ibid.,* p. 180). Since Hecate was associated with hares, this suggests that rabbits are in the Virgin Mary's Background. Given the parthenogenetic propensities of rabbits and given the reversal mechanisms of patriarchal myth, this association makes sense. We are also led to think about the identity of the familiar "Easter Bunny" (and about the reversal involved in the image of "Playboy Bunnies"). Finally, when considering Lilith, Hags should note that this name is said to be derived from the Babylonian-Assyrian word *lilitu,* meaning a "female demon, or wind-spirit." (See Robert Graves and Raphael Patai, *Hebrew Myths: The Book of Genesis* [Garden City, N.Y.: Doubleday, 1964], p. 68.) This is interesting in view of the fact that the name of the "Holy Spirit," who is believed to have impregnated the Virgin Mary, is derived from the Latin *spiritus.* Is the holy spirit trying to copy Lilith? Also fascinating is the thought that since, as we have seen, Yahweh is a derivative and reversal of the Goddess, one of whose primary names is Lilith, he is exposed as an imposter, a female impersonator, and a transsexed caricature of that Great Hag herself.

The adequate androcratic invasion of the gynocentric realm can only be total erasure/elimination of female presence, which is replaced by male femininity. Thus in the christian myth the divine son is re-born again and again without even the vestigial presence of the "Virgin Mother." One of his rebirths is his baptism by John the Baptist, at which time the Paternal Voice from heaven booms: "This is my beloved Son, in whom I am well pleased." (Matt. 3:17). This is later followed by the supreme rebirth, namely his resurrection from the dead. This theme of descent to the Underworld and emerging from the earth had of course been present in myths concerning the Goddess. Thus, for example, Persephone, Demeter's daughter and Self, was obliged to spend three months of each year in the underworld realm of her husband Hades, who had raped and abducted her. Although this earlier myth was male-manipulated and functioned to legitimate the transition to patriarchal control, it still contains remnants of the theme of the Goddess rising/emerging from the depths. In the christian tale, however, the feminine male god, the "Son of God" who has replaced the Daughter/Self of the Goddess, descends into "hell" (the earth's womb) and emerges on his own. There is no female presence involved in this Monogender Male Automotherhood.*

The autogestation of the androgynous Christ was completed by a sort of second "growing up" (going up) which was his ascension into heaven, where he rejoined his father (himself). Since Dionysus ascended into heaven and now sits at the right hand of Zeus, it is consistent that the christian Dionysus should have done the same thing.[29] As Kerényi points out, that Greek god conferred immortality upon his "mother," Semele, renamed her Thyone, "the ecstatically raging," and took her to heaven.[30] Roughly corresponding to this is the catholic dogma of "the Assumption," according to which Mary was taken up into heaven. Although protestants were alarmed at the papal proclamation of this dogma in 1950, the catholic myth-makers

* The only remnants of divine female presence in this resurrection story were the women at the tomb, whose words of witness were dismissed as worthless, as *trivia*.

undoubtedly sensed, at least subliminally, that this final gesture was no threat to the primacy of the self-mothered godman. Unlike Semele, Mary hardly appears to be ecstatically raging. Her dis-ease more nearly resembles catatonia. Dutifully dull and derivative, drained of divinity, she merits the reward of perpetual paralyis in patriarchal paradise. It is rage-provoking to recall that this assumed and assimilated holograph is an aftershadow of the great Moon-Goddess Marian, who is the counterpart of Neith and the original Athena. For here is the ravished remnant of Haggard Holiness in patriarchal history. Here is the crushed Crone, flaunted before us as the symbol of our tamed Fury.

This flaunting of the tamed Goddess, however, is not essential to christian myth. Although it was expedient in medieval christianity and still functions in catholicism, the use of this symbol is basically a sales promotion gimmick, a transitional trick/(de)vice. The real direction of religious rapism is toward absolute elimination of all vestiges of real female presence. Just as catholicism was an important stage in the refinement of phallocentric myth, protestantism represents a more advanced stage of "purification." Having eliminated Mary, the ghost of the Goddess, it sets up a unisex model, whose sex is male. Jesus, androcracy's Absolute Androgyne, is male femininity incarnate. Unlike Dionysus, whom he spiritually incorporates, he is not a member of a pantheon of female and male peers. He is the Supreme Swinging Single, forever freed from challenge by Forceful Furious Females. Moreover, the male-identified femininity of the unisex christian model does not negate male masculinity/sadism. Rather, it *accepts* this. This christian demolition of the Goddess and mythic establishment of male divinity has paved the way for the technological elimination of women through the application of modern medicine, transsexualism, cloning, and other forms of genetic engineering.

Here is the basic intentionality of this "Word made flesh." This "Word" is doublespeak that drives women M-A-D, violating cognitive boundaries, preparing the way for a phallotechnic Second Coming. It is the announcement of the ultimate Armageddon, where armies of cloned Jesus Freaks (christian and/or nonchristian) will range themselves against Hags/Crones, attempting the Final Solution to the "problem" of Female Force.

POSTCHRISTIAN EXTENSIONS OF CHRISTIAN MYTH

The majority of those who believe themselves to be sophisticated would probably deny that taking christian myth "seriously" has had any controlling effect on their behavior or beliefs. The fact is that the symbols of christian and prechristian patriarchy permeate Western culture and are actively promoted by Western technocracy. The messages of murderous misogynism are simultaneously superrefined and supercoarsened. Moreover, the christian church prepared the way for postchristian mental/moral dismemberment by morally coercing its members to believe the blatantly bizarre. The penalty for refusing such forced acts of "faith" was eternal damnation and hellfire. The descendents of christians (including former christians as well as those remotely controlled by the general heritage) have been trained to believe the unbelievable. Thus trained, they are ripe for the rapes of the professional bureaucratic and technological tyrants, the fabricators of texts and textiles that contort minds/bodies. In a particular way they are vulnerable to the violations of the media massagers, the subliminating ad-men.

Chilling Children's Tales

Postchristian mind-poisoning begins in earliest youth. Studies have demonstrated abundantly that infants are given gender identity messages even before they can understand words—messages which are conveyed through touching, voice intonations, choice of clothing.[31] It is not unusual for parents to use television as a tranquillizer for infants. While all of this is becoming recognized and documented, it is essential that Spinsters search out the symbolic content lurking behind obvious messages.

Children's books provide chilling evidence of mind-control through dismembering myth. Fairy tales are particularly gruesome examples. An apparently genteel contemporary type of disguised mind-dismembering myth for children is exemplified in *The Giving Tree,* by Shel Silverstein.[32] It is the story of a tree—consistently referred to by the pronoun *she*—who gives absolutely everything she has to a boy. This begins innocently enough, with her shade, leaves, and fruit. But, the boy grows up and cuts off her branches and then her trunk. Finally, in his old age, he uses her stump as a seat. As a result of all this nonreciprocated giving, the tree is "happy." The jacket blurb of this book, published in 1964 but still a big seller, describes it as "a tender story . . . . a moving parable for readers of all ages." The story, in fact, is one of female rape and dismemberment. It draws upon sources in the Background of female identity, taking the Tree of Life—who is the Goddess—and making her a willing participant in her own mutilation, which makes her "happy." Her degradation is total, for the "Giving Tree" wallows in self-destruction. Here is a model of masochism for female readers of all ages, and of sadism for boys of all ages. This chilling children's tale is an extension of christian myth. It is a superrefined, invasive, and deceptive offspring of self-satisfied secularists secure in their superiority to christian crudity. The saccharine sweet story of a little boy who "loves" a tree—a young Apollo who crowns himself with her leaves—has "healthier" appeal than overt S and M biblical tales of a dead godman crowned with thorns. Thus the post-christian (that is prechristian) parable has deceptive acceptability, extending its tentacles into unaware minds, guiding them to a more primal Fatherland, inhabited by paradigms of patriarchal matricide. It thus brings its parental purchasers and readers into unwitting compliance with primary programming for gynocide.

Whether or not the authors, illustrators, and promoters of such books "understand" that they are communicating gynocidal messages is beside the point. Since self-deception is of the essence of doublethink, they undoubtedly would respond with incredulity/amusement/indignation to such an analysis. For they themselves have been programmed not to recognize gynocidal reversals. Within the massive public relations business of patriarchy, the promotion of rape and dismemberment has top priority, and it is essential that the promoters make this fact invisible to everyone, especially to themselves. As George Orwell wrote of his character, Winston Smith, in *1984*: "For the first time he perceived that if you want to keep a secret you must also hide it from yourself." [33]

*Adult Entertainment/Amusement**

Misogynist mind-poisoning and dismemberment of adult as well as juvenile inhabitants of the Fatherland is managed by mass media programmers who coordinate and utilize the expertise of other professionals, e.g., medical, legal, psychiatric. This constitutes a veritable postchristian extension of the "theology of the Word" into the homes of millions. Such extensions/incarnations of the collectively supreme patriarchal Word (Lie) in secular as well as sacral society requires the discrediting of women's *own* words, although patriarchally instilled delusions will be accepted from the mouths of women after these have been tested and corroborated. This follows the tradition of the christian gospel: The words of the women who had "seen" the risen Christ were at first discredited, but the error of those who disbelieved the women was rectified when the reports were confirmed by male witnesses. The women's perseverance in perpetuating a patriarchal fantasy was finally rewarded. So also in postchristian secular society, where beliefs are managed by the mass media, women are still rewarded for perseverance in promoting male propaganda. It is when women speak our own truth that incredulity comes from all sides. Thus, in an accused rapist's trial, the raped woman's word is usually the chief evidence for the prosecution, and this is commonly evaluated as worthless.

A contemporary example of woman-dismembering, postchristian "theology of the Word" was the ordeal of Patricia

* According to Merriam-Webster, the "archaic" meaning of the verb *to amuse* is "to divert the attention of (as from the truth of one's real intent): DECEIVE, DELUDE, BEMUSE."

Hearst. Kathleen Barry points out that Hearst's status as an heiress did not cause her treatment by the patriarchy to be essentially different from that of the "ordinary" rape victim, welfare mother, or prostitute. As in all of the other cases, her *word* had no credibility without male corroboration. Steven Weed had publicly described the kidnapping of his then-fiancée. As Barry points out:

In this one instance, her word had been legitimately corroborated, and formal testimony wasn't necessary to believe her. For the rest of it—her life as a kidnap victim, as a fugitive—we have only her word, her testimony. Her life continues to hang on the worth of her word.[34]

That word, of course, is officially worthless.[35]

Barry gives an exquisite analysis of the idea of "lying" as it has been illustrated in the entire tragedy, including the trial:

It is argued that she lied to save her life; it is not argued that she told the truth to save her life; it is not argued that her attorneys gave her a story to fit their strategy; it is not argued that her defense attorneys developed a defense strategy based on her story.[36]

Patricia Hearst's truth was interpreted by the jury and the world at large as falsehood. Each of the jurors interviewed by Barry described her as listless and pale. Since she failed to entertain them with emotional outbursts against the SLA (Symbionese Liberation Army) and looked/spoke the way she really felt, it was assumed that she was lying *through her body* as well as her words. For, since the patriarchy requires women to be "made-up"—that is, lie through their bodies—this assumption that women are lying carries over to all physical appearance, however deviant. An alternate juror interviewed by Barry, Mary Neiman, credited Hearst's words, but *her* voice was not officially heard in the deliberations. This unheard woman acknowledged the listlessness, and interpreted it as a sign of truthfulness, stating: "She could have made herself look better if she were lying."

Here, then, is a succinct summary of the secular applied theology of the "Incarnate Word," according to which women are incarnate lies. The male-made lies are manifold and intertwined. Thus, the SLA was credited by the Left for "raising the consciousness" of an heiress, while the fact of the racist murder of Marcus Foster and the fact that a woman was beaten and raped were overlooked. "What mattered is that they got her to identify on tape with the plight of the oppressed." [37] The SLA used feminist rhetoric and forced Hearst into the public position of sex-role violator, thereby setting her up as a victim of sexist hatred by all classes. On one level of analysis it could be said that the SLA and the supporting Left were using Hearst to attack her rich father and his corporate power. In reality, they were impotent against him. A closer analysis shows that the SLA, the Left, the Establishment and its media were using his image and brand of power to attack and brand *her*. Through the manipulation of Patricia Hearst and of her image, seemingly opposed factions of men actively combined to brand and gang rape all women who persist in surviving. Because of her possession by the Hearst wealth, Patricia was hated by the less wealthy (almost everyone), and especially by righteous revolutionaries. Because of her enforced deviation from the role of well-brought-up feminine young woman, she was hated by the Establishment. The real effects of the media's symbolic identification of Patricia Hearst with all women—particularly those with a will to survive—should not be underestimated. The media-managed misogynist violation of this woman functioned to legitimate the escalation of violence against every woman.

Secular S and M

In christendom as well as in postchristian secular society, the words/expressions of female spirit are raped, twisted, tortured, dismembered. From the witch trials, brought about by the bonding of theologians and legal specialists, to the Hearst trial, effected by the bonding of secular theologians (psychiatrists) and attorneys, the dis-spiriting process is essentially the same. Whereas the christian cross glorified suffering as a means to purification and ultimate joy in the "Afterlife," the contemporary secular sadomasochistic gospel proclaims that female suffering *is* joy. Thus even the agony of Patricia Hearst was perceived by many as "a rich girl getting her kicks."

A Rolling Stones billboard atop Sunset Strip in Los Angeles in 1976 depicted a woman with hands tied together and legs tied spread apart, accompanied by the words, "I'm 'Black and Blue' from the Rolling Stones—and I love it!" The anonymous authors of a 1977 *Time* article entitled "Really Socking It to Women" paternally discuss some gimmicks of "kings of kink" who admittedly seek revenge against women. With Timely detachment they write of the men who shoot photos of women mutilating themselves, and describe the men who design albums with pictures of women chained, women hanged, women gang-raped. Predictably, they find a woman psychiatrist who is willing to claim that all of this corresponds to masochistic fantasies of independent women.[38] Thus the rape of the female mind/will, the message of the Virgin Mary's impregnation by the holy ghost, is repeated and completed in the "joyful" secular S and M resurrection of the torture cross.

I suggest that theologians have always fantasized a female hanging on the cross. Hannah Tillich, in her lucid autobiography, *From Time to Time,* describes the pornographic exploits of her husband, Paul Tillich, the famous theologian. She describes entering his room during his showing of a porn film for his own private entertainment:

> There was the familiar cross shooting up the wall. . . . A naked girl hung on it, hands tied in front of her private parts. . . . More and more crosses appeared, all with women tied and exposed in various positions. Some were exposed from the front, some from the side, some from behind, some crouched in fetal position, some head down, or legs apart, or legs crossed—and always whips, crosses, whips.[39]

Tillich was not atypical. He simply had a wife who was determined to publish the truth after his death, despite all the attempts of theologians, psychologists such as Rollo May, and other "friends" at first to stop her and later to discredit her.[40] His private life and fantasies reflected the essential symbolic content of his and other theologians' christology. Indeed, these sadomasochistic fantasies were the juice/sap of his impressive theologizing. Hannah, who after his death unlocked his drawers (supposed to contain his "spiritual harvest"), found the details of his sex-obsessed life:

> All the girls' photos fell out, letters and poems, passionate appeal and disgust. I was tempted to place between the sacred pages of his highly esteemed lifework those obscene signs of the real life that he had transformed into the gold of abstraction—King Midas of the spirit.[41]

Hannah Tillich thus helps to place the high symbolism and abstract rationalizations of christian theology of the cross in realistic perspective.

Torture for "higher causes," religious and secular, has always been legitimated by christian cross-bearers. In the fifteenth century witchcraft was defined as *crimen exceptum*, removing all legal limits to torture. Thus it is not surprising that the secular sadomasochistic society which has descended from christianity by no means restricts its brutality to the realm of advertising, pornographic films, and kinky sex orgies. There is abundant evidence that systematic torture of political prisoners is carried on by many—probably most—governments. Here the rationalization is not "joy in sex" but something like "national security." In the 1970s, Amnesty International, an organization devoted to the release of all political prisoners in the world, reported evidence that brutal political torture is a worldwide practice. While this reality is not new, and while the evidence of the horrors of the Nazi death camps and of American torture of Vietnamese is easily available, it is important to see this in the context of the superrefinement and simultaneous coarsening of postchristian secular extensions of christian myth.

Considering the horrors of the torture of heretics and witches in the beginnings of the patriarchal "modern" period, it would appear that the application of torture cross mythology could hardly get coarser. It does, in the sense that coarsening blends with superrefinement of technique. The most hideous/harsh/coarse torture is carried out with the sophisticated techniques of modern medicine, including "life-prolonging" machines and a variety of pharmacological means also used in hospitals. Indeed, the sadistic methods used in the Nazi death camps, in contemporary political prisons, and in hospitals, including "mental hospitals," bear striking resemblances to each other.[42] Each of these subcultures of sadism has its own hierarchy, apprenticeship, initiation rites, and its own language. The subculture of torture in Brazil is a bizarre example, with its "parrot's swing," its "dragon chair," its "spiritual seance," and its "advanced school of torture."[43] Moreover, women have a special role in these subcultures as subservient token torturers of other women. The "bitch of Buchenwald" and female torturers of female political prisoners in such countries as Argentina are illustrations of this traitor-token syndrome.

My point here is not that the sadosymbolism of christianity is the unique source for worldwide S and M. Sadomasochism is the style and basic content of patriarchy's structures, including those antecedent to and outside christianity. Rather, christianity, with its torture cross symbolism, has been one expression of this basic pattern. I am contending, however, that within Western culture this symbolism has provided legitimation and impetus for subsequent refinements/coarsenings of sadomasochism. Virtually all of modern patriarchal society has been influenced/shaped profoundly by the West, becoming a sort of Total Westworld. Thus, the ever more deceptively refined/coarsened/extended tentacles of the torture cross syndrome pervade the planet.

Contemporary Trinities

Another primary christian symbol which dominates secular society is the divine trinity, which, as I have noted, is the Model Merger, Supreme Stalemating. Episcopal bishop James Pike casually referred to it as "the committee god"—a remark intended and appreciated more for its wit than for its unwitting depth of perception. The quip expressed a profound truth—the fact that patriarchy has multiple anonymous, inseparable "heads." A popular song of the early 1970s referred to "the three men I admire the most—the Father, Son, and Holy Ghost." Such admirable/honorable men are the invisible computer-controlled controllers of the military industrial conglomerates that are killing the earth.

Significantly, the Los Alamos scientists who were building the atomic bomb in 1945 referred to the first test under the code name "Trinity." Commenting upon this, Robert Jungk wrote: "No clear explanation has hitherto been forthcoming as to why this *blasphemous expression* was employed, above all in such a connection [emphasis mine]." [44] That author, in choosing to perceive the use of the name "Trinity" in this connection as "blasphemous," manifests his complicity (probably unwitting) in the deceptive myth. Hags may recognize that this use of the divine name was indirectly blasphemous to the Triple Goddess, but this level of meaning was clearly beyond Jungk's intent.

The Goddess Iahu, as noted earlier, is the "exalted dove" who laid the Universal Egg. In christianity, not only has the Hebrew Yahweh replaced Iahu, but the One God has become also Three in One, and the "Third Person" enters the shell-like Virgin to lay "the Word." Now, we should ask/contemplate what sort of eggs are laid by the secular successors to this divine dove. Clearly, the "ultimate egg" would be the one with the power to destroy all that originally had been hatched from the Universal Egg of Creation. Within this context we can appreciate the appropriateness of Jungk's report on the language of the scientists anticipating the first atom bomb test. As the expectant fathers anxiously awaited the first complete bomb, they fantasized the appearance of a "dud" as the arrival of a "girl," a "success" as the arrival of a "boy." [45]

The use of trinitarian symbolism to describe the hellish stalemates of patriarchal necrophilia is not confined to esoteric code words of atomic scientists. In 1977 *Reader's Digest* saw fit to publish an article entitled "The 'Unholy Trinities' that Undermine America." The author, James Nathan Miller, describes these phenomena as three-cornered "power-cells" which are mutually self-serving. He informs the digesting reader that big government is "neither faceless nor monolithic." In fact it generally wears a collection of three stony faces (masks). After a fire in an Alabama nuclear plant in 1975 the Nuclear Regulatory Commission issued a "new" set of safety rules which were merely the same old rules in different language. Miller tried unsuccessfully to get the situation changed. He writes:

> There you have the typical unholy trinity: a Congressional committee responsible for recommending legislation in a particular area, the bureaucracy responsible for administering the legislation, and the private special interest group that's most directly affected. They are an incestuous family.[46]

Specifically, he points out that over 60 percent of NRC's top officials at the time (including the director of regulation, responsible for writing the "new" rules) "were hired directly from the nuclear industry."

The fact that such trinities are named "unholy" appears to separate them from the patriarchal god, but on another level are identified with him, for, like him, they are omnipotent/impotent. Just as the three-headed dog, Cerberus, is described by mythologists as a prechristian "infernal replica of the divine triunity," so we might see these congressional nuclear "watchdogs" as infernal replicas, preparing the way for the coming Inferno. In Greek myth, Cerberus is the guardian of dead souls in Tartarus, "charged with the task of preventing their return into the world above where atonement and salvation are still possible." [47] The "watchdogs" of Washington perform a similar function.

Modernized Mystical Bodies

So much for the three-headed leadership of the postchristian, secular, mystified Mystical Body. It may be useful to cast a glance at its mythic prototype—the catholic doctrine of the "Mystical Body." Explaining this, Pope Pius XII reiterates the Pauline doctrine that just as the faithful require the Head, so the Head requires the members. Indeed. Moreover, writes the pope, in the church "the individual members do not live for themselves alone, but . . . all work in mutual collaboration for their common comfort and for the more perfect building up of the whole Body." [48] The pope stresses the intimacy of the union between the Mystical Body and its Head. He also writes of the distinct internal principle of unification of this Body, which is vastly superior to the principle of union in a physical body or in a moral body (such as the State).[49]

According to catholic theology, entry into the Mystical Body is effected through the sacrament of baptism, the sacrament of "rebirth." As Emily Culpepper remarked, this involves a curious reversal of the birth process, which involves the exodus of the newborn from another's body.[50] Here is a clue to the tomb-like quality of this Body, which incorporates each new member. Moreover, baptism is said to imprint a "character" or indelible mark upon the soul. A typical theological authority on this subject explains the process in words that deserve to be read verbatim:

> Similarly, before man can enter into the organic union with Christ through incorporation, an inner transformation or structural change must take place within him. It is this very change which sacramental character is effective in bringing about. Through it we are made conformable to the Head and are enabled, as members, to assimilate the vivifying power of the mystical body and to cooperate with the work of the Head.[51]

The author of this passage stresses that this "mystery of Christ's body stands in organic relation to the great dogmatic truths of the Trinity, the Incarnation, grace, and the sacraments." [52] All of the sacraments contribute to the rise and growth of the Body. Moreover, "the Holy Spirit moulds the mystical body by imprinting the image of the Head upon the members so that His grace may overflow upon them." [53]

Ira Levin, in his popular dystopian novel, *This Perfect Day,* manifests uncanny comprehension of postchristian supersocialist extensions of this dogma.[54] In this negative utopian tale, in which the whole world is blissfully unified, all members of "the Family" function under the direction of a computer named Uni. The Unification of this mystical body/Family, whose heroes/saints/forefathers are Christ, Marx, Wood, and Wei, is total. The mark of the horrible head computer is the "nameber" which is stamped on each member's irremovable bracelet. His grace (the chemicals injected at everyone's monthly "treatments") flows through the veins of all. All are sustained by Totalcakes and Cokes—the only food and drink available—which is the daily communion of monotony for these dulled and dutiful truncated creatures, whose "excitement" consists in celebrating such holidays as Marxmas in Equality Park. Whereas the Head is immortal, the members are replaceable parts. Ultimately the goal is total removal of aggressiveness and deviance, building in helpfulness, docility, and gratitude—which in this supremely secular city of god will be achieved by genetic engineering.

Like the mystical body (church) and modern nation states, Levin's Unified Society has to deal with deviants. Its methods, however, are superrefined. Like priests, therapists, and deprogrammers, its advisors and doctors attempt to give heavier treatments to those suspected of deviancy, but chemistry has replaced confession and counseling. Moreover, the Unified Society has gone beyond the more obvious drastic means of "curing" deviants, such as witchburning and political "reeducation." Its techniques have advanced to absorbing and utilizing rather than merely eliminating the talents of strong deviants. In the surprise ending, the brightest and strongest resisters finally reach the innards of the hated computer with the intention of destroying this Super Machine, and find to their astonishment that they have passed the complicated series of tests/trials required for invitation to join the small ruling caste.

This fictionalized refinement of conversion represents the ultimate streamlining of patriarchal planning. Instead of wasting material by total elimination, the Head reincorporates would-be outsiders. This recycling and assimilation process, in which the Head eats the self-amputated members, surpasses the cruder religious scheme, which admits its failures through its doctrine of eternal damnation. Here, according to paternal plans, all are saved in one way or another—either as mystified members or as mystical masters.

It is profitable for feminists to read such "prophetic" dystopias, which certainly say as much about the patriarchal past/present as they do about the "future." This working out of theo-technology is a logical conclusion of the Bhagavad-Gita, the Talmud, Plato's *Republic,* Calvin's *Institutes,*

Hobbes's *Leviathan,* the Constitution of the United States, the Encyclical on the Mystical Body of Christ, the tenets of the Unification Church of Reverend Sun Myung Moon, B. F. Skinner's *Beyond Freedom and Dignity,* et cetera, ad nauseam. There is no active persecution of feminists in the ideal androcratic society, for there are no real feminists. All such problematic women will have been pacified/recycled in Perfect Fatherland, where Hags are not merely eliminated but assimilated alive. Such is the vampiristic aim of androcracy: to find a final resting place for the living dead (the undead).

Resurrections of the Dead

Within christian myth this dream is satisfied through the dreary dogma of "resurrection from the dead" (which should not be confused with profoundly cosmic consciousness of eternal life—a consciousness caricatured and cut short by the deadening dogma). Hope for "resurrection" is a felt necessity in those whose present life *is* dead or "only not dying." Phallotechnic extension and implementation of the resurrection theme is evident in efforts to achieve reproduction by cloning—a technological feat foreshadowed also by the myth of the Virgin Birth, as I pointed out earlier. Indeed, men can anticipate multiple future lives/selves through "xerox cloning." (The prospect of one hundred Henry Kissingers or one thousand Mick Jaggers is thought-provoking.)

For those not satisfied with succession by duplicates or centuplicates, there is the fascinating possibility of returning oneself—a combined resurrection/second coming/reincarnation through cryonics. The watchword of the cryonics movement (which advocates freezing at death, against the day when future science can thaw and revive those now defined as "dead") is: "Freeze—wait—reanimate." Robert C. W. Ettinger, who launched this movement in 1964 with his book, *The Prospect of Immortality,*[55] has acknowledged possible points of contiguity or similarity between cryonics and cloning, and has rejected the latter as having any interest for himself personally. Although Ettinger recognizes that after "resurrection" of a body that has been frozen for years it may be necessary to replace information stored in damaged parts of the brain, he does not like the idea of imprinting the old personality on a newly cloned duplicate brain. He is quoted as saying: "I wouldn't pay a nickel to have a twin of me built after my death." [56] However, since the one who has himself frozen at his nonfuneral has no guarantees about *who* will do *what* with his body or *when,* the state of dependency upon future godfathers implied in such technological hopes for resurrection is total.

The End of the World

Since myth functions as self-fulfilling prophecy, it is especially interesting to consider the fact that christian myth promises what is popularly known as "the end of the world." A common source for "information" about this impending disaster was the Book of Revelation. In this, the last book of the bible, John describes some of the wonders of his vision of what is to come in the future. Among these phenomena are earthquakes, drought, horrors in the heavens (stars falling, sun going black, blinding flashes of light), and plagues causing disgusting and virulent sores. Christians have commonly interpreted this prophecy of "the end" to include also a prediction of the conversion of the Jews. Finally, a major feature of this panoramic vision is the punishment of a famous prostitute (supposedly representing the large, wicked city of Babylon), who is stripped naked and eaten, and whose remains are thrown into the fire, according to god's intention.

In every age there have been christians convinced that they were living in Apocalyptic times—a reasonable assumption for a true believer, since the story had to come true some time and since patriarchy is ultimately self-destructive. The development of modern technology, however, has facilitated movement beyond mere passive expectation to active enactment of the envisioned horror show. Robert Jungk describes the first atomic explosion (in 1945) and the reactions of the scientists who created and witnessed it:

It is a striking fact that none of those present reacted to the phenomenon as professionally as he had supposed he would. They all, even those—who constituted the majority—ordinarily without religious faith or even any inclination thereto, recounted their experiences in words derived from the linguistic fields of myth and theology.[57]

He goes on to cite General Farrell, who spoke of "the sustained, awesome roar which warned of doomsday and made us feel that we puny things were blasphemous to dare tamper with the forces heretofore reserved to the Almighty." While Robert Oppenheimer was watching, a passage from the Bhagavad-Gita, the sacred epic of the hindus, flashed into his mind. As the gigantic cloud of destruction rose over "Point Zero" he recalled the line, allegedly uttered by Sri Krishna, the Exalted One: "I am become Death, the shatterer of worlds."

Here we see christian myth merge with the language of another sect of the religion which is Patriarchy. The message is Necrophilic Procession into Nowhere/Nothing. The point of Patriarchal Religion *is* Point Zero. Technologists from christian culture have led the way in acting out the Apocalyptic myth, making the magic mushroom cloud, fathering the fireball. Members and descendants of other religious bodies/families follow automatically in the atomic death march/funeral procession. Scientists are priests of patriarchy, performing the last rites. Typically, the justification for the atomic bomb in the 1940s was "to end the war." Translated, this means: To end the world.

Since Patriarchy *is* the State of War, it is interesting to consider the persistent propaganda concerning the "peaceful uses of nuclear energy." In the 1970s the Union of Concerned Scientists attempted to enlist cooperation in halting the funeral procession led by their more fanatic colleagues. In 1977 they sent out letters to selected "fellow citizens," pointing out the dangers of nuclear power plants and pleading for help in bringing these under control "while there is still time." They explained that a typical nuclear power plant contains an amount of radioactive material equal to the radioactive fallout from thousands of Hiroshima-size weapons, and they noted that in the next twenty-five years the nuclear industry plans to construct one thousand plants. Their fear is not that these will explode like an atomic bomb, but rather that the radioactive material will be accidentally released. In fact, no safe way has yet been found to dispose of the millions of gallons of lethal nuclear waste. Moreover, a typical nuclear power plant produces several hundred pounds of plutonium each year. One particle of plutonium produces lung cancer if inhaled, and it takes plutonium half a million years to lose its killing power. The concerned scientists pointed out that there are no adequate safeguards to prevent plutonium from being hijacked by terrorists. Moreover, the latter could use it to make atomic bombs.

The civilized governments of patriarchy, however, are run by terrorists. The plutonium, therefore, has already been hijacked. The Unholy Trinities are in charge of it. The powerful men are possessed by patriarchal myth and faithfully follow the blueprint in the Book of Revelation.

In the 1940s respected university professors, scientists, doctors, and industrialists of Nazi Germany carefully planned and executed the "conversion of the Jews" into soap, fertilizer, felt, and other by-products. In that same decade their respected scientific colleagues in America built the A-Bomb and dropped it "to end the war," thereby creating signs and wonders in the heavens, the horror of Hiroshima. In the decades that followed, more respected colleagues and their sons have busily prepared the way for the predicted earthquakes and drought. Through the "peaceful use of nuclear energy" and other forms of pure pollution they have paved the way for planetary plagues causing disgusting and virulent sores—radiation sickness and various forms of cancer.

In doing these things, the technological true believers of the Book of Revelation live their fatal faith, the faith of the Fathers. Knowing their own rightness/righteousness, they are participant observers in the stripping, eating, and burning of the "famous prostitute," the whore hated by god and by the kings (leaders) he has inspired. The harlot "deserves" to be hated and destroyed, of course, for she symbolizes the uncontrollable Babylon, the wicked city.* No one asks *who* are the agents of wickedness. It is enough to have a scapegoat, a victim for dismemberment. Everyone knows that the woman is at fault: the christian fathers have always spread this word, beginning with the story of Eve's "disobedience," and father Freud proved that it was true.

The ultimate contest was wrongly described in the Book of Revelation, however. The author in his vision failed to note the Holy War waged by Wholly Haggard Whores casting off the bonds of whoredom. These are Hags stripping away the last remnants of the harlotry imposed upon us, refusing to be eaten and burned, kicking away the disgusting beasts and "kings." Monique Wittig's "*guérillères*" shout the challenge:

> They [the women] say, put your legendary resistance to the test in battle. They say, you who are invincible, be invincible. They say, go, spread over the entire surface of the earth. They say, does the weapon exist that can prevail against you? [58]

The ultimately Holy War centers around the only genuine "energy crisis." Its focus is the wrenching free of female energy which has been captured and forced into prostitution by patriarchy, degraded into fuel for continuing its necrophilic processions. As Hags break from this bondage we break the spell of Deadly Deception. We break the myths of the masters.

In order better to understand how the spell can be broken we need to turn to further analysis of the ways in which mystifying myth is played out in patriarchy. This requires looking at the deadening dramas and rituals which program women into paralysis and into ultimate assimilation by the parasitic Processors, whose passion is focused on Point Zero, whose one deep desire is death.

* When Hiroshima was bombed, "she" was of course being treated like a "wicked" woman. The same imagery still controls the Japanese imagination. A character in a post-Hiroshima Japanese novel who is contemplating raping a woman who is wearing nylons makes a mental note of the fact that "the company making nylons is said to make atomic bombs also." As Robert Jay Lifton analyzes this passage: "The Americanized woman becomes both a betrayer of her race and a 'wearer' of the bomb." See: Robert J. Lifton, *Death in Life: Survivors of Hiroshima* (New York: Simon and Schuster, 1967), p. 418.

THE SECOND PASSAGE

THE SADO-RITUAL SYNDROME: THE RE-ENACTMENT OF GODDESS MURDER

Ti'âmat (and) Marduk, the wisest of the gods,
advanced against one another;
They pressed on to single combat, they approached for battle.
The lord spread out his net and enmeshed her;
The evil wind, following after, he let loose in her face.
When Ti'âmat opened her mouth to devour him,
He drove in the evil wind, in order that (she should) not
(be able) to close her lips.
The raging winds filled her belly;
Her belly became distended, and she opened wide her mouth.
He shot off an arrow, and it tore her interior;
It cut through her inward parts, it split (her) heart.
When he had subdued her, he destroyed her life;
He cast down her carcass (and) stood upon it.
After he had slain Ti'âmat, the leader,
Her band broke up, her host dispersed. . . .
The lord trod upon the hinder part of Ti'âmat,
And with his unsparing club he split (her) skull.
He cut the arteries of her blood
And caused the north wind to carry (it) to out-of-the-way places.
When his fathers saw (this), they were glad and rejoiced. . . .
The lord rested, examining her dead body . . .

from *Enûma elish* (The Babylonian Genesis)

The angel of the Lord declared unto Mary.
And she conceived of the Holy Ghost. . . .
Behold the handmaid of the Lord.
Be it done unto me according to thy word. . . .
And the Word was made flesh.
And dwelt among us . . .

from *The Angelus*

When I realized that they had made the Goddess into Mary and that the Annunciation scene was a depiction of the rape of the Goddess, I remembered that as a little girl I had been taught to recite "The Angelus" three times a day. I was horrified to realize that I had been taught to recite the rape of the Goddess and to cooperate in the mutilation and killing of my own self-image—of my Self.

Linda Barufaldi

These scholars
Translating ignorance into Latin and Greek. . . .
How easy to be king
When all your subjects are dead. . . .
Drone, drone
Drone your dreary dithyrambs
You stillborn, celibate intellects.
You fools, you frauds
You accumulated postules of useless learning. . . .
The curse of the makers upon you.

Rita Mae Brown,
from "Necropolis,"
The Hand That Cradles the Rock

PRELUDE TO THE SECOND PASSAGE

The Myth Masters are able to penetrate their victims' minds/imaginations only by seeing to it that their deceptive myths are acted out over and over again in performances that draw the participants into emotional complicity. Such re-enactment trains both victims and victimizers to perform uncritically their preordained roles. Thus the psyches of the performers are conditioned so that they become carriers and perpetrators of patriarchal myth. In giving the myth reality by acting it out, the participants become re-producers and "living proof" of the deceptive myths. The scene is set for the ritual de-legitimation and destruction of the be-ing of female-identified Furious women.

The idea that religious myth is *embedded* in ritual is common among sociologists, particularly those influenced by Durkheim.[1] The use of the term *embed* should be thought-provoking for anyone aware of the use of subliminal embeds in modern films, music, television, and printed media. The viciously exploitative technological embedding that infiltrates the modern psyche from all sides impresses the mind on levels beyond conscious awareness, profoundly affecting beliefs and behavior.[2] This sophisticated technological embedding has its antecedent in religious ritual which repeatedly rapes, kills, and dismembers women.

Nietzsche captured the essence of patriarchal ritual when he posed the question of how one can "create a memory for the human animal." The problem and solution, according to that philosopher, are as follows:

How does one go about to impress anything on that partly dull, partly flighty human intelligence—that incarnation of forgetfulness

—so as to make it stick? . . . "A thing is branded on the memory to make it stay there; only what goes on hurting will stick"—this is one of the oldest and, unfortunately, one of the most enduring psychological axioms. . . . Whenever man has thought it necessary to create a memory for himself, his effort has been attended with torture, blood, sacrifice.[3]

The use of such terms as *impress* and *brand* is significant. To *impress* is defined as "to apply with pressure so as to imprint." The term *brand* is derived from a Middle English term meaning torch, sword. The message is clear: The "thing" that is impressed/branded on the memory is forced into the mind by some violent and painful means, by pressing/cutting/invading. Such memory-creating is indeed, as Nietzsche said, "attended with torture, blood, sacrifice." This is the mind rape that accompanies male myth creation. It is not done only on a one-to-one basis, of course, but is inflicted by the representatives of patriarchy upon vulnerable individual women. That is, it is gang rape. Moreover, it is done over and over again.

It is important for Hags to ask just what sort of "memory" is being "created," and what is the purpose of this "memory." Moreover, why should it be necessary to "create" a "memory" by mind/spirit rape? Patriarchal myth itself provides us with basic clues. It is replete with stories of a primordial gynocidal "divine" act. For example, in the Babylonian creation myth, the *Enûma elish,* the god Marduk slays a marine monster, the Goddess Ti'âmat, and dismembers her body, splitting it in two, in order to create the cosmos. Eliade unwittingly elucidates the oppressive function of the rituals which re-create and re-enforce this primordial act. He writes that for all paleo-agricultural peoples "what is essential is periodically to evoke the primordial event that established the present condition of humanity [read: gynocidal patriarchy]."[4]

The following passage illustrates the ritual perpetuation of Goddess murder:

The true sin is forgetting. The girl who at her first menstruation spends three days in a dark hut without speaking to anyone does so because the murdered [divine] maiden, having become the moon, remains three days in darkness; if the menstruating girl breaks the tabu of silence and speaks, she is guilty of forgetting a primordial event.[5]

As Denise Connors has pointed out, this primordial event is the murder/dismemberment of the Goddess—that is, the Self-affirming be-ing of women.[6] It might seem confusing that in patriarchy "the true sin is forgetting" this deed, since its ideologies deny that there ever was, is, or can be female divinity, whose existence would be a prerequisite condition for her murder. However, since the fathers' ritual is the realm of reversals, such confusion should be expected. The purpose of such contrived confusion is to prevent us from committing the "true sin" against patriarchal rule/ritual, that is, remembering that as long as we are alive the Goddess still lives. The radical "sin" is re-membering the Goddess in the full sense, that is, recognizing that the attempt to murder her—mythically and existentially—is radically wrong, and demonstrating through our own be-ing that this deed is not final/irrevocable. The deed can be revoked by re-invoking the Goddess within, which involves "forgetting" to kill female divinity, that is, our Selves. Continual complicity in the crime of Goddess-killing is mandatory in the Man's world. Our refusal to collaborate in this killing and dismembering of our own Selves is the beginning of re-membering the Goddess—the deep Source of creative integrity in women.

In the following pages I will analyze a number of barbarous rituals, ancient and modern, in order to unmask the very real, existential meaning of Goddess murder in the concrete lives of women. I will focus upon five specific righteous rites which massacre women: Indian *suttee,* Chinese footbinding, African female genital mutilation, European witchburning, American gynecology. In examining these, I will seek out basic patterns which they have in common, and which comprise the Sado-Ritual Syndrome. Those who claim to see racism and/or imperialism in my indictment of these atrocities can do so only by blinding themselves to the fact that the oppression of women knows no ethnic, national, or religious bounds. There are variations on the theme of oppression, but the phenomenon is planetary.

My analysis of sado-rituals will include an unmasking of deceptive legitimations by scholars and "authorities." The scholars of patriarchy, despite protestations to the contrary, embrace and perpetuate the same Higher Order as the ritual performers/destroyers they are studying. Although they rarely publicly admit to this basic fraternity, it is evident in their own words. Understanding this aspect of the Sado-Ritual Syndrome is essential to understanding the universal sameness of phallocratic morality. The fact that patriarchal scholarship is an extension and continuation of sado-ritual is manifested—often unwittingly and witlessly—by its language. This language betrays, or rather, loyally and faithfully displays, the fact that the "authorities" are apologists for atrocities. It is an essential task of feminist metaethics to examine and analyze this language, untangling the snarls of sentence structure, unveiling deceptive words, exposing the bag of semantic tricks intended to entrap women.

This Passage is the most somber part of the Journey. Having uncovered the patterns of patriarchal myth, the Voyager must now dis-cover the global dimensions of its gynocidal re-enactments. As she moves through this Passage, she finds multiple manifestations of the lethal *intent* of patriarchy. Her increasing knowing of this intent and her facing its implications is radical exorcism. This knowing requires acknowledging the interconnectedness of the ritual atrocities, refusing to compartmentalize facts into stale and irrelevant "bodies of knowledge." Despite—and because of—the terrors and tragedies that must be faced in this part of the Journey, the Voyager senses a growing integrity of vision and purpose. As a consequence of her courage to see, she finds the focus of her anger, so that it fuels and no longer blocks her passion and her creativity. Thus this exorcising Passage gives her the right of passage into the Otherworld, the world of her own Enspiriting, Sparking, Spinning Ecstasy.

CHAPTER THREE

INDIAN *SUTTEE:* THE ULTIMATE CONSUMMATION OF MARRIAGE

Slow advancing, halting, creeping,
Comes the Woman to the hour!
She walketh veiled and sleeping,
For she knoweth not her power.

Charlotte Perkins Gilman,
from "She Walketh Veiled and Sleeping,"
In This Our World

"I have not deserved it. . . . Why must I die like this, alone with my mortal enemy?"

Willa Cather,
My Mortal Enemy

"Widow" is a harsh and hurtful word. It comes from the Sanskrit and it means "empty." . . . I resent what the term has come to mean. I am alive. I am part of the world.

Lynn Caine,
Widow

They speak together of the threat they have constituted towards authority, they tell how they were burned on pyres to prevent them from assembling in future.

Monique Wittig,
Les Guérillères

The Indian rite of *suttee,* or widow-burning, might at first appear totally alien to contemporary Western society, where widows are not ceremoniously burned alive on the funeral pyres of their husbands.* Closer examination unveils its con-

* Although *suttee* was legally banned in 1829, and despite the existence of other legal reforms, it should not be imagined that the lot of most Indian women has changed dramatically since then, or since the publication of Katherine Mayo's *Mother India* in 1927. The situation of most widows is pitiable. An article in an Indian paper, the *Sunday Standard,* May 11, 1975, described the wretched existence of the 7,000 widows of the town of Brindaban, "the living spectres whose life has been eroded by another's death." These poverty-stricken women with shaved heads and with a single white cloth draped over their bare bodies are forced every morning to chant praise (*"Hare Rama, Hare Rama, Rama Rama, Hare Hare, Hare Krishna"* . . . ad nauseam) for four hours in order to get a small bowl of rice. In mid-afternoon they must chant for four more hours in order to receive the price of a glass of tea. A not unusual case is that of a sixty-nine-year-old widow who was married at the age of nine and widowed at eleven, and has been waiting ever since for the "day of deliverance." Surveys carried out by an Indian Committee on the Status of Women revealed that a large percentage of the Indian population still approves of such oppression of widows.

An Indian woman need not be widowed to be victimized. Many are literally starved to death. An article in an Indian magazine, *Youth Times,* March 7, 1975, states: "Our marriage ceremony puts her two steps behind the sacrificial fire—like a puppy that must follow its master. It is a place that spells disaster for millions. For it is a medical fact that the malnutrition and anaemia that plague such a vast number of our women have a basis in the habit of the women eating after they have served their husbands, a practice which in poor homes means virtual starvation" (p. 23). A look at tables of age-specific death rates is revealing. In 1969, in rural India, it was estimated that 70.2 females per thousand under the age of four died, while the death rate for males was 58.3. Since infant mortality generally is higher among males, it is reasonable to believe that these girl children got less to eat or were purposefully starved. The death rate for females is significantly higher in each age group up to the age of thirty-four (Devaki Jain, ed., *Indian Women* [Publications Division, Ministry of Information and Broadcasting, Government of India, 1975], p. 148). A number of sources, including Jain, refer obliquely to the high rate of "suicide" among women. Jain suggests that suicide "must seem an attractive way out of an intolerable situation" (p. 77). Jain is here referring to victims of the dowry system. The bride is often tormented and pressured to extract more money from her parents. In some cases she is murdered by

nectedness with "our" rituals. Moreover, the very attempt to examine the ritual and its social context through the re-sources of Western scholarship demonstrates this connectedness. For the scholars who produced these re-sources exhibit by their very language their complicity in the same social order which was/is the radical source of such rites of female sacrifice.

The hindu rite of *suttee* spared widows from the temptations of impurity by forcing them to "immolate themselves," that is, to be burned alive, on the funeral pyres of their husbands. This ritual sacrifice must be understood within its social context. Since their religion forbade remarriage and at the same time taught that the husband's death was the fault of the widow (because of her sins in a previous incarnation if not in this one), everyone was free to despise and mistreat her for the rest of her life. Since it was a common practice for men of fifty, sixty, or seventy years of age to marry child-brides, the quantitative surplus of such unmarriageable widows boggles the imagination. Lest we allow our minds to be carried away with astronomic numerical calculations, we should realize that this ritual was largely confined to the upper caste, although there was a tendency to spread downward. We should also realize that in some cases—particularly if the widow was an extremely young child before her husband's unfortunate (for her) death—there was the option of turning to a life of prostitution, which would entail premature death from venereal disease.[1] This, however, would be her only possible escape from persecution by in-laws, sons, and other relatives. As a prostitute, of course, she would

---

her in-laws when her parents fail to come through. On January 13, 1977, the *New York Times* reported the details of one such murder of a twenty-year-old wife, who was strangled and burned in kerosene by her husband and in-laws. The article suggested that there are many such "dowry murders" in India each year, most of them disguised as kitchen accidents. These are occasionally reported in the Indian press in brief notices (as are cases of women murdered for not bearing sons). Although there was a Dowry Prohibition Act in 1961, according to the *Sunday Standard* (New Delhi, November 10, 1974), it is doubtful whether there has been even one instance of its enforcement. In addition to these horrors there is high maternal mortality resulting from extremely early marriage, too many pregnancies, maternal malnutrition, and unspeakably filthy and destructive methods of "delivery."

be held responsible for the spread of more moral and physical impurity.

If the general situation of widowhood in India was not a sufficient inducement for the woman of higher caste to throw herself gratefully and ceremoniously into the fire, she was often pushed and poked in with long stakes after having been bathed, ritually attired, and drugged out of her mind.[2] In case these facts should interfere with our clear misunderstanding of the situation, Webster's invites us to re-*cover* women's history with the following definition of *suttee*: "the act or custom of a Hindu woman *willingly* cremating herself or being cremated on the funeral pyre of her husband as an indication of her *devotion* to him [emphases mine]." It is thought-provoking to consider the reality behind the term *devotion*, for indeed a wife must have shown signs of extraordinarily slavish devotion during her husband's lifetime, since her very life depended upon her husband's state of health. A thirteen-year-old wife might well be concerned over the health of her sixty-year-old husband.

Joseph Campbell discusses *suttee* as the Hindu form of the widely practiced "custom" of sending the family or part of it "into the other world along with the chief member." [3] The time-honored practice of "human sacrifice," sometimes taking the form of live burial, was common also in other cultures, for example in ancient Egypt. Campbell notes that Professor George Reisner excavated an immense necropolis in Nubia, an Egyptian province, and found, without exception, "a pattern of burial with human sacrifice—specifically, female sacrifice: of the wife and, in the more opulent tombs, the entire harem, together with the attendants." [4] After citing Reisner's descriptions of female skeletons, which indicated that the victims had died hideous deaths from suffocation, Campbell writes:

> In spite of these signs of suffering and even panic in the actual moment of the pain of suffocation, we should certainly not think of the mental state and experience of these individuals after any model of our own more or less imaginable reactions to such a fate. For these sacrifices were not properly, in fact, individuals at all; that is to say, they were not particular beings, distinguished from a

class or group by virtue of any sense or realization of a personal, individual destiny or responsibility.[5]

I have not italicized any of the words in this citation because it seemed necessary to stress *every* word. It is impossible to make any adequate comment.

At first, *suttee* was restricted to the wives of princes and warriors, but as one scholar (Benjamin Walker) deceptively puts it, "in course of time *the widows* of weavers, masons, barbers and others of lower caste *adopted the practice* [emphases mine]." [6] The use of the active voice here suggests that the widows actively sought out, enforced, and accepted this "practice." Apparently without any sense of inconsistency the same author supplies evidence that relatives forced widows to the pyre. He describes a case reported in 1796, in which a widow escaped from the pyre during the night in the rain. A search was made and she was dragged from her hiding place. Walker concludes the story of this woman who "adopted the practice" as follows:

She pleaded to be spared but her own son insisted that she throw herself on the pile as he would lose caste and suffer everlasting humiliation. When she still refused, the son with the help of some others present bound her hands and feet and hurled her into the blaze.[7]

The same author gives information about the numerical escalation of *suttee*:

Among the Rājputs and other warrior nations of northern India, the observance of suttee took on staggering proportions, since wives and concubines *immolated themselves* by the hundred. It became customary not only for wives but for mistresses, sisters, mothers, sisters-in-law and other near female relatives and retainers *to burn themselves* along with their deceased master. With Rājputs it evolved into the terrible rite of *jauhar* which took place in times of war or great peril *in order to save the honour of the womenfolk of the clan* [emphases mine].[8]

Again the victims, through grammatical sleight of hand, are made to appear as the agents of their own destruction. The rite of *jauhar* consisted in heaping all the females of the clan into the fire when there was danger of defeat by the enemy. Thousands of hindu women were murdered this way during the muslim invasion of India.[9] Their masters could not bear that they should be raped, tortured, and killed by foreign males adhering to "different" religious beliefs, rather than by themselves.

The term *custom*—a casual and neutral term—is often used by scholars to describe these barbarous rituals of female slaughter. Clearly, however, they were religious rites. Some scholars assert that an unscrupulous priesthood provided the religious legitimation for the practice by rigging the text of the Rig Veda.[10] Priests justified the ritual atrocity by their interpretations of the law of Karma.[11] Furthermore, the typical mind-diverting orderliness of murderous religious ritual was manifested not only in the ceremonial bathing and dressing of the widows, but included other details of timing and placement. If the widow was menstruating, she was considered impure, and thus a week had to pass after the cessation of her period before she could commit *suttee*. Since impurity also resulted from pregnancy, *suttee* had to be delayed two months after the birth of the child.[12] For the event itself, the widow was often required to sit with the corpse's head in her lap or on her breast.[13] The orderliness is that of ritual: repetitive, compulsive, delusional.

This horror show was made possible by the legitimating role of religious rite, which allows the individual to distinguish between the real self, who may be fearful or scrupulous, and the self as role-performer.[14] This schizoid perception on the part of those participating in the ritual carries over to the scholars who, though temporally or spatially distanced from the rite, identify with *it* rather than with the victims. Joseph Campbell placidly writes of the tortured and sacrified woman:

> *Sati,* the feminine participle of *sat,* then, is the female who really *is* something in as much as she is truly and properly a player of the female part: she is not only good and true in the ethical sense but true and real ontologically. In her faithful death, she is at one with her own true being.[15]

Thus the ontological and moral problems surrounding female massacre are blandly dismissed. Campbell is simply discussing a social context in which, for a woman, to be killed is "good and true," and to cease to exist is to be. His androcratically attached de-tachment from women's agony is manifested in paragraph after paragraph. After describing the live burial of a young widow which took place in 1813, this devotee of the rites of de-tached scholarship describes the event as "an *illuminating,* though *somewhat* appalling, glimpse into the deep, silent pool of the Oriental, archaic soul . . . [emphases mine]." [16] What eludes this scholar is the fact that the "archaic soul" was a woman destroyed by Patriarchal Religion (in which he is a true believer), which demands female sacrifice.

The bland rituals of patriarchal scholarship perpetuate the legitimation of female sacrifice. The social reality, unacknowledged by such myth-masters, is that of minds and bodies mutilated by degradation. The real social context included the common practice of marrying off small girls to old men, since brahmans have what has been called a "strange preference for children of very tender years." Katherine Mayo, in an excellent work entitled with appropriate irony, *Mother India,* shows an understanding of the situation which more famous scholars entirely lack. Her work is, in the precise sense of the word, exceptional. She writes:

> That so hideous a fate as widowhood should befall a woman can be but for one cause—the enormity of her sins in a former incarnation. From the moment of her husband's decease till the last hour of her own life, she must expiate those sins in shame and suffering and self-immolation, chained in every thought to the service of his soul. Be she a child of three, who knows nothing of the marriage that bound her, or be she a wife in fact, having lived with her husband, her case is the same. By his death she is revealed as a creature of innate guilt and evil portent, herself convinced when she is old enough to think at all, of the justice of her fate.[17]

CHILD BRIDES

In order to understand the import of the distinction between a girl-child/virgin and a "wife in fact" we should realize that it has been traditional for hindu men to force intercourse on extremely young female children. The trauma, physical and mental suffering, and stunting of body and spirit that this would cause in a young girl-child can perhaps just barely be imagined by those who have not had to endure such an experience. With this effort of imagination a feminist should read and reread carefully such dis-passionate statements as the following from Vern Bullough's *The Subordinate Sex*. He writes:

> Even if the husband died before consummation, which was *not usually attempted until the girl was about ten,* the girl was regarded as a widow and could not re-marry [emphasis mine].[18]

"Not usually attempted until the girl was about ten." The words let the information just slide past consciousness that of course it was/is often "attempted" earlier. Since this is a text often used in Women's Studies courses and contains much useful information, this de-tached quality of the writing requires special attention. It is "writing that erases itself." [19] The style of patriarchal scholarship, even at its best, continues and participates in the Righteous Rites of female slaughter/erasure. In this instance what we are confronted with is not exactly untruth but a partially suppressed truth, which becomes absorbed, belittled, and discarded in the reader's mind.

Although the rape of female children by their fathers and other male relatives has been and is much more common in modern Western society than is generally acknowledged, those who do acknowledge the fact usually make some judgment about its morality, even though the criticism is often muted.[20] In reading about the Indian situation the Western reader has to shift mental gears in order to recognize that this violation has been considered legitimate because the older man was the child's husband. Bullough's language blurs the obvious identification with child abuse, so that the reader is almost compelled to think the husband was exercising virtuous self-restraint instead of raping a ten-year-old. Dirty-old-man behavior has social sanction. Upon the death of the dirty old man the girl-child could look forward to a life of perpetual misery, if she was spared *suttee*.

What about *before* his death? Mayo presented evidence of a horror show that defies description, citing medical evidence from the Indian Legislative Assembly Debates of 1922.[21] I will cite just four of the cases of child-wives brought to Indian hospitals, as described in Mayo's appendix:

A. Aged 9. Day after marriage. Left femur dislocated, pelvis crushed out of shape, flesh hanging in shreds . . .
I. Aged about 7. Living with husband. Died in great agony after three days . . .
L. Aged 11. From great violence done to her person, will be a cripple for life. No use of her lower extremities.
M. Aged about 10. Crawled to hospital on her hands and knees. Has never been able to stand erect since her marriage.

The list goes on. A female surgeon who took Katherine Mayo on a tour of a *purdah* hospital in northeast India showed her a small child who had been a very bright pupil in a government primary school before she was sent to the home of the fifty-year-old man to whom her family had married her. She was physically ravaged and had lost her mental balance. According to the doctor's account:

> I have never seen a creature so fouled. Her internal wounds were alive with maggots. . . . Meantime her husband is suing her to recover his marital rights and force her back into his possession.[22]

The case was a child of a well-to-do, "educated," city-dwelling family.

One might wonder what could be the reason/justification for these child marriages. Clearly, the brahmans have seen nothing wrong with child-brides. As one of them exclaimed during the Legislative Assembly Debates of 1925:

> To the Brahman girl-wife the husband is a greater, truer, dearer benefactor than all the social reformers bundled together![23]

Such godmen, of course, have the same urge to be "benefactors" of daughters, sisters, cousins, nieces. One of the justifications for child marriage and coitus with child-brides was the fact that the father dared not keep his daughter at home lest she be damaged before she was off his hands. In this warped sense her husband could be called her "benefactor," since he rescued her from male relatives.

BLAMING THE VICTIM

Western scholars have acknowledged this problem, but in such a way that they have succeeded perfectly in blaming the child victim. For example, a nineteenth-century catholic priest-scholar, the Abbé Dubois, wrote:

> Experience has taught that young Hindu women do not possess sufficient firmness, and sufficient regard for their own honor, to resist the ardent solicitations of a seducer.[24]

The evidence offered by the Abbé for his view of the situation was the fact that mothers admitted they were afraid to leave their eleven- and twelve-year-old daughters at home and accessible to male relatives. The christian priest thus perceives the situation through the lenses of his own tradition, which does not differ profoundly from the one he is observing.* The logic of the evidence which he offers for the "insufficient firmness" of hindu girls may seem strangely familiar to feminists of christian "background," who will recall being told repeatedly by their "confessors" and ministers that the onus of sexual responsibility was on the girl since males had "stronger sex drives."

It would be a mistake, however, to imagine that such ridiculous reasoning is restricted to the christian priesthood, for the priesthood of scholars devoted to the Rites of Re-Search has a more diverse membership. Thus David and Vera Mace,

* In the mid-sixties in Rome, during a conversation with roman catholic archbishop Roberts (one of the "radicals" at the Second Vatican Council) who had lived for years in India, he "informed" me that *suttee* is the "logical conclusion" of female nature. Although that prelate was not actively promoting the practice, he was clearly expressing a basic agreement with its underlying asssumptions—assumptions shared by his own particular sect of patriarchal religion.

commenting upon the Abbé's interpretation, appear to find nothing wrong with it, stating themselves that "from an early age, girls in the East were accustomed to the idea that they could not be trusted to guard their own virtue." [25] It requires cultivated obtuseness to fail to grasp the fact that an eleven- or twelve-year-old girl—particularly one who has had no training in self-defense and who has been trained to view males as gods—would hardly be able to fight off one or several full-grown rapist relatives.

Such horrors have not ceased.* Meanwhile, of the few women in "advanced" countries who have some idea of the facts of sexism and some knowledge of "women's history," far fewer glimpse the continued massacre that is masked by the rituals of re-search which repeatedly re-cover the interconnected crimes of planetary patriarchy. By the dogma of female worthlessness and the device of "blaming the victim" the priests of "objective scholarship" continue to justify a context in which *suttee* can be seen as reasonable and virtuous. From early childhood to old age, women are somehow made to appear at fault. Thus P. Thomas, describing the miserable life of an Indian widow in the house of her deceased husband, writes that "the mother-in-law, never too soft towards her daughters-in-law, could only look upon the widow as the virtual destroyer of her son who would not have died, according to *the then prevalent interpretations* of the law of Karma, if his wife was virtuous [emphasis mine]." [26] Subtly his style lays the blame on that traditional scapegoat, the mother-in-law. His use of the nominalized passive, "the then prevalent interpretations," hides the true agents of the atrocity by suppressing the question: Just *who* created and enforced these interpretations which could infect the minds of women who were cast into the role of "mother-in-law"?

Scholarly mystification continues to dull all sense of the unrightness of such rites as *suttee,* regarding them with detached interest and making them appear isolated and unre-

* Nor are they restricted to India. In April 1977 *Time* carried a story exposing a billion-dollar pornography industry in the United States specializing in children as subjects.

lated to "our" culture. It thus keeps minds/imaginations in a state of readiness to accept similar or comparable practices which carry out the same program—the killing of female divinity—ultimately requiring the extinction of female life and will to live.

Writing in 1960, David and Vera Mace masterfully muddied the issues illustrated in the rite of *suttee* for anyone searching in their book for insight. They wrote:

> Although *custom* and *duty* left many widows in the East no alternative but to suffer and even to die, it would be a grave *injustice* to explain all their sacrifices in these terms. In many, many cases the widow walked into the fire *proudly* and by *deliberate choice.* This was her way of showing the depth of her *affection,* her *devotion,* her *fidelity.* It was a strange way, and to us a gravely *mistaken* one. But leaving aside the *inappropriateness* of the action and looking at the motive, dare we say that these women of the East knew less of *true love* than their Western sisters [emphases mine]? [27]

The authors erase such obvious questions as: Why did not widowers walk "proudly" into the fire? And, what does "proudly" mean? At times, hundreds, even thousands, of women died in *suttee* for *one* royal male. Who could speak of "pride" in dying for such godmen? How could anyone continue to use such language in the face of such frank admissions as the following statement of a hindu, cited by Mayo:

> We husbands so often make our wives unhappy that we might well fear they would poison us. Therefore did our wise ancestors make the penalty of widowhood so frightful—in order that the woman may not be tempted.[28]

The fear expressed here is clearly a terror of deserved retaliation, for among other things, a wife risked receiving lethal doses of venereal disease by penile injection. The Maces' use of the term *injustice* to describe an attitude of horror and outrage at the widows' fate is worse than absurd. It throws the reader off the track of asking *who* was/is responsible for the real injustice which she finds so horrifying. She is tempted to feel guilty for not understanding women in "another culture."

Mistaken and *inappropriateness* are bizarre terms in this context. They suggest that there was a real choice involved, and they belittle/distort the horrible reality. As for *true love, devotion,* et cetera, one can speculate that true masochism may be an ideal cherished more by these Western authors than by the widows whose options were so desperately narrowed.

One can find endless examples of such patriarchal scholarship. My purpose here is to detect in these perpetuations of murder patterns whose effect is mental murder. This pattern-detecting—the development of a kind of positive paranoia—is essential for every feminist Searcher, so that she can resist the sort of mind-poisoning to which she must expose herself in the very process of seeking out necessary information. I have already suggested that the feminist Searcher must be particularly aware of subtle mystification through language in books which take a liberal feminist approach and which have become institutionally acceptable materials for Women's Studies. Another example from Vern Bullough illustrates this kind of trap. He writes:

> Nowhere was the concept of inferiority of women more exemplified than in the *custom* of suttee, the Hindu rite of *suicide* of widows by *self-immolation* [emphases mine].[29]

One might well ask whether any scholar would dare to describe the massacre of the Jews in Germany as a Nazi "custom." It is important also to note that even such a liberal scholar uses the terms *suicide* and *self-immolation*. It is abundantly obvious that if there was voluntariness, it consisted in "choosing" to jump from the frying pan into the pyre.

IDENTIFICATION WITH THE OPPRESSOR

If one seeks a probable explanation for such muddying language, I suggest that it may be found in the fact that the authors identify on some level with the agents of the atrocities, while being incapable of identifying with the victims—a subjective condition which is masked by the pose of "objective scholarship." Feminists have learned to expect such blunting of sensibilities in male scholars. Unfortunately, however, many female scholars also use similar language, for the temptation to identify with the male viewpoint—which is legitimated by every field—is strong, and the penalties for not doing so often intimidate women into self-deception. One also finds in teaching Women's Studies that some female students will at first resist seeing obvious implications of the material. A professor of Feminist Ethics described her experience in presenting gynocidal atrocities to her class of undergraduate women. Although most were able to respond intellectually and emotionally to the reality, a minority insisted that the women who died in *suttee* had "free choice." No amount of evidence or reasoning from the rest of the class could move them.[30] However, it is important to recognize that the reasons for women's resistance to consciousness are different from those of men who actually or potentially hold power. For a woman, to begin to allow herself to see is to begin the Feminist Journey, whose hazards she can intuit even before experiencing them.

Yet another dimension of the significance of androcracy's woman-killing rituals is illustrated by *suttee.* That is, the aftereffects—including both continued practice and scholarly legitimation of this—extend beyond official termination of the rite. Thus it is not surprising that "practical *suttee*" * has continued to occur among widows in India, even though the public ceremony was legally banned in 1829. Deceptively, this is called "suicide." The remarkable obtuseness of scholars regarding practical *suttee* is illustrated in the writing of Benjamin Walker, who apparently finds *suttee* disasteful only if the victim is "unwilling." He writes:

> Reports of eyewitnesses do record the *heroism* of some women who sought this form of death *of their own free will.* Quoting a number of instances from accounts of foreign travellers, Dr. A. S. Altekar speaks of his own sister who as late as 1946 *with indescribable*

* Katherine Mayo uses this expression to name instances where "the newly widowed wife deliberately pours oil over her garments, sets them afire and burns to death, in a connived-at secrecy" (*Mother India,* p. 83).

fortitude carried out her resolve, committing herself to the flames within twenty-four hours of her husband's death in spite of the pressing entreaties of her relations [emphases mine].[31]

Given the immense "knowledge" of this scholar concerning the attitudes toward widows in India, his ignorance is demonic, though typical.

It is enlightening to compare Walker's account of "heroic" *suttee* with Katherine Mayo's realistic assessment of the situation. She writes:

She has seen the fate of other widows. She is about to become a drudge, a slave, starved, tyrannized over, abused—and this is the sacred way out—"following the divine law." Committing a pious and meritorious act, in spite of all foreign-made interdicts, she escapes a present hell and may hope for a happier birth in the next incarnation.[32]

RESISTANCE TO FEMINIST SEARCHERS

Since Katherine Mayo stands as a startling exception among scholars who have written about women in India, it is interesting to look at what happened to her work from the perspective of fifty years later. *Mother India* was published in 1927. It aroused a storm of protest in the East and in the West. There was a flurry of books and articles, replies and counterreplies. Titles of volumes that appeared in the controversy include: *My Mother India; Sister India; Father India; Living India; Understanding India; A Son of Mother India Answers; Neighbour India; Unhappy India; India, Step-Mother; India: Its Character, A Reply to Mother India; Shiva or The Future of India.* Obviously Mayo had struck a nerve. As a result of her exploration and boldness, the literature multiplied. She herself wrote later books defending her position: *Slaves of the Gods* (1929) and *The Face of Mother India* (1935).

The sort of defensiveness which Mayo's exposé evoked is exemplified in *My Mother India* by Dalip Singh Saund. Defending the hindu married woman's condition, he pictures her as "dropping longingly into his [her husband's] embrace with almost divine confidence . . ." He speaks for his sister (who of course is not allowed to speak for herself):

And when the ideal of her childhood was realized, no wonder she found in his company that height of emotional exaltation which springs from the proper union of the sexes and is the noblest gift of God to man. The American girl thinks my sister married a stranger; but she had married an ideal, a creation of *her* imagination, and a part of her own being [emphasis mine].[33]

In fact, his sister had been trained to worship her appointed husband as a god. She had no choice. The contrast between such defensive rhetoric and Mayo's eyewitness account and analysis speaks for itself.

The evaluation of Mayo's work and its impact has been left to such scholars as the authors of *Marriage: East and West,* who write:

The dust finally settled. It *was conceded* that Katherine Mayo's *facts, as facts,* were substantially accurate. It *was recognized* that she had taken up a serious issue and drawn attention to it, which had helped in some measure to *hasten much-needed reforms.* But at the same time her book had done a *grave injustice to India,* in presenting a one-sided and distorted picture of *an aspect of Indian life* that could only be properly understood *within the context of the entire culture* [emphases mine].[34]

Thus Mayo is put in her place. We find here the familiar use of the passive voice, which leaves unstated just *who* conceded, *who* recognized. We find also the familiar balancing act of scholars, which gives a show of "justice" to their treatment of the attacked author. The qualifying expression, "as facts," added to "facts," has the effect of managing to minimize the factual. Women who counter the patriarchal reality are often accused of "merely imagining," or being on the level of "mere polemic." Here we have "mere" facts. Then the authors graciously concede that Mayo hastened "much-needed reforms," which gives the impression that everything has now been taken care of, that the messy details have been tidied up. Then comes the peculiarly deceptive and unjust expression "grave injustice to India." Mayo was concerned about grave injustice to living beings, women. Injustice is done to individual living beings. One must ask how it is possible to do injustice to a social construct, for example, India, by exposing its atrocities. We might ask such re-searchers whether they would be inclined to accuse critics of the Nazi death camps of "injustice" to Germany, or whether they would describe writers exposing the history of slavery and racism in America as guilty of "injustice" to the United States. The Maces go on to accuse Mayo of distorting "an aspect of Indian life." But what *is* "Indian life"? Mayo is concerned not with defending this vague abstraction (presumably meaning customs, beliefs, social arrangements, et cetera), but with the *lives* of millions of women who happened to live in that part of patriarchy called "India."

The final absurdity in this scholarly obituary is the expression "properly understood within the context of the entire culture." It is Katherine Mayo who demonstrates an understanding of the cultural context, that is, the *entire culture,* refusing to reduce women to "an aspect." Her critics, twenty years after her death, attempted to absorb the realities she exposed into a "broad vision," which turns out to be a meaningless abstraction.

Feminist Searchers should be aware of this device, commonly repeated in the re-searchers' rituals. It involves intimidation by accusations of "one-sidedness," so that others will not listen to the discredited Searcher-Scholar who refused to follow the "right" rites. The device relies upon fears of criticizing "another culture," so that the feminist is open to accusations of imperialism, nationalism, racism, capitalism, or any other "-ism" that can pose as broader and more important than gynocidal patriarchy. Thus the just accuser becomes unjustly sentenced to erasure. Her life's meaning, as expressed in her life's work, is belittled, reversed, wiped out.

Feminist Seekers/Spinsters should search out and claim such sisters as Katherine Mayo. Her books are already rare and difficult to find. It is important that they do not become extinct. Spinsters must unsnarl phallocratic "scholarship" and also find our sister weavers/dis-coverers whose work is being maligned, belittled, erased, deliberately forgotten. We must learn to name our true sisters, and to save their work so that it may be continued rather than re-covered, re-searched, and re-done on the endless wheel of re-acting to the Atrocious Lie which is phallocracy. In this dis-covering and spinning we expand the dimensions of feminist time/space.

In the process of seeking out these sister Seekers/Spinsters, it is essential to look at *their own* writings. Secondary sources, even those which one would hope to be just, are often misleading. The entry on Katherine Mayo by Mary F. Handlin in *Notable American Women,* for example, would throw the reader completely off the track.[35] Handlin gives a disproportionately small amount of space to Mayo's major work, *Mother India,* subtly discredits Mayo's motives, and gives no indication of the content or importance of the book. She distracts the reader by her use of pop psychology, stating that Mayo could confront her own sexual anxiety openly "only in writing about distant places and alien cultures." This is an unsubstantiated and irrelevant personality attack, a device which could be used on any scholar who studies a foreign culture. In order to recognize its inappropriateness, one could look at biographical entries concerning male historians and anthropologists and note the absence of such speculations, as well as the focus upon content and importance of their works. This ultimate burial of the Spinster (and Mayo was "unmarried," a point stressed snidely by Handlin) takes place quietly. Only ashes can be found in such "biographical entries," which softly intone the "last rites" in the series of cross-cultural rituals designed to make us *forget* the murder and dismemberment of the Goddess, that is, the killing of be-ing, of the creative divine life and integrity in concrete, existing women.

THE PATTERN OF THE SADO-RITUAL SYNDROME

In order to re-member female divinity, it is important for Hags/Spinsters to look carefully at the pattern of the maze of gynocidal ritual illustrated in *suttee* and its aftereffects. I have shown that there are a number of layers/levels of erasure. These are all designed to stop the Journey of women finding our Selves—a Journey which is quest-ing, be-ing. They are also designed to stop women from finding each other, for this is essential to finding our Selves. Thus feminist Searchers are blocked/divided from knowing their sisters who have been erased by ritual atrocities, and the rituals of re-search function to ensure this blockage, sending feminist would-be Searchers repeatedly down blind alleys. The few who find their way at last through the maze are often too far ahead of their sister Searchers for the latter to catch up. Meanwhile the re-searchers have time to spread propaganda discrediting these dis-coverers, and their findings are effectively re-covered. All of these elements are parts of the Sado-Ritual Syndrome. We are now in a position to perceive the operative pattern of this Syndrome, which is illustrated in the ritual of *suttee* and its aftereffects, and which we can find—if we look wildly, listen keenly—over and over again in the other ritual atrocities of androcracy.

I

In the Sado-Ritual we find, first, an obsession with purity. This obsession legitimates the fact that the women who are the primary victims of the original rites are erased physically as well as spiritually. These primary victims are often killed, as in the case of the rite of *suttee*. In other cases, such as Chinese footbinding, as we shall see later, they are physically and psychically maimed. This original erasure obviously keeps the primary victims from being witnesses. In the name of "purity," they are effectively silenced. Thus the widows' sexual purity is "safeguarded" by ritual murder. In preparation for this ultimate purification they are ceremoniously bathed, and care is taken to kill them at a "pure" time, that is, when they are not menstruating or pregnant. Thus "society" is purified of these "wicked" widows and also of all traces of female rebelliousness, for the women and girl-children who witness these events or hear of them must be perfectly brainwashed with terror of the same fate.

II

Second, there is total erasure of responsibility for the atrocities performed through such rituals. Those doing the destruction commonly have recourse to the idea that they are acting "under orders," or following tradition (serving a Higher Order). This allows the self as role-carrier to commit acts which the personal/private self would find frightening or evil.

III

Third, gynocidal ritual practices have an inherent tendency to "catch on" and spread, since they appeal to imaginations conditioned by the omnipresent ideology of male domination. Moreover, since the patriarchal imagination is hierarchical, there is a proliferation of atrocities from an elite to the upwardly aspiring lower echelons of society.

IV

Fourth, women are used as scapegoats and token torturers (for example, by the "setting up" of mothers-in-law as to blame for the widows' doom). This masks the male-centeredness of the ritualized atrocity and turns women against each other.

V

Fifth, we find compulsive orderliness, obsessive repetitiveness, and fixation upon minute details, which divert attention from the horror. In short, attention is focused upon what is proper and ceremonial, rather than upon the woman's horrible suffering and death.

VI

Sixth, behavior which at other times and places is unacceptable becomes acceptable and even normative as a consequence of conditioning through the ritual atrocity. Such value judgments are easily interchangeable in the swinging-pendulum society characterized by consciousness split into false opposites. Thus it is not surprising that the practice is desired and sometimes continued even after it has officially/legally been terminated, as in the recurring instances of "practical *suttee.*"

VII

Seventh, there is legitimation of the ritual by the rituals of "objective" scholarship—despite appearances of disapproval. The basic cultural assumptions which make the atrocious ritual possible and plausible remain unquestioned, and the practice itself is misnamed and isolated from other parallel symptoms of the planetary patriarchal practice of female maiming and massacre. Jan Raymond has suggested that such scholarship could be called *meta-ritual.*[36] The name is accurate, for this kind of writing not only "records" (erases) the original rituals but also provides "explanations" and legitimations for them, purporting to see beyond their materiality into their "soul" or meaning. This legitimation by the Rites of Re-search is an extension of the primordial gynocidal acts. The practitioners of these Last Rites re-enact the original rites by erasing their meaning and by effacing those Searchers who did weave their way through the mazes of re-search with integrity, dis-covering the forbidden fruit of their labors, that is, the *facts.*[37]

CHAPTER FOUR

CHINESE FOOTBINDING: ON FOOTNOTING THE THREE-INCH "LOTUS HOOKS"

If you care for a son, you don't go easy on his studies; if you care for a daughter, you don't go easy on her footbinding.

Chinese saying,
Ts'ai-fei lu

". . . a woman's heart must be of such a size, and no larger, else it must be pressed small like Chinese feet; her happiness is to be made as cakes are, by a fixed receipt." That was what my father wanted.

George Eliot,
Daniel Deronda

The bonsai tree
in the attractive pot
could have grown eighty feet tall
on the side of a mountain
till split by lightning.
But a gardener
carefully pruned it.
It is nine inches high. . . .
With living creatures
one must begin very early
to dwarf their growth:
the bound feet,
the crippled brain,
the hair in curlers,

the hands you
love to touch.

Marge Piercy,
from "A work of artifice,"
To Be of Use

Last week, in the bus, I was preoccupied with feet.
So many were in sandals, almost squinting
at a light, they rarely see.
One woman's toes, grotesque contortions cramped
beneath
a brave façade of purple polish—
I missed my stop, with staring.
Who could heal such feet?

Robin Morgan,
from "The City of God,"
Lady of the Beasts

Women, women limping on the edges of the History
of Man
Crippled for centuries and dragging the heavy emptiness
Past submission and sorrow to forgotten and unknown
selves.
It's time to break and run.

Rita Mae Brown,
from "The New Lost Feminist,"
The Hand that Cradles the Rock

The Chinese ritual of foodbinding was a thousand-year-long horror show in which women were grotesquely crippled from very early childhood. As Andrea Dworkin so vividly demonstrates, the hideous three-inch-long "lotus hooks" *—which

* It is thought-provoking to consider that the symbolism of the lotus in the East is comparable to that of the rose in the West. Like the rose, it is of course considered very beautiful and it is allegedly a

in reality were odiferous, useless stumps—were the means by which the Chinese patriarchs saw to it that their girls and women would never "run around." [1] All of the components of the Sado-Ritual Syndrome are illustrated in this atrocity.

I

First, there was the familiar fixation on "purity." In contrast to their counterparts in such countries as India, Chinese males did not have to confine their wives and daughters in *purdah* in order to protect their "purity," but saw to it instead that their prisoners were hopelessly crippled. The foot purification (mutilation) ensured that women would be brainwashed as well, since their immobility made them entirely dependent upon males for knowledge of the world outside their houses. Moreover, since torture and mutilation of a small girl was carried out by her mother and other close female relatives, the lesson of "never trust a woman" was branded upon her soul, and emotional dependency upon the seemingly less in-

---

natural symbol for all forms of evolution. The deception involved in naming the rotted "tiny feet" of Chinese women after a beautiful flower is evident. Moreover, the acquisition of "lotuses" by the maimed girls meant the end of hope for natural physical and mental "evolution." The fact that the "lotuses" were frequently named "lotus hooks" is also suggestive. In fact the maimed feet did resemble hooks, since the large toe was pointed upward, whereas the others were crushed and bent under the plantar. The Chinese male foot-fetishists were "hooked" on their perverted practices with the "adorable" tiny feet, and their female victims were painfully caught on the hook of this ritual, robbed of the normal means of escape—running away. For the symbolism of the lotus see C. E. Cirlot, *A Dictionary of Symbols* (New York: Philosophical Library, 1962), pp. 184–85.

For further clues concerning connections between the lotus and purity, see *Funk and Wagnalls Standard Dictionary of Folklore,* ed. by Maria Leach, Jerome Fried, asso. ed. (New York: Funk and Wagnalls, 1972), pp. 645–47. The entry on *lotus* discusses its meaning in China: "As elsewhere, it is the emblem of purity (because it rises unsullied, however muddied the waters, and does not grow in the earth)." Clearly, the mutilation of Chinese women's feet was intended to keep the victims "pure," that is, the unsullied property of their masters. Like lotuses, these feet could not be planted firmly on the ground.

volved males was guaranteed. She was not supposed to know that men were the real Master Minds of her suffering. Thus her mind was purely possessed, and it became axiomatic that the possessor of tiny feet was a paradigm of feminine goodness.

II

The second element of the syndrome—erasure of male responsibility—is evident in footbinding. From the Chinese male's point of view, there was no question of his blame or moral accountability. After all, women "did it to themselves." One man, cited by Howard S. Levy, described his sister's ordeal as a child, when she was forced to "walk" with bound feet:

> Auntie dragged her hobbling along, to keep the blood circulating. Sister wept throughout but mother and auntie didn't pity her in the slightest, saying that if one loved a daughter, one could not love her feet.[2]

There is a kind of ignorant arrogance in this man's assertion that the older women (the token torturers) felt no pity. According to his own account, they performed this ritual mutilation out of fear that otherwise the girl would not be marriageable. This was a realistic fear, since for a thousand-year period Chinese males—millions of them—required this maiming of female feet into "lotus hooks" for their own sadistic, fetishistic, erotic pleasure. One male is quoted by Levy as making the following comment:

> Every time I see a girl suffering the pain of footbinding, I think of the future when the lotuses will be placed on my shoulders or held in my palms and my desire overflows and becomes uncontrollable.[3]

Such male sadism, which dictated the creation of "golden lotuses," often masked itself as "compassion." Nan-kung Po, a Chinese historical novelist, relates the thoughts of one of his characters upon beholding a courtesan's "tiny feet":

> He couldn't help feeling compassion for her lower extremities. Compressing the feet in order to thicken the thighs must have been

the invention of a genius. And of course the inventor must have been a woman . . .[4]

Such feelings of "compassion" and "pity," which were often described by Chinese men as experienced at the sight of "tiny feet," contributed to their sadistic pleasure. It did not occur to them, it seems, that *they* were the agents behind the mutilation, demanding it and enforcing it, deceptively using their mindbound women to execute their wishes. This "compassion" was pure doublethink, pure abnegation of responsibility, made plausible by the visibility of women cast into the role of each other's torturers and mutilators.*

Yet another Chinese "genius," who signed himself as "Lotus Knower," blatantly expressed the same self-excusing illogic:

Women of antiquity regarded the tiny foot as a crystallization of physical beauty; it was *not* a product of lewd thinking [emphases mine].[5]

Yet, a few lines later he expresses his own lewd thinking:

The lotus has special seductive characteristics and is an instrument for arousing desire. Who can resist the fascination and bewilderment of playing with and holding in his palms a soft and jade-like hook? [6]

The examples can be multiplied. No one was guilty except the girls and women who attempted to disobey or escape. No one was to blame for the evil of maiming women, since the reality of evil and maiming was not acknowledged. There were only "beauty" and "the extremes of pleasure." Among the Chinese, footbinding was universally legitimated. Its apolo-

* This tactic is common enough. In the United States, for example, pimps use their older, tougher prostitutes to beat up young novices. While these trapped women mete out physical punishment, the pimps (like all top-dog bureaucrats) play the role of comforting compassionate Godfathers/"lovers." Moreover, we are all familiar with the subtle cultural messages which trick mothers into training their daughters to accept the many physical alterations required for the feminine role.

gists included philosophers, poets, authors of erotic literature, diplomats, and ordinary "honorable men."

III

Chinese gynocidal foot-maiming "caught on" rapidly and spread widely. The brutal rite (a family affair, "enjoyed" by all the members), which scholars say commenced in the period between the T'ang and Sung dynasties, spread like a cancer throughout China and into Korea. By the twelfth century it was widely accepted as correct fashion among the upper classes. The mothers who belonged to families claiming aristocratic lineage felt forced to bind the feet of their daughters as a sign of upper-class distinction. Not to mutilate their daughters was unthinkable to them, for it meant that men would find them unattractive and would refuse to marry them. Themselves physically and mentally mutilated, the mothers paradigmatically acted out the role prescribed for them as mutilators of their own kind.* As muted "members" of patriarchal society, their imaginations too were forced into hierarchical patterns. A mother who "loved" her daughter would have upwardly imitative ambitions for her, and the only possible expression of this would be ensuring that she would be made attractive to a suitable husband. Since one requirement for this high status was the possession of "golden lotuses," this sado-ritual spread downward, even to women of the lowest classes in some areas.[7]

IV

The use of women as token torturers is more obvious in Chinese footbinding than in *suttee*. The imprisoned, mutilated women had to believe that "if one loved a daughter one could

* Older and more skilled concubines were also used to bind the feet of young maids and concubines, while their lord enjoyed the painful spectacle. See Howard S. Levy, *Chinese Footbinding: The History of a Curious Erotic Custom* (New York: Walton Rawls, 1966), pp. 177–79.

not love her feet." Not only did the contemporary Chinese males choose to see this as something done *by* women, as if women were the truly controlling agents, but so also do modern Western scholars. Arthur Waley, for example, in his foreword to Howard Levy's book, writes of his "interest" in this, "as the most striking example of the strange things that women do or have done to them, in almost all cultures, in order to make themselves more attractive to men." [8] There is more. After mentioning that he has been "intrigued" for more than fifty years by such "propensities" of women, he gives cross-cultural examples.* He then gives fraternal praise to the author:

> One of the values of Mr. Levy's well-documented book on footbinding in China is that it will give material to anyone writing a general anthropological study of such *self-mutilations* or *self-modifications* in all parts of the world [emphases mine].[9]

One could ask, did Mr. Waley read Mr. Levy's book? Did he read there that seven-year-old girls mutilated *themselves?* What does "self" mean? That the mothers did it? But it is evident why they were *forced* to do it. The Myth-Masters and the other males who wielded economic and political power had decided that maimed female feet were essential for male approval and for marriageability.

Despite the blatant male-centeredness of this ritual, practitioners of the Rites of Right Scholarship allow themselves to write as if women were its originators, controllers, legitimators. This, of course, is the function of women used as token torturers in sado-rituals: to give plausibility to such deceptive misinterpretations and to perpetuate hate and distrust among

* Among his examples are African women who wear large round disks suspended from their lower lips. It requires no great effort of imagination to think of the usefulness of these disks to the lords and masters of these oppressed women to "keep them in line." Another example is the elongated necks of some African women. Waley neglects to mention that husbands punished these "giraffe women" by removing the neck rings (which Waley calls "necklaces") supporting their heads, causing excruciating pain.

women. For the use of female token torturers affects not only the primary victims of the original rituals, the maimed mothers and daughters, who are turned against each other. In addition to this primary level of dividing and conquering women, there are others. Women of "other" cultures are deceived by sado-scholarship which "proves" that women like to maim each other, documenting the "fact" that "women did it." This false knowledge fosters female self-loathing and distrust of other women. This deception affects not only the few women who read "primary" sources but also those exposed to derivative re-sources, such as grade-school textbooks, popular magazines, like *National Geographic,* and "educational" television programs.

V

The fifth element in the Sado-Ritual Syndrome—ritual orderliness—is illustrated in the thousand-year-long female massacre, Chinese footbinding, which was archetypically obsessive and repetitive. This ritual involved extreme fixation upon minute details in the manufacture and care of "tiny feet." There were rules for the size of the bandages, the intervals between applications of tighter and tighter bandages, the roles of various members of the family in this act of dis-memberment, the length of the correct "foot," the manner in which the foot-bound women should sit and stand, the washing of the re-formed feet (to be done privately because of smell and ugliness hidden by ointments and fancy shoes). There were also rites of fashion connected with the re-fashioned feet. "Beautiful" tiny shoes were designed for various occasions and ceremonies, and the women wore fashionable leggings to hide their monstrously misshapen ankles.

VI

All of this horror and dissipation/misfocusing of energy quickly became accepted as normal and normative, and it remained so for almost a thousand years. Moreover, the complete reversibility of "normality" in patriarchy is illustrated in the transition from the footbinding era to the New Order of "letting out the feet." Discussing the Kuomintang government of the late 1920s, Levy writes:

> Women with bound feet who lived during the transitional era suffered twofold. They endured the pain and discomfort of binding in tender childhood, only to be told in maturity that their sufferings had been in vain because of the demands of the Revolution and the change in aesthetic viewpoint.[10]

Thus the tiny-footed came to be humiliated and looked down upon.* Just as the natural-footed had formerly been called "unmarriageable," this epithet was now hurled at the possessors of lotus hooks. But for the latter, the unnatural had now become "normal." One can imagine the situation of a young woman of twenty with perfect three-inch "lotuses" in which the bones were hopelessly broken and deformed, being told to take off her bindings and walk. The fact was that she could not; she could hobble better in bindings than without them. Those with less "perfect" feet—somewhat longer ones, with the bones unbroken—did in some cases manage to let their feet out. The insensitivity of the new masters to the sufferings of these women manifested that this was hardly a gynocentric revolution. The following propaganda song was sung by revolutionaries in the villages to "recalcitrant" tiny-footed women who were too maimed to "let out" their feet:

> Big sister has big feet;
> See how fast she walks the street!
> Little sister has tiny feet;
> With each step she sways complete.

* Those "socialist feminists" who persist in crediting the Maoist regime with the ending of footbinding are doubly mistaken. First, they are chronologically off base, since by the late 1920s footbinding was on the wane, and "letting out the feet" was encouraged and often enforced under the Kuomintang. Second, they demonstrate inexcusable ignorance of the intent of the early Chinese revolutionaries (to get women into the work force) as well as of their Maoist successors, from whose perspective the idea of radical feminism is wholly absent.

Big sister grows vegetables, tills the fields
Takes cabbages to market on a carrying pole.
Little sister, who can do none of these,
Washes her bindings, kneeling at the river bank;
Everyone runs away when they smell the stank! [11]

Evidently, males were able to change *their* aesthetic standards for female beauty when *their* politics required this. Moreover, women got their cruel and insane orders from all sides, left and right. During the Japanese occupation of Taiwan in the early twentieth century, bureaucrats forced women to untie their bindings (often taking an obscene interest in this procedure), and in many cases this had disastrous results. For their extremely abnormal footbound condition had become the closest approximation to normality possible for these crippled victims.

VII

The final element of the Sado-Ritual Syndrome—legitimation of the gynocidal ritual by the Rites of Re-search—follows a variety of familiar patterns. Indifference, de-tachment, and minimizing of the sadistic nature of Chinese footbinding are glaringly evident in Waley's foreword to Levy's book. He writes:

> On the psychological side this book would have fascinated Havelock Ellis, who in discussing sexual abnormalities stresses the *attractiveness to some men of lameness or an uncertain gait in women.* There is no doubt that this and other *small perversions* became institutionalized in the cult of the bound foot in China [emphases mine].[12]

"Small perversions"! This expression refers to the torture and crippling of millions of women for the satisfaction of "some men." These men, as Levy points out and documents, enjoyed squeezing the stumps (golden lotuses) to the point of causing acute pain, smelling them, whipping them, stuffing them into their mouths, biting them, having their penises rubbed by them. These men stole "tiny shoes" in order to pour semen into them, and drank tea containing the liquid in which the stumps were washed.[13]

We should not imagine that the attraction of "some men" to lameness in women is restricted to the Far East. In *Rationale of the Dirty Joke,* G. Legman (this really *is* the author's name as indicated on the book) writes:

A woman . . . had lost a leg during World War II and had to wear an artificial limb, with the unexpected result that perverted men began following her in the subway and whispering sexual invitations to her . . .[14]

Moreover, William A. Rossi (who thoroughly approves of foot fetishism) points out that "female helplessness arouses many men," alluding to the fact that one extreme example—ankle bondage—goes back at least four thousand years.[15]

Clearly, Waley is aware of this widespread fixation, for he himself, in his pure scholarly way, participates in it. He is "interested" in women's mutilation and knows that Havelock Ellis would have been "fascinated." Moreover, the fact that Levy allowed this foreword to be published in his book—a foreword that completely negates the realities so explicitly exposed in the book—suggests that the author either concurs in the erasure or doesn't notice it. All of this boils down to about the same thing: doublethink and de-tachment from women's oppression. This doublethink is of a piece with that of the Chinese males who were moved to "compassion" at the sight of the tiny feet, which was a condition for sexual arousal.

Conventional scholarship contributes mightily to the "normalizing" of the atrocious ritual in people's minds after the fact, perpetuating and extending its mindbinding influence. This is accomplished repeatedly through the use of language that minimizes/belittles facts. Thus the very title of Levy's book puts footbinding in its place: *Chinese Footbinding: The History of a Curious Erotic Custom.** The adjective *curious* suggests the bland detachment of schizoid scholarship. The

* Nevertheless this is a well-documented and horrifyingly well-illustrated book—a fact no doubt due in large measure to the help of Levy's wife, Henriette Liu Levy, who is credited in the acknowledgments with giving "invaluable assistance, aiding me in reading and clearing up problem areas with a minimum of wasted time."

adjective *erotic* is deceptively innocuous sounding, for it fails to convey the fact that sexual desire is aroused precisely by mutilation. I have already discussed the lie that is embedded in the term *custom,* which suggests something as physically harmless as a handshake or the table manners of Emily Post. Another normalizer is Rossi who, writing in the United States in 1976, finds it possible to describe footbinding as "one of the most powerfully persuasive examples of the foot's *natural* eroticism [emphasis mine]." [16] The reversal is obvious.

Rossi's work is a veritable sourcebook for a study of legitimation of sado-ritual by the Rites of Re-search. It is full of examples whose grotesqueness would have to be rated as above average. The author asserts that the view of the "outside world," which judged this thousand-year-long "sex orgy" involving five billion Chinese (his estimate) as barbarous and cruel has been "naive and distorted." By way of elucidation, he explains that "the *Chinese* regarded the bound foot as the most erotic and desired portion of the entire female anatomy [emphasis mine]." [17] The use of the term *Chinese* here is pseudogeneric, for it was men who desired this portion of the mutilated female anatomy. Women, desiring to survive, were conditioned to believe that this maiming was essential to please the patriarchs. Rossi's deceptive usage of pseudogenerics is even more blatant in his assertion that "the *human species* prefers *itself* a little bent out of natural shape [emphases mine]." [18] The statement, of course, veils the fact that men prefer women to be bent badly "out of shape" on all levels—physical, mental, and spiritual.

Rossi describes the Chinese semi-amputees as "a *reigning* clan of *goddesses* with *sensual powers* not bestowed upon ordinary women [emphases mine]." [19] By now it is evident to the reader what sort of "powers" these "reigning goddesses" enjoyed. Rossi prefers not to know. When he uses the term *cruel* to describe the practice of footbinding, it is in quotation marks. Instead of using the term *pain,* he writes blandly of "discomfort" to which "the growing girl developed a good deal of immunity." [20] The unsuspecting reader of his book may be seduced into associating footbinding with something like the adolescent discomfort of wearing braces on one's teeth. Perhaps she is even lulled by the arrogant style of authority into forgetting to ask the most obvious questions, such as: Just how would *he* know? Thus she may nod in mesmerized agreement when he intones the familiar misinformation that "women have always had an affinity for fragile foundations and willowy walking." [21]

Anyone who thinks of contemporary Western stylish women's shoes and of the indoctrination women all receive from earliest childhood, about the "correctness" of such footwear, knows something about this "affinity" and its origins. We have all heard the familiar derisive remarks about "women who wear sensible shoes." The term *sensible,* meaning reasonable, is used as derogatory when applied to women's choice of footwear. An implication of this is that women should not be sensible/reasonable because this is de-sexualizing in men's eyes. The connection between the condition of one's feet and the state of one's mind is implied in this adjective, *sensible.* Hobbling on spiked heels or platform shoes, painfully smiling, women feel physically and emotionally unsteady. In such attire they are vulnerable physically, since it is at least difficult, if not impossible, to run from an attacker or participate in many ordinary—not to mention athletic—activities. They are also vulnerable mentally/emotionally, since such footwear keeps them aware, at least subliminally, of their victim status. Their response to this awareness is to send out signals of helplessness through tones of voice, nervous laughter, body language, and Self-depreciating speech and behavior.*

Another muddied approach to foot fetishism is to be found

* In reconsidering the pejorative attacks on "sensible shoes," it may also be enlightening to consider another definition of the term *sensible:* "capable of receiving impressions from external objects through the sense organs." Feet are our contact with the ground, the earth. Spinsters undertaking a dangerous and adventurous journey need to be balanced and sure-footed and capable of receiving impressions accurately. We therefore choose our equipment wisely, and this means choosing sensible shoes. To succumb to the dictates of foot "fashion" is to fail to break away from sado-ritual behavior. Such behavior creates the familiar "living proof" which supports mendacious assertions by the scholars of sado-ritual, such as Rossi, about women's "affinities."

in Ernest Becker's *The Denial of Death*. Becker, who argues that sadomasochism is "natural," sees the foot as "the absolute and unmitigated testimonial to our degraded animality, to the incongruity between our proud, rich, lively, infinitely transcendent, free inner spirit and our earth-bound body."[22] This combination of flesh-loathing and false transcendence is developed further in the same paragraph, when he states that "nothing equals the foot for ugliness or the shoe for contrast and cultural contrivance." After reading this, it is not too surprising to find the same author affirm that the practice of Chinese footbinding represents "the perfect triumph of cultural contrivance over the animal foot—exactly what the fetishist achieves with the shoe."[23] Thus the "infinitely transcendent, free inner spirit" and "cultural contrivance" are clearly identified with the male, while the "ugly, animal foot" over which the latter triumphs *is* the female. The mutilated female foot, then, is a triumph of patriarchal transcendence.

Becker hardly seems to know what he is saying, or how he unmasks patriarchal values. He goes on:

> One of the reasons that the fetish object is itself so splendid and fascinating to the fetishist must be that he transfers to it the awesomeness of the *other human presence*. The fetish is then the manageable miracle, while the partner is not [emphasis mine].[24]

Becker fails to make explicit the fact that "the other human presence" which the threatened male finds so awesome that he must reduce it to manageability is female. Also lacking is any recognition of the perversion involved in seeing the natural female foot as ugly and its mutilated substitute as "splendid." But then, this is consistent with Becker's belief that sadomasochism is "natural."

Another sterling example of sadoscholarship legitimating Chinese footbinding is R. H. Van Gulik's *Sexual Life in Ancient China*. Van Gulik dismisses as "far-fetched" the explanation that confucianists encouraged the "custom" because it restricted women's movements and kept them within the house. He misses the point that the explanation in terms of restriction of women's movements is not "far-fetched" but rather that it does not go far enough. Van Gulik dismisses footbinding as having something or other to do with "shoe-fetishism," but fails to see it as oppressive, despite the fact that he himself presents a truly horrifying drawing of a bound foot based on an X-ray. Following the usual pattern of doublethink, he is unable to see/name the significance of his own observation that "woman's small feet came to be considered as the most intimate part of her body, the very symbol of femininity, and the most powerful centre of sex appeal." [25] Failing to acknowledge that the mutilation/muting of women into "femininity" was/is sadism on the scale of massacre, he culpably misses the point of his own observation that the bandages were taken off only in seclusion when they were changed after the bath.[26] The point is, of course, that public exposure would destroy the illusion promoted by the euphemistic ritual of "tiny feet."

The blatancy of Van Gulik's de-tachment is illustrated in the following statement:

> As to the detrimental effects on women's health caused by footbinding, these are *often exaggerated*. For the general state of health of Chinese women, the secondary effects of footbinding were the most serious: bound feet *discouraged women's interest in dancing, fencing, and other physical exercises* popular with the weaker sex in pre-footbinding days [emphases mine].[27]

This is comparable to describing a leg amputation as "discouraging" figure skating, skiing, and ballet. One difference between footbound women and amputees is that the latter can, with prostheses, learn to walk, whereas perfectly footbound women could only fall from stump to stump and often had to be carried. Our author does seem to overcome his de-tachment enough to feel one serious regret, however:

> In the artistic field footbinding had the regrettable consequence that it put a stop to the great old Chinese art of dancing. After the Sung period . . . one hears less and less about great dancers.[28]

Indeed. And here the irony of the sado-ritual procession has come full circle. For the legend that had been employed to "explain," legitimate, and encourage the ritual tells that the

Emperor Li Yu had a favored palace concubine named Lovely Maiden who was a gifted dancer. He ordered her to bind her feet and dance in the center of a six-foot-high lotus constructed for this purpose. "She then danced in the center of the lotus, whirling about like a rising cloud." [29] This "event" was used to trick women into identifying beauty and *dancing* with bound feet. Clearly, no contradiction is too blatant to qualify as a sado-ritual legitimation. Indeed, the more blatant the contradiction/reversal, the more effective it seems to be as a mind poisoner. This is an essential characteristic of sado-ritual scholarship as well as myth.

Van Gulik, finally, provides an illuminating example of scholarly hypocrisy *about* scholarly hypocrisy, slapping the wrist of a nineteenth-century scholar who proclaimed that the minds and bodies of Chinese "people" are distorted and deformed by unnatural usages:

> That observer conveniently forgot that at about the same time his wife and female relatives at home were *bringing upon themselves* cardiac, pulmonary and other serious afflictions by the excessive tight-lacing of their waists. Footbinding caused much pain and acute suffering, but women of all times and races have as a rule *gladly borne those if fashion demanded it* [emphases mine].[30]

With his magic wand, the scholar brands all women as agents of their own affliction. The First Agent supposedly "demanding" this is "fashion." In this fascinating example of learned doublethink we find a right-thinking scholar conveniently using the universal oppression of women by patriarchal fashion designers as a weapon to chastise a member of the scholarly brotherhood. The latter came close to nonobservance of the rules by becoming too critical of the Chinese "custom." It is undoubtedly true, as Van Gulik insinuates, that the criticized scholar was a cultural chauvinist. Nevertheless, he had inadvertently taken a step too far in the direction of Searching rather than ritefully re-covering. Consequently, the right-thinking Van Gulik had to brand him as exemplifying "the smug attitude of 19th-century Western observers."

There are also more subtle/refined manifestations of scholarly mystification. In the case of Chinese footbinding, as in the case of Indian *suttee,* Vern Bullough provides examples of language which fails to *move* the reader, who then becomes a victim of "syntactic exploitation." [31] Thus, he describes footbinding as "a practice which made it *almost* impossible for women to move about *without great effort* [emphases mine]." [32] The combination of the adverb *almost* with the phrase *without great effort* has a completely nullifying effect. Each erases the point of the other. Had he eliminated either the adverb or the phrase, the statement would have been correct. Had he eliminated both, it still would have been accurate. By the use of both, he succeeds in watering down the reality to the point that the statement is simply wrong, for footbinding did indeed make it impossible for women to move about without great effort and without great *agony*. His choice of the bland term *effort* is deeply and subtly deceptive. If it conjures up any images at all, these are somewhere in the range of tight shoes, corns, bunions, or at worst a sprained ankle—hardly conveying the reduction of a woman's feet to putrescent three-inch stumps.

Bullough deceives by omission. He nowhere describes the horrible physical reality of footbinding, although he uses the same source (Howard S. Levy) as Andrea Dworkin, and therefore had available for use the very same graphic and detailed material. His terse statement that "there was a cult of foot fetishism" conveys nothing of the maiming of women. Rather he fulfills the expectations of Arthur Waley that Levy's book "will give material to anyone writing a general anthropological study . . ." Indeed, this is the Ritual of Re-search. Each book "gives material" for another. The more "general" the better. That is to say, the more blandly that it blends the "material," universalizing it all into vague abstractions, such as "customs," the safer, the better, the more scholarly. All that is missing is life/spirit/spinning process.

In contrast to the luminaries cited above, Andrea Dworkin —who uses Levy as her source—has written of footbinding with passion, with integrity of know-ing and feeling, with feminist consciousness. As a result she shocks the reader into awareness, helping her to *understand* holistically—that is, using mind/imagination/emotions—the significance of the facts of footbinding and their interconnections with other facts, such as contemporary American destruction of women in the name of "romantic love." Her book title, *Woman Hating,* and her chapter title, "Gynocide: Chinese Footbinding," quickly sweep the "material" off musty library shelves reserved for those who are "curious" about remote "erotic customs." The facts come alive, for the feminist author has no hidden agenda of hiding the horrors. Quite the contrary is the case. She deliberately unmasks them, showing the interconnectedness between this and other gynocidal practices and propaganda. Thus Dworkin helps the reader to know, sense, become incensed. Catching an essential thread of meaning in this "curious erotic custom," she shows it to the reader:

> It [footbinding] demonstrates that man's love for woman, his sexual adoration of her, his human definition of her, require her negation, physical crippling and psychological lobotomy . . . Brutality, sadism, and oppression emerge as the substantive core of the romantic ethos.[33]

Dworkin's work has received the usual "silent treatment" meted out to those who name atrocities and point out their interconnectedness. There has also been criticism of her lack of scholarship. This could only be justified if the same criteria were universally applied, rather than selectively used as an excuse for dismissing feminists, and if her book had been intended primarily as a work of conventional scholarship. Unlike male social critics (such as Marshall McLuhan, for example, who regards his books as "probes") her work has been judged without generosity or justice, dismissed without adequate cause. Yet women continue to be awakened by it because it breaks away from the rituals and makes thinking come alive.

Thinking that is alive involves seeing connections between seemingly different phenomena, for example, between fairy tales and gynocidal history. Crone-logical thinkers, then, will not be surprised to read in *Funk and Wagnalls Dictionary of Folklore* that the tale of Cinderella is originally an Oriental story. Indeed, "the earliest known version happens to be Chinese, from the 9th century A.D." [34] In the light of the history of footbinding, this isolated piece of information ominously "makes sense." Upon further reflection, the picture becomes more ominous. Hundreds of millions of children "know" the story of Cinderella. Most of us received it from the Brothers Grimm in a rather refined and adulterated form. Nevertheless we learned from it (or were supposed to learn) several important lessons: that tiny feet are essential to female beauty, that stepmothers (read: mothers) are cruel, that the ultimate female tragedy is not to be married. In order to realize the full implications of the Grimm tale of Cinderella, however, it is helpful to look at earlier versions, which are less delicate. One version, recounted by Jakob Ludwig Karl Grimm in the early nineteenth century (republished and translated in subsequent editions, as recently as 1975), has it that when the eldest sister unsuccessfully tried to fit her foot into the tiny golden slipper provided by the prince, her mother ordered her to cut off her big toe to make it fit. At first the prince was fooled, but the flow of blood made him aware that he had been tricked. Then the stepmother had her other daughter cut off a slice of her heel to get into the shoe, but she had the same bloody problem. Then, of course, Cinderella tried it on and it fit her tiny foot.[35]

The reader of this book will recall the account of the Chinese mother and aunt who said that if one loved a daughter, one could not love her feet. This, however, is no Oriental peculiarity. It is an idea legitimated not only in the obscure tomes and scholarly journals of specialists in "curious erotic customs" but in the "charming" fairy tales we heard as bedtime stories. From pre-kindergarten learning through graduate school "education" female foot-maiming and mind-maiming is re-covered, re-searched, re-hearsed. The literature, from the Brothers Grimm's tale to Van Gulik's opinionated prose, functions to perpetuate the Rite, to promote Right Thinking, above all to prevent women from putting the pieces together and running/dancing free.

CHAPTER FIVE

AFRICAN GENITAL MUTILATION: THE UNSPEAKABLE ATROCITIES

Have you ever risen in the night
bursting with knowledge and the world
dissolves toward any listening ear
into which you can pour
whatever it was you knew
before waking
Only to find all ears asleep
or drugged perhaps by a dream of words
because as you scream into them over and over
nothing stirs
and the mind you have reached is not a working mind
please hang up and die again? The mind
you have reached is not a working mind
Please hang up
And die again.

Audre Lorde,
from "A Sewerplant Grows in Harlem,
or;
I'm a Stranger Here Myself When
Does the Next Swan Leave,"
New York Head Shop and Museum

If a woman ignores these wrongs, then may women as a sex continue to suffer them; there is no help for any of us—let us be dumb and die.

Elizabeth Barrett Browning,
Letters of Elizabeth Barrett Browning

I have gained many sisters.
And if one is beaten,
or raped, or killed,
I will not come in mourning black.
I will not pick the right flowers.
I will not celebrate her death
& it will matter not
if she's Black or white—
if she loves women or men.
I will come with my many sisters
and decorate the streets
with the innards of those
brothers in womenslaughter.
No more can I dull my rage
in alcohol & deference
to *men's* courts
I will come to my sisters,
not dutiful,
I will come strong.

Pat Parker,
from "Womanslaughter,"
Womanslaughter

There are some manifestations of the Sado-Ritual Syndrome that are unspeakable—incapable of being expressed in words because inexpressibly horrible.* Such are the ritual genital

* I have chosen to name these practices for what they are: barbaric rituals/atrocities. Critics from Western countries are constantly being intimidated by accusations of "racism," to the point of misnaming, non-naming, and not seeing these sado-rituals. The accusations of "racism" may come from ignorance, but they serve only the interests of males, not of women. This kind of accusation and intimidation constitutes an astounding and damaging reversal, for it is clearly in the interest of Black women that feminists of all races should speak out. Moreover, it is in the interest of women of all races to see African genital mutilation in the context of planetary patriarchy, of which it is but one manifestation. As I am demonstrating, it is of the same pattern as the other atrocities I discuss.

mutilations—excision and infibulation—still inflicted upon women throughout Africa today, and practiced in many parts of the world in the past.* These ritualized atrocities are unspeakable also in a second sense; that is, there are strong taboos against saying/writing the truth about them, against *naming* them. These taboos are operative both within the segments of phallocracy in which such rituals are practiced and in other parts of the Fatherland, whose leaders cooperate in the conspiracy of silence. Hags see that the demonic rituals in the so-called underdeveloped regions of the planet are deeply connected with atrocities perpetrated against women in "advanced" societies. To allow ourselves to see the connections is to begin to understand that androcracy is the State of Atrocity, where atrocities are normal, ritualized, repeated.[1] It is the City of Atrophy in which the archetypal trophies are massacred women.

Those who have endured the unspeakable atrocities of genital mutilation have in most cases been effectively silenced. Indeed this profound silencing of the mind's imaginative and critical powers is one basic function of the sado-ritual, which

* Lest Westerners feel smugly distant from these rituals, it would be well to recall some facts of "our" culture. In a later chapter I will discuss the implications of the fact that clitoridectomies and other mutilations have been inflicted by American gynecologists. It should be noted also that slashing and mutilation of genitals are common features of contemporary gang rape, which is "as American as apple pie." Moreover, there has been a time-honored christian European tradition of infibulation and of the chastity belt. According to some, this was done in the same way as the infibulation of mares practiced in the veterinary profession, consisting of fastening together the labia by means of a ring, a buckle, or a padlock. According to Davis, the upper classes resorted less frequently to infibulation, but used instead the chastity belt, which was supposedly less painful. When one considers that some women were locked up in these for months or even years while their lords were away, the torture of accumulated excrement and of infection is beyond imagination. Such items are of course still on display in European museums, objects of merriment for guides and visitors, including female visitors who often do not comprehend their implications. See Elizabeth Gould Davis, *The First Sex* (New York: G. P. Putnam, 1971), pp. 163–67.

teaches women never to forget to murder their own divinity. Those who physically survive these atrocities "live" their entire lifetimes, from early childhood or from puberty, preoccupied by pain. Those women who inhabit other parts of the planet cannot really wish to imagine the condition of their mutilated sisters, for the burden of knowing is heavy. It is heavy not merely because of differences in conditions, but especially because of similarities which, as I will show later in this Passage, increase with the march of progress of phallotechnology.

The maze of lies and silences surrounding the genital mutilation still forced upon millions of young girls in many African countries continues to be effective. Yet it is becoming the subject of increasingly widespread attention.[2] Fran P. Hosken presents the following important definitions of the practices usually lumped under the vague and misleading expression, "female circumcision":

1. Sunna Circumcision: removal of the prepuce and/or tip of the clitoris.
2. Excision or Clitoridectomy: excision of the entire clitoris with the labia minora and some or most of the external genitalia.
3. Excision and Infibulation (Pharaonic Circumcision): This means excision of the entire clitoris, labia minora and parts of the labia majora. The two sides of the vulva are then fastened together in some way either by thorns . . . or sewing with catgut. Alternatively the vulva are scraped raw and the child's limbs are tied together for several weeks until the wound heals (or she dies). The purpose is to close the vaginal orifice. Only a small opening is left (usually by inserting a slither of wood) so the urine or later the menstrual blood can be passed.[3]

It should not be imagined that the horror of the life of an infibulated child/woman ends with this operation. Her legs are tied together, immobilizing her for weeks, during which time excrement remains within the bandage. Sometimes accidents occur during the operation: the bladder may be pierced or the rectum cut open. Sometimes in a spasm of agony the child bites off her tongue. Infections are, needless to say, common. Scholars such as Lantier claim that death is not a very common immediate effect of the operation, but often there are complications which leave the women debilitated for the rest of their lives.[4] No statistics are available on this point. What is certain is that the infibulated girl is mutilated and that she can look forward to a life of repeated encounters with "the little knife"—the instrument of her perpetual torture. For women who are infibulated have to be cut open—either by the husband or by another woman—to permit intercourse. They have to be cut open further for delivery of a child. Often they are sewn up again after delivery, depending upon the decision of the husband. The cutting (defibulation) and re-sewing goes on throughout a woman's living death of reproductive "life."[5] Immediate medical results of excision and infibulation include "hemorrhage, infections, shock, retention of urine, damage to adjacent tissues, dermoid cysts, abcesses, keloid scarring, coital difficulties, and infertility caused by chronic pelvic infections.*[6] In addition, we should consider the psychological maiming caused by this torture.

Yet this is an "unmentionable" manifestation of the atrocity which is phallocracy. The World Health Organization has refused for many years to concern itself with the problem. When it was asked in 1958 to study this problem it took the position that such operations were based on "social and cultural backgrounds" and were outside its competence. This basic attitude has not changed.[7] There has been a conspiracy of silence:

International agencies, the U.N and U.N. agencies, especially WHO and UNICEF (both devoted to health care), development agencies (such as U.S. Agency for International Development), non-governmental organizations working in Africa, missionaries and church groups concerned with health care, also women's organizations including World Association of Girl Guides and Girl Scouts, Y.W.C.A., and the Associated Country Women of the World, and others working in Africa, all know what is going on. Or they have people in Africa who know. This quite aside from the Health Departments and hospitals in African countries and the M.D.s, espe-

* Linda Barufaldi observed that the circumcision of the male requires only the removal of the foreskin, which not only leaves his organ of sexual pleasure intact but also makes him *less* susceptible to infection (conversation, Boston, January 1978).

cially gynecologists, who get the most desperate cases. . . . The doctors know all. But they don't speak.* [8]

It is important to ask why such a variety of organizations and professions have other priorities. Why do "educated" persons babble about the importance of "tribal coherence" and "tradition" while closing their eyes to the physical reality of mutilation? We might well ask why "female circumcision" was reinforced in Kenya after "liberation" and described by President Kenyatta, in his book *Facing Mount Kenya,* as an important "custom" for the benefit of "the people." [9] Hosken maintains that in the socialist countries in Africa clitoridectomy and infibulation are practiced on a vast scale without comment from the governments or health departments. Again, one must ask why. Why do anthropologists ignore or minimize this horror? Why is it that the catholic church has not taken a clear position against this genital mutilation (which is practiced upon some of its own members in Africa)? Why do some African leaders educated in the West continue to insist upon the maiming of their own daughters?

These questions are profoundly interconnected. The appearance of disparateness among these groups and of their responses (or nonresponses) masks their essential sameness. Even the above-named organizations whose membership is largely female are androcratic since they are willing to participate in the conspiracy of silence. Socialists, catholics, liberal reformers, population planners, politicos of all persuasions—all have purposes which have nothing to do with women's specific well-being unless this happens to fit into the "wider" aims.

I

The components of the Sado-Ritual Syndrome are present in African excision and infibulation. The obsession with purity is

* As Hosken shows, a few doctors have spoken out in recent years. The evidence is to be found in a few medical journal articles, some of which are cited in this chapter. Particularly useful are the articles of J. A. Verzin, A. A. Shandall, and G. Pieters.

evident. The clitoris is "impure" because it does not serve male purposes. It has no necessary function in reproduction. As Benoîte Groult points out, hatred of the clitoris is almost universal, for this organ is strictly female, for women's pleasure.[10] Thus it is by nature "impure," and the logical conclusion, acted out by the tribes that practice excision and infibulation, is purification of women by its removal. Furthermore, it is believed that excision encourages fidelity, that is, moral "purity," for there is a "decrease in sensitivity from the operation."[11] The term *decrease,* here, is a euphemism for *loss.* These women have been de-sensitized, "purified" of the capacity for sexual pleasure. The ideology among some African tribes which explains and justifies this brutal robbing from women of their clitoris—the purely female organ—displays the total irony of the concept of purity. There is a widespread belief among the Bambaras and the Dogons from Mali that all persons are hermaphroditic and that this condition is cured by circumcision and excision. Since they believe the boy is female by virtue of his foreskin and the girl is male by her clitoris, the sexes are purified (that is, officially distinguished) by the rites of puberty. Thus the removal of the purely female clitoris is seen as making a woman purely female. In fact, its purpose is to make her purely feminine, a purely abject object.

Infibulation goes even further, displaying yet other dimensions of the androcratic obsession with purity. For the "sewn women" are not only deprived of the organ of pleasure. Their masters have them genitally "sewn up," in order to preserve and redesign them strictly for their own pleasure and reproductive purposes. These women are 100 percent pure because 100 percent enslaved. Their perpetual pain (or the imminent threat of this) is an important condition for their perpetual purity, for pain preoccupies minds, emotions, imaginations, sensations, prohibiting presence of the Self.

II

The second component of the syndrome, erasure of male responsibility, is present by virtue of male absence at the execution of the mutilation. In most cases, it is not males who perform the brutal operations, although male nurses and surgeons now do it in some modern hospitals.[12] Moreover, there are comforting myths, ideologies, and clichés which assure political leaders and other males that they are blame-free. Together with the hermaphroditic myth, described above, there is the justification that "this is a way of teaching women to endure pain." There is also the belief among the Bambaras that a man who sleeps with a nonexcised woman risks death from her "sting" (clitoris). The Mossis believe that the clitoris kills children at birth and that it can be a source of impotence among men. A basic belief that justifies all, erasing all responsibility, is of course that these rites keep women faithful.[13] What is erased is the fact that these "faithful" wives have been physically reconstructed for male purposes. They have been deprived of their own sexuality and "tightened up" for their masters' pleasure—tightened through devices like wounding and sewing and through the tension of excruciating pain.* Erasure of all this on the global level occurs when leaders of "advanced" countries and of international organizations overlook these horrors in the name of "avoiding cultural judgment." They are free of responsibility and blame, for the "custom" must be respected as part of a "different tradition." By so naming the tradition as "different" they hide the cross-cultural hatred of women.

III

The massive spread of female genital mutilation throughout Africa has been noted by responsible Searchers. Accurate

* When reading this passage, Emily Culpepper pointed out the possibility that these genitally reconstructed women are designed to offer their masters a kind of sexual experience comparable to that obtained by anal intercourse with other men. These "tight" women are never allowed to become too loose, for this would decrease the strong stimulation of the penis which men experience in anal coitus. For the women's genital structure has been reduced and simplified to the dimension of a small hole. In a metaphorical sense, too, these women can never be "loose." This fact may give rise to the thought that in Western society both "tight" women ("dried-up old maids") and "loose" women ("dirty whores") are sexually *wrong* by male standards. For in fact female sexuality—as an expression of female be-ing—is essentially wrong by androcratic, heterosexist standards.

statistics are impossible to obtain, since the operation is usually performed in secret. Nevertheless the ritual, which is of ancient origin, is known to be widespread from Algeria in the north to the Central African Republic in the south, and from Senegal and Mauritania in the west to Somalia in the east.[14] Doctors working in Africa are in a position to know what is going on, since women suffering from complications connected with the operations are sometimes brought to them. Two physicians have given lists of countries in which female genital mutilation, in one form or another, is still practiced.[15] Fran Hosken, using these and other sources, and relying also upon her own personal investigations, concludes that some form of female circumcision is probably practiced in all countries of Africa today in at least some tribal groups.[16] Hosken believes that the practice started historically in Africa and was taken on by Arab conquerors and later islam.[17] Ashley Montagu maintains that infibulation and the successive operation—defibulation—are practiced among some Indian tribes in Peru and possibly elsewhere in South and Central America.[18] Montagu also holds that genital mutilation is still practiced in Australia.[19] It will require a massive effort to obtain detailed and accurate information. One point is certain: this ritual spread rapidly over a large geographical area, involving the torture and maiming of millions of women, condemning them to a living death, deadening the divine spark of be-ing, the Goddess within.*

In discussing the phenomenon of the spread of sado-rituals, in the "cases" of Indian *suttee* and Chinese footbinding, I have shown that there is a pattern of proliferation from an elite to the upwardly aspiring lower echelons of society. The case

* According to Hosken, female genital mutilation takes place in some tribes in the following countries: Kenya, Tanzania, Ethiopia, southern Egypt, Sudan, Uganda, northern Zaire, Chad, northern Cameroon, Nigeria, Dahomey, Togo, northern Ghana, Upper Volta, Mali, northern Ivory Coast, Liberia, Sierra Leone, Guinea, Guinea Bissau, the Gambia, Senegal, Mauritania. See Hosken, *WIN News,* Vol. II, No. 3 (Summer 1976), p. 22. Benoîte Groult states that excision in small girls still takes place in Yemen, Saudi Arabia, Iraq, Jordan, and Syria (*Ainsi soit-elle* [Paris: Grasset, 1975], pp. 93–118).

can be argued that this pattern has also existed in female genital mutilation. According to Strabo's *Geography,* Pharaonic Egypt was characterized by clitoral excision, meaning the cutting off of sections of the clitoris and of the labia minora.[20] Inspection of royal female mummies has led some authorities to conclude that these high-caste women of Egypt had been excised. Huelsman claims that in ancient Egypt, female genital surgery was performed between the ages of fourteen and fifteen years. He remarks brightly that "it seems probable that even the amorous adventures of Cleopatra may have been conducted *sans* clitoris." [21] Shandall suggests that genital surgery on ancient Egyptian women was limited to the female relatives of rulers and priests. He speculates that women from these social and economic classes may not have been able to inherit property unless they had first undergone some form of genital surgery.

Indeed, a large number of Pharaonically circumcised mummies have been discovered.[22] Since the privileged classes were mummified, it would appear that excision was a feature of female life among the royalty. Benoîte Groult claims that the mummies of both Cleopatra and Nefertiti lack clitorises.[23] Although Ashley Montagu seems to think that all girls in ancient Egypt were excised, there really is not much evidence to back this up.[24] The evidence points to the existence of rites of passage involving genital mutilation of upper-class girls. Since we know that at the present time it is practiced upon girls at all levels of society among many African tribes (and most likely in other parts of the globe)[25] it is logical to think that it did spread from royalty to lower strata of society, as well as expanding outward geographically. The spread of this atrocity was condoned, legitimated, demanded by the World Religion which is patriarchy. Although such sects as islam and christianity did not invent it, neither did they effectively stop it. More ancient than islam, it was practiced by pre-islamic Arabs. The "custom" was prevalent in widespread areas of the globe, in Aboriginal Australia, South America, India, Pakistan. Today it still massacres the bodies and spirits of millions of women in Africa, mostly women living in poverty, far removed from the palatial splendors that surrounded Cleopatra and other royal victims of sado-ritual.

IV

The use of women as token torturers is horribly illustrated in this ritual. At the International Tribunal on Crimes Against Women the testimony of a woman from Guinea was brought by a group of French women. The witness described seeing "the savage mutilation called excision that is inflicted on the women of my country between the ages of 10 and 12." In the instance she describes, which she saw with her own eyes, six women were holding down the victim, intoning prayers to drown her screams:

> The operation was done without any anesthetic, with no regard for hygiene or precautions of any sort. With the broken neck of a bottle, the old woman banged hard down, cutting into the upper part of my friend's genitals so as to make as wide a cut as possible, since "an incomplete excision does not constitute a sufficient guarantee against profligacy in girls."
>
> The blunt glass of the bottle did not cut deeply enough into my friend's genitals and the exciseuse had to do it several more times. . . . When the clitoris had been ripped out, the women howled with joy, and forced my friend to get up despite a streaming hemorrhage, to parade her through the town.[26]

The witness goes on to describe the "parade," in which the mutilated girl, dressed in a loin-cloth, her breasts bare, is followed by a dozen or so women singing:

> They were informing the village that my friend was ready for marriage. In Guinea, in fact, no man marries a woman who has not been excised and who is not a virgin, with rare exceptions.

This last sentence unmasks the male-centeredness of the entire ritual. It is men who demand this female castration, and possession in marriage is required in *their* society for survival. The apparently "active" role of the women, themselves mutilated, is in fact a passive, instrumental role. It hides the real castrators of women. Mentally castrated,* these women participate in the destruction of their own kind—of womankind—and in the destruction of strength and bonding among women. The screaming token torturers are silencing not only the victim, but their own victimized Selves. Their screams are the "sounds of silence" imposed upon women in sado-ritual.

The extent to which female token torturers have been used to mask the male master-minds of female genital mutilation is suggested in an account given by Montagu of female infibulation as practiced among tribes immediately south of the First Cataract of the Nile. Part of the procedure involves a visit to the bridegroom before the marriage by one of the women who performs the infibulation. The purpose of the visit is to obtain exact measurements of his "member." The following activity ensues:

> She then makes to measurement, a sort of phallus of clay or wood and by its aid she incises the scar for a certain distance and leaves the instrument wrapped round with a rag—in the wound in order to keep the edges from adhering again.[27]

Thus the master has his bride made to order to suit his "member." Montagu gives a similar account of a ceremony that was practiced among the Conibos of the Rio Ucalayi of Peru. He first describes the incision. Then:

> The old sorcerers rubbed some medical herbs into the bleeding parts, and after a while introduced an artificial penis, made of clay, into the vagina of the maiden, the thing being exactly the same size as the penis of the man betrothed to her. Thereafter she was considered properly prepared to marry, and was given over to her future husband.[28]

Again, the master is assured of a snug and pleasurable fit.

* In its origin, the term *castrate* is akin to the Sanskrit *śasati,* meaning, "he cuts to pieces." This describes precisely what is done to women's bodies/minds/spirits under patriarchy: they are divided and fragmented into disconnected pieces.

The fact that "women did it—and still do it—to women" must be seen in this context. The idea that such procedures, or any part of them, could be woman-originated is only thinkable in the mind-set of phallocracy, for it is, in fact, unthinkable.[29] The use of women to do the dirty work can make it appear thinkable only to those who do not wish to see. Yet this use of women does effectively blunt the power of sisterhood, having first blocked the power of the Self.

Most horrifying is the fact that mothers insist that this mutilation be done to their own daughters. Frequently it is the mother who performs the brutal operation. Among the Somalis, for example, the mother does the excising, slicing, and final infibulation according to the time-honored rules. She does this in such a way as to leave the tiniest opening possible. Her "honor" depends upon making this as small as possible, because the smaller this artificial aperture is, the higher the value of the girl.[30]

An indication of the strength of the stranglehold which tradition has upon the mother-daughter relationship is the fact that some women who by academic and professional standards would be considered educated also insist upon excision. The case is cited of a young Egyptian woman physician who was expecting a baby and was asked by a Danish scholar, Henny Harald Hansen, about the reasons for these mutilations. She informed him that "if the child she was expecting should be a girl she would circumcise her herself." The young woman gave several reasons. The first was religious: she was a muslim. The second was cosmetic: she wanted "to remove something disfiguring, ugly and repulsive." Third, the girl should be protected from sexual stimulation through the clitoris. The fourth reason was tradition. "The young doctor argued in support of her intention to respect tradition that the majority of husbands preferred their wives to be circumcised." [31] The fact that this woman was a physician might at first seem startling. Yet further reflection suggests that there is not such inconsistency as one might suppose, particularly in view of the facts of gynecological mutilation in present-day America, which will be discussed later in this Passage.

V

The fifth component of the syndrome, compulsive orderliness which misfocuses attention away from the fact of evil, is manifested even in the most primitive environment. Although the "surgical instrument" may be as crude as broken glass or a kitchen knife, the performance is itself highly ritualized. The "ceremony" in the Sudan is described by Montagu as "preceded with food and merriment." [32] Certain women are chosen to perform the rite. Often it is a relative who does the excising. The procedures differ among different tribes, but they always follow certain rules that have been handed down, which constitute "the way it has always been done." Thus, among the Nandi in Africa, there is a two-part horror show. The first day, stinging nettles are applied to the clitoris, so that it swells and becomes unimaginably large. The second day, an old woman chars it off with glowing coals. The mutilated girl is then sent to a convalescent hut, having been converted into property for her husband.[33] Another manifestation of the ritualized orderliness is the age of the victim: The mutilating rite takes place at different ages in different tribes, but the point is that each has its prescribed age, which often does not correspond to the individual girl's onset of puberty. It is claimed that some Arabs do it several weeks after birth, that the Somalis fix the age of mutilation at 3–4 years, that in southern Egypt it is done at 9–10 years, that in Abyssinia it is at 8 years or else 80 days after birth. Among the Malinkes and Bambaras the age is 12–15 years.[34] All of this indicates that the order imposed is the contrived order of ritual, having nothing to do with the physiological stage of development.

There are various ritual prescriptions in various places, but the obsessive repetitiveness and fixation upon minute details are clearly present. Thus, van Gennep describes some details of the ritual among the Masai of Tanganyika:

> The rites for the girls differ [from the boys'] in the following respects: several are excised at a time; their heads are shaved; they remain at home until scar tissue forms on the wound; they adorn their heads with grasses, among which they place an ostrich feather, and smear their faces with white clay; all of the women of the kraal eat a communal meal; and the marriage takes place as soon as the fiancé is able to pay what he owes on the dowry.[35]

Other tribes have other versions of this sado-ritual.[36] There are rules for the stages in the mutilation process, rules about festivity, about timing, about dress and "cosmetics," about seclusion, about relation of the maiming to marriage. These distract the attention of the participants (and of foreign specialists such as anthropologists) from the victimized women's physical agony, mutilation, life-long deprivation, deformity, pain, and premature death from complications.

VI

The sado-ritual of excision and infibulation bestows acceptability upon gynocidal behavior—even to the extent of making it normative. This is illustrated in the precept of the president of Kenya, Jomo Kenyatta, that "no proper Gikuyu would dream of marrying a girl who has not been circumcised," since this operation "is regarded as the *conditio sine qua non* for the whole teaching of tribal law, religion, and morality."[37] With these words, one chief in the Higher Order of phallocratic morality dictates its chief lesson: that women should suffer. Typically, the justification for the atrocious ritual under the reign of phallic morality involves a reversal in which the unnatural becomes normative. Only a mutilated woman is considered 100 percent feminine.* By removal of her specifically *female*-identified organ, which is not necessary for the male's pleasure or for reproductive servitude, she "becomes a woman." At first the reversal might seem astonishing, if one hears the term *woman* as representing a state of natural integrity. But if we understand this term to refer to an embodi-

* It is interesting to compare these attempts to feminize women with the feminization of male-to-constructed-female transsexuals. The latter, who consider themselves to be "women" (referring to "other" women as "native women") undergo operations which remove the testicles and penis and give them artificial vaginas, but no clitoris. Both of these mutilating attempts at feminization receive a large amount of legitimation by phallocracy. See Janice Raymond, *The Transsexual Empire: The Making of the She-Male* (Boston: Beacon Press, 1979).

ment of the feminine, which is a construct of phallocracy, then the meaning of the expression becomes clear.*

In *La Cité magique,* Jacques Lantier reports a conversation about clitoridectomy with a tribal chief and magician. The latter illustrates the way in which atrocious, sadistic behavior has come to be regarded as normative. According to this sage:

[God] has given the clitoris to the woman so that she can use it before marriage in order to experience the pleasure of love while still remaining pure. . . .

The clitoris of very little girls is not cut off because they use it for masturbating. The clitoris of girls is sliced off when they are judged ready for procreation and marriage. When it has been removed, they no longer masturbate. This is a great hardship to them. Then all desire is transferred to the interior. Thus they then attempt to get married promptly. Once married, instead of experiencing dispersed and feeble sensations, they concentrate all [desire] in one place, and the couples experience much happiness, which is normal.[38]

So much for brutish and monodimensional male wisdom and romance, the purpose of which is to negate the complexity of female experience. It is perfectly obvious who "god" is in this de-lightful tale (which has a number of variants). The legitimating myth not only erases pain and mutilation, but turns it all into the right, good, and fit. It is god's (man's) plan. Even the fact that "they feel deprived" is made to seem a marvelous prelude for the "great happiness" to come. By now we are in a position to guess the nature of this "happiness."

* It may be helpful in this connection to recall Simone de Beauvoir's famous axiom: "One is not born, but rather becomes a woman." (*The Second Sex,* trans. and ed. by H. M. Parshley [New York: Vintage, 1974], p. 301). In this book of course, I use the term *women* to refer to females generally and reserve the term *feminine* to connote the male-created construct/stereotype. However, *woman* is often used by others to refer to the androcratically constructed (destroyed) female, who is, of course, considered "natural." There is, for example, the "total woman" of Marabel Morgan, and the "true woman" of Pope Pius XII and Pope Paul VI.

But it is not necessary to guess. Dr. G. Pieters, a gynecologist who worked in a hospital in Somalia (1966–1968) explains that defibulation—the opening of the scar of the infibulated girl—is performed with a knife when she is married. The same author says that intercourse takes place immediately and it must be frequent during the first weeks of marriage, because otherwise the wound might close again.[39] The deception inherent in the magician's tale of female sexuality and marital bliss boggles the mind. Yet we should not fall into the trap of allowing ourselves to think that such religious/mythic legitimation is entirely foreign to "our" Western society. As Fran Hosken points out, the medical profession and especially Freud in the West "are enthralled by the same male-created misconception: that of vaginal orgasm."[40] This is the universal test of the "normal" woman. Moreover, the logical acting out of this misconception, brutal and unnecessary gynecological surgery, including clitoridectomies, is not unknown in nineteenth- and twentieth-century American medicine (a point to be discussed in Chapter Seven).

As I have shown in analyzing other ritual atrocities, the acceptability and normative character of the monstrous rite becomes so ingrained that it continues even after the circumstances of its original performance appear to have changed drastically. Thus "practical *suttee*," as we have seen, has continued to take place in India for more than a century after it was legally abolished. In the case of African female genital mutilation, in some countries the practice has moved from the arena of old women with broken bottles and kitchen knives in the forest to the sterile rooms of modern hospitals. This is the case in the Sudan, in Egypt, and throughout Somalia—but only, of course, for a small number of girls. According to Dr. Pieters, the wealthy do not use the hospitals, but have private surgeons. It does not require great imagination to realize that the medical profession, rather than rejecting these horrors, has even made a specialization out of them, to its own economic benefit.

Dr. Pieters, whose article I have cited above, observed these operations in a hospital of the European Common Market in Mogadishu, the capital of Somalia. It is clear that no religious rituals (in the commonly accepted sense of the term *religious*) are involved in the hospitals, although moslem leaders and parents oppose stopping the atrocity. What has happened is that the barbarous rites of religion have been replaced (for these "privileged" few) by the barbarous rites of modern medicine. In the latter, male nurses wear surgical gloves and gowns, and use disinfectants, (insufficient) local anesthetic, surgical scissors (for cutting off the labia minora and excising the clitoris), catgut (for suturing), silk (for sewing), and sometimes penicillin.[41] As in other parts of the world, refined, "white" destruction by the practice of "medicine" perpetuates and "purifies" the religious rituals of gynocide.

VII

Finally, we find the legitimation of the sado-ritual by the last rites of "objective" scholarship. Thus, for example, Felix Bryk, in a book entitled *Dark Rapture: The Sex Life of the African Negro,* introduces his telling description of female genital mutilation with a maze of deceptive expressions and manifestations of crass indifference. Alluding to the "gallant fight" being put up by missionaries to stop this "custom," he writes:

> It is hoped that the barbaric custom, *which is no less cruel than that of circumcision of the male*[!] may be gradually abolished through education and punishment. Personally I do not believe that punishment and education will do any real good in this instance because the custom is primarily practiced for erotic reasons [emphasis mine].[42]

Hags may well ask: "*Whose* erotic reasons?" The author's use of the expression "no less cruel" can be recognized as totally mendacious, when one compares excision and infibulation to the relatively minor operation of male circumcision. Had he written that male circumcision is "no less cruel" than female mutilation, this simply would have been a blatant lie. Instead, he performs a semantic trick, giving an illusion of justice or even of generosity toward the female sex in his assessment of the situation. Given the fact that this author himself presents a horrifying description of excision among the Nandi, it might seem astonishing that he can erase its reality in the same book. However, we have encountered this sort of gross contradiction in works of re-search concerning *suttee* and footbinding. The use of sensational materials, combined with erasure/denial of their significance, is a familiar pattern in patriarchal scholarship.

Bryk, who at the end of his foreword irrelevantly informs us that he is writing on Mount Elgon, "2,350 meters above sea level," is so high above the subject of his book, apparently, that he can give the de-tached opinion that "punishment and education" will not "do any real good"—a perspective which the physically and mentally mutilated women are in no position to refute. It is from this lofty perspective that he is able to interpret the Nandi bride's wedding night plea, "Let me be!" This comes, Bryk explains, "more out of passion than dread." [43] A few lines down we read a description of the scene to which she protests "more out of passion than dread":

> During the first night, among the Nandi, some of his friends wait to hold her down in case she refuses to obey her husband. If the hymen happens to be too tough for ordinary defloration, the husband pierces it with a knife *without letting her know* [emphasis mine].

Despite his bird-like perspective when writing the book on Mount Elgon, this scholar, in doing his re-search, was not above endangering the life of one of these young victims, whom he describes as "the poor, mutilated child." He writes:

> I recall how once, *driven by curiosity,* I crossed the door of the sacred sanctuary [where the recently circumcised girl was confined], in spite of all restrictions, at a time when no woman was around [emphasis mine].[44]

In that society, his seeing the child was a violation of taboo, and could have resulted in the girl's death—a fact of which he was aware.

It is important to note Bryk's views on sex differences and on race. One can imagine him looking down upon the earth from Mount Elgon with his telescope as he utters the following bit of wisdom about "woman" and "man":

Woman is forever woman, and man everywhere man; independently of race or color of skin—white, black, yellow, or copper-red; whether ugly or beautiful; despite youth or age; beyond good and evil.[45]

The universality of the patriarchal role-defined society is thus described and legitimized. It is "beyond good and evil." On the next page we read about racial differences:

They [Blacks] like to lie—particularly to the whites—just as children do, because, like children, they cannot comprehend the moral necessity for truthfulness.[46]

It is obvious, then, that Blacks are different from the author, who is a paragon of truthfulness. Women are also "forever" different from him, but all women of all colors are alike. It would be helpful if women of all races could hear this message of patriarchy with the deep understanding/hearing of the labyrinthine inner ear, for it describes succinctly the sexual caste system, pointing to its fundamentally same view of all women.

There is a danger presented by such unabashedly racist books that the underlying, universal misogyny will go unnoticed. Haggard criticism should enable women who have been intimidated by labels of "racism" to become sisters to these women of Africa—naming the crimes against them and speaking on their behalf—seeing through the reversal that is meant to entrap us all. It is truly *racist* to keep silent in the face of these atrocities, merely "studying" them, speaking and writing deceptively about them, applying different (male-created) standards to them, failing to see and name the connections among them. Beyond racism is sisterhood, *naming* the crimes against women without paying mindless respect to the "social fabric" of the various androcratic societies, including the one in which we find our Selves imprisoned.

Among the most mystifying practitioners of sado-ritual

scholarship legitimating female genital mutilation are "noted" anthropologists, for example Arnold van Gennep. First of all, the subject is erased in the index, having been lumped together with male circumcision under the single entry, *circumcision.* If one looks up this topic, one finds excision of the clitoris discussed incidentally. The following statement sums up the author's views:

> The length of the clitoris varies with individuals and races. In certain cases, the object of the excision may be to remove the *appendage* by which *the female resembles the male* (a view which is *correct* from an anatomical point of view), and the operation is nothing more than a rite of sexual differentiation on the *same order* as the first (ritual) assigning of *dress, instruments, or tools* proper to each sex [emphases mine].[47]

It might seem to require a special talent to assemble this much misinformation/deception in one brief footnote. In what sense is the idea that the clitoris is an "appendage" by which the female "resembles" the male "correct"? According to Merriam-Webster, the term *resemble* means: to be like or similar to. Leaving aside the fact that many women would consider this not only absurd but insulting, one might ask what the author could possibly have in mind in this "anatomical point of view." Would he agree that cutting off the penis is "nothing more" than a rite on the same order as "assigning of dress," et cetera? One can safely assume that he would not, and this throws some light on the implications of his use of the term *resembles* in this context. Van Gennep apparently sees the clitoris precisely *not* from an "anatomical" perspective, but for what it symbolizes/signifies: the potential in females for the independence, power, and prerogatives which are preserved exclusively for males by all the phallocratic "rites of sexual differentiation." For this reason he can minimize and erase the physical reality of female pain and mutilation.

We should not be surprised to read on the very next page not only the familiar remark that excision will "*diminish* sexual excitability," but also his inclusion of the clitoris among the organs which "because of their histological constitution, undergo all sorts of treatment without harming an individual's *life* or *activity* [emphases mine]." [48] The other organs which van Gennep compares to the clitoris are the ear and nose, but of course the "treatment" is not at all comparable. Our scholar has in mind such operations as "cutting off the ear lobe" or perforating it. He is of course not discussing the total removal of both ears or slicing off the nose, which would be comparable to total removal of the clitoris. Finally, the author fails to mention infibulation, which is the most horrifying part of female genital mutilation. This erasure completes his contribution to the vast body of ignorance about his subject, "the rites of passage."

The freudian psychoanalyst, Marie Bonaparte, also muddies matters in her famous "Notes on Excision" in her book, *Female Sexuality*. In this academic treatise she takes issue with Bryk's theory that "the Nandi males, in this way, seek to maximally feminize their females by doing away with this penile vestige, the clitoris, which, he adds, must result in encouraging the transfer of orgastic sensitivity from the girl's infantile erotogenic zone, the clitoris, to the adult erotogenic zone of the woman, which must necessarily be the vagina at puberty." [49] Bonaparte concludes that the Nandi men may have had such a wish, but that even such cruel excision would not achieve this aim. To support her response she cites cases of excised women who continued to refuse to "internalize [their] sexuality." Although she recognizes the cruelty of excision, Bonaparte's attitude toward these women is de-tached; she "studies" them.

Her analysis, moreover, is couched in the falsifying jargon and framework of freudian/fraudian theory, which assumes the reality of the "vaginal orgasm." Her language contains absurd phrases, such as "physical *intimidation* of the girl's sexuality by this cruel excision . . . [emphasis mine]." [50] The term *intimidation* is hardly accurate in this context. More freudian than Freud, Bonaparte lacks not only social perspective but the sensitivity and imagination to even begin to relate to the situation of these women outside the doctrinaire freudian framework. Thus she declares in passing that the "mutilations

. . . are delegated to the old women who doubtless enjoy thus revenging their age on the young." [51] Such terms as *doubtless, enjoy,* and *revenging* reflect the male-identified ignorance/arrogance of father Freud's acolyte and disciple. To say the least, they are not based upon evidence. Bonaparte's poverty of imagination about the feelings of other women is damning evidence of the mind mutilation of women in phallocracy.

Mircea Eliade also contributes generously to the body of ignorance in his book, *Rites and Symbols of Initiation,* which has a section entitled "Initiation of Girls." He is perfectly silent about genital mutilation, making no reference either to excision or to infibulation. He does note that "female initiatory rites—at least so far as they are known to us—are less dramatic than the rites for boys." [52] If we take the term *dramatic* to mean "showy," this is probably true. There is generally more ceremony surrounding the circumcision of a boy—more sound and fury. In the case of millions of mutilated girls, there is less "show" and far more reality in the initiation rites—horrible reality. This Eliade chooses to ignore (genuine ignorance in this case would seem to be impossible). He mentions that girls are "isolated" at menstruation and refers to dietary taboos. Focusing upon some Australian tribes, he points out signs which mark the *end* of female initiation, such as tattooing and blackening of the teeth. He writes: "The essential rite, then, is the solemn exhibition of the girl to the entire community." [53] Since this is written as a general statement, giving the impression that it applies generally to the initiation of girls in "ancient" stages of culture, it is essentially deceptive (skipping over excision and infibulation), erasing by its deceptiveness the essential patriarchal rite: dismemberment of female be-ing.

Just as Eliade fails to convey the physical/psychological mutilation which is the sado-ritual of "initiation of girls" into androcracy, so also he fails to see/name the ecstatic reality which is initiation and process in gynocentric be-ing. Yet, oddly and obtusely, he points to some clues. Thus on the symbolic level he gives information whose Background meaning must be lost on most of his readers, as it is on himself. He writes of the periods of seclusion which are part of girls' puberty rites, and remarks that they often learn such skills as spinning and weaving. Discussing the symbolism of these crafts, he says:

The moon "spins" Time and "weaves" human lives. The Goddesses of Destiny are spinners. We detect an occult connection between the conception of the periodical creations of the world (a conception derived from a lunar mythology) and the ideas of Time and Destiny, on the one hand, and on the other, nocturnal work, women's work, which has to be performed far from the light of the sun and almost in secret. In some cultures, after the seclusion of the girls is ended they continue to meet in some old woman's house to spin together.[54]

Spinsters reading such works of re-search can search and find lost threads of connectedness. Thus when Eliade goes on to say that "spinning is a perilous craft," which can be carried on only in special houses during particular periods and until certain hours, we hear the meaning of this peril in the deep recesses of the labyrinthine inner ear. And when he says that "in some parts of the world spinning has been given up, and even completely forgotten, because of its magical peril," we recognize the peril as our own, and know that we have neither given up nor forgotten. Indeed, in the face of the atrocities associated with phallocratic female initiation into femininity, we must respond not only with exposé. Nor is feminist analysis enough. Most importantly, we must live through the genuine initiation, which is not into femininity but into Self-centering female integrity. This means exorcising the atrocities not only by seeing/naming/acting against them, but also by refusing to remain fixated upon them, and by exercising our new and ancient craft of spinning. This is the initiation of Spinsters, our heritage and new beginning.

The words of Eliade convey something of this woman-centered quality of spinning:

In some places—Japan, for example—we still find the mythological memory of a permanent tension, and even conflict, between the groups of young spinning girls and the men's secret societies. At night the men and their Gods attack the spinning girls and destroy not only their work, but also their shuttles and weaving apparatus.[55]

The members of "the men's secret societies" throughout patriarchy have never ceased to fear and envy the gynaesthetic gift for Spinning.*

In the following chapter we will come to understand more deeply the perils which must be faced by women who have the talent and courage to Spin. We shall see how attackers destroyed the work and "weaving apparatus" of the women in "renaissance" Europe who were/are our foresisters, the witches.

* In the summer of 1976 I saw a living confirmation of this "mythological memory of a permanent tension" at a folklore festival in Heraklion, Crete. The theme of one of the folk dances was the theft of spindles from a group of young girls by some invasive "playful" males after which the latter danced around with these stolen spindles/sticks held between their legs in the position of erect penises.

CHAPTER SIX

EUROPEAN WITCHBURNINGS: PURIFYING THE BODY OF CHRIST

they don't have to lynch the women
very often anymore, although
they used to—the lord and his men
went through the villages at night, beating and
killing every woman caught
outdoors.
the European witch trials took away
the independent people; two different villages
—after the trials were through that year—
had left in them, each—
one living woman:
one.

Judy Grahn,
from *A Woman is Talking to Death*

Repeat the syllables
before the lesson hemorrhages through the brain:
Margaret Barclay, crushed to death with stones, 1618.
Mary Midgely, beaten to death, 1646.
Peronette, seated on a hot iron as torture
and then burned alive, 1462.
Sister Maria Renata Sanger, sub-prioress
of the Premonstratensian Convent of Unter-Zell,
accused of being a lesbian;
the document certifying her torture
is inscribed with the seal of the Jesuits,

and the words Ad Majorem Dei Gloriam—
To the Greater Glory of God.

What have they done to us?

Robin Morgan,
from "The Network of the Imaginary Mother,"
Lady of the Beasts

A woman's place is set like a tightly woven net
She's chained like a dog to her position.
But if by chance or fate she should happen to escape
She's a menace to the keepers of tradition.
So if you have the gift to heal but forget which way to
kneel
Get ready for a manmade Inquisition.

In the Witching Hour you come to your power
You feel it deep inside you, it's rising, rising
And you think it's a dream until you hear yourself
scream
Power to the witch and to the woman in me.

Willie Tyson,
from "The Witching Hour,"
Debutante (Urana Records)

A specifically Western and christian manifestation of the androcratic State of Atrocity was the European witchcraze.*

* I am not dealing here with the American witch trials, which are hardly comparable in scope to the European witchcraze. The most notorious trials in the United States occurred toward the end of the seventeenth century in Salem, Massachusetts, where a total of twenty persons—thirteen women and seven men—were executed. In addition, two women died in jail. (The reader should be warned, however, not to visit the witch museum in Salem, where the propaganda focuses entirely upon blaming the female victims.) Rhode Island did not officially eliminate hanging as the penalty for convicted witches until 1768. It is claimed that the final execution of a witch in an English-speaking territory was in 1730 in Bermuda, and that the victim was Sarah Bassett, a Black slave. See Sally Smith Booth, *The Witches of Early America* (New York: Hastings House, 1975).

During the fifteenth, sixteenth, and seventeenth centuries, the witchcraze spread throughout western Europe. In analyzing witchburning we can see basic similarities to other manifestations of the Sado-Ritual Syndrome which I have already discussed. However, it is essential also to be aware of some significant differences—differences embedded in contemporary androcratic Western-dominated society, on whose boundaries Hags and Crones are struggling to survive today. The following analysis will separate and examine these strands of dissimilarity as well as the threads of similarity which tie witchburning to the other atrocities.

I

It is well known that the witches were accused of sexual impurity. "All witchcraft comes from carnal lust which is in women insatiable," intoned the dominican priests, Kramer and Sprenger, authors of the *Malleus Maleficarum,* which was brought out in 1486 and remained the most important catechism of demonology.[1]

Clearly, the supposed sexual fantasies of these women were (are) archetypically male fantasies. Trevor-Roper writes:

> Anyone who supposes that the absurd and disgusting details of demonology are unique may profitably look at the allegations made by St. Clement of Alexandria against the followers of Carpocrates in the 2nd century A.D. . . . , or by St. Epiphanius against the Gnostic heretics of the 4th century A.D. . . . , or by St. Augustine against

---

I am also omitting here a study of witch-hunts in Africa, which are in a different (though in some ways comparable) social context. See Geoffrey Parrinder, *Witchcraft: European and African* (London: Faber and Faber, 1963), p. 9: "In other continents, from India to the Pacific, various forms of witchcraft appear. But it is in Africa that it is now most widespread. Witch-hunts are common there and witch-hunters are important members of society." Parrinder also indicates that the witches are usually believed to be women (although there are some men accused of witchcraft) and mainly elderly women (See Chapter Ten). In this century, women accused of witchcraft have been stoned to death in Africa. See S. F. Nadel, "Witchcraft and Anti-witchcraft in Nupe Society," *Africa: Journal of the International Institute of African Languages and Cultures,* Vol. VIII, No. 4 (October 1935), pp. 423–47.

certain Manichean heretics . . . , or indeed, at the remarks of Tacitus on the early Christians . . . , or of the orthodox Catholics on the Albigensians and Vaudois of the 12th century and the Fraticelli of the 14th. . . . In these recurrent fantasies the obscene details are often identical, and their identity sheds some light on the psychological connection between persecuting orthodoxy and sexual prurience. The springs of sanctimony and sadism are not far apart.[2]

So we see that male christian "saints" are in the forefront among the fantasy mongers. In the fifteenth, sixteenth, and seventeenth centuries, women accused of being witches became the projection screens for these hallucinations. Moreover, huge numbers of women were tortured to such an extreme degree that they confessed to anything and everything their tormentors lewdly desired, and thus they became living proof of these fantasies.

In order to get some perspective on these confessions, it is useful to read H. C. Lea's *Materials Toward a History of Witchcraft,* which, among other things, describes some individual cases. A typical example was that of a young woman of twenty, whose name was Agnes, who was tortured in Tettenwang, Germany, in 1600. On August 11 she was hoisted repeatedly in the strappado (defined in Merriam-Webster as a torture consisting of "hoisting the subject by a rope sometimes fastened to his [*sic*] wrists behind his back and letting him fall to the length of the rope"). According to Lea, she bore this heroically, confessing nothing and pardoning those who had falsely accused her, even though she had been hoisted eleven times, ten of them with a fifty-pound weight. Ten weeks later she was hoisted again and was told that her mother had accused her, and then "her courage gave way." Lea records the following information from Sigmund Riezler's *Geschichte der Hexenprozesse in Bayern*:

Four days later she made an unsuccessful attempt at suicide, and after this she told monstrous tales of herself—how she had had intercourse with the devil since she was eight years old, had killed numbers of children, 30 of whose hearts she ate, killed 8 old people by smearing them with ointment, raised 5 tempests, killed numerous cattle, been constantly to the Sabbat, renounced God and so forth. Both she and her mother were burnt, and she with others, to their confessors, withdrew their confessions and denunciations of others.

Commenting upon this account, Lea succinctly states: "It can readily be seen how few would escape when once on trial." [3] Indeed. And this was the reason for defining witchcraft as a *crimen exceptum,* a crime distinct from all others.

In order to understand the full implications of this "special status" of the so-called crime of witchcraft, and of the *intent* behind this, it is important to listen to the words of Jean Bodin, the sixteenth-century jurist, magistrate, political theorist, described as a "darling of the intellectual historians." [4] In reading the excerpt from Bodin that follows, it is illuminating to keep in mind that its author was lauded by historian Trevor-Roper as "the undisputed intellectual master of the 16th century," and described (with some puzzlement) by the same historian as "the Aristotle, the Montesquieu of the 16th century, the prophet of comparative history, of political theory, of the philosophy of law, of the quantitative theory of money, and of so much else, who yet, in 1580, wrote the book which more than any other, reanimated the witch-fires throughout Europe." [5] Here is part of what this "genius" had to say:

But those greatly err who think that penalties are established only to punish crime. I hold that this is the least of the fruits which accrue therefrom to the state. For the greatest and the chief is the appeasing of the wrath of God, especially if the crime is directly against the majesty of God, as is this one. . . . Therefore it is that one accused of being a witch ought never to be fully acquitted and set free unless the calumny of the accuser is clearer than the sun, inasmuch as the proof of such crimes is so obscure and so difficult that not one witch in a million would be accused or punished if the procedure were governed by the ordinary rules.[6]

The point of course, is not to punish crime, because there was no crime. The point is "to appease the wrath of God." By now, the reader knows who this cretin/christian "god" is, whose "majesty" is threatened by women, especially by independent women. Bodin knew that "ordinary rules" would not suffice for accusation and punishment. For, clearly, the intent was to break down and destroy strong women, to dis-member and kill the Goddess, the divine spark of be-ing in women. The intent was to purify society of the existence and of the potential existence of such women.* The purpose, as Bodin expressed it, was "to strike awe into some by the punishment of others, to preserve some from being infected by others, to diminish the number of evil-doers, to make secure the life of the well-disposed . . ." [7] In this masterpiece (*De la Demonomanie des Sorciers*) Bodin even enumerated fifteen filthy crimes of which every witch is guilty and argued that in default of proof, presumption should suffice for the sentencing of witches to death. He actually demanded death at the stake not only for witches but for all who (as Trevor-Roper summarized it) "do not believe every grotesque detail of the new demonology." [8] This is a truly "purifying" doctrine, and one that was enthusiastically carried out by professional men—priests, theologians, lawyers, physicians—and the thousands of thugs who carried out their Holy Orders.

We are now in a position to see that the motif of "purification" assumes different dimensions in European witchburning from those uncovered in the atrocities discussed in earlier chapters. The situation of those accused of witchcraft was somewhat different from that of the footbound Chinese girls

* There are no complete records of the numbers of women killed as witches. See Matilda Joslyn Gage, *Woman, Church and State* (2nd. ed.; New York: Arno Press, 1972), p. 247; edition first published 1893. Gage writes: "It is computed from historical records that nine millions of persons were put to death for witchcraft after 1484, or during a period of three hundred years, and this estimate does not include the vast number who were sacrificed in the preceding centuries upon the same accusation. The greater number of this incredible multitude were women." See also Felix Morrow's foreword to Montague Summers, *The History of Witchcraft and Demonology* (Secaucus, N.J.: Citadel Press, 1971), p. viii. He writes: "The figures of scholars estimating the number of witches put to death vary enormously, from 30,000 to several million, and it is really impossible to know, given the records of the times, but it is clear that substantial numbers were put to death." Rossell Hope Robbins, in *The Encyclopedia of Witchcraft and Demonology* (New York: Crown, 1959), p. 180, gives a typical conservative estimate of 200,000.

and of the genitally maimed girls and young women of Africa, for these were mutilated in preparation for their destiny—marriage. It was also somewhat different from the situation of the widows of India, who were killed solely for the crime of outliving their husbands. For the targets of attack in the witchcraze were not women defined by assimilation into the patriarchal family. Rather, the witchcraze focused predominantly upon women who had rejected marriage (Spinsters) and women who had survived it (widows). The witch-hunters sought to purify their society (The Mystical Body) of these "indigestible" elements—women whose physical, intellectual, economic, moral, and spiritual independence and activity profoundly threatened the male monopoly in every sphere.

Lest there be any doubt that the motive of the European witchcraze was to purify society, we need only examine the work of contemporary witch scholars. A fascinating example is H. C. Erik Midelfort, who, writing in 1972, shows himself not adverse to a widespread view which he terms "functionalism." * In his conclusion he writes:

> Turning briefly to the larger social question of function, we can concede that the small trials may indeed have served a function, delineating the social thresholds of *eccentricity* tolerable to society, and registering fear of a socially *indigestible group, unmarried women*. . . . Until *single women* found a more *comfortable* place in the concepts and communities of Western men, one could argue that they were a socially disruptive element, at least when they lived without family and without patriarchal control. In this restricted sense the small witch trial may have even been *therapeutic,* or functional [emphases mine].[9]

* See H. C. Erik Midelfort, *Witch Hunting in Southwestern Germany, 1562–1684: The Social and Intellectual Foundations* (Stanford, Calif.: Stanford University Press, 1972), p. 3. Basically, the idea which he intends to convey by this term, an idea which he claims to be shared by a number of scholars (e.g., George L. Kittredge, E. William Monter, Kai Erikson, Guy Swanson, George Rosen) is that "witchcraft accusations seem often to provide legitimate channels for aggression against persons otherwise immune." Although Midelfort asserts that such theories "yield confusion," and claims in his introduction to take a different position, by the time he reaches his conclusion he shows himself quite in agreement.

It would be unthinkable for scholars to refer to Jewish pogroms or to lynchings of Blacks as "therapeutic."

Midelfort mentions both widows and Spinsters as "defenseless" because of their "isolation" (read: independence). Women outside patriarchal control—Spinsters and widows—whose crime is independence (indigestibility) have always been intolerable to such intellectuals. Jean Bodin, for example, knew that these women are the real threat to the majesty of the christian god. It is interesting that such a contemporary scholar as Midelfort admits that "our common picture of the witch as an ugly old hag, living alone, and known for her eccentricities is not unlike the sixteenth or seventeenth century stereotype." He then immediately bemoans the fact that during the largest witch-hunts "the stereotype deteriorated dangerously, leaving all social classes and all types of *people* open to suspicion [emphasis mine]." [10] Clearly, then, the problem was that the craze had got out of hand, to the point that the witch-fires were consuming also the most docile and already socially "digested" women, and, unfortunately, men as well. To quote Midelfort once again:

> Men had lost . . . the ability accurately to *detect* witches. From their own experience men had learned that the attempt to purge the body politic was not worth the agony that resulted [emphasis mine].[11]

As Hags know, unfortunately men have not learned any such thing. However, Hags are re-membering and therefore understanding not only the *intent* of the Sado-State—the torture, dis-memberment, and murder of deviant women—but also the fact that this intent is justified and shared by scholars and other professional perpetrators of this State.

This obsession with purifying society of deviant/defiant women has been both the origin and manifestation of the secret bond between seemingly distinct and even opposed categories of men. Thus the members of the legal profession, who at first appeared opposed or at least indifferent to the witch-hunting propensities of priests, later became even more fervent persecutors. Thus also protestants, though bitterly opposed to catholicism, vied with and even may have surpassed their catholic counterparts in their fanaticism and cruelty during the witchcraze. Typically, each used the orthodoxy of the other to entrap women under the witch-label. Among some protestants, for example, Bishop Palladius, reformer of Denmark, the term *witch* was extended to include "those who used catholic prayers or formulas." [12]

This massacre of women, then, masked a secret gynocidal fraternity, whose prime targets were women living outside the control of the patriarchal family, *women who presented an option*—an option of "eccentricity," and of "indigestibility." The term *eccentric* is derived from the Greek *ek* (out of) plus *kentrum* (center of a circle). One definition in Merriam-Webster is "not having the same center, used of circles, cylinders, spheres, and certain other figures: opposed to *concentric*." It also means "deviating from some established type, pattern, or rule." The women hunted as witches were (are) in a time/space that is not concentric with androcracy. Hags are Self-centering, constituting the Society of Outsiders, defining gynocentric boundaries. This is the dreaded option of Dreadful, Dreadless Crones, the ultimate indigestible threat to the "majesty of God." Therefore in the name of god this Self-centering process must be halted and all Hag-centered process re-moved, sucked back into the dead center of patriarchal darkness.

The purification of society was legitimated as a cleansing not only of the "body politic" but, more specifically, of the Mystical Body of Christ. Since Christ was believed to possess not only his own body but also a Mystical Body—extended to include all members of his church—this Mystical Body had to be kept pure enough to perform the functions required by its divine Head. This extended Body symbolism had commonly been invoked by fathers and doctors of the church when confronted with the problem of heretics. The latter—like diseased members—had to be cut off (killed) for the good of the whole organism. This tradition provided a ready-made solution for the problem presented by the witches.[13] Moreover, while the argument had frequently functioned to legitimate the "amputation" of heretical male members, it was particularly appropriate in the case of deviant women, for there is something basically incongruous in trying to see women with any sense of Self as incorporated into The Male Mystical Body. This incongruity was partially and convolutedly expressed by Kramer and Sprenger when they declared that males were protected from so horrible a crime as witchcraft because Jesus was a man.[14]

It is important to note here an essential pattern in the maze of the witchcraze. On the symbolic level, the emphasis centers around god-the-son, "The Second Person of the Divine Trinity," who "became incarnate." Dogmatically speaking, "the Word became Flesh." Thus in christian doctrine, the "fact" that god-the-son became man (male), assuming a human—that is, male—body, enabled males to become gods. It prepared the way for the Brotherhood representing/replacing Yahweh & Son. Thus the original christian divine model for Big Brother in Orwell's *1984* is the godman, Jesus. It is significant that in this "futuristic"—that is, patriarchally past and contemporary—novel it is not Big Father who is the Head. For everyone knows on some level that this "divine" father is omni-absent, a figurehead as blatant as Archie Bunker, Idi Amin (Dada), Tricky Dick Nixon, or Pope Paul the Sicksth (VI; *sic*). Rather it is Big Brother who is omnipresent—seeing/knowing/controlling all, constantly purifying the body politic of deviants. Male (and male-identified) professionals and aspirants to political power have identified with this more accessible and "real" symbol.

II

The second element of the Sado-Ritual Syndrome—erasure of responsibility for the atrocities—is clearly in evidence in the witchcraze, and it is closely intertwined with phallocentric obsessions with purity. Since the demonologies accused the witches of lewd acts, their male persecutors were perfectly "justified" in destroying them. To this end, the good sons of the holy father projected their fantasies upon the accused women. It was believed that at the Sabbat the witches kissed the devil in homage, under the tail if he appeared as a stinking goat, on the lips if he were a toad. After this they allegedly threw themselves into promiscuous sexual orgies.[15] It was clear, therefore, that they *should* be tortured. Since their obscene "acts" were performed with the devil, god's enemy, their christian killers could feel totally religious and righteous.

It was clear to "everyone" during the witchcraze that the witchburners were doing god's will by slaughtering women. Even the title of the "authoritative" work of demonology, the *Malleus Maleficarum* (The Hammer of Witches) worked as a self-fulfilling prophecy, for of course "maleficarum" is the feminine form of the word for evil-doer/witch. Since this was published in 1486, in the early period of the witchcraze, it contributed mightily to the overwhelming focus on women during the following centuries. In order to grasp how thoroughly males justified their massacre it is necessary only to look through the *Malleus Maleficarum*. For example, in the ninth question of Part One, the priestly authors gravely pose the pregnant question: "Whether Witches may work some Prestidigitatory Illusion so that the Male Organ appears to be entirely removed and separate from the Body?" The learned response is that they can: "But when it is performed by witches it is only a matter of glamour; although it is no illusion in the opinion of the sufferer." [16] The term *glamour,* of course, means "a magic spell." *

Kramer and Sprenger gave abundant reasons to justify the gynocidal maniacs who controlled society and culture. They explained that witches turn men into beasts, copulate with devils, raise and stir up hailstorms and tempests. The witch/woman-killers appeared "perfectly" justified, since the priest

* This anxiety of the witch-hunters is understandable when we reflect upon the fact that the women they had in mind were mainly Spinsters and widows—women free from invasion by the "member," women who might even find the "Male Organ" laughable, unaesthetic, and, perhaps more importantly, uninteresting. We should not be surprised that such women today are often called "castrating bitches." As Jane Caputi has pointed out, the meaning of *glamour* has been reversed by the spell of modern grammar. "Glamourous" women are made up and done in. See her article, "The Glamour of Grammar," *Chrysalis: A Magazine of Women's Culture,* No. 4 (1978), pp. 35–43.

professionals had posed the question: "Why is it that Women are chiefly addicted to Evil Superstitions?" The question itself set the framework for the answer. The reader was informed that women are more credulous, that they are naturally more impressionable, have slippery tongues, are feebler both in mind and body, are more carnal than men (!) to the extent of having insatiable lust, have weak memories, are liars by nature. Then—without missing a beat, after hammering home their view that women are feeble in every sense—these Sado-Sages add that "nearly all the kingdoms of the world have been overthrown by women." [17]

Those who acted as henchmen in hunting out, torturing, and killing women as witches could argue correctly that they were serving the Higher Order of patriarchy and were acting "under orders." The papal Bull of Innocent VIII, Summis desiderantes affectibus (1484), was a document of the highest authority, giving the support of Rome to "Our dear sons," the dominican Inquisitors, Kramer and Sprenger, who were encountering opposition to the witch persecutions. This papal document had been purposefully solicited by the two dominicans to legitimate their attempt to launch the witchcraze in the Rhineland. As Trevor-Roper points out:

> Having obtained it, they printed it in their book, as if the book had been written in response to the bull. The book thus advertised to all Europe both the new epidemic of witchcraft and the authority which had been given them to suppress it.[18]

Here we see very conscious manipulation of legitimation from on high by the Inquisitors. Given the "go ahead" from Innocent, they had perfect justification for carrying out orders. More than that: Innocent had made it clear that "Our venerable Brother, the Bishop of Strasburg . . . shall threaten all who endeavor to hinder or harass the Inquisitors, all who oppose them . . . [with] terrible penalties." [19] Thus ecclesiastical power was used to erase responsibility for opposing the witch persecutions, even for speaking against them. Although Innocent's Bull itself refers to "many persons of *both* sexes" as having "abandoned themselves to devils, incubi and succubi," the authors of the *Malleus Maleficarum* manage to totally erase this idea, while at the same time retaining the full support of "Innocent" in their war against women. Thus the "dear Sons" —the real leaders of the witch-hunting brotherhood—were the power behind the throne of the Holy Father.

In the witchcraze, then, we can see the truth of Helen Diner's insight that "in Christianity the tree becomes the torture cross of the world." Under the Sign of the Cross good and wise women were tortured and burned to death. Trees were killed and their wood used to make the fires that would devour these women. Under the reign of the Torture Cross Society, the Tree of Life—the divine Self-centering life of independent women—was cut down and consumed. The citizens of the city of god created, staged, and acted out the christian hell on earth. Their theology expressd itself as demonology; their reigning philosophy became an ontology of the damned.[20] No one was responsible for this evil except the victims, who were perceived not as victims of their murderers, but of the devil. Innocent and his "dear Sons" were servants of god, burning with innocence.

III

As in the cases of the other gynocidal rituals, witchburning "caught on" and spread like wildfire. Trevor-Roper describes it as an "explosive force," and points out that "there can be no doubt that the witchcraze grew, and grew terribly, after the Renaissance. . . . The years 1550–1600 were worse than the years 1500–1550, and the years 1600–1650 were worse still." [21] The spread was geographically as well as numerically explosive. Originally the craze had been confined to the mountainous areas of Germany and Italy. With the printing of the *Malleus Maleficarum* it not only spread down the Rhine but through Italy, Spain, France, and countries in northern Europe.[22]

As Jane Caputi has shown, this colossal spread was fostered by the invention of the printing press.[23] The escalation of technology and of persecution goose-stepped together in the "march of progress." There appears to be some obtuseness on the part of scholars concerning the crucial function of printing in spreading the craze. Trevor-Roper writes of the "mere multiplication of the evidence after the discovery of printing," but does not stress the role of printing as a causal factor. Many historians simply ignore the connection.*

When we examine the role of printing as a means for spreading the witchcraze we see that it reinforced an evolving hierarchy based upon a developing technology and upon controlled access to officially acknowledged learning. Moreover, we should note that the original demonologies were printed in Latin, the language of formally educated, professional men. Thus it is not surpising to read the following:

> It [the craze] was forwarded by the cultivated Popes of the Renaissance, by the great Protestant Reformers, by the saints of the Counter-Reformation, by the scholars, lawyers, and churchmen of the age of Scaliger and Lipsius, Bacon and Grotius, Berulle and Pascal.[24]

Clearly, then, it was not merely the wealthy but the "cultivated"—and most specifically the rising professional power

* An exception is Jeffrey Burton Russell, *Witchcraft in the Middle Ages* (Ithaca, N.Y.: Cornell University Press, 1972); on p. 234 he writes: "The fact that the printing press could now disseminate the works of the witch theorists in a quantity hitherto undreamed of added enormously to the growth of the witch craze. . . . It was an unfortunate coincidence that printing should have been invented just as the fervor of the witch hunters was mounting, and the swift propagation of the witch hysteria by the press was the first evidence that Gutenberg had not liberated man from original sin." However, having made this connection, Russell lets it pass. Here, as in so many other works of scholarship, the author gives an important clue but fails to perceive or convey its significance. In fact, his own choice of the symbolic expression, "original sin" conjures up images of women as wicked Eves deserving of punishment, thus evoking the very myth which legitimated witchburning in the first place. This language diverts the reader's attention *away* from the *torturers* of the accused women and from the role of phallotechnology in their sadistic reign of terror. It is essential that Hags follow through in detecting the clues and connections which such scholars erase in their writing, so that we can expose the foundations of modern androcratic society as it was taking shape in the West, for the societal patterns hardening then remain to be a-mazed today.

block—who forwarded the witch-hunts. The latter led the battle against Hags:

Laymen might not accept all the esoteric details supplied by the experts, but they accepted the general truth of the theory, and because they accepted its general truth, they were unable to argue against its more learned interpreters. So the experts effectively commanded the field. For two centuries the clergy preached against witches and the lawyers sentenced them. . . . Confessors and judges were supplied with manuals incorporating all the latest information . . .[25]

This phenomenon of leadership and control by "experts" is familiar to inhabitants of modern Western society. It is not surprising, then, that there was not only a "body" of expert knowledge, but also popularized propaganda for the masses. Here again technology, in the form of printing, was an essential means of mental artificial insemination. A new genre of literature emerged in the form of *Teufelsbücher,* or "devil books," whose general effect was "to suggest that the devil was everywhere." [26] It is obvious *who* were considered to be the primary cohorts and agents of the devil in christian society. As Caputi points out, the message to the masses was imprinted especially through the woodcuts and engravings of the period.[27] One needs only to glance through a sampling to see that women are typically represented as dupes of the devil. One did not have to know Latin to read the German *Teufelsbücher,* and did not have to be literate at all to get the message of the woodcuts. Then, as today, the messages of the professional experts were professionally embedded in the minds of the masses through "mass market" editions. Phallotechnic society had launched its first massive campaign against dangerous women—a campaign whose escalated echoes haunt us today in the ubiquitous "mass media": the films, slick magazines, television, billboards, newspapers, textbooks, and other "literature" which carry overt and subliminal images of rape, dismemberment, and gynocide.*

* It is thought-provoking to read the following statement by the priest Montague Summers in his glowing introduction to the 1928 edition of the *Malleus Maleficarum:* "To effect the death of a man [*sic*] or to

We can now approach the question of just *who* were the women who were so horrifying to the learned experts who created, controlled, and legitimated the witchcraze. An essential clue is to be found in the abandonment, in the latter part of the sixteenth century, of the legal distinction between the "good" and the "bad" witch. In 1563 the Scottish witch-law dropped this distinction, and soon after, the laws on the continent and finally in England also changed. The purest expression of the ideology behind this legal change was uttered by the Cambridge preacher, William Perkins, who maintained that whoever has made a pact with the devil, even to do good, must die. Perkins declared that the "good witch [was] a more horrible and detestable monster than the bad." Thus, "if death be due to any . . . then a thousand deaths of right belong to the good witch." [28] The logic here is impeccable. On an overt level it expresses the fact that of course the christians will(ed) to destroy real female-identified goodness, that is, the independence, strength, wisdom, and learning through which Hags (healers, counselors, wise women, teachers) earned the respect of the people.

The import of the apparently convoluted thinking which saw the good witch as more evil than the bad witch should not be lost upon Hags. As Denise Connors has pointed out, since such women gained (and gain) respect for their work, their competence shows up the incompetence of the legitimated professionals.[29] The competition is intolerable, and the professionals cannot maintain their prestige.* Clearly they are not

---

injure him by making an image in his likeness, and mutilating or destroying his image, is a practice found throughout the whole wide world from its earliest years." See Heinrich Kramer and James Sprenger, *The Malleus Maleficarum,* trans. with introductions, bibliography, and notes by the Rev. Montague Summers (New York: Dover, 1971), p. xix, note. This, of course, is what is done to women by men through the mass production of "pin-up girls," *Playboy* centerfolds, et cetera, ad nauseam. These mutilate and destroy women's image, and the *intent* of this technological voodoo is to effect the *death* of the female-identified Self.

* It is enlightening to recall the "archaic" definition of the term *prestige.* According to Merriam-Webster, it meant a conjurer's trick:

willing to attribute such wisdom and healing power to the native talent and superiority of women. During the witchcraze the solution was to attribute female power to the "fact" that they were tools of the devil, the rival of the christian god, that is, of males themselves. Thus, the combination of spiritual and medical knowledge made good witches the epitome of "evil" to the christian persecutors.

Not only were these wise women misnamed "evil," but also "melancholic." Midelfort describes this "melancholy" as "a depressed state characterized occasionally by obscure or threatening statements and odd behavior." [30] Any Hag can recognize something familiar in this description. These women were deviant and threatening, and we can safely assume that they did not titter and smile in self-depreciation. No doubt they considered patriarchy a Depressing State.

I suggest, then, that just as the "elite" caste who perpetrated the witchburnings was in large measure an aspiring "intellectual" elite of professional men, so the hated targets were primarily a spiritual/moral/know-ing elite cross-section of the female population of Europe. This primal battle of principalities and powers was at heart concerned with the process of know-ing, which the professionals wanted to possess and control as their "body of knowledge." In this respect, the witchcraze differed from the atrocities studied in earlier chapters.

The economic status of the accused women varied. Information given by Monter supports the thesis that most accused witches were poor women.[31] In contrast to this, Montague Summers cites with apparent agreement Bodin's opinion "that there existed, not only in France, a complete organization of witches, immensely wealthy, of almost infinite potentialities, most cleverly captained, with centres and cells in every district, utilizing an espionage in every land, with high-placed adherents at court, with humble servitors in the cottage." [32] However, anyone with even the slightest experience of the

---

illusion, deception. It is helpful to remember this definition when hearing of the "prestige" of such institutions (and their products) as Harvard Medical School, Yale Divinity School, M.I.T., et al.

contemporary legal system of "justice" can affirm that such a discrepancy between ideology and practice is not unfamiliar. The paranoid delusions of the persecutors picture the "guilty" women as immensely wealthy, but in fact those with wealth are usually protected from and by the law. It is not surprising, then, if the records show that many women caught and tried were poor. Whatever may have been the delusions about the financial wealth of the persecuted witches, the real wealth that was feared was spiritual, mental, and moral.

In studying the witchcraze, then, we see that the victimizers belonged to a "higher" class of men, in the sense that they had professional legitimation and *officially recognized* knowledge. If we examine the status of the victims, it is clear that these women were not necessarily from the higher social and economic classes, but that they constituted a threat to the rising professional hierarchy precisely as possessors of (unlegitimated) higher learning, that is, of spiritual wisdom and healing—and of the highly independent character that accompanies such wisdom.

To affirm this primacy of the fear of spiritual power is not to negate the presence of an "economic" motive, however. This is evident when we consider that the witches were a threat not only to the prestige but also to the economic power of the rising professionals. No doubt they were troublesome in many ways. William Dufty points out in *Sugar Blues* that while witches advised people against eating sugar, the church had a vested interest in the sugar industry, beginning in the Middle Ages. Writing that "Christendom took a big bite out of the forbidden fruit," he adds:

> What followed was seven centuries in which the seven deadly sins flourished across the seven seas, leaving a trail of slavery, genocide, and organized crime.[33]

Dufty maintains that the healers correctly attributed many ills to the eating of sugar. He summarizes the situation of the witches in the face of sugar:

> Ancient civilizations such as those of the Orientals believed that all disorders of body and mind proceed from what we eat. . . . The

sorceress—wise woman—natural healer believed this too. However, by the time sugar was introduced widely in Europe, the natural healers were uncovered—practically overnight—as a declared enemy of church and state.[34]

While it would be simplistic to reduce the witchcraze to this one single cause—the conflict between the witches and sugar—as Dufty seems to do, the point is important. The vast and complex machine of Western macho religion fostered false physical and spiritual needs and false consciousness. To paraphrase Dufty, it left a trail of slavery, *gynocide,* and organized crime. In a typical reversal, it branded the women healers as the perpetrators of organized crime, scapegoating its enemies.

The extension of the witchcraze geographically has already been noted. Its extension over time is an even more complex and horrifying phenomenon. We have seen that the massacre reached its peak in the first half of the seventeenth century and then petered out when the stereotype "deteriorated" to the point of threatening to include too many "people." However, this was not the end of the horror. In order to begin to comprehend the temporal expansion of the effects of the witchcraze, it is vital to consider the use and abuse of children in connection with the witchburnings, for the horrors branded upon their memories must have carried over for many generations. We are informed that "by law, children who were said to have attended their mother to the Sabbat were merely [*sic*] flogged in front of the fire in which their parent was burning." [35] It is probable that the majority of these children were girls. These daughters saw their mothers burned alive.* This is the other side of the mother-daughter tragedy in patriarchy.

* In a discussion about the effects of this, one woman made the point that it must have broken the minds of small girls to such an extent that all female identification, all capacity for confident bonding with women, would have been effectively destroyed. Then someone else remarked that these daughters no doubt drew the logical conclusion that "it is better to marry than to burn." The ensuing laughter provided brief relief from the intensity of our realization of what had been done to our foresisters and consequently to us all.

Not only have daughters been maimed by their mothers, but they have from early childhood seen them in the process of being tortured and killed.

In the witch trials, moreover, children were often used as legal witnesses. As Ronald Seth pointed out, the witchcraft judge Jean Bodin "openly declared that he used children as witnesses because at a very young age they could without difficulty be persuaded or compelled to inform against the accused." [36] The word of children from seven upwards was regarded as sufficient testimony for fatal condemnation. This was part of the exceptional nature of the witch trials. As Seth writes:

> To make it possible for children to give evidence before the courts in witchcraft trials, the rules regarding children as witnesses, which applied to all other forms of judicial proceedings and laid down that no witness below the age of fourteen could be heard, were suspended.[37]

This enforced active/instrumental role of children sheds further light upon the demonic distortion of women's minds by the witchcraze. For a daughter to remember seeing her mother burned was one thing. To remember all her life that she had been used to accuse and condemn her mother to death, that she had in effect committed matricide, would have meant carrying a burden of self-loathing that is almost unimaginable. Such children would have branded this self-hatred upon their daughters and upon generations that followed. Thus the presence of young girls both as helpless "observers" at the burnings and as legal witnesses at the trials may effectively have perpetuated the lesson of the witchcraze down through the centuries into this, our "own," time. Without knowledge and consent women are trained to continue the ritual murder of female divinity, burning the witch within themselves and each other. In order to stop this silent continuation of the witchcraze—a continuation that has been foreseen and planned by such men as Jean Bodin—it is necessary to break the silences and deceptions of "history."

IV

We have already seen one aspect of the use of women as token torturers in the witchcraze: They were forced through torture to accuse each other:

> Once a witch had confessed, the next stage was to secure from her, again under torture, a list of all those of her neighbors whom she had recognized at the witches' Sabbat. Thus a new set of *indicia* was supplied, clerical science was confirmed, and a fresh set of trials and tortures would begin.[38]

One can see that the process of indictment under torture could and did progress *ad infinitum,* illusion building upon illusion, destruction upon destruction. Sister was used against sister, friend against friend, and—without doubt—lover against lover. The primary bond of love and trust, without which female-identification is difficult to establish—the bond between daughter and mother—was broken on the torture rack, burned in the purifying paternal fires.

Unlike the patriarchs who invented and legitimated footbinding and genital mutilation, however, the wholly christian fathers and sons generally did not use mothers as the primary instruments of the physical torture of their daughters. Rather, they used mothers and daughters as witnesses against each other. In addition, they vampirized the power inherent in the Mother as symbol, naming their persecuting institution "Mother Church." Thus on a mythic/symbolic level they attempted to warp the deepest feelings of women—all of whom are, of course, daughters—snarling these feelings into Self-contradictory love-hate. In the witchcraze, males used the Mother symbol to cover their own motives of sadism and control. Instead of using physical female bodies to carry out the acts of torture and murder, the christian fathers used the institutional Body of Mother Church. This Mystical Body, the church, which was also known as the "Bride of Christ," was/is the false "Mother" used to destroy female-identified Selves. In carrying out this destruction the fathers and sons invoked the "Mother of God"

—the robotized replica of The Goddess—who had been tamed and re-named, made into a reminder of their need to keep on maiming, raping, and killing female divinity.

V

The witch-killers employed the usual tactic of blocking all awareness of the horror of their deeds by focusing attention upon orderliness, repetitive procedures, and fixation upon minute details. These "great intellects" dwelled assiduously upon such infallible signs of guilt as the presence of a wart or mole, or of an insensitive spot which did not bleed when pricked, or of the ability to float when tied up and thrown into the water, or the inability to shed tears.

Anyone who might question the fact of compulsive orderliness in the witch trials need only peruse the Third Part of the *Malleus Maleficarum,* which is concerned with the judicial proceedings in both the ecclesiastical and the civil courts, "Containing XXXV Questions in which are most Clearly set out the Formal Rules for Initiating a Process of Justice, how it should be Conducted, and the Method of Pronouncing Sentence." [39] It is thought-provoking to compare the obsessive orderliness of this outline of judicial proceedings with the imaginative views concerning witches expressed by the priestly authors earlier in the same work. A sample should suffice to convey their state of mind:

> And what, then, is to be thought of those witches who in this way sometimes collect male organs in great numbers, as many as twenty or thirty members together, and put them in a bird's nest, or shut them up in a box, where they move themselves like living members, and eat oats and corn, as has been seen by many and is a matter of common report? [40]

The authors respond to their own question by explaining that "it is all done by devil's work and illusion." The split-minded combination of ritual orderliness and bizarre fantasies characterizes the mentality exemplified in these Inquisitors. Their superficial order of prescribed proceedings is an attempt to give the appearance of logic to the hideous holocaust—the world of their acted-out fantasies.

The particularized orderliness of the rules for judicial proceedings was matched by the meticulously detailed legal reports of the actual trials. By the combined ritualized fixations upon minutiae the witchburners were attempting not only to give an appearance of reason to their own dementia, but also to distract their minds from the horror of the acts which they instigated, condoned, encouraged, and commanded. The following description, cited by Henry Charles Lea, gives some idea of the christian hell masked by the Male Factor's ritualized logic:

There are men who in this art exceed the spirits of hell. I have seen the limbs forced asunder, the eyes driven out of the head, the feet torn from the legs, the sinews twisted from the joints, the shoulder blades wrung from their place, the deep veins swollen, the superficial veins driven in, the victim now hoisted aloft and now dropped, now revolved around, head undermost and feet uppermost. I have seen the executioner flog with the scourge, and smite with rods, and crush with screws, and load down with weights, and stick with needles, and bind around with cords, and burn with brimstone, and baste with oil, and singe with torches.[41]

Lea goes on to cite the same witness on geographical differences. He says:

In Italy and Spain torture is limited to an hour, but in Germany it will last anywhere from a day and a night to four days and four nights, during which the executioner never ceases his work, and the judge never omits to order him to renew it, and the executioner has full power to employ new methods.[42]

While the frenzy did reach exceptional heights among the orderly Germans,* illustrating vividly the connection between

* As Janice Raymond has pointed out, those who write and speak of the holocaust of the Jews in twentieth-century Nazi Germany never acknowledge the history of gynocidal holocaust. See her article, "Women's History and Transcendence," in *Religious Liberty in the Crossfire of Creeds,* Franklin H. Littell, ed., (Philadelphia: Ecumenical

compulsive methodicalness and maniacal sadism, this combination—characteristic of sado-ritual—was generally present throughout the European witchcraze. As Robbins points out:

During the torture it was the practice, following the *Malleus Maleficarum,* for the notary to "write down everything in his record of the trial, how the prisoner is tortured, on what points he [*sic*] is questioned, and how he answers." [43]

The torture and burning of women as witches became normal and indeed normative in "Renaissance" Europe. The male members of the Mystical Body, attempting to act out the resurrection myth of their symbolic Head, strove for "re-birth" through Goddess-murder, that is, through the violent elimination of Female Presence.* Their theology and their law required this massacre. Even to defend a witch was tantamount to declaring oneself a witch.

VI

The methods used to extort confessions from those accused of witchcraft were not legally "normal," as we have seen, for witchcraft had been defined as a *crimen exceptum,* outside all the ordinary rules of "just" judicial proceedings. Yet the basic methods of torture—those not considered extraordinary enough to "count" as torture—were quite normal for patriarchy. According to Robbins:

More likely, the woman, during her stripping, would be raped by the torturer's assistants, as happened to Frau Peller, the wife of

---

Press, 1978), pp. 47–52. The witch trials in Germany were characterized by extreme brutality combined with masterful meticulousness. Yet most authors, for example William L. Shirer, write about the massacre of the Jews as if such massive sadism were without this historical precedent.

* The fact that the Renaissance is exalted as the "rebirth of humanism" is a blatant indication that "humanism" is *not* universal, since it does not include women. Thus *humanism* functions as a pseudogeneric term, and it is comparable to such expressions as *human liberation*.

> a court officer, in her trial at Rheinbach in 1631. She had, incidentally, been accused of witchcraft because her sister had refused to sleep with the witch judge, Franz Buirmann. . . . So little regard was given this preliminary torture that many court records ignored it and simply stated, "The prisoner confessed without torture."[44]

Thus rape was not recognized as torture. Neither were degradation and humiliation (e.g., stripping).

The acceptability of witchburning in Renaissance society is evident in the absence of objections to the massacre in the writings of such prominent and prolific thinkers as Bacon, Grotius, Selden, and Descartes, who "flourished" in the early seventeenth century, the peak period of the witchcraze. The silence of these respected intellectual leaders was no doubt at least partially the result of cautious self-protection, or, more precisely speaking, cowardice. Certainly, we can assume that these "great men" justified to themselves their nonconfrontation with massive social evil. After all, the members of this fainthearted fraternity were concerned with more "important" matters than gynocide. In effect, their craven silence screamed their tacit approval. The silence of these pusillanimous men may well have done as much to fuel the foresisters' funereal fires as the depraved fanaticism of their more aggressive and vulgar colleagues.

It is not surprising that in this witchburning society, in which the massacre of women was deemed not only normal but also normative, the fires were difficult to stamp out. We have seen that in the warped "wisdom" of the theologians and jurists a good witch was deemed as "bad" and even "worse" than a "bad" witch. In the light (dark) of this misogynistic mentality, a return to justice was hardly to be expected. Indeed, the very nature of patriarchy inherently excludes justice. At the end of *Materials Toward a History of Witchcraft,* Henry Charles Lea noted that the *Vossische Zeitung* of April 28, 1888, had an account of a woman burnt as a witch in the marketplace of Bambamarca, Peru, after repeated scourgings.[45] The concluding words of this work, which was compiled during the first decade of the twentieth century, ominously ring true:

There is a revival in Protestant circles in Germany of belief in sorcery and pact with the devil. . . . The applause which these writings have met shows how numerous are those who are ready to revive the old superstitions.[46]

VII

One does not have to look for obscure writings by religious fanatics, however, to know "how numerous are those who are ready to revive the old superstitions." We need only look at the best known and most respected works of "objective" contemporary writings on the witchcraze to recognize the familiar phenomenon of legitimation by the rites of sado-scholarship. These works of re-search re-enact the gynocidal rites in a variety of styles and guises, reaffirming—sometimes blatantly, sometimes subtly—the same cultural assumptions which supported the witchcraze to begin with, erasing their significance.

For whole-hearted support of the witchcraze, no other twentieth-century scholar has quite matched the priest Montague Summers, editor of the English edition of the *Malleus Maleficarum.* In his introduction to the 1928 edition father Summers calls it a "great work," describing it as "one of the most pregnant and most interesting books I know in the library of its kind." [47] In his introduction to the 1948 edition, Summers displays even greater enthusiasm, affirming (accurately) the "modernity of the book." The following passage summarizes his sentiments:

One turns to it again and again with edification and interest: From the point of psychology, from the point of jurisprudence, from the point of history, it is supreme. It is hardly too much to say that later writers, great as they are, have done little more than draw from the seemingly inexhaustible wells of wisdom which the two Dominicans, Heinrich Kramer and James Sprenger, have given us in the *Malleus Maleficarum.*[48]

Father Summers's enthusiasm speaks for itself. This was written about a book which claims that witches turn men into beasts, cause the male member to disappear, copulate with devils, raise and stir up hailstorms and tempests. Hags should feel no astonishment, however, for the views expressed by father Summers are quite in accord with the traditional and contemporary androcratic attitude concerning women—an attitude which he shares with other twentieth-century professional men, including physicians, psychiatrists, attorneys, and acclaimed literary "genuises" such as Henry Miller and Norman Mailer. The "problem" of the witch-crazed priest is simply that he expresses his total complicity in gynocide in a naively old-fashioned way, leaving himself open to ridicule.*

In contrast to Summers, Trevor-Roper is deceptively sophisticated. Defending the silence of Bacon, Grotius, Selden, and Descartes, he asks the rhetorical question: "Why should they court trouble on a secondary, peripheral issue?" [49] He claims that the primary issue to which these thinkers all were dedicated and which supposedly ultimately destroyed the witchcraze was "the new philosophy, a philosophical revolution which changed the whole concept of Nature and its operations." [50] Thus Trevor-Roper hides gynocide behind the skirts of a fictional "new philosophy" (the same old philosophy trotted out in new costumes), belittling the reality and meaning of the events which he himself had so carefully re-searched. And so we read in his essay that the men who made this philosophical revolution "did not launch their attack on so marginal an area of Nature as demonology." [51] Trevor-Roper thus seduces the reader into believing that Demonology—always "marginal"—is now dead. It is precisely this belief, of course, which is the central dogma of modern Demonology, allowing it to control thought and behavior in a subliminal way, pervading the entire atmosphere of modern society as a colorless, odorless, and totally poisonous gas. Demonology (another name for theology) is still the King of the humanities and sci-

* Thus, for example, instead of dedicating his misogynistic works to his (nonexistent) wife, father Summers signed both of his introductions to the *Malleus Maleficarum* on catholic feast days of the Blessed Virgin Mary and signed the introduction to his own book, *The History of Witchcraft,* "on the feast of Saint Teresa, Virgin."

ences of patriarchy. As Trevor-Roper asserted earlier in his essay: "The more learned a man was in the traditional scholarship of the time [the period of the witchcraze], the more likely he was to support the witch-doctors." [52] This rule regulates the rites of sadoscholarship today, as the same author's remarks demonstrate.

It is enlightening to compare Trevor-Roper and Summers. The latter writes glowingly of "the voluminous and highly technical works of the Inquisitors and demonologists, holy and reverend divines, doctors *utriusque iuris*, hard-headed, slow, and sober lawyers—learned men, scholars of philosophic mind, the most honorable names in the universities of Europe, in the forefront of literature, science, politics, and culture . . ." [53] Unlike Trevor-Roper, father Summers finds nothing "sobering" in the fact that learned men wrote such works. On the contrary, he accepts every word, finding such obsession with sexual fantasies and such sadism altogether appropriate. Unlike Trevor-Roper, he feels no need to justify the silence of a Francis Bacon or a Descartes in the face of atrocity, for the only atrocity perpetrators are the massacred women. Summers's concern is to glorify the witchburners. For, unlike the dispassionate and sophisticated scholar, the impassioned priest is—to borrow a term employed by Felix Morrow, "forthright." With naive accuracy he displays the fundamental sameness of seventeenth-century and twentieth-century professional "approaches" to female deviancy.

There are, of course, diverse degrees of "forthrightness." While Summers definitely rates the Nobel Prize for Blatant Hag-Hating, Trevor-Roper is explicit enough to earn a medal of honor in this "field"—particularly if compared to the majority of historians of the witchburning period, who rarely admit that such a phenomenon even took place. Except for the few specialists who have made witch-hunting their field of "expertise," historians generally follow a policy of almost total erasure, wiping out the witches again and again through the subterfuge of silence. This does not mean that their misogynism is less intense than that of Summers or the witchcraze specialists, but only that it expresses (nonexpresses) itself in a different, though ultimately more effective, way. The method of historical erasure is, after all, consistent with the final solution of gynocide.

It is the custom of historians of the early modern period to omit discussion of the witchcraze. Usually the omission is almost, but not quite, absolute. This is more effective than complete nonmentioning of the subject, for it gives the impression that witch-hunting has been "covered"—which, of course, it has. Thus, for example, the third volume of the much used and highly respected *The Pelican History of the Church,* by Owen Chadwick, devoted to the "Reformation" and "covering" a significant part of the witchcraze period, contains two (2) references to *witch* in the index. I shall cite the passages in their entirety, so that the reader will not miss their import. Checking out the first reference, we find the following noninformation:

> Ill-regulated fervour could be superstitious or even demonic. In 1500 more witches were being tortured and burnt, more Jews were being persecuted. But superstition was no innovation.[54]

The statement, which lacks both content and meaningful context, is thoroughly stupefying. The phrase "more witches were being tortured and burnt" both raises and stifles the question: "More than how many?" The casual reader would be lulled into imagining that perhaps a few dozen persons were involved. However, even this thought would be blurred into meaninglessness by the sentence following, which erases the massacre of women by using the ephemeral and irrelevant abstraction, "superstition." While it may be true that "superstition was no innovation" (many would consider the persistence of christian beliefs to be abundant evidence of this), this truism is totally beside the point, distracting the reader from the unmentioned fact that the escalation of witchburning in the sixteenth century was more than superstition.

The second and only other indexed reference to witches (which is actually a reference to "witch-hunters") in this

Pelican's eye view of "church history" occurs more than two hundred and fifty pages later, where the Searcher finds the following illuminating statement:

> . . . the practitioners of Protestant medicine were hardly emancipated from material magics, their astronomers were still astrologers, their chemists were still alchemists, their witch-hunters were as zealous.[55]

Again, the author magically obliterates the most obvious questions by the alchemy of deceptive scholarship. He does not ask or answer: "As zealous *as whom* or *as what?* Thus he doles out to the reader a modicum of information which upon close examination proves to be misinformation, since the witchcraze had escalated during the first half of the seventeenth century, the period allegedly being described here. The witch-hunters, therefore, were not "as zealous" but more zealous than before. Such minimal mentioning of the term *witch-hunters* is more effective than complete silence, for it programs the reader to categorize the most monstrous atrocities under the title of "trifles." When such false knowledge slides into the unsuspecting student's mind, it occupies the mental space where genuine questioning takes place.

Just as "church history" erases the witchcraze, so do standard history texts purporting to deal with this period. A typical example is *The Foundations of the Modern World: 1300–1775* by Louis Gottschalk, L. C. MacKinney, and E. H. Pritchard. While it is difficult to imagine anyone reading this book, which has the flair of something composed by a computer, it is an esteemed tome, and is the fourth of a six-volume series accurately entitled *History of Mankind.* The series, sponsored by UNESCO, is described on the jacket of this volume as "the first global history, planned and executed from an international viewpoint." It is certainly planned from a woman-executing viewpoint. The index of this volume, a tome of some 1,133 pages which thoroughly "covers" the period of the witchcraze, mentions witchcraft in passing in exactly four (4) places.

The first brief reference merely announces that an "epidemic" of witch-hunting commenced during the last quarter of the fifteenth century, that death penalties for witchcraft rapidly became more common, that in the town of Como, Italy, several hundred women were burned.[56] The second reference to the subject, which consists of one paragraph and occurs some 300 pages later, provides the reader with such tidbits as the fact that the so-called heroic Jesuit Friedrich von Spee pleaded for an enlightened reconsideration of the subject in his *anonymous* work, *Cautio criminalis* (a shining example of male intellectual bravery). The reader learns that thousands "who had incurred official displeasure" were "imprisoned." When she reaches the end of the paragraph she knows that "a witch was burned in Switzerland as late as 1782, and two in Poland as late as 1793." What she does not learn is that hundreds of thousands—probably millions—of women were executed prior to these dates, during the period covered by this book.[57] Some 450 pages later the tome mentions that "waves" of witchcraft persecutions continued until the late seventeenth century, deceptively emphasizing the atypical and numerically small witchcraze in New England.[58] The fourth and final mention of the subject is the following informative sentence: "As a humanitarian Thomasius raised doubts about the justice of current court practices in connection with witchcraft and torture." [59] If the reader retains anything in connection with witches from *The History of Mankind* it will probably be the names of the "heroic" Jesuit von Spee and the "humanitarian" Thomasius. None of the massacred women is mentioned by name. No accurate image of the scope and horror of the witchcraze is conveyed. There is no hint of the true intent of the hunters nor of the true identity of their victims.

In addition to these general histories which cover and re-cover the period of the witchcraze, there are, of course, books purporting to deal specifically with women of this period. Repeatedly, the Searcher finds that these simply wipe out the witchcraze, either by not mentioning it at all, or by passing references to the "horrid" women who supposedly did abominable things deserving of recrimination. Erasure of witches and deletion of the witch-hunters is the name of the game in scholarship "about women" of the so-called Renaissance and Reformation period in Europe.[60]

There are, of course, many works specializing in the history of the witchcraze. I have already alluded to the enlightening study of Midelfort, who voices the view that the small witch trial may have been "therapeutic, or functional." Although he does not state *for whom* it was therapeutic, we may safely assume that it was not so for the murdered women.

Another form of scholarly mystification is illustrated in the work of social historian/anthropologist Julio Caro Baroja, *The World of the Witches*. In the last section of his book, adopting a modern "psychological" approach, Baroja presumes to describe "the personality of the witch." He sagely informs us that "a woman usually becomes a witch after the initial failure of her life as a woman; after frustrated or illegitimate love affairs have left her with a sense of impotence or disgrace."[61] Hags may successfully "double-double unthink" this statement to mean that "a woman usually becomes a witch after the initial success of her life in overcoming the patriarchally defined role of 'woman'; after seeing through the inherent contradiction of 'romantic love'—a clarifying process which enriches her sense of gynergy and grace." Baroja's book concludes:

> In conclusion, it seems to me, as a historian, that witchcraft makes one feel pity more than anything else. Pity for those who were persecuted, who wanted to do evil yet could not do it, and whose lives were generally frustrated and tragic. Pity, too, for the persecutors who were brutal because they believed that numberless dangers surrounded them.[62]

This pitiful analysis reveals the pitfalls of "pity." Since there is no reason to think that good witches—Spinsters, midwives, healers—"wanted to do evil," this "pity" is perverted and deceptive. Hags may well feel grief and anger for our tortured foresisters, but pity for their/our persecutors is not the appropriate response. Righteous anger is more in accord with the reality and can generate creative energy.

Just as social historian Baroja has recourse in the end to feeble psychologizing so also does moralist W. E. H. Lecky in his two-volume *History of European Morals*. He writes revealingly (in the sense of unveiling and re-veiling at the same time) of the conditions that drove some witches to suicide:

In Europe the act was very common among the witches, who underwent all the sufferings with none of the consolations of martyrdom.

Without enthusiasm, without hope, without even the consciousness of innocence, decrepit in body and distracted in mind, compelled in this world to endure tortures, before which the most impassioned heroism might quail, and doomed, as they often believed, to eternal damnation in the next, they not unfrequently killed themselves in the agony of their despair.[63]

This is a perfect description of the condition to which the lords of patriarchy *desire* to see defiant women reduced. It is an announcement of androcratic intent. How would Lecky know that the witches were "without even the consciousness of innocence"? The expressions "decrepit in body" and "distracted in mind" are deceptive because not accompanied by any description of the christian torturers' methods.

On the following page, this "historian of morals," having admitted the fact of unspeakable torture of witches, actually manages to write that "*epidemics* of purely *insane* suicide . . . not infrequently occurred [emphases mine]." Lecky here refers specifically to the women of Marseilles and of Lyons. He then goes on:

In that strange *mania* which raged in Neapolitan districts *from the end of the fifteenth to the end of the seventeenth century,* and which was attributed to the bite of the tarantula, the *patients* thronged in multitudes towards the sea, and often, as the blue waters opened to their view, they chanted a wild hymn of welcome, and rushed with passion into the waves [emphases mine].[64]

By naming this phenomenon a "mania" and failing to note the significance of the dates, Lecky makes its meaning invisible to most readers. Hags, however, knowing something about the history of The Burning Times, can see that this was a completely sane decision. Multitudes of women rushed into the sea, precisely because they refused to be "patients" for the witch doctors/torturers and chose to be agents of the one Self-affirming act possible under the Reign of Infernal Justice.* Otherwise, they would have been forced to submit their minds and bodies, to accuse themselves, their daughters, their mothers, their dearest friends, of impossible crimes. Moral historian Lecky legitimates this horror by deleting the context and the agents of gynocide from his text. He writes that such cases "belong rather to the history of medicine than to that of morals." Thus no one is to blame. The Fathers are exonerated, since there is nothing in this picture relevant to the history of "morals."

Since moral historians are willing to eradicate moral responsibility for witchburning, misfiling the matter under "medicine," it is to be expected that practitioners of the rituals of psychiatric re-search will continue this eradication. As Thomas Szasz points out, the possibility that some persons accused of witchcraft were "mentally ill" was voiced long before the beginnings of modern psychiatry, even during the witch-hunts, notably by Johann Weyer.[65] Szasz believes that Jean-Etienne-Dominique Esquirol (1772–1840) "did more than any other man to establish the view that witches were mentally deranged persons." [66] Thus the way was paved for the sado-rituals of psychiatric re-search, which erase and perpetuate the trials of Hags.

Among the psychiatric re-searchers, Gregory Zilboorg has been one of the most influential. Typically, he sees the witches/victims and not the witchburners/torturers as insane. He writes that "no doubt is left in our mind that the millions of witches, sorcerers, possessed and obsessed, were an enormous

* The words of the hymn, according to Hecker's *Epidemics of the Middle Ages* (London, 1844), are:

Allu mari mi portati	trans.:	Take me to the sea
Se voleti che mi sanati,		If you are willing that I be healed,
Allu mari, alla via,		To the sea, to the way
Cosi m'ama la donna mia,		Thus does my lady love me,
Allu mari, allu mari,		To the sea, to the sea,
Mentre campo, t'aggio amari.		While I live, I must love you.

mass of severe neurotics, psychotics, and considerably deteriorated organic deliria." [67] Zilboorg's ignorance is colossally distorting. Particularly malignant is his buttressing of christian bigotry. Commenting on the *Malleus Maleficarum,* he warns:

However, the sadistic details which are so shocking to the man of today, do not concern us here. A consideration of these would add nothing to our knowledge of human propensities and would, moreover, tend considerably to obscure the calm judgment of the facts under consideration.[68]

Clearly, the sadism of the christian persecutors does not concern this psychiatric son of the Holy Fathers. He has a good word for more than one demonologist, for example, Johannes Trithemius, a younger contemporary of Sprenger and Kramer, who shared their views. Johannes was a "very learned and very kind man." With complete credulity, Zilboorg accepts a contemporary's description of Johannes: "A goodness that could not be expressed in words rested upon his sturdy manly brow and . . . his pure and luminous eyes appeared to reflect a celestial light." In his *Antipalus Maleficarum,* Johannes wrote that "the number of such witches is very great in every province." He bemoaned the fact that there were not enough Inquisitors and Judges, while "man and beast die as a result of the evil of these women." [69] Not surprisingly, Zilboorg refers reverentially to "the Reverend Montague Summers, who today, like many of his predecessors in the fifteenth and sixteenth centuries, combines great and profound learning with no less great and no less profound belief in the existence of witches." [70]

Zilboorg's support of christian bigotry applies both to the past and the present. Of the past, he writes:

In other words, these witches were *actually* heretical; they actually sinned against the Sacraments . . . they actually either rebelled against or were afraid of the sign of the Cross—all this while mentally sick, of course.[71]

There is no criticism here of the concept of "sin," of "the Sacraments," or of "the sign of the Cross." There is no admission that such rebellion could be a sign of strength and health. His statements about contemporary "sacrilege" are consistent with this double-double think:

> It is known that in adolescents and in adults one of the most typical phases of a compulsion neurosis even today is a conscious or unconscious expression of sacrilege, as it were, a series of impulses directed against God, Christ, and the Church.[72]

The usual tactic of agent deletion through the use of the expression "it is known" gives the delusion of "the voice of authority." It is important for Hags to note this alliance of "profound" psychiatric re-search with christian orthodoxy. The issue here is not one of *belief* in "God, Christ, and the Church." The object of his attack is the *defiant* deviant who goes beyond mere disbelief, acknowledging and naming the deception of christian myth, exorcising its deception and journeying into the Background. Hags elicit the same nameless terrors in the Sprengers, Kramers, Summers, and zany Zilboorgs of Sado-Society. Hence the continued legitimation of witchburning—both in its past and in its present forms—by the rites of psychiatric writing.

The culpable ignorance of contemporary Crone-killers is ilustrated also in Alexander and Selesnick's *The History of Psychiatry*. They write:

> It must also be said that accused witches oftentimes played into the hands of the persecutors. A witch relieved her guilt by confessing her sexual fantasies in open court; at the same time, she achieved some erotic gratification by dwelling on all the details before her male accusers. These severely emotionally disturbed women were particularly susceptible to the suggestion that they harbored demons and devils and would confess to cohabitating with the evil spirit, much as disturbed individuals today, influenced by newspaper headlines, fantasy themselves as sought-after murderers.[73]

The context in which these contemporary witch doctors (i.e., doctors of witches) write this passage indicates that the distortions expressed here are not manifestations of simple ignorance. In the preceding pages they have outlined and discussed the *Malleus Maleficarum*. It is not possible that these wizards of modern psychiatry were unaware of the fact that women were tortured by their persecutors. Lists and pictures of the instruments and methods of torture are available in many sources, for example Robbins's *Encyclopedia of Witchcraft and Demonology*. There were eye-gougers, branding irons, spine-rollers, forehead tourniquets, thumbscrews, racks, strappados, iron boots for crushing legs, heating chairs, choking "pears." The torturers cut off hands and ears of their victims, imposed artificial sleeplessness, unendurable thirst (by feeding salted foods and refusing liquids), and "squassation," which completely dislocated hands, feet, elbows, limbs, and shoulders. I have already alluded to the fact that humiliation, stripping, and the usual gang rape were not counted as "torture."

In light of this easily available information, one should reread the statement quoted above from the good doctors Alexander and Selesnick. If there were a modicum of intellectual honesty the passage cited above *should* read more or less as follows:

> It is clear that the witches were physically and mentally mutilated and dismembered by their persecutors. A witch was forced to relieve her torture by confessing that she acted out the sexual fantasies of her male judges as they described these to her. The judges achieved erotic gratification from her torture, from the sight of her being stripped and gang raped, from seeing her mangled body, from forcing her to "admit" acting out *their* erotic fantasies, from her spiritual and physical slow death. These disturbing and sadistic men were creating the delusion of devils other than themselves—projecting their own evil intent onto these "devils" which were mirror images of themselves—much as sadistic psychiatrists today, influenced by myth, media and professional training, fantasy themselves as sought-after healers of the "sickness" which they themselves invent.[74]

When we double-double unthink the psychiatric historians' maze of reversals in this way, we focus attention upon the agents of the atrocities: the professional hunters and judges of the witches. In its convoluted and deceptive way the psychiatric literature calls attention to the central issue of sadomasochistic erotic fantasies. Hags can see the acting out and voyeurism of the torturers and judges as establishing a christian precedent for the "live porn" which men "enjoy" today. Such entertainment reaches its logical conclusion when the female "performer" is actually murdered—snuffed out. In a notorious underground porn movie shown in New York, an actual rape-murder was done to the unsuspecting "actress," and the popular movie *Snuff* simulated this original, capitalizing on the voracious voyeuristic appetite of film-goers. This kind of entertainment is enjoyed by judges, physicians, policemen, and other professionals today, all in the line of "duty," when women who have been victimized (rape victims, for example) come under their power. Nor is it only while "on duty" that men in power require action to fit their fantasies. The use/abuse of prostitutes is a favorite outlet.*

Although a variety of professional men act out the witch trial syndrome, the parallels between the witchburners and their modern psychiatric replacements are especially striking. Robbins points out that for the witch judges a voluntary confession did not suffice: "It had to be made under torture, for only then could it be presumed to come from the heart and be genuine." [75] This kind of "reasoning" prevails also in modern psychiatry, as Szasz has admirably demonstrated.[76] Mental

* A recent exposé of this acting out of sadomasochistic fantasies by men in power is *A Sexual Profile of Men in Power,* by Sam Janus, Barbara Bess, and Carol Saltus (Englewood Cliffs, N.J.: Prentice-Hall, 1977). Interestingly, these "powerful men," whose professional success requires sadistic behavior while "on duty," pay prostitutes to degrade them in every imaginable way, including urinating and defecating on them. The prostitutes refer to these johns as "the slaves," because they want to be treated as slaves. The behavior of such men (including Hitler, who was an extreme masochist) suggests that the "sadist" and the "masochist" are the same person assuming different roles. Thus the psychiatric historians' theory that the fantasies of women were being acted out in the witch trials is askew. Women were/are not the producers of the torture shows. Rather, the drama of the witch trials is the product of the fantasies of males, which are alternately sadistic and masochistic. The "men in power" are the playwrights who create and identify with the roles of both the victimizers and the victims. There is no evidence that any woman enjoyed the torture. However, the male torturers vicariously enjoyed the women's suffering.

patients are also tortured and scapegoated, and are expected to pay the costs. Robbins points out that the estate of the accused witch and of her relations had to pay the costs of the entire trial, including the fees for torture. The same rule applies today for shock treatments, psychosurgery, and incarceration in mental hospitals.

In all of the male-authored scholarship, however, from the worst to the best, there is something lacking: specifically, a Hag-identified vision. There is a general reluctance to state that most of the witches were women. Even though this is often grudgingly admitted, its implications are not made explicit. Robbins generally uses the pseudogeneric pronoun *he,* which any Hag can see is absurd. Only reluctantly is the strength and power of the witches, which threatened the Fathers, admitted. Perhaps Szasz comes closest to identifying the Malefactor, but he fails to isolate and expose the Male Factor. He does show that three institutions—the Inquisition, the *lettre de cachet,* and psychiatry—all rest upon principles of paternalism, their respective fathers being the holy father (the pope), the national father (the king), and the scientific father (the physician).[77] However, this still leaves the reader with the impression that things might be all right if the fathers would only behave better. Szasz does not unmask the inherent gynocidal intent of patriarchy itself.

Feminist analysis does this unmasking. Moving into the Background, it makes known the interconnectedness of things. Such an analysis was written in the nineteenth century by Matilda Joslyn Gage in her a-mazing book, *Woman, Church and State,* which was originally published in 1893, and which contains a learned and revolutionary chapter on witchcraft. Feminists today are, of course, working as Hag-ographers/Hag-ologists, uncovering our Prehistory, our Crone-ology. There has been a sense of dis-covery and shock as we have learned more about The Burning Times. Yet for some it has been almost as shocking to come upon the work of Gage, and to read this very perceptive and learned woman's study. It is infuriating to discover that this foresister, and others like her, had already gathered and analyzed materials which feminist scholars are just beginning to unearth again. As Jane

Caputi wrote: "It is painfully ironic to confront the erasure of Gage . . . [who] devoted the overwhelming portion of her energies towards reclaiming our past." [78] Such a painful discovery raises enraging questions: How could we—especially women historians, educated and legitimated by "degrees"—have been kept in such ignorance of our own tradition? And when women overcome this studied ignorance to some degree and publish our own works will these be as effectively concealed from our "educated" sisters of the future as the work of our foresisters has been hidden from us? One of the basic premises of Hag-ographers must be a promise to carry on the process, to create in such a way that our creativity cannot be silenced. This will require knowing deeply that The Burning Times continue, and that the Rites of Book Burning—in such sophisticated forms as bad reviews, poor publicity and distribution, letting feminist books go out of print, keeping them from getting into print—are raping women's minds.

A great Hag herself, Matilda Joslyn Gage wrote with impressive erudition and passion. Unlike male scholars, she was able to write with boldness, accuracy and pride of her *own* tradition:

> The superior learning of witches was recognized in the widely extended belief of their ability to work miracles. The witch was in reality the profoundest thinker, the most advanced scientist of those ages. . . . As knowledge has ever been power, the church feared its use in woman's hands, and leveled its deadliest blows at her.[79]

Gage thus names the game correctly: The church feared and hated women's knowledge and power. She correctly named women *the* healers, who were therefore hated by the church and its sons:

> The earliest doctors among the common people of Christian Europe were women who had learned the virtues and use of herbs. The famous works of Paracelsus were but compilations of the knowledge of these "wise women" as he himself stated. . . . But while for many hundred years the knowledge of medicine, and its practice among the poorer classes, was almost entirely in the hands of women and many discoveries in science are due to them, yet an acquaintance of

herbs soothing to pain, or healing in their qualities, was then looked upon as having been acquired through diabolical agency.[80]

Here the nineteenth-century scholar makes the point succinctly: The sons of the church had to erase women with the power to heal, not only by killing them, but by denying that they healed *of their own power*. It must have been "through diabolical agency," that is, through obedience to another—the "devil."

Gage recognized fully the church's horror of women's wisdom:

The Church having forbidden its offices and all external methods of knowledge to woman, was profoundly stirred with indignation at her having through her own wisdom penetrated into some of the most deeply subtle secrets of nature.[81]

She saw that the church wanted to claim for itself such "mysterious hidden knowledge . . . which it regarded as among its most potential methods of controlling mankind." [82]

Although there was much emphasis upon christianity in Gage's work, she recognized the universality of patriarchy. Discussing the torture of the witches, she points out that "under the laws of both Church and State they found their sex to be a crime." [83] Her chapter on witchcraft is presented in a context of interrelatedness, in a book which begins, appropriately, with a chapter entitled "The Matriarchate," establishing that matriarchy preceded patriarchy and that the latter is characterized by polygamy, infanticide, and prostitution.

Since Gage's perspective was gynocentric, the reality and meaning of her work is erased by historians. It is particularly ironic that her work is obscured in *Notable American Women*. The entry by Elizabeth B. Warbasse credits Gage's father (who is praised at some length in the short article) with "directing his daughter's education." [84] Had Warbasse been more sensitive to Gage's own writing, she would have noted that her father is not mentioned in the dedication to *Woman, Church and State*. Rather, Gage writes:

This Book is Inscribed to the Memory of my Mother, who was at once mother, sister, friend.

These words indicate who, in Gage's view, was the real educator of her life, but the author of the brief biographical sketch, overlooking this obvious clue, informs the reader only that Gage's mother "was a lady of refined tastes, whose handsome furniture and carpets enabled the Joslyns to begin housekeeping in comfortable circumstances." Significantly, the *Notable American Women* entry devotes a long paragraph to the details of Gage's marriage but allots exactly eight unilluminating lines to its description of her major work, *Woman, Church and State*. We are informed that Gage "never equaled the achievement" of Elizabeth Cady Stanton and Susan B. Anthony. Literally speaking, this is true. Gage was a revolutionary thinker who did not "equal" but rather outdistanced these reformers in the originality and creativity of her thinking, that is, in the time/space journey of metapatriarchal knowing.

In the first half of the twentieth century Margaret A. Murray argued in her extensively documented books that the witches represented the remains of a pagan religion which christianity was determined to stamp out.[85] She established this, eliciting hysterical rebuffs from Montague Summers, for her writings brought to light the fact that the newcomer on the religious scene, christianity, had taken over elements from the Old Religion. Since Murray had said that the witches' covens consisted of thirteen members, father Summers howls in outrage:

> . . . the demonologists are never tired of insisting that Satan is the ape of God in all things, and that the worshippers of evil delight to parody every divine ordinance and institution. The explanation is simple. The number thirteen was adopted by the witches for their covens in mockery of Our Lord and His Apostles.[86]

Apparently, father Summers is also shocked by Murray's "astounding and indecorous assertion" that "Joan of Arc belonged to the ancient religion, and not to the Christian." [87] To this priest demonologist, the Dianic cult is "imaginary," and "the witches' service is a hideous burlesque of Holy Mass." Thus he sees his scholarly antagonist as reversing everything, saying that "what Miss Murray suggests is that the parody may have existed before the thing parodied."[88] Reflecting upon this father's Fun House of distorting mirrors, Hags today may appreciate that Murray had struck a nerve. There is ample supporting evidence for her underlying thesis that remnants of the Old Religion survived and threatened the christian fathers.

From a feminist perspective, however, her work leaves much to be desired and can hardly be taken to represent the psychic dimensions of gynocentric living. An extremely serious problem with her work is the fact that she bases her assertions about the practices of the witches upon records of their trials. By now the reader will be aware of all that is wrong with this method. In her introduction to *The Witch-Cult in Western Europe,* Murray defends her use of these sources, even against the objection that the evidence was always given under torture, arguing that "in most of the English and many of the Scotch trials legal torture was not applied."[89] To the objection that the evidence of the witches at the trials is almost uniform in character, which implies that they were asked "leading questions," she suggests that the Inquisitors arrived at the form of the questionary as a result of knowledge, and that "the very uniformity of their confessions points to the reality of the occurrence."[90]

This argument might appear to make perfect sense if one were unaware of the extent of the torture and of the nature of some of the accusations: for example, the accusation of raising tempests. Yet it is not possible to dismiss all of Murray's evidence. It is most important for feminist scholars to realize that Murray is describing the cult in a late form, when "the worship of the male deity appears to have superseded that of the female."[91]

Perhaps one of the chief benefits to be derived from the problems connected with struggling over such works as those of Murray is the realization that the history and meaning of gynocentric creative, psychic, spiritual energy cannot be discussed adequately in the context of a "cult," or of an "organized religion," or as some call it, "the Craft." It is heartening to listen to the words of Matilda Joslyn Gage:

When for "witches" we read "women," we gain fuller comprehension of the cruelties inflicted by the church upon this portion of humanity.[92]

Feminists who identify their deep centering Selves with the term *witch* are not being merely metaphorical, or cute, or popularizing, or "trivializing." I suggest, rather, that the reverse is true: that to limit the term to apply only to those who have esoteric knowledge of and participate formally in "the Craft" is the real reductionism. This is the case particularly since the cult, as Murray demonstrated (perhaps inadvertently), has been strongly invaded by patriarchal influences.

Together with Robin Morgan, who has done so much both to elicit in women the wide and deep intuition of the meaning of *Witch* and to resist simplistic vulgarization, I hope that more feminists will give to the history of witches "the serious study that it warrants, recognizing it as a part of our entombed history, a remnant of the Old Religion which pre-dated all patriarchal faiths and which was a Goddess-worshipping, matriarchal faith . . . [reading] the anthropological, religious, and mythographic studies on the subject." [93] Hopefully, in doing so we will not sacrifice the original vigor and integrity that inspired the "New York Covens" in the late sixties to proclaim:

> You are a Witch by saying aloud, "I am a Witch" three times, and *thinking about that*. You are a Witch by being female, untamed, angry, joyous, and immortal.[94]

Many women have understood this identity of the Witch within, the Self who is the target of the fathers' attacks and the center of original movement. Barbara Ehrenreich and Deirdre English did much to spread knowledge among women of the role of the witches as midwives and healers, showing that their suppression coincided with the creation of a new male medical profession.[95] In the early seventies, Andrea Dworkin named the witchcraze for what it is: gynocide. She showed its interconnectedness with other horrors such as footbinding, fairy tales, rape, and pornography.[96] Others have searched out pieces of the mosaic which are not easy to find.

Such works should be valued for igniting the Spark which inflames the desire to search further. There is much to be done. Working with increased confidence and precision, Hags must continue in the spiritual tradition of such visionaries as Matilda Joslyn Gage, continuing to uncover our past and paths to our future. This will be possible to the degree that we continue with courage in the Journey of our own time/space. Seeing through the fraudulent re-presentations of the witchcraze will help us recognize the tactics of today's Male Midwives, the professional Wizards who have unsuccessfully "succeeded" the Wise Women—the Unhealers of Modern Medicine.

CHAPTER SEVEN

AMERICAN GYNECOLOGY: GYNOCIDE BY THE HOLY GHOSTS OF MEDICINE AND THERAPY

> John [my husband] is a physician, and *perhaps*—(I would not say it to a living soul, of course, but this is dead paper and a great relief to my mind)—*perhaps* that is one reason I do not get well faster. . . .
> There comes John, and I must put this away,—he hates to have me write a word.
>
> Charlotte Perkins Gilman,
> *The Yellow Wallpaper*

> Psychological testing . . . had revealed him as a boy with violent instincts, a fact that had at least partly determined the choice of both rugby and medical study for him; the demanding physical contest and the practice of surgery, it was thought, would help to channel his aggressive tendencies.
>
> Piers Paul Read,
> *Alive: The Story of the Andes Survivors*

> I will simply claim for myself the rights of the gynaecologist . . .
>
> Sigmund Freud,
> *The Case of Dora*

I have shown in the earlier chapters of this passage how women in various cultures—which are merely multi-manifestations of the overall culture of androcracy—have often been lulled/ lobotomized by the myths and habits of their particular social context. Drugged by the prevailing local dogmas and disabled physically, they have not always seen the intent behind the vicious circle of maiming and murder of mothers and daughters. In twentieth-century America, women are lulled by the myths and rituals of gynecology and therapy, believing that "doctor knows best." * We have entered the Ice Age of Gynocidal Gynecology.

A BRIEF CRONE-OLOGY

Many feminists have noted the significance of the fact that the massacre of the wise women/healers during the witchcraze was followed by the rise of man-midwives who eventually became dignified by the name "gynecologist."[1] Gynecology was slow to rise. Man-midwives of the sixteenth, seventeenth, eighteenth, and nineteenth centuries were under fire from woman midwives, such as Elizabeth Nihell, who described their instruments as "weapons of death." [2] Nevertheless, the nineteenth

* In this chapter I use the term *gynecology* broadly to refer to all those professions—including psychiatry and the other psychotherapeutic fields—which specialize in the "diseases and hygiene" of women's bodies and minds. I use the term *gynecologist* to refer to all members of those professions whose beliefs and behavior are motivated by loyalties to their patriarchally identified fields rather than by concern for women. As I have explained in the Introduction, some specialists in these fields are at times helpful to women, but such genuine helpfulness occurs *in spite of* the pervasive intent, ethos, and method of their professions. Moreover, in an increasing number of cases, the effectiveness of such healers consists in repairing damage caused by their colleagues, that is, iatrogenic damage.

Although in some cases women have no choice other than to turn to members of the gynecological professions, it is important to remember: (*a*) that in many instances, despite appearances, women do have other options; and (*b*) that frequently the best option is *not* to go to such specialists. Finally, even if these professionals are consulted out of necessity and with good short-term results, the long-term effects often include increased physical and psychological dependency, and consequent loss of autonomous creative energy needed for searching out woman-identified solutions.

century witnessed the erection of gynecology over women's dead bodies. By 1883—the year of the death of J. Marion Sims, the "father of gynecology" (known as the "architect of the vagina")—gynecologists could "apply their knives at will to the whole range of woman's being, reduced as it was to sex." [3]

As G. J. Barker-Benfield shows, the more notorious mid-nineteenth-century gynecologists were bent upon reducing women to their sex organs.[4] Sexual surgery became The Man's means of restraining women. J. Marion Sims, known for his hatred and abhorrence of female organs, remedied his problems (becoming very rich in the process) by ruthlessly cutting up women's bodies. He began his life's work "humbly," performing dangerous sexual surgery on black female slaves housed in a small building in his yard, but rapidly moved up the professional ladder, becoming the "moving spirit" behind the founding of the Woman's Hospital in New York, which provided him with bodies for his brutal experimental operations. It also provided him with a theatre, in which he performed his operations upon indigent women used as guinea pigs before an audience of men.

In his private practice, where he charged enormous fees to the rich, Sims used the "knowledge" gained through the pain and mutilation inflicted upon the poor patients at the Woman's Hospital.* There were plenty of victims for Sims and his ilk, for there were women suffering from fistulae and general bad health who were desperate enough to reach for any hope of help. The historical evidence suggests strongly that their "helper," Sims, did not differ essentially from his gynecological colleagues in intent, attitude, or method. He simply was more monomaniacal and ambitious than most men. Internationally famous, honored by his peers, he was an object of adulation at Harvard Medical School, where "the students recognized 'divinity' in Sims and counted him 'one of the immortals.' " [5] As Peggy Holland has remarked, such men are "immortal" in

* Mary Smith, an Irish indigent, suffered thirty of his operations between 1856 and 1859. The black slave Anarcha had suffered the same number in his backyard stable a decade before.

the sense that they pass on death and fear, their only true offspring.[6]

Such gynecological "holy ghosts" as Sims now haunt the history of women from generation to generation. The seeds of such ghostly/ghastly presences are iatrogenic diseases, and the daughters of women infected by such "divine" doctors carry in their bodies and minds the cancerous cells hidden there by these "helpers." * It is helpful for Hags to recall that one definition of the verb *to doctor,* given in Merriam-Webster, is "to conceal the real state or quality of by deceptive alteration (as with chemicals)."

Doctor Sims et al. inspired through their work certain essential qualities of American gynecology which, as I shall show, have metastasized during the march of modern medical progress. Barker-Benfield wrote of that field as it was defined and congealed in the nineteenth century:

> The spate of gynecological activity in America and America's international prominence in gynecology were characterized by flamboyant, drastic, risky, and instant use of the knife.[7]

As we shall see, the pattern has not changed. Rather, the doctored diseases have spread. The seeds which Sims and his colleagues sowed in the minds of their simian sons, the professional cultivators of that field, have ripened in a rich harvest of medicinally manufactured carcinomas, "cured" by the cutting edge of advanced sexual surgery. The mutilations and mutations masterminded by the modern man-midwives represent an advanced stage in the patriarchal program of gynocide. The supremely sterile, infinitely impotent "immortals" have brewed their final solution. Unable to create life, they are performing the most potent act possible to them: the manufacture of death. This production is a last attempt by these

* The plight of DES daughters manifests this phenomenon on a literal and physical level. The situation of daughters whose mothers' minds were "fixed" by Freudian analysis exemplifies the "evolution" of infection on a more subtle and spiritual plane. In the latter instance, the expression "cancerous cells" is metaphorical; the damage indicated by the metaphor is real.

holy ghosts and hospital hosts to erect a fitting temple/tumor for themselves, an appropriate embodiment for their word-made-flesh, a womb-tomb dedicated to the worship of Nothing.

It is essential for Crone-ologists to see that the specialized treatment for women known as gynecology arose in the nineteenth century as a direct response to the first wave of feminism. Significantly, the attempts of nineeenth-century urologists to constitute an "andrology" specialty, in contrast to gynecology, were abortive. For of course the purpose and *intent* of gynecology was/is not healing in a deep sense but violent enforcement of the sexual caste system.

Keeping this intent in focus, we can uncover the significance of some outstanding events in the history of gynecology. Thus, in 1848, the year of the first Women's Right's Convention, Dr. Charles Meigs was advising his pupils that their study of female organs would enable them to understand and control the very heart, mind, and soul of woman. Clitoridectomy, "invented" ten years later by the English gynecologist Isaac Baker Brown, was enthusiastically accepted as a "cure" for female masturbation by some American gynecologists. In 1852 Dr. Augustus Kinsley Gardner let out a battle cry against "disorderly women," including women's rightists, Bloomer-wearers, and midwives. In the 1860s Dr. Isaac Ray and his contemporaries proclaimed that women are susceptible to hysteria, insanity, and criminal impulses by reason of their sexual organs. The year 1873 marked the publication of Dr. Robert Battey's invention of "female castration," that is, removal of the ovaries to cure "insanity." *

* As Diana E. H. Russell and Nicole Van de Ven, editors of *The Proceedings of the International Tribunal on Crimes Against Women* (Millbrae, Calif.: Les Femmes, 1976), have noted on p. 150, it is more accurate to use the term *castration* to refer to clitoridectomy, excision, and infibulation, since these destroy women's sexuality. In a wide sense, however, I think it is also applicable to punitive/unnecessary ovariotomy and hysterectomy. Certainly it applies to lobotomy and to mind mutilation by therapists, for one definition of *castrate* is "to deprive of vigor and vitality." Since deprivation of vigor and vitality was clearly the intent of Battey and his followers who did ovariotomies, I use this term (as did they) to describe this operation, although I do not use it exclusively or primarily in this sense.

For the next several decades ovariotomy became the gynecological craze; it was claimed to elevate the moral sense of the patients, making them tractable, orderly, industrious, and cleanly. "Disorderly" women were handed over to gynecologists by husbands and fathers for castration and other forms of radical treatment. Such doctors as S. Weir Mitchell combined anesthesia and knife, forcing a "rest-cure" upon the castrated victims.[8] Only after the establishment of body-gynecology did psychoanalysis (the earliest form of mind-gynecology) take over. As Ehrenreich and English point out:

> Under Freud's influence, the scalpel for the dissection of female nature eventually passed from the gynecologist to the psychiatrist . . . It [Freudian theory] held that the female personality was inherently defective, this time due to the absence of a penis, rather than to the presence of the domineering uterus.[9]

As we shall see in the course of our study, mind-gynecologists* and body-gynecologists have been playing "musical chairs" ever since, combining and conniving to repress and depress female be-ing. Moreover, our Crone-logical analysis will show that the current escalation of murderous gynecological surgery (and of chemotherapy and psychotherapy) is no chronological coincidence. There is every reason to see the mutilation and destruction of women by doctors specializing in unnecessary radical mastectomies and hysterectomies, carcinogenic hormone therapy, psychosurgery, spirit-killing psychiatry and other forms of psychotherapy† as directly related to the rise of radical feminism in the twentieth century.

* Within the category of mind-gynecologists I include: psychiatrists, psychoanalysts, psychologists, and the proliferation of semiprofessional therapists and counselors trailing on *ad infinitum*.

† Throughout this chapter I will be using the term *psychotherapy* in a very broad sense, which includes not only therapy which relies upon psychological means, but also "somatic therapy." (The latter is defined by Kovel as including "all those therapeutic approaches which apply physical means—drugs, electric shock, etc.—to the body, as a strategy for altering an emotional state." I also include psychosurgery under "somatic therapy" as does Kovel in his text.) See Joel Kovel, M.D., *A Complete Guide to Therapy: From Psychoanalysis to Behavior Modification* (New York: Pantheon, 1976), pp. 264–65.

CHRISTIAN PARADIGMS FOR GYNECOLOGICAL GYNOCIDE

We have seen that in the West, the European witchcraze signaled the arrival of a new age of gynocidal processions. During that era the personifications of the Second Divine Person—the sons of god representing the Son of God—appeared on stage, forming the professional and corporate mystical mergers that required the massacre of "indigestible" women. In nineteenth- and twentieth-century America (and in other nations following American leadership) a further phase has been reached. This is the Age of the Holy Ghost and his ghostly representatives. The multiple holy ghosts of the Age of Gynecology (body-gynecologists and mind-gynecologists) follow the mythic model of the "Third Divine Person." We have seen in the First Passage that the original christian holy ghost was a mythic male mother, the spirtual single parent who impregnated Mary, the Totaled Woman. The latter was a reversal of the parthenogenetic goddess, who was thus reduced to a brainwashed receptacle/rape victim.

In studying the sado-rituals of the gynecological holy ghosts, it is useful to recall some of the theological lore associated with their christian theological archetype. The holy ghost, the feminine member of the divine trinity, was known as "the Spirit"—the one who inspires, or breathes into the souls of the chosen. In the ideal transsexual world of christian myth, "he" manages not only to impregnate Mary physically, producing the "Incarnate Word," but also to fecundate the souls/minds of the faithful, engendering "supernatural life" and inspiring them with "divine" ideas and images. It is important to realize the interconnection between these two aspects of the myth, for they are reflected in the emergence of the two classes of specialists "devoted" to women, that is, the body-gynecologists and the mind-gynecologists.

The various types of psychotherapists are the theologians of gynecology. These theologians and the specialized "ministering" physicians whom they legitimate represent the two complementary functions of the holy ghost. Both function to keep women supine, objectified, and degraded—a condition ritually symbolized by the gynecologist's stirrups and the psychiatrist's couch. By their combined efforts, these specialists keep many women in the state of perpetual patients whose bodies and minds are constantly invaded by foreign objects—knives, needles, speculums, carcinogenic hormone injections and pills, sickening self-images, festering fixations, debilitating dogmas.*

It is significant that certain male-defined feminine qualities are attributed to the holy ghost of christian theology. Thus he is called Helper and Healer—which makes him an appropriate paradigm for the "helping professions." He is also known by the name Gift.[10] The deceptiveness of such appellations is apparent to victims of theological/psychiatric/gynecological "help," who have learned the truth of the slogan: There is no such thing as a free lunch.

Finally, he is called Love.[11] In emulation of this model, spiritual pseudolove has been practiced by christians in the name of charity and is presently perpetuated by the therapeutic establishment in the name of psychological help. This detached, objectifying model of "Love" is also mirrored in the fetishism and genital fixations of body-gynecologists as well as mind-gynecologists, who symbolically and ritually make love lovelessly. To the extent that they are successful, their female patients are paralyzed by lack of Self-respect, for these doctors engender the debilitating disease of self-hatred.

All of this takes place on a deeply mythic level, in re-enactments of christian theological paradigms.[12] The medical and therapeutic establishments' adaptation/adoption of these mythic models is illustrated in their translation of the doctrines of "supernatural life" and of the virtues into their own ideology and practice. Thus, according to medieval theology (and contemporary roman catholic theology), the faithful receive from

* As we have seen, it is no coincidence that the establishment of gynecology was followed chronologically by the creation and spread of Freudian ideology and its offspring. The medical establishment soon found that its colonization of women's bodies required the concomitant conquest of their minds/spirits. The new theology of therapy has fulfilled this role, extending its tentacles into the privacy of minds and hearts.

the holy ghost a whole new level of supernatural life known as "sanctifying grace." * Together with grace, the baptized are believed to receive the virtues of faith, hope, and charity. In this belief system, faith makes it possible for the "reborn" christian to will to believe whatever is revealed by god. Hope is essentially for fulfillment in the afterlife. Charity allows the supernaturally reborn to love god above all things, including themselves.

In modern times, this doctrine of grace and virtue is reflected in the so-called helping professions, in which the gynecological holy ghosts infuse New Life into victim marys. The new supernatural life may be technological (for example, prostheses replacing breasts), chemical (for example, hormone replacement), or psychological (as when a woman is subjected to any of the various forms of behavior modification intended to replace deviancy with role-defined femininity). Hence, there is actually no natural (wild) state of femaleness that is legitimated/allowed in the Gynecological State, and this denial of female be-ing is the essence of its gynocidal intent. There are only two possibilities. First, there is a fallen state, formerly named sinful and symbolized by Eve, presently known as sick and typified in the powerless but sometimes difficult and problematic patient. Second, there is the restored/redeemed state of perfect femininity, formerly named saintly and symbolized by Mary, presently typified in the weak, "normal" woman whose normality is so elusive that it must constantly be re-enforced through regular check-ups, "preventive medicine," and perpetual therapy.

This man-made femininity, the normal state of feminitude, grows and swallows up the remnants of naturally wild femaleness by its supernatural/unnatural "life" (undeadness). It is force-fed by male foster mothers, the omnipresent holy ghosts. These healers help Unnature along by constant injections of the modern secular supernatural virtues, the vitamins of victimization. They instill ever greater faith in the doctor/god, in-

* This ideology allows no purely natural life for human beings, acknowledging only the "fallen" state and the "supernatural" state conferred through grace.

creasing the woman's will to believe (that is, inability to disbelieve) whatever he "reveals." After more and more injections, she willingly accepts not only all the standard doctored dogmas but also all the latest miracles of modern medicine. Her faith in the mind-gynecologist enables her to acquire ever greater faith in the body-gynecologist. These are, after all, only different masks (persons) of the same divinity. Moreover, all of these gynecological gods give her unnatural hope. This is not merely false—that is, unrealistic—hope. It is *wrong* hope, for it is warped. Its energy is dispersed into the blind alleys of the Masters' Maze. It is deeply distorted "hope" for Self-destructive solutions. Finally, the ghastly givers bestow upon their patient a remodeled version of christian charity, which inclines her to love them—god's ghosts—above all things, including herself. Under their tutelage she learns that she is lovable only to the extent that she can conform "to the image of god." In other words, she must allow herself to be modeled after their ghostly image of "woman."

THE SHRINKING OF FEMALE BE-ING

In the atrocities of this age of gynecological holy ghosts, the gynocidal intent of androcracy is acted out religiously, but more subtly and subliminally than in the sado-ritual sacrifices of "other" societies. The methods are refined to achieve ultimate ownership of female be-ing and power. The techniques are devised to achieve the final solution—*pre*possession. This is possession before a woman's original movement in be-ing can break through to consciousness. It involves depths of destruction that the term *possession* cannot adequately name. For someone to be possessed, she must first *be*. But the point here is precisely that the process of be-ing is broken on the wheel of processions. Prepossession means that be-ing is condensed to a static state, that it is frozen.

The condensation and freezing of female be-ing is nothing new. In the foregoing analyses of ancient and modern atrocities we have seen that gynocidal intent is endemic to patriarchy and its processions. However, in the new Ice Age of

Gynocidal Gynecology, the methods are "evolved" to execute this intent with maximum efficiency. One method used to reinforce the prepossession of women is *pre*occupation. The prepossessors invade and occupy a woman, treating her as territory before she can achieve autonomous, Self-centering process. Thus, the DES daughter whose mother had taken "harmless" drugs ordered by a gynecologist during pregnancy to prevent miscarriage has been preoccupied with cancerous (or potentially cancerous) cells. Her mind is preoccupied with anxiety—a preoccupation which increases with frequent check-ups, prescribed by "preventive" medicine, which function to increase anxiety and predispose her to sickness. Likewise, a woman subjected to compulsive breast examinations is preoccupied. So also is a woman preoccupied who obsessively examines herself in a mirror, seeing herself as a parcel of protuberances. She is looking through male lenses. Filled with inspired fixations, she checks to see if hair, eyebrows, lashes, lips, skin, breasts, buttocks, stomach, hips, legs, feet are "satisfactory." Thus the craving for cosmetics, including cosmetic surgery, should not be seen in isolation from the syndrome of gynecological preoccupation.

Gynecological/therapeutic/cosmetic preoccupation conceals the patient's emptiness from her Self. It drives the splintered self further into the state of fixation upon the parts that have become symbols of her lost and prepossessed Self. Reduced to the state of an empty vessel/vassal, the victim focuses desperately upon physical symptoms, therapeutically misinterpreted memories, and "appearance," frantically consuming medication, counsel, cosmetics, and clothing to cloak and fill her expanding emptiness. As she is transformed into an insatiable consumer, her transcendence is consumed and she consumes herself. This is enforced female complicity in gynocidal fetishism—the complicity of those programmed to repeat: "Let it be done unto me according to thy word."

Clearly, gynocide in the Age of Gynecology has deep roots in fetishism. Although fetishism has been a consistent feature in the sado-rituals of patriarchy (most obviously in Chinese footbinding and in African genital mutilation), it assumes omnipresent yet less obvious forms in the age of the holy helpers/healers of modern medicine. A-mazing the Sado-Ritual Syndrome as it manifests itself in American gynecology will require a preliminary analysis of this dis-order.

A feminist Searcher who reads definitions of fetishism in psychiatric encyclopedias and "studies" will find ejaculations of bias and self-contradictions everywhere. The authors of the entry on fetishism in the *Encyclopedia of Aberrations and Psychiatric Handbook,* for example, begin by discussing this as "a form of sexual deviation in which the *person's* sexual aim becomes attached to something that symbolizes that person's *love-object*" [emphases mine].[13] These sages go on to explain that the "something" may be an article of clothing or a non-genital (!) part of the body.* It is only later in the article that we find their admission that the fetishistic "person" is male and the "love-object" female, when we read that: ". . . the fetishist is attempting to escape from women. When he cannot do so he compromises by depreciating them. . . . he can then consider [his mate] superfluous." [14]

It would be a mistake for women searching for clues about fetishism to stop reading the article at this point, for we would be left with the knowledge that fetishists are male but might still assume that these constitute a perverted minority of males. Moving further into the maze of this analysis we come upon their admission that fetishism is so widespread in its implications that it includes acoustic stimulation, such as the pleasure obtained by listening to sexual stories. Immediately the processions of professional Peeping/Listening Toms appear before the feminist mind's eye, as we recall the parade of priestly, psychiatric, and ob/gyn Toms, whose main interests and concerns are sexual stories. By now we are ready to handle the concluding sentence of the article:

> Fetishism is quite often a *normal* and *necessary* component of the sexual lives of *all individuals* [emphases mine].

* It is typical of such literature that the "experts" restrict the meaning of the term *fetishism* to nongenital parts of the body, deceptively ignoring/denying the fact that men fetishize genitals.

A-mazing, we see not only that "individuals" means males, but that the "sexual deviation" described at the beginning of the article is considered "normal and necessary" for all males.

Searching for further clues concerning the nature of fetishism and its motivation, we can consult Rycraft's *A Critical Dictionary of Psychoanalysis*. The following description deserves some scrutiny:

> *Fetishists* can be said to regard their fetish as being "inhabited by a spirit," since the fetish is clearly associated with a *person* without being one, and as having "magical powers," since *its presence gives them the potency they otherwise lack* [emphases mine].[15]

Lest there still be any doubt concerning the sexual identity of the fetishist and of "the person" whose fetishized presence gives him the potency he otherwise lacks, one can consult other sources. The *Encyclopedia Britannica,* in its segment on psychiatric usage of the term *fetish,* is quite explicit:

> The condition occurs almost exclusively among men, and most of the objects used relate to the female body or female clothing.[16]

The question that arises, then, is: How do men within patriarchy manage to gain "potency" from fetishized female presence? Returning to Rycraft, we find the following helpful hint: ". . . the fetish has multiple meanings derived by CONDENSATION, DISPLACEMENT, AND SYMBOLIZATION from other objects."[17]

These three aspects of fetishism are threads to be traced through the analysis of the sado-ritual of American gynecology. At this point it is sufficient to note that the be-ing of women is condensed into particular parts/organs of her mind/body. A woman thus shrunken/frozen is manipulable/manageable. Her fetishizers feel potency/power which they otherwise lack, and exercise this negative and derivative potency to dis-place her energy further and further from her center, fragmenting her process, devouring her. Dis-placed, she becomes a consumer of re-placements, as in estrogen replacement therapy, cosmetic surgery, and psychiatric re-placement of her Self-identified natural history by man-made misinterpretations. These misinterpretations are magnified into a powerful symbol system which contains women, keeping them condensed and displaced, reducing them to replaceable replicas of the standardized Symbol: the Total/Totaled (fragmented) Woman, made and remade after the image projected by her god.

In order to see why the condensation, displacement, and symbolization syndrome has so important a function in the arsenal of ghostly gynecology, it is useful to consider Ernest Becker's statement that fetishism "merely encapsulates the general problem of making reality come alive for an organism with limited powers who must yet make contact with the world." [18] We should note that the fetishist, "the organism with limited powers," is by Becker's reluctant admission, male.[19] By wrenching this analysis out of Becker's context and applying it to gynecological fetishism, we can see that the fragmentation of female be-ing into condensed, displaced, highly charged symbolic parts is the method by which all the diverse gynecologists vampirize their feelings of effectiveness/potency from women.

I

Keeping the foregoing analysis in mind, I will discuss the rituals of American gynecology in relation to the pattern of the Sado-Ritual Syndrome. The obsession with purity is evident, and it is multileveled. There is, first of all, the obvious level of "cleanliness," or more precisely, asepsis (freedom from pathogenic microorganisms). Adrienne Rich has pointed out the stunning reversal which gynecological historians have inflicted upon our minds by referring to the "filthy" midwives who were replaced by antiseptic ob/gyns: "The midwife, who attended only women in labor, carried fewer disease bacteria with her than the physician." [20] Indeed. As Rich documents: "In the seventeenth century began a two centuries' plague of puerperal fever which was directly related to the increase in obstetric practice by men." [21] The hands of physician or surgeon often came directly from cases of disease to cases of childbirth. Hospitals were horror shows. Not until the second half of the nineteenth century, when doctors finally began to wash their hands, did the two hundred years of deadly blood-poisoning, euphemistically called puerperal or childbed fever, gradually come to an end.[22]

The current fixations upon asepsis, as they are manifested in the gynecological professions, are rooted in a much deeper level of obsession with purity. In the Gynecological Age, as in the past, women are identified as filthy and impure beings in the most radical sense. That is, we are stigmatized as ontologically impure and are therefore targets of hatred on this fundamental and all-pervasive level. Since this mythic mind-set controls the theories of doctors who "doctor" female flesh, these professional helpers continue to be carriers of iatrogenic disease. They still frequently bring the same sorts of "gifts" to their patients as their predecessors: infection, mutilation, and a slow, painful, degrading death. Thus, iatrogenic disease is *the* radical impurity endemic to the medical profession itself.

Ultimately, the intent of The Gynecologists is to purify women and society of our Selves. In other words, their intent is to castrate, that is, to deprive women of vigor and vitality, and finally of life itself. As I have noted, the term *castrate* is from the same root as the terms *chaste, chasten, chastise,* and *caste,* namely the Sanskrit *śasati,* meaning "he cuts to pieces." A powerful and indispensable means by which the gynecological purification/castration of women is accomplished is the fetishization of female parts. The gynecological holy ghosts, themselves faded and faked copies of the "Holy Ghost," who is the inverted mythic Copy of Female Divinity, cannot bear to stand respectfully before earthly manifestations of female creative power, that is, of the Goddess within women. Thus they put women *beneath* them, supine, on examination tables, delivery tables, psychiatrists' couches. Clearly, women should be in upright positions, in order to be *agents,* helping themselves. From their lewd, lofty positions the frustrated gynecological fetishists attempt to wrench from female power of be-ing a *feeling* of potency which they pervert into the negation and destruction of women.

In 1897 the *Encyclopedia Britannica* (as cited in the *Oxford English Dictionary*) explained: "If the wishes of the worshipper be not granted . . . the fetish . . . is kicked, stamped on, dragged through the mud." Applying this to the gynecological worshiper and would-be Goddess, we see that his wishes for female creativity are inevitably frustrated, since he cannot *become* female.* He then expresses his rage and frustration by technologically, chemically, and verbally kicking, stamping on, and dragging his fetish (fragmented parts of the female anatomy and psyche) through his medicinal and mind-molding muck.

An example of this fetish destruction is the recent hysterectomy epidemic in the United States fostered by the medical male mothers. Deborah Larned has pointed out that for several years gynecologists have been promoting this operation, which is major surgery, as "a simple solution for everything from backaches to contraception." [23] To legitimate this form of castration, well-known gynecologists resort to describing the uterus by such expressions as "a possible breeding ground for cancer" [24] and as "a potentially lethal organ." [25]

In this rapist society, which grants the hysterical hysterectomy advocates license to practice medicine, we must ask just *who* are the possessors of "potentially lethal organs," both biological and technological? This reversal is consistent with the symbol system of the world of holy ghosts fixated on technological and spiritual male motherhood. Under the tutelage of this system, doctors frequently bully women into believing that they "need" a hysterectomy, failing to tell their patients "that the death rate for hysterectomy itself . . . is, in fact, *higher* than the death rate for uterine/cervical cancer." [26]

Since, as we have seen, there is a lecherous link-up between body-gynecology and mind-gynecology, it is not surprising that in 1977 the executive vice-president of the American

* Transsexualism, which Janice Raymond has shown to be essentially a male problem, is an *attempt* to change males into females, whereas in fact no male can assume female chromosomes and life history/experience. The perpetual need of the castrated males known as transsexuals for hormonal "fixes" to maintain the appearance of femaleness is a sign of their contrived and artifactual condition. See *The Transsexual Empire: The Making of the She-Male* (Boston: Beacon Press, 1979).

Medical Association opined that hysterectomy is a cure for unmanageable fear. Dr. James Sammons told a congressional hearing that while tubal ligation (a minor operation) often will not relieve "pregnophobic" anxiety, hysterectomy will. He announced that "the absence of a uterus is *prima facie* evidence that pregnancy is impossible," and added that "the same anxiety relief justifies a hysterectomy for a woman with an extreme fear of cervical cancer." [27] Of course, the AMA official speaking for all the gynecologists who favor cutting out fear neglected to point out that the fear is to a large extent caused by doctors themselves. The doctors' doctrine that women should be purified even of anxieties by radical surgery is an important and deadly practical application of the murderous myth of female ontological impurity.

Yet another application of this myth is the medically masterminded maze of lethal "choices" among surgical, chemical, and mechanical solutions to The Contraceptive Problem. It is obvious to Hags that few gynecologists recommend to their heterosexual patients the most foolproof of solutions, namely Mister-ectomy. It is women who choose to be agents of be-ing who have pointed out that tried and true, and therefore, taboo, "method." The Spinsters who propose this way by our be-ing, liv-ing, speak-ing can do so with power precisely because we are not preoccupied with ways to get off the hook of the heterosexually defined contraceptive dilemma.

However, all females, from four-month-old babies to octogenarians, are potential victims in a rapist society whose male members function as "lethal organs." * It is therefore neces-

* This is not entirely metaphorical. Medical journals present evidence of the physical reality: "Since the observation that cancer of the uterine cervix is almost unknown in nuns, it has been established that sexual activity is a major factor in the genesis of cervical cancer." The author is referring specifically to heterosexual activity. See Valerie Beral, "Cancer of the Cervix: A Sexually Transmitted Infection?" *The Lancet,* May 25, 1974, pp. 1037–40. See also Albert Singer, Ph.D., Bevan L. Reid, M.D., and Malcolm Coppelson, M.D., "A Hypothesis: The Role of a High-Risk Male in the Etiology of Cervical Carcinoma," *American Journal of Obstetrics and Gynecology,* Vol. 126, No. 1 (September 1, 1976), pp. 110–15. The authors maintain that evidence has led them "to propose that a carcinogen is present in the male sperm" [of the

sary for Spinsters/Lesbians to provide the most lucid analysis possible in this State of Siege. Precisely as defiant deviants, as Daughters of the healers burned as witches because they were "indigestible," we can take on the label Impure as a badge of honor, for we defy the pure image of perfect femininity. As Anti-Marys whose prehistoric sources are the ante-Marian Goddesses, we are in a position to see Mary, Eve, Athena, the Total Woman as fetishes formed from fragmented female divinity. The Total Woman is the Total Fetish. Be-ing implies deviating from this fetid model, reclaiming independent female divinity. Spinsters who are choosing be-ing are ecstatically moving outside the space of the patriarchal holding pattern. From the vantage point of Journeyers into the natural Background of our Selves, we can expose and judge all pseudochoices and pseudosolutions foisted upon women by the foreground fetishists. In order to do so effectively, we must analyze the legitimating logic as well as the techniques employed by the purifiers/castrators of women.

The Mystique of "Moral Purity"

Clearly the project of purifying society of women has been problematic for gynecologists, since all women are ontologically impure according to the implicit assumptions of patriarchal myth. To follow through too rapidly on the logical conclusion of these assumptions—that is, the Final Solution—would mean premature extinction of women before technological replacements for us could be "discovered." Not surprisingly, therefore, the Planners (e.g., physicians, theologians, ethicists) formulated a flexible concept of impurity which functions to justify the *partial* cutting out of women from society through the magic of labeling. The concept of "moral impurity" (with variations on this theme) has served their purposes. In 1866, Dr. Isaac Ray stated:

"high-risk" male] which acts on a "target cell" in the cervix. For further evidence see the extensive bibliographies attached to both of these articles.

In the sexual evolution, in pregnancy, in the parturient period, in lactation, strange thoughts, extraordinary feelings, unseasonable appetites, criminal impulses, may haunt a mind at other times innocent and pure.[28]

Since "sexual evolution" takes place throughout the life-span (including fetal development) one wonders when the "other times," that is, of female innocence and purity, might be. Obviously, since according to such views all women hover on the edge of madness and crime, their self-appointed caretakers must be ready with knives at all times.

Ray was not an isolated case. We have already noted that in 1848 Dr. Charles Meigs had informed his gynecological pupils that the female organs exert "strange and secret influences" even on "the very soul of woman." He concluded from this that gynecological study must not be purely medical, "but psychological and moral." [29] The gynecologist as priest, guru, omniscient Understander and Guide of the female soul (condensed and displaced into her sexual organs) is thus given his Holy Orders and Great Commission to go forth and cut. Gardner and other gynecologists of his age saw masturbation, contraception, abortion, and orgasm as sexual transgressions which were in the ultimate analysis functions of faulty sexual organs. Their theme song and panacea was "cut it out."

Cutting it out has taken a number of lucrative forms, rewarding not only financially but also psychologically to sadistic surgeons. Clitoridectomies were approved among the doctors as their cure for female masturbation. Of course this functioned also as a basic cure for orgasm. This operation, wholeheartedly endorsed and practiced by such nineteenth-century male-factors of women as J. Marion Sims, was still performed well into the twentieth century.[30] Another operation, known as "female castration," or "oophorectomy" or "normal ovariotomy" (removing of ovaries), was a widespread medical mania between 1880 and 1900 and began to decline during the first decade of this century—although "women were still being castrated for psychological disorders as late as 1946." [31] Naturally—that is, unnaturally—this mutilation provided a solution to the problems of contraception and abortion. It was also a way of "taking care" of women deemed unfit to breed. Castration, like impregnation, functioned as a way to control women's sexuality and to punish them, causing pain and disablement.

In an astonishing article published in 1906, entitled "The Fetich of the Ovary," Ely Van de Warker, M.D., bemoaned the epidemic of unnecessary removal of ovaries, pointing out that this had become a "stock operation," and claiming that he had yet to see a woman made better in health by this procedure. His criticism of the practice reflects the ideology of purity in yet a different dimension. This doctor/savior of ovaries gave the following rationale:

> A woman's ovaries belong to the commonwealth; she is simply their custodian. Without them her life is stultified. Making a guess at figures I believe it to be within the mark to say that the one hundred and fifty thousand physicians of the United States have sterilized one hundred and fifty thousand women. Some of this large number have openly boasted, when the lunacy was at its height, that they have removed from fifteen hundred to two thousand ovaries. Assuming that each of these women would have become the mother of three chlidren, we have a direct loss of five hundred and fifty thousand for the first generation and one million six hundred and fifty thousand in the second generation.[32]

This "benefactor" of women had indeed fetishized ovaries, as had the physicians whose "lunacy" compelled them to castrate thousands of women. Unlike the castrators, whose intent was to condense female be-ing into ovaries and then obtain a sense of power by purifying society of these unwanted "objects," this fetishist wanted condensed female be-ing to serve a single pure purpose: breeding huge numbers for the "commonwealth." In both cases, that of the fanatic castrators of women and that of fanatic impregnators like Van de Warker, the intent is to keep women morally pure—that is, purified of an autonomous Self: Selfless. The pain inflicted upon women, both as mutilated "objects" and as professionally controlled breeders, is not even mentioned by these skilled practitioners of sado-ritual.*

The same fetishistic fixations on moral purity characterize contemporary gynecologists and the legitimating -ologists, who write about the "moral problems" posed by women in "society." Thus it is interesting to compare the 1906 statement cited above with the following statement concerning abortion, published by biologist Marc Lappé in 1975:

> If the mother's right to privacy overrides the fetus's right to survive prior to its ability to exist outside the womb, then it would seem that *the state has seriously reduced its prerogative to regulate other forms of maternal behavior* which may compromise fetal development, such as allowing her fetus to be subject to experimentation, or smoking, or taking harmful drugs or abortifacients, during the same period [emphasis mine].[33]

The author of this statement is of course concerned with protecting the "rights of the fetus." The context of his discussion was the U.S. Supreme Court's declaration that the fetus need not be considered a person in the whole sense prior to viability. Like Van de Warker, this contemporary caretaker of women's organs openly declares the (male-controlled) commonwealth/state to be possessor and regulator of women, whose be-ing is displaced and condensed into the function of breeding for the state. As in the case of the earlier author, his intent is to purify women of our autonomous Selves. Thus, forced fertility, like forced sterility, is used to break the wills of women, destroying vigor and vitality. That is, it is a means of castrating women.

We have seen that the ovariotomy mania was superseded by the hysterectomy mania. The earlier practitioners of female castration were followed by bolder butchers. Ovariotomy, de-

* According to Merriam-Webster, in its etymological roots the term *skill* is akin to the Goth. *skilja,* meaning "butcher," and to the Lith. *skélti,* meaning "to split." Although it is not intrinsic to skills as such that they be destructive, a necrophilic society "naturally" rewards those most adept at body-splitting and mind-splitting skills, e.g., surgeons, military scientists and strategists, and schizophrenically specialized academicians.

scribed by its critic Van de Warker as "ridiculously easy" (easy for whom?) has been replaced by a bigger castration business. This is given support and legitimacy by the psychiatric castrators, who, drawing upon their inexhaustible reversal reflex mechanisms, manipulate their female patients into believing that they, their mothers, and women in general are castrators of *men*. This reversal rivals the story of Eve's birth from Adam for top rank among the Great Hoaxes of history.

Contemporary gynecology is not content with purifying women of their uteruses. It is obvious that there is a breast surgery craze, and that this is connected with the breast fetishism of the entire culture. Sadistic surgery is targeted at that which symbolizes the female to the fetishist. It keeps women pure, that is, terrified, victimized, docile. However, this is not enough, for women thus mutilated must conform to the image of pure femininity by attempting to look "normal." Hence the market for specialists in "postmastectomy reconstruction of the breast." [34] Moreover, in the telling words of one plastic surgeon: "Plastic surgeons have wandered into the field of tumors of the female breast." [35] The same author, who opposes unnecessary mastectomies, offers the following cancer-promoting advice:

> Self-examination, regular examination by a qualified breast surgeon, mammograms, xerograms, and thermograms still remain the best defense against breast cancer.

This is, of course, an effective formula for keeping women in a state of prepossession and preoccupation.

While the Gynecological State requires that women be purified of their fetishized female "parts," it also frantically forces the possessors of such parts to labor at their assigned role of "reproduction" (a mechanical term which anticipates the ultimate in androcentric "motherhood": xerox cloning). The point here is not essentially whether an individual woman does or does not have babies, but that the True Parent, the holy ghost, represented by his reproduced xerox copies, the gynecological ghosts, maintains absolute control over her "choice." Women, particularly nonwhite and other low-income women, are the unwilling victims not only of sterilization but of forced motherhood—a fact demonstrated repeatedly, as in the 1977 U.S. Supreme Court decisions allowing Congress and state legislatures to ban funds for elective abortions.[36] Forced motherhood, like forced sterilization, is essentially female castration, for it means domestication and deprivation of female vitality, both physical and spiritual. As we have seen, this "cutting to pieces" of women's autonomous wills is deeply related to the perverse patriarchal will for male motherhood.

Chemical Cures for Moral Impurity

In recent decades, gynecology has further refined its methods for purifying women. Its High Priests have invented chemical cures for the disease of femaleness. High on the list of these is Diethylstilbestrol (DES), a nonsteroidal estrogen. Between 1943 and 1970, DES was widely prescribed in the United States to prevent miscarriage. Estimates of the numbers of women who received this drug range from 500,000 to possibly 2,000,000.[37] Although it was not effective for preventing miscarriage, in another sense it was horribly effective. It is now widely known that DES causes precancerous conditions and cancer in daughters of the women who took this drug during their pregnancies. Indeed, an estimated 90 percent of the young women exposed to DES have adenosis, the development of abnormal vaginal and cervical cells, a condition which may lead to cancer. It is not yet known to what extent these abnormal cells will be affected by pregnancy and menopause. Both the known effects of DES and the probability of further complications have been widely publicized. Thus pregnant women who were brainwashed into taking this drug to ensure having offspring are now chastised by the knowledge that they were unwittingly instrumental in the damaging of their daughters. Together with their daughters they exist in a state of anxiety.

The doctors whose fetishism took the form of fixation upon fertility (ensuring that women carried through on their pregnancies, conforming to the pure purpose of breeding) ceeded to some extent in "purifying" the daughters of these same women of their health, sense of well-being, and—in some cases—of life itself. All of the DES daughters have to a great extent been purified of their autonomy, for the anxiety implanted in their minds together with the abnormal cells implanted in their vaginas makes them dependent upon the godly gynecologists. Like the holy ghost, who was believed to inspire the faithful with the "Gift of Fear," these motherhood specialists ejaculate fear and fearful disease into their dependent prey.

Writing of nineteenth-century gynecologists, Barker-Benfield notes: "There is . . . ample evidence that gynecologists saw their knives cutting into women's generative tract as a form of sexual intercourse." [38] In the mid-twentieth century, this sadosexual intercourse assumed also more subtle forms through the "miracles" of chemistry, penetrating through one generation of women into the next (and the next and the next?). The sickening symbolic "semen" swallowed by DES mothers "under doctor's orders" has penetrated the vaginas of their daughters, as a deadly poison, engendering death. Moreover, this disguised ejaculation of chemical semen is the fatal foreplay preceding surgical sexual intercourse, that is, castration.* Ironically, many women cast into this chastened patient role feel gratitude to their professional "love-makers." [39]

There is, of course, more than this to the irony of the DES syndrome. Diethylstilbestrol, originally ordered by the Master Mothers as an antimiscarriage pill, is widely used in the 1970s as a postcoital pill to immediately interrupt pregnancy. Kay Weiss points out:

> Although vaginal cancer in daughters exposed to DES in utero provided the clinical evidence to secure a Food and Drug Administration ban on DES as an additive to cattle feed, the FDA approved a new use of DES as a "morning-after pill" contraceptive

* Of special importance, also, is surgical "caressing" of the breasts of women with knives. There is good reason to think that the miracles of modern chemistry produce the clientele required for this professional "petting."

even though the contraceptive contains 833,000 times the amount of DES banned for human consumption in beef.[40]

One of the excruciating twists in the history of the DES massacre is the fact that among the thousands of uninformed young women used as guinea pigs for the "morning-after pill" there were many DES daughters.* This group of young women, of course, were/are, in the bland jargon of the professional journals, "at particular risk." [41]

Yet another noteworthy feature of the DES destruction racket is the following fact: Women forcibly subjected to sexual intercourse, that is, rape victims, who go to hospitals in pain, degradation, and desperation after their experience of ultimate violation are "helped" with megadoses of this chemical. They are the beneficiaries of the treatment meted out to victims of a rapist society, receiving murderous medicine for the condition resulting from their "unchaste behavior."

From the very beginning of the damaging DES history there has been more male moralism at work than immediately meets the eye. The DES mothers were ordered to take this carcinogenic "cure" to prevent miscarriage, that is, to prevent involuntary abortion. Some pregnant women were given DES routinely, without being informed concerning its alleged purpose.[42] That is, the doctors and not they decided that there be no "spontaneous" abortion. Moreover, there surely were subtle psychic consequences for the "expectant mothers" who *were* informed that this medicine was prescribed because they "threatened to abort." As many women know, there is a subtle interflow of energy and intentionality between mind/spirit and body. It is highly probable that in many cases pregnant women who in the deep dimensions of their psyches do not want to bear a child (perhaps not at this time, perhaps never) solve their problem in a natural way, that is, through a spontaneous abortion, which requires no external act on the part of the woman—no "medicine," no instruments, no "accident" (such

* For years university "health services" and private physicians have liberally been dispensing DES without disclosing its experimental status.

as falling).* In such cases, the degree of "conscious" intentionality is not measurable or even relevant. When, however, the DES-dosing doctors named the condition ("threatening to abort") and prescribed "medicine," they preyed upon the false conscience/consciousness embedded in women by patriarchy's institutions, eliciting feelings of guilt and of "desire for a child" which such women "should" have.

Another variation on the theme of chemical cures for female impurity is the ritual of estrogen replacement therapy, contemporary gynecology's response to the threat presented to males by menopause. As Emily Culpepper has shown, the history of attitudes toward menstruation from ancient times to the present demonstrates male fear, envy, and hatred of women.[43] The menstruating woman is called filthy, sick, unbalanced, ritually impure. In patriarchy her bloodshed is made into a badge of shame, a sign of her radical ontological impurity. It is consistent with the logic of the woman loathers' doublethink that the cessation of menstruation is also horrifying. Since every woman's entire be-ing is fetishized by men, that is, condensed, displaced, and symbolized in her sexual organs and functions, the cessation of any of these functions implies Female Power of Absence. Since the frustrated "worshipper's" desire for control is threatened, fetishized menopausal and postmenopausal women must be "kicked, stamped on, and dragged through the mud."

When women become free of the possibility of impregnation, one of the time-honored means of imprisoning females is removed. What frustrates The Jailors is the fact that freedom is attained not by the "divine" acts of sadistic surgical castrators but by natural processes of female biology. Freedom from pregnancy is evil/impure in the Gynecological State if it is not "created" by the surgeon's knife or by the doctor's chemicals. The postmenopausal woman is a potential escapee, deviant, Crone. Therefore, she must be cured.

* I am not saying that this analysis applies to all women who have miscarriages. This assumption would be far too simple, and the point is that women *are* naturally complex and have many innate as well as learnable ways of problem-solving which are not only ignored but blunted and blocked by male medicine.

The woman perceived as threatening to become a free/wild Crone is inundated with propaganda to convince her that menopause is a sickness which must be "treated." However, in order to be adequately convincing, the persuaders must first persuade themselves. Thus an editorial in the *New England Journal of Medicine* pontificates that "the unaltered hormonal state of the *untreated menopause* [is a] possible contributory factor in the causation of cancer [emphasis mine]." [44] Implying that menopause is carcinogenic, the medical messiahs neglect to mention that this is a universal and natural process in women, found in areas of the globe where cancer is unknown. These physicians, who are themselves "contributory factors in the causation of cancer," use a malignant misconception of menopause to support the idea that more "knowledge" (i.e., experimentation upon women) is needed to find a "safe type of hormone replacement therapy."

Of course most of the women who are the gynecologists' guinea pigs do not read medical journals. Instead they are given patronizing bad advice and moronic reading material. A physician-authored booklet entitled *The Menopause: A New Life of Happiness and Contentment* is a typical example of such idiot-ology.[45] The booklet, illustrated with cartoons of middle-aged women, asks such questions as: "Does estrogen cause cancer?" The professional response, accompanying a cartoon of a woman happily popping a pill from a bottle marked "Estrogen," is "Only in mice." To the question, "How long should a menopausal woman take hormones?" the doctor responds to the smiling woman: "For the rest of your life." If the woman follows doctor's orders, this will probably not be long.

The pamphlet just cited was published in 1969. It might be objected that the major medical admission of the carcinogenic nature of estrogen replacement therapy did not occur until 1975, with the publication of "findings" in the *New England Journal of Medicine* linking the use of exogenous estrogen and endometrial carcinoma. However, it had long been known that estrogen replacement therapy was very risky.[46] Moreover, the response of gynecologists to the 1975 "findings" demonstrates that their views remained unchanged.

Particularly interesting was the comment of Dr. Donald C. Smith in the *New York Times* (December 4, 1975). He is reported to have said: "This is an extremely valuable drug and I hope they don't take it off the market, but we have to start using it more cautiously." *Dr. Smith had directed one of the studies revealing the carcinogenic properties of the drug and had co-authored one of the NEJM articles exposing it.*[47]

The *New York Times* (December 5, 1975) also reported views of other gynecologists around the country. All of the doctors contacted after the estrogen exposé refused to change their attitudes, despite the evidence. Moreover, all emphasized that every patient treated with estrogen should be thoroughly examined every six months. The ultimate aim, the purification of society by eliminating "indigestible elements," that is, potential Crones, is revealed (that is, both veiled and unveiled) in the following statement attributed to Dr. Rubin Clay:

> I think of the menopause as a deficiency disease, like diabetes. Most women develop some symptoms whether they are aware of them or not, so I prescribe estrogens for virtually all menopausal women for an indefinite period.

It is important for Crone-ologists to note that this false chronology is manufactured and inflicted upon women by the gynecological time-keepers.

It is also of obvious significance that other lethal purifying medicine is working to ensure an even earlier extinction of women. Now that the model of female moral purity has been converted into pure sexual availability, the Purifiers have produced The Pill. This is known to increase risks of thrombophlebitis, pulmonary embolism, cerebral thrombosis and hemorrhage, myocardial infarction, gallbladder disease. The Pill also causes a decrease in glucose tolerance and serious depression. There is every reason to suspect that it increases the risk of cancer.[48] Estrogens are now also offered to American women for a wide variety of other uses, including treatment of acne, excess facial hair, menstrual tensions, depressions, and excess breast milk.[49] Premenopausal Pill-popping thus prepares the way for premature death, the ultimate purification.

Purification by the Mind-Gynecologists

This syndrome of Male Motherhood and female castration—rooted in patriarchal myth, specifically in christian myth—is re-enacted in the sado-rituals of the mind-gynecologists, which I shall call by their common name, "therapists." In order to see how the first element of this syndrome—obsession with purity—is acted out by the therapists, it is helpful to call to mind some essentials of the christian sacramental system.

The first of seven sacraments officially recognized in the roman catholic system was baptism, or rebirth to supernatural life. As we have seen, the church taught that this sacrament caused the infusion of sanctifying grace and of the supernatural virtues, and this mythic paradigm is re-enacted in the various forms of gynecology. At this point in our Crone-logical analysis, it is important to understand how the "cleansing waters" of baptism have been translated into therapeutic ritual.

According to this belief system, although original sin is washed away by baptism, and sanctifying grace (New Life) is infused, the faithful thus redeemed are still in a precarious state. Baptism cannot wash away the remains of sin, that is, darkness of intellect, weakness of will, and inclination to concupiscence. Thus the faithful are by no means finally cured by this one treatment; they must remain under pastoral care throughout their earthly lives. They require continual fixes of actual grace* through reception of other sacraments, such as penance (confession) and holy eucharist, through prayers, and other good deeds. If they commit a mortal sin, they can be restored to the state of sanctifying grace through penance. Even if such a serious lapse does not occur, they require injections of actual grace as a spiritual preventive medicine.

Applying this paradigm to psychiatry and the various therapeutic professions, we see that a woman's initial surrender of her private Self to the mind-gynecologist is the condition for his cleansing of her original sin, that is, of her original Self-

* "Actual grace" is defined in the Baltimore Catechism as "supernatural help of God which enlightens our mind and strengthens our will to do good and to avoid evil."

moving Self. This Self-denial places her in a state of therapeutic grace, purified of Originality. She is reborn as a therapeutic creation, a nonself to be perpetually serviced by the holy ghost. She must re-turn to him regularly because she still (as long as she is alive) has the "remains of original sin," that is, of her original Self. Thus she still has "darkness of intellect" (read: occasional glimmers of insight), "weakness of will" (read: some potential to choose freedom), and "inclination to concupiscence" (read: inclinations to Self-identified integrity of sensuality). Thus she cannot be cured by a single treatment but must be strengthened—that is, debilitated—by constant infusions of therapeutic "actual grace." After her initial baptism into therapy, therefore, she must go to the secular holy ghost for repeated confession/cleansing, that is, erosion, of her soul. In connection with her ritual cleansings, she is fed the eucharist of her therapeutic host—deceptive words which are transformed into her own body and blood. If she responds well to these treatments, she expresses gratitude to her "helper." She is taught prayers (formulas) and good deeds (conditioned responses and behaviors) which will bring peace (death) to her soul.

Since no penitent/patient is thoroughly cleansed so long as she is living, there is always the possibility that she will lose therapeutic sanctifying grace through "mortal sin." According to the Angelic Doctor, Thomas Aquinas, most mortal sins can be forgiven, but there is one sin which is essentially unpardonable, that is, the sin of blasphemy against the "Holy Ghost." However, even in the cases of those who commit this "unpardonable sin," an all-powerful and merciful god "sometimes, by a miracle, so to speak, restores health to such men." [50] Blasphemy against the holy ghosts of gynecology, especially of psychiatry and psychotherapy, is also almost unpardonable. Yet we can be sure that the brain-scrubbing merciful Mister Cleans of these professions will try every miracle-cure, so to speak, to restore spiritual health to such women.* In their

* The reader will recall from the chapter on European witchburning that the contemporary witch-hunting psychiatrist, Gregory Zilboorg, allies himself with theologians in blaming the witches who "actually

efforts to work such miracles they enter into the sacrament of holy matrimony, the State of Holy Wedlock/Deadlock with the priests whose superstitious beliefs they openly despise and secretly embrace. The product of their union is the re-born robotized woman.

In order to effect this re-birth—that is, castration—of women, the therapeutic "mothers" know that it is essential to discredit real mothers. All Hags are familiar with the omnipresent "blaming the mother" syndrome among psychotherapists from Freud downward. C. G. Jung, whose theories are pernicious traps which often stop women in the initial stages of mind-journeying, displays with arresting arrogance another way of discrediting women who are mothers. He simply flattens them into projection screens. We read:

> My own view differs from that of other medico-psychological theories principally in that I attribute to the *personal mother* only a limited etiological significance. That is to say, all those influences which the literature describes as being exerted on the children do not come from the mother herself, but rather from the archetype projected upon her, which gives her a mythological background and invests her with authority and numinosity [emphasis mine].[51]

Having reduced women to nothing, Jung blames them for everything. The reader is subliminally led to accept the idea that mothers and not men (such as Jung) are the castrators of women. This renders invisible the fact of female castration by males. Thus, describing a daughter who has a "mother-complex," Jung writes:

> The daughter leads a shadow existence, often visibly sucked dry by her mother, and she prolongs her mother's life by a sort of continuous blood transfusion. . . . Despite their shadowiness and passivity,

---

muttered profanities in the churches" and describes sacrilege against "God, Christ, and the Church" as "typical phases of a compulsion neurosis" (*The Medical Man and the Witch During the Renaissance* [New York: Cooper Square, 1969], pp. 62–63). This alliance should be noted by Crone-ologists.

> they [these daughters] command a high price on the marriage market. First, they are so empty that a man is free to impute to them anything he fancies. In addition, they [these women] are so unconscious that the unconscious puts out countless invisible feelers, veritable octopus tentacles, that suck up all masculine projections; and this pleases men enormously.[52]

Jung's reversals should be obvious to Hags. He frankly admits that the daughters' condition of being "sucked dry" is a male requirement for marriageability. Just as footbinding was required by the men of China, so is mindbinding a universal demand of patriarchal males, who want their women to be empty so that they will be forced to suck male projections/ejections, becoming pre-occupied, pre-possessed. This deprivation of vitality is required by patriarchal males who "*command* [this] high price" which "pleases men enormously." On the level of body-gynecology we have seen what women are commanded to "suck up": The Poisonous Pill, carcinogenic exogenous estrogens, DES, et cetera, ad mortem.

It is clear that the discrediting of the "personal mother" by the therapist is required for his baptismal cleansing of the daughter, which makes her also vulnerable to chemotherapists and surgeons. Since the sado-rituals of the psychotherapist are deeply mythic, it is not surprising that Jung names his mortal enemy in mythic terms. He writes of Demeter (and those of her kind) that "she compels the gods by her stubborn persistence to grant her the right of possession over her daughter." [53] Thus the threatened therapeutic god expresses his horror that Demeter can *compel* the male divinities. At the same time he misnames the situation, calling her righteous wrath "stubborn," and her right to authentic relation to her daughter a "right of possession" which the gods grudgingly "grant her." Identifying with the gods, particularly with Pluto, who had abducted Demeter's daughter, Persephone, Jung says of the divine rapist husband that "he had to surrender his wife every year to his mother-in-law for the summer season." [54] With this semantic sleight of hand, the Divine Daughter is re-born as "his wife" and the Divine Mother is baptised as "his mother-in-law." Thus the therapist proclaims his solidarity with the rapist, identifying himself, as many women have noted, as the/rapist.

A primary goal of gynecology, as we have seen, is to purify society of Crones, that is, to prevent the becoming of Crones. This Compleat Castration requires a conspiracy of holy ghosts, a mating of body-gynecologists and mind-gynecologists. We have noted that the body-gynecologists were the first to institute the Great Castration Operation, arriving on the scene just in time to thwart the threat posed by the "first wave" of feminism, and later enlisting the aid of the specialized Mind Cleaners. The Body Men however, have never fully relinquished their early self-appointed prerogatives over "the very soul of woman," illustrated in the late nineteenth century by S. Weir Mitchell's combination cure for disorderly women, consisting of castration (ovariotomy) and "rest cure." * Barker-Benfield's description of the latter is arresting:

> Mitchell's "rest-cure" consisted of the patient's descent into womb-like dependence, then rebirth, liquid food, weaning, up-bringing and reeducation by a model parental organization—a trained female nurse entirely and unquestioningly the agent firmly implementing the orders of the more distant and totally authoritative male, i.e., the doctor in charge. The patient was returned to her menfolk's management, recycled and taught to make the will of the male her own.[55]

This "rest-cure" aspect of Mitchell's work has, of course, been assumed in large measure by the Mind Menders. But the

* It is horrifying to read in the autobiography of Charlotte Perkins Gilman that this great feminist activist, lecturer, and author was sent to Mitchell, the prominent "nerve specialist." He prescribed that she devote herself to domestic work and to her child, confine herself to, at most, two hours of intellectual work a day, and "never touch pen, brush, or pencil as long as you live." See *The Living of Charlotte Perkins Gilman: An Autobiography* (New York: Appleton Century, 1935), p. 96. One result of her medical experiences was her writing of the story, "The Yellow Wallpaper," an exquisite exposé of medicine. Most women thus treated, needless to say, did not survive to tell their story to the world and to struggle for the cause of women. In her autobiography, Gilman states that "the inevitable result" of Mitchell's treatment is "progressive insanity" (p. 119).

point is that the division of "labor" between these two classes of gynecologists is not altogether clear and distinct. The holy ghosts can separate and blend their shadowy forms according to the requirements of expediency. As shadows and reflections of each other, they perform the same purifying rites on different altars. Mitchell & Sons counsel and advise, enforcing various forms of rest cures. Psychotherapists, in their turn, follow the example of Freud, who wrote: "I will simply claim for myself the rights of the gynaecologist—or rather much more modest ones." [56] Obviously, the "modest" rights claimed by Freud were in fact even more exorbitant than those claimed by gynecologists. His aim was to invade women's minds, exposing their deepest secrets.

Both sorts of gynecological ghosts function as confidants for women, purifying them of their privacy. Since many women confide to their gynecologists and therapists private matters which they do not share with any woman, the team of holy ghosts keeps women from sharing secrets with each other and thus purifies society of female bonding. This team thus constitutes a modern secular church, blocking the way to feminist movement/communication. While the body doctors offer their faithful The Pill as daily holy communion, the mind doctors offer weekly confession.

As shadows of each other, the two branches of gynecological ghostdom trick the mind in parallel ways. We have seen that the Body Men offer a variety of bad choices to women within the maze of The Contraceptive Problem. Similarly, the mass proliferation of "schools" and forms of psychotherapy, many of which are in apparent contradiction to each, offers a variety of choices among therapies, but not the option to opt out of therapy altogether. So also, both convert the masses to their belief system, encouraging what theologians call a "leap of faith." The Pill-users, estrogen-takers, and surgical patients *will* themselves to believe the doctor. So also, the patients/clients of therapists *will* to believe the Mind-Molders. Both types of gynecologists encourage a false risk, the pseudorisk of always saying yes to the professional, rather than the risk of saying No to such authority and going on to find woman-identified solutions.

The mythic archetype of the psychotherapist is the feminine god Dionysus, the boundary-violator who invaded women's minds, driving them into the madness of forgetfulness and frenzy. These Dionysian doctors purify women's minds of their real history, fragmenting speech into frenetic babble. On the material plane their physician cohorts also coerce women into forgetfulness of their own Self-interest. Such coercion is exemplified in the forcing of harmful drugs upon women in labor—drugs which are described as pain relievers but in fact block memory. (Scopolamine, for example, erases the memory of pain while inducing frenzied behavior during labor.) The women thus drugged vow that they experienced no discomfort and continue with more pregnancies without knowledge of the pain—their pain and frenzy having been kept secret from themselves. The use of such Dionysian drugs is both legitimated and reflected by the therapy/theology of deep boundary violation.

II

The second aspect of the Sado-Ritual Syndrome—total erasure of their own responsibility by the ritual destroyers—is evident in both species of gynecologists. I shall begin by examining some self-absolutions of body-gynecologists. One obvious form which this takes is violent denial that physicians are agents of destruction. Thus Adrienne Rich discusses the brutal treatment meted out to such medical critics as Oliver Wendell Holmes and Ignaz Philipp Semmelweis when they exposed the fact that puerperal fever was carried from physician to patient to patient. The response of their profession was outrage at the very idea that the hands of the physician could be unclean.[57]

Another familiar method of erasure of responsibility in professional language is the tactic which Julia Stanley has named "agent deletion."[58] This can be achieved through the use of deceptive adjectives. For example, "*untreated menopause*" implies a need for treatment. Again, gynecologists apply the term *necessary* to a forceps delivery which becomes "necessary" only within the context of anti-woman ob/gyn practices. They also deceptively use constructions such as the passive voice.

Thus the physician who proclaims that "estrogen replacement therapy is required" neglects to explain *by whom* it is required.

The gods of gynecology also erase their own responsibility by obliterating women's own words and their context, and recording lies. Thus it is not unusual, in cases of patients who have been told that they "need" a hysterectomy, that their medical chart announces: "Patient requests hysterectomy."

The ideology which justifies such methods has several important threads, which I shall begin here to unsnarl. The most essential thread, to which all others are tied, can be simply summarized in the maxim: "It's God's will." In the judeo-christian tradition this mystification/mythification of sado-masochism is expressed in the biblical words of Yahweh (Genesis 3:16):

> I will multiply your pains in childbearing,
> you shall give birth to your children in pain.
> Your yearning shall be for your husband,
> yet he will lord it over you.

By now the reader is aware of the identity of god, both generally speaking, and specifically in the Gynecological Age.

Naturally, when the use of anesthesia in childbirth was introduced in the nineteenth century, there was great opposition, arising largely from the clergy, who represented Yahweh & Son. They claimed that it would "rob God of the deep earnest cries which arise in time of trouble for help." [59] Rich points out: "The lifting of Eve's curse seemed to threaten the foundations of patriarchal religion; the cries of women in childbirth were for the glory of God the Father." [60] As the church of the fathers faded and the gynecological ghosts moved into the foreground, more subtle drugs were found for women in labor. Thus the new drugs, by producing afteramnesia, satisfy god's representatives by nonstoppage of pain, while deceiving women.

The god-identified desire to see women—particularly feminists—suffer was expressed by the Reverend Richard Polwhele concerning Mary Wollstonecraft's horrible death from septicemia. As Adrienne Rich notes, he "complacently observed" that "she had died a death that strongly marked the distinction of the sexes, by pointing out the destiny of women, and the diseases to which they were peculiarly liable."[61] It would be difficult to find a more precise expression of the essential christian attitude toward feminists. We can note here also that the explicit use of god's name is not needed when the wording shifts to "destiny of women." Similar god-deleting "destiny of women" rhetoric is of course used also by anti-abortionists.

In contemporary times, "god" rhetoric and "destiny of women" rhetoric have been largely superseded by more lethal legitimations. Thus the rhetoric of re-search justifies the use/abuse of patients with such seemingly innocuous but profoundly ominous refrains as: "Further studies are needed." This bland statement legitimates the use of women as uninformed guinea pigs for such drugs as The Pill and the morning-after pill. The temptation might be to imagine that such destructive experimentation is confined to a particular time (the past) or to particular segments of the female population (e.g., low-income and nonwhite). While the latter are victimized in a special way, their "higher-class" sisters are taken care of in a different manner. Thus well-educated (miseducated) upper-middle-class women who "willingly" subject themselves (are subjected) to mutilating surgery and estrogen replacement therapy are uninformed objects in a refined sense; they are the victims of knowledgeable ignorance conforming to the model of the mentally raped and castrated Mary. The point is that experimentation on women's bodies is standard and universal gynecological practice and that it is legitimated by the divine right of professionals to "study." Even the more critical medical journal articles almost invariably call for "further research." The potential object of such studies is Everywoman.

To understand the highly effective erasure of professional responsibility in gynecology it is helpful to look at the ways in which erasure has been accomplished in all the sado-ritual atrocities studied in earlier chapters. Since in all of the other instances, we were analyzing events in other segments of patriarchy (temporal and/or spatial), it was possible to see that women's minds were dulled/hypnotized by the prevailing beliefs of their time and place. Since American gynecology is the here-and-now atrocity, it is both more obvious and more elusive. In order to gain distance/clarity concerning it, we can use insights already gained in the course of the voyage through this Passage.

We have seen that the religious legitimation for *suttee* involved blaming the widow for her husband's death. This may shed some light upon the unspoken justifications behind the gynecological crusade to shorten women's lives. Since women on the average survive men by a significant number of years, it should not be surprising that gynecology is functioning to remedy this unacceptable situation.[62] In both the Indian and the American cases there is an ideology of blaming the victim. In India, the husband's death supposedly resulted from his wife's wickedness. In American society it is claimed that men are worked to death to support parasitic women.

Another parallel to the Indian situation: Widows in that country have been described as "choosing" to be consumed by fire, when in reality Indian society makes life untenable for women left alone. Similarly, American women show signs of "willingness" to be consumed, in this case by gynecological "treatment." The doctors claim that women "ask for it" (without of course mentioning the lethal nature of the "it"). What is not mentioned is the fact that the patriarchs of this society also attempt to reduce women's potential for long and full living to (at best) merely not dying, and that their institutions especially militate against the survival of Crones.

In studying Chinese footbinding, we noted that the sadism and sexual arousal of the males who perpetrated the "curious erotic custom" was disguised as compassion for the possessors of tiny feet, the objects of male fetishism. The "compassion" of the gynecological helpers, particularly since it is linked with fetishism, should of course be suspect. As one member of that profession stated:

> I wouldn't want most of my patients to realize what an ego trip I get from taking care of them, because there's something selfish about enjoying the fact that a lot of women are dependent on you. . . . I think there are some in this specialty who like to punish women. Some doctors really get a kind of unconscious kick from seeing a woman in labor. There are doctors who are very sadistic.[63]

The doctors have plenty of material for ego trips and fanciful fetishism, as did the Chinese males surrounded by tiny-footed women whose maimed feet were meant to resemble vaginas and to make them totally dependent.

Another interviewee among gynecologists stated:

> My sex life hasn't changed but sometimes I get numb. I see thirty pelvises in a day. My cousin wants to know about all the pussy, but it really doesn't affect me. After a day's work I'm blown out.[64]

And another:

> That part of her body loses its identity. I could be examining a mouth. But I'm not. Now *it doesn't bother me at all* [emphasis mine].[65]

Having studied the footbinding ritual, we are in the privileged position of being able to see the significance of such numbing and of such denial of identity to the parts of a woman's body. We have seen that psychic numbness and sadism are deeply interconnected. Thus it should come as no surprise to find that the numb/fetishistic physician turns to violent and violating surgery to obtain a sense of potency/aliveness. And all of this in the name of the compassionate virtues: "helping" and "healing."

The legitimations used to erase male responsibility for African genital mutilation of women also can enable Hags to focus more sharply upon the justifications for gynecological genital mutilation. In Africa, clitoridectomy and infibulation are alleged to be justifiable because they are ways "for teaching women to endure pain." As we have seen, pain—and the dread of it—is also the Great American Gynecological Way of teaching women to be pre-occupied and pre-possessed. Other reasons given for mutilation in the African situation are religious belief and "custom." American women, like their African sisters, are also lulled into pain-full captivity by the prevailing beliefs and "customs."

African women, moreover, are mutilated for "aesthetic reasons," since the men of the tribes practicing these sado-rituals do not want their women to have anything "hanging down." Maiming for the alleged purpose of enhancing female beauty is standard practice in American cosmetic surgery. An example is mammaplasty, defined in *Dorland's Illustrated Medical Dictionary* as "plastic reconstruction of the breast, as may be performed to augment or reduce its size." A variation on this is mastopexy, which is performed to "correct a pendulous breast." This involves removal of breast tissue and filling the space with a silicone bag-gel prosthesis, often with additional maneuvers to reshape the breast so that it points upward. Women shocked by the pain and danger of infection inflicted upon millions of African women for "aesthetic" reasons should consider the parallels with the increasingly popular American way of deadly beautification.

Another illuminating argument given to erase male responsibility for African mutilations is that excision of the clitoris controls the female sexual appetite. We recall that the spate of clitoridectomies performed in the United States in the late nineteenth and early twentieth centuries was also justified on these grounds. If we look at other manifestations of the gynecological syndrome,we can see that controlling women's sexual appetite is still a strong element in the hidden agenda of justifications, although it is covered by deceitful reversals. The gynecologists are doing "everything possible" to make women "correctly" sexual—that is, Supersexy according to male-identified terms. Like the African sorcerer cited in Chapter Five who praised excision of the clitoris and the consequent alleged transferral of erotic feelings of the woman to "deep inside," the gynecologists also are true believers in the myth of the vaginal orgasm; that is, their treatments also are totally controlled by heterosexual suppositions, particularly by the idea that all "normal" women should think/live only in terms of sexual relations with men. The horrors of The Pill, the morning-after pill, estrogen replacement therapy, and cosmetic surgery all center around this controlling heterosexist supposition. Thus, although they parade themselves as being in the vanguard of "sexual liberation," the American Professional

Castrators have as their deep intent to control women's sexual appetite, to cut it down to the dimensions required by male-identified sexuality.

We have seen that the "primitive" African castrators of women believe that the clitoris causes impotence among men. The "sophisticated" gynecologists share this belief. The fact that their founding father, J. Marion Sims, performed clitoridectomies is significant. The fact that his ghostly heirs do not, merely means that so obvious a method as clitoridectomy is not the most efficacious means to achieve their purposes in the contemporary Ice Age. With the assistance of their psychotherapeutic colleagues, they need only make the option of woman-identified sexuality appear "sick," or, better still, to render it invisible. By leaving women genitally whole (with clitorises) while castrating them in other senses (both physically and psychically), they perform a more refined "female circumcision"—i.e., ritual initiation into patriarchal femininity (called "womanhood"). Like the Bambaras, they believe that a man who sleeps with a nonexcised woman risks death from her "sting." The professional solution/resolution is deep psychic removal of the "sting" in women, that is, of the vitality and vision needed to pierce through the thick veil of phallocentric myth and ritualized control of our lives. This is indeed the Ghostly Excision, appropriate to the time and space of the reign of the holy ghosts.

Finally, we should note that the familiar tactics for silencing criticism of African genital mutilation—i.e., accusations of "racism" and of "interfering with the fabric of another culture" —are not without their counterparts here. The best legitimation is, after all, enforced silencing of critics. I have pointed out that in christian theology the almost unforgivable sin is "blasphemy against the Holy Ghost." So also in the Gynecological Culture it is blasphemous to criticize the deep mythic dimensions of the professional sado-rituals. Women who dare to criticize on this deep level are labeled "paranoid" by the mind-gynecologists.

The ultimate irony occurs when a woman-identified woman who dares to counterattack these "helpers" of women is made to appear hostile to women.* This is most likely to happen when she pierces the whole fabric of the Gynecological Culture by exposing its underlying connecting thread of imposed totalitarian heterosexism. By doing this, she risks seeming not only anti-gynecological (which she is) but anti-woman (which she is not). The risk of being caught in this maze of reversals is comparable to that of the white woman who risks being called "racist" for exposing the ritual atrocities which victimize women in Africa. However, the stakes are higher, for the battle is in *this* segment of patriarchal space. The courage to be and to speak, in the age of the holy ghosts of gynecology, is, in the final analysis, the Courage to Blaspheme.

In Chapter Six we have seen that the legitimating theology of the witchburners, which erased their responsibility for the murder and torture of the witches, was Demonology. The witches were named victims, not of their torturers, but of the Devil, god's enemy. Since the Devil was the "real" enemy, the Inquisitors, as god's agents and representatives, were clearly acting for the good of the women they tortured and killed, for the good of other women (who were being given a bad example by the witches), for the good of men and children (the victims of the witches), and for the good of the church.

All of these elements shed light upon the gynecologists' erasure of their responsibility for gynocide. Gynecology is of course streamlined Demonology, and the Devil is Disease, to which women are especially susceptible. Patients are named victims, not of the physicians, but of Disease, the doctors' enemy. The "fact" that the patients are under the influence of Sickness is built into the very phrasing of "problems." Thus modern witch-hunters speculate about the "untreated menopause" as "a possible contributory factor in the causation of cancer" and about the uterus as "a possible breeding ground for cancer." Since Disease is the "real" enemy, the gynecologists, as god's agents and representatives, can present themselves as acting for the good of the women they torture and

* For example, such critics are sometimes accused of "putting down" women who go to gynecologists and of making *women* appear "at fault."

kill, for the good of other women (who will benefit from the re-search done upon uninformed/misinformed patients), for the good of men and children (who must endure the effects of these "sick" women's inability to perform their proper functions), and for the good of the state.

The Mind-Menders' Self-Absolutions

I shall now consider the basic threads in The Therapists' snarl of self-absolution for their responsibility in the psychiatric/psychotherapeutic ritual destruction of women. Two basic strands in this legitimating ideology are blaming the mother and blaming the patient/client. These are simply variations on the theme of blaming the victim.

A glance through one volume of *Psychological Abstracts* (Vol. 52, 1974) is sufficient to give searching Spinsters clues to the omnipresence of blaming the mother and to the vast array of "disturbances" alleged to be caused by mothers. A typical article describes the case of a thirty-two-year-old businessman who was treated for "profound fears of maternal engulfment," supposedly manifested in fantasies of homosexuality, voyeurism, exhibitionism, sexual masochism, transvestitism, and transsexualism. According to the abstract:

> During the course of psychotherapy, the patient exhibited repetitive, involuntary body contractions, interspersed with screaming, shrieking, and barking noises, apparently symptoms of Giles de la Tourette syndrome. It is suggested that these phenomena represented the conflict between succumbing to the devouring mother and an attempt to ward off this event . . .[66]

All because of Mother. To this list of mother-caused symptoms, the Searcher can add many others, gleaned from the same volume. These include schizophrenia, identity diffusion, auditory hallucinations, delusions of persecution and grandeur, trichotillomania (abnormal desire to pull out one's hair), suicide, feminine identification in males, hypermasculinity in males (exhibited in tough behavior such as drinking and weapon-carrying, and in emphasized sexual athleticism), delinquency, school-phobia (the result of maternal overprotectiveness), and heroin addiction.[67]

Thus the therapeutic holy ghosts continue to follow their mother-blaming inspirer, Freud, expanding the lists of maternally caused symptoms. They also continue to multiply tests which will prove their foregone conclusions. Thus, for example, mothers of hair-plucking children were given the "Rosenzweig Picture Frustration Test," which "proved" that these mothers induced such disturbed behavior in their children.[68] Of course, such tests are not necessary to legitimate mother-blaming for most people, since nearly everyone has been indoctrinated from infancy in the mother-hating myths of the controlling religion: Patriarchy. Fairy tales (for example, "Snow White" and "Cinderella") teach that the only good mothers are dead ones, thinly disguising living mothers as "evil" stepmothers. Folk "wisdom," the officially recognized religions, literature, and the media carry on from there, forming a firm platform for the processions of the therapeutic -ologies.

The other basic thread in the therapeutic snarl, that is, blaming the patient, is illustrated in one of Freud's "classic" works: *The Case of Dora.* In his disgusting discussion of Dora, who suffered from "hysteria," he re-lays her experience of being sexually assaulted at the age of fourteen and pontificates upon what she *should* have experienced. He describes the scene in which Herr K., an older man and friend of the family, having managed to get Dora alone, "suddenly clasped the girl to him and pressed a kiss upon her lips." Freud's profound analysis follows:

> This was surely just the situation to call up a distinct feeling of *sexual excitement* in a girl of fourteen who had never before *been approached.* But Dora had at that moment a violent feeling of disgust, tore herself free from the man, and hurried past him to the staircase and from there to the street door [emphases mine].[69]

Clearly, Freud assumes that any woman who "is approached," that is, sexually accosted, should respond with uncontrollable visceral desire for the male who mauls and violates her. Thus Dora's normal reaction of disgust and Self-salvation is negated. Freud drones on:

> In this scene . . . the behavior of this child of fourteen was already entirely and completely hysterical. I should without question consider a *person* hysterical in whom *an occasion for sexual excitement* elicited feelings that were preponderantly or exclusively unpleasurable; and I should do so whether or no the person were capable of producing somatic symptoms. . . . Instead of the genital sensation which would certainly have been felt by a healthy girl in such circumstances . . . Dora was overcome by the *unpleasurable feeling* which is proper to the tract of mucous membrane at the entrance to the alimentary canal—that is, *disgust* [emphases mine].[70]

In this maze of obscene babble the great mind-shrinker announces that any woman who does not enjoy rape is hysterical. He reduces deep existential disgust to an "unpleasurable feeling" in the mucous membrane. Freud's identification with Herr K., who seems to have been an *un*extraordinary dirty old man, is displayed in his note describing that child molester as "still quite young and of *prepossessing* appearance [emphasis mine]." [71] Indeed, any Hag can recognize here a description of a true pre-possessor presented by one who could easily recognize his own kind. Pre-possessor Freud's psychoanalytic babble is a paradigm of the/rapists' erasure of male responsibility for rape on all levels. The patient is not merely blamed for being a victim who "asked for it." She is blamed for being a victim who did *not* "ask for it," and who did *not* love being violated. This is the Disease of the Female Spirit which must be cured.

Thus Freud qualifies as Earthly Representative of the Divine Spirit-Eraser and as model for the procession of therapeutic erasers who have succeeded him, erasing as deeply as possible the pre-possessed patient's Self. By the very fact of misnaming and misdefining her reactions, he obscures his own active role in the repetition of her violation. This love-maker is centuries beyond the stage of the Dear Sons of Pope Innocent, authors of the *Malleus Maleficarum,* who merely accused women of insatiable carnal lust. Freud's refined technique negates female pride, warping his patient's disgust at male lechery into sickening feelings of shame for her own healthy, Self-assertive behavior.

III

The third element of Sado-Ritualism—an inherent tendency to spread—is also manifested in American gynecology. I shall first consider the expansion of body-gynecology. Although the patterns of spread are complex, the familiar thread of diffusion from an "elite" class of women to those in the lower echelons of society is not absent. It is enlightening to recall the history of the man-midwife, who began to appear on the scene in the seventeenth century, and of whom Rich writes:

> He appears first in the Court, attending upper-class women; rapidly he begins to assert the inferiority of the midwife and to make her name synonymous with dirt, ignorance, and superstition.[72]

Indeed, in seventeenth-century France, the few physicians "qualified" in obstetrics profited from this fad among the upper classes, and limited their practice to this specialty and to those who could pay their high fees.[73]

Ehrenreich and English point out that in nineteenth-century America it was convenient for physicians to see working-class women as inherently healthy and robust, and to regard affluent women as inherently sick. In reality, of course, the poor suffered far more from contagious diseases and complications of childbirth:

> Sickness, exhaustion, and injury were routine in the life of the working-class woman. Contagious diseases always hit the homes of the poor first and hardest. Pregnancy, in a fifth or sixth floor walk-up flat, really was debilitating, and childbirth, in a crowded tenement room, was often a frantic ordeal.[74]

In this social context we can see the calloused deceptiveness of the physicians who fostered the cult of invalidism among the upper classes:

But doctors reversed the causality and found the soft, "civilized" life of the upper classes more health-threatening and medically interesting than hard work and privation.[75]

Indeed, the economic motive behind this medically "interesting" focus upon rich women is obvious.

It is important for Hag-ographers to emphasize the fact that from the inception of their profession, gynecologists have used black, immigrant, and other poor women as guinea pigs, experimenting upon them without their informed consent, in order to later use the "expertise" thus gained in lucrative private practice. Yet a class analysis is inadequate here, for it falls short of explaining all of the dimensions of androcratic atrocities. The fact is that experimentation is part of the routine procedure of gynecology for women of all classes. As I have already indicated, poor and nonwhite women are usually totally uninformed of how they are being used for "study." So also middle- and upper-class women are often simply not told anything, or when they are given "information," their miseducation gives them the illusion of informed consent. There are, then, varying ways in which women serve as unwitting/unwilling "material" for gynecologists.

There are also varying ways in which women are targeted. Thus poor and nonwhite women are particularly singled out for sterilization. As Judith Herman pointed out, in a recent survey: "Ninety-four percent of gynecologists polled in four major cities said that they favored *compulsory* sterilization for welfare mothers with three or more 'illegitimate' children."[76] It is obvious that the concern here is not for the health of the women involved. In the mid-1970s HEW announced that states would pay 90 percent of the costs of sterilizations for poor women, but only 50 percent of the cost of abortion. As Herman writes:

This gives hospitals and clinics an incentive to promote an irreversible birth control method and to discourage the method which gives the individual woman the greatest amount of flexibility and personal control.[77]

Poor women, then, are seen as compulsive breeders who must be castrated for the good of "society" but denied abortions when they need and choose to have them.

It would be simplistic, however, to conclude that poor women are the essential targets of the *intent* of gynecological gynocide. Barker-Benfield observes that in the nineteenth century "the chief targets of gynecologic surgery aimed specifically at sexual discipline were the wives and daughters of rich, or at least middle-class, men." [78] Nor can this be explained solely by an economic motive. Such gynecologists as Augustus Kinsley Gardner "realized that the fashion-conscious, *leisured* woman was becoming the model for all women [emphasis mine]." [79] It was the leisure (read: potential freedom) of these women that deeply threatened the gynecologists, who feared that the model of freedom might catch on. Barker-Benfield concludes that the essential issue was "the surgical discipline of women deemed deviant, rather than simply considerations of class." [80]

"Surgical discipline" (combined with psychiatry and psychoanalysis) is the specific means of castrating/killing deviant women in America in the Age of Gynecology. However the *agents* of this punitive castration participate in the universal patriarchal ethos. Their intent does not differ from that of the Sado-Ritualists of other cultures. Their primary and proximate target is the woman who appears to be on the verge of breaking free and threatens to be a model of freedom for other women. Their essential target is Self/Spirit in all women. It is essential, therefore, to see in the Atrocity of Gynecology the basic and familiar pattern of victimization, which focuses upon an elite body of women and extends to the women caught in the ranks of the upwardly aspiring lower echelons of society.

The Metastasizing of Gynecology

In studying the sado-ritual of American gynecology, we must recognize a specific form of spread which is endemic to the atrocity proper to the age of the holy ghosts. I refer to the burgeoning of iatrogenic disease among women. We have already seen evidence of this in the discussion of such disasters as DES and preventive medicine. At this point I shall cite a few statements from medical journals which cautiously admit some hazards of gynecological medicine. The examples which follow illustrate both the content and the style of such admissions. The Searcher will have to peer closely through the fog of deceptiveness which their authors emit by the guarded, self-protective style of their writing.

An article entitled "A Biostatistical Evaluation of Complications from Mastectomy" states:

> Hospital death, chest wound infections, and some loss of skin graft were significantly higher when patients received preoperative or postoperative radiation than when they received none [in connection with mastectomies].[81]

The same article discusses "the morbid consequences of such a radical operation," and admits that sometimes "tumor cells [are] dislodged into the blood and lymph during surgical manipulation." They state rather quaintly: "The problems are ubiquitous." [82]

Another article (typically only four pages long but having three authors and written in computer-speak) discloses the following information: "Using a more sensitive statistical technique, this risk [of endometrial cancer] was calculated to be 7.5 times higher among estrogen users than among nonusers." [83] Ominously, the same article ends with the following statement: "Estrogen-exposed women should have periodic cancer screening examinations." [84]

Yet another group of re-searchers admit that gynecologists have been *culpably* ignorant for many years of the known connection between the taking of estrogens and the risk of cancer. They write:

> That systemic estrogens are associated with excess risk of uterine cancer should not be surprising. Gynecologists through the years have been concerned with the effects of estrogens in müllerian tissues and have been aware that estrogens may either initiate or promote growth of tumors of the uterus. Forty years ago Novak warned of the carcinogenic possibilities of estrogenic substances.

A few papers have reported cases which associate exogenous estrogens with endometrial carcinoma.[85]

Thus the recently publicized evidence of the carcinogenicity of estrogens, which drew great attention in the press in 1975, should have come as no surprise.

The same article abounds with clues which are available to the Searcher who can break through the obscure language. Thus we read:

> It has been estimated that in the near future 50% of women in the postmenopausal age range will have had a hysterectomy and therefore no longer be at risk for this disease.[86]

Here is a typical gynecological solution to gynecological iatrogenic disease: major surgery, which can have serious consequences, including death. The authors also reassure their colleagues with a comment upon the "high cure rate of this cancer" (which turns out to be not very high, and would be little consolation to the woman with cancer).

A gem of an article (illustrated) entitled "Use of Dermal-Fat Suspension Flaps for Thigh and Buttock Lifts" proposes a solution to the problems commonly associated with surgical procedures for establishing "desirable contours of the hips and thighs." The author points out that the prolonged bed-rest and lack of activity which are still prescribed "to minimize the risk of dehiscence [the parting of the sutured lips of a surgical wound] increase the risk of thrombophlebitis and pulmonary embolism." [87] What he is obliquely saying is that patients (referred to throughout the article as "she" and "her") may die as a consequence of such operations. The unspoken fact, buried in the interstices of professional jargon, is this: These women, seduced into surgery through implanted fear of unfashionable fat, risk death. Naturally, the author does not advocate exercise and a healthy diet to alleviate the "deformity," but rather a complex surgical procedure.

Another team of re-searchers published an article on "second cancers" in patients with ovarian cancer, indicating that the use of certain drugs (in a procedure referred to as "alkylating-agent therapy") causes acute leukemia in some cases. In the course of their discussion they say: "Although the carcinogenicity of alkylating agents in laboratory animals is well established, the effects in man are poorly defined." [88] The possible ominous implications of this might not become evident to the Searcher until she reaches the last sentence:

> Further studies are also needed to evaluate the carcinogenic effects that may result from interactions between different types of treatment, including radiation and alkylating agents.[89]

One distinctly has the impression that human beings will become the "subjects" for these "further studies."

In glancing through a one and one-half page article authored by four re-searchers, entitled "Maternal Death Resulting from Rupture of Liver Adenoma Associated with Oral Contraceptives," the Searcher will read that in July 1976, data was collated on sixty-seven cases of liver lesions associated with oral contraceptives.* There is a Catch-22 in the article: Women taking The Pill who as a consequence of this have a liver adenoma ("benign" tumor) are warned to stop taking it. However, it is by this time very dangerous for them to become pregnant:†

> . . . the potential effect of a subsequent pregnancy on a liver adenoma remains *unanswered*. The high levels of sex steroids and increased vascularity of the liver during pregnancy *seemingly* would increase the chance for liver rupture [emphases mine].[90]

Despite the insipidity of the style, despite the self-protective terms, *unanswered* and *seemingly,* the ominous implications are clear.

Such documentation can go on and on. The destruction

* This data is available at the Registry of Liver Tumors Associated with Oral Contraceptives, Department of Gynecology and Obstetrics, University of California, Irvine, California.

† Any Spinster/Lesbian could point the way out of the Catch-22, but it is too much to expect that the medical establishment would propose such a clear and direct solution.

wrought by gynecology is on display in medical journals. Moreover, so is the fact that it assumes the shape of continuing processions. Thus the plight of DES daughters, itself a manifestation of iatrogenic disease, is an invitation to further gynecological molestation. There is evidence that radiation directed at the vagina for treatment of adenosis can cause uterine cancer.[91] Moreover, local progesterone therapy is reported to have exacerbated growth of tumors. The processions of necrophilic medicine are endless.

The Multiplying of Mind-Menders

The tendency to spread is of course inherent also in mind-gynecology. It is clear that the ritual of psychotherapy has followed the pattern of diffusion from an "elite" group of victims to a wider circle, and that this sado-ritual spreads in the manner of iatrogenic dis-ease. The proliferation of "schools" and types of therapy has fostered its spread in both of these senses.

I shall first look at the spread of psychotherapy from well-to-do women to a wider segment of the female population. The progenitor of modern therapy was, of course, Freud. The fact that Freudian psychoanalysis as an institution has now been relegated to a minor role in actual therapeutic practice does not alter the fact of his mystical "mother" role in relation to all of them. As psychiatrist Joel Kovel acknowledges:

> It is striking to see work after work, new method after new method, define itself by reference to Freud, usually as an alleged breakthrough past his limits. Through the years, a thousand commentators, mostly long forgotten, have labeled Freud passé. Buried countless times, just as perpetually resurrected, the spirit of Freud continues to brood over contemporary therapy.[92]

Like the holy ghost, Freud multiplies himself, continuing to breed—and especially—to brood over his progeny, who resemble him even in their reactions "against" him. For in such re-actions they move, yo-yo-like, back and forth on his apron strings, eternally fixated upon his Word. The source of their movement/"life" is his breath, for he is their spirit, their basic re-source, whom they must constantly re-search, re-vise, re-fute, re-cover, and resurrect.

Freud focused upon females who "belonged" to the well-to-do classes, and so did the seemingly very divergent therapists who followed him, such as Jung, Adler, Rank, Reich, Fromm, and Perls. Gradually, the proliferation of clinics and the development of various forms of group therapy has made Mental Help and Healing available to Everywoman. The sheer volume of therapy has multiplied approximately fivefold since 1960.* Hags should note that the increase in volume has been accompanied by multiplication of forms. The following partial list may assist the haggard imagination to glimpse the dimensions of the "Triumph of the Therapeutic":

behavioral-directive therapy
behavior therapy
biofunctional therapy
encounter therapy
est (Erhard Seminars Training)
existential analysis
family therapy
game therapy
Gestalt therapy
hypnotherapy
mysticotranscendent therapy
primal therapy
psychoanalytic therapy
rational-emotive therapy
reality therapy
script therapy
sensitivity training
sex therapy
somatic therapy
transactional analysis[93]

This proliferation of therapies, which are like shadows, distorted reflections and resurrections of each other, has the effect of including everyone not only as patient but as mini-therapist. Thus, "virtually everyone who is touched by psychoanalysis identifies with it and soon wants to become a therapist himself." [94] The result is that therapy has spread not only from the "elite," selected for "the best" psychoanalytic treatment,

* Obviously some males also go to therapists, whereas gynecology is targeted specifically at women. However, the point to keep in focus here is that mind-gynecology has women as its essential targets, even when men are in the patient role, since therapy generally reinforces stereotyped gender roles and fosters woman hating. Thus a rapist who is sent to a therapist is frequently "helped to see" that "his problem" originated with his mother.

to the poor who are offered "budget" or government-dispensed therapies, but even to those who do not go to therapy sessions but who are friends or even casual acquaintances of those who do. Thus the contemporary religion of therapy has produced its own "priesthood of believers."

It is easy to recognize here an ominous resemblance to the proliferation of christian churches and sects, and to the consequent witnessing by the "born-again" laity. After the death of Jesus, the holy ghost started inspiring more and more "converts." These eventually formed different and seemingly opposed churches, and this doctrinal and structural variety functioned to seduce more and more into membership. These in turn profoundly affected the environment of nonmembers.

The diffusion of therapy, then, like that of religion, has been downward and outward, affecting all women. However, the contagion of mind-gynecology cannot be understood in socioeconomic or numerical terms only. Just as body-gynecologists spread iatrogenic disease, so also do therapists create a market for their "healing." A woman seduced into treatment is "inspired" with dis-ease she had never before even suspected. As she becomes more fixated upon her surfacing "problems" she becomes more in need of Help. The multiplicity of therapies feeds into this dis-ease, for they constitute an arsenal for the manufacture of many forms of semantic bullets used to bombard the minds of women struggling to survive in the therapeutically polluted environment. The bullets of "psychobabble" invade the ears of Everywoman, informing her in a thousand tongues of her Sickness and Need for Help. This invasion continues unchecked because it fixes women's attention in the wrong direction, fragmenting and privatizing perception of problems, which can be transcended only if understood in the context of the sexual caste system.

IV

The medical employment of women as token torturers is evident in the use of nurses, physiotherapists, and token women doctors. In the field of body-gynecology, the nurse, trained to be totally obedient to the Olympian Doctor, functions as the proximate and visible agent of painful and destructive treatment. Nurses shave women about to give birth and give enemas to women in labor. It is they who give injections and it is they who withhold pain medication begged for by the patient. Programmed not to answer women's questions, they sometimes magnify suffering by unreasonable silence and degrading nonanswers. Hags should note that most unpleasant procedures which nurses perform (for example, changing of dressings after surgery) are done while the woman is awake and aware of being hurt, whereas the deepest wounding—cutting in surgery—which is performed by doctors, is done under anaesthesia. Thus, as Peggy Holland has noted, within the hospital situation most procedures *experienced* as painful are done by women, whereas the doctors' actions—prescribing drugs which often have harmful effects, issuing orders from on high—are often not directly perceived.[95] The nurse, then, functions as token torturer in the primary sense of the term *token,* that is, as an outward indication or expression. She is both weapon and shield for the divine doctor in his warfare against The Enemy, Disease, to which the woman as patient is susceptible by her nature [*sic*]. Likewise, physiotherapists (most of whom are female) assume the token role, often forcing women to do excruciating exercise after surgery, for example, after mastectomies.

There are, of course, some women gynecologists, many of whom are far more sensitive to women's needs than their male colleagues, and some of whom (like some nurses) act in a genuinely healing manner despite the obstacles presented by their training and by the institutional set-up in which they participate. However, they have gone through the same indoctrination as male doctors (the same texts, instructors, internship), read the same medical journals, and continue to be subjected to pressures to conform. Paraphrasing a discussion with Dr. Mary Howell, Gena Corea summarizes the situation: "Female doctors who are 'honorary white males' don't defend female patients against harmful obstetrical practices, unnecessary surgery, unsafe contraceptives, and forced sterilizations." [96]

We have seen that in the other sado-rituals mothers are forced to function as token torturers of daughters. Clearly, this aspect is perpetuated in gynecology, in ways that are not only more refined but also more complex. The "cooperation" of the DES mothers in the mutilation of their daughters was elicited from them in a state of ignorance. Also to be counted among well-intentioned victimizers are those mothers who urge and even command their daughters to go for frequent, unnecessary gynecological check-ups and treatments. Such women are educated to be unaware that "any idea, seriously entertained, tends to bring about the realization of itself." [97] It is ironic that these mothers, whose insights have been blunted by fear and heavy bombardments of medical propaganda, display a less accurate awareness of the sources of danger than Joseph Chilton Pearce, author of *The Crack in the Cosmic Egg,* who writes of the cancer epidemic among females in his family:

> Few people understood my fury when the medical center that attended my wife requested that I bring my just-then-budding teenage daughter for regular six-monthly check-ups for ever thereafter, since they had found—and thoroughly advertised—that mammary malignancies in a mother tended to be duplicated in the daughter many hundred percent above the average. And surely such tragic duplications *do* occur, in a clear example of the circularity of expectancy verification, the mirroring by reality of a passionate or basic fear.[98]

The mothers who are pre-possessed and pre-occupied by instilled iatrogenic fears have a difficult time saying no to this circularity, precisely because they are themselves mesmerized both as victims and as token torturers. They function in the victimizer role ignorantly and often ambivalently by socializing daughters to be "popular"/sexy on male-identified terms, thus setting them up to become Pill-users, teenage mothers, or abortion candidates.*

* Obviously, I am by no means advocating the position that abortion is "morally wrong." Indeed, it is preferable to the agony of unwanted pregnancy and childbirth. This does not lessen the fact that it is a degrading and painful procedure which no woman should have to endure.

Likewise, from the very inception of mind-gynecology, women as token torturers have had an important role. Outstanding more-freudian-than-Freud women analysts included Helene Deutsch and Marie Bonaparte. Deutsch, whose morbid outpourings are continually reprinted and are often sold in the "Women's Studies" sections of bookstores (right next to de Beauvoir) was trained by Freud, having worked under him for years. A haggard Searcher will not expend too much energy unsnarling Deutsch's opinions. The following sample should suffice as a re-minder of the methods of her re-search:

> The theory that I have long supported—according to which femininity is largely associated with passivity and masochism—has been confirmed in the course of years by clinical observation.[99]

Certainly. And blackness has long been "associated" with the same qualities in racist societies. The point is brought up, re-hashed and re-futed in Sociology 101 at Everycollege every year. The problem is not simply that the argument is impeccably fallacious but that it came from a woman. Deutsch sustains her circularity to the bitter end of her work, *The Psychology of Women*. Writing of the "climacterium," she faithfully copies the tradition of the *Malleus Maleficarum,* when she says:

> The suggestibility of women in this life period increases markedly, their judgment fails, and they readily fall victim to evil counsellors.[100]

In the Age of Gynecological Holy Ghosts, however, the situation is more complex than it was in the days of Pope Innocent and his Dear Sons, Kramer and Sprenger. For the ranks of truly evil counselors have been expanded to include such Dear Daughters as Deutsch. Since the witches were Wise Women/Healers, it is particularly appropriate that the androcratic usurpers who erased them should later replace them with man-made women, legitimated as "counselors" and therapists. Nor need these adopted daughters of pathological patriarchs be as blind as Helene Deutsch or Marie Bonaparte.[101]

There have been female adlerians, rankians, reichians, frommians, and—ad nauseam—jungians. Particularly seductive is the illusion of equality projected through Jung's androcratic animus-anima balancing act, since women are trained to be grateful for "complementarity" and token inclusion. Tokenism is embedded in the very fabric of Jung's ideology—in contrast to the more obvious misogynism of Freud's fallacious phallocentrism. Thus it is possible for women to promote Jung's garbled gospel without awareness of betraying their own sex, and even in the belief that they are furthering the feminist cause.

Moreover, since the Age of the Holy Ghosts is a time of Dionysian boundary violation, it is predictable that the mantle of male motherhood will be shifted to the shoulders of more and more women deemed worthy by Dionysian men. The same incongruities that are inherent in the role of females who would be christian priests and ministers are ingrained in the functions of the newly ordained female priests of therapy. Moreover, the downward spread of therapy itself inevitably renders it more accessible as a respectable occupation for upwardly mobile women in male-monitored society. Thus the lower ranks of token victimizers multiply.

Nor is this all. For it is also inevitable that the monodimensional Great Sponge Society will soak up into its interstices women with a genuine desire and native ability to heal. Thus the Thoroughly Therapeutic Society must not only castrate potential witches as victims/patients. It must craftily con some of its stronger potential deviants into the role of unwitting token victimizers, in the name of Feminist Therapy.

I am *not* saying that genuinely woman-identified counseling cannot and does not take place, nor am I denying that, given the state of alienating structures in which we live, there is an urgent need for drop-in centers and other places for women to go *in crisis situations.* My criticism concerns therapy as a way of life, as an institutionalized system of creating and perpetuating false needs, of masking and maintaining depression, of focusing/draining women's energy through fixation upon periodic psychological "fixes." My criticism concerns the emotional, economic, and intellectual hooking of women into a perpetual procession of cyclic re-turning, which provides false security and prevents independent risking/questing. It concerns the woman-crippling triumph of the therapeutic over transcendence.*

There are many arguments that can be made for and against the variety of situations which generally are listed under the heading of "feminist therapy." Those who argue in favor of "feminist therapy" maintain that it departs entirely from the old freudian presuppositions. I suggest that this assumption be closely examined by A-mazing Amazons, for behind the more obviously misogynistic presuppositions of patriarchal psychotherapy (e.g., "penis envy" and blaming the mother) there is a more subtle agenda, which is difficult to uproot and which seems to be endemic to the therapeutic situation in its various forms.

This agenda contains, as a basic element, dependency upon agendas—in other words, addiction. The term *therapeutic* is from the Greek *therapeuein,* meaning "to attend, worship or treat medically." Just as roman catholics feel obliged to attend mass regularly and to worship the god of the church, and just as patients are regularly treated medically, the therapeutized re-turn. I suggest that the god of therapy is therapy itself. Moreover, as in the case of all religions, there is a fixation upon the act of worship itself, which tends to function as a shelter against anomie, against meaninglessness. For this reason, any criticism of therapy threatens/terrorizes the therapeutized.

A clue to the fact that this addictive quality is present in "feminist therapy" is the reaction of some readers/listeners who fixate defensively upon "feminist therapy" rather than expanding their vision to comprehend a long and complex

* In the Name of Feminist Therapy, and of Radical Feminist Therapy and of Wholly Lesbian Therapy, Women's Centers, originally the products of creative/wild woman-identified energy, are sometimes converted into Taming Centers, where independent gynergetic be-ing is treated as a source of disease.

analysis of androcratic atrocities and tactics. This limitation of focus is itself symptomatic of the fetishization and fragmentation inflicted by mind-gynecology. It suggests that the very concept of "feminist therapy" is inherently a contradiction. I hasten to add that gynergizing, en-couraging, healing communication among Hags/Crones is not a contradiction. Therefore, when this is taking place it should *not* be called "therapy." Moreover, I suggest that Hags dispense with the trappings of therapy.

Among these trappings/traps is stale therapeutic jargon, which arrests thinking, neatly labeling/limiting every impulse toward re-considering Original Movement. For example, we are told to "deal with" the issue of "feminist therapy." One who strives for Gyn/Ecological vision may be accused of "not dealing with" therapeutic problems (just as Lesbians/Feminists generally are accused of "not dealing with" men). Yet to satisfy the accusers' often insatiable need to "deal with" this issue would require falling into the very therapeutic trappings/trap which Gyn/Ecology transcends. It would mean settling for settling down in one blind alley of the Masters' Maze, putting on the blinders of tunnel vision. While there are sometimes needs for tunnels on our Journey, Journeying itself is not tunneling. Since Gyn/Ecological Journeying is not "feminist therapy," but rather is itself an entirely Other Way, Revolting Hags refuse the therapeutic society. We re-fuse our gynergetic Selves.

Refusing the triumph of the therapeutic is essential for the affirmation of transcendence. It will be objected that "feminist therapy" can be a means to transcendence. Without a doubt it does function at some times and in some cases to remove obstacles and to provide clues to transcendence. Yet the same can be said for the catholic church. Although Hags might want to evaluate these institutions in different ways, the fact is that both have the agenda of dis-couraging women into the state of dependency. While the symbol system and institutional intent of the catholic church is overtly oppressive, "feminist therapy" as an institution is covertly dis-couraging.

The point is that Hags should not have to resort to taking back from such institutions as religion and therapy the powers and tactics which were rightfully our own to begin with, and which have been warped and watered down after having been stolen by patriarchy. The situation is parallel to that of a woman who begs a robber to return her stolen and damaged possessions—except that women who turn to religion and therapy usually do not realize that they are attemping to reclaim stolen goods from thieves.

It will be objected that "feminist therapy" is a step toward re-claiming women's own healing powers. This is partially true, but I suggest that there are serious inherent difficulties (comparable to the difficulties inherent in the idea of "feminist religion"). For therapy, including the institution of "feminist therapy," resists being relegated to the role of a "step." Like religion, it tends to replace transcendence, assuming/consuming all process, draining creative energy, eliminating Originality, mislabeling leaps of imagination, shielding the Self against Self-strengthening Aloneness. The Self becomes a spectator of her own frozen, caricatured history. She is filed away, mis-filed, in file-cabinets filled with inaccurate categories. Thus filed, she joins the Processions of those who choose downward mobility of mind and imagination.

Symptomatic of such pseudo-feminist downward mobility is the Soap Opera Syndrome, whose one basic Program can be entitled, "How to Deal with Relationships." Like the heroines of 1940s radio soap operas and 1970s television soap operas, the therapeutized actress deals with her programmed problems before an audience of dealers. Like the radio and television heroines, she rehearses but does not create the script. She may try out for different roles, since everything can be coopted by therapy. Thus writing is therapeutic, swimming is therapeutic, painting is therapeutic, demonstrating is therapeutic. The script-follower forgets that writing is writing, swimming is swimming, painting is painting, demonstrating is demonstrating. Instead of creating, she deals and deals, struggles and struggles, relates and re-lates. She finds that her problems are endless, having the infinity of a closed circle. Everything becomes a problem. The situation of being Feminist and/or Lesbian adds to the problems but does not break the circle. Only Journeying breaks the circle. In Journeying/process, therapy is not the priority.

V

The fifth element common to the androcratic atrocities—compulsive orderliness, repetitiveness, and fixation upon details—is familiar to anyone who has been near a hospital or a doctor's office. In the case of physicians specializing in women's "diseases," the orderliness is obviously associated with fetishistic "worship" of female organs. Under the aegis of Professional Help, detachment and prurient interest are righteously combined in the rituals of examination and treatment. One gynecologist summed up his condition rather neatly:

> You have to be kind of crazy to go into the field, because it's a difficult, physically demanding residency. I had to be extremely obsessive-compulsive to get through it.[102]

To many women these words will ring absolutely true.

To understand the intent behind the specific forms of orderliness peculiar to gynecology, we should recall the historical origins of this profession in the nineteenth century. We already know that gynecologists saw themselves as having a mission to control the increasing "disorderliness" of women through such methods as clitoridectomy, ovariotomy, and "rest cure." The castrating doctors saw themselves as reimposing order upon women whose disorder consisted in deviation from the female role of subservience to their husbands and dedication to household duties. Thus it is appropriate that the Gynecological Guardians of Housekeepers should themselves exhibit extreme symptoms of obsessive compulsive orderliness, repetitiveness, and fixation upon detail. Since they are the Good Housekeepers in charge of housekeepers, since they are the liturgists and celebrators of genital fixation, they must themselves be caught up in routinized, ritualized behavior, riveted to the targets of their own fetishistic fixations.

The same components are evident in the psychotherapeutic syndrome. The therapeutic curers of disorder impose a false order (meaning) upon the histories of their patients/clients. Vying with the unnaturalness of the lithotomy (supine) position, of The Pill, of exogenous estrogens, of cosmetic surgery, this psychically dis-ordering order decomposes and dismembers women's personal histories, recomposing them to match the monotonous beat of the Masters' metronome. To achieve this disordered dominance of their Higher and Holier Order, the therapists routinize their patients, subjecting them to a false need for regular appointments and for repetitive reconstruction of their past. Perpetually pushed into this revised past, the patient patiently re-learns her history, which is reversed and rehearsed for the therapist's records. The patient learns to fixate upon herself as an object, to objectify and label happenings in her process until process is re-processed into processions of thoroughly impersonal, explainable events. She becomes the therapeutic watcher of her reinterpreted self. Her history repeats itself. Her sense of transcendence/wildness/adventure is tamed. She mistakes her convoluted gropings through this man-made maze for progress. To the extent that therapy mutes the call of the wild Self to transcendence, she fixates more and more upon the observation of details. If totally "cured" she is "terminated." Otherwise, she is maintained in her state of depression, reciting the litanies, novenas, and rosaries of her therapeutic salvation history. She participates in the Masses of Encounter Groups, hoping to receive the Spirit from those whose function is to dis-spirit her.

VI

Medical/therapeutic practices which in another age would have been unthinkable have become acceptable ("normal") and even normative, and this adaptation has been effected with sublime refinement. Examples abound. Concerning hospitalized childbirth, Suzanne Arms demonstrates the case: "A woman opting for the hospital may have asked for a normal birth, but she is going where she should know normal birth is least likely to occur." [103] Moreover, as Kathleen Barry points out, not only regular hospitalized childbirth but also " 'natural childbirth,' as we know it now, is nothing more than a romanticized means of helping women to better adjust to the abnormal and intensely painful delivery process mandated by men." [104]

The gynecological profession and the popularizing media have combined their efforts to make the poisoning of women appear acceptable. Just as popping The Pill is both "normal" and normative for younger women, so is estrogen replacement therapy for their mothers and older sisters. Elaborating upon the latter form of chemotherapy, medical re-searchers have obscurely revealed a particularly odd twist, namely that it is most dangerous for healthy women: "Our data also indicates that the exogenous estrogen-related risk is highest for women classified as normal—i.e., those with none of the "classic" predisposing signs." [105] They explain that the risk of endometrial cancer "associated" with estrogens is highest in patients *without* hypertension and obesity. The horrifying message is that precisely the asset of good health in women is warped by these wonder-workers into a predisposing condition for iatrogenic disease. The uncalled for "treatment" of such healthy women is but one illustration of the massive abnormality of the medical system, in which experimentation on healthy women has become normal. The routinization and normalizing of the mutilation of women has peaked to the point of glamorizing such mutilation.

This was first evident in the wonders of cosmetic surgery. In the mid-seventies, mastectomies became popularized when not only First Lady Betty Ford but also "Happy" Rockefeller had them. The prosthesis business has boomed. Symptomatic of the shift in controlled popular opinion was an article which appeared in 1977 in *People Weekly* entitled "Barbie Doll Developer Ruth Handler Offers a New Look to Mastectomy Victims." Ruth, whose last name unbelievably is Handler, is described as the woman who, "nearly 20 years ago, dared to put bosoms on Barbie Doll." Since then, much has happened. She has lost a breast and is described as "back in the breast business," with her new product, the prosthesis, "Nearly Me." The article begins tantalizingly with the following statement:

> She unbuttons her blouse to expose her brassiere and says, "Put your hands on both breasts, then give a good squeeze. Can you feel the difference?" she asks.

Apparently the handlers cannot, for: "Wherever Handler has

introduced Nearly Me . . . women have flocked in by the hundreds."[106] Indeed, if some gynecologists have their way, the flocks will multiply, and it will soon be abnormal for a woman over fifty to have her own breasts and/or uterus.*

We have already seen abundant evidence that the therapeutic game also consists largely in legitimating "normal," that is, lobotomized and tame behavior which is in fact indoctrinated, artifactual, man-made femininity. Thus Freud reversed the meaning of Dora's healthy reaction of disgust at sexual assault by naming it "hysterical." So also Jung slyly legitimates punitive measures against strong women, implying that strength of mind is abnormal. Writing of women who express strong arguments (women "ridden by the animus"), he states:

> Often the man has the feeling—*and he is not altogether wrong*—that only seduction or a beating or rape would have the necessary power of "persuasion" [emphasis mine].[107]

Women who have been seduced by jungian ideology might do well to consider the implications of this attitude.

Moreover, women who have been seduced, brow-beaten, and mind-raped by individual therapists or by gangs of mini-therapists in marathon encounter sessions should re-consider the meaning of "normality" in such a setting. A clue is to be found in the fact that whereas only a few decades ago anyone was stigmatized who was discovered going to a therapist, today the stigma is inflicted upon any woman who does *not* go to a therapist. Any institution which could so rapidly reverse its status, gaining power and prestige in the most "advanced" nation of a patriarchal planet, clearly must be serving the interests of patriarchy.

* The normalizing and popularizing of such maiming should not be seen in isolation from the increasingly popular phenomenon of transsexualism. As Janice Raymond points out: "Transsexualism has taken only 25 years to become a household word" (See her article: "Transsexualism: The Ultimate Homage to Sex Role Power," in *Chrysalis*, No. 3, fall 1977, pp. 11–23). Although, as Raymond points out, the majority who undergo "sex change operations" are men who want to become women, the same vested interests are being served here as in gynecology.

VII

The seventh component of the gynecological sado-ritual, that is, the meta-ritual of its legitimating re-search and scholarship, has been indecently exposed throughout this analysis. There are two points of particular importance to be emphasized here. The first is that gynecological re-searchers (like all ghosts) love the dark. The second is that they have a propensity to hook their prey with professional renditions of Catch-22.

Love for the Dark

The author of an editorial on "Risks and Benefits of Estrogen Use," which appeared in the *New England Journal of Medicine* in 1975 concluded:

> Unfortunately, questions regarding long-term drug safety can rarely be resolved in a short time. Despite the urgent need for answers, there is little choice but to remain in the dark for a few years more.[108]

In the same issue, the re-searchers who were credited with uncovering the evidence for the causation of cancer by exogenous estrogens boldly assert: "To the best of our knowledge, conclusive studies are unavailable." [109] The authors of another article on estrogens and endometrial cancer, after admitting the probability that one case of cancer would be expected to develop from among every nine women treated with estrogens, extinguish the light of this knowledge with the following gust of hot air:

> It must be evident that this type of estimate is only speculative based on the best information currently available and that there is no means to determine with certainty at present whether this is a cause-and-effect association, and, if so, the precise magnitude of the problem.[110]

Medical ethicists are also often engineers of intellectual blackout. Benjamin Freedman, writing on "A Moral Theory of Informed Consent," snuffs out the lamp with the following conclusion (which the editors found so illuminating that they emphasized it in large italics):

Our conclusion, then, is that the informing of the patient/subject is not a fundamental requirement of valid consent. It is, rather, derivative from the requirement that the consent be the expression of a responsible choice.[111]

By the obscurity of this statement the author deliberately shifts the focus from a patient's clearly informed choice to vague willingness to be experimented upon while being kept essentially in the dark.

Catch-22: Caught Coming and Going

The gynecological patient is frequently in a no-win situation, once she has been hooked. The authors of an article on breast cancer provide a strikingly usual example of this kind of set-up:

At present, prophylactic removal of nearly all the breast tissue appears to be the only way of preventing breast cancer in the obviously vulnerable woman.[112]

As another doctor put it:

Some advocate this approach as the most effective prophylactic procedure to high-risk patients, to say nothing of obviating the diagnostic radiation hazards.[113]

An article on "Giant Uterine Tumors" which reports the "management and surgical removal of a 65 lb. uterine tumor" begins with the sentence: "Surgery for massive abdominal tumors is interesting and challenging." [114] This professional piece placidly lists a series of hideous "procedures," to which the woman (described as a sixty-year-old, black, gravida 1, para 1) was subjected. We are informed that the patient was "afraid of the hospital and surgery." The woman, whose healthy fear had kept her away from the hospital, had lived with the tumor for fifteen years, but had suffered from low-back pain and had trouble "ambulating." After treatment, she had not only the same problems but others, infinitely more serious. She was subsequently hospitalized at a nursing home, where she died approximately seven months after her original admission to the hospital. It is safe to conclude that the surgery was not "interesting and challenging" for her.[115]

In the field of mind-gynecology, Catch-22 is the name of the game. Wolfgang Lederer, in a chapter entitled "Planetary Cancer?", writes with horror of overpopulation, leading to "the extinction of personality in a human glut," and savagely blames this entirely on women.[116] He writes of the "uterine hunger" in feminine (read: normal) women which renders birth control as futile as dieting, and describing motherhood as an "ominous inevitability," which results from the fact that "archaic woman [is] monomaniacally bent on nothing but the best breeding stock, faithful only to her biological mission, unbound by any man-made, father-made law." Lederer drones on that he is *not* only talking about women who are "pathologically fertile." Rather:

> In an overpopulated world, ordinary, "normal" woman may yet become the sorceress who inundates man with ever new creation, who keeps pouring forth a stream of children for whom there is neither role nor room, whose procreative instinct, irresistible, keeps producing like a machine gone mad . . .[117]

Lederer consistently conforms to the contorted logic of Catch-22, asserting just two pages later that:

> . . . there is hardly a woman, *not terribly sick,* who does not wish for at least one child, even though she be a Lesbian and intolerant of men [emphasis mine].[118]

Thus women who want children are called "normal" (in quotation marks) and those who do not are called terribly sick. The quotation marks around "normal," moreover, may be an unintended admission of his deception. Lederer leaves out of his absurd picture a few realistic details, such as the fact that women have always waged a fierce struggle against unwanted pregnancies. He leaves out the fact that men have constantly oppressed women by impregnating them against their will through legal and illegal rape and by denying access to safe abortion and birth control. He also neglects to mention that patriarchy attempts to enforce motherhood by bombarding women with propaganda that this is their inevitable destiny.

The lie embedded in Lederer's language about women also lies exposed in his babble about ecology. Thus we read:

> And in the end the balance of this globe may yet again have to be redressed by the Great Mother herself in her most terrible form: as hunger, as pestilence, as the blind orgasm of the atom.[119]

Just as this thoroughly therapeutic reverser blames the "planetary cancer" of overpopulation upon victimized women, so he falsely attributes patriarchally planned disasters to the "Great Mother." In reality, world hunger is to a large extent managed, and not merely accidental. Pestilence is largely the result of iatrogenesis and of environmental pollution. The sickening use of nuclear energy, that is, the rape of the atom, is preparing the way for a man-made holocaust, which Lederer blindly labels "blind orgasm." The reversal in this image is comparable to labeling the agonized screams of a rape victim "cries of ecstasy."

The final and ultimate Catch-22 of the therapeutic justifiers is their legitimation of psychosurgery, frequently known by such names as *cingulotomy* and *amygdalotomy*. Such operations are done far more frequently on women than on men. Jan Raymond has shown that they attempt a final solution to the patient's problems by irreversibly removing her capacity to confront and transcend problems.[120] This mentality is demonstrated in a journal article by Vernon Mark, Frank Ervin, and two of their colleagues, in which they report that psychosurgery performed on a woman patient was successful, despite the fact that she killed herself. Her suicide was interpreted as a sign that she was getting over her depression, a "gratifying" effect of the operation.[121]

The very title of Mark and Ervin's well-known book on psychosurgery—*Violence and the Brain*—is a specimen of doublethink. The feminist social critic who is at all aware of the horrors perpetrated in the name of psychosurgery could imagine this to be the title of a work on psychosurgical criminal violence. Of course, when she realizes the identity of the authors and looks through the (illustrated) book, she realizes the reversal that has been pulled off. These brain mutilators do not name themselves as perpetrators of violence, but rather brand their patients/subjects as "violent." They do not brand/blame the powerful planners/controllers of the War State who perpetrate mass murder and ecological disaster, but rather support them by destroying deviants.

The Catch-22 of the psychosurgeons' reversing logic hooks their prey into irreversible destruction. These holy ghosts represent the familiar blend of body-and-mind gynecology. They have gone far beyond the "nerve specialists" such as S. Weir Mitchell, however. In all probability, few of their victims can yet match the articulate criticism of Charlotte Perkins Gilman, after her escape from Mitchell's "cure." Still, like Connie, the mental patient in Marge Piercy's novel, *Woman on the Edge of Time,* some can find the deep Sources to know that "this is war" and to fight back. As Crones/Furies find again our new and ancient wisdom and psychic power, we can communicate the gynergy that will save our sisters from being captured and killed. This creation of Self-identified sense of reality is our most potent safeguard against the mind/body violators who offer the "gift of peace" at the price of living death.

CONCLUSION AND AFTERWORD TO CHAPTER SEVEN

NAZI MEDICINE AND AMERICAN GYNECOLOGY: A TORTURE CROSS-CULTURAL COMPARISON

i was sitting in the field behind the institution
& she came up from behind & said,
can i join you, this flower is for you.
how wide & glassy her eyes were, stiff-limbed
from the medicine.

it was only weeks before,
that she ran like a flame thru the locked ward.
i could tell from her screams
that the 6 orderlies had defeated her.
i felt the needle bite with its serpent's tongue
& the men, satisfied, walked away.

Evelyn Posamentier,
from "Sharon, in the Field,"
Chrysalis: A Magazine of Women's Culture

The birds sing summer above the head
of the granite Jew whose stone eyes stare
sweetly. . . .

. . . Red

are the cheeks of the children, smooth, well-fed,
the tourist children with golden hair
bright as the rain El Barrio shed.

Bored, impatient, they play hide-
and-seek in the ovens, laughing where
sweetly the furrows flower red,
bright as the rain my people shed.

Robin Morgan,
from "Dachau,"
Monster

The universities of Germany are her chief glory, and the greatest boon she can give us in the New World is to return our young men infected [*sic*] with the spirit of earnestness and with the love of thoroughness which characterizes the work done in them.

William Osler, 1890

In important ways American gynecology continues to reflect and to refine the professional "spirit" and methods of the medical faculties of Germany and Austria. As Thomas Neville Bonner points out:

The first sizable contingents of Americans interested in obstetrics arrived in Vienna in the years just after the Civil War. Vienna continued for many years to be the chief training ground for American obstetricians, while gynecologists were more likely to base their studies in Berlin. Americans were continually amazed by the unparalleled opportunities to study the processes of pregnancy and birth at Vienna.[1]

The Searcher would do well to wonder about these "unparalled opportunities," particularly in light of Rich's analysis of the conditions in the Vienna Lying-In Hospital in the nineteenth century. As she points out, there is testimony that in the 1840s the mortality there from "childbed fever" was so high that women were buried two in a coffin to disguise the rate of death. Moreover, in 1861, Semmelweis published a book establishing that poor women who literally gave birth in the streets of Vienna had a lower mortality rate than those giving birth in the First Clinic (staffed entirely by physicians and medical students) of the Vienna Lying-In Hospital. For his truthful exposé, that scholar was ostracized by his profession. Twenty years later, Semmelweis's plea for doctors to wash their hands finally became accepted practice.[2]

The women who suffered agonizing deaths from the filthy hands of medical re-searchers in Vienna doubtless were *not* "continually amazed by the unparalleled opportunities to study the processes of pregnancy and birth at Vienna." Indeed, as Rich states:

> Women knew that delivery in the hospitals meant a far greater likelihood of death than deliveries at home. . . . Many ran from the hospitals, others committed suicide rather than enter.[3]

As for the "spirit" of gynecological study which lured Americans to Berlin, we can get a slight hint of its "earnestness" and of its influence from Bonner's description of the gynecological clinic of August Martin, which in the late nineteenth century was "extremely popular among Americans." We read:

> Nowhere in Berlin . . . could such a variety of operations be seen as in his hospital, and his practical courses were always crowded. His students included some of the best known names in American gynecology and obstetrics . . .[4]

In order to imagine the probable context of the "variety of operations" which "could be seen" in such a medical circus, it may be helpful for the Searcher to recall the abominations performed in the operating theatre of J. Marion Sims in the Woman's Hospital in New York. It is also significant that German physicians admired Sims. Bonner writes:

> Europeans found something to praise, too, in the work of American gynecologists, especially that of Marion Sims, whose death in 1883 brought a front page obituary and tribute to the pages of the *Deutsche Medicinische Wochenschrift*.[5]

Gynecology is one of the few fields in which American medical re-searchers have not lagged far behind. The professional climate, in which the goals of "study and research" have overshadowed the will to heal and have perverted healing into hurting, was to a large extent imported. Rosemary Stevens states:

> It has been estimated that at least one-third and perhaps half of the best-known men and women [*sic*] in American medicine in that period [1870–1914] received some part of their training in Germany, including virtually the entire faculties of the medical schools at Harvard, Johns Hopkins, Yale and Michigan. The effect of this massive movement is still felt in the outlook and hierarchical structure of American medical schools.[6]

Although Stevens is hardly a strong critic of this "massive movement" or of its implications, she does point to the fact of the derivative nature of American re-search, indicating that "experimental research," which did not begin to get underway in the United States until the 1890s, was in large measure "stimulated by an outstanding cadre of German-trained Americans." [7]

Just as American body-gynecology is deeply influenced by the German and Austrian professionals, so also is mind-gynecology. Bonner points out that in the late nineteenth century, Americans were advised "to pursue nervous diseases in Heidelberg as well as Berlin . . ." [8] He also says:

> . . . in neurology, psychiatry, and psychoanalysis the German and Viennese impact on American thought and practice was decisive until well into the twentieth century. Even Sigmund Freud was involved at one time in an English language course for Americans in Vienna. Most of the key figures in the development of psychiatry in the United States . . . were either born in Central Europe or studied there.[9]

Moreover, Austrian and German specialists in these fields also came to America in the twentieth century. Freud, for example, gave a series of lectures at Clark University in 1909. Otto Rank (1884–1939), a favored pupil of Freud, had a considerable following in the United States and established a "functional" school of social work at the University of Pennsylvania. Other well-known analysts who worked in this country were Theodore Reik (1888–1969) and Wilhelm Reich (1897–1957).[10]

Finally, it is noteworthy that German psychiatrists whose ideas influenced and helped to promote the Nazi "euthanasia" program also came to have a particularly strong influence upon American specialists. One of these German psychiatrists was Alfred Hoche, who in 1920 co-authored the influential book, *The Release of the Destruction of Life Devoid of Value*—the book which provided the Nazi exterminators with a legitimating slogan and ideology. He also trained a number of eminent specialists who taught in America.*

The emergence of the Nazi party in Germany even contributed to German influence in America. Franz Alexander states:

> Under the political upheavals starting in the early 1930's in Europe both the Berlin and Vienna Institutes [of psychoanalysis] disintegrated. Most members of both institutes emigrated to England and to the United States.
>
> The development of organized training in the United States followed in principle the patterns established originally in Berlin and Vienna.[11]

Although we should assume that there was some difference of political opinion between those psychoanalysts who emigrated to the United States and those who stayed in Germany, the point is that there is an identity of origin, that is, of tra-

* Among these, according to Fredric Wertham, were Robert Wartenburg, professor of neurology in California, and Adolf Meyer, professor of psychiatry at Johns Hopkins. Another psychiatrist whose ideas contributed to the justification of the massacre of mental patients was Ernst Reudin, professor of psychiatry at Basel and at Munich. Reudin emphasized the alleged influence of heredity upon mental disorders, providing "scientific" reasons for the compulsory sterilization law which was the forerunner of the mass killing of mental patients. Like Hoche, Reudin influenced American psychiatry through his students. One of these was Eugen Kahn, who became a noted professor of psychiatry at Yale. See Fredric Wertham, M.D., *A Sign for Cain: An Exploration of Human Violence* (New York: Macmillan, 1966), pp. 161–63.

dition and training, which affected mind-set and methodology.

It is my intention here to show some threads of connectedness between manifestations of the medical re-search mania as it worked itself out in Nazi death camps and as it has manifested itself in gynecology practiced in America. There are striking similarities in style and method of perpetrating and legitimating atrocities. Thus the following analysis constitutes a fitting conclusion and afterword to the seventh chapter, and —for those who will face the horror and acknowledge the connections—a warning and source of clues to aid in a-mazing and in avoiding the traps set by the righteous Erasers/Defacers of Female Selves.

I

Like the body- and mind-gynecologists of America, the physicians and psychiatrists who justified and participated in the Nazi extermination and medical experimentation programs operated in the tradition of the Torture Cross society. Although their victims—mental patients and Jews—were of both sexes, all were cast into the victim role modeled on that of the victims of patriarchal gynocide, which is the root and paradigm for genocide.[12] This massacre was justified by an ideology of purity. Prior to the extermination of the Jews, when the targets for massacre were "Aryan" mental patients, the alleged object was purification of the race from the burden and contamination of defectives. The same ideology was extended to legitimate the elimination of Jews from the general population.

II

Since the Nazi Medical Erasers were allegedly acting "under orders," they were absolved of all responsibility. In the publisher's epilogue to *Doctors of Infamy* the following statement appears: "To the end, they [the major medical criminals] did not acknowledge that they had done any wrong." [13] Defendant Karl Brandt, one of the doctors convicted in the Nuremberg trials for cruel experimentation on prisoners, was an articulate spokesman for this pure state of mind. Asked by Judge Sebring whether in the war situation the institution which requires an experiment causing the death of involuntary subjects takes away responsibility on the part of a physician, Doctor Brandt responded:

> In my opinion it removes it from the physician, for from this moment on the physician is only an instrument, in about the same way as is an officer in the field who is ordered to take three or five soldiers without fail to a position where they will perish, fall.[14]

The military analogy is important. With Virginia Woolf, we should recall that military and academic processions are profoundly interconnected. The processors of these and other professional processions function as models and as erasers of responsibility. Thus a German physician who killed training-school boys and girls with intravenous injections of morphia stated in court: "I see today that it was not right. . . . I was always told that the responsibility lies with the professors from Berlin." [15] Another typical case was that of S.S. Captain Josef Kramer (the "Beast of Belsen") who in the so-called "Doctors' Trial" attributed his active role in medical experiments to orders received from Professor August Hirt, head of the Anatomical Institute of the University of Strasbourg. Kramer stated:

> I had no feelings in carrying out these things because I had received an order to kill the eighty inmates in the way I already told you. That, by the way, was the way I was trained.[16]

III

Following the pattern with which the reader is now familiar, the atrocity was planned by a medical professional elite and spread downward. Chief among the early leaders of these "men of science" were university professors of psychiatry and directors and staff members of mental hospitals. These men systematically planned and executed the massacre of mental patients, which began in 1939. Wertham estimates that whereas in 1939 there were about 300,000 mental patients in psychiatric hospitals, institutions, or clinics, in 1946 their number was 40,000.

Again and again the excuse has been given that psychiatrists were merely obeying a law or following an order. Hitler gave no order to kill mental patients indiscriminately. It wasn't necessary:

> Even if the psychiatrists were under orders, which they were not, it is noteworthy that their complete mobilization for killing patients went as speedily and as smoothly as the military mobilization of soldiers to fight the enemy.[17]

The final planning for the massacre of mental patients was done in July 1939. The planners included professors of psychiatry and chairmen of departments of psychiatry of the leading universities and medical schools of Germany: Berlin, Heidelberg, Bonn, Wurzburg.[18]

The extermination program was of course not limited to mental patients, nor were the medical exterminators restricted to the field of psychiatry. By 1945 there were more than a thousand concentration camps in Germany, Austria, and occupied countries. Besides Jews, who constituted the vast majority of those killed, the approximately seven million people killed included gypsies, Slavs, prisoners of war, political prisoners, and homosexuals. Their unspeakable agony was exacerbated by the infamous medical experiments, which Shirer describes as resulting from sadism, perpetrated by eminent members of the medical profession:

> It is a tale of horror of which the German medical profession cannot be proud. Although the "experiments" were conducted by fewer than two hundred murderous quacks—albeit some of them held eminent posts in the medical world—their criminal work was known to thousands of leading physicians of the Reich, not a single one of whom, so far as the record shows, ever uttered the slightest public protest.[19]

Of course, doctors were not the only ones involved in genocidal torture. Some of the cruel experiments were initiated by pharmaceutical firms, as are some of the gynocidal experiments carried on in America today. So also businessmen found that the supplying of crematories, gas furnaces, and chemicals for killing and disposing of bodies was a lucrative affair. The many large industries which knowingly employed slave labor from the death camps (for example, Krupp, I. G. Farben, Volkswagen, Continental Rubber, and Shell) also profited. The parallels between this profitable profusion and the spread of iatrogenic gynecology in America should not be ignored by Searchers. The architects and builders of hospitals, manufacturers of medical equipment—from hospital beds to surgical instruments to devices for electroshock treatment to prostheses—benefit financially. Although slave labor in the strict sense is not employed, the fact that millions of unpaid housewives and underpaid female workers are destined to "benefit" from such equipment after they have rendered their services to the system is thought-provoking. Moreover, the spread of Nazi medical atrocities, like the expansion of American gynecology, was rapid and efficient. As psychiatrist Leo Alexander admitted:

> Nazi propaganda was highly effective in perverting public opinion and public conscience in a remarkably short time. In the medical profession this expressed itself in a rapid decline in standards of professional ethics.[20]

IV

The use of women as token torturers is another familiar feature of Nazi demonology. As Wertham reports:

> . . . in 1941 the psychiatric institution Hadamar celebrated the cremation of the ten thousandth mental patient in a special ceremony. Psychiatrists, nurses, attendants, and secretaries all participated. Everybody received a bottle of beer for the occasion.[21]

Not only were there willing nurses, attendants, and secretaries; there were also token women doctors. Herta Oberheuser, M.D., camp physician at the Ravensbruck concentration camp for women prisoners, was the one woman defendant at the famous Doctors' Trial. Her behavior was cruel. The fact is, however, that her existence (like that of Frau Ilse Koch, the wife of the commandant of Buchenwald, nicknamed "the Bitch of Buchenwald") is used to mask not only the overwhelmingly male population of medical murderers, but also the fact that the originators and controllers of the operation were male.

V

The Nazi medical horror show was just as bureaucratic and methodical as the other aspects of their assembly-line extermination program, which as a whole represented the ultimate in streamlined orderliness, repetitiveness, and fixation upon details. As one survivor described this environment, it was "a fantastically well-organized, spick-and-span hell." [22] As we have seen, Searchers need not search far to see the "spick-and-span hell" aspects of gynecological medicine and brain-cleansing therapy.

An important point to note concerning such compulsive orderliness and methodical amassing of detail is the fact that the medical murderers showed a tendency to hang themselves with their meticulous records, note-keeping, and correspondence.* As we have seen in Chapter Seven, Searchers can also find abundant evidence against gynecological Bluebeards. Their self-condemning records are available not only in pro-

* Thus, for example, Wolfram Sievers (dubbed "the Nazi Bluebeard"), who collected severed Jewish heads for the august Professor August Hirt, head of the Anatomical Institute of the University of Strasbourg, kept a meticulous diary which, together with his correspondence, "contributed to his gallows end." (See William L. Shirer, *The Rise and Fall of the Third Reich: A History of Nazi Germany* [New York: Simon and Schuster, 1960], pp. 980–81). Another example of a self-damning letter-writer was Doctor Sigmund Rauscher, whose groveling letters to Himmler exhibit him begging to have professional criminals available for the infamous "high-altitude rescue experiments," in which the victims suffered excruciating deaths. (See Alexander Mitscherlich, M.D., and Fred Mielke, *Doctors of Infamy: The Story of the Nazi Medical Crimes* [New York: Henry Schuman, 1949], pp. 4–7.)

fessional books and journal articles, but also in personal correspondence.[23] The problem is not primarily one of availability of evidence, in a material sense, but rather it is one of developing our own ability to a-maze the material, which is grossly obvious (obviously gross) and yet eludes the untrained or mistrained eye.

VI

Clearly, in the Nazi medical atrocities, behavior deemed unacceptable by the righteous rest of the civilized world became acceptable and normative in Germany. We have seen that the planning and execution of the massacre and utilization of mental patients and death camp inmates went smoothly, and that an enormous number of killers (from "desk murderers" to rank-and-file torturers and murderers) were involved. It would be naive to think that the majority of these appeared evil to those around them. Eric Fromm rightly points out the error of believing that an evil man must be devoid of any positive quality, that is, that he must look like the devil. This "prevents people from recognizing potential Hitlers before they have shown their true faces." Fromm accurately states:

> Such devils exist, but they are rare. . . . Much more often the intensely destructive person will show a front of kindliness; courtesy, love of family, of children, of animals; he will speak of his ideals and good intentions. But not only this. There is hardly a man who is utterly devoid of any kindness, of any good intentions. . . . *Hence, as long as one believes that the evil man wears horns, one will not discover an evil man.*[24]

As the Searcher is prepared to recognize, the fallacy in Fromm's analysis lies in singling out such men as Hitler for "study," while failing to acknowledge that this description applies to a state of being which is common among the members of his own profession—as evidenced in the psychiatrists' massacre of mental patients in Nazi Germany and in less spectacular atrocities elsewhere. Such "good doctors" do not, of course, wear horns. Thus they are easily accepted and can set the standards/norms of conduct for their colleagues and underlings.

To describe such phenomena, Hannah Arendt provided us with her often quoted expression, "the fearsome, word-and-thought-defying *banality of evil.*" [25] In studying the material on the Nazi medical atrocities, we can see different forms of such banality, since there were different degrees of proximity to the actual physical events. Thus the psychiatrists who planned (or tacitly consented to) the "euthanasia program" and the other university professors, such as Hirt, who handed down orders to underlings in the death camps, masked their evil intent with ideological abstractions and bureaucratic statistics. Closer to the scene of the crimes were those who carried out orders and/or voluntarily carried out the atrocious experiments. In their case, a sense of ease/normality/banality was achieved by the technique of physically and psychologically degrading the victims. Such degradations contributed to the appearance of "otherness," fostering a sense of detachment from the victims destroyed in the name of "scientific research." We should not overlook the fact that this degradation, which undermined the victims' self-respect, diminished the potential for bonding among the prisoners. As Des Pres points out:

> How much self-esteem can one maintain, how readily can one respond with respect to the needs of another, if both stink, if both are caked with mud and feces? . . . Here was an effective mechanism for intensifying the already heightened irritability of prisoners towards each other, and thus for stifling in common loathing the impulse toward solidarity.[26]

The "banality of evil" is not an unfamiliar theme to women struggling to refuse all of patriarchy's bad medicine. We have heard the trite untruisms of medical and therapeutic professionals and of their colleagues in other professional/processional circles. We have witnessed and heard testimony concerning the acts of those who execute the Holy Orders of Helping and Healing. We have seen gynocidal practices and operations become acceptable to and accepted by women who are filled with self-loathing, and who are unable to bond with the loathed mirror-images of their decaying selves. Such fashioned and fashionable women are not caked with mud and feces, but are encrusted in the mold of man-made femininity. As I have already demonstrated, the conditions of actual physical filth are not necessary to make women feel dirty. This is accomplished in other ways. The entire "culture" of patriarchy continually generates messages of female filth, for example, through theology and pornography.[27] The degradation of women's organs and such functions as menstruation—promoted at present by medical, pharmaceutical, and therapeutic Mister Cleans—prepossesses the intended victims with "feminine hygiene," preoccupying them with such measures as excessive douching and use of deadly deodorants. The induced preoccupation with "fixing-up" the female body, the cosmetic caking of hair, face, and body with dangerous and expensive dyes, the molding of the female form into unhealthful shapes—all contribute to lack of Self-esteem and to common loathing.

The role of male obscenity in banalizing the massacre of women should not be overlooked. In common locker-room jargon, as Julia Stanley points out, there is usage of such illuminating terms as *piece of ass, fleshpot, broad, cunt, gash, pisspallet, slopjar, pig, bedbug.*[28] In all-male organizations—for example, the Marine Corps—every part of the female anatomy is used as a name-calling weapon of degradation to whip "boys" into "real men." Women are in fact conditioned by such talk, since it conditions the attitudes of males, whose contemptuous treatment deeply affects our self-images. More directly, these degrading views are conveyed through the vast technology of subliminal advertising.[29] All of this paves the way for efficient, smooth-running, gynecological gynocide. As Denise Connors has demonstrated:

> An analysis of the "Medical Profession" makes it blatantly clear who the Subject is, as well as the interchangeability of the words Woman . . . Patient . . . Object. The role of patients is patterned after the role of women—hence women patients are doubly cursed.[30]

Such objectification is reflected in common medical terminology. Although this is not obviously obscene, it insidiously degrades women. Thus, for example, a typical description of a female patient is "gravida 10, para 8, abortus 1." [31] This kind of language makes it difficult to realize that the subject/object thus described is a living, loving, sensitive woman, deserving dignity and respect.

Nowhere does the mechanism of banalizing of evil function more smoothly and insidiously than in gynecology. A symptom of this is the predictable re-action of outrage at an analysis which dares to expose the common roots and similarities between Nazi medical atrocities and American gynecological practice. Since the degradation of women is as commonplace and acceptable as the neighborhood drug store, this is perceived—if it is perceived at all—as minimally offensive. By contrast, the Nazi atrocities are recognized *as atrocities.* Yet the latter *are* belittled in the sense that they are seen as isolated events. Since their radical origin in patriarchal myth and social reality is not acknowledged, their deep roots are not eradicated. It is precisely the isolation of those genocidal atrocities from the reality of patriarchal gynocide, particularly in its most lethal modern manifestations, which should elicit outrage, for it minimizes the horror of the Holocaust, allowing its uneradicated roots to grow unnoticed, to sprout again elsewhere. This resistance to seeing connections, this scorn for integrity of vision re-presents/re-enforces the triumph of the banality of evil.

VII

It is important for Crone-ographers to note the role of scholarly legitimation of the Nazi psychiatric and medical atrocities. We have seen that there is much documentation in scholarly works which expose the medical experimentations carried on in the death camps. Generally these are seen as inexplicable atrocities, as if they sprang from nowhere. If connections are made with other mass killings, they are rarely made with the torture and massacre in the witchcraze which reached the greatest extremes in Germany.[32] Moreover, the Nazi medical atrocities are not examined by scholars as a logical development of the medical profession's methodology and its establishing of priority of "research and study" over healing.

The language of Dr. Andrew C. Ivy concerning the medical atrocities is illuminating. He writes: "It appears that fewer than two hundred German physicians participated directly in the medical war crimes; however, it is clear that several hundred more were aware of what was going on." [33] While this appears to be a broad condemnation of German medicine, it actually functions to disguise the enormity of the corruption. As we have already seen, Shirer estimates that *thousands* of German physicians knew. It is hard to imagine that there were many who did not know. Moreover, since the professional club of physicians/psychiatrists is hardly confined within national boundaries, it is evident that many non-Germans knew. Ivy castigates only Germans, however, suggesting that even if "one single courageous individual" could not have saved the honor of German medicine, "such an individual could have done something to mitigate the horrors which are related in this book." [34] He does not connect this idea with any information about the horrors perpetrated in the name of American medicine. Nor does he call for a courageous American physician to criticize his destructive and incompetent colleagues, or to expose the roots of medical massacre (such as perverted priorities and murderous methodology) which are transnational. His critique is limited, in more ways than one; certainly it is limited by national boundaries.

Indeed, Doctor Ivy fails to express an understanding of the interrelatedness of atrocities. He fails to acknowledge the existence of gynocide and its connection with genocide. Consequently, he makes the following re-veiling statement:

> Now it appears evident to me that this *"witches' sabbat"* of medical crime was only the logical end result of the mythology of racial inequality and of the gradual but finally complete encroachment on the ethics and freedom of medicine by the Nazis . . . [emphasis mine].[35]

It would be impossible, by now, for the Journeyer/Explorer of this Passage to ignore or to be surprised by the reversal involved in comparing the Nazi medical crimes to a witches' sabbat. Doctor Ivy was at least subliminally clued in to the connections between the witchburnings and the medical crimes in Nazi Germany and thus slipped in this stunning and precise reversal. Arguments about whether the reversal was "conscious" or "intentional" are useless. Whether Ivy wrote in "ignorance" or not, his odiously deceptive comparison is "true" to the tradition of patriarchal scholarship, functioning to perpetuate the persecution of Spinsters/Hags/Crones/Witches.

It is important to notice that the language of respected studies of the death camp atrocities (with the exception of psychiatric/psychoanalytic studies, as we shall see presently) does not erase or belittle the horror of the "experiments." We have seen that no one has had the gall to refer to the Holocaust of the Jews in Germany as a Nazi "custom" (although *suttee* is commonly called a hindu "custom"). The doctors who ordered and performed the infamous medical experiments are clearly labeled "doctors of infamy." In contrast to this, most gynecological experimentation upon women in the United States is not even acknowledged as experimentation, as we have seen in relation to The Pill, DES, estrogen replacement therapy, and various forms of gynecological surgery. When the deadly effects of such treatment become too obvious, the situation is commonly covered by the jargon of fair gamesmanship, in which "risks" are weighed against "benefits" of the procedures. Women who have been unnecessarily mutilated and who have died premature, agonizing deaths are often blandly described as having "benefited." The ominous implications of the usual re-solution to such problems—that is, the claim that "further study is needed"—elude the naive true believer in miraculous medicine.

If we look specifically at the major psychiatric atrocity of Nazi Germany, the massacre of hundreds of thousands of mental patients, the initial problem is that it is hard to see anything, since the facts are erased. First, the project was—and still is—euphemistically named the "euthanasia program." Second, the number of victims is erased. As Wertham notes:

. . . in none of the publications, books, or news reports of recent years is a more-or-less correct figure given. It is characteristic that without exception all the figures that are mentioned are far below the reality.[36]

Third, the fact that renowned professors of psychiatry and chairmen of departments of psychiatry in German universities participated in planning the program is erased. Again, Wertham makes the point: "Historians of medicine and sociologists will have a lot of work to do to explain this. So far they have not stated the problem or even noted the fact." [37]

Searchers should pay particular attention to this *silence* of scholars concerning the role of psychiatry in the Nazi massacre of mental patients. This deadly quiet stands in stark contrast to the cries of outrage (from physicians, historians, sociologists, theologians, et cetera) against the medical experiments carried on by physicians in the death camps. Although one may detect hypocrisy in the outraged insistence of American physicians that they are totally different from the death camp doctors, the *fact* that there were medical atrocities and that there were doctors who were agents of these is not in itself erased.

In contrast to this, the role of German psychiatrists has been erased. Yet, the fact is that leading professors of psychiatry from Germany's most prestigious universities were directly involved in the planning of the "euthanasia program." [38] Hags may well be suspicious about why American psychiatrists and their colleagues in allied fields de-emphasize—to the point of erasure—the Nazi psychiatrists' responsibility for massacre. In the light of the fact that psychiatrists were originators/planners of the euthanasia program which prepared the way for the escalation of mass murder in the death camps, we should reflect carefully upon the implications of their insidious omnipresence as guiding spirits of gynecology.[39]

I suggest that a basic clue to the deep kinship between the American mind-gynecologists and the Nazi mind-genecologists* is their shared belief in the rightness of blaming the

* I use the term *genecologist* loosely. Merriam-Webster defines *genecology* as "a branch of ecology concerned primarily with the species and its genetically variant subdivisions, with their position in nature and with

victim (although, of course, blame is not called "blame" and the victim is not called "victim"). We have already seen ample evidence of how this method is used against women (for example, in Freud's *The Case of Dora*). It is instructive to see how it operates in assessments of the death camp victims. As Des Pres points out, most psychoanalytic studies maintain that the prisoners "regressed" to infantile behavior:

> Here, as in general from the psychoanalytic point of view, context is not considered. The fact that the survivor's situation was itself abnormal is simply ignored. That the preoccupation with food was caused by literal starvation does not count; and the fact that camp inmates were *forced* to live in filth is likewise overlooked.[40]

Hag-ographers are all too familiar with this noncontextual kind of judging on the part of psychoanalysts, psychiatrists, and other therapists.

An illuminating example of such blind-think regarding death camp inmates is the work of Bruno Bettelheim. He describes the fact that new prisoners were given "nonsensical tasks, such as carrying heavy rocks from one place to another, and after a while back to the place where they had picked them up." He also admits that they were forced to dig holes in the ground with their bare hands even though tools were available. Then he makes the following assessment:

> They resented the senseless work, although *it should have been immaterial to them whether their work was useful or not.* They felt debased when they were forced to perform "childish" or stupid labor. They *felt* even more debased when they were hitched like horses to heavy wagons and forced to gallop. By the same token many prisoners hated singing rollicking songs by command of the SS more than being beaten by them [emphases mine].[41]

Although Bettelheim obliquely acknowledges that this degradation was planned, he writes of it as "an influence [*sic*] adding

---

the controlling genetic and ecological features." The genocidal Nazis were, of course, attempting to control genetic features of the species.

to regression into childhood," giving the impression that the prisoners' behavior was inherently regressive. Writing of their "masochistic, passive-dependent, and childlike attitudes," he says: "But as a psychological mechanism inside the prisoner it *coincided* with SS efforts to produce childlike inadequacy and dependency [emphasis mine]." [42]

Searchers will not find it too difficult to see parallels with women's situation in patriarchy. We often must "dig with our bare hands" although tools are available—but not available to us. This is clear to feminists who have worked to create Women's Studies programs, women's health clinics, women's businesses, and so on. Women also are commonly required to do senseless labor and to "sing rollicking songs" ("act happy") by command of their "bosses." The resentment, sense of inadequacy and dependency, and "childlikeness" which are caused in women by the male ruling caste are named by therapists "natural," "inherent," "feminine," "normal." At the same time, women are blamed for such "normality."

Such blaming of the female victim by mind-gynecologists is so omnipresent that it is thoroughly banal. Hags will note that Bettelheim is as deeply insightful about women in America as he is about the death camp prisoners. He tells us: "We must start with the realization that, as much as women want to be good scientists or engineers, they want first and foremost to be womanly companions of men and to be mothers." [43] Boringly, predictably, an objective predicament is twisted into an inherent "want."

A basic meaning of *banal* is "commonplace." The various modes of scholarly legitimation of Nazi medical atrocities, ranging from particularized, myopic outrage to deadly silence, exhibit the fact that such evil is commonplace, that it is common also to *this* time and place. The Holocaust of the Jews in Nazi Germany was a reality of indescribable horror. Precisely for this reason we should not settle for an analysis which fails to go to the roots of the evil of genocide. The deepest meanings of the banality of evil are lost in the kind of re-search which shrinks/localizes perspectives on oppression so that they can be contained strictly within ethnic and "religious group" dimensions.* The sado-rituals of patriarchy are perpetually perpetrated. Their plane/domain is the entire planet. The paradigm and context for genocide is trite, everyday, banalized gynocide.

* In a sample of New York City physicians, re-searchers found the following distribution of major religious groups: Catholics, 21 percent; Protestants, 13 percent; Jews, 53 percent; those of no religion, 13 percent. By comparison to this, the distribution of religious groups in a 1975 sample of New York psychiatrists was: Catholics, 7 percent; Protestants, 13 percent; Jews, 62 percent; those of no religion, 18 percent. See John L. Lally, "Selection as an Interactive Process: The Case of Catholic Psychoanalysts and Psychiatrists," *Social Sciences and Medicine,* Vol. 9 (1975), p. 158. See also W. E. Henry, J. H. Sims, and S. L. Spray, *The Fifth Profession* (San Francisco: Jossey-Bass, 1971). The authors maintain that in their recent survey of mental health professionals in the nation's three largest metropolitan areas, the percentage of Jews and of those who adhere to no traditional religion was disproportionately high in comparison to frequencies of Catholics and Protestants.

In the light of the anti-Semitic medical and psychiatric track record in Nazi Germany, one could be surprised at such figures. I suggest that they point to the fact that an ethnic or a "religious group" analysis of medical and therapeutic myths and atrocities is inadequate.

THE THIRD PASSAGE

GYN/ECOLOGY:
SPINNING NEW TIME/SPACE

There are words I cannot choose again:
humanism, androgyny

Such words have no shame in them, no diffidence
before the raging stoic grandmothers:

their glint is too shallow, like a dye
that does not permeate

the fibers of actual life
as we live it, now. . . .

My heart is moved by all I cannot save:
so much has been destroyed

I have to cast my lot with those
who age after age, perversely,

with no extraordinary power,
reconstitute the world.

Adrienne Rich,
from "Natural Resources,"
The Dream of a Common Language

Fancy! A great ear at the heart of the universe—at the heart of our common life—hearing women to speech—to our own speech.

Nelle Morton,
"Beloved Image!"
American Academy of Religion Workshop,
December 28, 1977

I am a woman committed to
a politics
of transliteration, the methodology

of a mind
stunned at the suddenly
possible shifts of meaning—for which
like amnesiacs

in a ward on fire, we must
find words
or burn.

Olga Broumas,
from "Artemis,"
Beginning with 0

PRELUDE TO THE THIRD PASSAGE

In the course of The Second Passage, Crone-ographers who have survived dis-covering the various manifestations of Goddess-murder on this patriarchal planet have become aware of the deep and universal intent to destroy the divine spark in women. We have seen that the perpetrators of this planetary atrocity are acting out the deadly myths of patriarchy and that this ritual enactment of the sado-myths has become more refined with the "progress of civilization." This refinement includes an escalation of violence and visibility and at the same time a decrease of visibility to those mesmerized by the Processions of fathers, sons, and holy ghosts.

The know-ing of this deadly intent has been necessary for our a-mazing process of exorcism. It is equally necessary for moving on the Labyrinthine Journey of Ecstasy, for this process is damaged/hindered by not knowing/acknowledging the dangers, traps, deceptions built into the terrain. As long as "knowledge" of the horrors of androcracy is fragmented, compartmentalized, belittled, we cannot integrate this into our know-ing process. We then mistake the male-made maze for our Self-centering way.

Since we have come through the somber Passage of recognizing the alien/alienating environment in which woman-hating rituals vary from *suttee* to gynecological iatrogenesis, we can begin to tread/thread our way in new time/space. This knowing/acting/Self-centering Process is itself the creating of a new, woman-identified environment. It is the becoming of Gyn/Ecology. This involves the dis-spelling of the mind/spirit/body pollution that is produced out of man-made myths, language, ritual atrocities, and meta-rituals such as "scholarship," which erase our Selves. It also involves dis-covering the sources of the Self's original movement, hearing the moving of this movement. It involves speaking forth the New Words which correspond to this deep listening, speaking the words of our lives.

Breaking out of the patriarchal processions into our own Gyn/Ecological process is the specific theme of this, The Third Passage. In a general sense, our movement through the preceding Passages has all been and is Gyn/Ecological Journeying. Moreover, since our movement is not linear but rather resembles spiraling, we continue to re-member/re-call/re-claim the knowledge gained in the preceding Passages, assuming this into our present/future. Hence, there is no authentic way in which the preceding Passages can be dissociated from the Third. Thus, Gyn/Ecology is not the climax or linear end point in time of the Journey, but rather it is a defining theme/thread in our Labyrinthine Journey of the inner ear, in the course of which we constantly hear deeper and deeper reverberations from all of the Passages and learn to be attuned to echoes, subtleties, and distinctions not attended to before. Yet, Gyn/Ecology is the proper name for The Third Passage, for it names the patterns/designs of the moving Female-identified environment which can only be heard/seen after the Journeyer has been initiated through The First and The Second Passages.

As the Spinster spins into and through this Passage she is en-couraged by her strengthened powers of hearing and seeing. By now she has begun to develop a kind of multidimensional/multiform power of sensing/understanding her environment. This is a Self-identified *synaesthesia:* it is woman-identified *gynaesthesia*. It is a complex way of perceiving the interrelatedness of seemingly disparate phenomena. It is also a pattern-detecting power which may be named positive paranoia. Far from being a debilitating "mental disease," this is strengthening and realistic dis-ease in a polluted and destructive environment. Derived from the Greek terms *para,* meaning beyond, outside of, and *nous,* meaning mind, the term *paranoia* is appropriate to describe movement beyond, outside of, the patriarchal mind-set. It is the State of Positively Revolting Hags.

Moving through all three Passages is moving from the state of anesthesia to empowering gynaesthesia, as dormant senses become awake and alive. Since, in The Second Passage, the Voyager became more aware not only of the blatancy and interconnectedness of phallocratic evil, but also of its reality, she is enabled to detect and name its implicit presence and therefore to overcome roadblocks in her dis-covery of be-ing. Empowered with positive paranoia she can move with increasing confidence.

We have seen that this is the age of holy ghosts, with particular reference to gynecology. It is an age of manipulation through/by invisible and *almost* insensible presences. Some of these might be called physical, such as radiation and "white noise." Others more properly may be said to belong to the realm of the spirit, of "ghost." We are dealing here with the realm of implicit or subliminal manipulation, of quiet, almost indiscernible, intent on the part of the manipulators and quiet, unacknowledged acceptance of their ghostly presences and messages by their victims. Hence, the first chapter of this Passage will be concerned with Spooking. The Haggard Journeyer will not be astonished to find that Spooking is multileveled. Women are spooked by patriarchal males in a variety of ways; for example, through implicit messages of their institutions, through body language, through the silences and deceptive devices of their media, their grammar, their education, their professions, their technology, their oppressive and confusing fashions, customs, etiquette, "humor," through their subliminal advertising and their "sublime" music (such as christmas carols piped into supermarkets that seduce the listener into identifying with the tamed Goddess who abjectly adores her son).

Women are also spooked by other women who act as instrumental agents for patriarchal males, concurring, with varying degrees of conscious complicity, in all of the above tactics. To the extent that any woman acts—or nonacts when action is required—in such complicity, she functions as a double agent of spooking, for politically she *is* and *is not* functioning as a woman. Since Hags/Witches have expectations of her—righteous expectations which are almost impossible to discard without falling into total cynicism and despair—she spooks us doubly, particularly by her absences/silences/nonsupport. Finally, Spinsters are spooked by the alien presences that have been inspired (breathed into) our own spirits/minds. These involve fragments of the false self which are still acting/nonacting in complicity with the Possessors. They also take the shape of nameless fears, unbearable implanted guilt feelings for affirming our own being, fear of our newly discovered powers and of successful use of them, fear of dis-covering/releasing our own deep wells of anger, particularly fear of our anger against other women and against ourselves for failing our Selves. Spinsters are spooked by fear of the Ultimate Irony, which would be to become a martyr/scapegoat for feminism, whose purpose is to release women from the role of martyr and scapegoat.

Faced with being spooked, Spinsters are learning to Spook/Speak back. This Spinster-Spooking is also re-calling/re-membering/re-claiming our Witches' power to cast spells, to charm, to overcome prestige with prestidigitation, to cast glamours, to employ occult grammar, to enthrall, to bewitch. Spinster-Spooking is both cognitive and tactical. Cognitively, it means pattern-detecting. It means understanding the time-warps through which women are divided from each other—since each woman comes to consciousness through the unique events of her own history. It means also seeing the problems caused through space-warps—since Hags and potential Hags are divided from each other in separate institutional settings, disabled from sharing survival tactics in our condition of common isolation, spooked by our apparent aloneness. Tactically, Spooking means learning to refuse the seductive summons by the Passive Voices that call us into the State of Animated Death. It means learning to hear and respond to the call of the wild, learning ways of en-couraging and en-spiriting the Self and other Spinsters, learning con-questing, learning methods of dispossession, specifically of dis-possessing the Self of possession by the past and possession by the future. It means a-mazing the modern witchcraze, developing skills for unpainting the Painted Birds possessed through the device of tokenism, exposing the Thoroughly Therapeutic Society.

Since Spooking cannot always be done alone, and since it is a primary but not complete expression of Gyn/Ecology, the second chapter of this Passage is concerned with Sparking. In order to move on the con-questing Voyage, Spinsters need fire. It is significant that witches and widows were burned alive, consumed by fire. For fire is source and symbol of energy, of gynergy. It is because women are known to be energy sources that patriarchal males seek to possess and consume us. This is done less dramatically in day-by-day draining of energy, in the slow and steady extinguishing of women's fire. Sparking is necessary to re-claim our fire. Sparking, like Spooking, is a form of Gyn/Ecology. Sparking is Speaking with tongues of fire. Sparking is igniting the divine Spark in women. Light and warmth, which are necessary for creating and moving, are results of Sparking. Sparking is creating a room of one's own, a moving time/spaceship of one's own, in which the Self can expand, in which the Self can join with other Self-centering Selves.

Sparking is making possible Female Friendship, which is totally Other from male comradeship. Hence, the Spinster will examine male comradeship/fraternity, in order to avoid the trap of confusing sisterhood with brotherhood, of thinking (even in some small dusty corner of the mind) of sisterhood as if it were simply a gender-correlative of brotherhood. She will come to see that the term *bonding,* as it applies to Hags/Harpies/Furies/Crones is as thoroughly Other from "male bonding" as Hags are the Other in relation to patriarchy. Male comradeship/bonding depends upon energy drained from women (its secret glue), since women are generators of energy. The bonding of Hags in friendship *for* women is not draining but rather energizing/gynergizing. It is the opposite of brotherhood, not essentially because Self-centering women oppose and fight patriarchy in a reactive way, but because we are/act for our Selves.

The term *comrade* is derived from a Middle French word meaning a group of soldiers sleeping in one room, or roommate. The concept of room here is spatial, suggesting links resulting from physical proximity, not necessarily from choice. The space is physical, not psychic, and it is definitely not A Room of One's Own. To the degree that it has been chosen, the choice has been made by another. The comrades do not choose each other for any inherent qualities of mind/spirit. Although this accidental and spatial "roommate" aspect does apply to all women insofar as all women are oppressed/

possessed, it does not apply to the deep and conscious bonding of Hags in the process of be-ing. Since the core/the soul-spark of such deep bonding is friendship, it does not essentially depend upon an enemy for its existence/becoming.

At first, it is hard to generate enough sparks for building the fires of Female Friendship. This is particularly the case since patriarchal males, sensing the ultimate threat of Female Sparking, make every effort to put out women's fires whenever we start them. They try to steal the fire of Furies in order to destroy us in their perpetual witchcraze. Like Cinderellas, Hags stand among the cinders, but we know that they are cinders of our burned foresisters. We know that the cinders still Spark.

Sparking means building the fires of gynergetic communication and confidence. As a result, each Sparking Hag not only begins to live in a lighted and warm room of her own; she prepares a place for a loom of her own. In this space she can begin to weave the tapestries of her own creation. With her increasing fire and force, she can begin to Spin. As she and her sisters Spin together, we create The Network of our time/space.

Gyn/Ecological Spinning is essential for entry into our Otherworld. The Voyager who does not Spin is in mortal danger. She may become trapped in one of the blind alleys of the maze which has been uncovered in The Second Passage. That is, she may become fixated upon the atrocities of androcracy, "spinning her wheels" instead of spinning on her heel and facing in Other directions. Or the nonspinner may make the fatal mistake of trying to jump over the atrocities into pseudo-ecstasy. As a result of this escapism, this blind "leap of faith," she can only fall into a tailspin.

The force of Spinsters' Spinning is the power of spirit spiraling, whirling. As we break into The Third Passage we whirl into our own world. Gyn/Ecology is weaving the way past the dead past and the dry places, weaving our world tapestry out of genesis and demise.

CHAPTER EIGHT

SPOOKING: EXORCISM, ESCAPE, AND ENSPIRITING PROCESS

I am still caught unawares
By ghosts lurking in my nightmares
That mock our revolution

With ancient loneliness
And ancient pain
And the old scars
And the old scars
Ache again.

Meg Christian,
from "Scars,"
I Know You Know (Olivia Records)

If I could make sense of how
my life is still tangled
with dead weeds, thistles,
enormous burdocks, burdens
slowing shifting under
this first fall of snow,
beaten by this early, racking rain
calling all new life to declare itself strong
or die,
if I could know
in what language to address
the spirits that claim a place
beneath these low and simple ceilings,
tenants that neither speak nor stir
yet dwell in mute insistence
till I can feel utterly ghosted in this house.

Adrienne Rich,
from "Toward the Solstice,"
The Dream of a Common Language

> I hazard the explanation that a shock is at once in my case followed by the desire to explain it. I feel that I have had a blow; but it is not, as I thought as a child, simply a blow from an enemy hidden behind the cotton wool of daily life; it is or will become a revelation of some order; it is a token of some real thing behind appearances; and I make it real by putting it into words. It is only by putting it into words that I make it whole; this wholeness means that it has lost its power to hurt me; it gives me, perhaps because by doing so I take away the pain, a great delight to put the severed parts together.
>
> Virginia Woolf,
> "A Sketch of the Past,"
> *Moments of Being*

In the course of this Voyage, we have seen that patriarchy is designed not only to possess women, but to prepossess/preoccupy us, that is, to inspire women with false selves which anesthetize the Self, breaking the process of be-ing on the wheel of processions. This condensing and freezing of be-ing into fragmented being is the necessary condition for maintaining the State of Possession. Condensation, or thing-ifying, makes "ownership" of Female Divinity possible, in the sense that it erases our awareness of this, our Process, and blocks our original movement. Yet it is not possible to own/possess Process itself. The confusion that is evoked in all women as a result of sensing simultaneously both the invincible reality of Female Process itself and its erasure/fragmentation in the foreground of our consciousness is the condition of being spooked. The antiprocess through which this alienation is achieved in androcracy is negative spooking. After examining this condition and this antiprocess we shall move on to the space where it is possible to Spook/Speak back at and beyond the spookers.*

* There is a peculiar form of spooking that haunts the radical feminist writer in her attempt to Spook/Speak back, that is, ahead. Adrienne Rich described it as follows: "Ordinarily one would associate the search

That is, we shall move on to Positive Spooking, which is our enspiriting process.

SPOOKING FROM THE LOCKER ROOM

We have seen that women are fetishized, and this involves condensation, displacement, and symbolization. The fetishizing of women through male obscenity condenses, displaces, symbolizes our be-ing into distorted fragments, in an endless series of acts of verbal violence. Although some women on some occasions have the "privilege" of being directly addressed by such names as *cunt* or *pussy,* most of the time this language is used in all-male environments. Yet it is the common male view of all women and, although most women do not hear it directly, we receive the message in a muted way. It is conveyed through silences, sneers, jeers, excessive politeness, paternalistic praise and disapproval, aggressive physical contact (an arm around the shoulder, a pat on the behind), invasive stares. Since women often do not *hear* the messages of obscenity directly, we are spooked. For the invasive presence and the intent are both audible and inaudible, visible and invisible.

Moreover, women are conditioned to pretend not to hear/see the constant and violent bombardments of obscenity, for we have been taught the lesson that since verbal violence is a "substitute" for physical assault, we should be grateful for such seemingly mild manifestations of misogynism.[1] Thus, spooking from the locker room, the unacknowledged noise of

---

for knowledge with eagerness, curiosity, the thirst to know. But for us, much of what we have to learn is depressing at least, sickening at worst. The *desire* for knowledge of our condition and in particular of gynocide and the enemy status to which we have been relegated is in direct conflict with the *burden* of horror and revulsion which that knowledge imposes on us. Several women who are now writing books on pornography, female child abuse, and female sexual enslavement have expressed to me the agony of working for hours daily with such materials, having literally to drive themselves to the sources of such knowledge. . . . In this pre-exorcistic state the terror of what one knows one is going to have to know paralyzes the Searcher. And there is the sense that once one has uncovered it—'After such knowledge, what forgiveness?'—in the words of T. S. Eliot, who little knew" (personal communication, January 1978).

omnipresent male obscenities, constitutes the "background music" which continually confuses and fragments consciousness. Exorcising this invasive presence requires acknowledging its existence and refusing to shuffle. This has the effect of bringing the spookers out into the open. Exorcism requires naming this environment of spirit/mind rape, refusing to be receptacles for semantic semen. As we become experienced in detecting the patterns of this apparently passive aggression, we become aware of its more sophisticated forms.

SPOOKING BY THE PASSIVE VOICE: GRAMMAR

The Passive Voice calls us from all sides. It is embedded in the voices of the secret agents, manipulators, possessors, who use passive forms not only to disguise *who* are the agents of androcracy, but also to pacify/passivize its victims/patients. We have already seen examples of agent deletion. In this Passage I will analyze this device as a method of spooking. Julia Stanley describes agent deletion lucidly:

> The passive and its related constructions theoretically permit the deletion of the agent in contexts where the reader can ascertain the deleted agent from the context. However . . . the agent may be deleted or never surfaced, and this deletion has the effect of creating an appeal to a universal consensus . . . so that the major proposition of the sentence appears to have more weight than it actually does. In other contexts, the agent is deleted in order to protect the agents responsible for the action.[2]

Deleting the agent by appealing to a presumed universal consensus is common. In "ethical" statements, for example, we find such specimens as the following:

> What determines when a being is human? When is it lawful to kill? These questions *are linked* in any consideration of the morality of abortion [emphasis mine].[3]

Since the statement does not say *who* links these questions, its author implies that they represent a general agreement about what are the central questions concerning abortion. The expression, "any consideration," of course does not include the consideration of millions of women who have had abortions.

B. F. Skinner, an agent-deleter in more ways than one, offers countless examples, such as the following:

> Is man then "abolished?" Certainly not as a species or as an individual achiever. It is the autonomous inner man [*sic*] that is abolished, and that is a step forward.[4]

The suppressed questions are, of course: *Who* is abolishing (or will abolish, if Skinner had his way) the "inner man"? *For whom* is this a "step forward"? By his style, this infamous advocate of behavioral technology even makes the reader forget to question. No agent is made to assume responsibility for the elimination of human autonomy.

Passive adjectives function in similar ways. Thus when we read of "*undesirable* behavior," the question that is suppressed is: *Who* does not desire this behavior? Similarly, the use of nominalized passives (verbs in the passive voice made into nouns, as in "behavior *modification*") hides the aggressive agents. Stanley explains: "A nominalized passive is an unqualified assertion about an event in the world, stripped of persons, time, and modality so that it *looks* like an objective statement." [5] Examples of the deceptive use of this device abound in professional literature and in the writings of "futurists." Alvin Toffler, at the end of his unshocking *Future Shock*, wrote that the "ultimate objective of social futurism" is "the *subjection* of the process of evolution itself to conscious human guidance [emphasis mine]." [6] Obliterated is the question: Just *who* will subject *whom*, under the guise of "human guidance"?

Of course, Hag-ographers, including this one, do use such constructions as the passive voice, and sometimes even passive adjectives and nominalized passives. The point is that we do not use these constructions in a way that hides the agents. Thus, to write of "the *subjection* of women by men" is hardly to delete the agent. When the context has made it abundantly clear who the agents are, it is not necessary to repeat "by men," "by androcrats," et cetera, in every sentence. This is quite different from the passive voice of writers who spook by implanting ambiguity and programming confusion in the minds of their readers through grammatical usage.

The mumblings of behaviorists, futurists, psychosurgeons, et al., bury the agent often in confusing combinations of passive forms with pseudogenerics. Clearly, even novice Hags are aware that *man* is no true generic term. But the problem is deeper and wider than this. There are no generics in English.[7] Terms such as *people, persons, individuals, children, workers, officers,* et cetera, are used to cover the absence of women as agents and our all too frequent presence as patients. Thus we hear that "faculty members and their wives attended the conference," and that "people were burned as witches." Those who attempt to "reform" language but stop at superficial levels (for example, by substituting *person* for *man* and moving no further) simply aid the phallocratic antiprocess of spooking by whitewashing the problems.

Hag-ographic analysis not only of "generic" nouns but also of supposedly inclusive pronouns uncovers the fact that these are elastic words. They function as rubber bands which can be stretched to include women when some weakness or deficiency is being discussed, as in the sentences: "People are gullible"; and "We failed in Vietnam." They can also be stretched to include women in a flattering and deceptive solidarity. Thus an expert on transsexualism, John Money, in a book coauthored with journalist Patricia Tucker (a confusing "we" in itself) writes:

> Since it's a safe prediction that the foregoing prenatal hormonal findings are going to be distorted out of all recognition by nativists, sex chauvinists, and the more emotional sex liberationists, it's essential that the rest of us be very clear about just what it is they show.[8]

"The rest of us" functions not only to establish the supposed sanity and rationality of the authors; it also seduces/intimidates/ spooks the reader into accepting the authors' ideology of sex differences. The reader who is bought by Money's "we" slides into passive inclusion in his expanding empire.

Of course, the elastic "we" and "us" snaps back to normal whenever the planetary Men's Association shows its hand.

Knowing this, Virginia Woolf proclaimed herself a member of the "Society of Outsiders," saying: ". . . as a woman I have no country. As a woman I want no country. As a woman my country is the whole world." [9]

Hags know that "the whole world" is precisely the Otherworld, which is our own whirling World. In order to express this, we must not only break the spell of the spooking "we." It is necessary also to break the spell of the "I" of phallocratic language, the Evil "I" which spooks the speaker/writer each time she speaks/writes. As Monique Wittig writes in the "Author's Note" at the beginning of *The Lesbian Body:*

> . . . The "I" [*Je*] who writes is alien to her own writing at every word because this "I" [*Je*] uses a language alien to her; this "I" [*Je*] experiences what is alien to her since this "I" [*Je*] cannot be *"un"* ecrivain. . . . *J/e* is the symbol of the lived, rending experience which is m/y writing, of this cutting in two which throughout literature is the exercise of a language which does not constitute m/e as subject. *J/e* poses the ideological and historic question of feminine subjects.[10]

Such devices as Wittig's breaking of the pronouns to display the woman-breaking effects of language are helpful for bringing spooks out into the light. Interestingly, the publishers of the English translation of *Le Corps Lesbien,* although they split m/e and m/y, include an introduction which "explains" that "the typographical implausibility of splitting our [*sic*] English monosyllabic 'I' is obvious. It has therefore been printed throughout as *'I.'* " [11] "Obvious" to whom? As Emily Culpepper remarked, it was not necessary to settle for the slanted *"I."* She pointed out that the crossed "I"—with a line drawn through it—would resemble a broken or cut phallus. Thus it would have been very plausible and effective to split "our" English monosyllabic "I." Too plausible.[12]

The process of materializing the spooks of grammar in order to break their spell will require constant vigilance. The false/evil "I" (the ghostliest pronoun) must be burned into impotence by the Evil Eyes of watchful Witches, who by the power of our glamour can cause such male "members" to disappear.

In order to re-member our dis-spelling powers, Hags must move deeper into the Background of language/grammar. However, we cannot expect to gain much insight from orthodox professional linguists.[13] Otto Jespersen expresses the common mentality of his colleagues. Women, he intones, build sentences "like a string of pearls, joined together on a string of ands and similar words." He refers to "the greater rapidity of female thought" (correct), but hastily adds that this is not "proof of intellectual power." [14]

Another demonstration of the "intellectual power" of professional linguists is provided by Noam Chomsky. It might be argued that the obtuseness of scholars like Jespersen can be explained by the fact that they are ivory-tower scholars, isolated from social and political problems. Therefore, it is particularly instructive to look at the writing of a scholarly linguist who is also an activist, such as Chomsky. In an essay entitled "Language and Freedom"—a topic which in itself continually keeps every Hag's mind spinning with ideas about interconnections, he begins with the following statement:

> When I was invited to speak on the topic "language and freedom," I was puzzled and intrigued. Most of my professional life has been devoted to the study of language. There would be no great difficulty in finding a topic to discuss in that domain. And there is much to say about the problems of freedom and liberation as they pose themselves to us and to others in the mid-twentieth century. What is troublesome in the title of this lecture is the conjunction. In what way are language and freedom to be interconnected? [15]

This introductory paragraph, written by a linguist who is also a "radical" social critic, a political activist of the Left, is not a rhetorical device or a joke. Chomsky's essay illustrates the split-consciousness syndrome common among academics and professionals. Chomsky is genuinely "puzzled and intrigued." The topic of "language and freedom," evidently suggested to him by someone else, suggests a connection he has never made. Moreover, by the time we reach the end of this short chapter it is evident that he still has not made it. In the last paragraph he writes: "I am no less puzzled by the topic 'language and freedom' than when I began—and no less intrigued." [16]

NEWSPEAK VERSUS NEW WORDS

The struggle against semantic spooking is essential for Hags escaping/overcoming the State of Possession. The courage to *try,* to risk ridicule, is essential for our encounter with the demons of timidity and other-directed "correctness." This is especially the case since a basic weapon in the arsenal of spookers is ridicule. The spookers make those who challenge their deception appear laughable, sometimes even to ourselves. They also make the Deep Background, which they hide and belittle through their spooking, seem unreal. This is an important tactic of the ghostly deceivers, for it serves their purposes to stop women who are coming close to the entry of the Labyrinth, the Background of our Selves.

Predictably, boringly, feminists who begin unspooking language are compared by linguistic "purists" to the originators of "Newspeak" in Orwell's *1984.* A classic example, on the *Time* magazine level, is a cutely titled article, "Sispeak: A Msguided Attempt to Change Herstory." [17] The author, Stefan Kanfer, compares feminist critiques and language changes to Orwell's "Newspeak," which, of course, is not recognized as prototypical Malespeak. Kanfer deserves to be nominated for the Reversal of the Century Award. In his caricature of women's efforts to break the bonds of rapist language, he equates our new words to the "breakdown of language" exemplified in the rapist film, *A Clockwork Orange.* Kanfer uses the power of "humor" to spook his female readers:

> As they [feminists] see it, William James' bitch-goddess Success and the National Weather Service's Hurricane Agnes are products of the same criminal mind.[18]

This weaponry is effective, because most readers "know" that naming a hurricane "Agnes" is not criminal, and at the same time do not know deeply enough that both such naming and such ridicule are, on a psychic level, at least as destructive to women as a hurricane. The spirit of deceptive mockery blasts into the minds of the intended victims; its aim is to destroy the balance of the novice Voyager.

Another *Time*-grimed trick exemplified in this essay is naming the problem in such a correct but at the same time deprecating way that its reality is erased in the reader's mind. Thus, Kanfer writes: "It is pathetically easy to spy in this [traditional] vocabulary a latent slavery, a cloaked prejudice aimed at further subjugating women in the name of language." This statement is exactly correct. However, the choice of such words as "pathetically easy," "spy," and "cloaked," manages to belittle and lampoon the women who have lucidly pointed out that it is pathetically easy to see through traditional language.

The same author is not above accusing feminists of crime:

> The feminist attack on social crimes may be as legitimate as it was inevitable. But the attack on words is only another social crime—one against the means and the hope of communication.

Thus feminists are permitted to "attack social crimes," but we must stop short of attacking the more insidious social crime of sexist language.

To break the spell of such revelatory reversals, Croneographers should remind our Selves that the Newspeak of Orwell's negative utopian tale is patriarchal Oldspeak. Since his "prophecies" are descriptions of what has already happened, we can follow through on his clues, naming the Missing Links/Agents overlooked by Orwell. He writes: "Newspeak was designed not to extend but to diminish the range of thought. . ." [19] This applies to male-controlled language in all matters pertaining to gynocentric identity: the words simply do not exist. In such a situation it is difficult even to imagine the right questions about our situation. Women struggling for words feel haunted by false feelings of personal inadequacy, by anger, frustration, and a kind of sadness/bereavement. For it is, after all, our "mother tongue" that has been turned against us by the tongue-twisters. Learning to speak our Mothers' Tongue *is* exorcising the male "mothers."

Orwell writes that "the special function of certain Newspeak words . . . was not so much to express meanings as to destroy them." [20] We need only think of such words as *feminine, unfeminine, womanly, unwomanly,* to recognize how certain words, particularly those that are supposed to name us, not only fail to express who we are but also destroy our identity. Moreover:

> These words . . . had had their meanings extended until they contained within themselves whole batteries of words which, as they were sufficiently covered by a single comprehensive term, could now be scrapped and forgotten.[21]

The doublebinding, falsely opposite words for women contain a great number of pejorative meanings, which the spooking speaker need not spell out. A single mystifying term will do the trick.

The crippling of thinking—mindbinding—by lack of words is expressed in another way:

> In Newspeak it was seldom possible to follow a heretical thought further than the perception that it *was* heretical; beyond that point the necessary words were nonexistent.[22]

Haggard Heretics are familiar with this thought-stopping aspect of the male-mothered tongue. Often Hags are worn down by this stupefying resistance of those who are unable to follow our thoughts further than the perception that they are heretical/heterodox/unacceptable. When we create New Words, re-call our Old Words, these are perceived/named Newspeak (read: trite, gimmicky, pretentious, nonintellectual) by the Newspeakers/spookers themselves.

In Orwell's *1984,* some words were euphemisms, such as *joycamp,* meaning forced-labor camp. Women can think of such haunting euphemisms as *homemaker, rest cure, finishing schools, intensive care, beauty parlor, the natural look, emotionally disturbed women.* Furthermore, in Orwell's dystopia, which we recognize as the patriarchal present, emphasis was placed upon short clipped words "which could be uttered rapidly and which roused the minimum of echoes in the speaker's mind." [23] In other words:

Ultimately it was hoped to make articulate speech issue from the larynx without involving the higher brain centers at all. This aim was frankly admitted in the Newspeak word *duckspeak,* meaning "to quack like a duck." [24]

Applying this ideal of political language to the realm of sexual politics, which are the most basic politics of patriarchy, we note the similarities between duckspeak and male obscenity: Words like *fuck, prick, cock, cunt, gash, slopjar, slut,* illustrate the point.

We should note that such mindless "duckspeak" is also used by certain professionals, particularly members of the military and medical professions, to refer to their enemies/victims. Thus American soldiers referred to the Vietnamese as *gooks.* Women spooked by false inclusion in the "we" of patriotic Americans have been prevented from seeing that the female sex is the hidden paradigm for such naming of "gooks." Indeed, male identifying of femaleness with *gook* (defined in Merriam-Webster as "sticky or gooey stuff") is shamelessly illustrated in existentialist philosopher Jean-Paul Sartre's long discussion of "the slimy," which he identifies with the Other, the female.[25] As Peggy Holland has demonstrated, Sartre's identification of women with "the hole" and "the slimy"—his proclamation of "the obscenity of the female sex" —is a philosophical "NO to women." In short: "Aligned with the slimy, the hole, and a precipice, she represents nothingness." [26]

It can also be illuminating for Hags to consider the slang/ "duckspeak" of modern medicine. Thus the staff of some hospitals refer to unconscious patients as *gorks* and "difficult" patients as *turkeys.* Female doctors and nurses haunted by the illusion of inclusion in male medicine are hindered from seeing that "normal" women are the primordial "gorks," that deviant women are the archetypal "turkeys." All male-instigated degradation of victims and enemies has as its hidden paradigm the female as Other, as victim.

Finally, there is "doublethink." Winston Smith, after torture in the Ministry of Love, came to understand that:

. . . if you want to keep a secret you must also hide it from yourself. You must know all the while that it is there, but until it is needed you must never let it emerge into your consciousness in any shape that could be given a name. From now onwards he must not only think right; he must feel right, dream right.[27]

We have seen many examples of doublethink in the preceding Passage. In order to understand spooking as it occurs in the environment of common, everyday gynocide, we should note that the broad aim of doublethink includes forcing us also to feel and dream right. The manipulation of feelings is accomplished through methods as seemingly varied as those of the psychotherapeutic establishment and of subliminal advertising. The "prolefeed" (which we might translate as "femfeed"), dished out by television, films, magazines, and best-sellers, programs women's dreams, setting up ghostly walls within the mind that block out the messages of the deep Background.

PAINTED BIRDS: THE STATE OF TOTAL TOKENISM

As Journeyers begin to see/sense the ghostliness of the fathers' foreground we must become aware of a more elusive type of spooking: tokenism. Through this device the spookers double and re-double the confusion of doublethink/doublefeel/doubledream into a maze in which there seems only to be re-turn. In order to begin A-mazing tokenism I will turn to the image of "The Painted Bird."

Jerzy Kosinski's novel, *The Painted Bird,* contains several passages about a man who vents his sexual frustration upon birds by painting their feathers. Commenting upon the poignant description of the tragedy, Thomas Szasz writes: "The Painted Bird is the perfect symbol of the Other, the Stranger, the Scapegoat." [28] Szasz's insight is useful. It is helpful as a springboard for a more difficult leap of insight/understanding by women coming to Self-consciousness. However, for Crones to stay at this level of analogy is to stay spooked. For we are moving into awareness of a condition which cannot be reduced to analogies with other scapegoat situations. This is the condition of Total Tokenism, of Totalitarian Tokenism.

In order to sense this condition, we might begin with the image of The Painted Bird. In the story, the tortured bird is given an artificial self; she is cosmeticized by her tormentor to such an extent that she is unrecognizable to her own kind. The latter turn upon her, torture and kill her. If directly applied to the situation of women under patriarchy, the image is inadequate and a reversal. For it is not the unusual woman who is The Painted Bird, the cosmeticized Freak. Rather, this is the common condition of women under patriarchy. The painted, cosmeticized artifacts (whether this is understood on the physical level or on the psychic level, or in both of these dimensions) are the creatures created by phallocracy, the artificial selves which prepossess all women, though in varying degrees. Thus it is not the man-painted bird-woman (who is reduced to an artifact) who is seen as "The Freak." Rather it is the woman who sheds the paint and manifests her Original Moving Self who appears to be The Freak in the State of Total Tokenism. It is she who is attacked by the mutants of her own kind, the man-made women. It is she who is threatened with ostracism and cruelty by those submerged in tokenism, those total women taken as tokens before they had a chance to be Selves.

In order to grasp this situation, we might begin with the common concept of "token woman doctor," or "token woman senator," or "token woman professor." These expressions clue us in to the fact that such women have been allowed into pieces of patriarchal territory as a *show of female presence*. They are understood to represent the female "half of the human species" in male terrain. The hidden agenda of their role includes thinking "like a man," that is, with the set limitations of patriarchal thought as prescribed for each situation, while at the same time behaving according to the feminine stereotype.[29] Women in this situation also participate, though perhaps without fully realizing it, in the "S" side which is the male prerogative in the "S and M" pseudodichotomy of roles.

We should next attempt to hear the expression "token *woman*" in a fuller context, realizing that a "token" is an outward sign. The token *woman* is the outer woman, Daddy's girl, the artifact. Add to this the realization that in the State of Totalitarian Tokenism the women who have escaped, to any significant degree, reduction to the artifact state—the condition of The Painted Bird—are a small minority. The majority of women, then, are in this condition of tokenism.

When we examine together the two senses of "token woman," as in "token woman on the committee" and in "token *woman*," we can immediately see the probability of a politically imposed combination of the two. Since men in power are the ones who choose their token women to represent the "female half of the species" in the territories of male prerogative, we can see the strong probability that those chosen for such roles will be drawn from the ranks of the token *women*—those most tokenized, cosmeticized, most identified with male purposes. This quasi-chemical combination equals "Athena." In a social situation in which there is pressure to nod approvingly in the direction of feminism, it is highly probable that the Athena will call herself a "feminist." We are then confronted with the presence of a triply compounded product of patriarchal ingenuity: a "token feminist." It is she who can best play the role which Robin Morgan has identified as "the ultimate weapon in the hands of the boys."

In the face and voice of such a construct, who is a doubly or triply Painted Bird, women who are in the process of peeling off the patriarchal paint can sense the snarl of phallic power. For here, in yet another guise, is the all too familiar token torturer, the woman who often unwittingly pleases her masters by selling out her own kind. She increases their pleasure by performing the acts which are less than gentlemanly, thus obscuring their role. She masks male responsibility and intent. Acting in the name of the Higher Order, she functions to tighten the bindings of her sisters' minds. The rulers repeatedly reproduce her: Her name is legion. Nor need she wait to be legitimated by scholars of a later age, for she is frequently condoned by contemporaries, even praised by them. As she turns her tricks in all the prescribed positions she does not perceive the meaning of this male approval, but only the fact that it *is* Approval, the flattering mirror upon which her identity depends. Since selective blindness is her primary role requirement, she does not suspect that this is the Archetypal Dirty Joke in which she plays such a crucial part. She does not know that the joke is on her Self.

Thus the doubly/triply tokenized woman, the multiply Painted Bird, functions in the antiprocess of double-crossing her sisters, polluting them with poisonous paint, making them less and less real in their own eyes and in the eyes of others. For unknowingly, she is herself a carrier of the paint disease, an intensifier of the common condition of women under patriarchy. Those women strong enough to resist the paint infection carried by this token torturer are carrying on a battle of will power, of gynergetic force, on a deep psychic level. Yet the battle consists not mainly in arguing, refuting, striking back at one who has become encased in an ever-hardening shell of paint, but rather in shucking off the shell of paint by which we ourselves have been partially paralyzed, deadened. For the less of this we allow to adhere to us, the smaller the chance that the new shower of paint will stick to our surface. Rather than hitting a surface like itself, this poison will be deflected, for the strong aura of the Self will protect the Self.

SPOOKING BACK: UNPAINTING

Women who have the strength to unpaint the Self are, by the same action, polishing our natural armor. This action is not the "show and tell all" personal revelation of therapy. In the State of Total Tokenism, women are vulnerable to the priests of the Thoroughly Therapeutic Society. Having been painted and repainted, women desperate to dis-cover the covered Self expose themselves to the tormentors who promise to take away the pain/paint. The result is commonly anesthesia rather than dis-covery of the powers of gynaesthesia, repainting rather than Unpainting. For Unpainting is a process which the Self must carry out. As Jan Raymond has remarked, it is not passive manifestation of "personal problems" but rather an active manifesto.[30] It is not the Self-victimizing striptease which is titillating to professional voyeurs. It is not peeling off the veneer in order to share one's pain—and consequently become more vulnerable.

The Unpainter is not "taking it off," but taking off, not re-turning to normal, but courage-ing to leave. She is coming into knowledge of her anger, which means getting ready for action. For, unlike depression, which is a defeated withdrawal from evil, and turning of one's energy against the Self, righteous anger is expression of creativity and hope. Manifesto-ing by strong women sends the paint flying back into the eyes of the soul-slayers, as our own Spirit-Selves soar with natural movement.

This soaring of the Unpainted Self takes us out of the circle of Father Time. We fly off the clock into other dimensions, to the boundary of the realm of Totalitarian Tokenism. In doing this Unpainting and Flying we may appear to the painters and the painted as Crazed Witches. What our Selves are doing in fact is breaking out of the maze and melting the maze by seeing it in perspective, by focusing our gynaesthetic power. We are thus A-mazing the spookers' society, the society of the perpetual witchcraze, that is, we are flying free.

DIS-POSSESSION I: THE ENSPIRITING SELF

In the State of Possession, the victim of psychic and physical invaders becomes autoallergic, re-acting against the body's own tissues, the spirit's own process. Pathologically re-acting against her own endogenous powers of resistance to invasion, she sides with her invaders, her possessors. Her false self possesses her genuine Self. Her false self blends with the Possessor who sedates his beloved prey. She turns against her sisters who, themselves invaded and carried into the State of Possession, turn against her Self and against their Selves. The divided ones, the self-Selves, shelve or sell their Selves. They become ever-hardening shells of their Selves, suffocating their own process. They become iron masks, choking their own becoming, hiding their own know-ing, substituting deception for know-ing.

So deep is the disease of autoallergy induced in women by the sedative seduction of the little Sir Sirens of Siredom, that women try to kill not only their Selves but their sister Selves even in the name of Sisterhood. Under the appearance of bonding there is binding. The mothers bind the feet and minds of daughters. The daughter is turned against the mother, the pseudosister is the re-sister of her Sister, standing against her. As her re-sister she is a reversed imitation, a mirror image, her "life-like" reproduction. She covers and re-covers the Sister until she can no longer find her Self, having forgotten to search for her Self. Trapped into re-searching she finds only the re-sister.

In order truly to search for the Sister it is necessary to see the dis-membered Sister within, the Sister Self, and to re-member her, coming into touch with the original intuition of integrity. Once mindful of the Sister, the Self need no longer resist her, her mind is full of her. She IS her. She is her Self. Re-membering is the remedy. The reign of healing is within the Self, within the Selves seen by the Self and seeing the Self. The remedy is not to turn back but to become in a healing environment, the Self, and to become the healing environment.

In this space the Self is not re-ligious, not tied back by old ligatures, old allegiances. She pledges allegiance to no flag, no cross. She sees through the lies of alleged allies. She re-veres no one, for she is free-ing her Self from fears. This space, the Self's holy environment, is the opposite of the re-covery rooms of the unnatural physicians of soul and body. It is dis-covery room.

In our dis-covery room our Selves dis-cover room, re-versing the refrains that have framed our know-ing into "knowledge." No need here to stay in the hearses the false physicians have made of our bodies, our minds, when they made us re-hearse each reversed truth, boxing them into coffins of deception, our false selves. No need to repeat the refrains of the rituals that restrain our Selves, that strain our Selves.

Breaking out of the rituals means refusing the role of penitent/patient, rejecting the virile virus of anti-biotic religion and medicine. No longer comatose, the Self refuses to be a "candidate" for such sacraments as confirmation or cosmetic surgery. She accepts neither the slaps in the face which are religiously and ritually administered to "confirm" the self as "soldier of Christ," nor the slashes in the face surgically administered to confirm the self in the medically mutilating rituals of femininity. The dis-covered Self refuses the white robes of these initiations into the rank ranks of the living dead.

The dis-covered Self washes her hands/mind of the antiseptic anti-Self, the internalized Possessor. She washes as she re-members her dis-membered Self. At first her handwashing/mindwashing may seem itself to be a ritual. If so, it is the right rite, the suitable ceremony of the one who has been named "unclean." She dispossesses her Self of the "purifiers" who muddy her mind, who try to master her mind. She re-calls Virginia Woolf's warnings against "adultery of the brain." [31] Re-calling also that the verb *adulterate* means "to falsify by admixture of baser ingredients," the Dis-possessing Self cleanses her thinking/feeling/dreaming of the base ingredients that were assimilated through coerced adultery. This cleansing/depolluting of the Self by the Self is essential to Gyn/Ecology.

It isn't enough for women who can see the State of Possession merely to "escape." The problem is not merely one of escape from the religious, technological, and medical Mafia. So long as we are only escaping, we are re-acting. The etymology of the term *escape* is enlightening. According to Merriam-Webster, it is derived from the Latin *ex,* meaning out, and *cappa,* meaning head-covering, cloak. Thus, as the word literally says, we are slipping out from our head-coverings or cloaks (ex-caping). In other words, as long as we are just escaping, we are simply un-veiling ourselves. Indeed, this is necessary for the Journey. It names the important process of women throwing off such alienating ideological "-hoods" as "womanhood." [32] Yet so long as the Voyager is only or primarily escaping, she is still looking back. So long as she is primarily escaping, re-acting, she is still haunted by the messages of the agents who spook in the Passive Voice.

When women unwind our veils, our winding sheets, our attention is at first fixed upon the unwinding. The task which next becomes visible, before us and around us, is the task of seeing/sensing/Self-moving in the directions which our dis-covering senses open out to us. This Self-conscious, Self-directed movement is springing free. As we do this we enspirit our Selves, freeing the life force that has been frozen, reified, fetishized.

As Jan Raymond has pointed out, the verb *enspiriting* says more than *escaping*.[33] It names the process of confronting and transcending the State of Possession. We are possessed to the degree that spirit is condensed by the fetishizing of matter, contained by matter.[34] The process of the Self enspiriting the Self is Dis-possession. The enspiriting Self is not anti-matter but pro-matter, freeing matter from its restricted/restricting role of vessel/container, unfreezing matter so that it can flow with spirit, fly with spirit. Enspiriting is breathing, be-ing.[35] The Self enspirits the Self and others by encouraging, by expanding her own courage, hope, determination, vigor. To enspirit is to be an expressive active verb, an Active Voice uttering the Self utterly, in a movement/Journey that spirals outward, inward. In this Active Voicing, the Self Spooks the spookers. She affirms the becoming Self who is always Other. She dis-covers and creates the Otherworld.

To the degree that the Female Self has been possessed by the spirit of patriarchy, she has been slowly expiring. She has become dispirited, that is, depressed, downcast, lacking independent vigor and forcefulness. As she becomes dispossessed, enspirited, she moves out of range of the passive voices and begins to hear her own Active Voice, speaking her Self in successive acts of creation. As she creates her Self she creates new space: semantic, cognitive, symbolic, psychic, physical spaces. She moves into these spaces and finds room to breathe, to breathe forth further space.

On a practical, tactical level women are using new words and transforming/re-calling meanings of old words. Hags are doing this verbally and with clothing and body language.[36] Hags dress comfortably, expressing our individuality and our responses to particular occasions, such as Halloween, Winter Solstice. Our clothing is useful for guerrilla tactics in situations of confrontation. Spinsters feel comfortable with our natural look, and thus do not require the cosmeticized "natural look." Women journeying learn to forget false body language and re-call the Self-confident styles of walking/standing/sitting/gesturing which express be-ing. Furious women learning Karate and various forms of Self-defense often experience a de-conditioning process, an escaping from the invisible bindings of femininity, and an enspiriting sense of power, control, and awareness of the immediate environment.

Such awareness of environment makes it possible to deflect both physical and semantic danger, to unspook the implicit messages coming from all sides. Thus Journeyers are developing ways of moving into different cognitive space, even when we are caught in male-controlled physical space. We are finding ways of "breaking set"—of focusing upon different patterns of meaning than those explicitly expressed and accepted by the cognitive majority. Thus, when we find ourselves physically confined in oppressive set-ups, we can concentrate upon implicit patterns in styles of communication, such as clothing, postures, gestures, eye-contact, speech intonation, choice of vocabulary, use of "humor," facial expressions, and—perhaps most importantly—silences.

Such pattern discovery, or positive paranoia, functions also to dis-spell the power of prevailing myths and symbols, a power which depends partly upon their hiddenness. This is not to say that patriarchal myths are not overt and blatant, but that their connections with our experience are masked. The connections are hidden from us so long as we accept the "acceptable" foreground patterns foisted upon us. When we break the patterns imposed upon our own thinking/imaging/acting/perceiving/speaking, we see and hear, that is, perceive gynaesthetically, the "plot" of the acts performed in patriarchal settings. This new perception allows us further freedom; we move further from the maze. As we A-maze, we are amazed. The spell of the underlying lies/symbols/myths is broken. We see their feeble derivative character and we recognize the omnipresent pattern of reversal. They are dis-credited.

This myth-breaking positive paranoia helps us move further into Hagocentric psychic space. De-tached from the mystifying myths, we move deeper into the Labyrinth. Depending less and less upon male approval, recognizing that such approval is more often than not a reward for weakness, we approve of our Selves. We prove our Selves. Such Self-approval attracts, and attracting Hags bond.

Out of this strong Self-centering bonding can come the physical spaces of which we dream. These will be unlike the earlier attempts to make women's spaces, which have reflected the unsureness of women in earlier stages of the Journey. For these attempts have often failed because the spectres of patriarchal presence have not been exorcized. Indeed, the physical absence of males often has added to their spookiness, when women have not recognized and rejected "the pig in the head." There is still bonding out of weakness—pseudobonding—when women are afraid to *be* alone. Rather than being empowering, places which reflect pseudobonding become disabling. They can cloak the processions of spooking in a way analogous to cloaking by timid "reformist" language which stops short of speaking in the Active Voice. Thus, "Women's Centers" which have not moved beyond very mild measures, such as "vocational counseling" which ignores all responsibility for criticizing the professions themselves, can be compared to linguistic reforms which do not imply radical analysis (for example, the use of the pronoun *she* to refer to the christian god within the context of christian religious services).

In contrast to such timid constructs, the new physical spaces—like the new semantic/cognitive/symbolic spaces—will be dis-covered/created further out/in the Otherworld Journey. The Hags who find and make them will have reached further beyond the boundaries of the Possessed State. They will have learned ways of Spooking the spookers. They will have learned Positive Spooking. They will come together because they are enspiriting, because they know how to be/travel Alone. These seasoned Spinsters will no longer be seeking the solace of domestication. They will be at home on the road.

Amazons who are breathing forth further space are looking with the Inner Eye (misnamed/reversed by the fearful as the Evil Eye). We are listening with the Inner Ear. Those who have continued the Journey know that the Basic Tactic is to keep moving. A moving target who moves fast enough becomes less and less visible to those who would target her, as she becomes more visionary, more visible to her Self. Hags know that the appropriate tactics present themselves to our consciousness when we are deeply conscious of the Journey. We know that there is not one tactic for each specific situation. At one time and place "outspokenness" may be more useful; at another time and place, camouflage. At all times, we are speaking our Selves, hearing and following the call of our undomesticated, wild be-ing.

DIS-POSSESSION II: THE CALL OF THE WILD

Enspiriting is hearing and following the call of the wild, which is in the Self. The call to wild-ize our Selves, to free and unfreeze our Selves is a wild and fantastic calling to transfer our energy to our Selves and to Sister Selves. To aid us in hearing/remembering the call of our wild, we can listen to the strange and improbable voice of the dictionary, which, in spite of itself, transmits this call.

Wild means "living in a state of nature: inhabiting natural haunts: not tamed or domesticated . . . being one of a kind not ordinarily subjected to domestication." It means "growing or produced without the aid and care of man: not cultivated: brought forth by unassisted nature . . . NATIVE." It means "not living near or associated with man." It means "not inhabited or cultivated." It means "not subjected to restraint or regulation: UNCONTROLLED, INORDINATE, UNGOVERNED."

Wild means "not amenable to control, restraint, or domestication: UNRULY, UNGOVERNABLE, RECKLESS." It means "(of a ship) hard to steer." It means "exceeding normal or conventional bounds in thought, design, conception, execution, or nature: EXTRAVAGANT, FANTASTIC, VISIONARY." It means "not acculturated to an advanced civilization: RUDE, UNCIVILIZED, BARBARIC." It means: "not yielding to a governmental authority: SAVAGE, INTRACTABLE, REBELLIOUS." It means "characteristic of, appropriate to, or expressive of wilderness, wildlife, or people [*sic*] in a simple or uncivilized society or environment."

Wild means "deviating from a natural or expected course, goal, or practice; acting, appearing, or being manifested in an unexpected, undesired, or unpredictable manner: RANDOM, ERRATIC." It means "not accounted for by any known theories."

Wild means "great in extent, size, quantity or intensity: EXTREME, PRODIGIOUS." It means (of a playing card): "having a denomination determined by the will of the holder."

Wild is the name of the Self in women, of the enspiriting Sister Self. The wildness of our Selves is visible to wild-eyes, to the inner eyes which ask the deepest "whys," the interconnected "whys" that have not been fragmented by the fathers' "mother tongues," nor by their seductive images or -ologies. These are the "whys" undreamt of in their philosophies, but which lie sleeping, sometimes half-awake, in the wild minds of women. These are the *whys* of untamed wisdom.

In order to ask these wild "whys" we must remove our Selves from the state of tameness, which is the State of Possession. Again, the dictionary names the intolerable truth of the female condition in the Land of the Fathers. Thus, the adjective *tame* means "reduced from a state of native wildness: made tractable and useful to man: DOMESTICATED." It means "maintained or displayed to serve the purposes of another: permitted to exist as a harmless specimen of its kind." It means "brought under control: HARNESSED." It means "made docile and submissive: MEEK, SUBDUED." It means "CULTIVATED." It means "lacking in spirit, zest, or interest: DULL, MILD, INSIPID."

In some ways the verb *to tame* more adequately expresses the fate of females spooked and possessed in the State of Feminitude. It means "to reduce from a wild to a domestic state: to make gentle or tractable: DOMESTICATE." It means "to subject to cultivation." It means "to bring under control: make manageable or usable." It means "to deprive of spirit, courage, or resistance: HUMBLE, SUBDUE." It means "to tone down, SOFTEN." The dictionary also informs us that in some English dialects *tame* means "to cut into; PIERCE, especially, BROACH."

In the tamed state, women are domesticated, dedicated to the cult of male divinity. They are seduced into disloyalty to the Self, into false loyalties that fragment, that lead them further and further away from the Self and more and more into unwholesome alliances, into alienating intercourse. Suavely persuaded of their own idiocy, they lose everything that is idiosyncratic, that is truly their own—personal, separate, distinct. Having lost touch with their Selves, they are impregnated by the holy spirit of alienation, the dis-couraging, dis-spiriting sperm that expels the Self. Thus vacated, their minds are on vacation. Such perpetual vacation, such self-lobotomization, which of course requires endless expenditure of energy, is the essential vocation of vacuous femininity.

Seeking out the wild questions, the interconnected "whys" unfragmented by the fathers' philosophies, is the way beyond mere escape and into enspiriting process. This requires hard work, for the categories of Aristotle, of Kant, of ancient myths and contemporary -ologies have shattered the deepest questions, making them seem disparate, unrelated. The questions—such as Why? If? When? Where? How? How come? Why not?—have been frozen. The natural flow among them has been intercepted. Males have posed the questions; they have *placed* the questions, tagged and labeled, into the glass cases of mental museums. They have hidden the Questions. The task for feminists now is con-questioning, con-questing for the deep sources of the questions, seeking a permanently altering state of consciousness.

In the beginning is the awakening awareness, which is spindled, spent, mutilated by false words. Our call of the wild is a call to dis-possess our Selves of the shrouds, the winding sheets of words. We eject, banish, depose the possessing language—spoken and written words, body language, architectural language, technological language, the language of symbols and of institutional structures—by enspiriting our Selves. The Sister Selves are the only Selves who can bond together and con-quest beyond, before, beneath, and around the seductive pseudowords. The pseudoselves within and outside us are bound in pseudosisterhood. The call of the wild is the call to dispossess our Selves of pseudobonding. This is essential, for through false bonding women hide from themselves the frightening absence of the courage to stand/move alone which is at the heart of the courage to bond. Such faint-heartedness is the ultimate trap of the entamed state, keeping women "harmless specimens" of our own kind. It also engenders the Ultimate Irony—the desertion of courageous Searchers/Spinsters by threatened pseudosisters, whose cowardice/absence casts strong women into the role of martyrs/scapegoats for feminism.

DIS-POSSESSION III: DAUGHTER-RIGHT

The fundamental lost bonding, as Furious women know, is the bond between mothers and daughters. It is the basic bonding, so important for Self-acceptance and the courage to be alone, which the professionals of the Thoroughly Therapeutic Society continue to destroy in the name of healing. The Usurpers/Male Mothers blind their victims to the deep reality of this relation, binding mothers and daughters together and apart in such a way that we cannot see each other's faces/Selves.

Blinded and dis-spirited by these mindbindings, daughters feel rage at their mothers' powerlessness against the patriarchal rule. Yet the pull toward the mother is always there; the daughter seeks her everywhere. Demeter and Persephone seek each other in all the wrong places, in strange faces, and, most tragically, in the male. Mothers transmit our divine wisdom to sons, husbands. Daughters seek from fathers, husbands, the birthright denied to us. Daughters seek the lost mothers in male surrogates, looking to them for the divine spark of encouragement which is not theirs to give, which is the rightful inheritance of our own kind.

Much has been written about the theft of Mother-Right through the establishment of patriarchy. A consequence of this theft has been the institution of patriarchal motherhood.[37] The destructive nature of this institution for mothers and daughters has in large measure been rendered invisible to women by the male supermothers who control and legitimate it. Haunted by the hidden controllers of this unnatural institution, women are manipulated as token betrayers and violators of their Selves, of each other.

One radical response of Revolting Furies to this insidious

destruction of the core of female bonding is the naming and establishment of what Jan Raymond has called Daughter-Right.[38] For, as she explains, daughterhood has a universality which motherhood lacks; clearly, *all* women are daughters. The word *daughter* is less suggestive of a role than of a given reality. Essentially, Daughter-Right names the right to re-claim our original movement, to re-call our Selves. It is this Self-centering identity that makes female bonding possible. Since it points to the original Self, it establishes the right to relate to other Selves. Thus, as Nelle Morton has pointed out, it is the Daughter with whom we can bond.[39] When we reach the Daughter within the mother we break the bindings of our false inheritance; we cut our ties to the institution of patriarchal motherhood. We strip away the treacherous "tradition" foisted upon mothers and daughters—our horrible false heritage of female infanticide, physical mutilations, mindbindings masterminded by Male Mother Superiors. When a woman comes to recognize the Daughter in her Self, in her mother, she comes into touch with her true tradition. She sees the face of her own divine promise. Sharing this recognition, mothers and daughters become sisters in struggle. They become friends again.

From this perspective of Daughter-Right women can ask the radical ontological questions, not only about the evil and pain inflicted upon our lives under the reign of fathers, sons, and holy ghosts, but also about our be-ing, our Journey into the Otherworld. The Divine Daughter demanding her rights is Nemesis. She denies and denounces the defilers and their disguises, their false mother-faces, their smothering "mothering." She repudiates their distortion of the mother into "the other."

BEWITCHING THE TIME WARPS I: EXPELLING THE PATRIARCHAL "PAST"

A time-honored trick of patriarchs is possession of and by "the past." Haggard Harpies and Crones struggling to live our Presence in the present are confronted with the spookers' efforts to invade/haunt our minds at every moment. As Andrée

Collard has remarked, they expropriate both memory and imagination.[40] Patriarchal expropriation of memory not only deprives women of our own past; it also negates our present and future. It pre-occupies women's minds, filling them with images which constantly re-generate confusion, guilt, and despair.

Every woman who has come to consciousness can recall an almost endless series of oppressive, violating, insulting, assaulting acts against her Self. Every woman is battered by such assaults—is, on a psychic level, a battered woman. As she moves on the enspiriting Journey she experiences a lessening of confusion, guilt, and despair, and an increasing sense of rage, of outrage. If she does not constantly convert the energy of this rage to creativity it pre-occupies her, pre-possesses her.

It is helpful to confront and name the reality and enormity of patriarchal possession/distortion of women's past. The Journeyer is by now aware of the prepossession of women's history. She must struggle to become aware of the ways in which the tentacles of the possessors attempt to snatch each new moment/movement, converting it into a dead and falsified past history. Thus, for example, *all* portrayals of "the women's movement" by the media are betrayals.

To see how our recent history has been betrayed, we might consider the nastiness of the media's "treatment" of radical feminists who have demonstrated commitment to the cause of women. We might then consider the use of media-made instant "feminists" who surface as critics and reviewers of genuinely feminist works. More significant still is the haunting phenomenon which we might call "Old is New," or "It's as if nothing had ever happened."

The spooking experience of "Old is New" is shared among Crones who have been consciously feminists since the late sixties (or longer) and who are now meeting a generation of young women—college students, for example—who have never read and never even heard of *A Vindication of the Rights of Woman, Three Guineas, The Second Sex, Sisterhood is Powerful, The First Sex* . . . Feminists who have been struggling to build Women's Studies courses and programs [illegible] to each other of this eerie experience, seeking confirmation of their own clear memories: "It's like beginning from square one." "It's like re-inventing the wheel." "It's as if nothing had ever happened." "They seem lobotomized." "We should have foreseen this." [41]

We *should* have foreseen this blackout and would have foreseen it, were it not for the fact that the wheel of patriarchal Processions repeatedly grinds down feminist accomplishments to unrecognizable fragments, demolishing our sense of our own tradition. Probably it would have been surprising for Matilda Joslyn Gage to see "the women's movement" starting from square one in 1969, for she had hoped, in the nineteenth century, that her work would be part of an ongoing female tradition. But by now we are able to know more about the mechanisms by which the masters devour the fruits of female creativity and attempt to grind them into oblivion. Armed with this knowledge, Crones/Hags will make every effort to remove our energy from allegiance to their systems, re-claiming our life force and our hidden, but never totally destroyed, traditions. As we re-create Hag-ography we will keep clearly in mind the fact that it is the patriarchs' possession and re-defining of "the past" that makes possible their possession of women *by* the male-defined "past."

Patriarchal expropriation of "the past" and of memory is accomplished by many means in addition to the media. Not only "history" but all academic fields erase and reverse women's history. The constant erosion/erasure/distortion of our past is accomplished also through art, through religious feasts and the ceremonies of civil religion, through music/muzak, through the repetitious rituals of family, school, and "social life."

Moreover, a particularly important theme of the program for the erasure of Crone-ology is the erasure of Crones.[42] We have seen that this has been accomplished through such measures as *suttee,* witchburning, and modern medicine. This erasure is accomplished also through the cooptation of Crone-Power by the institutions of phallocracy. Potential Crones are coopted as tokens by all the professions. Thus learned female professors dispense patriarchal propaganda as "the truth"; female criminal lawyers defend accused rapists; female physicians dispense poisonous medicine; female christian ministers preach female self-sacrifice . . . The list can go on. Crones working on the boundaries of the possessors' professions and institutions must struggle constantly to overcome the damage done by such tokens, and to avoid seduction into more subtle forms of the same behavior. Moreover, the visibility of coopted women defaces/erases awareness of Crone-Power, making those who are just starting the feminist Journey feel that there is no tradition, that they must become the first Crones to survive. The spookiness of this situation is intensified by the fact that women's minds are constantly being filled with debased images of Crones. These range from the "wicked stepmother" images injected through fairy tales and Halloween caricatures of witches[43] to the mother-in-law jokes that "enliven" parties and T.V. "situation comedies."

Hags can halt the processions of possessors of our past as they attempt to enter the doorways of our senses, but this will not be achieved by fixating upon blocking them out. We cannot always wear earplugs and blindfolds—and besides, their messages have already gained entry and have occupied chambers of our minds. Our primary method of demolishing the alien occupiers and of preventing their re-entry is movement out of their reach into our own time/space.

Hags/Crones struggling to overcome the possessors' attempts to distort our past can heed the advice of the women in *Les Guérillères*: "Make an effort to remember. Or, failing that, invent." [44]

The process of inventing/creating our Selves and our works *is* re-membering the past. This inventing in the present does not preclude the importance of Crone-ology, of our own Prehistory. Indeed, it makes possible the daring and vision not only to grasp the distortions of the patriarchal "past," but also to see through and beyond the distorting mirrors, to move through the looking-glass world of doublefeel/doublethink/doubledream into the Background.

The key to Dis-possession of the fabricated "past" projected by the fathers, sons, and holy ghosts, then, is female-identified creativity, through which we re-possess our energy. On a practical level this involves a constant struggle to re-affirm

Hags' own priorities, since the past-possessors/fabricators, the unrightful owners of our history/memory, use this stolen and damaged property as a weapon to confuse us about our priorities, to disorient our perceptions, and to thwart female process.

BEWITCHING THE TIME WARPS II: EXPELLING THE PATRIARCHAL FUTURE

In their house of mirrors, the past-owners/past-makers constantly bombard women's minds with false and insignificant choices in order to prevent us from seeing/facing the real choices that further our escaping, Self-enspiriting, and bonding with other women. The spookers attempt to possess and destroy the future by haunting women's minds *now*, preventing our Presence in our present. We have seen that they administer such preventive medicine by destroying and remaking the past, inspiring women with lies, with fears, with the disease of caution and self-contempt. There is no sharp line between the possessed "past" and the possessed "future," since both are illusions which constantly separate and re-blend, reflecting each other repeatedly, echoing each other endlessly. Keeping this blur in mind, Hags can crack the "future" mirror.

The basic form of the father's funereal "future" is fear. The necrophiliac Prince Charmings keep their Snow White spouses in the State of Sleeping Death with promises of a fear-free future. This blend of male-made fear and promise of release from fear is the recipe for the poison in the Poisoned Apples foisted upon females by the "Wicked Queens." Every Hag who has escaped from the glass coffin and dependent dwarfs intended for us has come to know the true identity of the poison-pushing Queen: "She," that is, he, is the archetypal Drag Queen, the male stepmother, the other side of Prince Charming's multiple personality, his holy ghost. He is able to trick the princess because he dissembles, falsely re-sembling the true Queen, the Wild Witch, the dis-membered Goddess.

Since the feigned future which is used to make women faint-hearted, faint-minded, fixed in a permanent faint is a shadow world, a world of deceptive lights and shadows, it is useless to strike at it directly. Instead of shadow-boxing, the gynaesthetic traveler learns to detect the deceptive light-projector, the shadow-caster. She detects the pattern that is behind his deceptive patterns; she dis-covers the necrophiliac nature of the fear in which he is fixated, which is also the fear he projects upon/injects into his snow white victims. This is *not* the fear of dying but the fear of living. As Valerie Solanas lucidly points out: "The male likes death—it excites him sexually and, already dead inside, he wants to die." [45] This statement would seem to be adequately substantiated/documented by the state of this male-controlled planet. If patriarchal males loved life, the planet would be different.[46]

Most precisely, the wicked drag queens' fear is fear of Female Living, of female-identified biophilic energy. For the release of this energy will mean the end of their blissful State of Sleeping Death. They therefore are compelled to use every means at hand to perpetuate the State of Paralysis. We have already discussed some of their tranquilizing treatments, their haunting holding patterns. One pattern common to all of these patterns is imposed poverty. The male queens perpetually try to keep women "blessed" by poverty of spirit. We have seen that they have starved women's minds through transmitting a poor vocabulary, a shabby symbol system, a genuinely impoverishing education. Hags can hardly afford to overlook the fact that they keep us chained to the wheel of mind-deadening work by keeping us economically poor. Our spiritual and physical deprivation/poverty nourish and support each other. The queens/prince charmings thus work to keep women roadblocked by the twin rocks of spiritual and economic poverty.

Depressed and angry over this unjust impoverishment, women at first turn our anger against ourselves and each other, blaming each other for being "richer" or "poorer" in different ways. Locked in mortal combat with ourselves and each other, we are kept from living in the Female Present/Presence. As long as this spooking trick works, the queens succeed in maintaining the State of Sleeping Death, where women are encased in the glass coffins of false past and false future.

Spinsters smash our way out of the mirror coffins by our courageous/contagious Revolting Risking. Our reckless Risking is unlike the ruthless "bravery" of the necrophiliac bomb-makers, planet-polluters, who try to turn the earth into their Poisoned Apple. The Life-loving Risking of Hags means loving our Selves and therefore turning our anger into propelling power for the Journey. Recognizing, finally, that we have all been possessed in the State of Possession, Furies can begin to stop misfiring our Fury at each other. Recognizing that we have been made falsely rich and truly poor in a vast variety of ways, we can learn to overcome the spooking confusion and Self-defeating conflicts over our diverse situations which are not of our own making. Not insipid "tolerance" but strong truthfulness about such complex conditions will enable Furious women to bond and to move deeper into the Background.

It is now our task to move further in understanding our aloneness and our bonding. As Enspiriting Furious Voyagers move deeper into The Third Passage we must re-call our original dis-covery of fire. This will happen as we re-member/invent Female Friendship, which is Sparking.

CHAPTER NINE

SPARKING: THE FIRE OF FEMALE FRIENDSHIP

And let the daughters of uneducated women dance. . . . and let them sing, "We have done with war! We have done with tyranny!" And their mothers will laugh from their graves, "It was for this that we suffered obloquy and contempt! Light up the windows of the new house, daughters! Let them blaze!"

Virginia Woolf,
Three Guineas

Mama, Mama, do you understand
Why I've not bound myself to a man?
Is something buried in your old widow's mind
That blesses my choice of our own kind?
Oh Mama, Mama.

Meg Christian,
from "Song to My Mama,"
I Know You Know (Olivia Records)

A strong woman is a woman at work
cleaning out the cesspool of the ages,
and while she shovels, she talks about
how she doesn't mind crying, it opens
the ducts of the eyes, and throwing up
develops the stomach muscles, and
she goes on shoveling with tears
in her nose.

A strong woman is a woman in whose head
a voice is repeating, I told you so,
ugly, bad girl, bitch, nag, shrill, witch,
ballbuster, nobody will ever love you back . . .

Marge Piercy,
from "For Strong Women,"
Chrysalis: A Magazine of Women's Culture

once upon a time there was a dream, a dream of women
turning the world all over and it still lives—
it lives for those who would be sisters

it lives for those who need a sister
it lives for those who once upon a time had a dream.

Pat Parker,
from "there is a woman in this town,"
Movement in Black

The rulers of patriarchy—males with power—wage an unceasing war against life itself. Since female energy is essentially biophilic, the female spirit/body is the primary target in this perpetual war of aggression against life. Gyn/Ecology is the re-claiming of life-loving female energy. This claiming of gynergy requires knowing/naming the fact that the State of Patriarchy is the State of War, in which periods of recuperation from and preparation for battle are euphemistically called "peace." Furies/Amazons must know the nature and conditions of this State in order to dis-cover and create radical female friendship. Given the fact that we are struggling to emerge from an estranged State, we must understand that the Female Self is The Enemy under fire from the guns of patriarchy. We must struggle to dis-cover this Self as Friend to all that is truly female, igniting the Fire of Female Friendship.

THE RADICAL ENEMY OF THE PATRIARCHAL WORLD WAR

The primordial, universal object of attack in all phallocratic wars is the Self in every woman. Nietzsche stated the ideal of this state of affairs in language that is more revealing/re-veiling than he and most of his readers could have understood: "Man should be trained for war and woman for the recreation of the warrior." [1] Indeed, the War State requires women for the re-creation of its warriors. This is true not only in the obvious sense that mothers produce sons who will be soldiers. It is true also on a deep psychic level: the psychic sapping of women in patriarchy functions continually to re-create its warriors.

The fact that warriors need the fetishized "recreational" presence of women to reactivate their depleted force is unintentionally substantiated in the writings of such authorities as Paul Fussell, author of *The Great War and Modern Memory*. Writing of World Wars I and II, Fussell states:

> In both wars alike a perennial rumor was that the enemy had women in his entrenchments. The women's underwear sometimes found in dugouts was assumed to belong to the residents rather than to represent gifts destined for home by soldiers hoping for leave.[2]

This fascinating piece of information is merely listed among "rumors originating in the Great War [which] have become standard for succeeding wars." However, viewing it from the perspective of positive paranoia, Amazons can perceive the significance of the persistent rumors that there were women in enemy entrenchments.

Fussell also furnishes unintended clues concerning militaristic perceptions of the enemy. He writes:

> What we can call gross dichotomizing is a persisting imaginative habit of modern times, traceable, it would seem, to the actualities of the Great War. "We" are all here on this side; "the enemy" is over there. "We" are individuals with names and personal identities; "he" is a mere collective entity. We are visible; he is invisible. We are normal; he is grotesque. Our appurtenances are natural; his, bizarre. He is not as good as we are.[3]

Amazons/Hags know that such "gross dichotomizing" is characteristic of patriarchal times, that it is traceable to the Great

War against the Female Self, which long predates World War I (a mere episode in the War State's chronic dis-ease). The archetypal "mere collective entity," consisting of "grotesque" beings whose "appurtenances" are "bizarre," is the dreaded Amazon Reality. For Female Selves are so terrifying to the patriarchal male that he must reverse/reduce them. This anti-process is the essence of the real Great War, of the endlessly re-turning reel of the Real War.

Fussell elaborates further upon the absolutism of militaristic dichotomizing. Describing "the binary deadlock, the gross physical polarization, of the trench predicament," he remarks: "Sometimes the shadowy enemy resembled the vilest animals." He alludes to a journalist who "was fond of speculating whether the enemy was human." [4] Here indeed is the all too familiar "binary deadlock" of patriarchy, unrecognized for what it is. Crone-ologists know the trench predicament all too well. We have read/heard/recorded endless comparisons of our Selves to "the vilest animals." We know that theologians have been fond of speculating whether women are human.

Clearly, the primary and essential object of aggression is not the "opposing" military force. The members of the opposing teams share the same values and play the same war games. The secret bond that binds the warriors together, energizing them, is the violation of women, acted out physically and constantly re-played on the level of language and of shared fantasies. In the absence of women, defeating the enemy is envisaged as making him into a woman. Yet the warriors always attempt to seal the ultimate victory by the actual rape, murder, and dismemberment of women.

In order to understand the misogynistic roots of androcratic aggression, we must comprehend that the perpetual War is waged primarily on a psychic and spiritual plane. This is not to minimize physical invasion/occupation/destruction, but to grasp the total horror. The most noxious forms of aggression are not reducible to the biological level alone, but involve also the fabrication of "symbolic universes in thought, language, and behavior." [5] *These universes are all present in each concrete violent act of aggression.*

Male authors have provided ample evidence that the bonding of androcratic aggressors is established and maintained through the fabrication of misogynistic symbol systems. Thus George Gilder, author of a confused and arrogant book supposedly dealing with feminism, becomes quite explicit when discussing his own sex. He writes of training in Marine Corps boot camp:

From the moment one arrives, the drill instructors begin a torrent of misogynistic and anti-individualist abuse. The good things are manly and collective; the despicable are feminine and individual. Virtually every sentence, every description, every lesson embodies this sexual duality, and the female anatomy provides a rich field of metaphor for every degradation.

When you want to create a solidary group of male killers, that is what you do, you kill the women in them. That is the lesson of the Marines. And it works.[6]

Thus the bonding of trained killers requires perpetual semantic degradation of women, in an effort to kill male weakness, which is misnamed "the women" in them.

The training described by Gilder was/is carried out in battle. In *A Rumor of War,* Philip Caputo, a marine infantry officer who "served" in Vietnam writes:

The tedium was occasionally relieved by a large scale search-and-destroy operation. . . . Weeks of bottled-up tensions would be released in a few minutes of orgiastic violence, men screaming and shouting obscenities above the explosions of grenades and the rapid, rippling bursts of automatic rifles.[7]

We can safely assume that the obscenities were *not* words referring to *male* anatomy. Rather, they echoed the misogynistic words of the drill instructors (DIs). Describing boot camp training, Caputo recalls that the recruits were no longer known by their own names, but were addressed by such epithets as "scumbag." He recounts the words of a DI whose voice "embedded itself in our minds until we could not walk anywhere without hearing it" as follows:

Square those pieces away SQUARE 'EM AWAY GIRLS. YOU, SHITHEAD FOURTH MAN IN THE FRONT RANK I SAID SQUARE THAT FUCKIN' PIECE, SQUARE IT AWAY Wan-tup-threep-fo.[8]

When the recruits thus addressed had their chance for orgiastic violence as "fighting men" in Vietnam, the voice of the drill instructor shouting misogynistic obscenities was no doubt still echoing in their minds and voices, as they turned their self-hatred upon "the enemy."

This use of verbal violence to unleash and support inclinations toward physical violence is operative also in the highest echelons of the military machine. On this level, too, male demonic destructiveness is clearly linked to hatred and contempt for women and all that men consider to be female. Thus, Lyndon Johnson was known to respect the value only of tough, "real" men. Only those who were confident and hawkish about Vietnam were listened to. David Halberstam writes:

> Hearing that one member of his Administration was becoming a dove on Vietnam, Johnson said, "Hell, he has to squat to piss." . . . Doubt itself, he thought, was almost a feminine quality, doubts were for women . . .[9]

Another example of this prevailing mentality was Spiro Agnew. Marc Fasteau points out that Agnew "compared then-Senator Charles Goodell to Christine Jorgensen, a man surgically changed into a woman [*sic*], literally an emasculated man, in describing Goodell's shift from hawk to dove." [10] Thus the male who is not willing to go forward blindly on the march of massive destruction is a "female." If he switches from hawk to dove, he is a "transsexual."

This idealization of necrophilia is linked to a sense of something lacking in the machine masters/members/themselves. Bruce Mazlish described Nixon as follows:

> He is afraid of being acted upon, of being inactive, of being soft, of being thought impotent, and of being dependent on anyone else.[11]

Such fear is also called fear of being "effeminate." It is supposedly horror of what Gilder calls "the women" in men. In fact, however, it has nothing to do with the reality of living women, but with an awareness on the part of males of an inherent weakness in themselves, which they name "femininity," or "effeminacy" or "woman"—and which they attempt to exorcise by projecting it upon really existent women as well as the women of their fantasies.

Valerie Solanas, in a blaze of insight, describes the situation:

> . . . the male is psychically passive. He hates his passivity, so he projects it onto women, defines the male as active, then sets out to prove that he is ("prove he's a Man"). . . . Since he's attempting to prove an error, he must "prove" it again and again.[12]

Solanas points out that the male is basically disgusted with himself for not being female (i.e., not having such qualities as emotional strength and independence, forcefulness, courage, integrity, vitality . . . which he misnames "male"), and that one effect of this is War:

> The male's normal method of compensation for not being female, namely, getting his Big Gun off, is grossly inadequate, as he can get it off only a very limited number of times; so he gets it off on a really massive scale, and proves to the entire world that he's a Man.[13]

Some male authors inadvertently confirm Solanas's analysis. Thus Gilder shamelessly describes male emptiness, using this information ultimately to justify male possession and draining of women. In spite of this misuse, his description parallels Solanas's perception:

> . . . unlike femininity [read: femaleness], relaxed masculinity [read: maleness] is at bottom empty, a limp nullity. While the female body is full of internal potentiality, the male is internally barren (from the Old French *bar,* meaning man).[14]

This awareness of emptiness has a causal relationship to the rigid role definitions required by patriarchal males, for the male, sensing his inner barrenness, is "deeply dependent on the structure of the society to define his role." [15]

Clearly, the basic paradigm and expression of the rigid societal structure and role definitions by which males attempt to cover their basic sense of emptiness is military. The military life provides "meaning" and the needed injections of "excitement." Caputo expresses this, proclaiming that "the heroic experience I sought was war; war, the ultimate adventure; war, the ordinary man's most convenient means of escaping from the ordinary." [16] Describing his reaction to his "honorable discharge" from the marines, the same author writes: "I felt as happy as a condemned man whose sentence was commuted, but within a year I began growing nostalgic for the war." [17] J. Glenn Gray, author of *The Warriors,* also describes the war experience as a cover for personal emptiness: "Peace exposed a void in them that war's excitement had enabled them to keep covered up." [18] The male sense of barrenness, then, breeds hierarchical structures of violence, epitomized in war. Even Lionel Tiger, who obscurely distinguishes aggression from violence, refers to male bonding as "the male equivalent of child reproduction, which is related to work, defense, politics, and perhaps even the violent mastery and destruction of others." [19] He admits that "it is presumably significant that the Nazi movement was an essentially male organization." [20]

Such organized aggression/violence of males filled with fear of their own emptiness and weakness is carried out against women in concrete acts of rape, dismemberment, and murder. These acts of violation/violence are expressions of the War State's essential identity as the State of Rapism, in which all invasions, occupations, destructions of "enemy territory" are elaborations upon the theme of rape/gynocide. We have seen that the female anatomy provides metaphors for degradation in military training, notably in the marines. Consistent with this mentality/training is the fact that porn films near military centers often depict violent attacks against women. Also consistent with these patterns of fantasy/behavior is the fact that such fantasies are acted out by military personnel in the form of violent abuse of available women and later converted into subject matter for stories upon return to the base after "liberty."

Not surprisingly, the fact that rapism is the essence of the perpetual World War is re-veiled by all the propaganda programmers. This re-veiling functions to re-cycle the Processions of Warriors/Rapists. Officially, rape is reported when committed by "the other side." Such selective reporting stimulates and justifies retaliation in kind by "this side." Necrophagous devourers of such rape propaganda feed upon the flesh of rape murderers' victims over and over again, storing up energy for their own turn. News of casualties caused by "this side" in "the casual continuing war against women" [21] is not usually included in All the News That's Fit to Print, having been deemed unfit according to delicate male standards. Susan Brownmiller shows that selective reporting of rape has provided an ideological excuse for men to rape women "belonging" to other men, and that since rape has frequently been a prelude to murder it has conveniently been minimized in reporting of the allegedly more serious act. Furthermore, the propagators of rape hide their responsibility (accomplish agent deletion) through the institution of prostitution. As Brownmiller indicates, moreover, rape has been perpetrated everywhere and always on all sides of patriarchal wars.[22] Finally, rape has been a source/form/confirmation of male bonding:

> Indeed, one of the earliest forms of male bonding must have been the gang rape of one woman by a band of marauding men. . . . It [rape] is nothing more or less than a conscious process of intimidation by which *all* men keep *all* women in a state of fear.[23]

This State of Fear is the State of War, the State of Rapism.

The War State's symbolic universes not only attack the Female Self as The Enemy, but also continually guise and dis-guise this fact. When women begin to show any signs of detecting the fact that we carry Enemy I.D.'s in our Selves, the War State bombards The Enemy's mind(s) with its familiar arsenal of tried and true weapons, such as erasure, reversal, false polarization, and false inclusion. These weapons are constantly in use against women's minds, but they are focused with special intensity against Furies/Crones who talk about The War.

Erasure: Casual, blatant admissions erase the reality by rubbing it in: "Naturally, there's a war between the sexes." Often, horrifying implications of the statement are turned into "humor" and those who reject them are pronounced "humorless." A powerful weapon in the arsenal of erasers is the mystique of romantic love. At times, however, the language of "love" erases its own erasures. Thus, a marine sergeant, describing a gang rape in Vietnam, concluded his narrative as follows:

But at any rate, they raped the girl, and then, the last man to make love to her shot her in the head.[24]

Nor is it even necessary to resort to the marines to hear a good Love Story. Important evidence is put forth by male novelists. Thus D. H. Lawrence, a rich source, describes a love scene between Gerald and Gudrun, two characters in his acclaimed novel, *Women in Love*:

Into her he poured all his pent-up darkness and corrosive death, and he was whole again. . . . This was the ever-recurrent miracle of his life, at the knowledge of which he was lost in an ecstasy of relief and wonder. And she, subject, received him as a vessel filled with his bitter potion of death.[25]

After describing Gudrun as receiving this death "in an ecstasy of subjection" (it never occurs to him that in real life such a woman might have been bored and faking) Lawrence goes on to describe the vampiristic scene:

As he drew nearer to her, he plunged deeper into her enveloping soft warmth, a wonderful creative heat that penetrated his veins and gave him life again. He felt himself dissolving and sinking to rest in the bath of her living strength. It seemed as if her heart in her breast were a second unconquerable sun, into the glow and creative strength of which he plunged further and further. . . . His blood, which seemed to have been drawn back into death, came ebbing on the return, surely, beautifully, powerfully.[26]

Lawrence indeed gives the whole show away. He describes Gerald after the act, "as he felt the full, unutterable sleep coming over him, the sleep of complete exhaustion and restoration." Our author continues: "*But Gudrun lay wide awake,* *destroyed into perfect consciousness* [emphasis mine]." * [27] Of course, the full horror of Gudrun's state is that it is not "perfect consciousness," nor is it the unconsciousness of blissful sleep. Rather, it is the dull aching state of one who has sold her body and soul and will continue to do so. It is a state of perfectly false consciousness. Lawrence seems to know this, for he describes the endless breaking "of slow sullen waves of fate [which] held her life a possession, whilst she lay with dark, wide eyes looking into the darkness." And still her false conscience keeps her from waking him:

> But she dared not make a light, because she knew he would wake, and she did not want to break his perfect sleep, that she knew he had got of her.[28]

Gudrun lies awake all night, waiting for the clock to strike five, when Gerald must go, "and she would be released. Then she could relax and fill her own place."

This style of rapism, this exchange of "the bitter potion of death" for life and strength is not quick killing; it is slow sapping. As Lawrence so precisely wrote of his character Gudrun: "She felt old, old." [29] Women possessed in this way by the mystique of romantic love are tamed, used. Dulled into Sleeping Death, they know, yet do not know, the identity of The Enemy.

Reversal: Even novice Furies are accused of thinking or saying that "men are the enemy." This is a subtly deceptive reversal, implying that women are the initiators of enmity, blaming the victims for The War. Its deceptive power is derived from the fact that the Fury in every woman does fight back against males and male institutions that target her as

* Adrienne Rich describes this common experience in "The Afterwake" (1961):

> Nursing your nerves
> to rest, I've roused my own; well
> now for a few bad hours!
> Sleep sees you behind closed doors.
> Alone, I slump in his front parlor.

The Enemy. The point is that she did not create The War, but rather finds herself in a set-up in which fighting is necessary for Surviving. An obvious consequence of this situation is the fact that patriarchal males are the enemies of women. However, the fighter role of Furies is a derivative status, necessitated by the fact that women are the primal objects of patriarchal attack.

False Inclusion: Without Furious Fighting, women are duped, doped, or demonically inspired into believing that they belong as "equals" or as Loved Ones in the centers of patriarchal power. Self-centering requires Self-defense. However, even this Furious response of the Self can itself be reduced to false inclusion if all our energy is drained in fighting, so that we are merely fighters. The fighting of Furies is effective only to the extent that we succeed in reversing the reversal that reduces our Selves to the condition of The Enemy. For all women have been "inspired," through forced false inclusion in the patriarchal "we," to view the Female Self as The Enemy.

Reversing this reversal means rejecting all identification with the myths, ideologies, and institutions which name our Selves The Enemy. The term *enemy,* derived from the Latin *in,* meaning not, and *amicus,* meaning friend, names the not-friend. Since Hags refuse to be included among those who treat the female Self as not-friend, we choose our own Selves as friends of our Selves. This involves also a choice of friends among other Female Selves who reject their imposed status as not-friend, as The Enemy. It does not imply friendship with those who hold up the reversing mirror, distorting our identity, destroying our integrity, our capacity for Female Friendship.

False Polarization: Women who accept false inclusion among the fathers and sons are easily polarized against other women on the basis of ethnic, national, class, religious, and other male-defined differences, applauding the defeat of "enemy" women. Haggard Journeyers have learned to see through this false enmity to the true identity of androcracy's Enemy. When this point has been reached, Crones know who we are. The time has come for rekindling the Fire of Female Friendship.

THE RADICAL FRIENDSHIP OF HAGS

Haggard Journeyers move alone and together away from the Haunted Houses and Zoos that are filled with mirrors/mirages/manacles intended to hold us in captivity.[30] "Together" does not mean in lockstep or simultaneously, but each according to her own Life-time. The moving presence of each Self calls forth the living presence of other journeying/enspiriting Selves. No doubt this is threatening to the Haunted House-Keepers, Zoo-Keepers. In a play written in the 1920s an unhappy husband wails:

> Under cover of friendship a woman can enter any household . . . she can poison and pillage everything before the man whose home she destroys is even aware of what's happening to him. When he finally realizes . . . it's too late—he is alone! Alone in the face of a secret alliance of two beings who understand one another because they're alike . . . because they're of a different planet than he, the stranger, the enemy! [31]

In this passage, one not unusual House-Keeper unknowingly acknowledges the horror of the situation which patriarchy has projected upon women, and which is now reflected back upon himself. No longer encased in the false identity of strangers to each other, of Enemy to the Self, and to each other, the two women have become friends—"two beings who understand each other because they're alike." The distraught male realizes that *his* home is no longer under his possessive power. The women are not *for* him. Since they have escaped, thrown off the cloak/cover of enmity toward their Selves, he perceives them as under the "*cover* [cloak] of friendship," for he perversely persists in his need to see friendship as alien to women.

In reality, their friendship is possible because they have come out from under the male-imposed veils/covers/identities, sparking forth their Selves. The projector must see this creative sparking, this re-claiming of female heritage, as poisoning and pillaging, for they have left the Prepossessor without his property—their Selves. By acknowledging their radical aloneness they have learned to bond in friendship and therefore left him to face the condition which he himself cannot bear: "He is alone!" Since his very existence has depended upon stolen female energy, he now faces ultimate horror. There is no comparison between the threat posed by female bonding and mere wifely infidelity with another man. The latter situation is mere usurpation of his property by another proprietor. However, *this* "secret alliance" of beings who are "of a different planet" is of another order: It challenges the caste of planetary proprietors by ignoring them. The bonding of Dreadless Hags is Dreadful. The result of this union is Nemesis.

It is Crone-logically important to re-call that the word *friend* is derived from an Old English term meaning to love, and that it is akin in its roots to an Old English word meaning free. The radical friendship of Hags means loving our own freedom, loving/encouraging the freedom of the other, the friend, and therefore *loving freely*. To those who might object that the word *friend* is an "old word," Crones who know what radical female friendship is can reply that it is indeed an Old Word and that we are re-calling it, re-claiming it as our heritage. The identity named by the Old Word *friend* is from our own Background. It names our Presence to each other on the Journey. It cannot be experienced by those who are under the spell of the Prepossessors. Nor can it be experienced by those who feel the need to prepossess others, for this need is evidence of inability to be radically alone, and thus of inability to be a friend. It is this lack that is hidden by the fraudulent claims of patriarchal males who name themselves The Proprietors of friendship itself, who propagate the Lie that "only men can be friends."

DOUBLE DILEMMAS AND THE DOUBLE AX

Crones journeying together find after a while that one of the most difficult parts of the journey is dis-covering the meaning of *together*. Those who have been journeying long enough to know Crone-ology can recall the euphoria experienced at the discovery of sisterhood. True, we had been "together" with women before we had learned to call our Selves feminists. But these prefeminist groupings had been essentially collections *of* women rather than *for* women. Then, with the rise of feminism, some women found each other, came to know each other in new ways. That was the beginning of our rough Voyage, which has proved—for those who have persisted—strange, difficult, unpredictable, terrifying, enraging, energizing, transforming, encouraging. For those who have persisted there is at least one certainty and perhaps only one: Once we have understood this much, there is no turning back.

Yet confusion/bafflement is experienced by Crones who are surviving the early euphoria over sisterhood, for nearly every aspect of our situation in the Land of the Fathers is contaminated by doublethink/doublefeel/doubledream. We have seen, for example, that the more we understand the State of Possession, the more anger is generated/awakened within us and the greater the danger that this will misfire in the direction of Sister Journeyers.

There are many experiences which throw women back into a sense of loneliness and isolation. For example, many women who have experienced, as a result of coming to feminist consciousness, a burning desire to study, have found that precisely because of this deep awareness, patriarchal "education" is almost too disgusting to endure. Others, having struggled with a passion for justice to attain certain goals, for example, professional careers, have found that their very success turns to ashes when they realize the shoddiness of the professions. Crones are tempted, then, to lean upon friends/lovers out of frustration. However, when women bond out of weakness, there is a danger of victimizing each other. Searching for words to analyze this dilemma, Crones find that we have inherited a contaminated language.

Words/labels often stop thinking/imagining/conquesting. We must break their mindbinding power. Sometimes it is necessary to reject them entirely; in other instances we prune them into adequate instruments, so that they will point the way into the Background, rather than blocking it. For this purpose, Crones need to sharpen our minds/wits so that they become the Sacred Double Axes of Amazons. The A-mazing Female Mind is the Labrys that cuts through the double binds and doublebinding words that block our breakthrough to understanding radical feminist friendship and sisterhood.

SISTERS AND FRIENDS

Women finding and creating deep bonds with each other seek to use the contaminated words of our patriarchal false heritage to express these. Women finding each other speak of sisters, friends, lovers. Yet the words often mysteriously bend back upon themselves, forming boomerangs rather than instruments for expression of bonding. Since the terms are all polluted with patriarchal associations, they function not only as means of expression, but also as mind pollutants.

Crones can begin to unsnarl the semantic problems that blind us into binding instead of bonding by examining some male definitions and distinctions. J. Glenn Gray offers the following enlightening distinction between male comradeship and friendship:

> The essential difference between comradeship and friendship consists . . . in a heightened awareness of the self in friendship and in the suppression of self-awareness in comradeship.[32]

Since brotherhood/fraternity are roughly equivalent to male comradeship, males also perceive a sharp contrast between the bonding designated by these terms and their "bonding" in friendship.

Women breaking away from the feminine condition often tend at first to imitate male comradeship, initially misperceiving sisterhood as something like the female equivalent of brotherhood. However, Crones who have persisted in the Otherworld Journey have come to know deeply that sisterhood, like female friendship, has at its core the affirmation of freedom. Thus sisterhood differs radically from male comradeship/brotherhood, which functions to perpetuate the State of War.

Since sisterhood is deeply like female friendship, rather than being its opposite (as in the case of male semantic counterparts) it is radically Self-affirming. In this respect it is totally different from male comradeship/brotherhood, in which individuals seek to lose their identity.[33] The difference between sisterhood and male comradeship, which is disguised by an apparent similarity of terms, would be almost impossible to exaggerate. An important clue to the essence of this difference is the fact that the epitome of male bonding in comradeship is experienced in war. Gray writes:

> In mortal danger, numerous soldiers enter into a dazed condition in which all sharpness of consciousness is lost. When in this state they can be caught up into the fire of communal ecstasy and forget about death by losing their individuality, or they can function like cells in a military organism, doing what is expected of them because it has become automatic.[34]

Such male merging in "the fire of communal ecstasy" or as "cells in a military organism" is necrophilic self-loss. In contrast to this, the Fire of Sisterhood results from the Sparking of Female Selves who are finding each other. It is the unleashing of biophilic energy. Furies spark new ideas, new words, new images, new feelings, new life, New Be-ing. This is the Fire of biophilic Self-finding. This Fire, unlike the male warrior's ecstasy, which causes him to stand outside himself, enables the Self-centering Spinster/Voyager to burn away the internalized false selves, so that she *is* deeper within her Self and outside the State of Possession, the fathers' foreground.

Since Sisterhood is the expression of biophilic energy burning through the encasements of the Necrophilic State of Staledom, it is more complex than mere male monogender merging. Since Bonding Furies are not primarily concerned with fighting, but with breaking boundaries, bounding free, our ecstasy is totally other than "war ecstasy." However, Crones also know that since the Female Self, who is Friend to her Self, is The Enemy of patriarchy, the bonding of our Selves is perceived by the warriors as the Ultimate Threat to be shot down with every big gun available. Given such conditions, besieged Furies *do* fight back, and thus there is a warrior element in Sisterhood. There is, then, an element in Haggard bonding which is "us versus a third," and which is Positively Furious. Yet Crones know that this warrior aspect of Amazon bonding becomes truly dreadless daring only when it is focused beyond fighting. Our inherited vocabulary is inadequate to express this complexity and its inherent priorities, since it has been dwarfed to accommodate the pale male experience of bonding.

In order to overcome this inherited vocabulary of idiotology, Hags/Harpies must use our Double Axes to hack away its false dichotomies, particularly the demonic opposition between Sister and Friend. For it is the Friend in the Sister who defines/limits/expands her role as warrior. It is the Free Friend who has no need to be consumed in the "fire of communal ecstasy," to melt/meld in mass murder/mergers. It is the Friend/Self who can define sisterhood as Other than brotherhood, who can aim the fire of Fury so that it transcends the state of enmity. It is she who can blaze the trails that will lead Journeyers away from the battleground, into the Background.

Far from being opposites, then, sisterhood and female friendship are not clearly distinct. A feminist thinks of her close friends as sisters, but she knows that she has many sisters—women extremely close in their temperaments, vision, commitment—whom she has never met. Sometimes she meets such women and some conversation unmasks the similarities between them. She may have an uncanny feeling that she has known these women for years, that the present conversation is merely one in a series of many with these women. The proximity that she feels is not merely geographic/spatial. It is psychic, spiritual, in the realm of inner life-time. She senses gynaesthetically that there is a convergence of personal histories, of wave-lengths. She knows that there is a network of communication present, and that on some level, at least potentially, it exists among women who have never met or heard of each other. Because of limitations of energy, time, space, these women are not actually her friends, but they are sisters, potential friends.

Only those who have the strength to be friends have the strength to bond in sisterhood. This sets sisterhood totally apart from male brotherhood or comradeship, which at best is a transitory and shallow substitute, dependent upon emergencies, upon violence, and upon the existence of The Enemy. Since the core, the Soul-Spark of sisterhood is friendship, it does not essentially depend upon an enemy for its existence and continued becoming. This friendship is the ultimate State of Enmity in relation to the War State, for it is the radical withdrawal of energy from warring patriarchy and transferral of this energy to women's Selves. Sisterhood exists precisely where women have found something better than the War State.

The A-mazing Female Mind must not only see through false distinctions between sisterhood and friendship, but must also cut apart The Fraternity's false combinations and identifications, such as the identification of "love" and comradeship, which are contrasted with friendship. Gray writes: "Friends do not seek to lose their identity, as comrades and erotic lovers do." [35] Further on, he states: "Erotic love can usually, though not always, find itself renewed when time has passed. The companionship of a lost friend is not replaceable." [36] Clearly, Gray is likening male comradeship and male erotic love, while separating both from friendship. Writing in a similar vein, Caputo describes "the intimacy of life in infantry batallions," asserting that there:

> . . . the communion between men is as profound as any between lovers. Actually it is more so. It does not demand for its sustenance the reciprocity, the pledges of affection, the endless reassurances required by the love of men and women.[37]

This lumping together of erotic love and comradeship is enlightening. Male-defined erotic love involves loss of identity and is inherently transitory. It involves hierarchies, ranking roles—like the military—on the model of S and M. While male erotic love is seen as similar to comradeship in these respects, it is experienced as weaker in intensity and depth. Woman-loving Spinsters/Lesbians who are finding integrity of gynaesthetic experience know that such splitting of erotic love from friendship and likening it to warrior-comradeship is symptomatic of the disease of fragmentation. This is the diseased State of Fraternity, and the well-being of sisterhood requires understanding that radically Lesbian loving is totally Other from this. For female-identified erotic love is not dichotomized from radical female friendship, but rather is one important expression/manifestation of friendship.

Women loving women do not seek to lose our identity, but to express it, dis-cover it, create it. A Spinster/Lesbian can be and often is a deeply loving friend to another woman without being her "lover," but it is impossible to be female-identified lovers without being friends and sisters. The Presence of Enspiriting Female Selves to each other is a creative gynergetic flow that may assume different shapes and colors. The sparking of ideas and the flaming of physical passion emerge from the same source. The bonding of woman-loving women survives its transformations because its source is the Sister-Self.[38] It survives because the very meaning of this bonding is Surviving, that is, Super-living. It is biophilic bonding.

INVITATIONS TO ASSIMILATION

In case there is any doubt that sisterhood is unlike male merging, Hags should *hear* the "authorities." D. H. Lawrence in an essay on Whitman expresses the patriarchal poetic vision of fulfillment: "Woman is inadequate for the last merging. So the next step is the merging of man-for-man love. And this is on the brink of death. It slides over into death." [39] Grateful for our "inadequacy," Amazons strive to step aside while the death-loving Mergers slide over the brink.

The problem is that the merging marchers want to pull women and all of life with them on the death march. Sensing that the Female Self will not willingly join this procession, since she is nonnecrophilic, they make every effort to deceive her, to drug her into an approximation of their own dulled-out state. This muted mental/emotional condition is described by Robert J. Lifton, who writes of the desensitization of G.I.'s: ". . . one merges with them [the men in one's unit] on a basis of shared psychic numbing." This, he says, is "collective psychic commitment to avoiding guilt, or at least an awareness of it . . ." [40] Caputo, writing of a marine in Vietnam who senselessly shot a woman, quotes him as follows: "I mean the thing that bothers me about killing her is that it doesn't bother me." [41]

This state of psychic numbing, of avoiding awareness of guilt, and specifically of shunning awareness of guilt for killing The True Enemy, is the condition which women are continually invited to share. The assimilation of Amazons as Athenas into The Army is an essential aim of androcracy. Merging by numbing is male-initiated. However, Ladies Are Invited. We should note the disguised/guised style of the invitations.

The basic form of absorbing women into The Army is, of course, tokenism, which is presented as the epitome and goal of feminism. President John G. Bowen of Princeton University made the following inviting statement:

The ultimate objective of Affirmative Action is to achieve a situation in which every individual, from every background, [feels] "*unselfconsciously included*" [emphasis mine].[42]

President Bowen feels that this is "an elusive objective, not attainable for many people in any full sense now." However, he deems it "a goal worthy of our best efforts."

Indeed. The goal of patriarchal institutions is "unselfconscious inclusion." This is the lethal inversion of the Outsiders' Society. It is the deceptive reversal of sisterhood—which means Self-conscious, Self-enspiriting Self-exclusion from the State of Possession—into male-identified comradeship/brotherhood. Of course, this "elusive objective" of tokenism, i.e., token merging in The Fraternity, is "not attainable for many people in any full sense now"—as President Bowen rightly points out. For the "ecstasy" of merging in omnipotent male groups is not the goal presented to most women as attainable by them.

What is offered to the majority of women is the ideal of self-sacrifice. Yet this, in a peculiar way, is also inclusion in brotherhood/comradeship. For, as Gray has shown, self-sacrifice is an important aspect of comradeship. However, in contrast to male modes of self-sacrifice, which are rewarded with the ecstasy of merging, the self-sacrifice imposed as an ideal upon most women is the radically unrewarding handing over of their identity and energy to individual males—fathers, sons, husbands—and to ghostly institutional masters. Thus, the two "ideals" of feminine fulfillment, namely "unselfconscious inclusion" (tokenism) and feminine self-sacrifice, both function to pollute the sense of sisterhood unless they are thoroughly exorcised.

The first of these false ideals, i.e., tokenism—which is commonly guised as Equal Rights, and which yields token victories—deflects and shortcircuits gynergy, so that female power, galvanized under deceptive slogans of sisterhood, is swallowed by The Fraternity. This method of vampirizing the Female Self saps women by giving illusions of partial success while at the same time making Success appear to be a far-distant, extremely difficult to obtain "elusive objective." When the oppressed are worn out in the game of chasing the elusive shadow of Success, some "successes" are permitted to occur—"victories" which can easily be withdrawn when the victim's energies have been restored. Subsequently, women are lured into repeating efforts to regain the hard-won apparent gains.*

Thus tokenism is insidiously destructive of sisterhood, for it distorts the warrior aspect of Amazon bonding both by magnifying it and by minimizing it. It magnifies the importance of "fighting back" to the extent of making it devour the transcendent be-ing of sisterhood, reducing it to a copy of comradeship. At the same time, it minimizes the Amazon warrior aspect by containing it, misdirecting and shortcircuiting the struggle.

This is a demonically double-sided trap, for of course reforms, such as legalization of abortion, aid many women in desperate situations. However, because the "changes" that are achieved are victories in a vacuum, that is, in a totally oppressive social context, they do not essentially free the Female Self but instead function to hide both the fact of continuing oppression and the possibilities for better options and for more radical freedom.† The Labrys of the A-mazing Female Mind

* Crone-ographers might re-view the history of such issues as the legalization of abortion, Affirmative Action, and the ratification of the ERA as illustrations of this phenomenon in the United States.

† The Journeyer has already confronted the fact that Lesbians/Spinsters have no need of abortions, unless forcibly raped (see Chapter Seven).

must cut through the coverings of these double-sided/multiple-sided situations, dis-covering the context, identifying the more radical problems, yet neglecting none.

A final point to consider about the "unselfconscious inclusion" of tokenism is its attempt to assimilate woman-for-woman erotic love. Tokenism/"Equal Rights" devours sisterhood, converting it into copied comradeship, and splitting it from its deep source, which is female friendship. Thus it also splits female sexuality from radical female friendship. When a woman has been divided in this way, her "sexual preference" is not ultimately important,[43] for the very meaning of sexuality has been dwarfed to fit patriarchal standards. She may be "heterosexual" or "bisexual" or "homosexual," but she is not Lesbian. In the final analysis, any woman who is "unselfconsciously included" is heterosexist, divided from her own Self and from other Female Selves. Since she is ultimately unthreatening to heterosexist institutions, her still male-defined sexuality is not ultimately threatening to them.

Women who are merely "gay" rather than Female-identified do, of course, find themselves in difficult circumstances in relation to heterosexist institutions. Some are hired as token "lesbians." Others are accepted/assimilated with the tacit agreement that they will remain "discreet," refusing to be proud examples of an Other way of living. Still others are persecuted, not because they are Furies/Feminists, but because their "sexual preference" is seen (correctly) by the Overseers as incipient, potential Fury. Yet as long as their struggle remains on the level of "gay rights" they do not actually pose the Ultimate Threat, which is female Self-accepting bonding, or sisterhood.

The second of the false ideals of feminine fulfillment, that is, self-sacrifice for the sake of men, also pollutes understanding/living of sisterhood. This is true on the obvious level that many women who want to be feminists are held back by primary loyalties to individual males. It is true also in the sense that women often have wrong expectations of strong women. That is, such women are expected to be Self-sacrificing for their sisters rather than Self-affirming. Thus, in a convoluted way, they are asked to be feminine in the name of female bonding. This unjust and contradictory demand is rooted in the residues of the patriarchal religious ethic, which still haunts Haggard minds. Therefore we must consider the problem of this mind-pollutant and its cure, that is, Self-acceptance.

REFUSING SELF-SACRIFICE: THE COURAGE OF SELF-ACCEPTANCE

Sparking the fire of female friendship requires recognizing the divine Spark in the Self and in other Selves and *accepting* this Spark. In order to understand this gynocentric courage of acceptance it is necessary to grasp what it is not. That is, Gyn/Ecologists must depollute the term *acceptance,* which has acquired overtones of passive acquiescence or resignation. One of the most blatant perversions of acceptance is the virtue which christian theologian Paul Tillich calls "the courage to accept acceptance." He writes:

> One could say that the courage to be is the courage to accept oneself as accepted in spite of being unacceptable.[44]

The problem with this, of course, is that it is precisely not a description of the courage to be in the full sense of accepting responsibility for one's process. Rather, the victim of this masochistic Pauline-Lutheran doctrine is condemned to live in a prison of mirror images, "knowing" that she is guilty and deserving of condemnation, but believing a loving god forgives her. Through such a belief system she is cut off from her own process, remaining forever worthless and forever accepted as such. There is no reason to change and no possibility of changing, only of wallowing. This wallowing Tillich calls "self-affirmation." He is explicit:

> . . . it is not the good or the wise or the pious who are entitled to the courage to accept acceptance but those who are lacking in all these qualities and are aware of being unacceptable. This, however, does not mean acceptance by oneself as oneself.[45]

This is the essence of religious self-deception, which in theological doublethink is called self-affirmation. Those religiously trained in such doublethink are adept at deceiving others because they are self-deceivers.

Such mythic/theological self-deception provides the paradigm for all distortions of self-acceptance. Tillich does not disappoint the reader who is looking for an explicit connection with medicine and therapy:

> In the communion of healing, for example, the psychoanalytic situation, the patient participates in the healing power of the helper by whom he [*sic*] is acceptable although he feels himself unacceptable.[46]

Here is the mythic/theological root of the triumph of therapy and of all the professions which keep the victim in a state of feeling unacceptable while pretending that she is affirming herself. Here also is the secret of the power to inflict the disease of "unselfconscious inclusion" upon tokenized women who are recruited into the Service of The Brotherhood. Finally, here is the mechanism which keeps women mesmerized by the mystique of self-sacrifice. For since those kept in a state of being unacceptable to themselves feel worthless, self-sacrifice is a logical conclusion of their condition. Since they have been trained to project the same evaluation upon other women, and since self-sacrifice is perceived as the highest ideal, they can expect and even demand this of the strong feminist women they most admire, while perceiving no contradiction in such expectations.

In contrast to this, the Enspiriting Self is acceptable to her Self. She knows that only she can judge her Self. Because she has a strong sense of her own worth, the Amazon who has the courage to accept her Self is not self-sacrificing. Having acknowledged the divine Spark in her Self and having accepted it as her own, she has no need to demand self-sacrifice of her sisters. This prospect is horrifying to her, for she cherishes their divine Sparks, their be-ing, as she cherishes her own, knowing that their combined combustion is the creation of Female Fire.

THE ULTIMATE THREAT OF FEMALE BONDING

We have seen that the Female Self is The Enemy targeted by the State of War. This Self becomes ultimately threatening when she bonds in networks with other Self-accepting Female Selves. Since we have been conditioned to think quantitatively, feminists often begin the Journey with the misconception that we require large numbers in order to have a realistic hope of victory. This mistake is rooted in a serious underestimation of the force/fire of female bonding. It occurs when Amazons fall into the trap of imagining that sisterhood is like male comradeship. Because of the inherent weakness of its cogs, the male machine does require large numbers of self-sacrificing comrades. Because of the inherent strength of a woman who is Friend to her Self, the force of female bonding does not require multitudes.

Ironically, patriarchal males show evidence of grasping this fact more readily than do many Hags, for the former know that their collective show of strength depends upon a colossal commitment to covering up their own individual weakness. Indeed, male bonding/comradeship requires the stunting of individuality. In contrast to this, female-identified bonding is based upon the highly individualized strength of Self-accepting Hags. It often takes time before Journeyers catch on to the force of our combined Sparking, for we have been socialized by the reversing doctrines of patriarchy into Self-depreciation. The effect of this socialization is entirely different from that of the male's conditioning to cover up his weakness and that of other men. When feminists break through to Self-knowledge we find our inherent strength which has been denied. In contrast to this, when the male attains insight about himself, he realizes that his role-defined "strength" has in large measure consisted in hiding his weakness. The male living the lie of role-defined masculinity has the cunning of one who constantly bluffs. He knows that he has everything to fear from the combination of even two or three Sparking Female Selves, for Sparking Spinsters confirm each other's sense of reality, burning through his lies. His fear of our converging power is the reason why strong female-identified women frequently find ourselves isolated in patriarchal institutions, surrounded by token women.

Knowing that whenever two or three Self-affirming women are gathered together in our own names we are lighting our Fire, Amazons can stop worrying about the false problem of numbers.* Our analysis can move from quantitative estimates to qualitative leaps of understanding and acting. From this position of known inherent strength we can consider the important issues of separation and separatism.

SEPARATION: ROOM OF ONE'S OWN

Writing of male bonding, J. Glenn Gray asserts: "While comradeship wants to break down the walls of self, friendship seeks to expand these walls and keep them intact." [47] Sisterhood has nothing to do with breaking down "the walls of self," but with burning/melting/vaporizing the constricting walls imposed upon the Self. Moreover, female friendship is not concerned with "expanding walls and keeping them intact," but with expanding energy, power, vision, psychic and physical space. Sisterhood and female friendship burn down the walls of male-defined categories and definitions. However, hagocratic separatism/separation is not essentially about walls at all. Rather, it is expanding room of our own, moving outside the realm of the War State, War Stare.

Having thus separated female bonding from male definitions, Crones can approach the questions of separation and separatism in new ways. The dictionary reports that we should understand the term *separate* to be derived from the Latin *se,* meaning apart, and *parare,* meaning to get ready, set. Without bothering to dispute the correctness of this etymology, it is still possible to look at the word another way, to see in it the

* Clearly, the issue of numbers is not false/unreal in every specific situation, especially in cases of physical violence. However, even in such circumstances the psychic combination of women's energies can significantly increase our power.

Latin word *se,* meaning self, and to see also that the Latin *parare* is the root of the verb *to pare*. When Spinsters speak of separatism, the deep questions that are being asked concern the problem of paring away from the Self all that is alienating and confining. Crone-logically prior to all discussion of political separatism from or within groups is the basic task of paring away the layers of false selves from the Self. In analyzing this basic Gyn/Ecological problem, we should struggle to detect whatever obstacles we can find, both internal and external, to this dis-covering of the Self.

It is Crone-logical to conclude that internal separation or separatism, that is, paring away, burning away the false selves encasing the Self, is the core of all authentic separations and thus is normative for all personal/political decisions about acts/forms of separatism. It is axiomatic for Amazons that all external/internalized influences, such as myths, names, ideologies, social structures, which cut off the flow of the Self's original movement should be pared away.

Since each Self is unique, since each woman has her own history, and since there are deep differences in temperament and abilities, Hags should acknowledge this variety in all discussions of separatism.* While it is true that all women have had many similar experiences under patriarchy, it is also true that there have been wide variations on the theme of possession and in struggles for dispossession. To simplify dif-

* I want to separate my position here from an attitude of "tolerance" for differences among women. A common definition of *tolerance,* given in Merriam-Webster, is "a permissive or liberal attitude toward beliefs or practices differing from or conflicting with one's own." This attitude of "different strokes for different folks," while appearing to support originality, is in fact often repressive. The tyranny of tolerance is often the source of silencing/erasure of strong-minded Hags—who are labeled "intolerant," "extreme," and "narrow." However, if we look at Merriam-Webster's first definition of *tolerance,* we find an interesting clue for an analysis of genuinely gynocentric respect for difference. *Tolerance* (which is derived from the Latin *tolerare,* meaning endure, put up with) is defined as "capacity to endure pain or hardship: ENDURANCE, FORTITUDE, STAMINA." The variety which Crones respect in each other has as its basic precondition and common thread the endurance/fortitude/stamina needed for persevering on the Journey.

ferences would be to settle for a less than Dreadful judgment of the multiple horrors of gynocide. It would also impoverish our imaginations, limiting our vision of the Otherworld Journey's dimensions. Finally, minimizing the variety in Amazon Journeyers' experiences, temperaments, and talents would blind us to the necessity for separating at times even from sisters, in order to allow our Selves the freedom and space for our own unique discoveries. Acknowledging the deep differences among friends/sisters is one of the most difficult stages of the Journey[48] and it is essential for those who are Sparking in free and independent friendship rather than merely melting into mass mergers. Recognizing the chasms of differences among sister Voyagers is coming to understand the terrifying terrain through which we must travel together and apart. At the same time, the spaces between us are encouraging signs of our immeasurable unique potentialities, which need free room of their own to grow in, to Spark in, to Blaze in. The greatness of our differences signals the immensity/intensity of the Fire that will flame from our combined creative Fury.

Whereas discussions of relations between men and women eulogize the so-called complementarity of opposites, an Amazonian analysis of female friendship/love dis-covers the fact that the basis of woman-identified relationships is neither biological differences nor socially constructed opposite roles. As Jan Raymond has observed, rather than accepting a standardized "difference" (femininity), Lesbians/Spinsters find in our authentic likeness to each other the opportunity to exhibit and develop genuine differences.[49] Rather than relying upon stereotypic role relationships, Amazon friends/lovers/sisters cast our Selves into a creative variety of developing relationships with each other. Since there are no models, no roles, no institutionalized relationships to fall back upon, we move together and apart in ever-varying patterns of relating. As each friend moves more deeply into her own Background she becomes both her earlier and her present Self. At times this re-membered integrity makes her appear Strange to her friends, and since the latter are also re-membering, the encounters of these older/younger Selves can be multiply Strange.

This Dreadful Strangeness is part of the terrain of the Otherworld Journey. It is essential to the Amazon adventure.

Women who have the courage to travel can see the absence of standardized roles as an asset, for such roles inhibit our struggle for truthfulness and fidelity. Heterosexist society does not reward Lesbians for friendship and fidelity to each other. Therefore, the way is clear for honest Amazon bonding. Since we know that our friendships will not in the final analysis yield social approval, we are free to seek Self-approval. We are free to follow our passion for Self-centering. As de Beauvoir correctly points out, men and women are always playing a part before one another. In contrast to this, Lesbians need not pretend. As she observes: "They [these liaisons] are not sanctioned by an institution or by the mores, nor are they regulated by conventions; hence they are marked by especial sincerity." [50]

Such sincerity involves risks. Since woman-identified relationships are unrestrained by mystification over biological and role-defined differences, there is often great intensity and turbulence in be-ing together. It has been observed that sisterhood involves stages when one seems to be stepping off a cliff, and that, mysteriously, the ground rises under the Journeyer's feet.[51] That ground is the Self's own confrontation with her reality, her truth—a confrontation made possible and unavoidable by her unprotected situation. Having defied the patriarchal protection racket, she finds her Dreadless Self.

Paradoxically, then, it is the likeness of women that makes room for our otherness, our wildness, our strangeness. The creation of separate female-identified psychic, mythic, semantic, physical spaces is necessary for likeness and wild otherness to grow. Each individual Amazon must have such room of her own, and she must be free to communicate the light and warmth generated in the privacy of her own room to the hearts/hearths of other Hags, and to receive their luminous energy.

Isolation of female-identified women from each other—a basic tactic of patriarchy—does not quench the individual woman's Spark, but contains it in a dampening environment. Each such woman, locked into the damp dungeon assigned to her by the misogynistic State, must struggle to maintain her own sense of reality against the prevailing lies. When she makes contact with even one other Sparking Self, the combination is conflagration. Each woman sees her own knowledge of reality confirmed in her sister. The possessors' spell is broken. Their prisons are reduced to ashes as these Sparking Selves energize and re-energize each other, giving each other the incendiary incentive.

Crones kindle the Fury of our own kind against the godfathers who burned our foremothers. The uprising of Cinderellas from the cinders/ashes of our mothers is the righteous Renaissance. In our rising together, Hags affirm the true identity of our foremothers who were burned as witches during the alleged "renaissance." We affirm the reality hidden by the "wicked stepmother" image—the reality of the women of Wicce, whose fire still burns in every Haggard heart. This uprising of Amazon Fire, our life-loving, be-ing, is the hellfire deserved and dreaded by the Grand Inquisitors. If its purpose were merely to consume them it would be less effective. In fact, it is simply the expression/expansion of gynergy for its own sake, and this transcendence of Fury itself is the Renaissance of Fire. In its light, the patriarchal male is forced to see his history of holocausts, to re-view the multitudes of women sacrificed as burnt offerings to his gods. This is his unbearable "beatific vision," his Last End.

As this Sparking communication occurs, Hags do not haggle over "equality," for we know there is no equality among unique Selves. Noting that one definition of the term equal is "capable of meeting the requirements of a situation or a task," Jan Raymond observes that what each asks of the other is that she be equal to the task at hand.[52] Crones expect and en-courage each other to become sister pyrotechnists, building the fire that is fueled by Fury, the fire that warms and lights the place where we can each have a loom of our own, where we can spin and weave the tapestries of Crone-centered creation.

CHAPTER TEN

SPINNING: COSMIC TAPESTRIES

I'm fundamentally, I think, an outsider. I do my best work and feel most braced with my back to the wall. It's an odd feeling though, writing against the current: difficult entirely to disregard the current. Yet of course I shall.

Virginia Woolf,
A Writer's Diary

This is what I am: watching the spider
rebuild—"patiently," they say,

but I recognize in her
impatience—my own—

the passion to make and make again
where such unmaking reigns

Adrienne Rich,
from "Natural Resources,"
The Dream of a Common Language

There are these women's faces, various
as dewprints sequined across my life's web,
every grain reflecting a different dawn.
The interlace of all my years shudders with such a
 weight
until each pod of moisture bursts,
flooding toward the center—
that hub of memory, itself unspeakable
from which is spoken all that moves us.

Robin Morgan,
from "The Network of the Imaginary Mother,"
Lady of the Beasts

we know no rule
of procedure,

we are voyagers, discoverers
of the not-known,

the unrecorded;
we have no map;

possibly we will reach haven,
heaven.

H. D. (Hilda Doolittle),
from "The Walls Do Not Fall,"
Trilogy

Spinsters spin and weave, mending and creating unity of consciousness. In doing so we spin through and beyond the realm of multiply split consciousness. In concealed workshops, Spinsters unsnarl, unknot, untie, unweave. We knit, knot, interlace, entwine, whirl, and twirl.[1] Absorbed in Spinning, in the ludic cerebration which is both work and play, Spinsters span the dichotomies of false consciousness and break its mindbinding combinations.*

SPANNING SPLIT CONSCIOUSNESS

Consciousness split against itself suffers from an inability to reach beyond externals. Thus patriarchally controlled consciousness is broken-hearted. Its impotence to reach beyond appearances expresses itself in reduction and fragmentation of be-ing. Such impotence manifests itself in leering at feminized victims everywhere, in attempting to penetrate, to pierce into an inner reality which the invader yearns to destroy, but cannot even find. The rapist breaks into matter, rips and tears,

* As we have seen, classic examples of such mindbinding combinations include the misbegotten ideas of "androgyny" and of "human [illegible]on."

yet moves further from the be-ing of his victim. As a consequence of his invasions, her consciousness is fragmented, so that she loses the thread of connectedness in her be-ing.

This culture of split consciousness is the world of sadomasochism. Even those social scientists who describe rather accurately some symptoms of this syndrome usually cut it off from the mainstream of "society," as if it were an oddity, an exception.[2] In fact this is the normal mode of existence of the patriarchal male, who is unable to relate to the inner mystery, integrity, Self of the Other, unable to connect with originally moving be-ing. In this state, he substitutes for genuine movement monotonous and predictable swinging back and forth between fixed points. The spirits of women who are attached/hooked to such pendulums, dulled and forced into dependence upon them, sway to and fro in an appearance of movement, marking time by the tick-tock of their ponderous, suspended existence. As long as women depend in this way, they are not Spinsters but merely swingers, rehearsing and reversing their positions again and again. Fixed and transfixed, spellbound, they are fascinated in their state of obsession.

Spinsters spinning out the Self's own integrity can break the spell of the fathers' clocks, spanning the tears and splits in consciousness. Spanning splits, however, involves something totally Other than attempting to fasten together two apparently opposite parts, on the mistaken assumption that these "halves" will make a whole. We have seen, for example, that attempts to combine masculinity and femininity, which are patriarchal constructs, will result only in pseudointegrity. Feminist theorists have gone through frustrating attempts to describe our integrity by such terms as *androgyny*. Experience proved that this word, which we now recognize as expressing pseudowholeness in its combination of distorted gender descriptions, failed and betrayed our thought. The deceptive word was a trap, hard to avoid on an earlier stage of the Journey. When we heard the word echoed back by those who misinterpreted our thought we realized that combining the "halves" offered to consciousness by patriarchal language usually results in portraying something more like a hole than a whole.[3] Thus *androgyny* is a vacuous term which not only fails to represent richness of be-ing. It also functions as a vacuum that sucks its spellbound victims into itself. Such pseudowholeness, which characterizes all false universalisms (e.g., humanism, people's liberation) is the deep hole—the chasm—which Spinsters must leap over, which we must span.

It helps to consider some definitions of the verb *to span*. There is one sense of this word which expresses precisely the mistake described above, namely: "to bridge over." Spinsters are not interested in building bridges between two undesirable and inimical "sides." However, we can consider the following definitions: *span* means "to grasp firmly: SEIZE." Spinsters grasp false opposites (e.g., *masculine-feminine*), that is, we understand that attempting to combine them creates not integrity but delusions of wholeness. We also grasp fallacious contradictions (e.g., *feminine-unfeminine, womanly-unwomanly*), comprehending that they are doublebinding traps.

Span means "to measure by or as if by the hand with fingers and thumb extended; *broadly*: to measure in any way." Spinsters make our own intuition of integrity the measure by which we judge the validity of the distinctions, divisions, separations, combinations, and all the categories through which patriarchal myth and language control consciousness.

Span means "to encompass with or as if with the fingers." Like the Minoan Snake-Goddess, the Spanning Spinster holds at arm's length the opposing mythic attackers that try to invade her senses. She grips them with the fists of her mind/spirit power. Caught in her grasp, they writhe, snake-like and venomous, but impotent. Unlike the crucified one, whose hands are nailed to the dead wood on which he dies, she is Living Power controlling the writhing "nails" that would transfix her. Unlike the suspended, crucified, self-sacrificing victim, she stands stably on the earth, Self-assuring and Self-centering.

An "obsolete" meaning of *span* is "to set a limit to." The Self-identified Snake-Goddess/Spinster sets a limit to the power of the would-be invading enemies. She sets her own boundaries by the stretch of her own imagination, the span of her re-membering Self. She contains her powers in the sense that she integrates and focuses them.

All of the definitions of *span* used thus far name Spinsters' means of resistance against the spirit-poisoners' weapons/instruments in the State of War. There is another meaning of the verb which suggests movement beyond the necessary fighting back/exorcism—movement into ecstatic be-ing: Thus, *span* also means "to swim along rising to the surface to breathe at more or less regular intervals—used of a whale." This suggests a complex, rhythmic mode of moving that involves taking in elements from the air and the water. This is an originally combining movement that has nothing to do with fighting off deception by false opposites, false contradictions, con-fusions. It is Gyn/Ecological movement.

We may find basic clues about the nature of this movement from considering the ways of whales and dolphins. These creatures are at home moving above the surface as well as in the depths. Their hearing is unimaginably keen and they communicate with each other in a complex musical language which we cannot completely hear and cannot comprehend. Their extraordinary hearing also helps them to orient themselves accurately on their long journeys. They apparently use a kind of sonar, an echolocation sense informing them of echoes bouncing off objects. Similarly, Voyagers developing gynaesthetic powers learn forms of ultrasonic speech and hearing. As the Journey progresses, these powers enable us to detect echoes from obstacles and from guideposts along the way.

SPINNING THREADS OF CONNECTEDNESS

Spanning requires spinning, in many senses of this term. Understood in a cosmic sense it describes the whirling movement of creation. According to Merriam-Webster, *spin* is connected in its origin to the Latin term *sponte,* meaning "of one's free will, voluntarily." Thus Spinning implies spontaneous movement, the free creativity that springs from integrity of be-ing. The first definition given in Merriam-Webster for the verb *to spin* is "to draw and twist thread: make yarn or thread from fiber." This immediately calls to mind the image of "spinning a yarn"—a creative enterprise of mind and imagination. *Spin* also means "to form a thread, web, or cocoon by extruding a viscous rapidly hardening fluid—used of a spider or silkworm." Gyn/Ecological creativity is spinning in this sense, too—dis-covering the lost thread of connectedness within the cosmos, repairing this web as we create.*

Spin means "to revolve or whirl rapidly: GYRATE, ROTATE." This comes even closer to naming Gyn/Ecological creating. Spinsters whirl and twirl the threads of life on the axis of our own be-ing. This be-ing is itself the spindle, the thread, the whirl. Spinning be-ing moves in many directions, with force and speed.

Spin means "to turn quickly on one's heel: face about in place." Women spinning counterclockwise counter the "wisdom" of Father Time with his time-killing time-clocks. Women whirling in be-ing shift the center of gravity. As vortices of thinking, imaging, feeling, we spin around, "face about in place." As the Masters' March of Time continues its monodirectional goose-stepping into oblivion, Spinsters are learning to re-direct energy. Turning quickly on our heels, facing many other directions, we spin away from the death march. As whirling dervishes we move backward, sideward, forward, upward, downward, outward, inward—transforming our time/space.

* This definition is helpful for double-double unthinking Sartre's intended demeaning of women by identifying "woman" with "the slimy" (*visqueux*). To cut through this snarl it is not enough simply to say that women are not "the slimy," or that Sartre and his kind are resentful of their origins in the "slime of the earth." (Matter and mother are etymologically connected.) It may well be true that "the slimy" is degraded by men because they envy female powers of fecundity. However, to see only this much is to see dimly, to have arrived at the first stage of reversing the reversal. To remain here is to be trapped. The next essential move is to see that the real unintended tribute contained in the intended insult is the acknowledgment of female creativity which is indescribably more than, but inclusive of, physical fecundity, and which *is* behind, above, around the intended degradation. This creativity of Crones is greater than the target of the degrader, who can see only as far as fecundity. As Valerie Solanas writes: "The male claim that females find fulfillment through motherhood and sexuality reflects what males think they'd find fulfilling if they were female." See Valerie Solanas, *Scum Manifesto,* with an introduction by Vivian Gornick (New York: Olympia Press, 1968), p. 6.

Another meaning of *spin* is "to stream or spurt . . . in a thread or jet." This image conveys the movement of women escaping from the "body politic" of patriarchy and from the christian "Mystical Body." This Spinning breakthrough is a surprise tactic (surprising sometimes also to those who do the Spinning), by which we spring free. Spinsters streaming forth find our threads of connectedness with the cosmos, the Life-lines that were lost in these "bodies."

Spin also means "to last out, extend." This names the tactic of biding one's time, that patient alertness which appears to be stillness but which comes from an inner movement that is so fast it is imperceptible to those who see only the "outsides" and cannot perceive inner reality. This enduring, easily mistaken by males for passivity, is an active power of secretly watching, planning, testing tactics for springing free. It is the inner whirl, gathering momentum to jet forth threads of gynergetic communication.

Significantly, when applied to a product of technology, *spin* sometimes has negative meanings. Thus one speaks of a car spinning its wheels and of an airplane falling into a tailspin. The power of Spinning cannot be reduced to the technological. It is spirit spiraling, whirling.

This movement may also be compared to a vortex. Merriam-Webster defines *vortex* as "a supposed collection of particles of very subtle matter endowed with a rapid rotary motion around an axis which is also the axis of a sun or a planet." Self-Centering Spinsters whirl around the axis of our own be-ing, and as we do so, matter/spirit becomes more subtle/supple. Adding that *vortex* also means "something resembling such rapid rotary motion," the same dictionary illustrates this definition with a sentence about looking forward to a time "when human beings shall have sloughed off the body and become vortices of thought." Spinsters need not "look forward" to sloughing off the body in order to become vortices. The whirling dance of be-ing *is* thinking/creating/transcending earlier movements of both mind and body.

Among other definitions of *vortex* is "a rapidly spiraling column of air: TORNADO, WHIRLWIND; especially, the eye of a cyclone." It also means "a rapidly spinning current of water:

MAELSTROM, WHIRLPOOL." * Spinsters *are* spiraling columns. At the same time, we are the eye of the cyclone—centering, seeing. This cyclone moves counterclockwise, countering the grandfathers' clocks that clog the movement of be-ing, chaining it to the pendulum that swings between opposites, moving nowhere.

The Spinning of Spinsters may also be compared to an eddy. *Eddy* means "a current of air or water running contrary to the main current; esp.: one moving circularly: WHIRLPOOL." Naturally, the dictionary offers some rather derogatory definitions of *eddy,* which connote stagnation. Thus, *eddy* is said to mean "a movement or school (as of thought or policy) that is static and unprogressive or that runs counter to the main trend." This is partially true of patriarchal "eddies" within patriarchal society. Male-led "revolutions" are indeed static and unprogressive, but they do *not* essentially run "counter to the main trend." Spinsters, who really counter the main current of phallocracy, would appear to be creating unprogressive eddies to those who see patriarchy as progressive. It is helpful for Hags unsnarling this confusion to know that the term *eddy* is derived from the Sanskrit *ati,* meaning "beyond." This names the true direction of the metapatriarchal journey of Spinsters.

THE CALLING OF SPINSTERS: SPINNING, NOT SWINGING

One of the most basic reversals of double-double think is the common contemptuous and pitying attitude toward "spinsters."

* In Greek myth, Charybdis, a daughter of Poseidon and Gaea, thrown into the sea off Sicily by Zeus, created a whirlpool by swallowing and spewing water. The whirlpool is also known by her name, and is supposedly located in the Straits of Messina, opposite Scylla (a dog-like, six-headed female monster on a rock who could seize six men at a time). Of course Charybdis—and Scylla—are dangerous and destructive only to the male-led crews of processors, such as that of Odysseus, whose pseudojourneys follow the pattern of separation and re-turn, going nowhere. Female Monsters are friendly to Spinster-Voyagers, their sisters. (One definition of *monster,* according to Merriam-Webster, is "one who deviates from normal behavior or character.") Moreover, Spinsters are at home in whirlpools.

We have seen that the first meaning given for *spinster* in Merriam-Webster is "a woman whose occupation is to spin." Another definition is "an unmarried woman—often used as a legal term." Moving on, we read that the term means "a woman past the common age for marrying or one who seems unlikely to marry—called also *old maid*." Next comes the term *spinsterhood*, whose definition comes right to the point: "the state or condition of being a spinster: OLD MAIDHOOD." Following this comes the term *spinsterish*, which is churlishly defined as "having the habits, appearance, or traits of a spinster: OLD-MAIDISH." In case anything should be left to the imagination, it is possible to look up *old maid*. We are informed that it means "a prim nervous person of either sex who frets over inconsequential details: FUSSBUDGET." The mendacious use of the expression "of either sex" is obvious, especially if one looks up *bachelor* and finds, of course, no reference to *old maid, old-maidishness*, or anything of the kind.

The functioning of the word *spinster* to contort women's minds into double-double think is clear. It has been a powerful weapon of intimidation and deception, driving women into the "respectable" alternative of marriage, forcing them to believe, against all evidence to the contrary, that wedlock will be salvation from a fate worse than death, that it will inevitably mean fulfillment. The alternatives, traditionally, have been the roles of prostitute, nun, or mistress. In more recent times, another alternative is the life-style of "swinging single," euphemistically called "bachelor girl." The process of re-claiming the meaning of *spinster* does not follow the route of affirming the "freedom" of the "swinging" bachelor girl, which is simply a variation on the theme of prostitute/mistress/wife. Instead it begins with reversing the reversal, seeing the basic unfreedom in all these feminine roles.

Like the women in *Les Guérillères*, Spinsters proclaim:

> The summer day is brilliant but more brilliant still is the fate of the young girl. Iron plunged into ice is cold but colder still is the lot of the young girl who has given herself in marriage. The young girl in the house of her mother is like seed in fertile ground. The woman under the roof of her husband is like a chained dog.[4]

In essence, the Spinster is a witch. She is derided because she is free and therefore feared. Since derision is not powerful enough to stop her spinning, she is the object of attack by propaganda.* Any cursory reading of a typical children's fairy tale book gives overwhelming evidence of the campaign against witches, which includes mothers, stepmothers, wicked queens, ogresses. It is not accidental that in the story of Sleeping Beauty, the princess is cursed to prick her finger on a spindle which causes her to fall asleep for one hundred years, until she is awakened by her prince. More adept Spinsters are not falling asleep, not waiting to be awakened, but awakening and waking each other by our Presence.

SPINNING AS AMPHIBIOUS/MULTIBIOUS BE-ING

Since patriarchy is the State of Schizophrenia, it is to be expected that those who show signs of integrity will be called "schizophrenic." Seeing through such labels, Spinsters can spin with intensified integrity. This integrity must be intense enough to make possible spinning in more than one dimension, spanning through more than one environment. Such moving integrity expresses itself in adaptability, flexibility, and inventiveness. This Spinning movement is living "on the boundary." [5]

Creative boundary-living energy is expressed and symbolized not only by whales and dolphins but by such amphibious creatures as the tortoise, famed for her longevity and her ability to live in the water and on the land. When she descends

* One escapee from a long indoctrination program in such propaganda is Linda Franklin who, after graduating from Boston College, remarked: "I have my Spinster of Arts degree" (conversation in Boston, summer 1975). Given the inanity of "higher education," this title was, of course, flattering beyond measure to the institution which gave her the "Bachelor of Arts" degree. The university did not/could not teach her to spin. Her spinning was possible because of her own native wit and the Presence of a few Spinsters. These Survivors managed, to some degree, to span the pseudowhole of the university's fragmented universe. They somehow spanned the black hole/void of its re-versing "education."

below the water's surface, the tortoise emits a series of bubbles. Thus her way of life passes through air and water and over the earth. Spinsters can see her as a symbol not merely of amphibious but of multibious be-ing, that is of living in several dimensions.

Moreover, the tortoise/turtle's shell can be seen as a moving house.* Spinsters, too, learn to be at home on the road. Our ability to make our spirits our moving shelters will enable us to dispense with patriarchal shelters, the various homes that house the domesticated, the sick, the "mentally ill," the destitute. Spinsters Spinning multibiously may be perceived as "crawling into our shells," but this is a reversal used to label our exit/exodus from the "houses of correction" which function to keep all life straight, monodirectional, and essentially only undead.

Another animal who offers clues about being at home on the road is the hermit crab. She exhibits the resourcefulness of a Survivor in her practice of moving into the discarded shells of other animals ("gastropods"), in which she comfortably travels while seeking larger shells to occupy as she increases in size. This ability to adopt as shelter and vessel whatever is at hand is important for Spinning Voyagers. Since the "gastropod" whose abandoned shell is "borrowed" by the Voyager no longer has need of this vessel, such occupation would seem to be a wise ecological move on the part of the hermit crab and should be of interest to Gyn/Ecologists.

Moving amphibiously/multibiously is not possible for a divided/fragmented self. This Spinning/Voyaging is multiform expression of integrity. Its warped mirror image is the fragmented existence of the token, who is doubly/multiply "merely not dying." She not only participates in the split-

* The word *shell,* of course, describes, on the material level, a hard covering of an animal. When applied to describe the protective aura—O-Zone—of the Voyager in the psychic realm the image is only partially accurate. For while the aura of gynergy resembles a shell in the sense that it protects, it does not protect in a static sense, as a mere encasement. It is not an armor. Rather, it is a kind of psychic force field, which not only protects but also communicates and affects the environment.

mindedness of the higher caste but also in the brokenness of femininity. These types of fragmentation are combined, locking the victim/token into a bind. They are also blended in an illusion of integrity often labeled *fulfillment*. It is enlightening to re-call that the archaic meaning of the verb *to blend* is "BEDAZZLE, BLIND, DECEIVE." The split-minded are bedazzled, blinded, deceived, divided by the boundaries of patriarchy.

In contrast to this, the multibious have the agility that comes from integrity of Self, which makes it possible to move on the dangerous boundary-zones of patriarchal institutions. The point is, of course, to gradually move out of these, leaving them to shrink into their own unreality. Moving out into new time/space will require spiritual metamorphosis, a process that is already taking place among adventurous Spinsters.*

SPINSTERS AS SPIDERS: FROM ARACHNE TO CHARLOTTE

Arachne, the most skillful weaver of Lydia, challenged Athena to a weaving contest. According to the *Standard Dictionary of Folklore*:

> Athena wove into her web the stories of those who had aroused the anger of the gods, while Arachne chose stories of the errors of the gods. Enraged at the excellence of the work, Athena tore Arachne's web to tatters. Arachne hanged herself in grief and was transformed by Athena into a spider.[6]

Robert Graves adds that the spider is the insect Athena hates the most, and also points out that the rope with which Arachne hanged herself was changed by Athena into a cobweb, up which the transformed Arachne climbed to safety.[7] Spinsters remember that Arachne *is* still safe and well, and that despite Athena's spiteful act we can still find her in our Selves. The myth gives important clues to aid in this discovery. We can begin by considering spiders.

* One spinning creature who metamorphoses is the silkworm, who spins silken fibers around her body and later emerges as a moth. She is a symbol of organic creation and regeneration.

Cirlot's *Dictionary of Symbols* reminds us that the spider is a symbol with three distinct, sometimes overlapping, meanings:

The three meanings are derived from: (i) the creative power of the spider, as exemplified in the weaving of its web; (ii) the spider's aggressiveness; and (iii) the spider's web as a spiral net converging towards a central point. The spider sitting in its web is a symbol of the centre of the world . . .[8]

The first meaning—the creative power of the spider—as well as the second, her aggressivity, are described in myths and stories from ancient times to the present. Thus Spider Woman in the Navaho myth of the Twin Warriors gave advice and protective charms. She taught them magic words. And, as even the scholars of patriarchy have recorded, it was believed that "Spider Woman with her web can control the movements of the Sun." [9] Spider Woman is, in fact, a symbol for the Cosmic Mother, whose creative aggressiveness is also protective.

In patriarchal myth, of course, the energies of the Spider are drained off in the enterprise of guiding and protecting males: "The hero who has come under the protection of the Cosmic Mother [Spider] cannot be harmed." [10] This theme recurs in so recent a tale as *Charlotte's Web,* a popular children's story by E. B. White. The story deserves the serious attention of Spinsters.

The hero of this story, a young pig named Wilbur, is saved from the dreadful fate of being butchered through the creative, aggressive work of Charlotte, a spider who inhabits the same barn. It should be mentioned that Wilbur has already been saved by Fern, the little girl who aggressively stopped her father from killing him because he was the runt of the litter. He is also aided continually by the advice of a wise old ewe who lives in the same barn. All of these female figures are, of course, goddesses aiding the hero.

When Wilbur grows older and the farmer who owns him plans to butcher him at Christmas, Charlotte saves him by performing a miracle, that is, by weaving into her web, which hangs over Wilbur's "bed" in the barn, the words "SOME PIG!" in block letters. The farmer, and people from miles around who come to see the web, conclude that Wilbur is "no ordinary pig." Only the farmer's wife has the wits to remark to her husband: "Well . . . it seems to me you're a little off. It seems to me we have no ordinary *spider*." [11]

Charlotte, a creative genius and PR expert, weaves other slogans for the "miraculous pig." He is "TERRIFIC" and "WITH NEW RADIANT ACTION," and "HUMBLE." As in the case of the Twin Warriors of the Native American Spider Woman story, the hero pig lives out the prophecy created by the cosmic Spider, for he believes it. Like all truly creative geniuses Charlotte is extremely versatile, being able to use whatever material is at hand in order to carry out her bewitching plans. Using the rat, Templeton, as messenger boy, she finds just the right way to employ the meager vocabulary he furnishes by bringing her ads from the dump. Thus, the very last slogan she weaves—"HUMBLE"—saves Wilbur from defeat by a larger pig in competition at the fair by eliciting empathy from the judges. Wilbur's miraculous nature is confirmed and he knows now that Mr. Zuckerman, the farmer, will never butcher him, but will keep him as long as he lives. Like Spider Woman in the Navaho story, Charlotte has saved the day by creating/weaving magic words. Like the Twin Warriors, who have been protected at the beginning of their hero journey by the Cosmic Spider against the dragon forces they must pass, Wilbur is protected by his encounter with Charlotte on his pig journey of ecstasy.

There are some serious hitches in all this, however. Near the end of *Charlotte's Web* we read:

> Nobody, of the hundreds of people that had visited the Fair, knew that a grey spider had played the most important part of all. No one was with her when she died.[12]

Although this is a marvelously written story, and although it conveys clearly just *who* is the creative and aggressive One—which brings it far beyond most children's and adults' stories—there is still the problem of its functioning at least partially to legitimate double-double think, as do Spider Woman stories in general. For part of the message is that women can rejoice in the secret knowledge that they are the real creative forces behind the apparently miraculous males. The message is generally dished out in platitudes ("The woman behind the throne . . ."; "Behind every great man . . ."; and so on). It is a not very subtle invitation to complicity and self-sacrifice for the sake of the always-male hero. The questions which the little girls reading *Charlotte's Web* are not invited to ask clearly enough are simply: Is Wilbur worth it? Moreover, what if the aided pig had been "Wilma" or "Wilhelmina"? In such a case Charlotte (Spider Woman) would have come to the aid of a sister, who could then more easily have gained Self-esteem. What if Charlotte's gynergy had been shared with another female? *

Having seen that mythic Spiders—from Arachne to Spider Woman to Charlotte—have been renowned for their creativity and aggressiveness, Spinsters should note another manifestation of these qualities in the lives of spiders, that is, their method of distributing themselves over wide areas. This is called "the flight of spiders" or "ballooning." In discussing this remarkable trait, entomologists sometimes become almost lyrical. Cloudsley-Thompson writes of the "adventure and risk" in the life of the spider, and describes the trip. When the spiderlings have left the egg sac, they climb over the stems of plants and up the leaves of grasses, stringing their threads as they go:

Soon a tangle of webs springs up, crossing in all directions and covering the vegetation. When the young spider has reached the

* Significantly, entomologists feel compelled to use the generic "she" quite consistently when writing of spiders. The natural importance of the female can hardly be questioned. Moreover, although it is not my purpose to dwell upon the mating habits of spiders, the reader should be aware that the literature on the subject is enormous. One entomologist summarizes the situation, stating that "mating must be a hazardous undertaking fraught with real danger, particularly to the male who is usually smaller and weaker than his intended mate" (J. L. Cloudsley-Thompson, *Spiders, Scorpions, Centipedes and Mites* [New York: Pergamon Press, 1968], p. 219).

summit of the nearest promontory—a weed, a bush, or a fence—it turns to face the wind, extends its legs so that it appears to be standing on tiptoe and lets air currents carry the silk from its spinnerets. When the friction of the currents against the threads exerts sufficient pull, the spider loosens its hold and usually sails away: at the take-off, at least, it is dragged backwards.[13]

The Flight/Journey of Spinsters is also "backwards." However, as we have seen, "backwards" in relation to the necrophilic death procession is the direction of survival. When we leap "forward" it is in directions which are completely Other. Moreover, our take-off into this Other time/space requires the construction of our own Network, which is at first a "tangle of webs." Later, as Spinsterlings move further into the time/space of Crone-ocracy each will spin the web of her own creation, which we might compare to the spider's "spiral net converging."

THE SPIDER'S WEB AS SPIRAL NET CONVERGING

Having examined the Spider's/Spinster's creativity and aggressivity, Searchers can turn to the third symbolic meaning attached to spiders, or rather to the products of their creativity—their webs. Looking at the complex and fascinating web of the spider and following its thread, Spinsters can spin ideas about such interconnected symbols as the maze, the labyrinth, the spiral, the hole as mystic center, and the Soul Journey itself. In order to think of these interlacing themes, Hags must be able to weave and unweave, dis-covering hidden threads of connectedness. Such activities have deep sources in our Background. As Helen Diner writes: "Knitting, knotting, interlacing, and entwining belong to the female realm in Nature, but so does entanglement in a magic plot . . . and the unraveling of anything that is completed." [14]

There is an ineffable difference between Crones' creative weaving and the contrived combinations, the inorganic sticking together of things which is the "genius" of androcratic art, technology, and academic/professional -ologies.[15] Unspeakable also is the contrast between Crones' creative unraveling and the virulent/virile violation and tearing of nature's webs. Helen Diner proclaims:

> All knowledge of Fate comes from the female depths; none of the surface powers knows it. Whoever wants to ask about Fate must go down to the woman. This is the reason for the female predominance in the realm of the mysteries. There never were mysteries of Zeus. Of the female mysteries of Eleusis, Adesius wrote to the Emperor Julian: "Once you have participated in the mysteries, you will feel ashamed to have been born a mere man." [16]

Only those who risk Voyaging into our Background can know the secret combinations of the cosmos. Ecologists such as Barry Commoner can summarize "laws of ecology," but it is something else to intuit the deep mysteries, to spin the threads of an analysis that is constantly in touch with these mysteries. On the whole, ecologists have not been successful in following the thread of connectedness. We have seen that female prophets such as Rachel Carson, who in 1962 warned about DDT, have—like Cassandra—gone unlistened to, even by "environmentalists." It is the task of Gyn/Ecologists to continue to initiate the Journey into participation in the mysteries, threading our way through the Dreadful labyrinthine ways beyond the maze, knotting and unknotting when necessary, following the spiral net converging toward the mystic center of creation.

Whether or not we will "be heard" is not the central question. What matters is that Hags ourselves hear, and hear our Selves. In order to hear, we must find/wind our way back through the labyrinthine ways of the Internal Ear to the center of knowing. This stage of the Journey will require a-mazed alertness and balance, as we wend our way along perilous cliffs, balancing between the multiple pairs of false opposites which threaten to crush Amazon spirits.

The spider's web as spiral net converging is a natural/symbolic re-minder of the importance of positive paranoia, of seeing/making new patterns of perception as preparation for the later/deeper stages of Journeying. Cirlot notes:

> . . . the spiral is associated with the idea of the dance, and especially with primitive dances of healing and incantation, when the pattern of movement develops as a spiral curve. Such spiral movements . . . may be regarded as figures intended to induce a state of ecstasy and to enable man [*sic*] to escape from the material world and to enter the beyond, through the "hole" symbolized by the mystic Centre.[17]

The "incantation" that accompanies the spiraling dance is essential to the process. We have learned that Hags break through to the Background of language, breaking dead silence and breaking the deadening babble. We know that Spider Woman knows magic words, and we know that singing has always been associated with spinning. In spinning cultures, the average woman was so familiar with her task she could easily walk and chatter as she spun, and "singer" became a byword for the spinner. This combination is natural, for "spinning—like singing—is equivalent to bringing forth and fostering life." [18] And, as Louise Bernikow remarks: "We have, from the first, been singers, always." [19]

Hags will not fail to note that the converging patterns move toward dis-closing the mystic center, which is "the hole," the symbolic way of entry into the Otherworld. To know this fully, we must break the spell of male obscenity. This is the common phallocentric view of reality. It is articulated by Sartre, the philosopher of the obscene:

> The obscenity of the feminine sex is that of everything which "gapes open." It is *an appeal to being* as all holes are. In herself, woman appeals to a strange flesh which is to transform her into a fullness of being by penetration and dissolution.[20]

Sartre continues the thrust of his argument: "Beyond any doubt her sex is a mouth and a voracious mouth which devours the penis—a fact which can easily lead to the idea of castration." [21] *Whose* idea of castration? As Peggy Holland has pointed out, Sartre is wholly off. She knows that there is no reason for the vagina to appear to the female as a "voracious mouth," since "it is not going to devour any part of her body, but is, rather, a part of it." [22]

Free of the unbalancing castration anxieties which beset those with such fragile protrusions, Spinsters possess the inner capacity to spin, spiral, dance, and sing. Not compelled by obsessions with plugging up holes, Amazons can pass through and beyond these cultural fixations, entering through the "hole" (gateway) that leads past the obsessions of patriarchal culture.

Neumann notes: "Because of its dangerous character, the labyrinth is . . . frequently symbolized by a net, its center as a spider." [23] Our Journey is inward toward the Center, but this inwardness is not dichotomized from "outward." Moreover, Hags' movement inward is not crawling into an alien being and/or space, nor is it toward a "dead center." Spider Woman who is Isis/Ishtar/Daughter/Self is Be-ing. When we find her we have not merely reached The End but The Beginning, who spins and spirals outward, inward, in all directions.

THE LABYRINTH OF ENTRY INTO THE OTHERWORLD

This Amazon movement through our gateways is utterly Other from patriarchal males' projections of holy holes. Joseph Campbell enthusiastically cites Euripides (in *The Bacchae*): "Come, O Dithyrambos, Enter this my male womb." Campbell comments: "This cry of Zeus, the Thunder-hurler, to the child, his son, Dionysos, sounds the leitmotif of the Greek mysteries of the initiatory second birth." [24] It would not occur to this scholar, or to most of his colleagues who thrill to such words, that the idea of entering a hallucinatory male womb or of going through an initiatory second birth is neither necessary, nor thrilling, nor mysterious to Searchers. For Hags this image is not ageless and archetypal, as Campbell claims, but aged and boring. Women, born of women, do not invent a false need to be reborn from, of all things, men.

Yet phallic culture drones and drums this irrelevant theme incessantly. It is a basic blind alley of the man-formed mythic maze. The term *maze* is from the old English *masian,* meaning to confuse. The mythic maze hides the entry to the Otherworld by confusing and baffling women, reducing our imaginations to the dimensions of holey phallic projections, paraded as sacred "mysteries." Hags, re-membering our memories, stare in a-mazement at these blinding "mysteries."

Spinning through and past these projections means overcoming bafflement. According to Merriam-Webster, among the meanings of the verb *to baffle* are: "CHEAT, TRICK." It also means "to reduce to ineffectiveness." It means "to defeat or check (as understanding, plans, efforts, actions) by confusing or puzzling: DISCONCERT, PERPLEX, FRUSTRATE." To baffle also means "to check or break the force of: deflect or stop the flow of . . ." Journeying Hags can recognize all of these definitions as descriptions of the forces attempting to stop us. We can recognize also as descriptive of a basic style of phallic attack the following "obsolete" meaning: "To subject to a disgraceful punishment or infamy." Spinning past such bafflement means rejecting such undeserved "disgraceful punishment," making its falseness visible; exorcising it. When it comes from pseudosisters, from re-sisters, the Spinster does not pay it back or play it back. Instead, she Spins, which awakens the Sister.

More interesting still for Amazons is the noun *baffle*. It means: "something for deflecting, checking, or otherwise regulating flow." It means "a device or structure . . . for preventing the passage of, deflecting, or regulating the intensity of light." It means "a device or structure for deadening, preventing the transmission of, or deflecting sound." The baffles set up to prevent Spinning are intended to check and regulate the flow of gynergy so that it is detached from our own process and fills insatiable male needs. They are also intended to deflect light away from what we need to see, regulating its intensity so that it is too glaring or too dim for Searching. The implanted baffles are also intended to deaden/distort the sounds of Searchers speaking to each other. The Bafflers try to reduce our roars to titters, our wails to whines. They try to baffle the New/Old Words of Crone-speech, blending it with their own babble. The intent of The Bafflers is to block Journeyers. A *baffle gate* is, according to Merriam-Webster, "a gate that permits passage in one direction only." The baffle gate is Babel, the "gate of god," which permits passage only on the plane of the fathers' foreground, and which is intended to straighten out the spiraling process of Spinsters into linear, predictable processions, to herd us into the predators' game preserves.

Genuine Spinning is spiraling, which takes us over, under, around the baffle gates of godfathers into the Background. One definition of the term *spiral* is "a three-dimensional curve (as a helix) with one or more turns about an axis.* Interestingly, one meaning of *helix* is "the incurved rim of the external ear." The metapatriarchal journey begins with hearing the dissonant voices of the foreground and dis-spelling them. As we spiral into the Background Hags *hear* the Background. One meaning of the term *labyrinth* is "the internal ear." Indeed, there is a *labyrinthine sense,* which is defined as "a complex sense concerned with the perception of bodily position and motion . . ." Hags hearing into the labyrinth beyond the foreground hear new voices—our own voices. We learn to sense our own new position and motion; we learn delicate balance. Hearing/moving through this intricate terrain we find our way from the entrance of the labyrinth deeper into the center of the homeland, of the Self. We become ever more skillful in using the labrys, our double ax, to ward off the demon wardens implanted/embedded even here, near the Center. We cut down the baffling demons with our double ax of imperial might, slashing from side to side, swinging and swirling with this weapon/wand so aptly contrived for the Amazon. As she cuts down the baffles/demons with her labrys she moves deeper into the labyrinth leading to the moving center, the Eye of the cosmic cyclone, the "I" who says *I am.*

The speed of Spinsters journeying into the Background is spirit-speed. Helen Diner proclaims that "the woman is the possessor of the most secret arts of knotting." [25] By this art, Amazons can avert disaster. Only those who know the secrets of knotting can unknot, and unknotting can be seen as making our way through the labyrinth. Cirlot points out: "To undo the knot was equivalent to finding the 'Centre' which forms

* Gyn/Ecologists will not overlook the fact that DNA, the mysterious substance which is the basis of all life on earth, and which determines the nature of every living organism, is in the form of an interlocking or "double" helix.

such an important part of all mystic thought. And to cut the knot was to transfer the pure idea of achievement and victory to the plane of war and of existence."[26] Journeying to the Center is undoing the knot, not cutting the knot. To try to cut the knot is merely to take a misleading short-cut. It is to remain fixated in the foreground, the place of the patriarchal War State.

The knotting which is Journeying implies a bond of union. Cirlot states: "The 'slip-knot' is a determinative sign in the Egyptian language, entering into the composition of words such as calumny, oaths, or a journey. The meaning must have originated in the idea of keeping in touch with someone who is far away . . ."[27] Spinsters' knotting/journeying involves "keeping in touch" with other Selves who may be at different points in their Spinning. It also requires paying just enough attention for adequate defense against those who would calumniate us, but not enough attention to distract our focus from the Background. Knotting also requires defeating those who take oaths, solemnly calling upon their gods to legitimate their Crone-destroying calumnies. But our primary "keeping in touch" must be with those who continue moving/hearing into the Center, the Centering Self.

Knotting also expresses the concept of binding and fettering. Hags can think of our Original powers of spellbinding; we must re-member these powers. In our own charm schools, grammar schools, and glamour schools we must re-claim the "obsolete" meanings of our own words, the words of our silenced Fore-Spinsters.[28] These are the incantations which can baffle the bafflers, binding them in their own double binds.

There are nonknots which should not be confused with knots. These should be recognized as snarls. Unlike a knot, a snarl is without harmony, order, sense. Unlike a knot, it is not characterized by the complexity of integrity, but by inherent confusion. One definition of the verb *to snarl* given in Merriam-Webster is to "ensnare by arts and wiles as if by a noose." In this sense, women's minds and bodies have been snarled. A definition given as "obsolete" is "STRANGLE." Spinning requires cutting the stranglers' noose. *Snarl* also means "to growl with a snapping or gnashing of teeth." As Hags become more attuned to our Selves, hearing more deeply into our Otherworld, we detect more accurately the sounds of those who can merely snarl (no matter how deceptively and seductively) from the sounds of Spinsters singing. Predictably, our singing will sound like snarling to the snarlers, who will hear the teeth of Spinsters snapping the bonds and double binds intended to impede our unknotting and knotting Journey through the labyrinth.

The images conjured up by the expression "nautical knot" function better than the flat, linear concept of the mile to describe the Journeyer's process. Knotting is magic. As symbol for the labyrinth and as symbol for infinity, the *knot* conveys the Spinning, Surviving quality of the Otherworld Journey. As symbol of "a pure connection" (Cirlot), it expresses the profound relational aspects of Journeying. Crones are mindful also of the fact that knots are found in trees, and that they are formed at the point where a branch grows out of the trunk. Knots, then, are signs of the flourishing and spreading of the Tree of Life, who is the Goddess within the Journeyer.

SPINNING AS SPOOKING I: WEAVING AND UNWEAVING

As the Spinner moves/senses more deeply toward her Center, she is attacked by the spookers in ever more subtle ways. Having been a feminist for a significant period of time (measured Crone-logically), she knows the atrocities of The Second Passage. She finds that she must confront yet other atrocities, many of which are demonic baffles embedded in her own psyche and in the minds of her Sister Journeyers. Despite her increasing clarity, she feels increasingly baffled. Moreover, the spooking baffles cannot be simply divided into those "inside" and those "outside" her own mind. Nor are the haunting Passive Voices only male voices. As the Journeyer becomes more radicalized—that is, moves more deeply into touch with her own roots/sources—she distinguishes more and more female/feminine Passive Voices. These are the voices of the Painted Birds engendered by the ghostly male pseudomothers. These token voices sometimes call themselves "feminists"; they may even say they are sisters.* Confronting such spooking by male sirens and by female agents, who are "the ultimate weapon in the hands of the boys," [29] requires both weaving and unweaving.

Crones must constantly weave. As Denise Connors has pointed out, each has a loom of her own—her own Self/Substance—which is her Weapon against the spookers' weapons. With this loom she can weave her way past their baffles by creating visible/audible/tangible replicas, images, and caricatures of them.[30] For this ongoing task, she will be fortified by the words of Fore-Spinster Virginia Woolf, who describes "shocks" which, as a child, she had believed to be "simply a blow from an enemy hidden behind the cotton wool of daily life." As she later realized: "it [the existential shock] is a token of some real thing behind appearances; and I make it real by putting it into words. It is only by putting it into words that I make it whole; this wholeness means that it has lost the power to hurt me . . ." [31] She also puts it another way, writing that "explanation blunts the sledge-hammer force of the blow" of "exceptional moments" in which "they seemed dominant; myself passive." [32] This is a way of talking about Spinning as Spooking back, or as Positive Spooking.

Amazons can overcome the "sledge-hammer force" of the baffling spookers by naming them and by very explicitly analyzing/explaining their games. In this way we weave them into visibility/audibility/tangibility. We force them out of the shadows into our sight; we magnify the volume of their eerie whispers—removing their haunting inaudible mystery; we cool down their ghastly gases into puddles of liquid, so that we can bottle and label them, disable them. By this righteous objectifying of those whose intent is to objectify us we come to *know* the limits of their reality. This process is totally Other from their objectification/fetishization of Female Reality, by which

* Emily Culpepper has suggested that one problem inherent in the word *sister* is the fact that some women may think they are bonding with women under the aegis of this term, while failing to confront the fact that they continue to act as daughters of the fathers, giving their primary allegiance and obedience to the male parent.

they *impose* limits upon our be-ing. Spinsters also impose limits by our weaving, but what we are limiting is the antiprocess of the aggressors, their destruction. To do this we may weave caricatures in our fits of Haggard Humor. Unlike the Jock-Jokers' caricatures of Crones and Hags, however, our cartoons are simply accurate portrayals. Precisely speaking, they *appear* to be caricatures to the extent that they are historically/hysterically precise.

Spinsters must also constantly unweave the ghostly false images of ourselves which have been deeply embedded in our imaginations and which respond like unnatural reflexes to the spookers' unnatural stimuli. Unweaving involves undoing our conditioning in femininity. This means unraveling the hood of patriarchal woman-hood. As we spin more deeply into the labyrinth we must also learn to unravel the hood of pseudo-sister-hood, to distinguish tokens from Hags, to separate the token selves from the Hag Self within.

SPINNING AS SPOOKING II: EARTHQUAKES

Crones spinning closer and closer to the Center of our Centering Selves sometimes speak to each other of a certain experience which I shall call "the earthquake phenomenon." This is not precisely the same as the experience of "stepping off a cliff," which is known even in earlier stages of the Journey.[33] The earthquake phenomenon happens unexpectedly, just when Crones feel surefooted, just when we know we are moving with spirit-speed and power. In earlier times we might have called such occurrences "attacks of existential anxiety." This is not altogether inaccurate but it is simply too general and abstract to describe the familiar yet strangely new experience of earthquake. Sometimes this simply takes the form of tremors of the spirit. Since Hags love the earth, who is of our own kind, the image which naturally comes to mind to describe this cosmic sense of shakiness is that of an earthquake. As Gyn/Ecologists, we feel a deep communion with our natural environment. We share the same agony from phallocratic attack and pollution as our sister the earth. We tremble with her.

Sometimes the quaking sensation is deeper, more drastic and

sudden. A Crone may be moving swiftly over solid ground and find/feel to her horror that it gapes open before her; there is a chasm at her feet. She must focus very quickly in order to strike a new balance. She holds fast until the horror passes, converting the necessary effort of resistance into increasing assertion of her energy and dis-covery of latent powers. She attempts to perfect her sense of balance and to Spin with greater sureness and precision. She knows that the greatest peril would arise from ceasing to Spin. Spinning is Surviving (superliving). Ceasing to Spin is subviving.

When Crones speak to each other of this phenomenon we are often confirmed in our shared experience. Yet it is of the nature of the earthquake phenomenon that it is always endured alone. The Crone is essentially Alone when the ground splits and when it comes together again. At the time, and afterward, she is tempted to accuse herself of "instability." The Passive Voices embedded in her mind jeer: "Unstable." They echo: "Unable."

Since Hags are Daughters/Lovers of the earth, it is helpful to consider what transpires during her earthquakes. The crust of the earth, the outside layer of solid rock, is not always still; it is subject to strain and stress. There are lines of structural weakness in the earth's crust. An ordinary encyclopedia describes "the edges of . . . depressions [which] are lines of weakness in the crust . . ." [34] Hags/Crones are all too familiar with "the edges of depressions" which are the results of damage inflicted upon us in phallocracy. The encyclopedia revealingly rambles on: "The shock produced by the sudden fracture sets up vibrations in the solid matter of the earth's crust, and these vibrations, waves or tremblings travel long distances . . ." [35] Indeed. And Crones, like Virginia Woolf, feel the shock. We have many Sister Journeyers dispersed at great distances, both physically and psychically. We feel their vibrations as well as our own. We read on:

Earthquakes are not to be expected where there are extensive plains, but wherever the slope of the land is very steep the rocks tend to slip and give rise to earthquake shocks. [This occurs where] the coast lands . . . are . . . tilted very sharply; deep water is close to the seashore and high mountains rise close to the coast . . .[36]

We have seen that the terrain of the Otherworld Journey is rough. Moreover, Journeying is amphibious/multibious moving. Hence we travel where the slope of the land is very steep, where the deep water is close to the seashore and high mountains rise close to the coast. Hags know the heights and the depths; earthquakes, then, are to be expected. A final point to note is the following: "Usually the shock lasts for a little longer than a minute; the amplitude of the vibration diminishes with distance from the origin." [37] In Crone-logical time/space, "a little longer than a minute" cannot be measured. Yet we can know that the quake is finite. Since we are moving into the Origin, however, the amplitude of the vibration can be expected to *increase* as we Spin deeper/further.

The resolution of this dreadful prospect cannot be to turn back. Crones who know the earthquake phenomenon know that it is already too late for that. Moreover, we have seen that it is fatal to stop Spinning, for this is equivalent to stopping living.[38] We should listen again to the prophet, Virginia Woolf: ". . . it gives me, perhaps because by doing so I take away the pain, a great delight to put the severed parts together. Perhaps this is the strongest pleasure known to me. It is the rapture I get when in writing I seem to be discovering what belongs to what . . ." [39]

The resolution of the earthquake phenomenon is not resignation. It is the dis-covery/creation of integrity. The adequate response to the experience of fragmentation is to unbreak the brokenness, the fragmentation of our minds/bodies. Hags overcoming the effects of mind-rape are not merely "coping." We find ecstasy/rapture. And this ecstasy happens when we weave the fragments together. Woolf affirms her "background conception" that "there is a pattern hid behind the cotton wool." She continues:

And this conception affects me every day. I prove this, now, by spending the morning writing. . . . I feel that by writing I am doing what is far more necessary than anything else.[40]

The earthquake, the rending of the Spinster's spirit is the ultimate challenge. Our resilient response is Spinning/Weaving the pattern behind the fragmentation. Crones compose cosmic tapestries, expressing/reflecting/creating the integrity of our be-ing.

The mindbinders and those who remain mindbound do not see the patterns of the cosmic tapestries, nor do they hear the labyrinthine symphony. For their thinking has been crippled and tied to linear tracks. Spiraling/Spinning is visible/audible to them only where it crosses the straight lines of what they call thinking. Hence the integrity of Spinning thought eludes them, and what they perceive is merely a series of fragmented breaks/crosses, which might appear like an irregular series of dots and dashes.[41] Since they do not understand that creativity means seeing the interconnectedness between seemingly disparate phenomena, the mindbound accuse Hags of "lumping things together." Their perception is a complete reversal.

Nelle Morton, who weaves cosmic tapestries, precisely describes the speech of a woman who had survived earthquakes and whose thought was spiraling: "Her story took on fantastic coherence." [42] What makes such fantastic coherence possible is deep hearing by sisters. Nelle Morton explains:

> I knew I had been experiencing something I had never experienced before. A complete reversal of the going logic in which someone speaks precisely so that more accurate hearing may take place. This woman was saying, and I had experienced, a depth hearing that takes place before the speaking—a hearing that is far more than acute listening. A hearing engaged in by the whole body that evokes speech—a new speech—a new creation. The woman had been heard to her own speech.[43]

The deep hearing of Journeyers in the labyrinth is hearing in the labyrinthine internal ear. It is this hearing which makes it possible to spin, to weave The Network. The Network which Spinsters spin, alone and together, can break our fall at those times when the ground opens up *right under us*. Like an acrobat's net, The Network catches us and springs us into new space, transforming our movement into ever more transcendent Spinning, when this most drastic form of the earthquake phenomenon takes place.

SPINNING: FROM IGNORANCE TO INNOCENCE

The Otherworld Journey begins with a loss of ignorance.[44] The term *ignorance* is derived from the Latin *ignorare*, meaning "not to know." The Journey begins with following Lilith's invitation to eat of the Tree of Knowledge, which is to participate in the life of the Goddess within, that is, in be-ing/know-ing. The Spinster comes to know more and more, both of horror and of ecstasy. Her Journey is itself the weaving of patterns of "fantastic coherence." As in the case of the spider, her spinning movement is her spinner's creation. As she travels, she makes her knowledge visible. To other Spinners her Network is a paradigm of creation. To her enemies it is a lethal trap. As Neumann notes: "The labyrinthine way is always the first part of the night sea voyage, the descent of the male following the sun into the devouring underworld, into the deathly womb of the Terrible Mother. This labyrinthine way . . . leads to the center of danger . . ."[45] Patriarchal males have always dreaded and feared the labyrinthine know-ing of women. The Beatific Vision of Hags and Harpies means mortal danger to the foreground fathers, who see this as a descent into hell.

As Voyagers move away from ignorance we begin to discover innocence. The term *innocence* is derived from the Latin *in,* meaning not, and *nocere,* meaning hurt, injure. We do not begin in innocence. We begin life in patriarchy, from the very beginning, in an injured state. From earliest infancy we have been damaged, no matter how "happy" our child-hood appeared to be. Even before birth we injured our mothers, albeit unwillingly, draining their energy, and even by the fact of being born we caused and experienced pain. Once damaged by "education," we began our sub-conscious complicity in the damage, injuring others. The Voyage is not one of re-gaining "lost innocence," but of learning innocence.

Spinning is creating an environment of increasing innocence. Innocence does not consist in simply "not harming."

This is the fallacy of ideologies of nonviolence. Powerful innocence is seeking and naming the deep mysteries of interconnectedness. It is not mere helping, defending, healing, or "preventive medicine." It must be nothing less than successive acts of transcendence and Gyn/Ecological creation. In this creation, the beginning is not "the Word." The beginning is hearing.[46] Hags hear forth new words and new patterns of relating. Such hearing forth is behind, before, and after the phallocratic "creation." It is truly, as Nelle Morton has said, "a complete reversal of the going logic."

As Hags hear forth cosmic tapestries, re-membering the Original creation of the Goddess, there is a cacophony of cackles. Harpies harp; Hags haggle; Spinsters sputter; Crones croon; Furies fume. There is Dreadful dis-order. Some attempt to imitate/learn from the language of "dumb" animals, whose nonverbal communication seems so superior to androcratic speech.[47] Thus, in the midst of the cackling there can be detected meowing, purring, roaring, barking, snorting, twittering, growling, howling. The noise of these solemn assemblies functions to distract the would-be invaders, baffling them. In fact, however, the tactic of distracting is not even a major intent of the singing Spinners. Our sounds are sounds of spontaneous exuberance, which the demon wardens vainly try to translate, referring to their textbooks of Demonology and Female Psychology.

Since the bafflers attempt to interpret the Crones' Chorus by the rules of the going logic, they remain baffled. Since they can hear only sounds but cannot hear hearing, they cannot break the code of the Gyn/Ecologists' Un-Convention, whose participants are hearing ever more deeply into the secret chambers of the labyrinth. Since the bafflers are only gamesters, they are unable to perceive the high creativity of Crones, which is playful cerebration.

THE VERTIGO OF CREATION

The term *vertigo* is from the Latin *vertigo*, meaning "the action of whirling." Thus it obviously has relevance to the spinning of

Spinsters. According to the *Oxford Dictionary of English Etymology* the term means "swimming in the head." This makes the word all the more significant for amphibious Amazons. Merriam-Webster defines *vertigo* as "a disturbance which is associated with various known diseases or due to unknown causes and in which the external world seems to revolve around the individual or in which the individual seems to revolve in space." Self-centering Hags revolving in space can recognize our Selves in this definition. Since the term *disturbance* is derived from the Latin *dis* plus *turbare,* meaning "to throw into disorder," we can find this term appropriate to describe our creative acts, and thus appropriate the term. For Crone-ographic creativity throws the imposed holy higher orders into dis-order. The roots of the term *order* are from the Latin *ordiri,* which means "to lay the warp, begin to weave." Since the prevailing order is warped, dis-ordered, we unweave it as we begin to weave. Since it is a source of our known dis-ease, we unweave it with increasing ease, uncovering its previously unknown causes.

Vertigo is also defined as "a dizzy confused state of mind: a state in which all things seem to be whirling around: mental bewilderment or confusion." Creative Crones can expect to be labeled by patriarchs as "dizzy dames." We are also labeled "confused." Since *confused* is from the Latin *confundere,* meaning "to pour together," it is a fitting name for Amazonian alchemists who pour strange elements together, melting the base metals compounded by the Mix-Masters, transmuting them into our Original Gold. The bafflers choose to perceive us as "in a state of bewilderment." The term *bewilder,* according to the *Oxford Dictionary of English Etymology,* is "perhaps a back-formation from wilderness," meaning "to lose one's way." Spinsters have not lost our way, however. We have chosen to *be* wilder; we have chosen the wilderness for our works of wild creation.

Wild Crone-centering creation is rigorous play/work, which is utterly Other than the ritualized rigor mortis of gamesmanship exhibited in phallocratic plays and works. Becker solemnly describes and at the same time unwittingly displays in his scholarship the rituals of rigor mortis:

In ritual the weighty sounds resonate through the head, music pierces the still air; with his measured body movements, in the ritual dance or procession, man takes command of space . . . claims it for man; banners, colors, flames flood the world. . . . To the natural mystery of quiet nature, with its strange neutrality, man adds his own mystery, which stems from his unique abilities to manipulate symbols and things.[48]

It would be hard to imagine a more satisfactory satire of androcentric asininity—except that its author has no satirical intent. He cannot imagine that the "strange neutrality" and "quiet" of nature are reflections of cosmic boredom at the "mystery" which man "adds." Piercing the still air, Becker proclaims, like gamesters Huizinga and Simmel before him, that all of society is a game which man plays.[49]

Crone Woolf, who knows the mysteries of quiet nature as well as man's "unique ability to manipulate symbols and things" cackles:

Now you wear wigs on your heads; rows of graduated curls descend to your necks. Now your hats are boat-shaped, or cocked. . . . Sometimes gowns cover your legs; sometimes gaiters. Tabards embroidered with lions and unicorns swing from your shoulders. . . .

Here you kneel; there you bow; here you advance in procession behind a man carrying a silver poker; here you mount a carved chair; here you appear to do homage to a piece of painted wood; here you abase yourselves before tables covered with richly worked tapestry.[50]

Woolf in her wildness sees through the acts of the gamesters/gangsters. She sees these actors abase themselves before their god, who is, as the medieval theologians defined him, nothing other than "Pure Act" [i.e., the ultimate Act].[51] His unique ability is the creation of nothing out of nothing.

Bewildered by beholding the Processions of Nothings, Crones become wilder. We spin higher/deeper into the vertigo of our own creation. Like the women in *Les Guérillères:*

They say that they leap like the young horses beside the Eurotas. Stamping the ground they speed their movements. . . . Begin the dance, step forward lightly, move in a circle, hold each other by the hand, let everyone observe the rhythm of the dance. Spring forward lightly. The ring of dancers must revolve so that their glance lights everywhere.

They say that they foster disorder in all its forms.[52]

As Spinsters whirl we continue to unweave the prevailing dis-order, weaving our way deeper into the labyrinth. In our creative Journeying, we resemble argonauts. The argonaut, a variety of nautilus, is a remarkable animal. Also known as the "paper nautilus," she is defined in Merriam-Webster as "related to the octopus and like it having eight arms two of which in the female are expanded at the tips to clasp the thin fragile unchambered shell." The ancients were attracted by the argonaut's apparently miraculous way of moving on the surface of the sea. According to Elmer G. Suhr:

The male is smaller than the female; he develops no shell and hence was not so important in the ancient view. The female, it was assumed, raised a pair of arms into the air and expanded them into a shell to be used as a sail, while the two appendages in the water functioned as oars—hence the picture of the argonaut as a sailor. The shell, known for the beauty of its spiral-like lines, is actually secreted from the expanded arms for the purpose of carrying her eggs, a feature which distinguishes her from other mussels. She has an ingenious way of discharging water through a siphon to drive her body backward over the water's surface.[53]

Any Spinster can readily see her Self in this description. After some experience on the Journey we all know how to raise a pair of arms into the air and expand them into a shell which can be used as a sail. Since the male has no sail, he is not so important in our new and ancient Amazon view. Moreover, we all know how to use our two appendages in the water as oars. Needless to say, our shells (auras) have beautiful, spiral-like lines and can be used for carrying eggs and other treasures. Finally, since we often move backward—like eddies—it is quite natural that we have developed ingenious methods for driving our bodies/minds against the current. As we drive our Selves in this way our vertigo becomes more intense; our creativity increases; our capacity for hearing heightens. We spin/sail further, together and apart.

THE DISSEMBLY OF EXORCISM*

At our Un-Conventions, Crones cackle at the crude Deceptions of the Demons who persist in trying to blend their voices into our Hearings. A-musing Amazons unravel the twisted tales of androcratic "argonauts" who allegedly sailed with Jason on a ship named *Argo* in quest of the Golden Fleece. Furies fume at the fact that these misnamed imposters tried to kill Amazons. Crone-ographers crack up reading that the term *argonaut* is used specifically to name those men "who went to California in 1849 in search of gold." The whole gathering of Gyn/Ecologists agrees that the Processions of deceptive demons must be woven into disposable tapestries to be made visible/tangible. Once distinguishable, they will be extinguishable, and can be consumed in the Flames of our Fury.

As the convocation unweaves more deceptions, the Procession of demons comes ever more glaringly into view. We recognize them, having encountered all of them numerous times in the course of our Voyage. We perceive ever more distinctly that they are ghostly personifications (masks) of the Deadly Sins of the Fathers.† Since we are ready for them now, we invoke them by weaving their previously hidden presences into visibility/audibility. We contain our cackles as more demon wardens appear in our labyrinthine conference chamber. More than once the Chaircrone finds it imperative to call the dissembled Hags back into Dis-order, since many are tempted to tweak the noses and twist the tails of the dissembling demons. Some of the more spirited Harpies have to be hindered from clawing the invoked visitors before the latter have had ample opportunity to expose themselves. A few Furies must be restrained from setting fire to the costumes and uniforms of the

* The word *dissembly,* according to Merriam-Webster, is an "obsolete" term meaning "assembly."

† The Voyager of this book is familiar with the demons' manifestations. However, she may wish to spin back to the Introduction for a brief refresher course in Haggard naming/listing/defining of the Sins of the Fathers, which the demons re-present.

ghastly guests. As the Amazonian Dissembly is hushed into readiness, the final contingent of infernal infiltrators materializes in the filled chamber. Suddenly seeing where they are, the demons react with routinized reflexes. Pompously approaching the Chaircrone in groups, they offer to address and advise the Dissembly. The calculating Crone accepts the entertaining offer of the unsuspecting spooks. Each group is allotted three moments of Crone-time. It is noticeable that the Infernal Imposters wear a variety of uniforms, but that each group includes some wearing business suits and/or casual sportswear.*

The first group to address the convocation are the Professionals, the personifications of Deadly Pride. Some wear black robes, some red robes and ermine capes. Others wear white coats, and among these, some have masks and rubber gloves and some have adorned themselves with stethoscopes and speculums. Still others wear the gowns and hoods of academia. Their spokesperson (as he calls himself) offers various kinds of Help to the crowd of Voyagers. Speaking for his colleagues, he offers an array of Aids for Amazons: rest-cures for the haggard ones; religion and psychotherapy for the psychic ones; hormones for the healthy ones; affirmative action for the Self-affirming ones; equal rights for the superior ones (i.e., *all* the ones); courses in re-search and re-covery of women's history for the wise ones. When he finishes there is thunderous silence. Then some of the younger Hags begin hooting. The Chaircrone remarks that there are some owls in the eaves of the chamber and calls for Dis-order.

The second group to approach the Chair are the Possessors, the personifications of Avarice. Their spokesperson proposes various health insurance plans, family insurance plans, social security plans, retirement plans, life insurance plans, and afterlife insurance plans. The latter take the form of memberships in a variety of religious groups, tailored to match a variety of

* Many movie-monitoring Hags note the resemblance of this attire to the apparel of the husbands who are the casual killers of *The Stepford Wives*.

personalities. A Harpie snarls; a few Crones snore. He has barely finished when he is pushed off the platform by the next group, the Aggressors.

The Aggressors, the personifications of virile violence, "explain" to the crowd that the labrys is obsolete. They offer what they describe as a modernized improvement: the "protection racket." They proclaim that Amazons need no longer possess weapons of our own and they offer their special services. It is noticeable that some demons in this group wear police uniforms and some wear military uniforms, whereas others wear plainclothes. Before they are finished a labrys flies through the air and grazes the horns of their chief spokesperson, which had been hidden by a policeman's hat. The Chaircrone explains that it must have dropped from the ceiling and calls for Dis-order.

The fourth group, the Obsessors, approach the platform carrying a variety of objects which they flash before the crowd. Among their articles are footwear (tiny shoes, nylons, and spiked heels), cosmetics (such as vaginal deodorants and "Placenta" hair conditioner) jewelry (such as gold crosses on chains, "chokers," and earrings), magazines for swinging singles (including *Cosmopolitan, Penthouse,* and *Playgirl*), girdles (Free Spirit), and The Pill. It is noted that some members of this group wear T-shirts and buttons which proclaim: "I like dykes." It is also noted that among this faction there are some who appear to be eunuchs. One is carrying a placard which reads: "I am a lesbian-feminist male-to-female transsexual. Take me in." As they begin to file off the platform two Harpies swoop down into their midst, causing them to stumble and stagger in all directions. The Chaircrone comments that there are a few bats living in the chamber who must have been awakened by the speech-making. She again calls for Dis-order.

The fifth demonic delegation appears more sophisticated than the preceding Processors. These are the Assimilators, the specialists in gynocidal gluttony and vampirism. They offer what they call Job Opportunities for Assertive Women. Their spokesperson describes their auxiliary organization: "Athena's Associates." He announces that the time has come for unselfconscious inclusion of women and minorities in business and in the professions. He advertises career-counseling conferences. While he is talking, a Black Widow who has been spinning a web just above the platform swings down and bites his throat. He collapses suddenly and is carried off by his cohorts.

Next come the demonic Eliminators of Hags, whom the crowd knows to be specialists in the Deadly Sin of Envy. The audience, many of whom have suffered acutely from the vicious tactics of these demons, listen intensely and with a sense of irony, as the Eliminators make their pitch. Pretending to offer salvation for the "desperate situation" of feminism, they point out some pseudoproblems. They suggest, for example, that there is a scarcity of talented feminist writers. They point out that most feminist publications are "embarrassingly mediocre," and that even "feminist" critics are obliged in honesty to give them bad reviews. Attempting to appear sympathetic, they suggest a more gradualist approach, which will give women "more time to prove themselves in their fields." Crone-ographers, acutely aware of the fantastic abundance of creativity among Crones, whose greatest works are erased by these Erasers, groan audibly. Hags begin a long steady hissing which assumes the proportions of a gale. The Eliminators cling to each other to prevent being blown off the platform. The Chaircrone announces that the chamber is too drafty and requests that the doors and windows be shut. Reluctantly, the Revolting Hags stop hissing and wait for the last delegation.

The Fragmenters—experts and practitioners in the Deadly Sin of Sloth—are as arrogant and obtuse as the other members of the Infernal Fraternity. Unaware of the hostility of their hearers, they suggest that Spinning is a waste of energy. They advise the listening Spinsters to "divide and conquer." "First," they say, "divide into fields; divide into classes; do not lump unrelated concerns together." Their second rule is: "Be sure not to confuse work and play: lose yourself in your work and lose yourself in recreation." Their third axiom is: "Divide the personal from the political." Finally, they drone: "Face the fact that this is a competitive world, in which there is a scarcity of commodities and a scarcity of ideas. Find your own niche and learn to play the game." They suggest seeking out robots as Self-replacements.[54] While this infernal babble has been taking place, a number of Spinsters have been energetically joining the Black Widow hanging from the ceiling who had finished off the Assimilators' spokesperson. Together they furiously spin several strong nets. As the Fragmenters begin to file off stage they walk into an enormous sticky cobweb which closes itself around them. The last words they are able to shriek are: "Stop Spinning." Since the webs muffle their voices, however, they seem to be gasping: "Stop Sinning." The entire Dissembly, unable to contain mirth any longer, begins to roar. Some roll in the aisles. Some fly around.

Having seen the fate of the Fragmenters, the members of the other demonic delegations attempt a quick escape, but the roaring of the Revolted Hags engulfs them, stopping them dead. Instead of running, they begin to unravel. The black and red robes, the white coats, the academic gowns, the police uniforms, the business suits—all unravel rapidly. The demons try to cling to each other for support, but each is more unsolid than the next; each has Nothing to hang on to. The Un-Convention gazes in a-mazement, noticing that the unraveling costumes contain Nothing. The Watching Witches and Hearing Hags realize that the demons will re-materialize. But no one present will ever forget this scene. We will tell it on the mountains and in the valleys. We will tell it to the Daughters of the Daughters of Crones, who will re-member our history and how the spell of the Demons is broken. In the times of storms and earthquakes we will re-member the story of The Great Unraveling.

THE CELEBRATION OF ECSTASY

Having seen, heard, and understood the Rite of Unraveling, the Gyn/Ecologists re-gather gynergies. Furies rush forth and collect the shreds of the deadly deceivers' costumes. We throw the threads and shreds into a heap. We toss onto the pile the combustible samples displayed by the Obsessors, such as magazines and bras. We set the pile afire with the flames of our combined Fury. Harpies fan the fire with our great wings. The fire crackles and roars. In the Background of its roaring can be heard the voice of Fore-Crone Woolf howling: "Let it blaze, Daughters! Let it blaze!"

In the light of the fire Amazons gather the pieces of jewelry from the display cases of the Obsessors—the gold crosses and chains, wedding rings, S and M "chokers," and earrings. We melt them in the great fire and mold the molten metal into a labrys. We say: "Let this be the symbol of our Amazon powers of alchemy. Let this double-edged weapon signify our invincible wildness." Grasping it and holding it high as she Spins on her heel a Spinster cries: "Let this be the symbol of our whirling movement of creation."

Sounds of joy echo through the chamber, and reverberate through other and deeper chambers of the labyrinth. The Voyagers glimpse our Paradise that is beyond the boundaries of patriarchal paradise, the Playboys' Playground. We hear the call of our wild. We play games to end their games. Those who have been called bitches bark; pussies purr; cows moo; old bats squeal; squirrels chatter; nags whinny; chicks chirp; cats growl; old crows screech. Foxy ladies chase clucking biddies around in circles.

The play is part of our work of unweaving and of our weaving work. It whirls us into another frame of reference. We use the visitation of demons to come more deeply into touch with our own powers/virtues. Unweaving their deceptions, we name our Truth. Defying their professions we dis-cover our Female Pride, our Sinister Wisdom.[55] Escaping their possession we find our Enspiriting Selves. Overcoming their aggression we uncover our Creative Anger and Brilliant Bravery.[56] Demystifying/demythifying their obsessions we re-member our Woman-loving Love. Refusing their assimilation we experience our Autonomy and Strength. Avoiding their elimination we find our Original Be-ing. Mending their imposed fragmentation we Spin our Original Integrity.

As we feel the empowerment of our own Naming we hear more deeply our call of the wild. Raising pairs of arms into the air we expand them into shells, sails. Splashing our legs in the water we move our oars. Our beautiful, spiral-like designs are the designs/purposes of our bodies/minds. We communicate these through our force-fields, our auras, our O-Zones. We move backward over the water, toward the Background. We gain speed. Argonauts move apart and together, forming and re-forming our Amazon Argosy. In the rising and setting of our sister the sun, we seek the gold of our hearts' desire. In the light of our sisters the moon and stars we rekindle the Fore-Crones' fire. In its searing light we see through the fathers' lies of genesis and demise; we burn through the snarls of the Nothing-lovers.

In the beginning was not the word. In the beginning is the hearing. Spinsters spin deeper into the listening deep. We can spin only what we hear, because we hear, and as well as we hear. We can weave and unweave, knot and unknot, only because we hear, what we hear, and as well as we hear. Spinning is celebration/cerebration. Spinsters Spin all ways, always. Gyn/Ecology is Un-Creation; Gyn/Ecology is Creation.

NOTES

PREFACE

1. See Mary Daly, *Beyond God the Father: Toward a Philosophy of Women's Liberation* (Boston: Beacon Press, 1973).

2. See Mary Daly, *The Church and the Second Sex: With a New Feminist Postchristian Introduction by the Author* (New York: Harper Colophon, 1975).

3. Daly, *Beyond God the Father*, pp. 41–42.

4. Marilyn Frye, "Some Reflections on Separatism and Power," *Sinister Wisdom*, summer 1978.

5. *Sinister Wisdom* is available at feminist bookstores, and by writing to P.O. Box 30541, Lincoln, Neb. 68503.

6. See Simone de Beauvoir, *The Ethics of Ambiguity*, trans. by Bernard Frechtman (Secaucus, N.J.: The Citadel Press, 1972), pp. 82–83. She points out that "if all it [life] does is maintain itself, then living is only not dying."

7. Virginia Woolf writes of the delight and rapture she experienced in putting the severed parts together. See her *Moments of Being: Unpublished Autobiographical Writings*, ed. by Jeanne Schulkind (New York: Harcourt Brace Jovanovich, 1976), p. 72. I owe the idea of "threads of connectedness" to Fran Chelland, who has developed many threads in her thinking and writing, particularly in an unpublished paper entitled "Mind over/versus Matter: The Spiritual Reversal."

8. There are continuing efforts by academic bureaucrats to reduce Women's Studies to "basket weaving," through the usual devices of tokenism, legal intimidation (e.g., accusations of "reverse discrimination"), economic sanctions, psychological harassment of women who are "too extreme."

9. Since the number of feminist journals can hardly begin to be adequate as outlets for the flood of creativity, feminists—Lesbian feminists in particular—are devising alternative methods of distributing and sharing our works. One such enterprise is *Matrices, A Lesbian/Feminist Research Newsletter*. Subscriptions to *Matrices* are available by writing to: Julia P. Stanley, Department of English, University of Nebraska-Lincoln, Lincoln, Nebraska 68588. A number of valuable articles and papers by subscribers are available for subscribers.

10. Virginia Woolf, *Three Guineas* (New York: Harbinger Books, 1938), p. 80.

11. See Veronica Geng, "Requiem for the Women's Movement," *Harpers*, November 1976, pp. 49–56, 61–68. Geng's article is deceptive because full of partial truths based on "inside" knowledge. It served

the patriarchs of publishing well, being a sophisticated pronouncement by a woman that "the women's movement" is dead. When and if they choose to resurrect this "movement," Journeyers will be aware that such re-births have no more reality than such deaths.

Introduction THE METAPATRIARCHAL JOURNEY OF EXORCISM AND ECSTASY

1. See Morton W. Bloomfield, *The Seven Deadly Sins: An Introduction to the History of a Religious Concept, with Special Reference to Medieval English Literature* (Michigan State University Press, 1967), especially pp. 7–27. Bloomfield discusses the tradition of the Otherworld Journey in connection with the Deadly Sins. On p. 12 he writes: "The Sins are a by-product of an eschatological belief which has been called the Soul Drama or Soul Journey. . . . The seven cardinal sins are the remnant of some Gnostic Soul Journey which existed probably in Egypt or Syria in the early Christian centuries. But the Soul Journey is itself part of a much vaster eschatological conception, the Otherworld Journey. . . ."

2. This listing became common in catholic doctrine. The number seven came to be favored for the cardinal sins, although there have been many different lists of the sins. See Bloomfield, *The Seven Deadly Sins.*

3. See Dolores Bargowski, "Moving Media: The Exorcist," *Quest: A Feminist Quarterly,* Vol. 1, No. 1 (summer 1974), pp. 53–57.

4. Conversation, Boston, October 1976.

5. See Mary Daly, "The Qualitative Leap Beyond Patriarchal Religion," *Quest: A Feminist Quarterly,* Vol. 1, No. 4 (spring 1975), pp. 20–40.

6. Françoise d'Eaubonne uses the term *phallocratisme* in her book, *Le Féminisme ou la mort* (Paris: Pierre Horay, 1974), especially pp. 113–24.

7. Conversation, Boston, September 1976.

8. Adrienne Rich, *Of Woman Born: Motherhood as Experience and Institution* (New York: W. W. Norton, 1976), p. 95.

9. See Daly, "The Qualitative Leap."

10. See Mary Daly, *Beyond God the Father: Toward a Philosophy of Women's Liberation* (Boston: Beacon Press, 1973), passim.

11. D'Eaubonne, *Le Féminisme,* pp. 213–52.

12. Rich, *Of Woman Born,* p. 153.

13. See Monique Wittig, *Les Guérillères,* trans. by David Le Vay (New York: Viking Press, 1971).

14. Conversation, Boston, December 1975.

15. See Adrienne Rich, "Women and Honor: Some Notes on Lying," *Heresies: A Feminist Publication on Art and Politics,* No. 1 (January 1977), pp. 23–26; reprinted by Motheroot Publications/Pittsburgh

Women Writers, available from Anne Pride, 214 Dewey Street, Pittsburgh, Pa. 15218.

16. Barbara Starrett, "I Dream in Female: The Metaphors of Evolution," *Amazon Quarterly,* Vol. 3, No. 1 (November 1974) pp. 13–27.

17. Emily Culpepper, "Female History/Myth Making," *The Second Wave,* Vol. 4, No. 1 (spring 1975), pp. 14–17.

18. See Harold H. Titus and Morris Keaton, *Ethics for Today* (New York: D. Van Nostrand, 1973), p. 366.

19. See Robert Graves, *The Greek Myths* (Baltimore, Md.: Penguin Books, 1975). I,9. *d, 9.1.* See also Jane Harrison, *Prolegomena to the Study of Greek Religion,* 3rd ed. (Cleveland and New York: World Publishing Company, 1966), pp. 302–3.

20. Catherine Nicholson, "How Rage Mothered My Third Birth," *Sinister Wisdom,* Vol. 1, No. 1 (July 1976), pp. 40–45.

21. Contemporary christian "theologians of hope," such as Jürgen Moltmann, have attempted to apply the idea of "call to an open future" to the judeo-christian god. The results are incongruous and unconvincing. See Jürgen Moltmann, *Theology of Hope: On the Ground and Implications of Christian Eschatology,* trans. by James W. Leitch (New York: Harper and Row, 1965).

22. Crones can well be suspicious of dictionaries which, in listing possible etymologies for *crone,* suggest that it is derived from a term meaning carrion. The *Oxford English Dictionary* discusses this possibility, but also suggests that *crone* is probably from *carogne,* meaning "a cantankerous or mischievous woman." This meaning seems somewhat appropriate. It is noteworthy that Merriam-Webster gives as the etymology of *crony* the Greek *chronios,* meaning long-lasting, which in turn is from *chronos,* meaning time. It would seem eminently logical to think that *crone* is rooted in the word for "long-lasting," for this is what Crones are.

23. Conversation with Denise Connors, Watertown, Mass., November 1976.

24. Julia P. Stanley and Susan W. Robbins, "Going through the Changes: The Pronoun *She* in Middle English," *Papers in Linguistics,* Vol. 9, Nos. 3–4 (fall 1977).

25. Monique Wittig, *The Lesbian Body,* trans. by David Le Vay (New York: William Morrow, 1975); author's note, pp. 10–11.

26. Rich, *Of Woman Born,* pp. 235–37.

27. See, for example, Barry Commoner, *The Closing Circle: Nature, Man, and Technology* (New York: Bantam, 1972), p. 200. Commoner makes only one brief reference to Rachel Carson, crediting her with unearthing the ecological facts about DDT and drawing them to public attention. The brevity and limitation of his acknowledgment of her work is a subtle kind of erasure, putting her in her unrightful place.

28. For an illuminating analysis of integrity, see Janice Raymond, "The Illusion of Androgyny," *Quest: A Feminist Quarterly,* Vol. 2, No. 1 (summer 1975), pp. 57–66.

29. This name, appropriately, is the title of a feminist journal—*Chrysalis: A Magazine of Women's Culture.*

30. Daly, *Beyond God the Father,* pp. 7–12.

31. Mary Daly, *The Church and the Second Sex: With a New Feminist Postchristian Introduction by the Author* (New York: Harper Colophon Books, 1975), p. 49.

32. The term *chairperson* does not disclose the sexual identity of the "person." The solution to the problem presented by this word's inadequacy does not lie in the direction of regressing to the pseudogeneric *chairman.* Rather, Hags—if we are interested in "chairs" at all—will be specific. A Hag holding a chair is a *chairwoman,* or a *chaircrone.* Males can be *chairpersons* or *chairmen*—it doesn't matter.

33. Gertrude Stein, "Poetry and Grammar," in *Gertrude Stein: Writings and Lectures 1909–1945,* ed. by Patricia Meyerowitz, with an introduction by Elizabeth Sprigge (Baltimore, Md.: Penguin Books, 1974), p. 133.

34. For a good analysis of these terms see Sarah Hoagland, "On the Status of the Concepts of Masculinity and Femininity," *Transactions of the Nebraska Academy of Sciences,* Vol. 5 (August 1977), pp. 169–72.

35. Edwin Newman, *Strictly Speaking: Will America Be the Death of English?* (Indianapolis: Bobbs-Merrill, 1974), p. ix.

36. Conversation, Wellesley, Mass., August 1976.

37. The following are some basic feminist sources not already cited: Phyllis Chesler, *Women and Madness* (Garden City, N.Y.: Doubleday, 1972); Elizabeth Gould Davis, *The First Sex* (New York: G. P. Putnam, 1971); Simone de Beauvoir, *The Second Sex,* trans. and ed. by H. M. Parshley (New York: Vintage, 1974); Kate Millett, *Sexual Politics* (Garden City, N.Y.: Doubleday, 1970); Robin Morgan, ed., *Sisterhood Is Powerful: An Anthology of Writings from the Women's Liberation Movement* (New York: Random House, 1970).

38. In addition to the works cited above, see: Susan Brownmiller, *Against Our Will: Men, Women and Rape* (New York: Simon and Schuster, 1975); Gena Corea, *The Hidden Malpractice: How American Medicine Treats Women as Patients and Professionals* (New York: William Morrow, 1977); Barbara Ehrenreich and Deirdre English, *Complaints and Disorders: The Sexual Politics of Sickness* (Old Westbury, N.Y.: Feminist Press, 1973) and *Witches, Midwives and Nurses* (Old Westbury, N.Y.: Feminist Press, 1973); Ellen Frankfort, *Vaginal Politics* (New York: Quadrangle Books, 1972); Linda Gordon, *Woman's Body, Woman's Right: A Social History of Birth Control in America* (New York: Penguin Books, 1977); Barbara Seaman, *The Doctors' Case Against the Pill* (New York: Avon Books, 1970); Barbara Seaman and Gideon Seaman, M.D., *Women and the Crisis in Sex Hormones* (New York: Rawson Associates, 1977).

39. See notes to Chapters Three to Seven of this book.

40. In addition to the sources cited above, see Diana E. H. Russell

and Nicole Van de Ven, *Crimes Against Women: Proceedings of the International Tribunal* (Millbrae, Calif.: Les Femmes, 1976).

41. Irene Peslikis, "Resistances to Consciousness," *Sisterhood is Powerful,* p. 337.

42. Bloomfield, *The Seven Deadly Sins,* p. 13.

43. Virginia Woolf, *Three Guineas* (New York: Harcourt, Brace, 1938), p. 63.

44. Ibid., p. 99.

45. Ibid., p. 74.

PRELUDE TO THE FIRST PASSAGE

1. See Thomas Aquinas, *Summa theologiae,* III, q. 66–q. 69. According to catholic tradition, believers participate in the divine life through the sacraments, which are instrumental signs that confer grace. Sanctifying grace is conferred initially through baptism. If it is lost through "mortal sin" it is restored through the sacrament of penance. All of the sacraments bestow "actual grace," which is a supernatural help from god that enlightens the mind and strengthens the will. It supposedly increases sanctifying grace, that is, the degree of participation in the divine life. In other words, it intensifies the believer's participation in the divine processions.

2. See Chambers' *Etymological English Dictionary,* ed. by A. M. MacDonald (Paterson, N.J.: Littlefield, Adams, 1964).

3. Thomas Aquinas, *Summa theologiae,* I, q. 37.

4. Conversation with Jane Caputi, Boston, May 1977.

5. See Robert Graves, *The Greek Myths* (Baltimore, Md.: Penquin Books, 1975), I, 24 *c–m.*

6. Virginia Woolf, *Three Guineas* (New York: Harcourt, Brace, 1938), p. 36.

Chapter One DEADLY DECEPTION: MYSTIFICATION THROUGH MYTH

1. See, for example, Karl Jaspers, "Myth and Religion," in *Kerygma and Myth: A Theological Debate,* ed. by Hans-Werner Bartsch, trans. by Reginald H. Fuller (London: S.P.C.K., 1962), Vol. II, especially pp. 143–45.

2. Paul Tillich, *Dynamics of Faith* (New York: Harper and Row, 1957), p. 42.

3. Mircea Eliade, *The Sacred and the Profane: The Nature of Religion,* trans. by Willard R. Trask (New York: Harper Torchbooks, 1961), p. 96.

4. Ibid., p. 99.

5. Virginia Woolf, *Three Guineas* (New York: Harcourt, Brace, 1938), p. 19.

6. Ibid., p. 21.
7. Conversation with Linda Barufaldi, Boston, January 1978.
8. Monique Wittig, *Les Guérillères,* trans. by David Le Vay (New York: Viking Press, 1971), p. 89.
9. See Bronislaw Malinowski, *Magic, Science, and Religion* (Garden City, N.Y.: Doubleday-Anchor, 1954), pp. 28–29. See also Emile Durkheim, *The Elementary Forms of Religious Life,* trans. by Joseph Ward Swain (Glencoe, Ill.: Free Press, 1954).
10. See Max Weber, *The Theory of Social and Economic Organization,* trans. by A. M. Henderson and Talcott Parsons; Talcott Parsons, ed. (New York: Oxford University Press, 1947), passim. See Rudolf Otto, *The Idea of the Holy,* trans. by John W. Harvey (New York: Galaxy Books, 1958).
11. See Durkheim, *The Elementary Forms of Religious Life,* passim.
12. See G. Van der Leeuw, *Religion in Essence and Manifestation* (New York: Harper Torchbooks, 1963), Vol. I, p. 43. See Rudolf Otto, *The Idea of the Holy,* passim.
13. Otto, *The Idea of the Holy,* p. 26.
14. Virginia Woolf coined this expression. See *Three Guineas,* p. 106.
15. The terms *hologram* and *holograph* are both used by writers on this subject. They are interchangeable terms.
16. Conversation in Newport, Rhode Island, July, 1975.
17. *Boston Evening Globe,* July 17, 1975.
18. Associated Press news release, *Newport Daily News,* July 17, 1975.
19. A United Press International news release, printed in the *Boston Herald American,* July 22, 1975, described the Russian "re-entry" as follows: "Leonov and Kubasov—shaky with fatigue and emotion, but in good health—crawled from their bell-shaped capsule to greet recovery teams with bear hugs and smiles." The same release announced that "Soviet leaders called for new space exploits 'in the name of lasting peace on earth.' " The unintended message clearly is that lasting peace could be attained if "both sides" would only leave the earth.
20. An Associated Press news release, printed in the *Boston Globe,* July 18, 1975, described the astronauts and cosmonauts as "gathered around a green metal table in the Soyuz . . . for a July picnic in space." It goes on: "There was good food, good talk, and picture-taking for the folks back home." Together with such mind-boggling euphemisms, phallic fixations filled the language of the news releases then, as now. An Associated Press news release, printed in the *Newport Daily News,* July 17, 1975, mused: "If the economy were a spaceship, now would be the time for lifting off with the massive machine ready to push upward or collapse back to earth. The signs now are that the economy is pointing upward, but hasn't yet gathered the thrust to rise to where it was before the recession set in. Industrial production is up, but lightly. Auto production is depressed, but gaining . . ."

21. Simone de Beauvoir, *The Ethics of Ambiguity*, trans. by Bernard Frechtman (Secaucus, N. J.: Citadel Press, 1948), p. 40.

22. Ibid., p. 42.

23. Ibid., pp. 82–83.

24. Ibid., p. 83.

25. Ibid.

26. Conversation, Boston, September 1977.

27. Conversation, Boston, May 1977.

28. See de Beauvoir, *Ethics of Ambiguity*, p. 82.

29. See Ellen Frankfort, *Vaginal Politics* (New York: Quadrangle Books, 1972), p. 94.

30. Ibid., p. 94. A striking admission of male identification with fetuses is made by Jean-Paul Sartre in *Being and Nothingness*, trans. and with an introduction by Hazel E. Barnes (New York: Washington Square, 1966), p. 198: "We can conceive of the ontological meaning of this shocking solidarity with the foetus, a solidarity which we neither deny nor understand."

31. Mary Daly, *Beyond God the Father: Toward a Philosophy of Women's Liberation* (Boston: Beacon Press, 1973), pp. 106–14.

32. Frankfort, *Vaginal Politics*, p. 95.

33. Philip E. Slater, *The Glory of Hera: Greek Mythology and the Greek Family* (Boston: Beacon Press, 1968), p. 233.

34. Ibid., pp. 234–35.

35. Ibid., p. 233.

36. Erich Fromm, *The Anatomy of Human Destructiveness* (Greenwich, Conn.: Fawcett, 1975), p. 383. Despite the useful insights on necrophilia offered by Fromm, he himself displays the necrophilic mother-blaming tendencies common to his profession. On p. 376 he writes about "the mother who is always interested in her child's sicknesses, his [*sic*] failures, and makes dark prognoses for the future; at the same time she is unimpressed by a favorable change . . ." After further explicitation, Fromm makes *his* dark prognosis that, although "she does not harm the child in any obvious way, yet she may slowly strangle his joy of life, his faith in growth, and eventually she will infect him with her own necrophilous orientation." Thus the eminent psychologist succeeds in putting the blame for necrophilic male behavior, which is harmful to girls/women in obvious as well as subtle ways, upon "the mother." Of course he does not universalize and say that *all* mothers infect their children, that is, sons, with necrophilia, for this might be too obvious. Besides, it isn't necessary, for his use of the "example" triggers the mother-blaming mechanism that has already been programmed into most of his readers' minds. One such ambiguous undocumented "example" is enough to let all males off the hook.

37. See Robert Graves, *The Greek Myths* (Baltimore, Md.: Penguin Books, 1975), I, 14.*2*. Graves admits that this is the usual view of the derivation of *Apollo*, but suggests that it might be derived from the root *abol*, meaning apple.

38. Jane Ellen Harrison, *Mythology* (New York: Harcourt Brace, 1963), p. 94.

39. Jane Ellen Harrison, *Prolegomena to the Study of Greek Religion,* 3rd ed. (Cleveland and New York: World Publishing Company, 1966), pp. 394–95.

40. C. Kerényi, *The Gods of the Greeks,* trans. by Norman Cameron (London: Thames & Hudson, 1951), p. 51.

41. Ibid., p. 138.

42. Slater, *The Glory of Hera,* p. 139.

43. Ibid., p. 141.

44. Thorkil Vanggaard, *Phallós: A Symbol and Its History in the Male World,* trans. by the author (New York: International Universities Press, 1972), p. 30.

45. Ibid., pp. 23–24.

46. Sam Keen, "Manifesto for a Dionysian Theology," in *Transcendence,* ed. by Herbert W. Richardson and Donald R. Cutler (Boston: Beacon Press, 1969), p. 32.

47. Ibid., p. 51.

48. Harrison, *Mythology,* p. 97.

49. Keen, "Manifesto," p. 52.

50. G. Rachel Levy, *Religious Conceptions of the Stone Age; and Their Influence upon European Thought* (New York: Harper Torchbooks, 1963), p. 292.

51. Slater, *The Glory of Hera,* p. 211.

52. Graves, *The Greek Myths,* I, 14. *c.*

53. Ibid., I, 14 *b.*

54. See Slater, *The Glory of Hera,* p. 233.

55. Norman O. Brown, *Love's Body* (New York: Random House, 1966), p. 116.

56. Graves, *The Greek Myths,* I, 27.*g.* See Janice Raymond, *The Transsexual Empire: The Making of the She-Male* (Boston: Beacon Press, 1979). Raymond discusses the phenomenon of male-to-constructed-female transsexuals who claim to be "lesbian feminists." Although the majority of men who "become women" act out the feminine stereotype, a significant minority does invade the feminist community. Like the eunuchs of all periods of history, they gain access to women's private spaces and secret meetings, appearing innocuous because of their castration.

57. Raymond, *The Transsexual Empire.*

58. Ibid. See also David M. Rorvik, "The Gender Enforcers," in *Rolling Stone* (October 9, 1975), pp. 52 ff. Rorvik discusses the UCLA "Child Gender" Program, funded by the National Institute of Mental Health, where the mothers of boys who display feminine behavior are trained to re-train their sons, thus "preventing" them from becoming transvestites, transsexuals, and/or effeminate homosexuals.

59. Conversation, Boston, January 1978.

60. Male-to-constructed-female transsexuals cannot menstruate; they

lack clitorises; they cannot give birth; they require continual hormone fixes; they are without female history and Background.

61. Honor Moore, "Polemic #1," *Amazon Quarterly*, Vol. 3, No. 1, pp. 28–29.

62. C. Kerényi, *The Gods of the Greeks*, p. 273.

63. Mary Shelley, *Frankenstein: Or, the Modern Prometheus* (New York: New American Library, 1965), pp. 52–53.

64. For an example of electronic male motherhood, with illustrations, see José M. R. Delgado, M.D., *Physical Control of the Mind: Toward A Psychocivilized Society* (New York: Harper Colophon Books, 1971).

65. Shelley, *Frankenstein*, p. 124.

Chapter Two DISMEMBERMENT BY CHRISTIAN AND POSTCHRISTIAN MYTH

1. See Robert Graves, *The Greek Myths* (Baltimore, Md.: Penguin Books, 1975), I, 25. *2*.

2. Ibid., I, 8. *1;* II, 154.*5*.

3. Ibid., I, 24.*3*.

4. Ibid., I, 16. *1*.

5. See Jane Ellen Harrison, *Prolegomena to the Study of Greek Religion,* 3rd ed. (Cleveland and New York: World Publishing Company, 1966), p. 274. This pattern of course recurs in patriarchal myth in images of male mythic persons. Thus Zeus and Dionysus are father and son and yet are also the same person. Moreover, in the christian trinitarian dogma the father and son, although they are distinct persons, have one and the same divine nature. They are consubstantial, and are distinct from each other only as "relations." See Thomas Aquinas, *Summa theologiae,* I, q. 39–40.

6. Graves, *The Greek Myths,* I, 24. *3*.

7. Ibid., I, 1. *a, b, 1,* Graves adds the information that it was as a dove that Marduk symbolically sliced the Goddess in two at the Babylonian Spring Festival, when he inaugurated the new world order. This is interesting in view of the fact that the holy ghost is traditionally portrayed as a dove.

8. Ibid., II, 131. *3–9*.

9. See C. Kerényi, "Kore," in C. G. Jung and C. Kerényi, *Essays on a Science of Mythology: The Myth of the Divine Child and the Mysteries of Eleusis,* trans. by R. F. C. Hull, Bollingen Series XXII (Princeton, N.J.: Princeton University Press, 1969), p. 112.

10. See Martin Puhvel, "The Mystery of the Cross-Roads." *Folklore,* Vol. 87 (1976), pp. 167–77. The tradition of the meeting of roads as the place for the cure of warts is reflected in *Tom Sawyer*. Robert Frost's poem, "The Road Not Taken" is a modern expression of the mystery of the crossroads.

11. Helen Diner, *Mothers and Amazons, The First Feminine History*

of Culture, ed. and trans. by John Philip Lundin, introduction by Brigitte Berger (Garden City, N.Y.: Anchor Books, 1973), p. 45.

12. See G. Rachel Levy, *Religious Conceptions of the Stone Age, and Their Influence upon European Thought* (New York: Harper Torchbooks, 1963), p. 122. See also Erich Neumann, *The Great Mother: An Analysis of the Archetype,* trans. by Ralph Manheim, Bollingen Series XLVII (Princeton, N.J.: Princeton University Press, 1972), p. 241. The Searcher should also see E. O. James, *The Tree of Life: An Archeological Study* (Leiden, Netherlands: E. J. Brill, 1966), especially chapter six, "The Female Principle." Writing of the Tree of Life, the embodiment of the Goddess, James points out that "in the Middle Minoan period (c. 2100–1700 B.C.), largely under influences from the Ancient Near East, she emerged as an individualized anthropomorphic figure in her threefold capacity of the Earth-mother, the Mountain-mother and the chthonic divinity." He adds that she became "the Great Mother of many names," and that "her appropriate emblems [symbolized] the awakening life" (pp. 163–64). If the Searcher can find it, she should look at Mrs. J. H. Philpot, *The Sacred Tree,* or *The Tree in Religion and Myth* (London and New York: Macmillan, 1897). It is saddening to read in the author's preface: "The reader is requested to bear in mind that this volume lays no claim to scholarship, independent research, or originality of view. . . . In so dealing with one of the many modes of primitive religion, it is perhaps inevitable that the writer should seem to exaggerate its importance . . ." A Hag who peruses this book will see that it displays extraordinary scholarship, independent research, and originality of view. She will also find that it takes no great effort of imagination to grasp the circumstances under which this devoted author labored—conditions which drove her to apologize for seeming to exaggerate the importance of the Sacred Tree and of her Self. Since she does not tell us her own name, we are left with the quaint label, "Mrs. J. H. Philpot," signifying the burial of this courageous foresister. Her book contains many important illustrations of Tree Goddesses. She discusses christian "adaptations" of the May Tree and of what came to be known as the "Christmas Tree." She causes the reader to reflect upon gynocentric origins of such biblical images as that of Yahweh speaking to Moses from the burning bush, pointing out that the sacred sycamores of Egypt were believed to be inhabited by such Goddesses as Hāthor and Nuit.

13. Diner, *Mothers and Amazons,* p. 45. Gyn-ographers should not fail to note that christmas trees are also dead.

14. Neumann, *The Great Mother,* p. 251.

15. Ibid., p. 252.

16. Ibid., p. 256.

17. J. E. Cirlot, *A Dictionary of Symbols,* trans. by Jack Sage (New York: Philosophical Library, 1962), p. 38.

18. Neumann, *The Great Mother,* p. 288.

19. Adrienne Rich, *Of Woman Born: Motherhood as Experience and Institution* (New York: W. W. Norton, 1976), p. 99.
20. Cirlot, *A Dictionary of Symbols,* p. 38.
21. See Thomas Aquinas, *Summa theologiae,* III, q. 28.
22. Diner, *Mothers and Amazons,* p. 4.
23. Anne Dellenbaugh, "Parthenogenesis: Why We've Never Heard About It," unpublished paper.
24. Ibid.
25. Robert T. Francoeur, *Utopian Motherhood: New Trends in Human Reproduction* (Garden City, N.Y.: Doubleday, 1970), p. 138.
26. Graves, *The Greek Myths,* I, 14. *1.*
27. As Linda Barufaldi pointed out: "In the christian myth the Virgin Mary does nothing, wants nothing, feels nothing, enjoys nothing, cannot relate to her 'lover.' She is the perfect 'lover' for a necrophiliac and is a living dead woman in the life of the myth."
28. Daly, *Beyond God the Father: Toward a Philosophy of Women's Liberation* (Boston: Beacon Press, 1973), pp. 82–92.
29. Graves, *The Greek Myths,* I, 27, *k.*
30. C. Kerényi, *The Gods of the Greeks,* trans. by Norman Cameron (London: Thames and Hudson, 1951), p. 259.
31. See, for example, Ann Oakley, *Sex, Gender, and Society* (New York: Harper Colophon, 1972), especially chapter seven.
32. Shel Silverstein, *The Giving Tree* (New York: Harper and Row, 1964).
33. George Orwell, *1984* (New York: New American Library, 1961), p. 231.
34. Kathleen Barry, " 'Did I Ever Have a Chance?' Patriarchal Judgment of Patricia Hearst," *Chrysalis: A Magazine of Women's Culture,* No. 1, (1977), p. 9.
35. If the Searcher looks up the verb *testify* in the *Oxford Dictionary of English Etymology* she will find that it is from the Latin *testis,* meaning witness. If she looks up *testicle* she will find that it is said to be from the Latin *testiculus,* "diminuitive of *testis:* witness (the organ being evidence of virility)." Since women do not have testicles, they cannot really be qualified to testify—give evidence—in patriarchal courts. Moreover, the christian bible appropriately is comprised of two divisions called *testaments.* This term, of course, is also derived from *testis.* Clearly, the idea of a woman swearing on the bible is incongruous. Her testimony (also from *testis*) does not count.
36. Barry, " 'Did I Ever Have a Chance?' " p. 10.
37. Ibid., p. 14.
38. *Time,* February 7, 1977.
39. Hannah Tillich, *From Time to Time* (New York: Stein and Day, 1973), p. 14.
40. See Elliott Wright, "Paul Tillich as Hero: An Interview with Rollo May," *The Christian Century* (May 15, 1974), pp. 530–33. The

psychologist's arguments against Hannah Tillich's account of her life with Paul Tillich are fascinating. May complains: "The things that make Tillich significant are left out. What this does, unless the reader already knows him, is to give a warped portrait; another dirty old man." Indeed, and Hannah Tillich knew him well. May goes on with impeccable illogic, explaining that he had tried to persuade Hannah not to publish this book, which would be "most humiliating *to her* [emphasis mine]." May was asked if he thought his version was "more factual on the sensual side of Tillich." He responded: "I do. An admiring student may not be the most objective judge of a teacher, but a wife is considerably less reliable. No man is a hero to his valet." May goes on to explain some of Hannah Tillich's chores as "valet," such as always driving the car and making travel arrangements. With psychological acumen he comments: "At times I felt sorry for her. Yet she seemed to enjoy it; she liked to meet the important people she met because she was Mrs. Paul Tillich."

41. Hannah Tillich, *From Time to Time,* p. 241.

42. For analysis of the horror of modern medical techniques, see Ivan Illich, *Medical Nemesis: The Expropriation of Health* (New York: Pantheon, 1976). Illich discussed the use of "medicine," including life-prolonging equipment, in the torture of political prisoners, in a talk at Harvard University in 1976. For an unwitting self-exposé by psychiatric torturers, see Vernon Mark and Frank Ervin, *Violence and the Brain* (New York: Harper and Row, 1970). Even the title of Mark and Ervin's book is a reversal of the fact that *they* are the perpetrators of violence against their patients. The Nazi death camps will be discussed in The Second Passage of this book.

43. See *Amnesty International Report on Torture* (London: Duckworth, in association with Amnesty International Publications, 1973), p. 61.

44. Robert Jungk, *Brighter than a Thousand Suns: A Personal History of the Atomic Scientists,* trans. by James Cleugh (New York: Harcourt, Brace, 1958), p. 197.

45. Ibid., p. 197.

46. James Nathan Miller, "The 'Unholy Trinities' that Undermine America," *Reader's Digest,* March 1977, p. 62.

47. Cirlot, *A Dictionary of Symbols,* p. 39.

48. Pope Pius XII, *Mystici Corporis Christi: Encyclical Letter on the Mystical Body of Christ* (New York: Paulist Press), par. 16.

49. Ibid., par. 66.

50. Conversation, Boston, March 1977.

51. Friedrich Jürgensmeier, D.D., *The Mystical Body of Christ: As the Basic Principle of Religious Life,* trans. by H. Gardner Curtis (London: Geo. E. J. Coldwell, 1939), p. 101.

52. Ibid.

53. Ibid.

54. Ira Levin, *This Perfect Day* (New York: Fawcett, 1970).

55. Robert C. W. Ettinger, *The Prospect of Immortality*, revised and updated by the author (New York: Macfadden Books, 1966).

56. Albert Rosenfeld, *Prolongevity* (New York: Alfred A. Knopf, 1976), p. 181.

57. Jungk, *Brighter than a Thousand Suns*, p. 201.

58. Monique Wittig, *Les Guérillères*, trans. by David Le Vay (New York: Viking Press, 1969), p. 137.

PRELUDE TO THE SECOND PASSAGE

1. See Emile Durkheim, *The Elementary Forms of Religious Life*, trans. by Joseph Ward Swain (Glencoe, Ill.: Free Press, 1954), passim.

2. See Wilson Bryan Key, *Subliminal Seduction: Ad Media's Manipulation of a Not So Innocent America* (New York: New American Library, 1974). See also by the same author, *Media Sexploitation* (Englewood Cliffs, N.J.: Prentice-Hall, 1976).

3. Friedrich Nietzsche, *The Genealogy of Morals*, in *The Birth of Tragedy and the Genealogy of Morals*, trans. by Francis Golffing (Garden City, N.Y.: Doubleday-Anchor, 1956), pp. 192–93.

4. Mircea Eliade, *The Sacred and the Profane: The Nature of Religion*, trans. by Willard R. Trask (New York: Harper Torchbooks, 1961), p. 101.

5. Ibid., pp. 101–2.

6. Conversation, Boston, June 1977.

Chapter Three INDIAN *SUTTEE*: THE ULTIMATE CONSUMMATION OF MARRIAGE

1. See Katherine Mayo, *Mother India* (New York: Blue Ribbon Books, 1927), esp. pp. 81–89, 51–62.

2. See P. Thomas, *Indian Women through the Ages* (New York: Asia Publishing Company, 1964), p. 263. This author describes the situation in muslim India of widows who tried to escape cremation, writing that "to prevent her escape, she was usually surrounded by men armed with sticks who goaded her on to her destination by physical force."

3. Joseph Campbell, *The Masks of God: Oriental Mythology* (New York: Viking Press, 1962), p. 62.

4. Ibid., p. 60.

5. Ibid., p. 65.

6. Benjamin Walker, *The Hindu World: An Encyclopedic Survey of Hinduism*, 2 vols., (New York: Praeger, 1968), Vol. II, p. 461.

7. Ibid., p. 464.

8. Ibid., pp. 462–63.

9. Thomas, *Indian Women*, p. 233.

10. Many scholars claim that by changing the Sanskrit word *agre*

to *agneh,* the priests converted a sentence from "Let the mother advance to the altar first," to "Let the mothers go into the womb of fire." See Edward Thompson, *Suttee: A Historical and Philosophical Enquiry into the Hindu Rite of Widow Burning* (London: Allen and Unwin, 1928), esp. pp. 16–17. As Peggy Holland pointed out, such scholars may be overzealous in their efforts to defend the "pure" and "original, sacred text" (Conversation, July 1977). The perverse perspective which she had in mind is illustrated in the following statement by Thompson: "*Suttee* reached its most *magnificent* and least squalid form among the Rājputs [emphases mine]" (*Suttee,* p. 42).

11. Thomas, *Indian Women,* p. 297.

12. Vern L. Bullough, *The Subordinate Sex: A History of Attitudes Toward Women,* with a final chapter by Bonnie Bullough (Baltimore, Md.: Penguin Books, 1974), p. 241.

13. Thompson, *Suttee,* p. 40.

14. Peter Berger discusses the effect of religious legitimation as "allowing the individual to differentiate between his 'real self' (which is afraid or has scruples) and his self qua role-carrier (warrior, hangman, and what-not, in which roles he may act the hero, the merciless avenger, and so on)." See *The Sacred Canopy: Elements of a Sociological Theory of Religion* (Garden City, N.Y.: Doubleday, 1967), p. 45.

15. Campbell, *The Masks of God,* p. 66.

16. Ibid.

17. Mayo, *Mother India,* p. 81.

18. Bullough, *The Subordinate Sex,* p. 235.

19. Conversation with Jane Caputi, Boston, November 1976.

20. See Florence Rush, "The Freudian Cover-Up: The Sexual Abuse of Children," *Chrysalis: A Magazine of Women's Culture,* No. 1, pp. 31–45.

21. Mayo, *Mother India,* pp. 411–12. Since the publication of Mayo's book in 1927, the laws in India have changed but, as I indicated at the beginning of this chapter, legal changes mean very little. Although the Sarda Act of 1929 raised the legal age of marriage for girls to 14 years, in 1961 it was reported that 28.8 percent of girls between 10 and 14 were married. See Rhoda L. Goldstein, *Indian Women in Transition: A Bangalore Case Study* (Metuchen, N.J.: The Scarecrow Press, 1972), p. 53. According to the 1971 census figures, 17.5 percent of females in the 10–14 age group were married. See *Youth Times* (A Times of India Publication), March 7, 1975, p. 24. Legally, the minimum age of marriage for women was raised again, from 14 to 16, but this does not correspond to deep or widespread changes in women's lives. Marriages of female children are still common. Nor is child marriage the only method by which female lives are stunted in India. The same issue of *Youth Times* reported that 21.5 percent of females are now literate, as contrasted with 45.3 percent of males. It also asserted that 48.9 percent of rural births and 33.4 percent of urban births are attended by untrained "*dhais.*" In order to understand the full implica-

tions of this dry statistic, the reader should consult Mayo's *Mother India* for a lengthy description of the "unspeakable" *dhais*, "midwives" from the "untouchable" caste to whose filthy, brutal, grotesque, and frequently murderous ministrations the woman in childbirth is subjected (See pp. 90–110). Since most females in India do become pregnant, whether they want to or not, the reality of *dhais* must be noted in order to comprehend the condition of female life. The following brief excerpt is from p. 95: "Such labor may last three, four, five, even six days. During all this period the woman is given no nourishment whatever—such is the code—and the *dhai* resorts to all her traditions. She kneads the patient with her fists; stands her against the wall and butts her with her head; props her upright on the bare ground, seizes her hands and shoves against her thighs with gruesome bare feet, until, so the doctors state, the patient's flesh is often torn to ribbons by the *dhai*'s long, ragged toe-nails. Or, she lays the woman flat and walks up and down her body, like one treading grapes. Also, she makes balls of strange substances, such as hollyhock roots, or dirty string, or rags full of quince-seeds; or earth, or earth mixed with cloves, butter and marigold flowers; or nuts, or spices—any irritant—and thrusts them into the uterus, to hasten the event." Lest the reader misinterpret the fact that the *dhais* are females, imagining that this employment of the filthiest and most ignorant women to attend women in childbirth is not patriarchal in its context and intent, it is important to see the connections. Mayo writes of the total contempt for women's bodily functions, particularly her sexual functions: " 'Unclean' she [the young wife] is, in her pain—unclean whatever she touches, and fit thereafter only to be destroyed. In the name of thrift, therefore, give her about her only the unclean and the worthless, whether human or inanimate" (p. 92).

22. Ibid., p. 54.

23. Ibid., p. 37.

24. Abbé J. A. Dubois, *Hindu Manners, Customs and Ceremonies*, trans. by Henry K. Beauchamp, 3rd ed. (Oxford: Clarendon Press, 1928), p. 210.

25. David and Vera Mace, *Marriage: East and West* (Garden City, N.Y.: Doubleday, 1960), p. 70.

26. Thomas, *Indian Women*, p. 297.

27. Mace, *Marriage*, pp. 246–47.

28. Mayo, *Mother India*, pp. 82–83.

29. Bullough, *The Subordinate Sex*, p. 240.

30. Conversation with Jan Raymond, Amherst, Mass., December 1976. Another professor of Feminist Studies noted that students who resist such information often will use any cliché to avoid seeing the facts and their implications. Some common expressions of resistance are: "There must have been a reason"; "Things are different today"; "I guess I'm just lucky, but . . ." (conversation with Andrée Collard, Boston, January 1978).

31. Walker, *The Hindu World,* II, p. 462.
32. Mayo, *Mother India,* p. 83.
33. Dalip Singh Saund, *My Mother India* (Stockton, Calif.: Pacific Coast Khalsa Duvan Society, 1930), pp. 59–60.
34. Mace, *Marriage,* p. 175.
35. Mary F. Handlin, "Mayo, Katherine," *Notable American Women, 1607–1950: A Biographical Dictionary,* ed. by Edward T. James, Janet Wilson James, and Paul S. Boyer, 3 vols. (Cambridge, Mass.: Harvard University Press, 1971), Vol. II, 515–17.
36. Conversation, Boston, June 1977.
37. Feminist Searchers continue to unearth facts. ISIS, the bulletin of Women's International Information and Communication Service, reported the following in its March 1976 issue, p. 10: "In a rural area of E. Tanjore, in 1972, untouchable women could not walk on the same road at the same time as the Brahmins. Through the organization of a woman's movement, by the CP (M), untouchable women had gained confidence to do this. The landlords and the Brahmins of the community were enraged by the blatant revolt against all caste rules. As a token of 'revenge,' to set an example and to maintain their class position, *44 women and children were put in one hut and burned alive.*" (ISIS can be obtained from 1915 Glenwood Ave., Raleigh, North Carolina.)

Chapter Four CHINESE FOOTBINDING: ON FOOTNOTING THE THREE-INCH "LOTUS HOOKS"

1. Andrea Dworkin, *Woman Hating* (New York: E. P. Dutton, 1974), p. 103.
2. Howard S. Levy, *Chinese Footbinding: The History of a Curious Erotic Custom,* with a foreword by Arthur Waley (New York: Walton Rawls, 1966), p. 219.
3. Ibid., p. 179.
4. Ibid., p. 187.
5. Ibid., p. 169.
6. Ibid.
7. Ibid., chapter two, especially pp. 52, 54; and chapter nine.
8. Arthur Waley, foreword to *Chinese Footbinding: The History of a Curious Erotic Custom,* by Howard S. Levy, p. 7. It is interesting that Waley is a much admired translator of Chinese poetry and a poet himself. Hags might consider what this says about the so-called sensitivity of the poet.
9. Ibid.
10. Levy, *Chinese Footbinding,* p. 208.
11. Ibid., p. 206.
12. Waley, foreword to *Chinese Footbinding,* p. 7.
13. Levy, *Chinese Footbinding.* See especially pp. 173–79, and pp. 182–84. In fact, see the whole book.

14. G. Legman, *Rationale of the Dirty Joke: An Analysis of Sexual Humor* (New York: Castle Books, 1968), p. 16.

15. William A. Rossi, *The Sex Life of the Foot and Shoe* (New York: Saturday Review Press, E. P. Dutton, 1976), p. 209.

16. Ibid., p. 28.

17. Ibid.

18. Ibid., p. 29.

19. Ibid., p. 28.

20. Ibid., p. 32. It is fascinating to discover that the same author many years ago published a book entitled: *Your Feet and Their Care* (New York: Emerson Books, 1955). In this earlier tome Rossi had written (p. 3): "Someone coined the expression, 'When your feet hurt, you hurt all over.' Every foot sufferer will vouch for the truth of that statement. Abe Lincoln, who wore a 14B shoe and suffered greatly with his feet, said more than once, 'I cannot think if my feet hurt me.' He had a private chiropodist who attended to his feet regularly.

"An aching foot can distress your whole being, put a raw edge on your disposition, annihilate your peace of mind, create nausea, dissipate your vigor. If the foot ill becomes serious and chronic, its gnawing persistence can produce sharp changes in your whole personality, harmfully affect posture, poise and carriage."

21. Ibid., p. 36.

22. Ernest Becker, *The Denial of Death* (New York: Free Press, 1973), p. 237.

23. Ibid., p. 240.

24. Ibid., p. 241.

25. R. H. Van Gulik, *Sexual Life in Ancient China* (Leiden, Netherlands: E. J. Brill, 1961), p. 218.

26. Ibid., p. 222.

27. Ibid.

28. Ibid.

29. Levy, *Chinese Footbinding,* p. 39.

30. Van Gulik, *Sexual Life,* p. 222.

31. Julia P. Stanley, "Syntactic Exploitation: Passive Adjectives in English," unpublished paper, 1972.

32. Vern L. Bullough, *The Subordinate Sex: A History of Attitudes Toward Women,* with a final chapter by Bonnie Bullough (Baltimore, Md.: Penguin Books, 1974), p. 259.

33. Dworkin, *Woman Hating,* p. 112. See Dworkin's entire chapter six: "Gynocide: Chinese Footbinding," pp. 95–117.

34. Maria Leach, ed., and Jerome Fried, asso. ed., *Funk and Wagnalls Standard Dictionary of Folklore, Mythology, and Legend* (New York: Funk and Wagnalls, 1972), p. 233.

35. See *The Complete Grimm's Fairy Tales,* with an introduction by Padriac Colum and folkloristic commentary by Joseph Campbell (London: Routledge & Kegan Paul, 1975), pp. 121–28.

Chapter Five AFRICAN GENITAL MUTILATION: THE UNSPEAKABLE ATROCITIES

1. Theologians such as Paul Tillich have noted that while there may in some sense be "sins," in a more original sense there is Sin, which is a state. However, Tillich and other theologians of patriarchy are not in a position to name this State accurately. This is demonstrated in Paul Tillich's *Systematic Theology,* 3 vols. (Chicago: University of Chicago Press, 1951–63), Vol. II, pp. 44–47.

2. See *Women's International Network News,* ed. by Fran P. Hosken (187 Grant Street, Lexington, Mass. 02173), Vol. 1, No. 3 (June 1975), Vol. 1, No. 4 (October 1975), Vol. 2, No. 1 (January 1976), Vol. 2, No. 2 (spring 1976), Vol. 2, No. 3 (summer 1976). In the last-mentioned issue, Hosken gives an extensive bibliography. The reader is advised to consult *WIN News* for up-to-date information.

3. See Hosken, *WIN News,* Vol. 2, No. 1 (January 1976), p. 30. See also J. A. Verzin, M.D., "Sequelae of Female Circumcision," *Tropical Doctor,* October 1975, p. 163. I have cited only the first three of the types of circumcision described by Verzin. He lists a fourth type, which he believes is practiced only among the Ditta Pitta tribes in Australia: "*Type IV: Introcision.* This is the cutting into the vagina or splitting of the perineum, either digitally or by means of a sharp instrument, and is the severest form of female circumcision." Verzin maintains that Type III (Pharaonic circumcision) is practiced throughout the Sudan, Ethiopia, and Somaliland.

4. Jacques Lantier, *La Cité magique et magie en afrique noire* (Paris: Librairie Arthème Fayard, 1972), p. 279.

5. Ibid., pp. 279–80. Lantier describes marriage among the Somali. When the bride goes to her husband's house he takes off her clothes and beats her until the blood flows. Since he cannot "deflower" her (that is, break the scar) with his penis, he uses a knife. Before using the knife, he forces a piece of wood, "specially tailored," into the vaginal orifice—a precaution designed to protect the perineum, in order not to cause a fistula on the rectum. Then he plunges in the knife before having intercourse with her. There is more:

"Selon la tradition, le mari doit avoir durant huit jours des rapports réiterés et prolongés. Ce 'travail' a pour objet de 'fabriquer' un vestibule en empèchant la cicatrice de se refermer. Pendant ces huit jours, la femme reste étendue et bouge le moins possible afin de tenir la plaie béante. Au lendemain de la nuit des noces, le mari fixe sur son épaule son poignard ensanglanté; il va faire des visites afin de recueillir l'admiration générale. Cette 'formalité' remplie, il rentre aussitôt chez lui reprendre son ouvrage."

Another source on infibulation and defibulation is Eugenio Lenzi, "Damage Caused by Infibulation and Infertility," *Acta Europaea Fer-*

tilitatis, Vol. 2, No. 47 (1970), pp. 47–58. Asim Zaki Mustafa, in his article, "Female Circumcision and Infibulation in the Sudan," *Journal of Obstetrics and Gynaecology of the British Commonwealth,* Vol. 73, pp. 302–6, discusses infibulation in the Sudan, with an emphasis upon resultant complications. He imparts the interesting information that an individual named Tiggani, who was the only psychiatrist in the Sudan for several years, in a personal communication in 1965 conveyed his opinion that circumcision provides a "happy social occasion" for Sudanese women who normally enjoy little in the way of entertainment. This psychiatrist maintains that "had it been unpleasant or unacceptable it would have perished long ago." Mustafa also informs us: "Rectal intercourse not infrequently takes place in error because the vaginal introitus has been obliterated" (p. 305). See also M. F. Ashley Montagu, "Infibulation and Defibulation in the Old and New Worlds," *American Anthropologist,* n.s. 47 (1945), pp. 464–67: Allan Worsley, "Infibulation and Female Circumcision: A Study of a Little-Known Custom," *Journal of Obstetrics and Gynaecology of the British Empire,* Vol. 45 (1938) pp. 686–91.

6. See Hosken, *WIN News,* Vol. 2, No. 1 (January 1976), p. 36. See also Verzin, "Sequelae of Female Circumcision"; Mustafa, "Female Circumcision"; Lenzi, "Damage Caused by Infibulation." See also the article (unsigned), "Excision in Africa," *ISIS International Bulletin,* No. 2 (October 1976), pp. 12–15. ISIS is a collective of women providing an information and communication service for the women's movement internationally. The address in Switzerland is Case Postale 301, 1227, Carouge, Switzerland. Money orders can be sent to this address. Subscriptions for individual women and women's groups are $10.00; for libraries and other institutions, $20.00.

7. See Hosken, *WIN News,* Vol. 1, No. 3 (June 1975), p. 41.

8. Hosken, *WIN News,* Vol. 2, No. 1 (January 1976), p. 30.

9. Jomo Kenyatta, *Facing Mount Kenya: The Tribal Life of the Gikuyu,* with an introduction by B. Malinowski (New York: Vintage, 1965), p. 125 ff. In his introduction, the prestigious scholar Malinowski writes: "As a first-hand account of a representative African culture, as an invaluable document in the principles underlying culture-contact and change; last, not least, as a personal statement of the new outlook of a progressive African, this book will rank as a pioneering achievement of outstanding merit."

10. Benoîte Groult, *Ainsi soit-elle* (Paris: Bernard Grasset, 1975), p. 96. The entire fourth chapter of this book, entitled "La Haine du C.," pp. 93–118, is worth reading. Since the author does not document her work, however, the Searcher will want to consult also more primary sources, such as those indicated in these notes.

11. "Excision in Africa," *ISIS,* p. 14. See Lenzi, "Damage Caused by Infibulation," p. 55; Worsley, "Infibulation and Female Circumcision," p. 688. Hosken in "Genital Mutilation of Females in Africa: Summary/Facts," a fact sheet available from *WIN News,* points out

that in the Sudan, where most of the women, including city-dwellers, are infibulated, the ceremony is called *tahur,* which means "cleansing."

12. G. Pieters, "Gynécologie au pays des femmes cousues," *Acta Chirurgica Belgica,* No. 3 (May 1972), p. 180. This article, on gynecology "in the country of the sewn women," is extremely valuable.

13. "Excision in Africa," *ISIS,* pp. 12–14.

14. Ibid., p. 12.

15. See Verzin, "Sequelae of Female Circumcision," in which he maintains that "circumcision" is done not only throughout Africa, but in Brazil, Eastern Mexico, Peru, several Asian countries, Australia, and, in Europe, among the Skopsi, a christian Russian sect, to ensure "perpetual virginity." Another strong argument for wide geographical distribution is given by Dr. Ahmed Abu-El-Futuh Shandall, in his article "Circumcision and Infibulation of Females," in *Sudan Medical Journal,* Vol. 5, No. 4 (1967), pp. 180–81. See also Ben R. Huelsman, "An Anthropological View of Clitoral and Other Female Genital Mutilations," in *The Clitoris,* ed. by Thomas P. Lowry, M.D., and Thea Snyder Lowry, M.A. (St. Louis, Mo.: Warren H. Green, 1976), p. 121.

16. Hosken, *WIN News,* Vol. 2, No. 1 (January 1976), p. 30.

17. Ibid., p. 32.

18. Montagu, "Infibulation and Defibulation," pp. 464–67.

19. M. F. Ashley Montagu, "Ritual Mutilation among Primitive Peoples," *Ciba Symposia,* Vol. 8, No. 7 (October 1946) pp. 421–36.

20. Huelsman, "An Anthropological View," p. 123.

21. Ibid., p. 124.

22. Shandall, "Circumcision and Infibulation," pp. 178–79.

23. Groult, *Ainsi soit-elle,* p. 94.

24. Montagu, "Ritual Mutilation," p. 434.

25. See Huelsman, "An Anthropological View," p. 121.

26. Diana E. H. Russell and Nicole Van de Ven, eds., *The Proceedings of the International Tribunal on Crimes Against Women* (Millbrae, Calif.: Les Femmes, 1976), p. 151.

27. Montagu, "Infibulation and Defibulation," pp. 465–66.

28. Ibid., p. 466.

29. There are other details of the infibulated woman's life that support the evidence concerning who is behind the scenes controlling the gynocidal set-up. Thus Pieters points to the fact that in some parts of Arabia salt is stuffed into the vagina after childbirth in order to shrink the orifice so that intercourse will be more pleasurable for the husband. A common result of this is vaginal stenosis. See Pieters, "Gynécologie au pays," p. 189. Pieters refers to B. M. L. Underhill, "Salt Induced Vaginal Stenosis in Arabia," *Journal of Obstetrics and Gynaecology of the British Commonwealth,* 1963, Vol. 71, No. 293.

30. Lantier, *La Cité magique,* p. 278: "La mère achève son intervention en veillant à ménager un orifice très étroit, destiné a ne laisser passer que les urines et les menstrues. Il y va de son honneur que le

trou soit le plus petit possible, car, chez les Somali, plus le passage artificiel est étroit et plus la femme est considerée."

31. Henny Harald Hansen, "Clitoridectomy: Female Circumcision in Egypt," *Folk,* Vol. 14–15 (1972/73), p. 18.

32. Montagu, "Infibulation and Defibulation," p. 465.

33. Felix Bryk, *Dark Rapture: The Sex-Life of the African Negro,* English version by Dr. Arthur J. Norton (New York: Walden Publications, 1939), pp. 89–90.

34. Arnold van Gennep, *The Rites of Passage,* trans. by Monika B. Vizedom and Gabrielle L. Caffee (Chicago: University of Chicago Press, 1960), p. 71.

35. Ibid., p. 86.

36. Ibid., p. 87.

37. Kenyatta, *Facing Mount Kenya,* pp. 127–28. On page 130, Kenyatta expounds upon his thesis as follows: "For years there has been much criticism and agitation against *irua* [genital mutilation] of girls by certain misinformed missionary societies in East Africa, who see only the surgical side of the *irua,* and, without investigating the psychological importance attached to this custom by the Gikuyu, these missionaries draw their conclusion that the *irua* of girls is nothing but a barbarous practice and, as such, should be abolished by law.

"On the other hand, the Gikuyu look upon these religious fanatics with great suspicion. . . . The abolition of *irua* will destroy the tribal symbol which identifies the age-groups, and prevent the Gikuyu from perpetuating that spirit of collectivism and national solidarity which they have been able to maintain from time immemorial."

38. Lantier, *La Cité magique,* pp. 271–72: "(Dieu) a donné le clitoris à la femme pour qu'elle puisse l'utiliser avant le mariage afin d'éprouver le plaisir de l'amour tout en restant pure. . . .

"On ne tranche pas le clitoris des toutes petites filles puisqu'il leur sert à se masturber. On tranche celui des jeunes filles que l'on juge disposées à la procréation et au mariage. Quand on leur a enlevé le clitoris, elles ne se masturbent plus. Cela les prive beaucoup. Alors tout le désir se porte vers l'intérieur. Elles cherchent donc à se marier promptement. Une fois mariées, au lieu d'éprouver des sensations dispersées et faibles, elles concentrent tout au même endroit et les couples connaissent beaucoup de bonheur, ce qui est normal."

39. Pieters, "Gynécologie au pays," pp. 182–83.

40. Hosken, *WIN News,* Vol. 2, No. 1 (January 1976), p. 35.

41. Pieters, "Gynécologie au pays," pp. 180–81.

42. Bryk, *Dark Rapture,* pp. 87–88.

43. Ibid., p. 100.

44. Ibid., p. 90.

45. Ibid., p. 27.

46. Ibid., p. 28.

47. Van Gennep, *The Rites of Passage,* p. 72, note 2.

48. Ibid., p. 73.
49. Marie Bonaparte, *Female Sexuality* (New York: International Universities Press, 1953), p. 191.
50. Ibid., p. 204.
51. Ibid., p. 207.
52. Mircea Eliade, *Rites and Symbols of Initiation: The Mysteries of Birth and Rebirth,* trans. by Willard R. Trask (New York: Harper Torchbooks, 1965), p. 42.
53. Ibid., p. 43.
54. Ibid., pp. 45–46.
55. Ibid., p. 46.

Chapter Six EUROPEAN WITCHBURNINGS: PURIFYING THE BODY OF CHRIST

1. Heinrich Kramer and James Sprenger, *The Malleus Maleficarum,* trans. with introductions, bibliography, and notes by the Rev. Montague Summers (New York: Dover, 1971); first published 1928.
2. H. R. Trevor-Roper, *The European Witch-Craze of the Sixteenth and Seventeenth Centuries and Other Essays* (New York: Harper Torchbooks, 1969), p. 127.
3. Henry Charles Lea, *Materials Toward a History of Witchcraft,* arranged and edited by Arthur C. Howland, with an introduction by George Lincoln Burr, 3 vols. (New York: Thomas Yoseloff, 1957), Vol. III, 1127.
4. Julia O'Faolain and Lauro Martines, eds., *Not in God's Image: Women in History from the Greeks to the Victorians* (New York: Harper and Row, 1973), p. 209.
5. Trevor-Roper, *The European Witch-Craze,* p. 122.
6. From *De la Demonomanie des Sorciers* (Paris, 1580), quoted in Alan C. Kors and Edward Peters, eds., *Witchcraft in Europe, 1100–1700: A Documentary History* (Philadelphia: University of Pennsylvania Press, 1972), p. 215.
7. Ibid.
8. Trevor-Roper, *The European Witch-Craze,* p. 122.
9. H. C. Erik Midelfort, *Witch Hunting in Southwestern Germany, 1562–1684: The Social and Intellectual Foundations* (Stanford, Calif.: Stanford University Press, 1972), pp. 195–96.
10. Ibid., pp. 1–2.
11. Ibid., p. 196.
12. Trevor-Roper, *The European Witch-Craze,* p. 143.
13. Thomas Aquinas, for example, had provided a theological legitimation for the extermination of heretics as decayed flesh. *Summa theologiae* II–II, 11, 3.
14. Kramer and Sprenger, *Malleus Maleficarum,* Part I, Question 6, p. 47.
15. Trevor-Roper, *The European Witch-Craze,* pp. 94–95.

16. Kramer and Sprenger, *Malleus Maleficarum,* Part I, Question 9, p. 58.
17. Ibid., Part I, question 6, pp. 41–47.
18. Trevor-Roper, *The European Witch-Craze,* p. 101.
19. Innocent's Bull is reprinted in Summers's edition of the *Malleus Maleficarum;* see pp. xliv–xlv.
20. Conversation with Emily Culpepper, Boston, May 1977.
21. Trevor-Roper, *The European Witch-Craze,* p. 91.
22. Julio Caro Baroja, *The World of the Witches,* trans. by O. N. V. Glendinning (Chicago: University of Chicago Press, 1973), p. 250.
23. Jane Caputi, "The Influence of Print upon the European Witch-Craze," unpublished paper, 1977.
24. Trevor-Roper, *The European Witch-Craze,* p. 91.
25. Ibid., p. 96.
26. Midelfort, *Witch Hunting in Southwestern Germany,* p. 69.
27. Caputi, "The Influence of Print."
28. Trevor-Roper, *The European Witch-Craze,* p. 142.
29. Conversation with Denise Connors, Boston, October 1976.
30. Midelfort, *Witch Hunting in Southwestern Germany,* p. 185.
31. E. William Monter, *Witchcraft in France and Switzerland* (Ithaca, N.Y.: Cornell University Press, 1976), p. 118.
32. Kramer and Sprenger, *Malleus Maleficarum.* See Montague Summers's introduction to the 1948 edition, p. vii.
33. William Dufty, *Sugar Blues* (New York: Warner Books, 1975), p. 31.
34. Ibid., p. 52.
35. Trevor-Roper, *The European Witch-Craze,* p. 152.
36. Ronald Seth, *Children Against Witches* (New York: Taplinger, 1969), p. 13.
37. Ibid.
38. Trevor-Roper, *The European Witch-Craze,* p. 121.
39. Kramer and Sprenger, *Malleus Maleficarum,* p. iii.
40. Ibid., Part II, Question 1, Chapter VII, p. 121.
41. From Johann Matthäus Meyfarth quoted in Lea, *Materials,* II, 735.
42. Ibid.
43. Rossell Hope Robbins, *The Encyclopedia of Witchcraft and Demonology* (New York: Crown, 1959), p. 503.
44. Ibid., p. 502.
45. Lea, *Materials,* III, 1548.
46. Ibid.
47. Kramer and Sprenger, *Malleus Maleficarum.* See Montague Summers's introduction to the 1928 edition, p. xl.
48. Ibid. See Montague Summers's introduction to the 1948 edition, p. ix.
49. Trevor-Roper, *The European Witch-Craze,* p. 181.
50. Ibid., p. 180.

51. Ibid.
52. Ibid., p. 154.
53. Montague Summers, *The History of Witchcraft and Demonology* (Secaucus, N.J.: Citadel Press, 1971), p. 1.
54. Owen Chadwick, gen. ed., *The Pelican History of the Church,* Vol. III: *The Reformation,* by Owen Chadwick (Middlesex, England: Penguin Books, 1964), p. 23.
55. Ibid., pp. 295–96.
56. Louis Gottschalk, Loren C. MacKinney, and Earl H. Pritchard, *The Foundations of the Modern World 1300–1775, History of Mankind: Cultural and Scientific Development,* Vol. IV (New York: Harper and Row, 1969), pp. 216–17.
57. Ibid., pp. 522–23.
58. Ibid., p. 982.
59. Ibid., p. 1003.
60. See for example R. de Maulde la Clavière, *The Women of the Renaissance: A Study of Feminism,* trans. by George Herbert Ely (New York: G. P. Putnam, 1901); and Roland H. Bainton, *Women of the Reformation in Germany and Italy* (Boston: Beacon Press, 1974).
61. Baroja, *World of the Witches,* p. 256.
62. Ibid., p. 257.
63. William E. H. Lecky, *History of European Morals From Augustus to Charlemagne,* 2 vols. (2nd ed.; New York: D. Appleton, 1919), Vol. II, p. 54.
64. Ibid., p. 55.
65. Thomas S. Szasz, *The Manufacture of Madness: A Comparative Study of the Inquisition and the Mental Health Movement* (New York: Harper and Row, 1970), p. 70.
66. Ibid., p. 72.
67. Gregory Zilboorg, *The Medical Man and the Witch During the Renaissance* (New York: Cooper Square, 1969), p. 73.
68. Ibid., p. 9.
69. Ibid., pp. 23–26.
70. Ibid., p. 26.
71. Ibid., p. 62.
72. Ibid., p. 63.
73. Franz G. Alexander and Sheldon T. Selesnick, *The History of Psychiatry: An Evaluation of Psychiatric Thought and Practice from Prehistoric Times to the Present* (New York: Harper and Row, 1966), p. 68.
74. Conversation with my Self, Boston, June 1977.
75. Robbins, *The Encyclopedia of Witchcraft,* pp. 500–1.
76. Szasz, *Manufacture of Madness;* see especially chapters 5, 6, 7, and 8.
77. Ibid., p. 48.
78. Jane Caputi, "Matilda Joslyn Gage: Philosopher of Feminism," unpublished paper, 1974.

79. Matilda Joslyn Gage, *Woman, Church and State* (2nd ed.; New York: Arno Press, 1972), p. 243; edition first published 1893. The Arno Press edition is part of their series: American Women: Images and Realities.
80. Ibid., p. 240.
81. Ibid., 233.
82. Ibid.
83. Ibid., p. 270.
84. Elizabeth B. Warbasse, "Gage, Matilda Joslyn," *Notable American Women 1607–1950: A Biographical Dictionary*, ed. by Edward T. James, Janet Wilson James, and Paul S. Boyer, 3 vols. (Cambridge, Mass.: Harvard University Press, 1971), Vol. II, 4–6.
85. See Margaret A. Murray, *The Witch-Cult in Western Europe* (Oxford: Oxford University Press, 1921) and Margaret A. Murray, *The God of the Witches* (New York: Oxford University Press, 1970). See also Christina Hole's work *Witchcraft in England* (New York: Collier Books, 1966), first published in 1947, which also presents useful material. Her analysis is partially in the tradition of Margaret Murray. However, like Murray, she lacks a woman-identified perspective.
86. Summers's *History of Witchcraft*, p. 40.
87. Ibid., p. 34.
88. Ibid., p. 43.
89. Murray, *The Witch-Cult*, p. 16.
90. Ibid.
91. Ibid., p. 13.
92. Gage, *Woman, Church and State*, p. 291.
93. Robin Morgan, *Going Too Far: The Personal Chronicle of a Feminist* (New York: Random House, 1977), pp. 71–72.
94. Robin Morgan, ed., *Sisterhood Is Powerful: An Anthology of Writings from the Women's Liberation Movement* (New York: Random House, 1970), p. 540.
95. Barbara Ehrenreich and Deirdre English, *Witches, Midwives and Nurses: A History of Women Healers* (2nd ed.; Old Westbury, N.Y.: Feminist Press, 1973).
96. Andrea Dworkin, *Woman Hating* (New York: Dutton, 1974). See chapter seven: "Gynocide: The Witches," pp. 118–50.

Chapter Seven AMERICAN GYNECOLOGY: GYNOCIDE BY THE HOLY GHOSTS OF MEDICINE AND THERAPY

1. See, for example, Adrienne Rich, *Of Woman Born: Motherhood as Experience and Institution* (New York: W. W. Norton, 1976). See also Barbara Ehrenreich and Deirdre English, *Witches, Midwives and Nurses: A History of Women Healers* (2nd ed.: Old Westbury, N.Y.: Feminist Press, 1973).
2. G. J. Barker-Benfield, *The Horrors of the Half-Known Life:*

Male Attitudes Toward Women and Sexuality in Nineteenth Century America (New York: Harper and Row, 1976), p. 81.

3. Ibid., p. 119.
4. Ibid., pp. 80–132.
5. Ibid., p. 100.
6. Conversation, Boston, August 1977. An extremely useful critique of modern medicine is to be found in Ivan Illich, *Medical Nemesis: The Expropriation of Health* (New York: Random House, 1976). Hagographers should not overlook Illich's well-documented analysis, which can serve as a springboard for a woman-identified analysis, despite the fact that Illich shows no inclination to acknowledge the specific targeting of women as victims of medicine. (The term *gynecology* does not even appear in the index of this book.) See also Rick J. Carlson, *The End of Medicine* (New York: John Wiley, 1975). Denise D. Connors, in a paper entitled "Medicalization of Society: The Sickness Unto Death," delivered in Boston, May 1976, discusses the necrophilic and iatrogenic realities of modern medicine from a woman-identified perspective.
7. Barker-Benfield, *Horrors of the Half-Known Life,* p. 90.
8. Ibid., pp. 80–132.
9. Barbara Ehrenreich and Deirdre English, *Complaints and Disorders: The Sexual Politics of Sickness* (Old Westbury, N.Y.: Feminist Press, 1973), pp. 43–44.
10. See Thomas Aquinas, *Summa theologiae,* I, q. 38.
11. Ibid., I, q.37.
12. This has been demonstrated by Janice Raymond, in a lecture entitled "Medicine as Patriarchal Religion," given at Boston College, April 1975.
13. Edward Podolsky, M.D., ed., *Encyclopedia of Aberrations and Psychiatric Handbook* (New York: Philosophical Library, 1953), p. 220.
14. Ibid., p. 221.
15. Charles Rycraft, *A Critical Dictionary of Psychoanalysis* (New York: Basic Books, 1968), p. 51.
16. "Fetishism," *Encyclopedia Britannica,* 1965, Vol. IX, p. 217.
17. Rycraft, *Encyclopedia of Aberrations,* p. 52.
18. Ernest Becker, *The Structure of Evil: An Essay on the Unification of the Science of Man* (New York: George Braziller, 1968), p. 180.
19. Ibid., p. 180.
20. Rich, *Of Woman Born,* p. 138.
21. Ibid., p. 151.
22. Ibid., pp. 151–55.
23. Deborah Larned, "The Greening of the Womb," *New Times,* December 27, 1974, p. 36.
24. Robert A. Wilson, M.D., *Feminine Forever* (New York: M. Evans, 1966), p. 138. On the same page Dr. Wilson opines: "A woman

who has had her uterus removed but retains her ovaries thus appears fortunate indeed. . . . She is truly an emancipated woman." On the next page he coos: "If your uterus has been removed, estrogen therapy will provide all its benefits without the annoyance of menstrual bleeding. You are a lucky woman indeed."

25. This description is attributed to Dr. Ralph C. Wright of Connecticut by Deborah Larned, in "The Greening of the Womb," p. 37.

26. Ibid.

27. Cited in the *Boston Globe,* May 10, 1977.

28. Barker-Benfield, *Horrors of the Half-Known Life,* p. 83.

29. Ibid.

30. Ibid., p. 120. Barker-Benfield maintains that clitoridectomy was performed in the United States "at least until 1904 and perhaps until 1925." He adds: "In the U.S. it coexisted with, and then was superseded by, the circumcision of females of all ages up to menopause: circumcision continued to be performed here until 1937 at least. Both clitoridectomy and circumcision aimed to check what was thought to be a growing incidence of female masturbation . . ." In fact, it has been pointed out to me that female circumcision (removal of all or part of the "hood" of the clitoris) is still practiced in the United States (conversation with Laura Brown, Boston, October 1977).

31. Barker-Benfield, *Horrors of the Half-Known Life,* p. 121.

32. Ely Van de Warker, M.D., "The Fetich of the Ovary," *American Journal of Obstetrics,* Vol. 54, No. 3 (September 1906), p. 371.

33. Marc Lappé, "The Moral Claims of the Fetus," *The Hastings Center Report,* Vol. 5, No. 2 (April 1975), p. 13. The unreality of such "rights of the fetus" rhetoric is demonstrated in Linda Gordon, *Woman's Body, Woman's Right: A Social History of Birth Control in America* (New York: Penguin Books, 1977); see especially pp. 35–39.

34. See Kenneth A. Marshall, M.D., "Postmastectomy Reconstruction of the Breast," *Surgery, Gynecology and Obstetrics,* Vol. 144, No. 1 (January 1977), editorial, pp. 77–78.

35. Reuven K. Snyderman, M.D., Commentary on Vincent R. Pennisi, M.D. and Angelo Capozzi, M.D., "Incidence of Obscure Carcinoma in Subcutaneous Mastectomy," *Journal of Plastic and Reconstructive Surgery,* Vol. 56, No. 2., p. 208.

36. *Boston Evening Globe,* June 29, 1977. The federal government allots much more money for sterilizations of poor women than for abortions. See Judith Herman, "Fighting Sterilization Abuse," *Science for the People,* Vol. 9, No. 1 (January/February 1977), pp. 17–19.

37. Jan Worthington, "The Cancer Time Bomb: Did Your Mother Take DES?" *Ms.,* March 1977, p. 16.

38. Ben Barker-Benfield, "Sexual Surgery in Late-Nineteenth Century America," *International Journal of Health Services,* Vol. 5, No. 2 (1975), p. 285. See Barker-Benfield, *Horrors of the Half-Known Life,* pp. 80–132.

39. Conversation with Denise Connors, Boston, September 1977.

40. Kay Weiss, "Vaginal Cancer: An Iatrogenic Disease?" *International Journal of Health Services,* Vol. 5, No. 2 (1975), p. 235.

41. Ibid., p. 245.

42. Worthington, "The Cancer Time-Bomb," p. 16.

43. Emily Culpepper has produced a number of important studies of menstruation. See: "Zoroastrian Menstruation Taboos: A Women's Studies Perspective," *Women and Religion, 1973 Proceedings,* edited by Joan Arnold Romero (Tallahassee, Fla.: American Academy of Religion, Florida State University, 1973), pp. 94–102. See also "Exploring Menstrual Attitudes," in *Women Look at Biology Looking at Women,* ed. by M. S. Hennifin, et al (Cambridge, Mass.: Schenckman Publishing, 1978). This chapter is comprised of two papers previously delivered by the author. She discusses hebrew menstruation taboos, and presents a "menstrual social/science fiction fantasy." Together with Esther Rome, she co-authored in 1977 a women's health information pamphlet entitled *Menstruation* (available free by sending a self-addressed stamped envelope to: Boston Women's Health Collective, Department B, Box 192, West Somerville, MA 02144). She has produced a ten-minute, 16 mm. film, *Period Piece,* exploring attitudes, experiences, and images of menstruation. For rental information write to: Culpepper, 64 R. Sacramento St., Cambridge, MA 02138, or to Insight Exchange, P.O. Box 42594, San Francisco, CA 94101.

44. Kenneth J. Ryan, M.D., "Cancer Risk and Estrogen Use in the Menopause," *New England Journal of Medicine,* Vol. 293, No. 23 (December 4, 1975), p. 1200.

45. Lindsay R. Curtis, M.D., *The Menopause: A New Life of Confidence and Contentment* (Bristol, Tenn.: Beecham-Massengill Pharmaceuticals, 1969), pp. 31, 36. On the back of this pamphlet are printed the words: PUBLISHED AS A SERVICE TO THE MEDICAL PROFESSION.

46. See Laman A. Gray, Sr., M.D., "Estrogens and Endometrial Carcinoma," *Obstetrics and Gynecology: Journal of the American College of Obstetricians and Gynecologists,* Vol. 49, No. 4 (April 1977). The authors of this article admit that forty years ago there had been warning of the carcinogenic possibilities of estrogenic substances. Feminists, of course, are aware that the Women's Health Movement had been pointing out the dangers of estrogen use for years before the doctors began publicly to expose themselves in the mid-seventies.

47. Donald C. Smith, M.D., et al., "Association of Exogenous Estrogens and Endometrial Carcinoma," *New England Journal of Medicine,* Vol. 293, No. 23 (December 4, 1975), pp. 1164–67.

48. A lengthy list of pill-related diseases can be found in *Physicians Desk Reference* (31st. ed; Oradell, N. J.: Medical Economics Company, a Litton division, 1977), pp. 1152–53. For specific discussions of the pill as cause of cancer see Barbara Seaman, *The Doctors' Case Against The Pill* (New York: Avon Books, 1969) pp. 128–38; Barbara Seaman and Gideon Seaman, M.D. *Women and the Crisis in Sex Hormones* (New York: Rawson Associates, 1977), pp. 93–94. In order to

understand something of the social climate which dis-courages women to such an extent that they continue to accept such poisons, the reader can find useful information in Linda Gordon, *Woman's Body, Woman's Right.*

49. Weiss, "Vaginal Cancer," p. 248.

50. Thomas Aquinas, *Summa theologiae* I, q. 14, a. 3.

51. C. G. Jung, *Psychological Aspects of the Mother Archetype,* in *The Basic Writings of C. G. Jung,* ed. with an introduction by Violet Staub de Lazlo (New York: Modern Library, 1959), pp. 334–35.

52. Ibid., p. 341.

53. Ibid., p. 339.

54. Ibid., p. 342.

55. Barker-Benfield, *Horrors of the Half-Known Life,* p. 130.

56. Sigmund Freud, *Dora: An Analysis of a Case of Hysteria, 1905,* trans. by Alix and James Strachey, in *The Case of Dora and Other Papers* (New York: W. W. Norton, 1952), p. 14.

57. See Rich, *Of Woman Born,* pp. 153–55.

58. See Julia P. Stanley, "Passive Motivation," *Foundations of Language,* Vol. 13, pp. 25–39; "Syntactic Exploitation: Passive Adjectives in English," paper delivered at Southeastern Conference on Linguistics, Atlanta, Georgia, 1971. See also Julia P. Stanley and Susan W. Robbins, "Truncated Passives: Some of Our Agents are Missing," *Linguistic Theory and the Real World,* Vol. 1, No. 2 (September 1976), pp. 33–37.

59. Cited in Rich, *Of Woman Born,* p. 168.

60. Ibid.

61. Ibid.

62. In 1974 it was reported that the average length of life of males in the United States was 68.1, whereas that of females was 75.8. See U.S. Department of Health, Education, and Welfare, *Vital Statistics of the United States, 1974,* Vol. II, section 5, life tables.

63. Lyssa Waters, " 'Why I Became a Gynecologist . . .': Four Men Tell All," *Ms.,* February 1977, p. 54.

64. Ibid., p. 91.

65. Ibid., p. 92.

66. Abstract of article by Charles W. Socarides, "Sexual Perversion and the Fear of Engulfment," *Psychological Abstracts: Nonevaluative Summaries of the World's Literature in Psychology and Related Disciplines* (Washington, D.C.: The American Psychological Association) Vol. 52, No. 5 (November 1974), n. 10339.

67. *Psychological Abstracts,* Vol. 52 (July–December 1974). See abstracts n. 1094, 1095, 1210, 1230, 5529, 10339, 10413, 12862.

68. Ibid., n. 1095. This is an abstract of an article illuminatingly entitled "Contribution to the Etiology and Pathogenesis of Trichotillomania with Special Consideration of Mother-Child Relations."

69. Freud, *Dora,* p. 36. See Florence Rush, "The Freudian Cover-Up," *Chrysalis,* No. 1 (1977), pp. 31–45. Rush exposes Freud's hy-

pocrisy concerning the sexual abuse of girl-children, referring to his early correspondence with Wilhelm Fliess in which he admits the reality of widespread sexual abuse of young girls, later to be denied in *Dora.*

70. Freud, *Dora,* pp. 36–37.
71. Ibid., p. 37.
72. Rich, *Of Woman Born,* p. 135.
73. Ibid., p. 139.
74. Barbara Ehrenreich and Deirdre English, *Complaints and Disorders,* p. 46.
75. Ibid., p. 12.
76. Herman, "Fighting Sterilization Abuse," p. 18.
77. Ibid.
78. Barker-Benfield, "Sexual Surgery in Late-Nineteenth Century America," p. 289.
79. Ibid.
80. Ibid.
81. Carlos C. Say, M.D., and William Donegan, M.D., "A Biostatistical Evaluation of Complications from Mastectomy," *Surgery, Gynecology, and Obstetrics,* Vol. 138, No. 3 (March 1974), p. 370.
82. Ibid., pp. 370–71, 374.
83. Peter Greenwald, M.D., et al., "Endometrial Cancer after Menopausal Use of Estrogens," *Obstetrics and Gynecology,* Vol. 50, No. 2 (August 1977), p. 241. In addition to this information, it is important to note that researchers admit that the "risk-ratio estimate" increases with duration of exposure. Thus women who have been conjugated estrogen users for seven or more years have a calculated risk of 13.9 times that of nonusers. See Harry K. Ziel, M.D., and William D. Finkle, Ph.D., "Increased Risk of Endometrial Carcinoma among Users of Conjugated Estrogens," *New England Journal of Medicine,* Vol. 293, No. 23 (December 4, 1975), pp. 1167–70.
84. Peter Greenwald, M.D., et al., "Endometrial Cancer," p. 243.
85. Laman A. Gray, Sr., M.D., "Estrogens and Endometrial Carcinoma," p. 388.
86. Ibid.
87. Joseph Agris, M.D., "Use of Dermal-Fat Suspension Flaps for Thigh and Buttock Lifts," *Plastic and Reconstructive Surgery,* Vol. 59, No. 6 (June 1977), p. 817.
88. Ronald R. Reimer, M.D., et al., "Acute Leukemia after Alkylating-Agent Therapy of Ovarian Cancer," *New England Journal of Medicine,* Vol. 297, No. 4 (July 28, 1977), p. 179.
89. Ibid., p. 180.
90. Deryck R. Kent, M.D., et al., "Maternal Death Resulting from Rupture of Liver Adenoma Associated with Oral Contraceptives," *Obstetrics and Gynecology,* Vol. 50, No. 1 (July 1977; supplement), p. 5s.
91. Weiss, "Vaginal Cancer," p. 240.

92. Joel Kovel, M.D., *A Complete Guide to Therapy: From Psychoanalysis to Behavior Modification* (New York: Pantheon, 1976), p. 63.

93. See Glossary of Kovel, *A Complete Guide,* pp. 261–65. Definitions of some of these forms of therapy are provided.

94. R. D. Rosen, *Psychobabble: Fast Talk and Quick Cure in the Era of Feeling* (New York: Atheneum, 1977), p. 6.

95. Conversation, Boston, June 1977.

96. Gena Corea, *The Hidden Malpractice: How American Medicine Treats Women as Patients and Professionals* (New York: William Morrow, 1977), p. 55. For an excellent feminist analysis of twenty-seven gynecology texts, see Diane Scully and Pauline Bart, "A Hard Day at the Orifice: Women in Gynecology Texts," *Changing Women in a Changing Society*, ed. by Joan Huber (Chicago: University of Chicago Press, 1973), pp. 283–88.

97. Joseph Chilton Pearce, *The Crack in the Cosmic Egg: Changing Constructs of Mind and Reality* (New York: Pocket Books, 1973), p. 7.

98. Ibid., p. 8.

99. Helene Deutsch, M.D., *The Psychology of Women: A Psychoanalytic Interpretation,* Vol. I: *Girlhood* (New York: Bantam, 1944), p. 225.

100. Helene Deutsch, M.D., *The Psychology of Women,* Vol. II: *Motherhood* (New York: Bantam, 1945), p. 483.

101. See Marie Bonaparte, *Female Sexuality* (New York: International Universities Press, 1953), for a treasury of misogynism, e.g., p. 81: "Masochism in woman is far stronger than in man. . . . And since woman, above all, remains always more or less dominated by her positive, passive, masochistic Oedipus complex, turned on the father . . . she remains, throughout life, more subject to her infantile libidinal urges than is man."

102. Lyssa Waters, "Why I Became a Gynecologist," p. 54.

103. Suzanne Arms, *Immaculate Deception: A New Look at Women and Childbirth in America* (New York: Bantam Books, 1975).

104. Kathleen Barry, "The Cutting Edge: A Look at Male Motivation in Obstetrics and Gynecology," unpublished paper, copyright 1972 by Kathleen Barry.

105. Donald C. Smith, et al., "Association of Exogenous Estrogen and Endometrical Carcinoma," *New England Journal of Medicine,* Vol. 293, No. 23 (December 4, 1975), p. 1166.

106. Lucretia Marmon, "Barbie Doll Developer Ruth Handler Offers a New Look to Mastectomy Victims," *People Weekly* (April 11, 1977), pp. 80–82.

107. C. G. Jung, *Aion: Contributions to the Symbolism of the Self,* in *Psyche and Symbol: A Selection from the Writings of C. G. Jung,* ed. by Violet S. de Lazlo (Garden City, N. Y.: Anchor Books, 1958), p. 14.

108. Noel S. Weiss, M.D., editorial: "Risks and Benefits of Estrogen Use," *New England Journal of Medicine,* Vol. 293, No. 23 (December 4, 1975), p. 1201.

109. Donald C. Smith, M.D., et al., "Association of Exogenous Estrogen," p. 1166.

110. Peter Greenwald, M.D., et al., "Endometrial Cancer," p. 242.

111. Benjamin Freedman, "A Moral Theory of Informed Consent," *The Hastings Center Report.* Vol. 5, No. 4 (August 1975), p. 35.

112. Vincent R. Pennisi, M.D., and Angelo Capozzi, M.D., "Incidence of Obscure Carcinoma in Subcutaneous Mastectomy: Results of a National Survey," *Plastic and Reconstructive Surgery,* Vol. 56, No. 1 (July 1975), p. 11.

113. William V. Dolan, M.D., letter to the editor, *Journal of the American Medical Association,* Vol. 238, No. 4 (July 25, 1977), p. 306. The author of this letter, a franciscan friar, also mentions that "the woman with a bilateral chronic cystic mastitis and a strong family history of breast carcinoma is an *ideal candidate* for subcutaneous mastectomy [emphasis mine]." This is, of course, typical medical jargon, and no more original than typical theological jargon about women. The usual meaning of *candidate* is, of course, one who aspires to an office, position, membership, right, or honor. It is derived from the Latin *candidatus,* meaning, clothed in white. The woman in this situation hardly feels like an "ideal candidate" for anything. The surgeon, clothed in white (like the candidates for office who wore white togas in ancient Rome), no doubt projects his own identity through this stunning reversal upon the victim, who provides him, at her expense, with an ideal opportunity for his aggrandizing of power, success, and more favored membership in his profession. Even her death, especially if it can be delayed, will not detract from this success.

114. Harry S. Jonas, M.D., and Byron J. Masterson, M.D., "Giant Uterine Tumors: Case Report and Review of the Literature," *Obstetrics and Gynecology,* Vol. 50, No. 1 (July 1977), p. 2s.

115. This observation was made by Peggy Holland during a conversation in Boston, August 1977.

116. Wolfgang Lederer, M.D., *The Fear of Women* (New York: Harcourt Brace Jovanovich, 1968), p. 248.

117. Ibid., p. 246.

118. Ibid., p. 248.

119. Ibid.

120. This kind of treatment is discussed by Janice Raymond, in "Women as Victims: The Fall and Rise of Psychosurgery," Boston College *Heights,* November 25, 1974, pp. 7, 15. Raymond shows that this kind of surgery represents the final absurdity of the "individual solution" to social ills.

121. Vernon H. Mark, M.D., Herbert Barry, M.D., Turner McLardy, M.D., and Frank R. Ervin, M.D., "The Destruction of Both Anterior Thalamic Nuclei in a Patient with Intractable Agitated De-

pression," *Journal of Nervous and Mental Disease,* Vol. 150, No. 4, pp. 266–72.

122. Vernon H. Mark, M.D., and Frank R. Ervin, M.D., *Violence and the Brain* (New York: Harper and Row, 1970).

Conclusion and Afterword to Chapter Seven
NAZI MEDICINE AND AMERICAN GYNECOLOGY: A TORTURE CROSS-CULTURAL COMPARISON

1. Thomas Neville Bonner, *American Doctors and German Universities: A Chapter in International Intellectual Relations, 1870–1914* (Lincoln: University of Nebraska Press, 1963), p. 93.

2. Adrienne Rich, *Of Woman Born: Motherhood as Experience and Institution* (New York: W. W. Norton, 1976), pp. 151–55.

3. Ibid., p. 152.

4. Bonner, *American Doctors,* p. 93.

5. Ibid., p. 10.

6. Rosemary Stevens, *American Medicine and the Public Interest* (New Haven: Yale University Press, 1971), p. 39.

7. Ibid., p. 9.

8. Bonner, *American Doctors,* p. 32.

9. Ibid., p. 96.

10. Silvano Arieti, ed., *American Handbook of Psychiatry,* Vol. I, *The Foundations of Psychiatry* (2nd ed.; New York: Basic Books, 1974), p. 57.

11. Franz Alexander, M.D., *Psychoanalysis and Psychotherapy: Developments in Theory, Technique and Training* (London: Allen and Unwin, 1957), p. 176.

12. See Mary Daly, *Beyond God the Father: Toward a Philosophy of Women's Liberation* (Boston: Beacon Press, 1973), esp. pp. 117–20.

13. Alexander Mitscherlich, M.D., and Fred Mielke, *Doctors of Infamy: The Story of the Nazi Medical Crimes,* trans. by Heinz Norden, with statements by Andrew C. Ivy, M.D., Telford Taylor, and Leo Alexander, M.D. (New York: Henry Schuman, 1949), p. 147.

14. Ibid., p. 161.

15. Fredric Wertham, M.D., *A Sign for Cain: An Exploration of Human Violence* (New York: Macmillan, 1966), p. 160.

16. William L. Shirer, *The Rise and Fall of the Third Reich: A History of Nazi Germany* (New York: Simon and Schuster, 1960), p. 982.

17. Wertham, *A Sign for Cain,* p. 168.

18. Ibid., p. 169.

19. Shirer, *Rise and Fall,* p. 979.

20. Leo Alexander, M.D., statement, in Mitscherlich and Mielke, *Doctors of Infamy,* p. xxxi.

21. Wertham, *A Sign for Cain,* p. 157.

22. Ibid., p. 139.

23. An example of self-damning correspondence is provided in

Freud's letters to Wilhelm Fliess, which Freud wanted destroyed, but which were smuggled out of Vienna by the devoted Marie Bonaparte during the Nazi invasion. Many years later these were used by Florence Rush to demonstrate that Freud had been aware of the widespread sexual abuse of girl-children by their fathers and other males and later deliberately covered this up in his published writings. She refers to this Freudian cover-up as "refusal to name the offender." See Florence Rush, "The Freudian Cover-Up," *Chrysalis,* No. 1 (1977), pp. 31–45. The letters are in Marie Bonaparte, Anna Freud, and Ernst Kris, eds., *The Origins of Psychoanalysis, Letters to Wilhelm Fliess, Drafts and Notes: 1887–1902,* trans. by Eric Mosbacher and James Strachey (New York: Basic Books, 1954).

24. Erich Fromm, *The Anatomy of Human Destructiveness* (Greenwich, Conn.: Fawcett, 1973), p. 480.

25. Hannah Arendt, *Eichmann in Jerusalem: A Report on the Banality of Evil* (New York: Viking Press, 1963), p. 231.

26. Terrence Des Pres, *The Survivor: An Anatomy of Life in the Death Camps* (New York: Oxford University Press, 1976), pp. 60–61.

27. Spin back to Chapter Two.

28. Julia P. Stanley, "Paradgmatic Woman: The Prostitute," *Papers in Language Variation,* ed. by David L. Shores and Carole P. Hines (Birmingham: University of Alabama Press, 1977), pp. 303–21.

29. See Wilson Bryan Key, *Subliminal Seduction: Ad Media's Manipulation of a Not So Innocent America* (New York: New American Library, 1973). See the same author's more recent book, *Media Sexploitation* (Englewood Cliffs, N. J.: Prentice-Hall, 1976).

30. Denise D. Connors, "Medicalization of Society: The Sickness Unto Death," paper delivered in Boston, June 1976.

31. Translated, this means that the woman thus described, i.e., objectified, conceived ten times, bore eight viable offspring, and aborted once.

32. Wertham at least mentions withchburnings in a list of mass killings of "civilians" in the world but he shrinks/falsifies the number of witches killed in all of Europe to "at least 20,000." See *A Sign for Cain,* p. 140.

33. Mitscherlich and Mielke, *Doctors of Infamy,* p. x.

34. Ibid., p. xi.

35. Ibid., pp. x–xi.

36. Wertham, *A Sign for Cain,* p. 157.

37. Ibid., p. 169.

38. Among such outstanding professors cited as involved were Dr. Max de Crinis of the University of Berlin; Dr. Werner Villinger of the University of Breslau; Dr. Carl Schneider of the University of Heidelberg; Professor Paul Nitsche who was successively director of several state hospitals; Dr. Werner Heyde of the University of Wurzburg; Dr. Friedrich Tillman, director of orphanages in Cologne; Dr. Berthold Kihn of the University of Jena. It has been noted that C. G. Jung, al-

though Swiss, was for several years co-editor (together with Dr. M. H. Goering, a cousin of Marshall Hermann Goering) of the Nazi-coordinated *Journal for Psychotherapy*. See Wertham, *A Sign for Cain*, pp. 171–79. See also Mitscherlich and Mielke, *Doctors of Infamy*, esp. pp. 90–116.

39. Even Dr. Andrew C. Ivy's muted statement contains the following important message: "Had the profession taken a strong stand against the mass killing of sick [*sic*] Germans [read: by psychiatrists] before the war, it is conceivable that the entire technique of death factories for genocide would not have materialized." See Mitscherlich and Mielke, *Doctors of Infamy*, p. xi.

40. Des Pres, *The Survivor*, p. 56.

41. Bruno Bettelheim, *The Informed Heart: Autonomy in a Mass Age* (Glencoe, Ill.: Free Press, 1960), p. 134.

42. Ibid., p. 131.

43. Bruno Bettleheim, "The Commitment Required of a Woman Entering a Scientific Profession in Present Day American Society," *Woman and the Scientific Professions*, MIT Symposium on American Women in Science and Engineering, 1965.

Chapter Eight SPOOKING: EXORCISM, ESCAPE, AND ENSPIRITING PROCESS

1. See Ashley Montagu, *The Anatomy of Swearing* (New York: Macmillan, 1967), especially chapters five and fifteen. Montagu is basically arguing that swearing and obscenity ("four-letter words") are substitutes for violent physical acts. He shows no understanding of psychic violence done to women by male obscenity or of the fact that verbal violence creates an atmosphere that encourages the "acting out" of physical violence.

2. Julia P. Stanley, "The Stylistics of Belief," a paper delivered at the Conference on College Composition and Communication, Anaheim, California, April 4–6, 1974.

3. John T. Noonan, Jr., "An Almost Absolute Value in History," *The Morality of Abortion: Legal and Historical Perspectives*, ed. by John T. Noonan (Cambridge, Mass.: Harvard University Press, 1970), p. 1.

4. B. F. Skinner, *Beyond Freedom and Dignity* (New York: Alfred A. Knopf, 1971), p. 215.

5. Julia P. Stanley, "Nominalized Passives," a paper delivered at the Linguistic Society of America, Chapel Hill, North Carolina, 1972.

6. Alvin Toffler, *Future Shock* (New York: Random House, 1970), p. 429.

7. Julia P. Stanley, "Prescribed Passivity: The Language of Sexism," a paper delivered at the Southeastern Conference on Linguistics, Nashville, Tennessee, March 20–21, 1975.

8. John Money and Patricia Tucker, *Sexual Signatures: On Being a Man or a Woman* (Boston: Little, Brown, 1975), p. 72.
9. Virginia Woolf, *Three Guineas* (New York: Harcourt, Brace, 1938), p. 109.
10. Monique Wittig, *The Lesbian Body,* trans. by David Le Vay (New York: William Morrow, 1975), Author's Note, pp. 10–11.
11. Ibid., introduction by Margaret Crosland, p. 7.
12. Conversation, Boston, October 1977.
13. For an excellent annotated bibliography, see Barrie Thorne and Nancy Henley, eds., *Language and Sex: Difference and Dominance* (Rowley, Mass.: Newbury House, 1975). Together with the bibliography, this work contains a number of useful articles on language. The bibliography is reprinted under the title *She Said/He Said: An Annotated Bibliography of Sex Differences in Language, Speech, and Nonverbal Communication* (Pittsburgh, Pa.: Know, 1975). The address of Know, Inc. is P.O. Box 86031, Pittsburgh, Pa. 15221.
14. Otto Jespersen, *Language: Its Nature, Development and Origin* (London: Allen and Unwin, 1922), chapter thirteen, "The Woman." This chapter is so loaded with non-sequiturs, faulty analysis, and arrogant misnaming, that it should be read in its entirety by Searchers as an exercise in exorcism. Jespersen's academic asininity is exemplified in his use of sentences attributed to female characters in male-authored plays and novels to "prove" that women's use of language is superficial.
15. Noam Chomsky, *For Reasons of State* (New York: Pantheon, 1970), p. 387.
16. Ibid., p. 406.
17. Stefan Kanfer, "Sispeak: A Msguided Attempt to Change Herstory," *Time,* October 23, 1972, p. 79. Another article in the same vein and of the same vintage was L. E. Sissman, "Innocent Bystander: Plastic English," in *Atlantic Monthly,* October 1972, pp. 32–37.
18. Kanfer, "Sispeak," p. 79.
19. George Orwell, *1984* (New York: New American Library, 1961), p. 247.
20. Ibid., pp. 250–51.
21. Ibid., p. 251.
22. Ibid., p. 252.
23. Ibid., p. 253.
24. Ibid., p. 254. An interesting analysis of such words can be found in Casey Miller and Kate Swift, *Words and Women* (Garden City, N. Y.: Anchor Books, 1976). This entire work of Miller and Swift deserves careful study by the serious Searcher.
25. Jean-Paul Sartre, *Being and Nothingness: An Essay on Phenomenological Ontology,* trans. by Hazel E. Barnes (New York: Washington Square, 1966), especially pp. 765–84.
26. Peggy Holland, "Jean-Paul Sartre as a NO to Women," *Sinister Wisdom,* No. 6 (Summer 1978).
27. Orwell, *1984,* p. 231.

28. Thomas S. Szasz, M.D., *The Manufacture of Madness* (New York: Harper and Row, 1970) p. 292. The novel which is the source of the metaphor, and whose plot and basic assumptions are totally unrelated to my use of the image, is Jerzy Kosinski, *The Painted Bird* (Boston: Houghton Mifflin, 1976).

29. For an excellent analysis of how tokenism works, see Judith Long Laws, "The Psychology of Tokenism: An Analysis," *Sex Roles,* Vol. 1, No. 1 (1975), pp. 51–67.

30. This distinction was made by Jan Raymond in a class lecture at the University of Massachusetts, fall 1976, in which she also developed her own concept of "manifesto-ing."

31. Virginia Woolf, *Three Guineas,* pp. 93–94.

32. This sense of *womanhood* was noted by Emily Culpepper during a conversation in October 1977. Clearly, such terms as *widowhood* can be heard in the same way.

33. Conversation, Greenfield, Mass., October 1976.

34. For a fascinating medieval discussion of the unifying "containment" of matter by spirit, which would be quite the opposite of the disintegrating containment of spirit by matter which characterizes fetishism, see Thomas Aquinas, *Summa theologiae,* I, q. 75–76.

35. The term *spirit* is derived from the Latin *spiritus,* meaning spirit, breath.

36. An important study of body language from a feminist perspective is Nancy M. Henley, *Body Politics: Power, Sex, and Nonverbal Communication* (Englewood Cliffs, N. J.: Prentice-Hall, 1977).

37. This institution is analyzed in depth by Adrienne Rich, in *Of Woman Born: Motherhood as Experience and as Institution* (New York: W. W. Norton, 1976).

38. Conversation, Amherst, Mass., December 1975.

39. Conversation, Madison, New Jersey, December 1975. See Nelle Morton's excellent article, "How Images Function," *Quest: A Feminist Quarterly,* Vol. 3, No. 2 (fall, 1976), pp. 54–59.

40. Conversation, Boston, December 1977.

41. The "Old is New" phenomenon was illustrated by an article by Laurie Downey, "Women's History at Harvard: Feminist Leads Exodus from Memorial Church," in *Seventh Sister: Radcliffe's Monthly Magazine,* December 1977. This story, written by a Radcliffe undergraduate in 1977, is an account of the Harvard Memorial Church walk-out of November 14, 1971. The student, attempting in the repressive late seventies to find out something about women's history, stumbled upon the fact that the once-famous "Exodus" had taken place—a fact that was not transmitted by any faculty members. In her interview with Emily Culpepper, Laurie Downey learned something about the erasure of women's history at such institutions as Harvard. For an account of the "Exodus," see Mary Daly, "Radical Feminism, Radical Religion," in *Women and Religion,* ed. by Elizabeth Clark and Herbert Richardson (New York: Harper and Row, 1977), pp. 259–71. See also

Daly, *Beyond God the Father: Toward a Philosophy of Women's Liberation* (Boston: Beacon Press, 1973), pp. 144–45.

42. Emily Culpepper made this observation in a conversation in Boston, December 1977.

43. The caricaturing of witches as part of the celebration of Halloween is of course a classic erasure and reversal. Halloween was/is a remnant of one of the great Sabbats, or feasts, of Wicce, the old Religion. It is interesting to observe, however, that despite the caricature, many women express the fact that we have always had a particular sense of wonder and excitement associated with Halloween, deep feelings and intuitions which christmas and easter do not elicit.

44. Monique Wittig, *Les Guérillères,* trans. by David Le Vay (New York: Viking Press, 1969), p. 89.

45. Valerie Solanas, *SCUM Manifesto,* with an introduction by Vivian Gornick (New York: Olympia Press, 1968), p. 36.

46. This observation was made by Andrée Collard during a conversation in Boston, September 1977.

Chapter Nine SPARKING: THE FIRE OF FEMALE FRIENDSHIP

1. Friedrich Nietzsche, *Thus Spoke Zarathustra,* trans. with an introduction by R. J. Hollingdale (New York: Penguin Books, 1969), p. 91.

2. Paul Fussell, *The Great War and Modern Memory* (New York: Oxford University Press, 1975), p. 120.

3. Ibid., p. 75.

4. Ibid., p. 77.

5. Erich Fromm, *The Anatomy of Human Destructiveness* (Greenwich, Conn.: Fawcett, 1973), p. 212, note.

6. George F. Gilder, *Sexual Suicide* (New York: Quadrangle Books, 1973), pp. 258–59.

7. Philip Caputo, *A Rumor of War* (New York: Holt, Rinehart, 1977), p. xiii.

8. Ibid., p. 9.

9. David Halberstam, *The Best and the Brightest* (New York: Random House, 1972), p. 532.

10. Marc Feigen Fasteau, *The Male Machine* (New York: Delta Books, 1975), p. 184.

11. Bruce Mazlish, *In Search of Nixon* (New York: Basic Books, 1972), p. 116.

12. Valerie Solanas, *SCUM Manifesto,* with an introduction by Vivian Gornick (New York: Olympia Press, 1970), pp. 5–6.

13. Ibid., p. 7.

14. Gilder, *Sexual Suicide,* p. 18.

15. Ibid., p. 18.

16. Caputo, *A Rumor of War,* p. 6.
17. Ibid., p. xiv.
18. J. Glenn Gray, *The Warriors: Reflections on Men in Battle* (New York: Harper Torchbooks, 1967), p. 217.
19. Lionel Tiger, *Men in Groups* (New York: Random House, 1969), p. 191.
20. Ibid., p. 188.
21. Susan Brownmiller, *Against Our Will: Men, Women and Rape* (New York: Simon and Schuster, 1975), p. 103.
22. Ibid., pp. 114 ff., 75–76, 107.
23. Ibid., pp. 14–15.
24. Ibid., p. 110.
25. D. H. Lawrence, *Women in Love* (New York: Viking Press, 1960), p. 337.
26. Ibid., p. 337.
27. Ibid., p. 338.
28. Ibid.
29. Ibid., p. 341.
30. Adrienne Rich pointed out that in the Apes' House in the Bronx Zoo there is a mirror accompanied by the following label: "This is the World's Most Dangerous Animal." Since women as well as men look into this mirror, they feel accused of crimes they have not committed (personal communication, January 1978).
31. Jeannette Foster, *Sex Variant Women in Literature,* with a new afterword by Barbara Grier (Baltimore, Md.: Diana Press, 1975), p. 212.
32. Gray, *The Warriors,* p. 90.
33. Ibid.
34. Ibid., p. 102.
35. Ibid., p. 90.
36. Ibid., p. 94.
37. Caputo, *A Rumor of War,* p. xv.
38. Adrienne Rich has pointed out: "Spinsters/Lesbians who have at one point been lovers often continue to be lifelong deeply loving friends. This phenomenon is virtually unknown in heterosexual romance, or, if known, it cannot have the same resonance, since female-to-female friendship is of a wholly different order" (personal communication, January 1978).
39. D. H. Lawrence, *Studies in Classic American Literature* (New York: Viking Press, 1964), p. 169.
40. Robert Jay Lifton, *Home from the War* (New York: Simon and Schuster, 1973), p. 109.
41. Caputo, *A Rumor of War,* p. 314.
42. John G. Bowen, in *Princeton Alumni Weekly,* September 26, 1977.
43. Susan Leigh Star has noted that the expression "sexual preference" contains the false implication that most women actually have a

free choice between heterosexuality and Lesbianism (conversation, Chicago, December, 1977).

44. Paul Tillich, *The Courage to Be* (New Haven: Yale University Press, 1952), p. 164.

45. Ibid., p. 165.

46. Ibid.

47. Gray, *The Warriors,* p. 90.

48. Emily Culpepper has discussed this in an unpublished paper entitled "On the Boundary of Sisterhood," May 1974.

49. Jan Raymond, class lecture given at University of Massachusetts at Amherst, fall 1976.

50. Simone de Beauvoir, *The Second Sex,* trans. and ed. by H. M. Parshley (New York: Vintage, 1974), p. 468.

51. See Mary Daly, *Beyond God the Father: Toward a Philosophy of Women's Liberation* (Boston: Beacon Press, 1973).

52. Jan Raymond, class lecture, fall 1976.

Chapter Ten SPINNING: COSMIC TAPESTRIES

1. See Helen Diner, *Mothers and Amazons: The First Feminine History of Culture,* ed. and trans. by John Philip Lundin (Garden City, N.Y.: Anchor Books, 1973), pp. 16–18.

2. See, for example, Ernest Becker, *The Structure of Evil: An Essay on the Unification of the Science of Man* (New York: George Braziller, 1968). See also Erich Fromm, *The Anatomy of Human Destructiveness* (Greenwich, Conn.: Fawcett, 1975).

3. Early evidence of misinterpretation and cooptation was the use (abuse) of Adrienne Rich's poem "The Stranger," in which she uses the term *androgyne,* by James Nolan in his article, "The Third Sex," *Ramparts,* December 1973.

4. Monique Wittig, *Les Guérillères,* trans. by David Le Vay (New York: Viking Press, 1969), p. 108.

5. See Mary Daly, *Beyond the God Father: Toward a Philosophy of Women's Liberation* (Boston: Beacon Press, 1973), passim.

6. Maria Leach, ed. and Jerome Fried, asso. ed., *Funk and Wagnalls Standard Dictionary of Folklore, Mythology, and Legend* (New York: Funk and Wagnalls, 1972), p. 69.

7. Robert Graves, *The Greek Myths* (Baltimore, Md.: Penguin Books, 1975), I, 25, *h.*

8. J. E. Cirlot, *A Dictionary of Symbols,* trans. by Jack Sage (New York: Philosophical Library, 1962), p. 290.

9. Joseph Campbell, *The Hero with a Thousand Faces,* Bollingen Series XVII (Princeton, N.J.: Princeton University Press, 1968), p. 71.

10. Ibid.

11. E. B. White, *Charlotte's Web* (New York: Harper and Row, 1952), p. 80.

12. Ibid., p. 171.

13. J. L. Cloudsley-Thompson, *Spiders, Scorpions, Centipedes and Mites* (New York: Pergamon Press, 1968), p. 194.

14. Diner, *Mothers and Amazons,* p. 16.

15. The genius of androcatic art is expressed by the "artist" Jasper Johns in his notebooks, cited in an ad for Philip Morris Incorporated in *Saturday Review,* April 15, 1978, pp. 52–53: "Take an object. Do something to it. Do something else to it. Do something else to it."

16. Diner, *Mothers and Amazons,* pp. 17–18.

17. Cirlot, *A Dictionary of Symbols,* pp. 291–92.

18. Ibid., p. 290. Independent women have traditionally survived through various modes of spinning. Women writers, such as Louisa May Alcott, for example, have spun yarns out of their experience. In the twelfth to fifteenth centuries the Beguines, who were sort of "free lance" nuns who lived without vows and escaped male authority before they were wiped out in the fifteenth century, frequently earned their livelihood by spinning wool thread. They did not require spinning wheels but carried spindles, which meant they could travel lightly, settle anywhere and find work. See Gracia Clark, "The Beguines: A Medieval Women's Community," *Quest: A Feminist Quarterly,* Vol. 1, No. 4 (spring 1975), pp. 72–80.

19. Louise Bernikow, ed., introduction, *The World Split Open: Four Centuries of Women Poets in England and America, 1552–1950* (New York: Vintage, 1974), p. 47.

20. Jean-Paul Sartre, *Being and Nothingness,* trans. by Hazel E. Barnes (New York: Washington Square, 1966), p. 782.

21. Ibid.

22. Peggy Holland, "Jean-Paul Sartre as a NO to Women," *Sinister Wisdom,* No. 6 (summer 1978).

23. Erich Neumann, *The Great Mother: An Analysis of the Archetype,* trans. by Ralph Manheim, Bollingen Series XLVII (Princeton, N.J.: Princeton University Press, 1963), p. 177.

24. Campbell, *The Hero with a Thousand Faces,* p. 142.

25. Diner, *Mothers and Amazons,* p. 17.

26. Cirlot, *A Dictionary of Symbols,* p. 165.

27. Ibid.

28. See Jane Caputi, "The Glamour of Grammar," *Chrysalis: A Magazine of Women's Culture,* No. 4, pp. 35–43. Caputi discusses these and other related terms.

29. Robin Morgan, "The One That Got Away, or The Woman Who Made It," *Monster* (New York: Vintage, 1972), p. 70.

30. The idea of "a loom of one's own" by which we "weave the way out" was suggested to me by Denise Connors in a conversation in Boston, October 1977.

31. Virginia Woolf, *Moments of Being: Unpublished Autobiographical Writings,* ed. and with an introduction and notes by Jeanne Schulkind (New York: Harcourt Brace Jovanovich, 1976), p. 72.

32. Ibid.

33. This experience was discussed at various points in my book, *Beyond God the Father,* often by the use of such terminology as "confronting the experience of nonbeing." The earthquake phenomenon is another mode or aspect of the appearance of nonbeing.

34. *Grolier Encyclopedia* (New York: The Grolier Society, 1957), Vol. VII, p. 230.

35. Ibid.

36. Ibid., pp. 230–31.

37. Ibid., p. 231.

38. Conversation with Peggy Holland, Boston, March 1978.

39. Woolf, *Moments of Being,* p. 72.

40. Ibid., p. 73.

41. This image was suggested to me by Emily Culpepper during a conversation in Boston, March 1978.

42. Nelle Morton, "Beloved Image!", paper delivered at the National Conference of the American Academy of Religion, San Francisco, California, December 28, 1977, p. 4.

43. Ibid.

44. The idea that ignorance is what is lost whereas innocence must be found was suggested to me by Andrée Collard during a conversation in Cohasset, Mass., December 1977.

45. Neumann, *The Great Mother,* p. 177.

46. Nelle Morton has made this point eloquently on innumerable occasions and to countless women. An earlier published article in which the idea is central to her thought is "The Rising of Woman Consciousness in a Male Language Structure," *Andover Newton Quarterly,* Vol. 12, No. 4 (March 1972), pp. 177–90.

47. A number of nonverbal conversations with "dumb" animals have re-enforced my appreciation of Spinning. To translate and credit just a few: "It's fun to spin": Spinner, a Belgian Shepherd bitch, Wellesley, Mass., June 1976.
"We spin together": Wild-Eyes and Wild-Cat, two female cats (sisters), Watertown, Mass., October 1976.
"I am the familiar of a Spinster": Kali, a cat living in Cambridge, Mass., May 1977.
"Spinning is deep": Moira, a cat living in Somerville, Mass., March 1978.

Since I cannot cite at length all the animals whose communications contributed to my concept of Spinning, I will name but a few (whose real names are known only to themselves): a silver-hued and agile cow encountered in the Alps at Kleine Scheidegg, Switzerland; a blackbird in Bergen, Norway; a group of sheep near Heraklion, Crete; some goats in the vicinity of Fribourg, Switzerland; a monkey in Venice, Italy; a hermit crab in Onset, Mass.; a brown-and-yellow-shelled turtle in Onset, Mass.; a dog and three horses in Lyndonville, Vt.

48. Becker, *The Structure of Evil,* p. 213.

49. Ibid., p. 173. See also J. Huizinga, *Homo Ludens: A Study of the*

Play-Element in Culture (Boston: Beacon Press, 1955); Kurt H. Wolff, ed., *Georg Simmel, 1858–1918* (Columbus: Ohio State University Press, 1959).

Within the gamesters' society there is little room for real creativity. The following statement by Dr. Willard F. Libby, who won a 1960 Nobel prize in chemistry, illustrates the dwarfed idea of "creativity" in androcracy: "Scientific creativity is scientific discovery through scientific research. . . . Science is the study of nature by the scientific method to discover new facts and truths eventually to be formulated as natural law. . . . This is the method which has proven so singularly effective in attacking natural secrets. . . . The experienced scientist knows that nature yields her secrets with great reluctance and only to proper suitors." See Willard F. Libby, "Creativity in Science," *Creativity: A Discussion at the Nobel Conference,* ed. by John D. Roslansky (Amsterdam and London: North Holland Publishing Company, 1970), pp. 35–52. See the whole book for other examples of scientific "literacy" and "logic."

50. Virginia Woolf, *Three Guineas* (New York: Harcourt, Brace, 1938), pp. 19–20.

51. Thomas Aquinas, *Summa theologiae,* I, q. 1–q. 26.

52. Wittig, *Les Guérillères,* p. 93.

53. Elmer G. Suhr, *The Spinning Aphrodite: The Evolution of the Goddess from Earliest Pre-Hellenic Symbolism through Late Classical Times* (New York: Helios Books, 1969), p. 48.

54. *Boston Evening Globe,* March 31, 1978, p. 5, carried a UPI photo of a domestic android known as Klatu (U-Talk spelled backward): "The robot will soon be available for $4000 to watch the children, answer the door, and take telephone messages. Quasar Industries of Rutherford, N.J., plans to mass market the android in 10 months. Klatu demonstrates his [sic] ability to serve coffee . . . and paint ceilings."

55. *Sinister Wisdom* is, of course, the name of a well-known Lesbian-Feminist journal.

56. Creative Anger and Bravery are rooted in a passion for Justice. As Dr. Elizabeth Farians has demonstrated, both in her writings and in her actions: "Justice is an active virtue. One must do something about justice." See her article, "Justice: The Hard Line," *Andover Newton Quarterly,* Vol. 12, No. 4 (March 1972), pp. 191–200.

INDEX OF NEW WORDS

Although many of these words are not new in the old sense, they are new in a new sense, because they are heard in a new way. The page numbers for the most part indicate where the words are first used or first defined.

GENERAL INDEX